Praise for **The Wolves of K Street**

"If you want to understand how American democracy went off the rails, all you need to do is read this book."

—Christopher Leonard, *New York Times* bestselling author of *The Lords of Easy Money*

"A fast-paced deep dive into a world of greed and ambition, inhabited by a uniquely fascinating group of wheelers and dealers. *The Wolves of K Street* is a history of not only how money and power have influenced American politics but also how the work of lobbyists touches the life of every American."

—Kate Andersen Brower, *New York Times* bestselling author of *The Residence*

"A not-so-guilty pleasure. . . . The Mullins brothers cleverly set up their story as a mystery . . . with considerable narrative skill and novelistic detail."

—James B. Stewart, *New York Times*

"Engrossing. . . . Smoothly written, meticulously researched, *The Wolves of K Street* informs and mesmerizes."

—*Guardian*

"An instant classic—deeply reported, powerfully told, and profoundly important. It's one of the best books I've read on Washington in many years."

—Peter Baker, *New York Times* bestselling coauthor of *The Man Who Ran Washington*

"However nefarious you think the lobbying industry is in Washington, Brody and Luke Mullins have news: It's worse. Not even during the Roaring Twenties and the Gilded Age did corporate America wield so much influence. In their deeply reported, compelling new book, the Mullins brothers track how that happened and the disastrous consequences."

—Susan Page, *New York Times* bestselling author of *The Matriarch*

"Absorbing. . . . This is the deep state."

—Franklin Foer, *Atlantic*

"Like many of the best stories, *The Wolves of K Street* opens with a corpse, which sets the Mullins brothers off to investigate what may be a more important mystery than any whodunit: How did corporations come to dominate the American political system?"

— Sasha Issenberg, author of *The Victory Lab*

"One of the most amazing developments in modern American politics is how Donald Trump's Republican Party seems to have supplanted FDR's Democratic Party as the political home of the 'working man.' . . . Anyone who wants to understand this transformation should read Brody and Luke Mullins's new book."

— *Washington Free Beacon*

"Although corporate lobbyists certainly fleece the American public . . . they put at least as much effort into fleecing the corporations that hire them. That comes across loud and clear in *The Wolves of K Street*."

— *Washington Post*

"This is nothing less than the definitive history of how corporate lobbyists took over Washington. The Mullins brothers have brought us the story of how Washington really works—and for whom."

— Jonathan Martin, *New York Times* bestselling coauthor of *This Will Not Pass*

"The Mullins brothers promise to untangle the intricate—and ultimately, pathetic—story of the selling of the American republic, and they have succeeded brilliantly."

— Duff McDonald, *New York Times* bestselling author of *Tickled*

"A vivid, brilliantly told tale that unfolds like a novel, this is the most potent portrait of the Washington swamp you will read."

— Ken Auletta, *New York Times* bestselling author of *Googled*

"Deeply reported and punchily written, this is an entertaining—and disturbing—account of the devious subversion of democracy."

— *Publishers Weekly* (starred review)

The Wolves of K Street

The Secret History of How Big Money Took Over Big Government

Brody Mullins and **Luke Mullins**

Simon & Schuster Paperbacks

New York   Amsterdam/Antwerp   Toronto   London   Sydney/Melbourne   New Delhi

Simon & Schuster Paperbacks
An Imprint of Simon & Schuster, LLC
1230 Avenue of the Americas
New York, NY 10020

For more than 100 years, Simon & Schuster has championed authors and the stories they create. By respecting the copyright of an author's intellectual property, you enable Simon & Schuster and the author to continue publishing exceptional books for years to come. We thank you for supporting the author's copyright by purchasing an authorized edition of this book.

No amount of this book may be reproduced or stored in any format, nor may it be uploaded to any website, database, language-learning model, or other repository, retrieval, or artificial intelligence system without express permission. All rights reserved. Inquiries may be directed to Simon & Schuster, 1230 Avenue of the Americas, New York, NY 10020 or permissions@simonandschuster.com.

Copyright © 2024 by Brody Mullins and Luke Mullins

All rights reserved, including the right to reproduce this book
or portions thereof in any form whatsoever. For information, address
Simon & Schuster Paperbacks Subsidiary Rights Department,
1230 Avenue of the Americas, New York, NY 10020.

First Simon & Schuster trade paperback edition May 2025

SIMON & SCHUSTER PAPERBACKS and colophon are
registered trademarks of Simon & Schuster, LLC

Simon & Schuster strongly believes in freedom of expression and stands against censorship in all its forms. For more information, visit BooksBelong.com.

For information about special discounts for bulk purchases,
please contact Simon & Schuster Special Sales
at 1-866-506-1949 or business@simonandschuster.com.

The Simon & Schuster Speakers Bureau can bring authors to your live event.
For more information or to book an event, contact the Simon & Schuster Speakers Bureau
at 1-866-248-3049 or visit our website at www.simonspeakers.com.

Interior design by Ruth Lee-Mui

Manufactured in the United States of America

1   3   5   7   9   10   8   6   4   2

Library of Congress Cataloging-in-Publication Data has been applied for.

ISBN 978-1-9821-2059-7
ISBN 978-1-9821-2060-3 (pbk)
ISBN 978-1-9821-2061-0 (ebook)

For Mom and Dad

Patton Boggs was built on the idea that the law can be changed to achieve client objectives . . . We see the law as a dynamic process, not as immutable rules and procedures.

—Marketing materials for the Washington
lobbying firm of Patton Boggs

Contents

Prologue 1

Introduction 5

Part I: The Inside Game (1972–1999) 17

Chapter 1 19

Chapter 2 52

Chapter 3 66

Chapter 4 106

Chapter 5 128

Chapter 6 150

Chapter 7 165

Chapter 8 186

Part II: The Outside Game (2000–2015) 213

Chapter 9 215

Chapter 10 240

Chapter 11 263

Chapter 12 277

Chapter 13 312

Chapter 14 331

Chapter 15 359

Chapter 16 378

Part III: The Reckoning (2015–Present) 385

Chapter 17   387

Chapter 18   409

Chapter 19   426

Chapter 20   439

Chapter 21   460

Chapter 22   472

Chapter 23   480

Chapter 24   493

Chapter 25   495

Epilogue   505

Acknowledgments   509

Notes   515

Index   591

Prologue

July 9, 2015
Gainesville, Virginia

It was after ten o'clock at night when the cops arrived at the Robert Trent Jones Golf Club in Gainesville, Virginia. Pulling up to the majestic, Georgian-style mansion that serves as the clubhouse, two officers from the Prince William County Police Department located a member of the staff who agreed to take them to the scene. The employee led the police officers away from the redbrick clubhouse, down past the azaleas and the presentation lawn, toward the banks of Lake Manassas. They reached a spit of land between the eighteenth green and the shoreline, where a collection of white Adirondack chairs were arranged in a semicircle around a fire pit. The secluded, serene spot was popular with the club's members, who liked to gather here after finishing their rounds of golf.

"He's sitting in a chair behind that tree,"[1] the employee said.

Through the darkness and the foliage, the police officers could make out a solitary figure slumped onto one of the chairs. The man was perfectly placid, facing the water. He was a large man—six foot one, maybe 215 pounds—and his clothes reflected the upscale sensibilities of an exclusive private club that cost about $150,000 to join. The man wore a black sports jacket, a white dress shirt, gray slacks, and black loafers. On the left arm of the chair was a burnt cigar. On the grass next to him was an empty bottle of Petrus, a rare wine produced on a twenty-eight-acre estate in Bordeaux, France, that cost $1,500 at the club.

As the police approached the fire pit, they noticed bloodstains on the man's shirt. They spotted a gunshot wound in his head, and they saw a silver Smith & Wesson .357 pistol. One of the officers put her fingers on the man's neck, to check his pulse. His skin, she found, was stiff. And despite the humid air of the summer's evening, the man's body was cold to the touch.[2]

Nestled thirty-seven miles west of Washington, DC, the Robert Trent Jones Golf Club is an august social sanctuary for America's ruling elite. The eighteen-hole course is carved out of a breathtaking stretch of suburban Virginia that runs along the banks of Lake Manassas, near the foothills of the Shenandoah Mountains. It is considered the magnum opus of legendary golf course architect Robert Trent Jones Sr.,[3] whose body of work includes the original White House putting green[4] and a pitch-and-putt course at Camp David,[5] the presidential retreat in Frederick County, Maryland. Upon opening in 1991, the club hosted the first four Presidents Cup matches ever held in the United States; superstar golfers such as Tiger Woods and Phil Mickelson walked the club's pristine fairways as the nation's commanders in chief performed ceremonial duties as honorary chairmen.[6] Along the way, the club's membership expanded to include some of the most illustrious names in Washington. President Barack Obama joined[7] the Robert Trent Jones Golf Club upon departing the White House in 2017.

On this day—July 9, 2015—the club's employees were hustling to prepare the grounds for a nationally televised PGA golf tournament hosted by Tiger Woods that would take place in just three weeks.[8] It was the biggest golf event of the year in the Washington area. Then the body of one of its members was found in a lawn chair behind the eighteenth green.

Back at the fire pit, the police were taking photographs of the body and carefully collecting evidence from the scene. The revolver was secured by removing the unused bullets from the cylinder. One of the officers walked back up to the clubhouse and began interviewing witnesses.

The staff had no trouble identifying the deceased man. He was a Washington lobbyist, a frequent golfer, and a familiar face at the club. As a server explained to the police, who documented it in their report,[9] the lobbyist had arrived at the club around three o'clock that afternoon, entered the bar, and ordered a bottle of Petrus. He left quickly, saying that he had work to do. His temperament, the server noted, had seemed a bit "short."

After reserving three rooms in the club's cottages, which are available to members wishing to stay the night, the lobbyist walked down to the fire pit. He took a seat in an Adirondack chair, opened his bottle of Petrus, and peered out at the 770-acre man-made lake. Around five o'clock, the server came down to the area.

Will you be joining us for dinner, he asked.

No, the lobbyist replied, I'm wiped.

At about seventy-thirty, an hour or so before sunset, a different club employee was standing on the eighteenth green when a gunshot pierced the silence. Roughly thirty seconds later, a second blast. The employee thought it must have come from a hunter on the other side of the lake. He went to the top of a hill, maybe fifty yards from the fire pit, and saw the lobbyist sitting alone with a bottle of wine. Assuming that the man had merely passed out, the employee returned to the clubhouse. At ten o'clock he sent the server back down to light the fire pit for another club member.

Realizing that the lobbyist hadn't moved in several hours, the server went over to check on him. There was a red substance dribbling out of the lobbyist's mouth, which, at first, the server figured was wine. He shook the man but couldn't rouse him. He called the police.

Within an hour, a team of county officials had descended on the golf club. Police located the lobbyist's white Porsche sports car in the parking lot and searched it for clues. A detective entered the room where the lobbyist was staying. Before long, a medical officer came down to the fire pit, examined the body, and, at 10:52 p.m., pronounced the lobbyist dead.

About a month later, after the autopsy had been performed and the body had been buried, things took an unexpected turn. On August 12, 2015, a detective from the Prince William County Police Department received a call from a criminal investigator with the federal Department of Justice.[10] The case, it seemed, was about more than a single dead lobbyist.

Though few outside of Washington had ever heard of the now-deceased man, in the capital of wheeling and dealing, he was among its most gifted operators. By pioneering an advanced set of influence-peddling tactics, he'd achieved crucial policy victories for his clients, secured windfall contracts from the federal government, cozied up to key officials in Congress and the White House, and financed a lifestyle of vacation homes, golf memberships, Rolex watches, fancy wine, and cigars.[11] But when lawyers at his company received an anonymous letter a few months before his death alleging wrongdoing, internal investigators began scrutinizing the lobbyist's business activities stretching back an entire decade. The allegations would touch off a years-long case handled by the Federal Bureau of Investigation and the US Attorney's Office in Washington involving millions of missing dollars, a second Beltway operative, and the murky ethics of DC's political-influence industry.[12] The suspicions would also set in motion the lobbyist's demise. A few weeks after the allegations first surfaced, his body was discovered behind the eighteenth green at the Robert Trent Jones Golf Club.

Introduction

Since the founding of America, powerful business interests have sought to exercise influence over Washington's political machinery. Back in the 1850s, the gun magnate Samuel Colt attempted to secure a federal patent extension with the help of young women who'd been enlisted to entertain elected officials.[1] "To reach the heart or get the vote, the surest way is down the throat"[2] is how a congressional committee characterized the philosophy of Colt's top lobbyist. Two decades later, a sitting congressman passed out corporate stocks to about a dozen influential lawmakers as part of an effort by the firm set up to build the Union Pacific Railroad to ensure the passage of railroad legislation.[3] By the opening decades of the twentieth century, the Standard Oil Company had a senator on retainer, J. P. Morgan & Co. had bankers ghostwriting federal legislation, and top executives at U.S. Steel had congressmen regularly sending them intelligence on key developments in the nation's capital.[4]

Yet despite these feats of corruption, for much of Washington's history, America's business establishment was unable to achieve the sort of enduring political clout that it so desired. Rather, this central struggle of our democracy—the prerogatives of industrial capitalism versus the best interests of ordinary men and women—played out in a back-and-forth fashion, with periods of corporate excess and abuse inspiring eras of consumer reform.

The industrial exploitation of the Gilded Age, for instance, led to the Progressive Era of the late nineteenth and early twentieth centuries,[5] when

Washington enacted measures outlawing child labor, establishing an eight-hour workday (at least for some employees), regulating the drug and meat-packing industries, and endowing public officials with the power to break up abusive monopolies. Following the indulgence of the Roaring Twenties and amid the trauma of the Great Depression, Congress passed a series of New Deal reforms[6] that, among other things, set a federal minimum wage, gave workers the right to form unions, insured customers' deposits against bank failures, and created new rules against Wall Street predation. When the post–World War II economic boom produced new hazards to employees, consumers, and the environment, the political system rallied to prevent workplace injuries, reduce car crashes, limit air pollution, and keep unsafe toys out of the hands of children.[7]

Among the first to recognize the tendency of American history to organize itself this way was the historian Arthur M. Schlesinger Sr. "A period of concern for the rights of the few has been followed by one of concern for the wrongs of the many," he wrote in 1939. "Emphasis on the welfare of property has given way to emphasis on human welfare."

But as contemporary intellectuals have pointed out, this once-predictable pattern—periods of laissez-faire indifference triggering eras of activist government—has thus far failed to materialize in the modern era.[8] In the face of banking catastrophes, environmental disasters, and the implosion of a once-thriving manufacturing sector, America's political leaders have not enacted the sort of broad-based reforms that followed previous crises.[9] A nearly century-long tradition of relatively evenly matched political debates between the forces of Big Business and the interests of ordinary citizens vanished. Instead, during the 1970s, Washington entered a new era: a nearly four-decade-long stretch in which the corporate capitalists of Wall Street, Big Pharma, and Silicon Valley exercised as much control of the political system as did their Gilded Age predecessors—with far less risk of accountability and reform.

How did this happen?

America's Founding Fathers were clear-eyed about the corrupting potential of special interests, says Bowdoin College professor Andrew Rudalevige. After all, many of the country's first colonists had fled to what is now

Massachusetts in order to escape religious persecution in England. With this ugly history in mind, the framers designed our democracy to withstand the political pressures of church authorities, bankers, merchants, and anyone else who might prioritize their own narrow interests above those of the general public. In 1787 James Madison, who is considered the father of the Constitution, described the "regulation of these various and interfering interests" as "the principal task of modern legislation."

In "The Federalist No. 10," one of the eighty-five essays—known as *The Federalist Papers*—that he and other founding fathers wrote to drum up support for the ratification of the US Constitution,[10] Madison outlined the young nation's tools for limiting the power of interest groups, or "factions," as he called them. Since any effort to abolish them would be an attack on liberty itself, Madison argued that all interest groups should be free to compete with one another in an open market of ideas. Small interest groups—or minority factions—posed little danger to democracy. But if a particular interest group were to gain favor with enough lawmakers, forming a so-called majority faction, it could, in Madison's view, "sacrifice to its ruling passion or interest both the public good and the rights of other citizens."

While drafting the Constitution, Madison and other framers erected a critical firewall against the formation of a majority faction: the nation would be governed by a body of elected representatives. And since these lawmakers would need to cultivate the support of numerous competing interests in order to get elected, it was unlikely, in Madison's view, that any single interest could achieve undue influence over a particular member of Congress, let alone the entire legislature. Beyond that, the sheer size of the republic—then a 420,000-square-mile expanse from New Hampshire to Georgia—would prevent the coordination required to establish a majority faction.

"The influence of factious leaders may kindle a flame within their particular States, but will be unable to spread a general conflagration through the other States," Madison wrote. "A rage for paper money, for an abolition of debts, for an equal division of property, or for any other improper or wicked project, will be less apt to pervade the whole body of the Union than a particular member of it; in the same proportion as such a malady is more likely to taint a particular county or district, than an entire State."

In 1792, five years after Madison wrote these words, America witnessed its first act of lobbying, a term derived from the cajoling and arm-twisting that took place in the lobbies of the seventeenth-century British Parliament. Following the American Revolution, a group of Continental army veterans from Virginia hired a former military officer, William Hull, in a largely unsuccessful effort to convince members of the recently formed Congress to grant them additional benefits.[11] As the US economy became more industrial, the number of business lobbyists in Washington gradually increased. Yet for the most part, the political struggle between industry and consumers remained more of an equal contest than a rout. The ambitions of business leaders were kept in check by a network of equally powerful groups with starkly opposing agendas—what the economist John Kenneth Galbraith called "countervailing" forces. At the turn of the twentieth century, railroad magnates and robber barons were outmatched by the political influence of progressive activists. The New Deal was powered by the muscle of organized labor. The reforms of the 1960s and early 1970s reflected the awesome strength of unions, environmental groups, and consumer advocates. Nearly two centuries after the publication of Federalist No. 10, Madison's framework for healthy interest group competition appeared to be flourishing.

Then, in the 1970s, everything changed.[12]

Fearing that increased government authority and widespread anti-business sentiment had imperiled the future of capitalism, industry leaders resolved to crush their political adversaries in the labor, consumer, and environmental movements once and for all. They incited a revolution in corporate political activism, inventing new strategies for deploying their clout—in areas such as campaign finance and think tank scholarship—and transforming Washington's once sleepy corporate lobbying community into the most powerful influence-peddling machine in American history. "My job used to be booze, broads, and golf,"[13] remarked one lobbyist in 1979. "Now it's organizing coalitions and keeping information flowing."

The political awakening of corporate America fundamentally altered the nature of interest group conflict in Washington, as neither labor unions nor consumer activists had the financial resources to restrain the ascendant power of Big Business.[14] From 1967 to 2007, the number of registered lobbyists in Washington—the vast majority of whom represented business interests—exploded from some five or six dozen to nearly fifteen thousand.[15] Washington was getting bigger too. But this rate of growth outpaced even the rapid expansion of federal government spending, which ballooned from about $15 billion to roughly $2.7 trillion over the same period.[16] By 2012, for every $1 spent by consumer groups or environmental activists to influence federal policy, corporations and their allies were spending $86.[17] That same year, the political scientist Lee Drutman conducted interviews with sixty lobbyists while researching his 2015 book *The Business of America Is Lobbying*. Not one of them cited a labor union, consumer group, or environmental organization as his or her leading opponent in a specific policy debate. Business lobbyists still had to worry about the political power of rival companies or opposing industries, but they no longer had much to fear from the labor leaders and consumer advocates who had represented the interests of ordinary citizens in Washington.

After holding up for nearly two centuries, James Madison's framework for healthy interest group competition had collapsed under the weight of the modern corporate influence-peddling apparatus. Using their financial superiority and advanced tactics, corporate lobbyists would deliver for business executives a period of sustained, entrenched influence over Washington policy making that lasted well into the twenty-first century.[18] In 2014 Princeton University professor Martin Gilens teamed up with Professor Benjamin I. Page of Northwestern University to examine which forces had the most impact in Washington over time: average citizens, economic elites, business interests, or mass-based groups, such as consumer or environmental organizations. "The central point that emerges from our research," they concluded, "is that economic elites and organized groups representing business interests have substantial independent impacts on US government policy, while mass-based interest groups and average citizens have little or no independent influence."[19]

The unusually strong position of corporations in Washington made tough-minded consumer reforms nearly impossible.[20] The major laws that did pass—such as the 2010 Dodd-Frank Wall Street Reform and Consumer Protection Act, which sought to crack down on Wall Street abuses, and President Barack Obama's national health care bill the same year—weren't fundamental overhauls of hopelessly broken industries but rather legislative compromises drafted in collaboration with business lobbyists. And key portions of these measures were subsequently watered down by judges, rolled back by lawmakers, or weakened during the federal rulemaking process. But the goal wasn't just kneecapping reform. More significantly, corporate lobbyists used their clout to bend the trajectory of federal policy making in a decidedly and actively pro-business direction. As the journalist Thomas Edsall wrote in his 1984 book *The New Politics of Inequality*, during the nearly fifty years following the 1932 election of Franklin Delano Roosevelt, the country's tax and spending policies were guided in large part by the principle of equity. New Deal liberals viewed federal power as a cushion against the destructive potential of corporate capitalism; assertive regulators worked to curb excess corporate power in the marketplace, progressive tax policies moderately redistributed income downward,[21] and robust social safety nets protected the poor, elderly, and unfortunate during times of hardship. But following their political awakening in the 1970s, corporate interests forged a pro-business alliance—among Republican *and* Democratic lawmakers—that pursued a radically different vision for the economy: government shouldn't restrict the power of capitalism, it should amplify it. "Government is not the solution to our problem," as Ronald Reagan famously said in his 1981 inaugural address, "government *is* the problem." As these free-market evangelists saw it, increasing economic efficiency would enable corporations to lower the price of goods for consumers, boost wages for workers, and grow the economy for all. The framework appealed to conservative Republicans as well as business-minded Democrats on Capitol Hill, who were just then scrambling for new ideas to address the "stagflation" panic of the 1970s. With remarkable speed, Washington set itself to drastically reduce anything that stood in the way of maximum economic efficiency, such as unions, regulations, taxes, and social welfare spending. "In short," Edsall wrote, "the goal became to influence government policy so as to supplant, in an economic sense, equity with efficiency."[22]

This new lodestar of economic policy making—efficiency, as opposed to equity—would guide Washington's political leaders for most of the next four decades. It was a fractious path; rival companies and competing industries continued to wage vicious lobbying battles with one another over the details of specific bills.[23] But over time, the broad parameters of federal economic policy would come to reflect the priorities of the modern corporate boardroom: lower taxes, fewer regulations, freer trade, weaker unions, and less commitment to social spending. For many leaders of Big Business, government was no longer an obstacle to growth, it was a partner in a more profitable future.[24] In the words of one lobbyist, "It's gone from 'Leave us alone' to 'Let's work on this together.'"[25]

Washington's pro-business policy consensus would lay the groundwork for a period of astonishing wealth creation. Yet it would also unleash a cascade of economic disruption and social discord for Americans in both political parties. Federal policy makers raced to reposition the US economy away from manufacturing and toward the financial and knowledge-based fields of their corporate benefactors. Millions of blue-collar workers—who didn't fit into the new paradigm of high-skilled labor and globalized trade—were left behind, shackling entire regions of the country with high unemployment, low social mobility, and endemic despair. Subsequent failures to adequately address a range of pressing concerns, such as stagnant wages, unaffordable health care, astronomical prescription drug prices, predatory home loans, and digital monopolies, kindled popular discontent with the political system.[26] All the while, as Jacob Hacker and Paul Pierson demonstrate in their 2010 book, *Winner-Take-All Politics*, Washington's corporate-friendly agenda was widening the current gulf between the rich and the poor[27] to levels not seen since the 1920s[28]—a development that fueled political polarization, inflamed class and ethnic resentments, and broadened the appeal of the extremist elements of our society.

Economic inequality is a particularly destabilizing condition, one that scholars have cited as a factor in everything from the fall of the Roman

Empire to the outbreak of World War I. "We may have democracy, or we may have wealth concentrated in the hands of a few," as Supreme Court Justice Louis Brandeis once said, "but we can't have both." During the thirty-five years between the 1940s and the mid-1970s, a time when unions and consumer groups were vibrant enough to restrain the ambitions of Big Business, the gap between the rich and the middle class was either shrinking or stable. But by 2021, four decades after corporations came to power in Washington, the United States had become more economically unequal than just about any other developed country in the world—a nation where the top 1 percent of all households held fifteen times the combined wealth of those in the bottom 50 percent.[29] And while more recent research suggests that the gap in income inequality in America may have peaked[30]— thanks to the labor market disruptions that accompanied the pandemic recovery[31]—it remains alarmingly wide.

Academics have found evidence indicating that economically unequal nations can be less socially cohesive, more politically polarized, less stable, and more vulnerable to revolution—the sorts of places where a mob of extremists might internalize a lie about a stolen election, storm the seat of government, and violently attempt to prevent the transfer of power to a duly elected president. Indeed, as the roughly forty years of outsized corporate influence worked to decouple the actions of America's policy makers from the opinions of its citizens, people of all political persuasions began to surrender their faith in democracy.[32]

No one ever called the corporate lobby a majority faction, the way James Madison might have. But it did garner a nickname. By the early 1980s, Washingtonians began referring to the modern, pro-business influence- peddling machine by the downtown thoroughfare along which many of the city's marquee lobbying firms were located, K Street. Still, as the writer John Judis noted, K Street's rise was not an inevitability. Nor did anything quite like it exist in other advanced democracies, such as those of Japan and Western Europe, he wrote in his 2000 book *The Paradox of American Democracy.*[33] K Street is a unique manifestation of American ambition, corporate power, and Washington ingenuity. It had to be constructed from the ground up, without blueprints or scale models.

This is a book about the men—for they were almost exclusively men—who built K Street. It follows three lobbying dynasties—one Republican, two Democratic—over the critical period from the 1970s to today, when the modern lobbying industry was created, corporate interests came to power in Washington, and the nature of our economy was fundamentally changed. The patriarch of the first Democratic lobbying dynasty, Tommy Boggs, was the cigar-chomping son of a powerful congressman who set aside his own political ambitions for a life of influence peddling. His prized pupil, Evan Morris, was a wide-eyed upstart determined to surpass the legend of his mentor. Meanwhile, a contemporary of Boggs's, the avant-garde political fixer Tony Podesta, used his experience as a brass-knuckled liberal activist to advance the interests of Wall Street and Silicon Valley. For more than a half century in the nation's capital, these men would help unify a previously fractured business advocacy community, ignite an explosion of political spending in Washington, develop close ties to the administrations of Bill Clinton and Barack Obama, and lead the Democratic Party away from its old friends in organized labor and toward a new set of allies in corporate America.

During this same era, four conservative political operatives—Charlie Black, Paul Manafort, Roger Stone, and Lee Atwater—used their links to the Reagan revolution to erect Washington's signature GOP house of lobbying. Each member of the partnership had his own distinct role: Atwater, the vicious character assassin; Stone, the Watergate-era dirty trickster; Manafort, the Machiavellian mastermind; Black, the elder statesman. Working as a team of campaign strategists and lobbyists, the men would bridge the divide between corporate executives and conservative activists, develop a radical new approach to influence-peddling tactics, provide critical guidance to a young Donald Trump, and help pull the conservative insurgency from the GOP fringes to the Republican mainstream. Decades later, a second-generation member of the family, Jim Courtovich, helped advance the influence industry once again through the newspaper reporters and cable-news celebrities he cultivated while serving as elite Washington's favorite cocktail party host.

Together, the three dynasties represent the triumph and tragedy of

Washington's lobbying industry. In the face of repeated legislative efforts to limit the political clout of corporations, these men helped facilitate K Street's evolution from a tiny club of well-connected insiders to an integrated, state-of-the-art business that was more secretive, lucrative, and effective than ever before. Rather than trying to reach individual members of Congress through envelopes of cash delivered in smoke-filled rooms, modern influence peddlers developed sophisticated strategies for winning the votes of lawmakers by shaping the opinions of their constituents back home in their districts. These innovations transformed what had been a business of personal connections and inside-the-Beltway access into one that deployed advanced media tactics to target ordinary Americans living thousands of miles outside of Washington. As K Street moved away from traditional "inside game" strategies in favor of this more advanced "outside game" approach, old-fashioned shoe-leather lobbyists began teaming up with a full sweep of related professionals—PR gurus, social media experts, political pollsters, data analysts, grassroots organizers—to further the interests of big US corporations and their executives.

While helping to enshrine a nearly four-decade-long period of entrenched corporate influence in Washington, the members of these dynasties succeeded in torpedoing one consumer reform effort after another, killing legislative measures that would have reduced prescription drug prices, expanded access to lower-cost home mortgages, and created a system of national health insurance, among many others. At the same time, they helped Rupert Murdoch establish America's first conservative cable news network, facilitated the emergence of "Too Big to Fail" banks on Wall Street, and assisted the transformation of a politically naïve tech start-up—Google—into the most influential company in Washington. Before long, some of them were exploring their talents outside of the United States, assisting brutal dictators from Zaire to Haiti, securing arms for a guerrilla leader in Angola, and helping a pro-Russian political party rise to power in Ukraine. In return for their efforts, the members of these dynasties achieved social acclaim and opulent wealth. They advised presidents, joined exclusive golf clubs, and amassed collections of modern art, rare wine, and expensive cigars.

But by 2016—amid a groundswell of right-wing populism, left-wing progressivism, and anti–Big Tech fervor—the pro-business alliance that had governed Washington since the late 1970s began coming unglued. The collapse of this pro-business policy consensus was, in a sense, propelled by the extraordinary success of the corporate influence-peddling machine. The same Big Business lobbyists who managed to shape federal policies so as to maximize corporate profits also fueled an angry backlash among the millions of ordinary Americans with neither the clout nor connections to get Washington to pay attention to them. And as this anticorporate blow-back gathered steam, industry lobbyists would be forced to confront the most treacherous political landscape in a generation.

The discord on K Street would coincide with a series of crises for key members of the lobbying industry's foremost dynasties. By the time President Donald Trump left office in January 2021, nearly all of these once high-flying influence peddlers would experience dramatic falls—succumbing to professional miscalculations, personal betrayals, or criminal allegations. One of the lobbyists had his namesake firm ripped away by his own colleagues. Another watched his business shut down altogether. Five came under the scrutiny of federal prosecutors or FBI agents. One went to prison. And, in a tragic illustration of the legacy of K Street, one was found dead at a private golf club located thirty-seven miles outside of Washington, with a bottle of rare wine at his feet and a gunshot wound in his head.

Part I

The Inside Game

1972–1999

October 16, 1972
Chevy Chase, Maryland

It was dark by the time Tommy Boggs got back to his home in Chevy Chase, an upscale enclave located just north of the Washington border. Pulling his car up to the front of the house, he came upon something unusual. A young man was standing alone in his driveway. Tommy recognized him. He was a former aide from Tommy's unsuccessful campaign for Congress. He had an urgent message.

"You probably haven't heard," the former aide said.

"No," Boggs replied, "I haven't heard."[1]

The encounter put an abrupt end to what, until then, had been a delightful evening for Tommy and his wife, Barbara. They'd spent the prior few hours at the seven-acre estate of one of DC's premier young power couples, Wyatt and Nancy Dickerson. Nancy, the pioneering television journalist, and Wyatt, the dashing real estate investor, had established themselves atop the city's glitterati[2] eight years earlier when they'd purchased their thirty-six-room mansion on the banks of the Potomac River, in McLean, Virginia. Situated just thirteen miles northwest of the US Capitol, the property, known as Merrywood, had been the childhood home of Jacqueline Kennedy Onassis; the future First Lady had grown up smacking a fuzzy ball across its tennis courts and splashing in its pool. It was here that John F. Kennedy, then a Massachusetts senator with his eye on the White House, is believed to have written *Profiles in Courage*, the book that would later earn him a Pulitzer Prize,[3] while he was confined to bed following back surgery. After renovating the mansion and adorning it with European antiques, the Dickersons made Merrywood the site of some of the era's most exclusive social events.[4] Invitations to their cocktail and dinner parties were coveted by Washington's social and political elite.

At thirty-two, Boggs was just starting his career as a Washington power broker. His waistline was heavy but not yet bulging. His neatly combed hair was still full and dark. It would be years before descriptions such as "superlobbyist," "the most influential lawyer in the nation's capital," and "the fattest of fat cats" would be attached to his name. Still, even back then, Washington society had good reason to make sure he was on the guest list. Tommy was the only son of Hale Boggs, the Democratic congressman from Louisiana who also served as majority leader, making him the second-highest-ranking member of the House of Representatives. Hale's standing was expected to increase even further in the coming years, when—as Capitol Hill insiders predicted—he succeeded Carl Albert as Speaker of the House.

Arriving at Merrywood, Tommy and his wife entered the redbrick, federal-style mansion and greeted their hosts. The event was a gathering of investors in the Palm restaurant, a New York City steakhouse that, at the suggestion of George H. W. Bush, then the US ambassador to the United Nations, had decided[5] to open a location in an emerging center of US economic power: downtown Washington. Following its launch two months later, in December 1972, the Palm would become Washington's premier power lunch spot and the preferred watering hole for Boggs and other A-list power brokers. After an evening of stiff drinks and insider gossip with the Dickersons and their guests, Tommy and Barbara said their good-byes and returned to their car. They departed the sweeping estate, headed east into the Maryland side of the Washington suburbs, and arrived back at their home in Chevy Chase.

It was then that Tommy found the young man in his driveway with an urgent message:

"Your dad's plane is missing."[6]

Carl Albert had been trying to reach Tommy all night. The House Speaker was desperate to make sure that Tommy's mother, Lindy Boggs, heard the news from one of her children and not some TV news anchor.[7] To track down Tommy, Albert had even conscripted the White House operators, who were famous for being able to locate public officials during all manner of emergencies: in October 1962, when President John F. Kennedy needed Hale Boggs at the White House to help the administration manage the Cuban missile crisis, the operators got ahold of him while he was on a fishing boat in the Gulf of Mexico.[8] But since the Boggs's babysitter didn't know where Tommy and Barbara had spent their evening, no one could find the couple. Around nine o'clock, the Speaker couldn't wait any longer. He had to call Lindy.

Lindy and Hale Boggs lived in a white brick house on a leafy boulevard in Bethesda, Maryland, just two and a half miles west of Tommy's place. Alongside their white-columned, center-hall colonial was a half acre of secluded land where Hale grew his sweet corn and the couple hosted their annual garden parties. Earlier that year, some 2,100 guests—lawmakers, aides, journalists—had crammed into their backyard for what was considered, at the time, the largest private party in the region's history. President Lyndon B. Johnson had once led a team of Secret Service agents onto this same lawn, turning up for the wedding reception of Lindy and Hale's oldest daughter, Barbara.[9]

While Tommy was at Merrywood, Lindy was writing letters at her kitchen table, according to a detailed account in Burt Solomon's book *The Washington Century*. As she waited to hear from her husband, the family dog had fallen asleep at her feet.[10] A day earlier, Hale had reluctantly flown to Anchorage to headline a pair of fund-raisers for a Democratic colleague who was facing a difficult election, Alaska representative Nick Begich. Hale hated the thought of adding the 3,500-mile journey to his already exhausting workload, but as the majority leader, he told a lobbyist at a dinner the night before the trip, "it's my duty." The trip would be quick, at least; just two days long. Hale was scheduled to return home that night. But as the evening wore on with no word from him, Lindy grew drowsy from the warmth of the fireplace and put her head down on the table. The ring of the telephone jolted her awake. It was Speaker Albert. He explained how he'd tried to reach Tommy and that he hated to be the one to tell her this, but there was a problem with Hale's plane.[11]

Hale's first fund-raising event in Alaska, which took place the prior evening, had been a nice success, bringing in $22,500 for Begich's campaign coffers. The speeches, however, had gone on longer than expected, and the next morning the congressmen were too tired to catch their commercial flight to Juneau, where the second fund-raiser was being held. Instead, Hale and Begich drove to the airport later that day and chartered a private jet for the 570-mile trip to the Alaskan capital. The flight should have taken an hour and a half. But their twin-engine Cessna had never arrived in Juneau. By the time Speaker Albert reached Lindy, Hale had been missing for eight hours. No messages had been received from the pilot. And the weather had turned nasty.

"Oh, Carl!" Lindy responded.[12]

As soon as the former campaign aide told him what happened, Tommy sped down Bradley Boulevard and turned into his parents' long, winding driveway. He found his mother in her bed. She was stunned—not fully capable of absorbing the news. Tommy explained how sorry he was that he hadn't been able to deliver the news himself. "Oh, Mom," he said. "It's so unfair to you."[13]

After details of Hale's missing plane were broadcast on the ten o'clock news, the Boggs house came alive with activity, as Lindy recalled in her memoir, *Washington Through a Purple Veil*. The disappearance of the second most powerful man in the House of Representatives was the biggest news story in America. Liz Carpenter, who served as press secretary for former First Lady "Lady Bird" Johnson, drove over and began fielding questions from the reporters who showed up at the front door.[14] The family's parish priest, Father Gingrich, arrived. Lindy spoke with the US Air Force and Coast Guard officials who were coordinating the search; so far, they'd been able to get only one plane in the air before the fog grew too dense.

Before long, a crowd of friends, neighbors, and family was stirring anxiously beside the framed photographs of Hale with Lyndon Johnson and Hale with John F. Kennedy. The phone rang nonstop, and a second line was soon installed. Former vice president Hubert Humphrey and Massachusetts Senator Edward Kennedy each called, separately, to say they'd flown with the man piloting Hale's plane. He was a top-notch navigator, they insisted. Alaska's first-term Republican senator, Ted Stevens, phoned to urge the family not to give up hope, explaining that he'd survived a plane crash in Alaska himself.* Another Republican, Michigan congressman Gerald Ford, who would become president in less than two years, called frequently to check in on Lindy and the family.[15]

As pots of black coffee brewed in the kitchen, Lindy summoned the strength to reassure her worried guests. President Richard Nixon was arranging for a military jet to fly the family to Alaska, and the federal government was set to deploy seventy aircraft, four Coast Guard ships, as well as mountaineers and divers in its effort to bring Hale to safety. It would be the largest search-and-rescue mission in American history. "Look, now," Lindy told the crowd of friends and family, "they're going to find him."[16]

By daybreak, the house had finally emptied. Lindy poured herself a glass of sherry and took a seat in the den. Tommy rested on the sofa beside her. For Hale's wife and son, it must have seemed like a particularly cruel time for all this to happen. After all the gossip and bad press, the burdens that once imperiled Hale's career had finally lifted. Over the past year and a half, the FBI had wrapped up its corruption probe, prosecutors had decided against bringing an indictment, and the fifty-eight-year-old congressman had found a way to manage his drinking. When he left for Dulles Airport less than forty-eight hours earlier, Hale Boggs wasn't just the future Speaker of the House, he was a happy man once again. But now Lindy and Tommy were wide awake at dawn, wondering if they'd ever see him again.

Eventually Lindy walked out of the room and left Tommy alone with his thoughts. He clenched his fists and grunted in anger.

"Son of a bitch," he muttered.[17] "Son of a bitch."

• • •

*In 2010 Stevens would die in a plane crash in Alaska himself.

Although he had not yet established himself as "the King of K Street," Tommy Boggs's insider pedigree had already set him apart from other DC lobbyists. With his mother's ancestors having held public office since the early seventeenth century,[18] and his father serving as an influential member of Congress, Tommy had grown up amid the romance of post–World War II Washington. He'd watched presidential State of the Union addresses from the House gallery, skipped school to attend important congressional debates, and found figures such as House Speaker Sam Rayburn and Texas Senator Lyndon B. Johnson sitting around his childhood dinner table.[19] In college, Tommy landed a part-time job as the private elevator operator for the Speaker of the House. To the lawmakers on Capitol Hill, he was known simply as "Hale's boy."[20]

After leaving public service, Tommy found another way to make an imprint on Washington. By studying how government power had transferred from the White House to Congress in the years after the Watergate scandal and learning how to organize rival business interests into unified lobbying coalitions, he helped lead the political-influence industry out of its primitive state. He would empower corporate executives to confront—and ultimately vanquish—their political adversaries in organized labor, consumer activism, and the environmental movement. "In some ways," as the *New York Times* put it in 1979, "Mr. Boggs now has as much influence over the decision-making process in Washington as if he had been elected."[21]

His power of persuasion was the stuff of legend; Boggs once convinced a senator to tank a major piece of legislation through a conversation at the lawmaker's wife's bedside in a Washington-area cancer ward. Yet despite his soft-spoken charisma and passion for the nuances of policy, Tommy's effectiveness as a lobbyist was rooted in his illustrious family tree. As the only son of Congressman Hale Boggs, Tommy acquired the influential friends, interpersonal gravitas, and political wisdom needed to broker complex legislative compromises. "Everything I know," Tommy once told a colleague, "I learned from my dad." The disappearance of Hale's plane, somewhere over the Alaskan wilderness in the fall of 1972, would serve as the defining trauma of Tommy's life. "Tommy was old enough and Hale was young enough that they had a relationship other than just father and son," his wife, Barbara, said in an interview with the author Burt Solomon for his book *The Washington Century*.[22] Then came an incident that "was so traumatic and unexpected and unnecessary."

Said Linda Lipsen, the head of the trial lawyers lobby and a longtime client of Tommy's: "It was a hole that was never filled."

The episode was more than a personal tragedy. Over the prior thirty years, Congressman Hale Boggs had worked to burrow the values of New Deal liberalism deep into the Washington firmament. With the backing of a then thriving union movement, Hale helped his Democratic colleagues erect a succession of brand-new regulatory bodies—from the Environmental Protection Agency (EPA) to the Occupational Safety and Health Administration (OSHA)—and provide public officials with a more muscular set of tools to rein in the power of free-market capitalism. In the wake of his father's disappearance, Tommy would pursue the opposite agenda, using his clout as a corporate lobbyist to roll back regulations, increase the political influence of business executives, and discredit the very notion that the government had a legitimate role to play in the private economy.

Though it didn't seem so at the time, it was then, during the first few agonizing hours of waiting for updates on the search for Hale's plane, that the Boggs family's legacy began to change. As a three-decade-long tradition of government activism and consumer reform vanished into the Alaskan skyline, the Boggs name would soon find itself affixed to Washington's premier Democratic lobbying dynasty. And through the efforts of Tommy, it would eventually become synonymous with PAC donations, duck hunting trips, and the outsized sway of corporations in Washington.

"I love the game," Boggs once told a reporter. "Always loved the game."

It began on a fraternity dance floor. During the opening week of rush season in 1934, Lindy Claiborne arrived at the Beta Theta Pi house at Tulane University, in New Orleans, for a fraternity dance. Then a sixteen-year-old freshman at Tulane's sister school, Newcomb College for women, Lindy was a petite southern lady of impeccable manners and understated moxie; she lied about her age to Newcomb's admissions officer in order to gain entry a year earlier than allowed. Her grace and pluck were rooted in imperial stock. Her earliest ancestor in the New World, William Claiborne, had emigrated from England to Jamestown, Virginia, in 1621, and he later became the first white settler to colonize Maryland. From there, each subsequent generation of Claibornes had sent at least one family member into public office. Thomas Claiborne, a congressman from Virginia, had fought with General Andrew Jackson in the Creek War of 1813–14. William Charles Cole Claiborne was the first governor of the Louisiana Territory. At the fraternity house, Lindy began dancing with a tall, handsome young man with blue eyes and wavy, brown hair. He guided her awkwardly across the floor, and then, in a soft voice, he made a daring promise: "I'm going to marry you someday."[23]

Lindy was speechless. When their dance ended and the two parted ways, according to her memoir, she wondered aloud, "Who was that crazy boy?"[24]

At eighteen, Hale Boggs was also just starting his freshman year of college. He'd been the golden boy of Long Beach High School, in Mississippi, just across the Gulf from New Orleans, earning high marks, arguing at the statewide debate championship, and serving as president of his senior class. Hale won the New Orleans *Times-Picayune*'s essay contest so frequently that the newspaper had to implement a rule preventing first-prize winners from submitting entries in consecutive weeks.[25] When Tulane's president saw Hale's academic record and learned of his family's financial troubles, he awarded him a four-year scholarship. Hale's family had once been nearly as prominent as Lindy's. One early ancestor, who owned an island in the Gulf of Mexico, had alerted Andrew Jackson to the British warships that were cruising toward New Orleans in 1814. Hale's father, though, was less commercially minded; he worked as a farmer, a dairyman, and then a bank cashier, but he could never bring in enough to make Hale and his five siblings comfortable. Eventually the Great Depression put Hale's father out of work,[26] and the family moved from one neighborhood to the next, ducking angry landlords when they couldn't scrape together the rent.[27]

Lindy and Hale got to know each other better through their work on Tulane's campus newspaper, the *Hullabaloo*; she was the women's news editor, and he was the editor in chief. Among his fraternity brothers, Hale earned the nickname "the Senator," and, on the editorial page, he regularly blasted Louisiana's iron-fisted political boss, Huey Long.[28] After college, Hale and Lindy got married and had a little girl, Barbara. To support his young family while he decided what to do with his life, Hale took a job at one of New Orleans's local newspapers, the *Daily States*. But when he told the editor he wanted a full-time position, the man said, "Too bad. You're fired." Hale's talents would be wasted in journalism, he was told.[29]

After graduating from Tulane University's law school, Hale decided to take on Long's corrupt political empire more directly. In 1940 he challenged Representative Paul Maloney, a five-term incumbent backed by the Long machine, for the congressional seat representing New Orleans. Wearing a white linen suit and casting his deep baritone voice, Hale lambasted Maloney as a "tool of the Long dictatorship" with nothing to show for his decade in Washington.[30] Amid a wave of reformist energy, Hale took the election by a comfortable margin.

Eight days later, Lindy gave birth to her second child, Tommy. It had been a difficult delivery, as little Tommy's breathing was strained, and his legs were weak. Doctors found a problem with his thymus gland and recommended what was then a novel treatment: radiation. "It was a difficult decision for Hale and me to make," Lindy wrote later.[31] "But we took a chance with the hope of a normal life for Tommy." The gamble paid off: Tommy soon began putting on weight and gaining strength. Before long, the little boy was, as his mother put it, "as round as he is tall." At just twenty-six, Hale was set to become the youngest Democrat in the House of Representatives. But even more than that, he and his young family were about to realize the campaign slogan that he'd borrowed from the popular 1939 Jimmy Stewart movie: "Mr. Boggs Goes to Washington."[32]

On a sunny, frigid morning in January 1941, Hale and Lindy crammed into a crowd of spectators near the East Portico of the US Capitol Building, about a block off the National Mall, as the infantry troops and West Point cadets strutted down Pennsylvania Avenue.[33] Lindy and the kids had joined Hale in Washington just in time for the third inauguration of the couple's political hero, President Franklin D. Roosevelt. The brand-new congressman and his wife had been inspired by the unprecedented measures that FDR had taken to rescue the economy from the Great Depression, and they looked on with approval as members of two popular New Deal jobs programs, the National Youth Administration and the Civilian Conservation Corps, marched in the inaugural parade.[34] As war raged in Europe and draft-age Americans worried about their futures, President Roosevelt appeared atop the marble steps of the Capitol. He needed both hands to steady himself at the podium, on account of his legs, long since paralyzed by polio, as he tried to encourage a jittery nation. "Democracy," he insisted, "is not dying."

Though their first election victories were eight years apart, both FDR and Hale Boggs had arrived in Washington by way of the same political riptide. In 1932, during the doldrums of the Depression, a diverse assortment of previously unallied Americans—union members, Blacks, religious minorities, recent immigrants, and southerners[35]—had joined forces to effectuate the most consequential political realignment since the Civil War. This so-called New Deal coalition would put FDR in the White House, precipitate an almost fifty-year stretch of nearly uninterrupted Democratic control of both chambers of Congress, and provide the popular support for an extraordinary expansion of the federal enterprise. It was during this period that voters grew increasingly enamored with politicians like Hale Boggs—Democrats who believed that government should use its power to protect ordinary citizens from the excesses of capitalism and help improve the lives of the disadvantaged and the poor.

While juggling the duties of a congressional spouse and mother of two, Lindy became accustomed to the unique rituals of political life in Washington. When she arrived late to a White House garden party—a serious embarrassment—Lindy apologized repeatedly to Eleanor Roosevelt and explained that she'd had to care for her little boy, Tommy, who was suffering from teething pains. "I'm glad somebody has her priorities straight," the First Lady responded.[36] Lindy made friends with the wives of other southern Democrats, such as Lady Bird Johnson and Pauline Gore, the wife of Senator Al Gore Sr. and mother of future Vice President Al Gore Jr. At the end of the workday, she often picked up Hale from his congressional office in the family's Pontiac. One evening, while she waited for her husband to finish up, she walked onto the lawn and stared admiringly at the Capitol dome. Then she heard a man's voice beside her: "Isn't that the most beautiful sight in the world?" It was Sam Rayburn, the Speaker of the House—one of the most influential men in Washington at a time when power was concentrated in the hands of the president and a few congressional leaders. He liked to step outside and gaze up at the rotunda when the pressures of leadership got to him.[37]

Rayburn, a taciturn Texan, had spotted potential in Hale the moment he stepped onto Capitol Hill. The freshman lawmaker was a soaring orator with magnetic charisma. He handed out sweet corn from his garden to his aides,[38] and the congressional secretaries—whom Hale always addressed as "Beautiful"[39]—once voted him the most charming member of the House. But in Hale, the Speaker found something even more valuable: loyalty. He considered the young southerner a dutiful soldier who could be counted on to vote for the Speaker's priorities. Rayburn began inviting Hale to his "Board of Education" meetings,[40] where a small group of Democratic lawmakers convened around five o'clock several days a week in the Speaker's hideaway office to drink liquor, play cards, and discuss votes. Over time, the childless and unmarried Rayburn became something of a surrogate father to the upstart lawmaker. "He more or less adopted me," Hale said.[41]

The Boggs children, who grew to three in number with the birth of their youngest sibling, Corrine "Cokie" Boggs, were raised on insider politics. Decades before becoming a cohost of ABC-TV's Sunday political talk show *This Week*, Cokie celebrated her seventh birthday in the Speaker's dining room, and towering Washington figures were constantly dropping by their house. Texas congressman Lyndon B. Johnson, whom Hale got to know through Rayburn's "Board of Education," was a frequent dinner guest. After Cokie's pet chicken, Charlie, was killed by a stray neighborhood dog, Speaker Rayburn—"Mr. Sam" to the kids—presided over the backyard funeral.[42] And when Lindy was confined to bed after contracting hepatitis from a blood transfusion, Hale decided to cheer her up by bringing over one of his buddies from Congress who'd recently recovered from the same illness: John F. Kennedy.[43]

Strong personal relationships were central to Hale's growing influence in Washington. As a close friend of both Kennedy and Johnson, he played a decisive, behind-the-scenes role in forging their historic political partnership. On the day that Kennedy received the Democratic nomination for president, at the party's 1960 convention in Los Angeles, Hale learned that Johnson had been offered the vice presidency. There was just one catch: Johnson would accept the position only if Speaker Rayburn supported the decision. Rayburn, however, thought the move would be disastrous; Americans would never elect a Catholic president, he believed, and Johnson's ties to the doomed campaign would imperil his career. It was Hale who changed Rayburn's mind,[44] arguing that by joining the presidential ticket, Johnson could deliver the South for Kennedy and keep Richard Nixon out of the Oval Office.

As his pals moved into the White House, Hale ascended the congressional leadership ladder. When Rayburn died from cancer in 1961, House Speaker William McCormack made Hale his majority whip, the third-ranking member of the House leadership. Other Boggs family members gained influence as well. Lindy served as cochair of Kennedy's inaugural ball,[45] and the couple's eldest daughter, Barbara, joined Kennedy's staff, where she wrote letters to constituents and performed other tasks.[46] On one occasion, at Barbara's behest, Kennedy's aides borrowed Lindy's silverware in order to prepare a proper southern breakfast for the Yankee president.[47] In November 1963 Hale and other House leaders had breakfast with JFK in the White House, and, afterward, the president took Hale and Lindy outside[48] to show them the recently redesigned Rose Garden.

"Lindy," Kennedy asked, "how long do chrysanthemums bloom in Washington in the fall?"

"Well, until the first frost."

"Oh, I hope the first frost comes late this year."[49]

Two weeks later, the president was dead, assassinated in Dallas. Hale was among the handful of somber congressmen assembled at Andrews Air Force Base, just hours after the shooting, in suburban Maryland, when Air Force One returned from Dallas carrying Kennedy's body and America's new president, Lyndon Johnson. Standing on the tarmac, Hale watched officials slide the coffin into an ambulance as Jacqueline Kennedy disembarked from the plane in a bloodstained pink suit. Around seven thirty that evening, Hale and eight other congressional leaders met Johnson in the Old Executive Office Building, next to the White House. "I am president in a way that no man would ever want to become president," Johnson told them.[50] "But I am president."

When the meeting ended, Hale wished his old friend well. "God bless you, Mr. President."[51]

Though Tommy Boggs had known Lyndon Johnson for the better part of his life, he hadn't really become friendly with the tall, swaggering Texan until his father arranged a part-time job for him in Congress in the late 1950s. His job as an operator of a private elevator[52] for Speaker Sam Rayburn put him on a first-name basis with lawmakers all over Capitol Hill. Boggs ran into Johnson, then the majority leader in the Senate, nearly every day. When Congress was in session, Johnson liked to stop by Rayburn's hideaway office around eight thirty at night for a couple of drinks. After an hour or so of chatting, Johnson would fix himself a final, tall glass of Cutty Sark scotch—"one for the road,"[53] in Boggs's telling—say good-bye to his colleagues, and walk back toward the elevator.

"Come on, Tommy," Johnson would say. "Carry this out to the car with me. I don't want to be seen running around Congress with a glass of [scotch] in my hand."[54] Tommy would hold the drink as discreetly as possible, as he walked Johnson down to the parking garage and then watched the future president drive off.

Like his father and his Claiborne ancestors, Tommy Boggs wanted a life in politics. After having developed the chummy relationship with Johnson, Tommy started doing advance work for his unsuccessful 1960 presidential campaign. Though not yet old enough to vote, he traveled with Johnson's team to New York and convinced volunteers to campaign on commuter trains so that they could reach more people. When he finished college in 1961, he joined the staff of the Senate's Joint Committee on Economics, while also attending Georgetown Law School at night. But he soon drifted back to Johnson's orbit, joining the White House in January 1964. Though technically a special assistant to the head of the Office of Emergency Planning, he functioned as a political aide to the president, spending most of his time handling logistics for Johnson's public appearances.

One of his first assignments was to help organize the new president's 1964 trip to Appalachia[55] as part of his war on poverty. That fall, Tommy traveled to Harrisburg, Pennsylvania, to prepare for the first public event of Johnson's reelection campaign. However, not even the Boggs family name could protect him from Johnson's temper. After Tommy was quoted giving details of the president's Harrisburg visit to a local newspaper, he received an irate phone call at six o'clock in the morning.

"*I'm* supposed to announce what I'm doing!"[56] Johnson barked. "Not you!"

Nevertheless, Tommy loved the work; it gave him a firsthand look at the scope of the White House's power. On one occasion, he used his authority to uproot a tree[57]—over the objections of the town's mayor—that would have blocked the president's view of spectators. Between the contacts he made in the White House and his family friends in Congress, he was developing into one of Washington's best-wired young operators. There was just one problem: the salary. Tommy had married his wife at age twenty while still in college; his mother and her best friend had set them up in what Tommy's sister once called "the only arranged marriage in the twentieth century." Now twenty-six, he and Barbara had two children and a third on the way, and he didn't think he could continue to support them on $10,500 a year. "[I] needed to make some money," he told a journalist.

In 1966, after fifteen months in the job, Tommy told the president he was leaving the White House for a more lucrative career.

Johnson wished his young sidekick "all the luck in the world."[58]

At the time, Washington's influence business was ruled by a small collection of masters-of-the-universe-type insiders who slipped in and out of government and called in favors from their powerful friends. While they couldn't introduce amendments or call up a bill for a vote, members of this permanent shadow government could bend federal policy in their clients' direction through a well-timed phone call or a private chat at a cocktail party. Tommy "the Cork" Corcoran, for example, was a Wall Street lawyer turned trusted aide to Franklin D. Roosevelt. During his seven years in the administration, he accompanied FDR to social events, drafted Depression-era banking laws, and crafted some of the president's most enduring speeches. It was Corcoran who authored the celebrated line from Roosevelt's 1936 address to the Democratic Convention in Philadelphia: "To some generations, much is given. Of other generations, much is expected. This generation has a rendezvous with destiny."[59]

Upon leaving the White House in 1940, Corcoran emerged as one of DC's first mega lobbyists. He derived his power from his ties to the men who ran Washington; during his years in the White House, Corcoran had played a role in the hiring of virtually every senior administration official, and he'd established a close personal relationship with President Roosevelt himself—indispensable friendships for an influence peddler on the make. The Cork didn't advertise his business, he kept his number out of the phone book, and he worked out of a small office with no nameplate above the door. Still, businessmen seeking help in Washington learned how to find him. One of his early clients, the industrialist Henry Kaiser, came to Corcoran looking for a way to profit off the American mobilization for World War II. Corcoran used his government contacts to broker a meeting between Kaiser and the US War Production Board that resulted in $645 million worth of federal contracts to build shipyards.[60] Corcoran earned $90,000 from that deal alone, and he went on to make a then-staggering sum of $1 million in his first year in business.

When Presidents Kennedy and Johnson took office, each sought Corcoran's guidance as one of the few Washington operatives with years of experience running the White House. Over the following decades, Corcoran used those relationships and his detailed knowledge of how to work the federal bureaucracy to benefit giant American companies such as Pan American Airways, El Paso Natural Gas Company, and United Fruit Company. His most effective tactics remained his most straightforward. In the early 1970s, representatives of a tool and die company arrived at Corcoran's office and explained that due to a welding problem, they were in jeopardy of losing their contract to make barrels for the US Department of Defense.

"Let me make a telephone call," Corcoran told the men, according to David McKean's *Tommy the Cork: Washington's Ultimate Insider from Roosevelt to Reagan.*

"Should we leave?" one of the executives asked.

"No, no. Stay put," Corcoran said, waving at them to sit down.

Corcoran picked up the phone, asked to be connected to a Defense Department official, had a brief conversation, and hung up.

"It's settled," he said. "Your problems are over."

The executives left his office, and, days later, they received an invoice for $10,000 payable to Tommy Corcoran.

The tall, dashing Clark Clifford was another legendary influencer of the era. A native of President Harry Truman's home state of Missouri, Clifford ran his own law practice before enlisting in the navy during World War II. When Truman tapped a friend from Missouri to serve as his naval aide, Clifford tagged along to Washington. He joined the White House as its legal counsel, became a close confidant of the president's, and drafted the legislation establishing the secretary of defense and creating the Central Intelligence Agency. Perhaps more important to his future career in lobbying, Clifford was put in charge of Truman's regular poker game.[61] He arranged for a rotating cast of Washington luminaries—Supreme Court Chief Justice Fred Vinson, Commerce Secretary W. Averell Harriman, Lyndon Johnson, among others—to float down the Potomac River on the presidential yacht, the USS *Williamsburg*, as they sipped bourbon, cracked jokes, and played cards. Truman, FDR's new running mate in 1944, had served as vice president for only three months when Franklin D. Roosevelt died suddenly of a cerebral hemorrhage in April 1945, catapulting Truman into the presidency. He was widely expected to lose reelection in 1948. But after Truman pulled off an upset victory over New York governor Thomas Dewey, Clifford was credited as the campaign's strategic mastermind and came to be viewed as the central nervous system of the White House.

Departing the administration in 1950, Clifford opened a legal practice and fashioned himself into the quintessential Washington wise man for hire. Before long, he was raking in lucrative fees from an elite roster of clients, including General Electric Co., Trans World Airlines, and Standard Oil of California.[62] In the early 1960s he tapped his vast network of allies in the Kennedy administration to slip a change into the law that saved $500 million in taxes for chemical conglomerate DuPont by allowing the firm to write off a huge fine, according to *Friends in High Places*, by Douglas Frantz and David McKean. Clifford's fee: nearly $1 million.[63] Though Clifford, like Corcoran, remained an effective political problem solver into the early 1970s, his playbook never changed; his entire business model revolved around his ability to land favors from influential friends in the executive branch. On one occasion, according to K Street lore, an attorney for a Midwest corporation reached out to Clifford and asked what his company should do about a tax bill that was pending in Congress.

Several weeks later, Clifford sent the lawyer a telegram with his response: "Do nothing." He then sent the company a bill for $20,000.

The attorney was furious. He demanded a more thorough explanation of the do-nothing strategy. Clifford sent another response: "Because I said so."

He followed up with a bill for an additional $5,000.[64]

Despite the outsized clout of a handful of well-connected men, Washington's influence business was still in its Stone Age. In 1961 a total of only 130 American companies had retained lobbyists of any kind. Of those, just 50 opened offices in Washington[65] to give their lobbyists a base of operations; most of these firms were in heavily regulated industries, such as telecommunications, broadcasting, and defense contracting, which required frequent contact with the government. These influence peddlers largely ignored the lawmakers on Capitol Hill. One study published in 1964 found that of the 166 large companies that the researchers examined, only 22 percent had made any contact at all with Congress during the prior two years.[66] The bulk of corporate representatives in Washington were there not to influence lawmakers but to try to sell products to Uncle Sam.[67] At most corporations, postings in the nation's capital were among the least desirable. "The Washington office," a Conference Board researcher wrote of this period, "used to be the place where you shipped your soon-to-retire executive." The small amount of lobbying that businesses did conduct was carried out primarily through trade associations,[68] which pressed government officials—mostly unsuccessfully—to rein in new industry regulations and curb the strength of organized labor unions. But the business community's leading advocacy groups, the US Chamber of Commerce and the National Association of Manufacturers, had small staffs, little funding, and even less influence on political decision-making.

Corporate America's disregard for Washington was, at the time, perfectly rational. The country's unprecedented economic boom of the 1950s and 1960s had wiped away nearly all major political threats to corporate profit growth.[69] As Europe and Japan struggled to rebuild their infrastructures and economies from the devastation of World War II, America's fast-growing manufacturing sector[70] made it a global economic powerhouse; from 1947 to 1973, the nation's gross domestic product exploded by a factor of six and the median income doubled.[71] In this twenty-six-year stretch, the average American family accumulated more purchasing power than it had gained during all 197 prior years of the country's history combined.[72] Some historians refer to this period as the Golden Age of Capitalism. Edward Heath, Great Britain's prime minister in the early seventies, called it "the greatest prosperity the world has ever known." As corporate revenues soared, the leading business executives in the United States reached a pivotal conclusion. They decided that their interests would be best served by making peace with their traditional adversaries.[73]

Since the start of the Industrial Age, the struggle between organized labor and corporate management had been the defining conflict of America's economy. But not long after World War II, the battle began to de-escalate. In 1950, for example, GM's leadership chose to accommodate—rather than fight—its largest labor union, the United Automobile Workers, reaching a historic compromise that came to be known as the Treaty of Detroit. In return for pledging not to strike, workers received an unusually generous five-year contract that provided annual wage increases, cost-of-living adjustments, health care benefits, a pension, and other perks.[74] Such agreements became increasingly common at US manufacturing firms, and they emerged as a defining feature of the "capital-labor accord" that marked the post–World War II era.[75] Corporate managers "wanted to make the labor movement tolerable and manageable," wrote the historian Howell John Harris, "and then to live with it, not to destroy it."[76]

Likewise, throughout most of American history, wealthy industrialists had fiercely resisted efforts to widen the government's authority. Even during the Great Depression, when the public was desperate for assistance, some business leaders maintained their opposition. But many others revised their thinking and became willing to back—or at least accept—the New Deal's historic expansion of the federal enterprise.[77] The corporate community's accommodation of Washington's growth continued during and after the Second World War. As President Johnson pushed to enact his Great Society initiatives, for example, Big Business chose to avoid open conflict with the government. Instead, corporate executives resolved not to resist—and in some cases even support—the key increases in federal power that accrued in the mid-1960s.[78] No major corporate leader opposed the passage of Medicare, federal aid to education, or the war on poverty. With the exception of those in the South, most businesses didn't try to stop the passage of the landmark 1964 Civil Rights Act,[79] despite the cumbersome new restrictions it placed on the handling of internal personnel matters.[80] The country's most sweeping protections for the air and water were signed into law by a Republican president, Richard Nixon, who created the Environmental Protection Agency. Top executives at twenty-two firms—including Standard Oil of California, General Electric, and Chase Manhattan Bank—signed a letter supporting a 1966 bill providing federal funds to redevelop urban slums.[81] And in 1970 a survey of 270 Fortune 500 CEOs found that nearly 60 percent believed that government environmental regulatory activities should actually be *increased*.[82]

As Richard Barber wrote in the *New Republic* in 1966, "a new breed of corporate executive is on the scene, professionally trained and more oriented to the science of management than to the perpetuation of an ideology which looks upon government as intrinsically evil. The modern company officer accepts government (much like he accepts the labor movement) and works actively with it."[83]

The corporate accommodation of labor unions and the government was a linchpin of the so-called liberal consensus[84] that emerged during the postwar years. As the economy continued to boom, activist federal regulators and a thriving labor movement served as "countervailing" forces that checked the power of corporations and compelled business executives to recognize—albeit grudgingly[85]—the legitimacy of collective bargaining, the welfare state, and federal intervention in the economy.[86] Though this measured detente[87] was brokered by a corporate establishment that was more moderate and pragmatic than today's, CEOs also had the best of all reasons to share power with their rivals. "What the hell," one executive told *Newsweek* magazine. "Business is making money."[88]

It was as close to James Madison's vision for healthy interest group competition as the United States had ever achieved.[89] But in the very same year that Tommy Boggs departed the White House, this equilibrium of power began to unravel. And it all became clear by way of an upstart consumer activist and an improbable case of mistaken identity.

During a trip to Des Moines, Iowa, in January 1966, Ralph Nader began to grow suspicious. The same man, he noticed, kept reappearing at different times and in different locations inside the Kirkwood Hotel, where he was staying. Nader spotted the man two times on the hotel's ground floor and once upstairs, near the door to his room. It wasn't only the multiple sightings that unnerved Nader, but also the stranger's ominous demeanor. Nader began to wonder if he was being followed.[90]

For most of his thirty-one years, Nader, a lanky Harvard-trained lawyer, had attracted little notice. But just six weeks before he arrived in Des Moines, the publication of his book *Unsafe at Any Speed: The Designed-in Dangers of the American Automobile*, had touched off a public relations nightmare for one of America's most powerful industries. At a time when traffic fatalities were climbing to record highs, Nader's book argued that a particular model of General Motors vehicles, the Chevrolet Corvair, was more likely to spin out of control due to a suspension flaw. Through meticulous research, he argued credibly that Detroit's auto giants were accumulating their massive revenues at the expense of customers' lives. In 1965, for example, Senator Robert Kennedy of New York forced the chairman of General Motors, Frederic Donner, to admit in a committee hearing that, a year before, GM had turned a $1.7 billion profit but spent just $1.25 million on vehicle safety.[91] The book's revelations generated a wave of media coverage,[92] increased congressional scrutiny on the auto industry, and turned Nader, almost overnight, into Detroit's most recognizable critic.

At the invitation of Iowa's attorney general, Nader had come to Des Moines to testify at a series of vehicle safety hearings. He was so rattled by his encounters with the man in his hotel that he reported his concerns to the attorney general. When Nader returned home to Washington, DC, other curious events started to occur.[93] In the days leading up to his appearance at a US Senate hearing on auto safety, he began getting bizarre phone calls, even though his number was unlisted.

"Why don't you change your field of interest?"

"You are fighting a losing battle. You can't win. You can only lose."

"Why don't you go back to Connecticut, buddy boy?"[94]

Around this time, Nader also started receiving phone calls and letters from old professors, colleagues, and classmates congratulating him on his new job opportunity. Nader, confused, inquired as to what they were talking about. As it turned out, a handful of his former teachers and coworkers had been contacted by a man who claimed to be conducting a background investigation of Nader on behalf of a company that was considering hiring him. One former law school classmate was visited by the investigator at his office in Boston. The investigator had thick-framed glasses, and he carried a tan attaché case. He refused to identify the company he represented, and he asked questions that didn't seem to have any bearing on Nader's professional qualifications. He inquired as to whether Nader was involved with any left-wing groups and, referencing his incorrect belief that Nader was of Syrian descent, wondered if he'd ever expressed anti-Semitic views. (Nader's parents were from Lebanon.) He also asked why Nader, a man in his early thirties, had never been married.

"Are you asking me if he's a homosexual?" the friend said.

"Well," the investigator replied, "we have to ask about these things."[95]

No, the friend told the investigator. Nader wasn't gay.

Back in Washington, Nader suddenly found himself attracting more attention from women. While perusing a magazine rack in a drugstore not far from his rooming house, he was approached by a pretty brunette in her twenties. "I know this sounds a little forward," she began, "but can I talk to you?"[96]

She was on her way to meet a group of friends to "discuss foreign affairs,"[97] she claimed. Would Nader like to join? The exchange alarmed Nader; he suspected that he was being lured into a compromising situation. He tried to decline the invitation politely, but the woman was so insistent that he had to walk away. Days later, it happened again. While Nader was shopping at a nearby grocery store, another attractive young woman, a blonde this time, came up to him. She asked if Nader would be kind enough to give her a hand moving "something heavy"[98] into her apartment, which, conveniently, was right around the corner. Though the store was full of other unaccompanied men, she claimed that "there's no one to help me."[99] His suspicions again stirred, he told the woman he had a meeting to attend.

In mid-February 1966 the odd events unfolding around Nader became public through an equally unlikely incident. When Nader entered what is now the Dirksen Senate Office Building for a television interview, a Capitol Police officer noticed two men following him. Police questioned the men and ordered them to leave the building. One officer, however, later mistook a *Washington Post* reporter for Nader. In his confusion, the officer told the reporter that Nader had been under surveillance. "There are a couple of detectives who were tailing a guy who's been writing about auto safety," the cop said.[100]

The *Post* subsequently ran an article about the surveillance of Nader, and other outlets published follow-ups. As the media pressure ratcheted up, General Motors's top executives admitted in March 1966 that they'd initiated a "routine investigation" of their chief critic. The investigation, in fact, had been carried out by a team of former FBI agents, and the attorney who'd orchestrated the probe said that GM wanted "to get something, somewhere, on this guy to get him out of their hair and shut him up."[101] The story exploded into a national scandal, forced GM's president to apologize to a panel of senators,[102] and energized the already spirited effort to regulate the automobile industry. Within six months, President Lyndon Johnson had signed into law the National Traffic and Motor Vehicle Safety Act.

It was a landmark political defeat for America's signature industry. GM, at the time, was the largest corporation in the world, employing a half million people in the United States alone. Yet on Capitol Hill, it had been bested by a single pain-in-the-ass lawyer who rallied American consumers into a powerful political force. Until then, GM and other vehicle manufacturers had been free to decide for themselves whether or not to equip cars with safety features, which they viewed primarily as selling points to attract new customers—not so different from leather seats and dashboard radios. With the passage of the National Traffic and Motor Vehicle Safety Act, the federal government wasn't simply tightening existing oversight; as the author David Vogel pointed out, it was imposing a sweeping new supervisory regime on a business that had never been regulated by the federal government before.[103] The legislation established, for the first time, rigorous national motor vehicle safety standards and resulted in innovations like headrests and shatter-resistant windshields. "The giant, fearsome, incredibly wealthy automobile industry," wrote the journalist Elizabeth Drew, "reluctantly lumbered into the unfamiliar political arena, [and] turned out to be a paper hippopotamus."[104]

How could an economic colossus like GM have been so powerless in Washington? Like the best corporate minds of their generation, the company's leaders had for years viewed federal politics as irrelevant to their firm; they simply couldn't comprehend how DC bureaucrats could impact their bottom line. "One of the serious problems in our industry is provinciality," an auto executive remarked at the time. "The sun rises in Dearborn and sets in Detroit."[105] As such, they'd seen little reason to invest in political influence. Indeed, when Nader's auto safety campaign got under way, GM—the very symbol of American industrial conquest—did not have a single lobbyist in the nation's capital.[106]

It was an unfortunate time for America's business establishment to lack political strength. The National Traffic and Motor Vehicle Safety Act was, as it turned out, the opening salvo in what would become a historic expansion of federal authority over corporate behavior.[107] From 1965 to 1977, Congress passed, and the president signed, forty-four major regulatory bills[108] that imposed strict constraints on how business executives could build their products, manage their employees, and treat the environment. Between 1970 and 1975, spending by social regulatory agencies nearly tripled to $4.3 billion,[109] while the size of the *Federal Register*—which details the country's laws and regulations—exploded from twenty thousand pages to sixty thousand.[110] Vigorous new bureaucracies, such as the Occupational Safety and Health Administration, the Environmental Protection Agency, and the US Consumer Product Safety Commission, brought an unprecedented level of federal scrutiny into boardrooms and factories. This wave of legislation was, David Vogel observed, an extension of the Great Society's social welfare objectives into the commercial sector, and it structurally changed the government's role in the economy. Officials in Washington were now telling soup manufacturers how to label their ingredients on cans, determining how banks could explain loan terms to borrowers, deciding which pieces of equipment coal executives could install in their mines, and choosing which products could be advertised on television and the radio. (Alcohol, yes; tobacco, no.[111]) "The government is now present," the editors of *Fortune* magazine wrote, "at every major business meeting."[112]

Unlike the New Deal, this period of government growth didn't spring from a specific crisis; it was triggered by revelations about a range of systemic harms that accompanied the ascent of corporate capitalism. Nader's research into GM helped jump-start the public interest movement, while Rachel Carson's 1962 book about the dangers of the pesticide DDT (dichloro-diphenyl-trichloroethane), *Silent Spring*, energized environmental advocates. The public interest and environmental movements swelled into powerful political crusades, disrupting the balance of power that corporations had achieved with the labor unions and the state. Though neither effort had much of a following to speak of in the 1950s, within a decade and a half, Washington was home to more than a hundred public interest groups, and between 1970 and 1971, the country's three leading environmental organizations saw their memberships swell by a third.[113] Alongside their allies in the labor movement, public interest and environmental advocates served as the organizational muscle behind the effort to build out the regulatory state, leading grassroots campaigns, rallies, and other initiatives to increase the government's role in the economy. But the advocates couldn't realize their political agenda on their own. They needed allies on Capitol Hill, and they found a crucial partner who shared similar aims in Louisiana congressman Hale Boggs.

• • • •

In October of 1972, Hale Boggs climbed atop the podium on the House floor to deliver what would turn out to be one of his final sets of formal remarks. It was Hale's duty to address the House chamber at the end of each year to celebrate the body's most significant achievements, and on this day, he lauded his fellow lawmakers for their commitment to environmental protection. "If there is one area in which this Congress can take a greater measure of pride than another," he said, "it lies here." Of particular significance, Hale noted, was the passage of the National Environmental Data System Act, which enhanced the sharing of environmental research; the Pesticide Control Act, which regulated the production and sale of potentially harmful pesticides; and the Federal Water Pollution Control Act Amendments of 1972, which authorized the large-scale funding of clean water programs. "The American people have awakened to the environmental dangers from abuse and neglect," Hale told his colleagues. "We in Congress, sharing that awareness and empowered to protect the general welfare, have responded with an outpouring of legislation over the past few years." Just a few days later, Hale's plane disappeared over the Alaskan wilderness.

During his more than a quarter century in Congress, Boggs often pressed his fellow lawmakers to shield the vulnerable elements of our nation—be it factory workers in Detroit or rivers in Montana—from the destructive power of corporate capitalism. In 1966, for example, he urged his colleagues to pass legislation that would have expanded the federal minimum wage to include an additional eight million Americans. This "is a bill that affects the people, affects human beings, affects families," Hale said on the House floor as lawmakers prepared to vote on it. "It is a minimum bill in a society described as an affluent society. I would hope this House will accept this conference report." In 1969, he touted the Federal Coal Mine Health and Safety Act, saying that by "setting limits on the amount of coal dust permitted in a mine, we have curtailed the threat of black lung disease, incurable and a major cause of death." On another occasion, he extolled the Consumer Product Safety Act, the Auto Safety Act, and the Public Health Cigarette Smoking Act.

More significant than Hale's advocacy for any individual bill, though, was his role in the broader, decadelong effort to expand the federal government's authority. At the time, power in Congress was held mostly by party leaders who took the lead in writing the nation's laws. But those leaders needed rank-and-file lawmakers to vote in large numbers in support. As House majority whip, it was Hale's job to make sure they did. He was responsible for much of the vote counting, arm-twisting, and behind-the-scenes horse trading needed to realize this unprecedented increase in federal power over corporations. David Bunn, a former member of President Johnson's congressional liaison team, described Hale's contribution to the effort as even more critical than the House Speaker's. "It was really Hale Boggs," Bunn recalled, "who produced the votes not only in terms of getting people to the floor but also in pointing out to them all the reasons why they should support the president's program."[114] Said congressional aide Richard Rivers, "He would move through the members in the chamber like a lion through high grass."[115]

While Hale pushed Congress to increase the government's authority over corporations, his son, Tommy, was doing the exact opposite. After graduating from law school and leaving the White House in 1966, Tommy had no trouble breaking into Washington's legal community. Thanks to his father's connections, he had his pick of the city's top law offices; in all, seventeen different firms offered to hire him. But it was a little-known, five-lawyer operation that Tommy found most appealing.

Just four years earlier, a former CIA agent named Jim Patton Jr. had left the city's most esteemed white-shoe firm, Covington & Burling, to launch his own outfit focused on international law. In its early days, Barco, Cook, Patton & Blow provided advice to American companies on their overseas investments. But in the mid-1960s Patton had watched a client's business deal collapse after a competing company pulled strings in Washington and convinced the Export-Import Bank of the United States to withdraw its support. In the deal's implosion, Patton saw an opportunity. He went searching for a different type of legal mind; someone just as comfortable in a congressman's office as they were in a law library. A contact on Capitol Hill gave him Tommy Boggs's name.[116]

This combination of law and policy was perfectly suited for Tommy, and the idea of growing a small firm excited him. But when he told his father his decision, Hale was furious.

"It doesn't make any sense," Hale told him. "You [should] practice law with a major firm in town!"[117]

After making partner, Tommy registered as a lobbyist in 1968 and began working to shield businesses from the onslaught of new regulations that his father was helping to orchestrate. Among his earliest clients was a New Jersey chemical firm that needed assistance managing the Washington bureaucracy and an association of yacht manufacturers that was worried about an onerous new water pollution bill. Tommy approached the US secretary of the interior about tariff issues on behalf of petrochemical companies, and he went to Congress to oppose import quotas for Central American sugar producers.[118] Initially, his influence-peddling efforts weren't terribly aggressive, due in part to his reluctance to use his family connections. "I was very skittish about lobbying when he was there," Tommy said. "I never represented Louisiana clients."

Such apprehensions were not unique to the rookie lobbyist. At the time, the business establishment was largely defenseless against the political power of unions, environmentalists, and public interest advocates. While industry had begun to build out its influence-peddling capabilities, corporations and business groups were still disorganized and ineffective, and they'd responded to the new legislation with confusion and apathy. "The truth is," GM CEO Thomas Murphy told an audience of other top executives, "we have been clobbered."[119]

At the root of this historic expansion of federal regulatory authority was a central faith—on the part of the public, consumer advocates, politicians, and even corporations themselves—that the commercial sector could continue to churn out strong profits even in the face of additional expenses.[120] But as the new regulations began touching every corner of the economy, the costs of compliance became increasingly onerous. Business spending to meet the new air pollution requirements, for instance, surged by 150 percent from 1970 to 1974. That same year, manufacturing firms allocated nearly 11 percent of their capital expenses to pollution controls and safety equipment, a nearly threefold jump from 1969. In other industries, such spending accounted for more than 20 percent of capital budgets.[121]

Higher regulatory costs were just one of the frustrations facing business executives. During the social upheaval of the 1960s, the public began to sour on corporate America; from 1968 to 1970, the share of citizens who agreed with the statement "Business tries to strike a fair balance between profits and the interest of the public" plunged from 70 percent to 33 percent.[122] On college campuses, students increasingly rejected careers on the corporate ladder, which many came to view as conformist, profit obsessed, and indifferent to the plight of the poor. "The field of business is a great wasteland," one student told researchers at Young & Rubicam, the New York–based marketing giant, "inhabited by men of narrow horizons and personal interest, where anticreativity and anti-idealism is the rule and not the exception."[123] In 1966 no more than 18 percent of Stanford University undergraduates planned to launch careers in business. At Princeton University, only 7 percent of seniors intended to take corporate jobs.[124]

As the anti–Vietnam War movement escalated, this distrust of corporations turned hostile. "Why . . . do we continue to demonstrate in Washington as if the core of the problem lay there?" asked the activist Staughton Lynd. "We need to find ways to lay siege to corporations."[125] In the late 1960s, university students organized 183 protests aimed at banning Dow Chemical, which mass-produced the bomb ingredient napalm, from recruiting on campus.[126] "In frequency and consistency of attack," a Dow spokesman said at the time, "this is a record unmatched over the past two years even by recruiters for the US armed forces."[127] The 1970 annual meeting of Honeywell Corp., which manufactured fragmentation bombs, was broken up after only fourteen minutes when demonstrators stormed the conference room and shouted down its president. Security personnel used mace to disperse the activists.[128]

In 1970 and 1971, protestors damaged at least thirty-nine Bank of America branches across the United States, using explosive devices at twenty-two locations and firebombs or arson at another seventeen.[129] Small bombs were detonated at the corporate headquarters of IBM, in Armonk, New York, and Mobil Oil Corp., in Irving, Texas.[130] Following a speech by an antiwar activist on the campus of the University of California at Santa Barbara in 1971, a mob of students set fire to a nearby Bank of America branch. "It was," said one student, "the biggest capitalist thing around."[131]

Of greater concern to executives, however, was the sharp deterioration of business conditions. In the mid-1970s the foundation of the economic boom began to wobble.[132] After emerging from the rubble of World War II, manufacturers in Germany and Japan started outcompeting American firms; by 1979, for example, foreign automobile companies accounted for one-fifth of all car sales in the United States.[133] More broadly, the American share of the world's economy was shrinking—and fast—nose-diving from roughly 40 percent in 1950 to 22 percent by 1980.[134] When the economy tipped into recession in 1973, concern turned to panic, as a collection of Middle East nations suspended the export of oil to the United States in retaliation for America's backing of Israel in the Yom Kippur War.[135] Gasoline prices soared, cars backed up for blocks outside fueling stations, and an already troubling rise in consumer prices ballooned into double-digit inflation. The American economy had become submerged in "stagflation," a combination of slowing growth and rising inflation so pernicious that many economists didn't believe it could actually occur.

Not since the Great Depression had America's business leaders felt so helpless.[136] Amid a confounding economic crisis, corporate profits dropped by more than one-third between the mid-1960s and mid-1970s.[137] As inflation cut into paychecks, labor unions went on strike to demand higher wages, upending the tense equilibrium between management and labor. Resentment of business was at the heart of the cultural zeitgeist, and the government was expanding its authority over corporations more aggressively than ever before. "At this rate, business can soon expect support from the environmentalists," one executive quipped. "We can get them to put the corporation on the endangered species list."[138]

Another businessman put it differently: "The American capitalist system is confronting its darkest hour."[139]

Those close to Tommy and Hale often remarked at the similarities between the two men. "The physical resemblance is startling," said Tommy's wife,

Barbara. In addition, Tommy seemed to unconsciously adopt many of his father's mannerisms, such as rocking the podium back and forth while delivering a speech. When it came to the important things, Hale always turned to Tommy for help. And in 1970, after the announcement of House Speaker John McCormack's retirement led to a vacancy in the majority leader post, father and son teamed up for a campaign to elect Hale to the position. The congressman needed the support of more than half of the Democratic caucus, and Tommy regularly came by Hale's office to help with the effort. He reached out to other lawmakers and tabulated the number of expected votes for and against his father.[140] Victory was far from assured, given the gossip and bad headlines that had been swirling around Hale of late.

About a year earlier, the FBI had opened a bribery and corruption probe involving the elder Boggs. Agents were looking into allegations that Hale had authorized a Baltimore builder, Victor Frenkil, to collect $5 million in cost overruns on a congressional parking garage project in return for favors worth more than $20,000 for Boggs.[141] Frenkil was friendly with the Boggs family; he'd mingled with Hale and Lindy at the Preakness Stakes horse race in Baltimore, and he'd attended at least one garden party at their home. More suspiciously, Frenkil's company had done a renovation of the Boggs's kitchen valued at $48,083 but charged the congressman only $21,000.[142] Tommy sat with his father through some of his FBI interviews. Though Nixon's Department of Justice ultimately decided against an indictment, details from their confidential investigation were leaked to the newspapers, casting a pall of embarrassment over the Boggs family and igniting inside Hale a bitter resentment of the FBI's longtime director, J. Edgar Hoover.

More troubling still were the whispers, then made only in private and behind closed doors, of what one congressman described as Hale's "bizarre and erratic behavior."[143] Colleagues began to notice that Hale seemed exhausted, and his face looked fleshy. Once one of Capitol Hill's most persuasive orators, his speeches became rambling and incoherent. Tommy admitted later that besides helping with the leadership campaign, there was another reason he was spending so much time in his father's office, "babysitting."[144] As he recalled, "When he was in a manic mood, I'd just hang around him."

In the end, Hale's close relationships with influential Big City Democrats—such as his good friend Tip O'Neill Jr., a long-serving Democratic Speaker of the House from Boston—handed him the election despite simmering questions about his fitness for the role.[145] After his promotion to majority leader, though, his conduct worsened. In March 1971, at the white-tie-and-tails dinner for Washington's exclusive and all-male Gridiron Club, Hale got into a drunken brawl with a former congressman in the men's bathroom. The episode left him bloodied and mumbling to himself on the bathroom floor.[146] Later, at a banquet in Florida, he was so intoxicated and belligerent that he had to be restrained by police and locked out of the ballroom.

"Gestapo!" the majority leader yelled. "Storm troopers!"[147]

There was a rumor about him screaming in a senator's face during a dinner party, and there was gossip about a heated altercation with a congressman at the Madison Hotel. It got so bad that Speaker Albert stopped taking trips outside of the Beltway for fear of what might happen if Hale were left alone to run the House.[148] Then, in April 1971, Hale's emotional decline burst into public view, when he took to the House floor and—still smarting from the FBI's investigation—accused J. Edgar Hoover of tapping lawmakers' phones. "The time has come," Hale told lawmakers, "to ask for the resignation of Mr. Hoover."[149]

The accusation, which Hale could never substantiate, became front-page news, alarming elected officials on both ends of Pennsylvania Avenue. President Richard Nixon called Hale's Republican counterpart, House minority leader and future president Gerald Ford, to ask, "What's the matter with your opposite number?"

"He's nuts," Ford replied.

"My God," Nixon said. "He's on the sauce, isn't that it?"

"I'm afraid that's right."

"Or he's crazy?"[150]

Losing confidence in the majority leader, the president stopped sharing with Hale the confidential information he provided to other congressional leaders. Meanwhile, inside the Democratic caucus, there was chatter about stripping Hale of his leadership duties. With his career in jeopardy, Hale finally listened to his family and friends and sought help. He met with doctors at the Bethesda Naval Hospital to address his drinking problem, and he began taking a medication that federal regulators had recently approved for the treatment of manic depression, lithium.[151] The drug improved Hale's mental state, and, while he continued to drink heavily, he behaved better in public. In October 1972, when Hale appeared on the House floor to deliver his closing remarks for the congressional session, his well-being and career were intact once again. "It is time to say farewell to more than fifty of our colleagues," Hale said, "who will not be returning to these halls for the Ninety-Third Congress."[152]

Soon after, Hale left Washington for a short campaign trip to Alaska.

The evening after Hale went missing, the entire Boggs family traveled to Elmendorf Air Force Base, in Anchorage, where the search was being coordinated. Defense Secretary Melvin Laird, a family friend, committed all available resources to the effort. As planes, boats, divers, and mountaineers scoured a 325,000-square-mile grid of the Alaskan backcountry, the Boggs family attended mass each morning and, when permitted, went out looking for Hale themselves. Family members trudged along the icy mountain ranges where the aircraft was believed to have gone down, and Lindy circled the tundra in a search plane flown by a Civil Air Patrol pilot.[153] Psychics reached out to offer their assessments; one told Tommy's wife that Hale was alive on a mountaintop with a broken leg and had just days to live. Tommy, meanwhile, used his inside knowledge of Washington to aid the effort: he persuaded the military officials in charge of the search to deploy the Lockheed SR-71 Blackbird,[154] a high-altitude spy plane whose existence was still a state secret. The massive search-and-rescue effort eventually turned up a World War II–era plane that had been lost for decades. But there was no sign of Hale. After days passed without progress, the family returned to Washington, heartbroken.

The effort was called off the day after Thanksgiving[155]—about a month after Hale's disappearance—and he was officially declared dead five weeks later.[156] Vice President Spiro Agnew, First Lady Patricia Nixon, Lyndon and Lady Bird Johnson, and Senator Hubert Humphrey of Minnesota were among the mourners who gathered at Saint Louis Cathedral in New Orleans to say good-bye.[157] For weeks, Tommy was despondent. "I was mad," he recalled later. "[I] thought it was unfair. People forget he was still very young; just fifty-eight years old."

Boggs talked to colleagues about leaving Washington and heading back to Louisiana.[158] It was only after Lindy decided to run for Hale's seat in Congress that his gloom began to lift. Remarkably, even though he was missing and thought to be dead at the time, Hale Boggs had won his race in November 1972. Later, in a special election, New Orleans voters chose Lindy to serve in her late husband's congressional seat.

The development took Tommy's mind off the tragedy. He soon turned back to his work and recommitted himself to growing his lobbying practice. Before long, the partners were so pleased with his effort that they added his name to the firm;[159] it would eventually come to be known simply as Patton Boggs.

Meanwhile, as Tommy continued to grieve, other events were taking place in and around Washington that would soon enable the young lobbyist to have a bigger impact on American policy than even his late father had.

2

Summer 1971
Richmond, Virginia

Lewis Powell was growing alarmed. From his home in Virginia's historic capital city, located 110 miles south of Washington, the sixty-four-year-old corporate lawyer and Harvard Law School graduate had been closely following the turmoil in corporate America. He'd cut out and saved op-eds in the local newspaper, the Richmond *Times-Dispatch*, which noted that nearly half of the students surveyed at a dozen American universities supported the socialization of key American industries, according to Kim Phillips-Fein's 2009 book *Invisible Hands*. Powell read an article in *New York* magazine about the public's growing skepticism of concentrated wealth and power. And in the financial news publication *Barron's*, he'd seen that a sinister-sounding organization, the Socialist Scholars Conference, had recently met in New York City.[1]

After three decades of representing commercial firms in court, Powell had emerged as a distinguished member of Richmond's business establishment. He served on the boards of a handful of major corporations, such as the tobacco giant Philip Morris, and he'd once been president of the American Bar Association. As a proponent of unfettered capitalism, he considered the free market to be Washington's best tool for growing the economy and raising the standard of living. He viewed the developments he saw in the news as a fundamental threat to the country's prosperity.[2]

Powell's old friend and neighbor, a department store owner named Eugene B. Sydnor Jr., shared his concerns. He'd once sent Powell a *Wall Street Journal* editorial calling on GM executives to respond more forcefully to Ralph Nader's claims.[3] In addition to running his company, Sydnor was also a director of the oldest corporate advocacy group in Washington. Headquartered in a handsome Beaux Arts building situated directly across from the White House, the US Chamber of Commerce was founded in 1912 in response to President William Howard Taft's call for a new advocacy group "that could speak with authority for the interests of business."[4] Over the ensuing decades, however, the Chamber was unable to staunch the flood of costly new regulations, and Sydnor had grown concerned about the business community's weakness in Washington. Eventually he asked Powell to draft an analysis of what corporate executives could do to confront the many challenges they faced.[5] In August 1971 Powell delivered a thirty-one-page document—labeled "Confidential Memorandum"—to Sydnor. He titled it "Attack on American Free Enterprise System."[6]

American capitalism, Powell began, has been the subject of criticism since the founding of the republic. "But what now concerns us is quite new," he wrote. "We are not dealing with episodic or isolated attacks from a relatively few extremists or even from the minority Socialist cadre. Rather, the assault on the enterprise system is broadly based and consistently pursued." Indeed, he continued, some of the harshest criticism has been leveled by "respectable elements of society," including college students, journalists, pastors, intellectuals, artists, and politicians.

Rather than fighting back, he noted, the business community has been content to ignore or appease its detractors. "They have shown little stomach for hard-nose contest with their critics, and little skill in effective intellectual and philosophical debate." In some ways, the flaccid response was understandable; after all, businessmen spend their days focusing on the management of their companies, and they've never been "trained or equipped to conduct guerrilla warfare with those who propagandize against the system." But as the threats to corporate capitalism multiplied,

Powell believed that executives could no longer afford to remain passive. "The time has come—indeed, it is long overdue—for the wisdom, ingenuity, and resources of American business to be marshaled against those who would destroy it."

What, exactly, should executives do? "The overriding first need is for businessmen to recognize that the ultimate issue may be survival—survival of what we call the free enterprise system." To save capitalism from extinction, Powell urged corporate executives to expand their responsibilities beyond their traditional duties of selling products and growing profits. "If our system is to survive, top management must be equally concerned with protecting and preserving the system itself." Action by individual corporations wouldn't be sufficient to protect against these threats. "Strength lies in organization, in careful long-range planning and implementation, in consistency of action over an indefinite period of years, in the scale of financing available only through joint effort."

Powell offered a list of suggestions for how businesses could work together to improve the standing of capitalism: create a panel of pro-business scholars to review and critique university textbooks in the hopes of presenting students with a more favorable perspective of private enterprise; closely monitor television shows and alert federal regulators and journalists to programming that unfairly or inaccurately criticizes business; establish a community of pro-business intellectuals who lecture and publish articles on the benefits of capitalism. At its core, though, Powell's memo was a plea to America's corporate titans to ramp up their political activities.

"Business has been the favorite whipping-boy of many politicians for many years," he wrote. "As every business executive knows, few elements of American society today have as little influence in government as the American businessman, the corporation, or even the millions of corporate stockholders." In order to change this, business leaders should study the legislative successes of the labor, environmental, and consumer movements. "This is the lesson that political power is necessary; that such power must be assiduously [sic] cultivated; and that when necessary, it must be used aggressively and with determination—without embarrassment and without the reluctance which has been so characteristic of American business." He continued, "There should be no hesitation to attack the Naders," or others "who openly seek destruction of the system. There should not be the slightest hesitation to press vigorously in all political arenas for support of the enterprise system. Nor should there be reluctance to penalize politically those who oppose it," according to the memo.

"It is time for American business—which has demonstrated the greatest capacity in all history to produce and to influence consumer decisions—to apply its great talents vigorously to the preservation of the system itself."

Though other businessmen had made similar arguments in the past, the Powell Memo, as it came to be known, represented the most urgent, articulate, and enduring expression of the corporate establishment's fears. It drew the attention of executives at companies large and small,[7] especially after Powell was sworn in as a Supreme Court justice in 1972. Key business leaders who read the document later credited it for sparking their political awakening. Inside the Chamber of Commerce, it had an immediate impact: in 1972 the organization set up a task force dedicated to turning Powell's call to arms into a blueprint for accumulating political influence.[8] Based on the recommendations of the task force, as well as the suggestions of other executives, the Chamber targeted its attention on four distinct areas: scholarship, campaign finance, indirect lobbying, and direct lobbying. And it was by building institutional capacity in these four areas that America's corporate establishment would, before the decade was through, begin its ascent to power in Washington.[9]

Among the Chamber's first initiatives was to create its own think tank, the National Chamber Foundation, to carry out and publish academic and other research on public policy matters from industry's perspective.[10] Executives had for years blamed liberal college faculties for fomenting anti-business sentiment. The charge wasn't completely meritless; at the time, the political views of social science professors at the nation's top universities were notably more liberal than those of the general public.[11] As a result, corporations and their allies lacked the research machinery to substantiate their pro-business ideology. "It takes about twenty years for a research paper at Harvard to become a law," Citibank CEO Walter Wriston said. "There weren't any people feeding the intellectual argument on the other side."[12]

Outside of the Chamber, the memo inspired other wealthy business-men to invest in pro-business scholarship. The document "stirred"[13] Joseph Coors Sr., of the beer brewing empire, and in 1973 he funded the creation of the Heritage Foundation,[14] a conservative think tank whose annual budget would grow to $5.2 million within a decade.[15] In a letter to the president of the American Enterprise Institute, another Washington-based conservative think tank, the chemical and munitions magnate John M. Olin said, "The Powell Memorandum gives a reason for a well-organized effort to reestablish the validity and importance of the American free enterprise system."[16] Olin's foundation endowed a chair at AEI,[17] and its budget surged by a factor of 10 during the 1970s. More broadly, neoconservative journalist William Kristol urged corporations to become more activist in their charitable donations, calling it "absurd"[18] for businesses to donate money to universities, foundations, or charitable causes with anticapitalist views. William Simon, a conservative businessman and former Treasury secretary, argued in his 1978 book, *A Time for Truth*, that "American business was financing the destruction of free enterprise," as he beseeched corporations to instead "funnel desperately needed funds to scholars, social scientists, writers, and journalists who understand the relationship between political and economic liberty."[19]

The Powell Memo task force also recommended that the Chamber make donations to the Business-Industry Political Action Committee (BIPAC), a nonpartisan group founded in 1963 to support pro-business congressional candidates. Though still too skittish to involve itself directly in elections, the Chamber moved to allocate $25,000 to an arm of BIPAC that educated the public about the democratic process without funding specific candidates.[20] Over time, though, leaders of the Chamber and other corporate interests became increasingly willing to back individual candidates financially. While corporations were barred by law from donating money directly to members of Congress, they were permitted to route cash to political candidates through separate fund-raising entities known as political action committees. These PACs, as they're called, were funded by voluntary contributions from business executives and senior-level employees. In the aftermath of a 1975 decision by the Federal Election

Commission that officially allowed companies to form them,[21] PACs became the preferred campaign financing vehicle for the corporate establishment. Between 1974 and 1978, the number of corporate PACs skyrocketed from 89 to 784,[22] and in the 1976 congressional elections, corporations outspent labor unions for the first time in modern American history.[23] By 1980, the number of corporate PACs had reached nearly 2,000, as Republicans and Democrats alike were growing increasingly dependent on this pipeline of campaign cash.

The Chamber also enhanced its indirect lobbying capabilities by launching another new organization, Citizens Choice,[24] to marshal support from allies out in the states. Through a monthly newsletter, a toll-free hotline, and occasional "action alerts," Citizens Choice staffers worked to convince local business leaders and their employees to contact their congressmen on behalf of the Chamber during key legislative battles.[25] Here again, corporations were reading from their rivals' playbooks. Both the public interest and environmental movements had relied on grassroots tactics—energizing ordinary Americans to pressure their representatives—to realize their political objectives. As the decade came to a close, though, it was corporations that were making the most effective use of these strategies.[26]

Finally, in response to the Powell Memo, the Chamber changed its leadership structure in order to improve its direct lobbying capacity; instead of rotating in various company executives for one-year terms as leader, the board voted to hire the organization's first-ever permanent, full-time president.[27] The decision came as trade associations throughout the country began redeploying resources to Washington in an effort to counter the legislative successes of unions, consumer advocates, and environmentalists. In 1972, for example, the National Association of Manufacturers announced plans to move its headquarters[28] from New York City to the nation's capital. In making the announcement, NAM's chairman, Burt Raynes, said that the group had been headquartered in New York for nearly a hundred years because it had considered the city to be the center of American commerce. "But the thing that affects business most today is government," Raynes wrote. "The interrelationship of business with business is no longer so important as the interrelationship of business with government."[29]

All of a sudden, the same corporate CEOs who had previously avoided Washington at all costs were diving into the political process. "If you don't know your senators on a first-name basis," one executive remarked at the time, "you're not doing an adequate job for your stockholders."[30] In 1972, leaders of GE and Alcoa helped launch the Business Roundtable, an organization made up of corporate CEOs who traveled to Washington to personally lobby lawmakers during legislative battles. By the end of the decade, the group represented more than half of the two hundred largest firms in the country.[31] As Bryce Harlow, a Procter & Gamble lobbyist who helped form the new organization, said: "We had to prevent business from being rolled up and put in the trash by Congress."[32] Meanwhile, as corporate trade associations strengthened themselves from the inside, CEOs also sought help from another source of power in Washington: political influencers.

But some lobbyists, of course, were more useful than others.

By the mid-1970s, Tommy Boggs was occupying a unique space in Washington's legal community. Conventional corporate attorneys relied solely on the filing of lawsuits and petitioning regulatory agencies to address their clients' concerns. But Tommy wasn't just a lawyer, he was also a lobbyist. And, as such, he took a wholly different approach to the law. Tommy recognized that the judiciary wasn't the only branch of government that businesses could turn to for redress. If an executive had the assistance of the right fixer—someone who knew how Washington really worked—he could also get help from officials in the executive branch or congressmen in the legislative branch.

"Patton Boggs was built on the idea that the law can be changed to achieve client objectives," the firm wrote later in promotional materials. "We will work with you to develop solutions that are not limited by conventional legal concepts—in the belief that our wider focus will help you find answers others might overlook." The firm continued, "We see the law as a dynamic process, not as immutable rules and procedures."[33]

Tommy put it more succinctly. "Why litigate, when you can legislate?"

If the beleaguered business community was going to reassert its authority in Washington, it needed a political influencer who could navigate the recent changes to the structure of Congress. And now it had its man. Some five years after the disappearance of his father's plane, a more experienced and confident Tommy Boggs found himself at the center of a legislative fight that would serve as the tip of the spear in corporate America's efforts to rein in the reach of the government—a fight that would help alter the balance of power in American politics.

In 1977, Ralph Nader, who by then had emerged as the most renowned consumer advocate in America, gave President Jimmy Carter a suggestion as to who should head Washington's marquee consumer protection agency, the Federal Trade Commission.[34] During his thirteen-year career on Capitol Hill, Michael Pertschuk had earned a reputation as a powerful Senate aide and a committed consumer advocate. From his desk in the Senate Commerce Committee, he'd helped craft many of the consumer safeguards that Washington had realized over the prior decade, from the legislation requiring warning labels on cigarettes to the launch of the National Highway Traffic Safety Administration. Lawmakers referred to him as "the 101st senator."[35] At Nader's recommendation, the president nominated Pertschuk for the post,[36] and, during a White House ceremony in April 1977, Supreme Court Justice William Brennan Jr. swore him in as the forty-fourth chairman of the FTC.

Right away, Pertschuk aroused the business community's suspicions. He wasn't your typical Washington bureaucrat. Born in London, Pertschuk preferred turtleneck sweaters over starched white shirts and dark blue suits. And although he was already among the least affluent officials ever to lead the agency, he had no plans to cash in on his government service. He insisted that when his FTC tenure was over, he wouldn't scurry over to a big Washington law firm and start representing corporations before the agency,[37] like many of his predecessors had done. For business leaders, however, Pertschuk's most alarming quality was his ambition. Shortly after starting at the agency, he pledged to make it "the best public interest law firm in the country."[38]

Pertschuk had arrived at a decisive point in the FTC's history. The agency had been founded more than sixty years prior, following the breakup of John D. Rockefeller's Standard Oil monopoly, as a Progressive Era bulwark against corporate abuse. President Woodrow Wilson signed the Federal Trade Commission Act in 1914, establishing a regulatory body and law enforcement agency with a broad mandate to protect Americans from unfair business practices. By the early 1960s, though, the FTC's unwillingness to exercise its consumer protection authority had made it the target of ridicule. A report from Ralph Nader and a study from the American Bar Association—compiled at President Nixon's request—lambasted the FTC as complacent, rudderless, and controlled by the very businesses it was supposed to regulate. Jokes about the agency's irrelevance began circulating in Washington: What are the three museums on Pennsylvania Avenue? The National Gallery of Art, the National Archives, and the Federal Trade Commission. Other critics dismissed the agency as "the little old lady of Pennsylvania Avenue."[39]

During the late 1960s and early 1970s, as consumer protection issues captured Washington's attention, the agency reclaimed its spine with the support of both Democrats and Republicans. A succession of chairmen reorganized the FTC's structure and reinvigorated its mission. They cleared out lethargic staffers and hired a contingent of eager, young attorneys and economists who viewed FTC service as a way to make a real difference in the lives of ordinary Americans. In 1975 and 1976, after Congress granted the FTC more authority to review corporate mergers and crack down on unfair and deceptive business practices, the agency embarked on a sweeping rule-making push to impose new consumer protection requirements on a variety of products and associated sales practices that, in many cases, had never been federally regulated before, including: mobile homes, eyeglasses, used cars, hearing aids, health spas, funeral homes, gas station lotteries, protein supplements, and cellular plastics.[40] By the late 1970s, this once-laughed-at coterie of lawyers and policy wonks was pursuing one of the most aggressive regulatory agendas in Washington. When Pertschuk took charge, the FTC became even more assertive.

Early in his tenure, Pertschuk grew concerned about the risks of obesity, tooth decay, and other long-term negative health effects that sugary foods posed to children. He directed his indignation at the corporate producers of cereals and candy bars who, he argued, targeted children with television commercials designed specifically to hook them on sugar. Their still-developing brains, he argued, weren't capable of telling the difference between advice from an adult and a sales pitch from a multinational conglomerate. "Commercial exploitation of children," Pertschuk told the audience at the Action for Children's Television Conference, "is repugnant in a civilized society." In the fall of 1977 his staff began working on a rule that would limit food producers' ability to advertise directly to children on television,[41] and Pertschuk moved to expedite the proposal so that it could be implemented without the typical delays.

The proposal jeopardized hundreds of millions of dollars in sales for food manufacturers and advertising revenues for broadcasters. A decade earlier, a CEO facing a similar threat might have thrown up his hands and swallowed the loss. But with corporate profits declining and regulatory costs rising, executives chose to fight back. As one Washington lawyer put it at the time, Pertschuk's effort to regulate children's advertising "awoke a sleeping giant."[42]

It was Tommy Boggs who united rival companies and disjointed business interests into a single, integrated campaign to kill the proposal, as detailed in Rick Perlstein's 2020 book *Reaganland*.[43] One of his clients, Mars Inc.—the maker of M&M's, Snickers, and Milky Way candies—stood to lose big if the rule took effect. So, Tommy reached out to other affected firms and built a coalition of thirty-two different television networks, food manufacturers, and other companies to lobby against the proposed rule. Together, the firms raised a war chest of as much as $30 million—a sum roughly equal to half of the FTC's annual budget.[44] Next, in an effort to shape the public debate surrounding the proposal, he sent materials outlining the companies' complaints to Meg Greenfield, the top editorial page editor at the *Washington Post*.[45] Despite the *Post*'s liberal tradition, it proved to be an ingenious maneuver. On March 1, 1978, Washington's newspaper of record, which was read diligently by the city's top decision-makers, published a searing editorial titled "The FTC as National Nanny."

"So the proposal, in reality, is designed to protect children from the weakness of their parents—and parents from the wailing insistence of their children," the *Post* declared.[46] "That, traditionally, is one of the roles of a governess—if you can afford one. It is not the proper role of government."

That two-word phrase—"National Nanny"—proved devastating. Corporate lobbyists would soon deploy "National Nanny" as a slogan not just to discredit the children's advertising rule, but also to delegitimize federal regulation more broadly. "Consumer advocates and regulators," Pertschuk lamented in a 1981 lecture to the University of California at Berkeley business school, "had lost our hold on the symbols of the debate." He continued, "Now it was the Commission—not amoral business—that allegedly threatened to undermine the moral fiber and authority of the family."[47] More significantly, the idea of a National Nanny crystalized in the minds of lawmakers and voters a growing suspicion that Washington's incursion into the economy had extended too far and that, on account of this overreach, government officials were no longer helping to solve the problems associated with corporate capitalism. Instead, the public came to view Washington's regulatory zeal as a root cause of the bankruptcies, layoffs, and inflationary spiral that were ravaging the country. "I need not tell you," Pertschuk admitted, "how politically wounding the *Washington Post*'s 'National Nanny' editorial was."[48]

After using the media to shift the public debate in his client's favor, Tommy was ready to attack the proposal itself. It was here that his proficiency in the inner workings of Washington proved most valuable. The distribution of political power had changed dramatically over the previous few years. For most of American history, real political power was concentrated in the hands of a select few elected officials: the president, the Senate majority leader, the Speaker of the House, and a small number of congressional committee chairmen. But in the aftermath of Nixon's Watergate scandal, lawmakers in the mid-1970s passed a series of reforms that served to decentralize this power.[49] Among other things, the measures added a raft of new committees and subcommittees to Congress, which drastically increased the number of elected officials with meaningful authority over public policy decisions. By 1979, for example, every Democratic senator except one chaired a committee or a subcommittee.[50] Each of these chairmen had tremendous control over the rules and regulations for the various industries under his or her jurisdiction.

The development brought to an end the masters-of-the-universe era of lobbying, when insiders such as Tommy "the Cork" Corcoran and Clark Clifford could shape federal actions with a single phone call.[51] "Instead of ten committee chairmen," Tommy explained, "you now have seventy people running the House and a hundred people running the Senate. In the past, a lobbyist needed to only know about ten people on the House side. He could call the Speaker of the House or Sherman Adams [an aide to President Dwight D. Eisenhower] at the White House and say, 'Help me.' All that has changed as power has dispersed."[52] With so many different members of Congress now in charge of various committees and subcommittees, effective lobbyists needed to reach lawmakers up and down the congressional food chain. On top of that, they had to have a detailed understanding of the tedious, arcane process by which legislation moves through Capitol Hill. As Tommy himself put it, instead of requiring just one well-connected lobbyist, "now you need a law firm to use the whole system." As a result, Tommy's lawyer-lobbyist model soon became the most effective vehicle for political influence. But the decentralization of federal power also created new opportunities for influence peddlers, since there were now many more lawmakers whom lobbyists could call upon for assistance in killing undesirable pieces of legislation.

In this new power structure of Washington, Boggs found his opening to tank the FTC's proposal. Since the children's advertising rule hadn't been formally enacted, he could neither challenge it in court nor block it in Congress. There was, however, the question of funding. In order for the FTC to carry out the proposal, it needed to spend money and resources to implement it. So, Boggs went to the congressional committees that controlled the agency's funding and persuaded them to prohibit the FTC from spending any money to enforce the rule. It was the first time a lobbyist had thought to use the congressional appropriations process to subvert an agency's rule-making authority—and it worked spectacularly. Without the necessary funding, the FTC's proposal died right there in Congress.[53]

Still, for the Federal Trade Commission's enemies in the food manufac-turing and broadcasting industries, a single, quiet political victory wouldn't do. They resolved to make an example out of the do-gooder agency and its meddling chairman. So, even though the FTC was not allowed to imple-ment the children's advertising proposal, General Mills—the maker of Lucky Charms and Count Chocula cereals—sued the agency to repeal the rule permanently. As the legal case advanced, lawyers for the company convinced a federal judge in November 1978 to bar Pertschuk from having any participation in the rule-making process for the children's advertising issue because, in the opinion of the court, the FTC chair had "prejudged" the facts when he supported the regulation so stridently.[54] During Senate oversight hearings on the FTC's activity, both Democratic and Republican lawmakers—who'd been targeted by the multimillion-dollar lobbying blitz by Boggs and others—unloaded on Pertschuk.

"I think this preoccupation with what children hear . . . is a waste of taxpayers' money," Connecticut Republican Senator Lowell Weicker told the FTC chairman. "I'm not going to have a bunch of idiots going around trying to discover the sugar content of cereal."[55]

"It's a good thing they passed the antilynching laws before you got ap-pointed," said South Carolina's Democratic senator, Fritz Hollings. "You're like the cross-eyed javelin thrower: you never hit anything, but you sure keep a lot of folks on the edge of their seats."[56]

Then, with his allies on Capitol Hill deserting him, Pertschuk suffered a final indignity. After refusing to appropriate the cash needed to imple-ment the children's advertising proposal, Congress moved separately to block funding for the entire agency. On two occasions—May 1 and June 2, 1980—the FTC was forced to close its doors for twenty-four hours because it didn't have enough money to operate.[57] It was a watershed moment in corporate America's struggle to win power in Washington. Food produc-ers and broadcasters hadn't just killed a regulatory proposal they didn't like; they had turned the FTC's chairman into a political pariah, shut down one of Washington's oldest consumer protection agencies, and delivered a resounding message to regulators throughout the federal bureaucracy.[58] "Other agencies that have not yet provoked Congress may not want to stir up that hornet's nest," a consumer advocate said at the time. "Regulators will have to keep more than one eye on what special interests they're antagonizing."[59]

The FTC was just one casualty in what had become, by the late 1970s, a fiery backlash against any and all regulations from Washington—a revolt fueled by corporate lobbyists, who were growing in number and influence each year. By the early 1980s, nearly 2,500 companies were paying lobbyists in Washington, up from fewer than 200 a decade earlier.[60] Lobbying spending, which totaled about $100 million in the mid-1970s, would soon reach into the billions. And many of these newcomers would learn the influence-peddling game by studying Tommy Boggs.

On account of the public's growing concerns over the economy, and the business community's increasingly unified and sophisticated lobbying efforts, corporate interests quickly achieved a series of landmark victories even though Democrats controlled the White House and both chambers of Congress. In 1977, lawmakers in the Democratic-run House of Representatives voted down organized labor's top legislative priority: a bill that would have allowed common situs picketing, or sympathy strikes arising from a single subcontractors' dispute.[61] The following year, lawmakers blocked the creation of a standalone consumer protection agency.[62] After intense pressure from industry lobbyists, Congress gave companies additional time to come into compliance with existing air-and-water pollution laws,[63] cut tax rates on capital gains and corporate profits,[64] and successfully pressured the Occupational Safety and Health Administration to repeal hundreds of pages of regulations.[65]

As the decade drew to a close, the balance of power in Washington had inverted. Unions, consumer groups, and environmentalists no longer had the clout to drive the legislative agenda. Instead, after fifteen years on the defensive, corporate power was on the march.

3

April 1, 1991
Columbia, South Carolina

In the late afternoon of an early spring day, stretch limousines and federal agents began to converge outside the majestic towers of Trinity Episcopal Cathedral in Columbia, South Carolina.[1] One by one, the giants of Republican politics emerged from their vehicles and walked into the 179-year-old church. Wearing dark suits and somber expressions, they stepped through the arched oak front doors, proceeded past the stained-glass windows, and took their places among the bereaved. It was a display of power that rarely convenes outside of Washington. Vice President Dan Quayle was trailed by a Secret Service detail. Secretary of State James A. Baker III had flown in on a private jet. White House Chief of Staff John Sununu, Defense Secretary Dick Cheney, South Carolina Senator Strom Thurmond, and South Carolina governor Carroll Campbell all had VIP seats. Earlier in the week, organizers had grown concerned that there might not be enough limousines in Columbia to accommodate all the dignitaries, so they'd arranged to have additional ones brought in from Tennessee.[2] At around four o'clock, the congregation turned to the back of the church and watched a group of pallbearers carry a wooden casket down the center aisle and set it next to the altar.[3] "Politics wasn't his business," Vice

President Quayle told the crowd of several hundred mourners. "It was Lee Atwater's calling in life."[4]

Of that, there was no doubt. At the time of his death, at age forty, Atwater was the defining campaign operative of the era. A key engineer of the Republican Party's supremacy in presidential politics during the 1980s, he'd helped to steer Ronald Reagan to two terms in the Oval Office and George H. W. Bush to one.[5] But as he mastered the art of manipulating the electorate, he unleashed a new age of political ugliness. Atwater was, in the words of an opponent, the "Babe Ruth of negative politics."[6] He pioneered the use of "wedge" issues—such as gay rights, abortion, school prayer, and, most notoriously, race—to drive once-reliable Democratic voters to the Republican Party.[7] No attack was too vicious, no smear too shameful. Back in 1980, while managing the reelection campaign of Republican congressman Floyd Spence, Atwater had arranged for allegedly independent pollsters to contact white suburbanites in South Carolina and falsely inform them that Spence's opponent, Tom Turnipseed, was a member of the NAACP—an association that chased away many of the state's white voters. Atwater then tipped off the media to a painful episode in Turnipseed's past: as a sixteen-year-old, Turnipseed had undergone electroshock therapy to treat a case of depression that was so serious he'd become suicidal.[8] Atwater dismissed Turnipseed as "mentally ill," and, he gleefully told the press, "they hooked him up to jumper cables."[9] His most infamous act came in 1988, when Atwater was spearheading George Bush's presidential campaign against former Massachusetts governor Michael Dukakis. With Bush down by 17 points in the polls three months before the election, Atwater helped elevate Willie Horton, a Black convicted murderer who committed rape after being furloughed from a Massachusetts prison,[10] into a national figure[11] as part of an effort to discredit Dukakis as weak on crime and activate the racial prejudices of white voters. "By the time we're finished," Atwater boasted, "they're going to wonder whether Willie Horton is Dukakis's running mate."[12] In the aftermath of Bush's convincing White House victory, he ascended to the highest post in the Republican Party: the chairmanship of the Republican National Committee.[13] In the days following Atwater's death, a delegation of GOP royalty traveled to South Carolina to pay its respects to the man who'd put them in power. "If anybody in heaven has a need for a political adviser," Governor Campbell said during his eulogy, "they have the best."[14]

On account of his vicious tactics, Atwater was reviled by Washington's liberal establishment. But, as John Brady notes in his 1996 biography, *Bad Boy: The Life and Politics of Lee Atwater*, even his enemies couldn't have crafted a crueler demise. At age thirty-nine, while serving as RNC chairman—the apex of his career ambitions—doctors discovered a tumor in his brain that was, as Atwater put it, "the size of a hen's egg."[15] Over the next thirteen months, during his slow march to certain death, the GOP's most feared political enforcer devolved into a feeble and desperate man. Surgery left him unable to use most of his body's left side; it took two people to move him from the bed to the wheelchair. He had violent seizures that could last as long as twenty minutes.[16] As a result of the medication, his hair fell out in clumps, and his face became so bloated that he was difficult to recognize. When physicians were unable to restore his health, Atwater searched elsewhere for answers. Tibetan monks examined his urine and prescribed vitamins and creams. Therapists analyzed his dreams, and a psychiatrist explored his subconscious. At the direction of an alternative healer, he stopped wearing black T-shirts and started sporting red underwear.[17] Yet still the disease progressed. During one six-week period, Atwater was hospitalized on five separate occasions. He broke down in sobs of anguish, and he shrieked at night from the pain. The morphine drip triggered bouts of delusion in which Atwater became convinced that someone was trying to kill him. He demanded that visitors be frisked for weapons, and he asked an aide to carry a gun for his safety.[18] Eventually he called his mother in South Carolina and asked her to come to Washington and sleep next to him in his hospital room. At one point, he made a hopeless request. "I want to die," he said. "Just get a gun and shoot me, Mama. You're the only person who can do it."[19]

After Atwater's diagnosis became public, the biggest names in politics and culture made grand gestures of sympathy. Presidents George Bush and Ronald Reagan visited him. NBC News anchor Tom Brokaw called to wish him well. Actor and future California governor Arnold Schwarzenegger sent a bouquet of flowers, along with a note reading, "From one terminator to another."[20] However, over the many months of his treatment, Atwater's increasingly unpleasant condition worked to keep most people away. Day by day, the countless Reagan and Bush administration aides and party officials who owed their careers to Atwater gradually disappeared from his life. "Lee couldn't do anything for these people anymore," said Linda Reed, a former Republican aide whom Atwater had hired as a caregiver. "It was Washington politics at its purest. This is the meanest town in America."[21] Instead, Atwater relied on his oldest friend in Washington, Charlie Black, to guide him through his terminal illness.

Though he was also a GOP operative with Southern roots, Black, then forty-four, was in many ways Atwater's opposite. While Atwater was an impulsive hooligan—he once answered the door for an *Esquire* magazine interview wearing only boxers and socks[22]—Black was a devout Christian who played golf and made time to read novels.[23] During their many years of working together on campaigns and as business partners in Washington, Black had come to serve as an older brother to Atwater. "I've sort of been his alter ego," as Black once put it.[24] He provided the sober-minded counsel that Atwater needed to negotiate the various professional pitfalls and marriage blowups that encumber the life of a high-end campaign operative. Upon learning of the diagnosis, Black organized a group of fellow GOP strategists to analyze cancer research and help determine the best course of treatment. Once Atwater became too weak to carry out his duties at the RNC, Black took over as the party's top spokesman. And when Atwater expressed an interest in religion, Black gave him a Bible.[25]

Facing the end, Atwater announced that he'd experienced a spiritual awakening. "I have found Jesus Christ,"[26] he told a reporter in November 1990, nine months after his diagnosis. The "bad boy" of Republican politics declared that he was through with the negativity, and he pledged to lead the rest of his life according to the strictures of the golden rule: Do unto others as you would have them do unto you. "I don't hate anybody anymore," he said. "I have nothing but good feelings toward people. It's just no point in fighting and feuding."[27] He preserved his thoughts by speaking into a small tape recorder. "Let this be the first day of the new Lee Atwater, the thoughtful Lee Atwater," he said in one recording. "I want everybody to be proud of me because I've got to show that Lee Atwater really is Lee Atwater and that I am an honest, decent guy with no hidden agenda, with no selfish agenda."[28]

At the suggestion of a spiritual counselor, Atwater compiled a "list of regrets," and he contacted some of the people he'd harmed to express contrition. He wrote "forgiveness letters" to two Democratic candidates whose careers he'd destroyed on the campaign trail. Writing to Tom Turnipseed, Atwater said it was a mistake to have weaponized his experience with depression in the South Carolina Senate race a decade earlier. "It's my hope," Atwater wrote, "that you'll grant a sick man a favor and forget it."[29] Later, in a *Life* magazine article, he apologized for some of the things he'd said about Michael Dukakis during the 1988 presidential campaign, tying him to the convicted murderer Willie Horton.[30] More broadly, Atwater said he'd reconsidered the way he'd slashed and burned himself to the summit of Washington power in the 1980s. "My illness has helped me to see that what was missing in society is what was missing in me: a little heart, a lot of brotherhood," he wrote. "The 1980s were about acquiring—acquiring wealth, power, prestige. I know I acquired more wealth, power, and prestige than most. But you can acquire all you want and still feel empty. What power wouldn't I trade for a little more time with my family. What price wouldn't I pay for an evening with friends. It took a deadly illness to put me eye to eye with that truth, but it is a truth that the country, caught up in its ruthless ambitions and moral decay, can learn on my dime."[31]

In the early morning hours of March 29, 1991, while rain came down over Washington, Atwater's body finally gave out.[32] Over the next several days, Black worked with Atwater's family and White House officials to arrange the funeral services in Washington and South Carolina. From the crowded pews inside Trinity Episcopal Cathedral, Black watched Vice President Quayle appraise the legacy of his old friend. "Today the world spins in new directions," Quayle said, "and Lee Atwater played a vital part in making all of that history."[33] For Black, however, the death of Atwater represented more than the loss of a singular campaign operative. It was the conclusion of one of the most consequential partnerships in Washington history.

Nearly two decades earlier, Black and Atwater—two GOP operatives from the South—had crossed paths with a pair of Republican consultants from the Northeast: Roger Stone and Paul Manafort. Before long, these four brash, young politicos teamed up in a series of overlapping political and lobbying ventures that would, over the course of the 1980s, change the way Washington worked and fundamentally alter the relationship between the government and the economy. "They are," as former Reagan campaign manager John Sears put it in 1985, "the best and brightest Republican operatives today."[34]

The four men arrived in Washington in the late 1970s as young conservative rebels determined to dismantle liberal control of the city, and they came to embody a new archetype of political insiders—professional campaign strategists—who used polling data, TV ads, and relationships with reporters to influence voters and elect politicians. "We're all hardball; we'll do anything and everything within legal boundaries to win," Atwater once said. "We don't blink. We don't flinch. The other guy usually does, and when he does, we know exactly what to do."[35] By employing an unusually savage array of tactics, the partners helped implant the values of the corporate political revolution into the Washington mainstream: facilitating the ideological hardening of the Republican Party, populating Capitol Hill with more right-wing lawmakers, forging alliances between the GOP's populist and capitalist wings, helping to uproot from DC the nearly half-century-long tradition of New Deal liberalism, and assisting the reorientation of federal policy making around a new set of pro-business ideals.

After helping to put Ronald Reagan in the White House, the men struck out on their own, creating a new type of political-influence operation that allowed them to bring their talents as election operatives to the stuffy world of lobbying. "If politics has done anything," Manafort once said, "it's taught us to treat everything as a campaign."[36] By the time the decade was through, the firm had emerged as the premier lobbying shop in the city—the go-to destination for anyone with a political problem that needed to be solved in Reagan's Washington. Like the corporate behemoths that would come to define the economic landscape, the firm pioneered an integrated business model that expanded the scope of its work far beyond what had traditionally been handled by lobbying firms. When the architects of history needed political advice, they turned to Charlie Black, Paul Manafort, Roger Stone, and Lee Atwater. On any given day, the glass doors of their office might push open for a future US president, a Wall Street tycoon, a third world guerrilla leader, an aspiring senator, a media mogul, or an industrial titan.[37] It was, in the words of *Time* magazine, "the ultimate supermarket of influence peddling."[38]

While Tommy Boggs drew his clout from the old-line establishment of New Deal liberals, this new dynasty of Republican influencers amassed its power through the conservative revolution. In this sense, Black, Manafort, Stone, and Atwater became to Republican Washington what Tommy Boggs was to Democratic Washington. Now, regardless of which party was in power or their own political persuasions, anyone with enough money could find a talented lobbyist to help them get what they needed out of our democracy.

Fourteen years before Atwater's funeral, in the spring of 1977, Paul Manafort Jr. arrived in Memphis for the biennial convention of the Young Republicans National Federation.[39] Walking into the Holiday Inn–Rivermont,[40] a fifteen-story tower overlooking the Mississippi River, he found hundreds of other youthful GOP loyalists slumped in various states of anguish and despair. It was a dark time for the party of Lincoln. Just six months earlier, on November 2, 1976, Republicans had suffered a full-blown catastrophe when voters elected former Georgia governor Jimmy Carter president and kept Democrats in control of both chambers of Congress; the government's entire policy-making apparatus was now under liberal control. The dismal election results were only the latest disaster for a Republican Party that had been in slow-motion collapse since the Watergate scandal rocked the electorate. Indeed, as eight hundred budding politicos converged in Memphis for the Young Republicans convention,[41] the GOP's very survival seemed in doubt. "Trying to avoid extinction as a party," PBS newsman Robert MacNeil told viewers at the start of the convention, "is one of the main themes of this sober gathering."[42] But Manafort hadn't traveled all the way from Washington, DC, to console his political allies. He had bigger plans.

At the time, the Young Republicans wasn't just a social club for eighteen-to-forty-year-old political obsessives; it was a decisive force in internal GOP politics.[43] Through the enthusiasm of thousands of members around the country, the group had the clout to influence the agenda for the entire party. In 1964, for example, fiery support from the Young Republicans had helped deliver the GOP's presidential nomination to Barry Goldwater.[44] The organization also functioned as a critical farm system for future Republican elites; House Speaker Kevin McCarthy,[45] former defense secretary Robert Gates,[46] and countless other lawmakers and top officials had gotten their start there. Moreover, the federation was an official arm of the GOP; the group's leaders worked from offices at the Republican National Committee's headquarters in Washington. For Manafort, seizing control of the Young Republicans was an irresistible opportunity to make a name for himself in the party. So, even though former president Gerald Ford and ex-California governor Ronald Reagan were each scheduled to address the convention, it was the election of the organization's next chairman that brought Manafort to the Holiday Inn–Rivermont that spring.

Manafort hadn't come to Memphis alone. In his master plan to take over the Young Republicans, he'd enlisted his buddy Roger Stone, a twenty-four-year-old operative whose history of Watergate-era skullduggery had already stirred controversy. The plan was straightforward: Stone would enter the election as a candidate for chairman of the Young Republicans, and Manafort would work behind the scenes as his campaign manager.[47] At twenty-eight years old, Manafort had a bushy mustache, thick sideburns,[48] and a fondness for custom-tailored suits. Though only a handful of years into his career, he'd already become an authority in the messy art of convention-floor politics; he was preternaturally well suited for the gossip gathering, promise trading, and loyalty enforcement needed to orchestrate election victories at chaotic mass gatherings.[49] In Memphis, according to Franklin Foer's 2018 exposé in the *Atlantic*, Manafort turned his hotel suite into the command center for Stone's campaign. He worked at a folding table stacked high with "whip books," or dossiers of information that he'd compiled on every single delegate in attendance. He had several additional phone lines installed in the room, and he used walkie-talkies to direct his battalion of deputies, or whips, who were rallying support for Stone throughout the hotel grounds. Manafort rented a riverboat and organized a booze cruise on the Mississippi River, where uncommitted delegates couldn't escape the pressure of his whips. Before long, the GOP diehards who'd gathered in Memphis started referring to Manafort's loyalists simply as "the Team."[50]

Manafort needed every vote he could muster for what became a convention-hall knife fight. Rivals circulated a newspaper column claiming that Stone was "waist-deep in 1972 Nixon campaign dirty tricks," attacks that so enraged Manafort he refused to allow Stone to pose for a photograph with his challenger.[51] In the end, the Team's muscle proved too much. The opposing candidate, twenty-eight-year-old car dealer Rich Evans of Kentucky, withdrew from the race and led three hundred convention delegates in a walkout, insisting that the election's outcome had been "scripted in the backrooms." The machinations of his opponents, Evans argued, "is not the image of the Young Republicans."[52] The development thrilled Manafort and Stone; the twentysomething duo was now at the wheel of their own political machine. But victory provided them something more personal as well. The two young operatives had arrived at the convention still bearing the wounds of the painful professional setbacks they'd recently endured back in Washington. By assuming control of the Young Republicans, they had found their path to redemption.

Manafort had acquired his political instincts as a boy in New Britain, Connecticut, a once-lively mixture of blue-collar immigrant communities—Polish, Irish, Ukrainian, Italian[53]—that, on account of the Stanley tools factory in town, came to be known as "Hardware City." The family had deep roots there. Upon emigrating from Naples, Italy, in the early 1900s, Manafort's then ten-year-old grandfather landed at Ellis Island without knowing a word of English. He made his way north to Connecticut, where he started his own demolition company, New Britain House Wrecking, while his wife ran a bootleg distillery in the basement of their home. Over the coming decades, the demolition company—later renamed Manafort Brothers—would emerge as a powerhouse in the local construction industry, building train stations and roads all over the state. The family's name means "strong hand" in Italian.[54]

Manafort's father, Paul Manafort Sr., served as a combat engineer in the army during World War II and, upon returning home from Europe, joined the family business and gravitated into Republican politics. Unlike most members of New Britain's GOP, Manafort Sr. was a working-class figure without a college degree. When he and his wife had their first child, Paul Jr., they lived in a tenement apartment across the road from a ball bearing factory.[55] Nevertheless, Manafort Sr. landed a seat on the city's board of aldermen and, in 1965, launched a long-shot campaign for mayor. Though he ran as a Republican in a liberal stronghold, Manafort Sr. radiated the kind of grip-and-grin charisma that won over skeptical voters. Spending time with the elder Paul Manafort "was like going to the bar with your grandfather," said former New Britain City Council member Paul Carver. "He would stick his hand out and buy a round of drinks. He knew almost everybody in town."[56] He was elected to three terms as mayor, served as Connecticut's deputy public works commissioner, and, through his affiliation with twenty-eight different community institutions—including St. Ann Church, Sons of Italy Lodge 2165, and New Britain General Hospital—he remained involved in civic affairs long after he retired from public office.[57] He was so popular in New Britain that, in 1994, city leaders named a half-mile stretch of road Paul Manafort Drive.[58]

Manafort Jr. grew up worshiping his father. "It was from watching my father that I got my first window into politics," he recalled.[59] As a teenager, Paul Jr.—or P. J., as his friends called him—pitched in on his dad's mayoral campaigns, and he served on a mock city council in high school. Around this time, he entered a student election to become mayor of New Britain for a day, and, after an enthusiastic campaign, he believed he'd convinced enough students to vote for him to ensure his victory. At the last minute, though, another student—a relative, no less—went behind his back, cut a deal with other students, and, according to Manafort's memoir, won the election. For Manafort Jr., the defeat offered two distinct lessons. "The first was that having the votes isn't enough until the people have voted," as Manafort would later write in his memoir. "More importantly, it got me thinking about the organizational and management aspects of politics, not just the service."[60] Despite the setback, there was no denying the potential of this teenaged politico. "He was the kind of guy you met, and you almost knew instantly he was going to be successful at whatever he chose to pursue," said former New Britain mayor Donald DeFronzo, who attended high school with Manafort Jr. and is a distant cousin. "He had that aura. He was confident."[61]

The style of politics that Manafort Sr. modeled for his son, however, was less benevolent than his legacy. "[His] outsize capacity for charm," as the *Atlantic* explained, "made him the sort of figure whose blemishes tend to be wiped from public memory."[62] And there were plenty of blemishes to erase. "Throughout his more than 20 years in public life," the *Hartford Courant* reported, "he has been the focus of controversy and several accusations of wrongdoing."[63] In 1968, during Manafort's second term as mayor, a complaint filed with the US Department of Housing and Urban Development alleged that he'd directed city redevelopment contracts to Manafort Brothers, which he still partly owned at the time of the actions in question.[64] Manafort subsequently sold his stock in the firm, and HUD ruled his actions were aboveboard.[65] In 1975, after he helped a group of Florida businessmen improperly obtain the environmental license they needed to build a sports arena in Bridgeport, Connecticut, he became embroiled in one of the state's most notorious scandals.[66] Other players in the deal were subsequently accused of fraud, bribery, and associating with organized crime. One of the Florida businessmen, David Friend, reportedly told Connecticut investigators that he'd obtained the license through a $250,000 payment to a local political figure. A grand jury couldn't substantiate the claim,[67] and charges of perjury and larceny did not result in convictions, but state officials forced Friend to relinquish his gaming license.[68] Though Manafort was never indicted, the family construction business admitted that it had charged inflated fees for its work on the project in order to kick back money to the International Brotherhood of Teamsters union,[69] whose pension fund had bankrolled the arena's construction. Neither the firm nor the union was charged in the case.[70] In another incident, a former municipal official testified that he'd delivered to Manafort Sr.'s house an envelope containing the questions and answers to New Britain's employment exam for would-be police officers, which, the former official alleged, a relative of

Manafort Sr.'s then passed along to two applicants. Manafort Sr. admitted receiving the envelope, though he claimed to never have looked inside.[71] The same man also testified that Manafort Sr. had told subordinates that he was looking to put a "flexible" employee in charge of his personnel office so that the department could operate "not one hundred percent by the rules."[72] And in 1981 Manafort Sr. was arrested and charged with perjury for the testimony he gave during an investigation into New Britain's cops.[73] In the wake of the probe, a city police captain pleaded guilty to accepting weekly bribes over nearly eight years from Joseph "Pippi" Guerriero, a member of the New Jersey–based DeCavalcante crime family, in return for tipping off the mobster to upcoming gambling raids.[74]

Once again, Manafort Sr. escaped serious consequences. The perjury charge didn't stick, and the statute of limitations prevented his prosecution in the alleged test-fixing episode.[75] Still, the incidents reveal the astonishing levels of corruption that seeped through New Britain's government in the 1960s and 1970s.[76] More than two dozen people were arrested, including the police chief, the head of the detectives office, two different fire department chiefs, the city's personnel director, and the chairman of the Civil Service Commission.[77] "It was a dark chapter," said New Britain's former city clerk, Richard T. Murphy. "Unfortunately, that's what happens when people get a little greedy."[78] Local leaders eventually retained an outside lawyer, Palmer McGee, to investigate how the city became so consumed by corruption, and McGee put the blame squarely on New Britain's favorite son.[79] "The facts cause us to conclude," he wrote, "that the person most at fault was . . . Mayor Paul Manafort."

It was in this mucky culture of graft and self-dealing that the mayor's eldest boy, Paul Jr., received his education in politics. "Some of the skills that I learned [in New Britain] I still use today," he told a reporter years later. "I was about fifteen, sixteen years old when my father first ran for mayor, and that's where I cut my teeth."[80]

The younger Manafort's ambitions were far too big for his New England hometown. At his first opportunity, he set off for the bright lights of Washington, DC, enrolling at Georgetown University—Tommy Boggs's alma mater—and becoming the first member of his large Italian family to attend college.[81] Though he arrived on campus as a business major, he quickly plunged into Republican politics. Manafort landed a leadership role at the College Republicans of DC, and he became a founding member of the Kiddie Corps, a group of rookie GOP activists who helped elect Republican congressman Thomas Meskill as governor of Connecticut.[82] "I started getting really into the *politics* of politics, not just the governance of politics," he recalled.[83] "While my friends were watching *Star Trek* and *Wild Wild West*, I was working the phones and going to all these College Republicans events." In 1970 Manafort returned to Connecticut for the state's Young Republicans convention, where he hoped to build support for Meskill's campaign. It was there that he met one of his future lobbying partners.

As other youthful GOP politicos began to arrive, a friend introduced Manafort to a scrawny, eighteen-year-old high school student who'd come to the convention with no place to stay. Could Manafort help him find a room? By then, Manafort was a highly regarded figure in the Connecticut Young Republicans; he was just the man to see for a favor like this. But before agreeing to assist the new guy, Manafort wanted to know if he was worth helping. He decided to test him—to determine if he was backing Manafort's preferred candidate, Meskill, or his rival for the GOP nomination, Lowell Weicker.

"Hey, kid. How ya' doin'?" Manafort said to Roger Stone. "Why are you supporting Weicker?"

"You think I give a fuck about Weicker?" Stone replied. "I'm here to elect Meskill."

Manafort was impressed. Though the hotel was mobbed with convention-goers, he managed to secure a room for his new friend.[84]

Like Manafort, Stone was born in Connecticut, though he grew up just across the border in Lewisboro, New York. It was a lonely, rural community. There were no children Stone's age around, and his father, who worked as a well digger, came home from work too exhausted to toss around the football with his only son. While neither his father nor his mother, who wrote for the local newspaper, had much interest in elections, young Stone found in politics a way to entertain himself. In 1960, when his elementary school held a mock presidential election, he campaigned for John F. Kennedy using the kind of tactics that would one day make him notorious. Stone, then eight, pulled aside his classmates in the cafeteria line and told them that, if elected, Kennedy's Republican opponent, Richard Nixon, would extend the school week to include Saturdays. The disinformation propelled Kennedy to victory. "It was my first political trick," Stone said.[85] He had decided to back Kennedy because of their shared Catholic faith, but his support for liberals was short lived. A few years after the mock election, a neighbor gave Stone a copy of a skinny, 123-page book by Arizona Senator Barry Goldwater. The boy was never the same.[86]

The publication of *Conscience of a Conservative*, in 1960, was a pivotal breakthrough for America's right flank. Only a few years earlier, the nation's conservative movement had been a loose affiliation of disjointed activists—libertarian economists, anti-Communist crusaders, traditionalist thinkers,[87] among others—struggling to breach the perimeter of mainstream America. But with *Conscience of a Conservative*, Goldwater, in his silver hair and clunky glasses, delivered for the first time a compelling treatment of conservative political philosophy to a mass audience. While the book covered everything from spirituality to the Soviet menace, it was animated by what Goldwater viewed as a dangerous imbalance of power: the enormous expansion of the federal government, which began with the New Deal and accelerated after World War II, was now, he argued, crushing individual freedoms and strangling economic prosperity. According to one study included in the book, Uncle Sam had become the "biggest landowner, property manager, renter, mover and hauler, medical clinician, lender, insurer, mortgage broker, employer, debtor, taxer, and spender in all history." The care and feeding of this massive bureaucracy, he wrote, required businessmen to surrender to capricious federal regulators, farmers to submit to government-imposed crop quotas, and workers to relinquish a growing share of their wages to tax collectors. "The result is a Leviathan," Goldwater concluded, "a vast national authority out of touch with the people and out of their control."[88]

The book catapulted onto the best-seller list, established Goldwater as a conservative folk hero, and served as a call to arms for a generation of young right-wingers, like Roger Stone. "I was immediately transformed into a zealot," Stone said of reading the book. "At twelve years old, I thought the world was going to hell."[89] He began arriving at school with a Goldwater for President button pinned to his shirt, and, when the school day was over, he would pedal his bicycle to the local GOP headquarters to stuff envelopes.[90]

Central to Goldwater's appeal was his contempt for the Republican Party's moderate establishment. The colossal federal budget, he argued, was the fault not only of the New Deal liberals who created the welfare state but also of the centrist Republicans who accommodated its growth. He dismissed the accomplishments of President Dwight Eisenhower—a moderate Republican who'd expanded Social Security, erected the Department of Education, and built the Interstate Highway System—as a "dime store New Deal."[91] Goldwater's brand of conservatism was too uncompromising for many business leaders; a survey by the Research Institute of America found that twice as many business executives planned to vote for the Democrat in the 1964 presidential election compared with the prior election. Still, his attacks electrified the Far Right. After defeating his moderate challenger, New York governor Nelson Rockefeller, in the GOP primaries, Goldwater took to the stage at the Republican National Convention outside of San Francisco, as the first authentically conservative presidential nominee of a major party since Republican William Howard Taft in 1912. "Extremism in defense of liberty is no vice," he famously roared from the podium. "Moderation in pursuit of justice is no virtue."[92]

Stone watched Goldwater's ascent with glee. He decorated his room to look like the campaign's headquarters, lining the walls with posters of Goldwater and his running mate, conservative New York congressman Bill Miller, along with bumper stickers and red-white-and-blue bunting. On November 3, 1964, when Lyndon Johnson massacred Goldwater with 90 percent of the electoral votes, Stone collapsed into tears. "I didn't eat for days," he said.[93] Voters had rejected Goldwater as too extreme, and the national media considered his humiliation to be the death knell for the moment. "Barry Goldwater not only lost the presidential election," wrote James Reston, the *New York Times*'s Washington bureau chief, "but the conservative cause as well."[94]

But in fact, the revolution grew stronger. In the aftermath of the election, the young insurgents that Goldwater had radicalized, like Stone, stormed into Republican political party organs determined to end the GOP's legacy of moderate accommodation and rebuild its future upon resolute conservative principles.[95]

After meeting Paul Manafort at the Connecticut Young Republicans convention in 1970, Stone graduated high school and moved to Washington, DC, where he enrolled at George Washington University. On a campus that pulsed with anti–Vietnam War passions, Stone stood out. He had intense eyes, a slender waist,[96] and a dandy's preoccupation with his appearance. He preferred double-breasted suits—he claims he stopped buying off the rack at age seventeen[97]—with silk handkerchiefs popping from his blazers. "Roger's big ambition in college was to have gray hair," said his first wife, Ann "Bitsey" Stone. "He couldn't wait to be thirty."[98] According to the story she would later tell at Washington social functions, Bitsey first met Stone when she came back to her room at George Washington University and discovered him in bed with a girlfriend. While things with that woman didn't last, Stone and Bitsey soon connected over conservative politics. When Bitsey decided to run for secretary of the College Republicans, Stone managed her campaign. They were married a few years later and spent their honeymoon chaperoning the youngsters who came to Washington, DC, for a Teenage Republican Leadership Conference.[99]

At George Washington University, Stone went about pursuing a career in Republican politics. He joined a handful of GOP groups and was elected president of the local chapter of the Young Republicans.[100] As Richard Nixon's 1972 reelection campaign got under way, he invited Jeb Magruder, the deputy director of the Committee to Re-elect the President, to speak to his organization. Following the talk, Stone approached Magruder about a job, and Magruder arranged for the nineteen-year-old college student to come work for Nixon's reelection campaign.[101] It was here that Stone's reputation for political subterfuge was born. During the workday, Stone was a junior aide in the campaign's scheduling division. But "by night," he explained, "I'm trafficking in the black arts."[102] Over the course of the Nixon campaign, Stone participated in a series of efforts to snoop on, trip up, and embarrass the president's enemies. Once, when Nixon officials wanted to discredit Pete McCloskey, a congressman from California who was challenging Nixon for the Republican presidential nomination, a senior campaign aide gave Stone $135 and instructed him to go to New Hampshire and make a donation to McCloskey's campaign on behalf of the Gay Liberation Front. Stone did as directed; he traveled to the Granite State and delivered the contribution, though he did so in the name of a different Far Left group, the Young Socialist Alliance.[103] Stone proved particularly adept at this type of work—"ratfucking," as Nixon's team called it. For his mission to New Hampshire, he took care to convert the cash into small bills and coins, so that the contribution would appear to have come from small donors. After returning to Washington, he drafted an anonymous letter and sent it, along with a photocopy of the contribution's receipt, to a New Hampshire newspaper, the deeply conservative *Manchester Union-Leader*, in an attempt to substantiate McCloskey's supposed ties to leftists.[104]

In a subsequent operation, Stone went undercover—adopting the pseudonym "Jason Rainier"—and flew to Kentucky to recruit a former parole officer, Michael McMinoway, to spy on the campaigns of Nixon's Democratic opponents. Stone dispatched McMinoway to Wisconsin to infiltrate the presidential campaign of Maine Senator Ed Muskie. Posing as a Muskie supporter, McMinoway joined the campaign as a volunteer and gained access to its headquarters, where he obtained information on the campaign's finances, staff, and schedule. But McMinoway wasn't just there to gather intelligence; he also worked to disrupt the campaign's operations. On a day when he was supposed to be supervising the distribution of Muskie-for-President pamphlets, he convinced his fellow volunteers to blow off work and head out for beers. On another occasion, after working his way into the Pennsylvania campaign of presidential hopeful Hubert Humphrey, he manipulated the instructions to the campaign's phone bank staffers so that they began placing repeated calls to Humphrey's volunteer leaders. Some of the volunteers got so fed up with the nonstop ringing of their phones that they quit the campaign.[105]

In his most impressive feat, McMinoway infiltrated the campaign of

Nixon's Democratic opponent in the general election, Senator George Mc-Govern of South Dakota. During the 1972 Democratic National Convention in Miami, McMinoway landed a position as a security guard on the penthouse floor of the Doral Hotel, where McGovern was staying. From this post, he met top campaign officials and overheard sensitive conversations; at one point, he watched the television coverage of the convention's proceedings with McGovern himself. "It is amazing how easy it would be to be right in the midst of all the operations and planning and yet be an enemy," McMinoway wrote in his diary.[106] McMinoway, who was paid $1,500 a month for several months of work, sent written summaries of the information he obtained to Stone through a post office box in Washington. Stone then passed the reports up the Nixon campaign's chain of command, all the way to the president's chief of staff, H. R. "Bob" Haldeman.[107]

Stone even had a backstage view of the Committee to Re-elect the President's most infamous operation. In the early morning hours of June 17, 1972, burglars linked to the Nixon campaign broke into the Watergate Hotel complex in a botched attempt to bug the sixth-floor headquarters of the Democratic National Committee. Stone, then renting a room from senior Nixon campaign aide Bart Porter, who was away for the night, fielded phone messages from characters like G. Gordon Liddy, one of the five burglars arrested in the history-making debacle.[108]

For Stone, this work was far more exciting than anything he could find in the university's lecture halls. "My academic studies," he recalled, "went right into the toilet."[109] He eventually dropped out of school. But when it came to starting a career in Washington, his experience on the Nixon campaign proved better than a college degree. Following Nixon's landslide victory, Stone joined the administration's Office of Economic Opportunity and then, in December 1973, landed a position in the office of Kansas Republican Senator Bob Dole. At just twenty-one years old, Stone's future in Republican politics looked promising. He'd made powerful friends and secured influential posts; the kid from Lewisboro, New York, was in the big leagues.

But then the past caught up to him. Six months after taking his new job in the Senate, Stone's escapades as a Watergate-era dirty trickster were exposed by the syndicated columnist Jack Anderson.[111] He was fired by Dole's office,[110] and no one else would hire him. As Republican elites scrambled to distance themselves from the stench of Watergate, Stone went from GOP wunderkind to political pariah. "It was tough to get a job for a couple of years," he later recalled.[112]

Around this same time, Paul Manafort was also experiencing a hard fall from the top. After graduating from Georgetown Law School in 1974, he had landed the kind of job that budding power players dream about. He joined the White House in the personnel office of President Gerald Ford, who'd assumed the presidency upon Nixon's resignation on August 9, 1974.[113] The personnel office was responsible for filling hundreds of sought-after positions throughout the administration, and it was up to Manafort to help decide who got these jobs and who didn't. As wealthy Republican donors and party officials crammed into his office with requests for federal appointments, Manafort emerged, at age twenty-six, as an influential broker of patronage and status.

In 1976 he joined President Ford's reelection campaign and became a student of the legendary Republican operative, and future secretary of state, James A. Baker. In August 1976 Manafort traveled to the Republican National Convention, in Kansas City, Missouri, where he hunkered down with Baker in a trailer next to the Kemper Arena.[114] During the bitter convention-floor battle that followed, Manafort and Baker did everything they could to persuade a critical group of undecided delegates to support the renomination of the GOP establishment's preferred candidate, President Ford, who was fending off a fierce push from the backers of his conservative challenger, Ronald Reagan. Working with Baker, Manafort assembled dossiers on the Reagan-aligned delegates who he believed could be turned into Ford supporters, in what proved to be the more accurate vote-counting operation of the two campaigns. Each tally sheet included the delegate's name, age, profession, home state and which candidate they were expected to support. "He was like a Soviet spy," said one confidant. "He used information as leverage." One Reagan delegate recalled that, shortly before the final vote, an ally of Manafort's had offered him a position at a DC law firm if he'd switch his allegiance from Reagan to Ford.

The effort proved successful, as Manafort and Baker managed to arm-twist just enough delegates to deliver a narrow victory to Ford. The experience gave Manafort the inside track on a senior position in Ford's second administration. But the promotion never came. That November, President Ford narrowly lost his reelection bid to Democrat Jimmy Carter.[115]

For Manafort, it was a crushing development. When the new administration moved into the White House, his influential standing evaporated. His phone calls were no longer returned, and he was deeply wounded by the supposed friends who turned their backs on him. "He always remembered the calls he didn't get—the people who didn't call him back," said John Donaldson, a friend and future lobbying colleague. The bitterness had a profound impact on the way Manafort looked at Washington. He came to view loyalty as the city's most elusive and valuable commodity; in the coming years, as he built his lobbying empire, he hired only employees whom he believed would remain faithful to him at all costs. There was another, more fundamental lesson that he took from this painful episode. "The thing he learned," Donaldson said in an interview, "was what happened when you win, and when you lose." It was with these stakes in mind that Manafort teamed up with his old friend Roger Stone and, in the spring of 1977, flew to Memphis for the annual convention of the Young Republicans. By wresting control of the organization, Manafort was able to recover the clout he'd surrendered in Ford's defeat, and Stone, the once radioactive Watergate saboteur, was able to return inside the GOP's power structure. These two aspiring kingmakers had been cast into the wilderness. Now they were back in the game.

Manafort and Stone assumed the leadership of the Young Republicans at a time of fundamental changes inside the American body politic. In the mid-1960s middle-class voters had been the principal base of support for expanding federal regulations on businesses.[116] But amid the economic panic of the late 1970s, many began to reconsider their views on the government's role in the market.[117] Years of sky-high inflation had undercut wage growth, squeezed the middle class's standard of living, and, according to *BusinessWeek* magazine, "all but destroyed its confidence in the traditional

American dream that if you work hard, you will get ahead."[118] With policy makers unable to diagnose the root cause of stagflation, the mysterious economic malaise was stoking fears of an even darker future ahead; a report authored by two radical economists predicted that the United States faced a 60 percent chance in 1978 of collapsing into a 1930s-style depression.[119]

At the same time, a thriving network of conservative think tanks— some of which were bolstered by donations from business leaders who'd been inspired by Lewis Powell's infamous call to arms—was deluging lawmakers, editorial writers, and other opinion makers with academic research identifying the growth of the federal bureaucracy as the primary source of the economy's stupor. For suddenly anxious baby boomers, many of whom had abandoned the 1960s-era counterculture for jobs on the corporate ladder, these conservative explanations made sense. After all, the government's long reach had become an increasingly intrusive feature of their lives. For example, the Truth in Lending Act of 1968, which Congress passed to protect mortgage borrowers from abusive bankers, turned the home buying process into a labyrinth of confusing paperwork. The bottles that pharmaceutical companies were forced to manufacture in order to comply with the Poison Prevention Packaging Act of 1970 made it nearly impossible for many elderly and arthritic citizens to open their medicines.[120] And in 1978 the Supreme Court put a stop to construction on the Tellico Dam outside of Knoxville, Tennessee, after concluding that the $100 million Tennessee Valley Authority project would destroy the habitat of a tiny species of fish, the snail darter, and was therefore in violation of the 1973 Endangered Species Act.[121] The Tellico Dam controversy came to serve as a caricature of liberal overreach, helping to fuel a burgeoning backlash against the federal bureaucracy. As the pain of stagflation dragged on, the public's resentment of the government began sparking antitax protests in various parts of the country.[122]

The most notable such uprising was California's so-called Tax Revolt of 1978, where a ragtag band of irate home owners attracted national attention for their ultimately successful campaign to enact a statewide initiative cutting property taxes and capping future increases. Americans' growing disdain for high taxes and bureaucracy produced an unlikely area of agreement between many middle-class voters and corporate America.[123] "It seems that nobody loves government anymore," NBC News anchor David Brinkley told viewers on the eve of the Proposition 13 tax initiative vote in California, which was overwhelmingly approved. "It is possible this might be bringing something like a second Whiskey Rebellion. Going far beyond California, and perhaps eventually to Washington."[124]

While middle-class Americans were turning against New Deal liberalism, the conservative movement was acquiring new allies. Disillusioned by what they viewed as Democrats' weak response to Communist aggression, an influential collection of liberal intellectuals broke from the Democratic Party and began working with Republicans to construct a more muscular American foreign policy; they would come to be known as neoconservatives. And in 1979 fundamentalist preacher Jerry Falwell founded an organization called the Moral Majority, which used social issues such as abortion and school prayer to rally evangelical Christians into a titanic political force. Although these activists joined the conservative movement's free-market ideologists in pushing for dramatic cuts to the federal enterprise, corporate lobbyists in Washington were initially reluctant to align with them. "To the business community, the social and cultural right wing was a fringe group, treacherously unsophisticated, and, as such, a political liability," Thomas Edsall wrote in his 1984 book *The New Politics of Inequality*. Moreover, conservative economic principles weren't always good for profits; the handful of right-wing hard-liners serving in Congress in the early 1970s were hostile to government giveaways in any form—whether they were tax perks for corporations or food stamps for poor children. Industry lobbyists preferred to steer clear of these new radicals and continue partnering with the moderate Republicans and conservative Democrats who'd been their allies as of late.[125]

Over time, though, corporate lobbyists came to recognize the value of the Far Right. In the business community's struggles against consumer groups and organized labor, conservatives proved particularly useful. In 1976, for instance, it was a conservative senator from Utah, Orrin Hatch, who led the effort to tank a union-friendly labor reform bill that industry groups had identified as the number one threat to their interests.[126] There was another factor behind the corporate lobby's embrace of the conservative movement: by the late 1970s, conservatives were arriving on Capitol Hill in growing numbers, thanks in part to the efforts of two young GOP operatives from the South.

The way Roger Stone tells the story, it all happened by chance. In the fall of 1978 the Republican operative was standing in the checkout line at D'Agostino, a grocery store not far from his apartment in New York City, holding a box of frozen tacos. While waiting on the cashier, according to Stone's account, he grabbed a newspaper off of the counter and began flipping through the pages. An article stopped him dead in his tracks. He dropped the tacos, dashed out to a pay phone, and placed a giddy call to his friend Lee Atwater.

"You're not going to believe this!" Stone said.[127]

At the time of the call, the twenty-seven-year-old Atwater was in South Carolina, scouring for dirt on a political opponent. As the field director for the reelection campaign of Strom Thurmond, the former segregationist turned Republican senator from South Carolina, Atwater had found himself in the middle of a surprisingly tough race. Thurmond's youthful and well-liked challenger, an ex–Harvard University football player named Charles "Pug" Ravenel, was running neck and neck with the four-term incumbent. As Election Day approached, Atwater and his colleagues were struggling to undercut Ravenel's support. If they couldn't find a way to discredit him soon, Ravenel might very well pull off the upset.[128]

It was for this reason that Stone had reached out, explaining to Atwater that he'd stumbled across a newspaper article with incendiary implications for Ravenel's campaign. The article, Stone said, reported that Ravenel had recently been in New York City for a fund-raiser hosted by a pair of his Ivy League classmates. While there, Ravenel was overheard saying that he was embarrassed to be from South Carolina and that if he were elected to Congress, he'd be more like a third senator from New York.[129]

Atwater could barely contain his excitement; he felt like he'd found a $100 bill on the top of a skyscraper.[130] "You've got to get that down to me,"[131] he said.

Stone said he mailed the article to South Carolina,[132] where Atwater fed it to the local media and convinced a state lawmaker to appear in a televised campaign ad about it. "This year we've got something more important than party," the state lawmaker told viewers. "We need Strom Thurmond, instead of a third senator from New York."[133]

Ravenel insisted he'd never made the comment. Indeed, given Stone's penchant for mischief making, Washington insiders have long suspected that Stone made up the story about Ravenel's comments and planted it in the New York media himself. In any event, there was little that Thurmond's challenger could do to defend himself against it. In the wake of Stone and Atwater's attack, Ravenel's unfavorable rating blasted from 12 percent to 43 percent, and Thurmond went on to win the election decisively by 11 points.[134]

Atwater was raised in the middle-class suburbs of Columbia, South Carolina, a sticky-hot state capital that was just then beginning to desegregate its lunch counters. His father worked as an insurance agent and his mother raised the children, clipping coupons to keep the family's budget for meat at dinner under a dollar a day. In the fall of 1956, five-year-old Lee experienced the defining event of his childhood. His mother was making doughnuts in the kitchen while his little brother, Joe, played near the stove. As the cooking oil crackled to a boil, Joe climbed onto a trash can and tried to peek inside the deep fat fryer.

"Joe, get down!" his mother scolded. "That grease is hot."

Suddenly the trash can gave way. Joe tumbled to the floor, grabbing the cord to the deep fat fryer as he fell. The fryer spilled over, sending the sizzling-hot oil onto Joe. Atwater heard the screams and raced in. There, on the kitchen floor, he found his three-year-old brother shrieking in desperation, as his skin began to peel off.

The family covered the boy in bedsheets and hurried him to the hospital. The oil had burned up most of Joe's tiny frame, incinerating his right eye. His hysterical mother remained in the hospital room throughout the night as her youngest child faded away.

"Mama, please don't cry," Joe said at one point. "Please don't cry."[135]

In the years following Joe's death, Atwater turned his grief inward.

Though he would say later that he could hear Joe's screams every day for the rest of his life, he refused to discuss what happened with anyone. Once, when a high school friend noticed a picture of Atwater and Joe hanging above the sofa in his living room, Atwater said only, "Oh, that's my little brother. He died."[136]

By then, Atwater had developed into a prankster and hell-raiser at A. C. Flora High School. During his senior year, he notched his first victory as a campaign consultant after convincing a buddy, David Yon, to enter the election for student body president. "I made up a whole lot of phony issues for him to run on," Atwater recalled. "Free beer on tap in the cafeteria, unlimited cuts, no grades less than Bs. We made up a whole list of credentials, including the fact that Yon had led an Arctic expedition and was the winner of the International Hairy Legs Contest."[137] Although Atwater delivered the win, the principal invalidated the results. Nevertheless, the episode served as a critical lesson in how to manipulate voters.[138] Later, while studying at tiny Newberry College, near Columbia, Atwater became active in national politics. He joined the College Republicans, in part as an act of rebellion. "I decided I wanted to be a Republican simply because I was always an antiestablishment-type guy, and all the establishment-type people on campus and in the state were Democrats," he said. "The young Democrats in South Carolina were an elite group that went around in three-piece suits, Gant shirts, and smoking cigars, acting like big shots."[139]

During his sophomore year at Newberry, Atwater landed a summer internship in Strom Thurmond's Senate office. While in Washington, Thurmond—who in 1957 had conducted a filibuster more than twenty-four hours long in an effort to tank civil rights legislation—became something of a mentor to the young intern. He educated Atwater in "the game, the competition, the show" of politics.[140] Following the internship, Atwater returned to Newberry and put his talents for spectacle and subversion to work for the senator. Whenever Thurmond's opponents in the 1972 Senate race came to campus, Atwater would write a series of hot potato questions on index cards, distribute the cards to his friends, and direct them to read the planted questions during live events. He then watched in delight as

Thurmond's rivals fumbled through their responses.[141] Over the following years, as he developed into a seasoned political consultant, Atwater grew increasingly ruthless. He became convinced that the key to winning an election was "driving up the opposition's negatives."[142] He once told a reporter, "When I first got into this, I became a polling junkie. . . . I just stumbled across the fact that candidates who went into an election with negatives higher than thirty or forty points just inevitably lost. One of the conclusions I've reached is that in a two-man race, if one of the candidates can't win, and the other one is yours, you are going to come out all right."[143]

Because the demographics in the South favored Democrats, Atwater argued that negative tactics were the only way to build a durable Republican majority in the region. "You had to make the case that the other guy, the other candidate, is a bad guy," he said. "You simply could not get out in a universe where sixty percent of the people were Democrats and twenty-eight percent Republican and win by talking about your issues."[144] Weaponizing race was the linchpin of his approach. Years later, in an interview that he believed was anonymous, he detailed the "Republican Southern Strategy" for exploiting racial prejudices to win elections below the Mason-Dixon Line. "Y'all don't quote me on this," Atwater began. "You start out in 1954 by saying, 'N[——], n[——], n[——].' By 1968, you can't say 'n[——]'—that hurts you. Backfires. So you say stuff like forced busing, states' rights, and all that stuff. You're getting so abstract now [that] you're talking about cutting taxes, and all these things you're talking about are totally economic things, and a by-product of them is [that] blacks get hurt worse than whites. And subconsciously maybe that is part of it. I'm not saying that. But I'm saying that if it is getting that abstract, and that coded, that we are doing away with the racial problem one way or the other. You follow me—because obviously sitting around saying, 'We want to cut taxes, we want to cut this,' is much more abstract than even the busing thing, and a hell of a lot more abstract than "N[——], n[——].' So, any way you look at it, race is coming on the back burner."[145]

During his senior year of college, Atwater traveled to Miami for the 1972 Republican National Convention. For three days, he served as a GOP delegate, worked as Strom Thurmond's driver, and got to know another up-and-coming conservative operative from the South.[146] Charlie Black had grown up in Wilmington, North Carolina, a middle-class community of God-fearing Baptists, where his father worked as a dairy salesman and his mother cared for the family. Like most whites in the South at the time, Black's parents had been loyal Democratic voters for years. But the efforts of liberals in Washington to combat racial injustice by enacting the Civil Rights Act of 1964—which Lyndon Johnson signed when Black was seventeen—triggered a dramatic reshuffling of the region's political alliances, as voters from Richmond, Virginia, to Biloxi, Mississippi, fled the Democratic Party for the GOP. "There was a general feeling of resistance or rebellion among white southerners to LBJ, to the things he was doing," Black recalled. "I wasn't conversant with the policies, or why the Civil Rights Act was bad, but it caused me to focus."[147] When Barry Goldwater became the subject of his family's dinner table conversations, Black read *Conscience of a Conservative* and was instantly converted. At the University of Florida, he became a regular reader of the conservative movement's leading magazine, the *National Review*. He joined the Young Republicans, worked as a poll watcher for Richard Nixon's 1968 presidential campaign, and moved to Washington, DC, eventually dropping out of American University Law School for a job with the Young Americans for Freedom, an influential conservative group.[148]

Though Black and Atwater became close friends, they contrasted in style and demeanor. Atwater was an impulsive bomb thrower who played the part of an overgrown frat boy. Black was more disciplined. With his conservative suits, meticulously parted hair, and thank-you-ma'am manners, he projected the image of "a prosperous Sun Belt banker,"[149] as the *New York Times* put it. Still, beneath Black's gentle disposition was the same killer instinct that Atwater possessed. "Charlie's the kind of guy, who if he came home and found somebody making out with his wife on a rainy day,"[150] said Roger Ailes, the former advisor to President Richard Nixon and chairman of Fox News, "he'd break the guy's umbrella and ask him to leave, and then have him killed a year later. . . . Lee would blow the house up." Unlike Atwater, who reveled in the public's attention, Black was more comfortable in the shadows. When he was hired to manage a campaign, he rarely surfaced in the press; instead, he remained cloistered in his office, contemplating how best to destroy his opponent between long drags of his cigarette.[151]

Years later, in 1984, Black was in Texas, working to elect Phil Gramm to the US Senate, when he picked up a piece of information about his Democratic opponent, Lloyd Doggett, that was sure to offend the state's conservative sensibilities. "Doggett got the endorsement of the big gay PAC in San Antonio," Black recalled. "That wasn't unusual, but then we got onto the fact that the gays had a male strip show at some bar, and Doggett takes that money."[152] Black turned the news of this $500 donation collected at a gay strip club into the centerpiece of a series of attack ads,[153] and Gramm steamrolled his way to the first of his three terms in the Senate. "Sure, they play hardball, but everyone plays hardball," said James Carville, a Democratic operative then working for Doggett who later became a key architect of Bill Clinton's 1992 presidential campaign. "They just do it better than anyone else."[154]

As Black and Atwater ascended the ranks of southern Republican politics, they helped turn the conservative movement into a legitimate force on Capitol Hill. Black engineered the 1972 Senate election victory of Jesse Helms,[155] bringing to Washington the former conservative talk radio host and antigovernment crusader who would, during his three decades of representing North Carolina in the upper chamber, establish himself as a bulldog of right-wing politics and, as the *Washington Post*'s David Broder put it, "the last prominent unabashed white racist politician in this country."[156] Meantime, Atwater helped Strom Thurmond win reelection in 1972 and 1978. These and other victories contributed to the growing clout of right-wing ideologues in Washington. In 1975 there were only four young and aggressive conservative senators in the Republican conference, but after the elections of 1978, that figure increased to eleven. In the House of Representatives, the ranks of conservatives swelled by twenty in the 1978 election alone.[157] The additional troops changed the way corporate lobbyists viewed conservatives. "From the point of view of the politically active business community," Edsall wrote in *The New Politics of Inequality*, "these elections converted the right wing of the Republican Party from a small and strategically insignificant minority into a substantial block of votes, of crucial importance if brought in on the side of business." As a result, Washington trade associations began working in partnership with the conservative activists they'd once dismissed. Corporations, which had traditionally split their political contributions evenly between Democrats and Republicans, started redirecting a growing share of their political spending to GOP candidates, in an effort to alter the partisan makeup of Congress.[158] In the 1980 election, Republicans received more than 60 percent of the donations from business PACs.

Stone and Manafort had met Atwater and Black in 1972 through the Washington, DC, chapter of the Young Republicans. Before long, the four men began teaming up. Sharing a right-wing ideology and preference for hard-nosed campaigning, they became die-hard confederates in the effort to advance the conservative movement. In 1975 Black joined with Stone, Manafort, and others to launch the National Conservative Political Action Committee.[159] The organization was among the first to exploit a provision in campaign finance laws that allowed PACs to spend massive sums of money to support the election of political candidates.[160] Over the rest of the decade, the group would become the country's largest conservative PAC,[161] plowing nearly $8 million into congressional races in 1980 alone. It was a precursor to the so-called Super PACs that would eventually allow billionaires, labor unions, and corporations to spend millions of dollars to elect their preferred candidates. And in another omen of America's political future, the group that Black and Stone helped create spent much of its money on vicious attack ads against Democrats and moderate Republicans. One of the benefits of a PAC, as another cofounder, Terry Dolan, explained to a reporter, came from the organization's legal structure. "Groups like ours are potentially very dangerous to the political process. We could be a menace, yes. Ten independent expenditure groups, for example, could amass this great amount of money and defeat the point of accountability in politics. We could say whatever we want about an opponent of a Senator Smith, and the senator wouldn't have to say anything. A group like ours could lie through its teeth, and the candidate it helps stays clean."[162] That's because, unlike political candidates themselves, PACs don't face the accountability of voters on Election Day.

Black and Stone then went to work for Reagan's 1976 presidential campaign, which came within 118 votes of defeating the sitting commander in chief, Gerald Ford, at the GOP convention. In 1977 Black advised Manafort and Stone during their successful takeover of the Young Republicans.

As a group, Black, Manafort, Stone, and Atwater advanced a more hotheaded, populist brand of conservatism that became known as the New Right movement. Its adherents weren't conservatives so much as "radicals working to overturn the present power structure in this country,"[163] according to Paul Weyrich, one of the movement's leaders. Members of the New Right, for instance, came to believe that, by the late 1970s, even Barry Goldwater had sold out to the Republican establishment.[164] Among their central objectives was to reorient the machinery of conservatism around the working class, or, as the writer Kevin Phillips put it, create "a cultural siege-engine out of the populist steel of Idaho, Mississippi, and working-class Milwaukee, and then blast the eastern liberal establishment to ideological-institutional smithereens."[165] In 1977 the New Right's more belligerent approach to politics was articulated by a former West Georgia College history professor who was then making his third attempt at a congressional seat. "One of the great problems we have in the Republican Party is that we don't encourage you to be nasty," Newt Gingrich said at the time. "We encourage you to be neat, obedient, and loyal, and faithful, and all those Boy Scout words, which would be great around the campfire but are lousy in politics. . . . You're fighting a war. A war for power. . . . What we really need are people who are willing to stand up in a slug fest."[166]

Together, these four young operatives would help build a pivotal, if tenuous, alliance between the GOP's New Right insurgents and its Big Business advocates—two wings of the party that had long viewed each other with contempt. In the summer of 1978, for example, Roger Stone and fellow conservative activists gathered at the home of New Right pioneer Richard Viguerie for a coordinating meeting that—in an unusual development—also included trade association officials, corporate lobbyists, and representatives of the US Chamber of Commerce and the Business-Industry Political Action Committee.[167] Following this gathering, the share of corporate PAC spending going to Republicans spiked to 71 percent in

October 1978.[168] The New Right's leaders "had previously bragged about their contempt for 'big business'; big business kept the New Right at a distance, as extremist yahoos," as Rick Perlstein wrote in *Reaganland*. "Now they would be working in harness."[169] Gradually, over the following years, this pragmatic accord would work to align the party's working-class populists and its free-market capitalists in a crusade to reduce the government's role in the economy—an essential milestone in the conservative takeover of the GOP as well as the rise of corporate power in Washington.

At the time, however, the nascent alliance remained fractious and uneasy, filled with tension, mistrust, and backstabbing. And even with the tentative support of certain members of the business community, conservative revolutionaries such as Black, Manafort, Stone, and Atwater hadn't been able to wrest complete control of the Republican Party away from the GOP's more liberal, East Coast elites. Meanwhile, Ronald Reagan's ascent had turned the long-running feud between the party's moderate establishment and its conservative wing into a full-blown civil war. To the Far Right, Reagan was the long-awaited savior: a former Hollywood leading man, union president, and New Deal evangelist who'd converted to the religion of free-market capitalism, became the folksy, budget-slashing governor of one of the country's most diverse states, and emerged as a national leader in the crusade against high taxes and federal power.[170] Though he had called FDR his "true hero," Reagan adopted his antigovernment identity during the eight years he spent at General Electric, where he hosted a TV show that spotlighted the company's appliances—*General Electric Theater*, it was called—and served as a goodwill ambassador for the industrial giant. Through his "postgraduate course in political science," as he called his time at GE, Reagan came to see efforts of unions, consumer groups, and environmental advocates to expand the government's authority as a critical threat to free enterprise.[171] Before long, he was articulating his worldview in homespun punch lines: "Government's view of the economy could be summed up in a few short phrases: If it moves, tax it. If it keeps moving, regulate it. And if it stops moving, subsidize it."[172] But to the more liberal members of the party's eastern establishment, Reagan was simply a more polished version of Barry Goldwater—an antigovernment fanatic whose appeal rested far outside the American mainstream. Supporting "the Gipper" for president, the moderates insisted, would be an act of self-destruction: Reagan wouldn't just blow the 1980 election, he would portray the entire Republican Party as a coterie of dangerous extremists.

As the swashbuckling new leaders of the Young Republicans, Manafort and Stone played a pivotal role in this intraparty struggle. As soon as they acquired control of the organization, they refashioned it into a vehicle for advancing the right-wing rebellion. Manafort and Stone worked to unmoor the Young Republicans from the party's moderate establishment and convert the group's legions of energetic activists[173] into shock troops for the Reagan campaign. For Stone, a die-hard conservative since age twelve, supporting Reagan was the natural extension of a deep-seated conviction. He'd been with Reagan since the 1976 election, when he served as the campaign's national youth director. For Manafort, however, backing Reagan for president was a 180-degree reversal. Less than two years earlier, he'd been a Gerald Ford loyalist doing everything he could to crush Reagan's White House aspirations. Manafort was viewed with suspicion by other conservatives on account of his shifting allegiances. But unlike Stone, Manafort had never been ideologically driven. He was a canny tactician who rigorously studied the trend lines of power. And by the late 1970s, he'd concluded that Reagan provided the best opportunity for the Republican Party, and for himself.[174]

Manafort and Stone ran the Young Republicans as black-hearted patriots of the conservative cause, using scorched-earth tactics to exterminate any whiff of moderate influence inside the group. "These guys were nut-cutting, tough operatives," says one former Young Republicans member from this era. Manafort and Stone were guided by an old political maxim: "The first thing you do when a fire starts in your house is not to get a bucket of water to put it out; you start a fire in your neighbor's house."[175] Neal Acker, for example, was a thirtysomething Alabama attorney who'd been a faithful lieutenant to Manafort during the 1977 convention in Memphis, working to persuade southern delegates to vote for Stone as Young Republicans chairman. In return for his help in securing the victory, Acker joined the organization's leadership team as its general counsel, and Manafort and

Stone pledged that at the following convention, in 1979, they would put their political muscle behind his bid to succeed Stone.[176] Manafort even promised to manage Acker's campaign himself. A week before the convention, everything was set; Acker was the only candidate in the race. But then things changed. When rumors surfaced that Acker wouldn't endorse Reagan's presidential campaign, Manafort confronted him with an ultimatum.[177] As the attorney recounted to a reporter, "He told me, 'Support Reagan or else.'"[178] When Acker refused, explaining that he preferred to defy tradition and remain neutral in the race, Manafort made his once loyal ally the target of a vicious political hit.[179]

According to a former member of the Young Republicans who attended the 1979 convention, Manafort and his allies leaked to delegates what they claimed was an embarrassing secret from his past; Acker, who was married at the time, had engaged in an affair with an also-married woman who worked at the Republican National Committee. Next, Manafort and others arranged for a second candidate—who hadn't expressed any prior interest in chairing the organization—to enter the race as Acker's challenger. This second candidate, Rick Abell, said later that he was "shocked" when, just a few days before the convention, he received a call from Acker's opponents informing him, "We want you to run."[180] Manafort then signed on to manage the challenger's campaign, urged delegates once loyal to Acker to vote for his opponent instead,[181] and watched in delight as his Manchurian candidate swept the election by a margin of 465 to 180.[182] "In an unprecedented 11th-hour move," the Associated Press reported, "the Reagan supporters steamrolled the defeat of Neal Acker, who up until a week before the group's annual convention was the unopposed candidate for national chairman."[183] It was a thundering assertion of power; the once-future chairman of the Young Republicans was now a cautionary tale about what happens when you get crossways with Paul Manafort. Its impact reverberated far beyond this individual campaign. By maintaining pro-Reagan control of the Young Republicans, Manafort further embedded conservative ideology into the organization's firmament. By employing a style of cutthroat, negative campaigning—which hadn't been widely used in internal races in the Republican Party—he helped foster the more ruthless tradition of electioneering that would come to define American politics over the coming decades. As a result, the thousands of eager activists who joined the Young Republicans—the pipeline of future party leaders—received a political training that was more ideologically conservative and tactically savage than it had been in the past. It was among the developments that helped facilitate the GOP's evolutionary hardening from Dwight Eisenhower's 1950s-era moderation to something altogether different. What's more, the Team's control over the Young Republicans apparatus put pro-Reagan leaders in charge of the influential group just as the conservative hero was gearing up for his next run for president.

In November 1979, a few months after Paul Manafort aligned the Young Republicans behind Ronald Reagan, Charlie Black accompanied Reagan to the New York Hilton, where the former California governor would formally announce his candidacy for president. Stepping into the ballroom packed with about a thousand well-to-do supporters,[184] each of whom had made a $500 campaign donation in exchange for admittance, Reagan flashed his tanned-and-creased smile and offered a simple way out of an economic crisis that had baffled the nation's intellectual establishment. The country could conquer inflation and put people back to work, he insisted, but only by liberating private enterprise from the tyranny of Uncle Sam.[185]

"The people have not created this disaster in our economy; the federal government has," Reagan told the crowd. "It has overspent, overestimated, and overregulated."[186] The following day, he set off on his first campaign swing of the race: a five-day tour through the Northeast region's early primary states.[187]

Four years after nearly pulling off the biggest upset in Republican primary history, Reagan was back in the race for the White House, this time as the front-runner. Among the first people he hired was Black, who would serve as the campaign's national political director, essentially the second-highest-ranking position on his staff. For Black and the other members of this new generation of antigovernment radicals, the Reagan campaign was the opportunity of a lifetime. Not since Barry Goldwater had an authentic conservative been so well positioned to capture the White House. With the country's most ambitious conservative operatives scrambling to join the team, Black helped secure positions for his pals. Roger Stone was put in charge of the effort to gather support for Reagan in the Northeast region, while Paul Manafort and Lee Atwater handled the southern states. It was the first time that the four young operatives had worked together on a single campaign. As the race got under way, though, Reagan's route to the nomination proved more treacherous than expected. In the first contest of the primary calendar, the Iowa caucuses, Reagan suffered a startling loss to George H. W. Bush, the Yale-educated champion of the GOP's establishment. The humiliating defeat triggered recriminations inside the Reagan campaign's already divided leadership. Over the following weeks, Reagan's California-based set of advisors convinced the former governor that the blame for the defeat lay with his strategists in Washington. They urged him to fire his DC-based campaign manager, John Sears, who was Black's boss.

The next test for Reagan was the New Hampshire primary, in February 1980. While traveling to a campaign event on the Friday before the vote, Reagan called Black to join him at the front of the campaign bus. As Black recalled later in an interview, the future president asked how he would respond to the ouster of Sears. "If I had to do something about John," Reagan said, "would you stick with the campaign?"

It was a delicate question. Sears wasn't just Black's longtime friend and ally; he was the most influential advisor on the staff. If he were fired, Reagan's West Coast advisors would begin calling the shots for the rest of the staff, undercutting the authority of Black and his counterparts in Washington. "No, Governor," Black told Reagan. If Sears was fired from the campaign, he would depart as well. "I think John and his strategic ability is too important, and you might not be able to win without him." It was an act of tactical loyalty—a calculated bet that Reagan wouldn't risk losing two of his top staffers over an internal power struggle. It backfired.

On the morning of the New Hampshire primary, Reagan pulled aside Black and Sears at the hotel where they were all staying. "Can you come to the suite?" he asked.

Upon entering the room, Black and Sears were greeted by Reagan and his wife, Nancy. William Casey, a former SEC chairman and Reagan advisor, sat off in a corner.

"Listen, guys," Reagan began, "we've been having some problems, and I have to put an end to it." With that, Reagan handed a sheet of paper to Sears, who began reading the document to himself. Black was furious. He recognized, correctly, that the document was a press release announcing that he and Sears had been fired from the campaign, and he was not about to end this chapter of his career that way. So, when Sears finished reading the paper and passed it over to him, Black placed the document facedown on the coffee table.

"Governor, I don't know what this is for," Black said, barely suppressing his anger, "but I want you to know that I resign."

Black and Sears left Reagan's hotel suite in silence. It was all over. Moments earlier, Black had been a top aide to a future president. Now he was an unemployed political consultant in need of a ride home to Washington.

William Casey was soon named the new manager of Ronald Reagan's campaign, and Black caught a commercial flight back to DC.

The embarrassing exit turned out to be a stroke of good fortune. When Black returned to Washington and began searching for a way back into the action, he reached out to Paul Manafort and Roger Stone about forming a three-man consulting shop that would help elect conservative political candidates. Though Manafort and Stone continued to work for the Reagan campaign, they agreed to join Black's new venture as well. Atwater chose to remain inside the campaign full-time. Before long, the partners signed the Reagan campaign as one of their first political clients, performing many of the same tasks they'd done prior to Black's firing. The launch of Black, Manafort & Stone, which took place on April 1, 1980[188]—Paul Manafort's thirty-first birthday—was immaculately well timed. Three of the country's best-connected young conservatives were going into business for themselves just as the tectonic plates of power in Washington were undergoing an epochal shift.

Corporate executives initially considered Reagan too radical and inexperienced to guide the country out of the economic darkness. During the GOP primary, they were more comfortable donating money to moderate figures such as George Bush, an eastern establishment Republican, and former Texas governor John Connally, who'd been a Democrat for most of his career. However, after Reagan bounced back from his Iowa loss and emerged as the party's presumptive nominee, the business community rallied behind him with generous financial support.[189] Industry leaders also accelerated their efforts to push Congress's ideological center of gravity to the right. In 1980, business PACs plowed nearly $40 million into congressional races, a sixfold increase from what they'd spent during the 1976 campaign. In some instances, businesses took the politically risky step of sending more money to Republican challengers than they did to the Democratic incumbents they were running against.[190]

On November 4, 1980, just over eight months after Black was fired from the campaign, Reagan routed President Jimmy Carter by a margin of 489 electoral votes to 49, in what would prove to be the most consequential election in fifty years. In the face of an economic catastrophe that was crushing the American spirit, voters chose as their commander in chief neither a liberal Democrat nor a moderate Republican, but a hard-line conservative. The results of the congressional elections were just as earth-shaking. In addition to capturing the White House, Republicans picked up a dozen seats in the Senate, enough to take control of the upper chamber. Three of these new Republican senators had been elected with the help of Black, Manafort & Stone. In the House, Republicans gained thirty-four seats. It was an astonishing feat. For nearly a half century, Democratic majorities on Capitol Hill had been an unremarkable fact of life in the nation's capital. With the exception of two brief stretches, Democrats had controlled both houses of Congress since 1933. Now, suddenly—and without warning—Capitol Hill was home to what David Vogel called "the most conservative Congress in a generation."[191]

Such a dramatic realignment of power had occurred only once before in the United States. Back in the early 1930s, voters sent Franklin D. Roosevelt and his liberal allies to Washington to extract the country from the Great Depression. Over the next four decades, the so-called New Deal Coalition—union workers, Blacks, women, southerners, and recent immigrants—provided lawmakers with the political support for the sweeping expansion of the federal enterprise, including increased government authority over business. Now, forty-eight years later, and with the financial backing of America's corporate giants, Reagan had assembled an equally powerful alliance of voters: southern whites who had left the Democratic Party because of its support for civil rights; blue-collar workers who'd also defected from the Left; evangelical Christians; Catholics concerned about abortion rights; business owners; and white-collar professionals. In November 1980 this "Reagan coalition" delivered a historic rejection of New Deal liberalism, sending a free-market ideologue to the White House with a mandate to dismantle the federal bureaucracy and unleash the full force of American capitalism.

Although the Reagan campaign had benefited from a range of social, economic, and political forces, Lee Atwater attributed the election of America's first conservative president to one critical development. "For one hundred fifty years, the establishment has always been business," Atwater told a reporter later. "Roosevelt came in and established another establishment, and it was the government. So, for the first time, you have two establishments." He continued, "I read the *National Enquirer* every week. The *National Enquirer* readership is the exact key, swing voter I am talking about. If you read those *National Enquirer* stories, there'll be about four or five about wasteful government projects, spending $400,000 to study some flying tree lizard. But at the same time, there'll be some stories in there about some millionaire that has five Cadillacs and hasn't paid taxes since 1974, or so-and-so Republican congressman who never paid taxes. It's which one of these establishments that the public sees as 'the bad guy' that determines which party wins elections." In the 1980 presidential campaign, he said, "we were able to define the establishment, insofar as it is bad, as government, not big business."[192]

The emergence of businessmen as *good guys* was part of a broader change rippling through the country at the time of Reagan's victory. During the economic slog of the late 1970s, when many young, college-educated professionals were revisiting their once-critical assessments of capitalism and embracing the benefits of the free market, America's cultural values began to shift. "No more radical chic," as *BusinessWeek* reported. "Instead . . . making money was in. Business, viewed with contempt by some in recent years, is now popular."[193] On college campuses, students stopped protesting the injustices of capitalism and began enrolling in business courses. From 1973 to 1983, the percentage of American students who graduated with business degrees surged nearly twofold, and from 1975 to 1985, the number of master of business administration (MBA) degrees conferred by graduate schools jumped by 87 percent.[194]

At the same time, the new decade witnessed the rise of an unlikely set of celebrities: American CEOs. Chrysler chairman Lee Iacocca achieved a level of star power typically reserved for Hollywood leading men after he rescued the auto giant from bankruptcy—thanks partly to a 1979 federal bailout engineered by Tommy Boggs—and returned it to profitability. His autobiography sold more copies than any other nonfiction title for two years straight, and he was soon ranked among the most admired men in America.[195] Other businessmen basked in the public's admiration as well. T. Boone Pickens, a swaggering oil-and-gas magnate and corporate raider from Texas, was on the cover of nearly two dozen magazines in the 1980s.[196] When billionaire software entrepreneur H. Ross Perot funded a daring rescue of two of his employees from an Iranian prison, it became the subject of an NBC TV movie.[197] And in 1987 a forty-one-year-old New York real estate developer named Donald Trump achieved national attention for his best-selling book *The Art of the Deal*.[198] "Never before has the business of business been such a cultural preoccupation," wrote the television producer Norman Lear. "America once found their heroes, for the most part, in Congress or the entertainment world or sports; now more and more people find them in business."[199]

While corporate leaders were encouraged by the public's less hostile attitudes toward business, they were elated by the results of the 1980 election. "Wall Street and the business community yesterday welcomed the election of Ronald Reagan," the *New York Times* reported, "amid predictions that the president elect would oversee the most pro-business administration since that of Dwight D. Eisenhower."[200] *BusinessWeek* suggested that the new administration might very well "end the long adversary relationship between business and government in the US."[201] Indeed, Reagan's triumph christened a new era in Washington.[202] In the mid-1960s, when Capitol Hill was controlled by New Deal liberals and moderate Democrats, such as Congressman Hale Boggs, America's business leaders were losing ground. Overmatched by the political power of labor unions, consumer groups, public interest attorneys, and environmentalists, CEOs could only watch helplessly as liberal lawmakers enacted a flood of new regulations on their activities. In the early 1970s, business leaders were able to gather political strength in Washington and, with the help of skilled lobbyists like Tommy Boggs, began fighting back against the additional regulatory and pro-union initiatives coming out of Congress. The 1980 election strengthened the corporate community's hand even further; executives now had a free-market advocate in the White House, a Republican majority in the Senate, and a growing number of pro-industry allies in the House. After nearly two decades on their heels, corporate interests in Washington were ready to go on the attack. "It's time for us," one official with the National Association of Manufacturers said, "to put our legislative muscle where our rhetorical mouths have been for the last twenty years."[203]

In January 1981, business leaders from around the country flocked to Washington for Reagan's inauguration. They spent the week toasting the capitalist president at black-tie parties that were often paid for by corporations, such as Exxon, General Motors, and IBM. A few weeks after Reagan was sworn in, hundreds of Big Business lobbyists packed into a fourth-floor room of the Old Executive Office Building, next door to the White House, where presidential aide Wayne Valis explained what the corporate community could expect from the new administration. "Like the Confederacy, you have only won defensive victories. That leads to defeat," Valis told the crowd. "If you will march with us this time, you will win offensive victories."[204]

The lobbyists broke into applause.

4

Following Reagan's victory, Charlie Black, Paul Manafort, and Roger Stone
worked to grow their business from a rented town house in Alexandria,
just across the Potomac River from the nation's capital. At first, they intended the firm to focus exclusively on helping conservative candidates
win elections. Before long, though, a new opportunity emerged.

America's leading corporations were eager to reap the benefits of Reagan's pro-business agenda. In order to do so, they needed the assistance
of lobbyists with friends in the new administration—officials who could
tweak a rule in their favor, steer a government contract their way, or head
off an undesirable regulation. But who should these corporations hire?
Washington's existing political-influence community was ill suited to the
task. Because liberals had ruled Congress for most of the prior fifty years,
Washington's stable of lobbyists consisted largely of Democrats, and the few
GOP influence peddlers in the city had little to offer. The Watergate scandal
had expelled the best-connected Republican fixers from the Beltway,[1] and
those who remained were just the sort of moderate establishment figures
the new administration despised. Black, Manafort, and Stone were different. As conservative revolutionaries who'd helped put Reagan in the Oval

Office, they had close relationships with the antigovernment crusaders who'd taken control of Washington. Stone and Manafort had even helped manage the new administration's transition effort, deciding which officials to install at agencies throughout the city.[2] And their buddy Lee Atwater had been named a deputy political director in Reagan's White House, where his job was, among other things, to ensure that the president remained popular with his base of industry executives, religious groups, and blue-collar workers. Soon corporate executives began approaching Black, Manafort & Stone about representing them as lobbyists before the new administration.

"Why in the hell would we want to do that?" Black asked his partners. "It's boring as hell!"

Manafort assured Black that the work wasn't all that dull. Besides, he said, "It paid well."[3]

What emerged was the signature political-influence firm of 1980s Washington—an amalgam of traditional lobbying, modern electioneering, and old-fashioned hustle. It was built on a straightforward innovation. As a result of the deluge of money that began flowing into politics in the 1970s, the nation's capital had become home to a bustling economy of specialized service providers, such as lobbying shops, campaign consulting firms, polling companies, and public relations outfits. The partners' central breakthrough was to merge all of these services into a single enterprise:[4] a fully integrated political-influence firm that resembled the diversified conglomerates it advocated for. Technically, the business had two distinct entities: Black, Manafort & Stone, which handled the corporate lobbying work, and a political consulting firm, eventually called Black, Manafort, Stone & Atwater. In Washington, the two entities were known simply as Black Manafort.[5]

Black Manafort was a lobbying shop that could secure a tax break for a multinational corporation. It was a campaign consulting outfit that could get a politician elected to Congress. It was a public relations agency that could spin a journalist. It was even an international advocacy business that could line up federal funding for an overseas despot.[6] By combining these disparate skill sets with their network of well-placed contacts, the partners created a new type of lobbying operation that revolutionized K Street. "If someone asked me the most important ingredient in how we built the firm," says Scott Pastrick, a lobbyist who joined the company in 1984, "it wasn't just the relationships, but how these guys thought."

Before long, Black Manafort was advancing the political interests of the era's most iconic companies and tycoons: media mogul Rupert Murdoch, pioneering investment bank Salomon Brothers, corporate raider Carl Icahn, pharmaceutical giant Johnson & Johnson, Wall Street financier Ron Perelman, industrial titan Bethlehem Steel, and an up-and-coming New York City real estate magnate named Donald Trump. At the firm's headquarters in Alexandria, staffers grew accustomed to unplanned run-ins with America's ruling elite—spotting George W. Bush[7] in the hallway or stumbling upon Lee Iacocca in the kitchen at the firm's annual holiday party. The firm's explosive ascent reflected the ambitions of its partners. Black, Manafort, and Stone—aged thirty-two, thirty-one, and twenty-seven, respectively, when the business launched—stormed into the political-influence industry with the same swagger that they'd brought to the campaign trail. "They were political guys and hustlers," says one former colleague. "They didn't and couldn't follow rules." While accumulating the trappings of inside-the-Beltway success—car phones, golf club memberships, first-class seats on the Concorde—they crashed through ethical guidelines, triggered congressional investigations, and achieved a level of notoriety that was unusual for K Street operators.[8] Amid the haze of money and testosterone, the firm developed a hard-partying culture that featured weekend-long booze binges at pricey golf resorts, casual misogyny at the office, and paid performances by dwarfs at company functions. "We were smoking cigars in the middle of the day and drinking and having sex with hot secretaries," says one former firm employee.

Despite the rule-breaking instincts of its partners—or, perhaps, because of them—Black Manafort's legacy would stretch far beyond Washington. The firm helped reengineer the American economy to better suit its corporate clients, clearing away the regulations and tax burdens that cut into quarterly profits. It laid the groundwork for the launch of the country's first conservative news network, Fox News. It helped redraw the world map in the final decade of the Cold War, supporting guerrilla revolutions in some parts of the globe and propping up iron-fisted despots in others. And it orchestrated Donald Trump's first incursion into Washington politics—a critical, early step in his evolution from New York playboy to national political firebrand.

"Paul and Charlie and Roger were really masters of the universe—masters of the Beltway," says one former lobbyist at the firm. "It was intoxicating."

The firm's initial growth was rooted in the same type of insider-access lobbying that Tommy Boggs had practiced, this time with the newly empowered Republicans who controlled Washington. Among the first clients to reach out to Black Manafort was the tiny oil company Tosco Corporation.[9] The California-based firm had developed a new way to extract oil from shale rock, and its executives believed that the innovation would allow it to access the vast, untapped oil reservoirs in the western slope of the Rocky Mountains in Colorado. It was a profitable opportunity but also a massive undertaking. So, Tosco partnered with oil giant Exxon Corp., and the two firms pursued the project as a joint venture. Reaching the oil would be expensive. Tosco and Exxon would need to purchase a stockpile of sophisticated drills, specialized trucks, and other equipment for the project, which was expected to cost a total of more than $3 billion. The companies wanted help from Washington. As a result of the 1970s energy crises, the federal government had begun working to increase oil production in the United States, and the Tosco and Exxon executives wondered if the Reagan administration might be willing to lend a hand with their project. They decided to seek a $1.1 billion loan guarantee from the US Department of Energy.

At first, the Tosco executives approached Patton Boggs for assistance. But a lobbyist at the Democratic firm told them they'd have better luck navigating the Reagan administration if they hired Black Manafort. It was excellent advice; as it turned out, the firm had a valuable friend at the Energy Department.

In the weeks before President Reagan was sworn in, Charlie Black had received a phone call from an old pal. It was Jim Edwards, the former Republican governor of South Carolina whom Black had known for years through conservative political circles. Edwards had just learned that he would be nominated to serve as Reagan's secretary of energy.

"What the hell do I do?" Edwards asked in disbelief, according to Black. "I don't know anything about this."

"Well," Black responded, "the first thing you need to worry about is getting confirmed."

Black promised to do everything he could to help. The following day, Black and Paul Manafort flew to Charleston, South Carolina, to meet with the nervous Edwards. After explaining the details of the confirmation process, the two operatives mapped out a strategy for winning Senate approval that relied on getting to know the lawmakers who would be most influential in his confirmation vote. Returning to Washington, they chaperoned Edwards to meetings with politicians such as Tennessee Senator Howard Baker, the incoming Senate majority leader and a member of the Senate Committee on Energy and Natural Resources. Under Black and Manafort's guidance, Edwards was confirmed easily. He took over as energy secretary a few days after Reagan's inauguration.

The following year, when Black was hired to obtain the loan guarantee for Tosco and Exxon, he turned to Edwards's agency for assistance. According to Black, he guided the oil executives through the sprawling bureaucracy, helping them to file their application with the appropriate division. At the same time, other Black Manafort lobbyists persuaded members of Colorado's congressional delegation to write letters urging the Energy Department to approve the loan guarantee. Black said he never spoke directly with Secretary Edwards about the issue because he didn't want to take advantage of his personal friendship. But he didn't have to. On the occasion when paperwork got hung up inside the department, Black or a colleague contacted one of Edwards's deputies to make sure the application moved along. Almost everyone who worked for Edwards knew that Charlie Black was one of the reasons Edwards had the job in the first place. Within a year, the agency had approved the $1.1 billion loan guarantee.[10]

Victories like this helped burnish Black Manafort's image as the best-connected lobbying firm in Reagan's Washington—a reputation that turbocharged demand for its services. In 1984 Black received a call from Rupert

Murdoch, the Australian media executive whom he'd come to know during Reagan's 1980 presidential campaign. Murdoch's tabloid newspaper, the *New York Post*, had emerged as a key ally of the president's—providing Reagan with its formal endorsement as well as a dependable supply of unflattering articles about his political rivals. In the final month before the 1984 election, for example, the *Post* published no fewer than ten negative front-page stories about Geraldine Ferraro—the running mate of Reagan's Democratic opponent, Walter Mondale—many of which linked her to organized crime. One smear was so vicious that it reportedly caused Ferraro to break down in tears.[11] Murdoch summoned Black to New York for a discreet meeting, Black said in an interview. A few days later, Black arrived in a spacious Manhattan office and listened as the budding media mogul laid out a top-secret new venture. "I am going to build a fourth TV network," Murdoch said.

The plan, Murdoch explained, was to buy up a movie studio as well as a string of local TV stations and tie them together as a nationwide network. It was an audacious proposal. Despite his thriving media conglomerate in Australia, Murdoch still wasn't terribly influential in America. At the time, his US holdings were limited to a few local television stations and some second-tier newspapers, like the *Post* and the *Chicago Sun-Times*. In attempting to start a new TV network from scratch, he would face savage competition from the three incumbent networks—ABC, CBS, and NBC— and intense scrutiny from officials in Washington. The media business was among the most heavily regulated industries in America, and Murdoch would have to overcome a number of legal and regulatory obstacles in order to realize his vision. For one thing, the Federal Communications Commission barred foreign nationals, like Murdoch, from owning large media companies. Beyond that, Murdoch's planned acquisition spree would violate federal rules limiting the number of TV stations that could be owned by a single entity, as well as restrictions on the ownership of newspapers and TV stations in the same market. When Murdoch explained his plan to Black, the lobbyist was incredulous. "That's crazy," Black thought. "How is this guy going to pull this off?"

Still, according to Black, Murdoch was confident that he could muscle his new network into existence. "I can handle the business side," he told

Black. "I need you guys to give me a road map of how to go about the governing side." He asked Black to gather intelligence on the challenges his effort would face in Washington and provide introductions to key Reagan administration officials. Everything had to be carried out in secret, Murdoch insisted. If executives at ABC, CBS, or NBC learned of his ambitions, they would dispatch their own lobbyists to sabotage his plans.

When he returned to Washington, Black assigned a mid-level lobbyist to gather the intelligence that Murdoch had requested. The lobbyist went about obtaining the information through casual conversations with government sources. Over lunch with a senior FCC official, she asked about the regulatory obstacles to creating a fourth network. During a midday meal with a former lawmaker, she inquired as to how Congress would react if Murdoch tried to acquire a movie studio. And while having lunch with a top congressional aide, she asked how the Democratic chairman of the House Commerce Committee felt about Murdoch.

Once the lobbyists had a handle on the political landscape, Black began connecting Murdoch with top federal regulators in the Reagan administration. In January 1985 he arranged for Murdoch to have dinner in Washington with Mark Fowler, the conservative media lawyer whom President Reagan had installed as chairman of the FCC. "He is exactly the type of person you need the support of," Black told Murdoch. In a strategy session beforehand, Black counseled Murdoch to describe his plan for a fourth television network in terms that reflected the Reagan administration's free-market ideology. They agreed on a message to drive home: competition benefits everyone. During his dinner with Fowler, Murdoch argued that a fourth TV network could invigorate the staid television market and provide Americans with more entertainment choices.

Murdoch's pitch appealed to Fowler, who, by the end of his term, would take to calling himself "Mr. Deregulation."[12] In the first four years of the Reagan administration, Fowler and his FCC colleagues had been loosening its decades-old restrictions on media ownership put in place in the 1930s to prevent foreign powers from using the media to disseminate propaganda in the United States. Fowler's moves were part of a broader effort to eliminate regulations and disrupt the monopoly of the three existing networks.[13] To

Fowler, Murdoch's gambit was just what the broadcast industry needed. "It was creating competition and a new choice for America's eyeballs," Fowler recalled. At dinner and over the subsequent months, the powerful regulator guided Murdoch as the media mogul cleared the way for his new venture. It was unusual, but not illegal, for a corporate executive to work with an agency chief to deconstruct regulations they each opposed. Fowler offered advice on how to sidestep the regulatory roadblocks, suggesting to Murdoch that he could get around the prohibition on foreign ownership by simply becoming a US citizen. Murdoch then worked with Fowler and the FCC to obtain years-long waivers on rules that would have prevented him from buying TV stations in the markets where he already owned newspapers: New York, Chicago, and Boston. Meantime, Reagan's FCC was relaxing its media concentration rules, allowing Murdoch to finalize his acquisitions of dozens of local TV stations around the country and complete its purchase of a 50 percent stake in the parent company of 20th Century Fox Film Co.[14] In October 1985, with the deregulatory efforts in full tilt, Murdoch unveiled his plans for his new nationwide network to the public. Borrowing a name from his recently acquired movie studio, he called it Fox News.

The favors granted to Tosco and Rupert Murdoch weren't isolated perks. They exemplified how the Reagan administration was reimagining the relationship between the American state and its economy. For most of the prior half century, Washington policy makers had viewed the federal government as a muscular check on the awesome power of capitalism. Through their control of the nation's capital, New Deal liberals empowered regulators to curb abuses in the market and, as Thomas Edsall pointed out, they deployed tax and spending policies to promote equity and modestly redistribute income down the economic food chain.[15] But through their efforts in the late 1970s, this confederation of corporate lobbyists and conservative ideologues rallied support for a competing vision. Washington shouldn't restrict the power of the free market, they argued. Rather, policy makers should amplify it by eradicating any and all barriers to maximum economic efficiency, such as unions, regulations, taxes, trade protections, and social welfare spending—which required taxes to sustain and bureaucrats to administer. As soon as he took power, Reagan used his authority to implement this pro-business vision, enshrining efficiency, as opposed to equity, as the animating principle of economic policy making[16] by working to cut corporate taxes, reduce regulations, and remove trade barriers.

Although Jimmy Carter had selected public interest advocates to run his federal agencies, Reagan turned to business leaders and antigovernment activists. These free-market-oriented appointees went about enfeebling the very agencies they were charged with leading. From 1981 to 1982, Reagan slashed the Consumer Product Safety Commission's budget by nearly 40 percent, cut the FTC's budget by nearly 30 percent, and reduced the National Highway Traffic Safety Administration's budget by 22 percent.[17] He shrank the number of employees at the Office of Surface Mining Reclamation and Enforcement by 37 percent and cut a quarter of the EPA's staff.[18] More significantly, Reagan's pro-business regulators adopted a permissive attitude toward enforcement. EPA officials referred 84 percent fewer cases to the Justice Department in 1981 than they had the previous year. At the Occupational Safety and Health Administration, the number of citations issued to business owners for serious hazards dropped by 47 percent, and fines plummeted by nearly 70 percent.[19] Thorne Auchter, a former construction executive whom Reagan installed as OSHA director, explained that "our philosophy is one of safety and health and not one of crime and punishment."[20]

Agency officials also worked to undo the legacies of their liberal predecessors. During Carter's four years in office, his administration had listed 150 species as endangered; in Reagan's first year, his administration listed only one.[21] Interior Secretary James Watt, a lifelong critic of federal land preservation efforts, opened up thousands of acres of public land to drillers and engineered the largest coal deal in American history—selling off 2.24 billion tons of coal from the Powder River Basin of Montana and Wyoming.[22] That's enough coal to fill a set of rail cars stretching more than 225,000 miles long.

While the Reagan administration was opening doors for business owners, it treated unionized workers with open contempt. After Reagan's appointees joined the National Labor Relations Board, a five-member body that adjudicates disputes between workers and management, the board became far more sympathetic to industry's priorities. Between 1983 and 1984, the NLRB sided with businesses in 72 percent of its decisions in representation cases, a dramatic reversal from eight years earlier, when it had ruled in favor of workers 65 percent of the time.[23] As this once-robust protection against employer abuse withered, America's unionized labor force shrank to its lowest level since the 1930s.[24]

Through their lobbying efforts for US corporate leaders, the partners at Black Manafort secured valuable political favors for individual companies and facilitated these foundational changes to the nation's economy. They helped deregulate the natural gas industry on behalf of a leading oil-and-gas trade association. They won a lucrative tax perk for the iconic Wall Street brokerage house Salomon Brothers. They assisted the cosmetics giant Revlon, which was owned by business magnate Ron Perelman, in fending off FDA regulators. They helped the famed corporate raider Carl Icahn fight new regulations from Congress and the Transportation Department after his 1986 hostile takeover of Trans World Airlines. They helped Sprint Corp. win part of a multibillion-dollar contract to provide phone service to federal agencies by finding a senior lawmaker to block the government from awarding the contract to a competing company. They changed US Interior Department rules to allow a client to rent snowmobiles in national parks. They rallied support to keep an aging helicopter fleet in operation even after the US Navy sought to kill it.

These services came at a steep cost. When a foreign-owned oil company needed a change in tax law to help wealthy investors, Black Manafort arranged for a face-to-face meeting with the head of the House's tax committee. The fee: $40,000.

In the mid-1980s the partners at Black Manafort left their original town house office and moved to a new headquarters that better reflected their standing in Washington. The handsome redbrick building was perched on the Alexandria waterfront. Black's desk overlooked the Potomac River. Manafort's office had a private balcony. At Monday morning staff meetings, the firm's two dozen lobbyists huddled around a mahogany conference table. Just five years after its founding, Black Manafort had emerged as the toast of K Street. The *Washington Post* described the firm as "a major new presence in the capital" run by "the cream of Republican inside operatives."[25] *Time* magazine called it "The Slickest Shop in Town."[26] As lobbying fees flooded in—$100,000 a year from Kaman Aerospace,[27] $180,000 from Rupert Murdoch, $72,000 from Salomon Brothers—the partners upgraded their aesthetics to match their estimated half-million-dollar annual salaries. They secured memberships at exclusive Washington-area country clubs and obtained a fleet of luxury vehicles. Black bought a Cadillac, Stone purchased a Jaguar, Manafort got a Mercedes. Stone began peacocking through Washington wearing $800 custom-tailored suits[28]—double-breasted with suspenders. He hosted lawn parties featuring French chefs and decorated with flower arrangements curated by a professional floral consultant.[29] Manafort became a connoisseur of silk ties and shiny watches. He had a pool built at his home in the tony suburbs of Virginia, and then, only a few years later, according to what Manafort told friends, he paid tens of thousands of dollars to have the pool demolished and reinstalled just a few feet from its original location. He jetted back and forth to Europe on the Concorde,[30] he arrived at one company event in a chopper, and, as payment for the lobbying work he did for the luxury British automobile manufacturer, he received a brand-new Aston Martin sports car. For a group of hustlers who'd arrived in Washington as part of a working-class revolution, business was booming. "I must confess," Atwater told a reporter, "I'm delighted with my new lifestyle."[31]

Atwater was an on-and-off presence at Black Manafort, working at the firm between stints at the Reagan White House and the 1988 presidential campaign of George H. W. Bush. Among the full-time partners, it was the responsibility of Black—the senior statesman of the group—to provide the adult supervision of his more impulsive colleagues. With a hair-trigger temper and an impatient disposition, Manafort was always running late but never at fault. Each partner had access to the firm's pool of young drivers, or "wheelmen," who chauffeured them around Washington. When Manafort was picked up for an appointment that he was already behind schedule for, he would offer a stern greeting to the driver: "I'm ready to be at my meeting." He seethed at drivers who ran into traffic, according to former employees of the firm; on one occasion, he demanded to be driven the wrong way down a one-way street in order to escape a congested section of Washington. If his driver was cut off by another vehicle, Manafort sometimes rolled down the window and screamed at the offending commuter, "You're a motherfucker!" Once, when his driver got lost on the way to an appointment, Manafort kicked him out of the vehicle and drove himself—forcing a second young staffer to retrieve the driver from the side of the road. "If I wanted to be lost, I could do it myself," Manafort huffed.

At the firm's headquarters, he could be equally volatile, former employees say. From outside his office, staffers occasionally heard him explode during billing disputes with credit card companies. "He would get someone on the phone," says a former staffer, "and say, 'Do you know who I am? I could buy your company!'"

Manafort demanded absolute obedience from his staff. Young employees hoping to ascend the firm's ranks were often put through one of Manafort's "loyalty tests." Manafort once tasked a pair of junior staffers with getting someone who could impersonate Billy Barty—a three-foot, nine-inch actor—to appear at a company party on just twenty-four hours' notice. (Somehow, they did it.)[32] Those who violated Manafort's trust faced his wrath. One former Black Manafort lobbyist recalls that when he informed the partners that he was leaving to start his own lobbying venture, Manafort became irate. "You'll never work in this town again," he hissed. (In fact, the young man grew up to be a top lobbyist for Wall Street.)

Roger Stone, meanwhile, worked to cultivate his reputation as the firm's Bad Boy. After a lifetime of political chicanery, he was despised by Washington's consultant class. Yet he relished his image as an inside-the-Beltway villain. Stone boasted that during a visit to the Palm restaurant, he'd noticed that the caricature of his face on the wall had been stabbed through with a steak knife.[33] "Roger likes the aura of having done something bad in his past," said his then-friend David Keene, referring to his Watergate subterfuge. "You get the feeling that he's sorry it was so minor."[34] He was impeccably dressed at all times, and he could be vicious to staffers who didn't share his sartorial values. One former Black Manafort lobbyist recalls wearing a short-sleeve button-down shirt, dress shoes, and a Brooks Brothers suit when he first met Stone.

"Anyone who wears a shirt with no sleeves has no class," Stone told him, according to the former Black Manafort lobbyist.

After asking to see the man's shoes, Stone tossed them out of the third-floor window. He then instructed the stunned lobbyist to head to Britches of Georgetown, an upscale men's clothing store, and speak with Stone's tailor.

"He'll take care of you," Stone said.

Riva Levinson endured even harsher treatment. She was in her mid-twenties when she joined the firm as one of its only female employees. Because her starting salary was so meager, Levinson sometimes applied Vaseline to her eyelashes instead of shelling out for mascara. Stone didn't approve, telling her that it looked like she had sex lubricant in her eyes. On another occasion, Levinson arrived at the office wearing the first formal professional outfit she'd ever purchased, a red-and-white checkered suit. "Riva," Stone said, "you look like you could be on the cover of a box of Purina Dog Chow."[35]

The partners worked long hours—at the office as early as five in the morning, and out hobnobbing with business executives, administration aides, and lawmakers until late at night. When it came to drinking, they were just as intense. Around five o'clock each Friday during the summer, a partner would dispatch a junior staffer to pick up liquor for the office happy hour. "The rule was: you can only have too little," recalls a former employee. The firm organized an annual weekend retreat of golf and debauchery called the "Boodles Classic,"[36] an homage to a brand of gin. The boozy days on the course might end with a golf cart in a pond or a foursome of plastered lobbyists diving into the pool while wearing their golf shoes. Manafort, who led the firm's "social committee," provided a different theme for the event each year; they included "Excess," "Exceed Excess," and "Excess Is Best."[37] The get-togethers were so unruly that the partners had to find a different golf resort to host them nearly every year, because the venues rarely allowed them back.[38]

Additional revelry took place around the holidays. According to former employees, Manafort handed out bottles of Dom Pérignon for Christmas, and the whole firm gathered in one of the partners' elegant homes for seasonal celebrations. During one such event, a staffer was giving a toast from a makeshift stage when he was drilled in the face with a champagne bottle, losing his front teeth. At a St. Patrick's Day party, a group of employees arranged for a dwarf dressed as a leprechaun to sing "Has Anybody Here Seen Kelly?" to a lobbyist named Peter Kelly.

Things weren't as much fun for the women in the office. Divina Westerfield, a former lobbyist at the firm, accused Manafort in a since-deleted blog post of making repeated advances toward her during the year she spent there. When she complained about the behavior to management, Westerfield said, she was fired. She described the lobbyists at Black Manafort as "the worst womanizers I had ever experienced."[39]

In the 1980s, the country's power elite felt right at home at the firm's headquarters. A son of Republican Senator Phil Gramm was an intern at Black Manafort. The daughter of Chrysler CEO Lee Iacocca was an account executive. And an array of US presidents—past and future—walked through the firm's glass doors. When George H. W. Bush hired Lee Atwater to prepare for his 1988 presidential campaign, the vice president sent his son—future president George W. Bush—to work in the Black Manafort offices to keep tabs on Atwater.[40] Despite the disgrace of Watergate, Stone continued to idolize Richard Nixon, going so far as to give his dog the former president's middle name, Milhous.[41] In the 1980s Stone became Nixon's unofficial DC press secretary, dispatching one of the firm's wheelmen to pick up the former president at the airport and chauffeur him around Washington.[42] At one point, when Stone was rumored to be considering running for Congress in New Jersey, Nixon told an employee of the firm, "I told [Roger] I'd be for him or against him—whatever he needed."

Another future president was a Black Manafort client. Roger Stone had met Donald Trump during the 1980 presidential race through Roy Cohn, the ruthless New York City attorney and ex-counsel to Senator Joseph McCarthy in the 1950s. At the time, Stone was looking to build support for Reagan in the Empire State. "So, Roy set up a meeting for me with Donald,"

Stone told an interviewer. "Donald said, 'Okay, give me the pitch,' and I told him why Reagan would win."[43] Trump became a Reagan backer, providing the campaign staff with the use of his plane, office space, and phones.[44] After the election, Stone persuaded Trump that the new firm could serve as his "eyes and ears" in the nation's capital, and the thirtysomething real estate playboy signed on with Black Manafort.[45] From there, Stone set himself to removing the various bureaucratic impediments to Trump's business ambitions and jet-setting lifestyle.

At one point, Trump purchased a 285-foot yacht—the third largest in the world—from the billionaire Saudi arms dealer Adnan Khashoggi. At $31 million, the yacht's interior had a distinctly Trumpian aesthetic: onyx floors, mahogany walls, gold-plated pillars, a private elevator, and an on-board disco.[46] There was just one problem: the *Trump Princess* was too big for the marina in Atlantic City, New Jersey, where Trump wanted to dock it. So, Stone worked his political contacts and secured the necessary permits from the US Army Corps of Engineers to have the harbor dredged deep enough for the ship to pass through. "Those permits can take years," Stone recalled. "I got it done in months."[47]

In 1985 Trump paid $10 million for the eighteen acres of land and property in West Palm Beach, Florida, that would become his private resort, Mar-a-Lago. Eventually, however, he became annoyed by all the airplanes buzzing overhead—Palm Beach International Airport is two and a half miles away—so he dispatched Black Manafort in an unsuccessful effort to get the air traffic rerouted.[48] When Trump purchased the struggling Eastern Airlines and rebranded it as the Trump Shuttle, he hired Stone to help create a media campaign that would lure customers away from its rival, the Pan Am Shuttle, in the Washington–New York–Boston corridor. "This is like a political campaign," Stone said. "Two candidates fighting for at least a fifty-one percent share, using the same tools: TV, radio, print, direct mail, telephones."[49] Stone's work as a political consultant benefited Trump as well. After Stone guided Republican Tom Kean to victory in the 1981 New Jersey gubernatorial election, he pressed the new governor to help Trump expand his casino business in Atlantic City, according to Stone's former colleagues. In addition, Stone told friends that he was among those who persuaded the Reagan White House to nominate Trump's sister—Maryanne Trump Barry—to be a district judge in New Jersey.

Black Manafort also organized Trump's original foray into Washington politics. The firm introduced the aspiring mogul, who was a Democrat at the time, to key members of the 1980s liberal establishment, such as Maryland congressman Steny Hoyer and Ron Brown, a former Patton Boggs lobbyist who in 1989 was named the chairman of the Democratic National Committee, becoming the first Black person to lead either national party. In the late 1980s Trump's Atlantic City casino empire—Trump Plaza, Trump's Castle, and Trump Taj Mahal—was facing a new threat. The Indian Gaming Regulatory Act of 1988, which enabled tribes to open their own casinos,[50] led to the construction of a number of new casinos on Native American lands, including a massive one in Connecticut, less than 270 miles north of Atlantic City.[51] To protect his gaming empire from this unwanted competition, Black Manafort assisted Trump in creating an organization called the Casino Association of New Jersey to lobby state and federal lawmakers. Stone assisted Trump in suing the secretary of interior alleging that the Indian Gaming Act unfairly disadvantaged non-tribal casinos and was therefore unconstitutional.[52]

In 1993 Trump traveled to Washington to testify before a House panel in support of efforts to sharply restrict gaming on tribal land. On the day of the hearing, a team of Black Manafort lobbyists escorted him to Capitol Hill, where he observed the proceedings until it was his turn to address the lawmakers. The policy experts at Black Manafort had spent days preparing for Trump's appearance—crafting a thoughtful, nuanced set of remarks for him to deliver. But as he waited for more than two hours while supporters of Indian gaming argued their points, Trump grew increasingly annoyed. By the time Trump was permitted to take his seat before the House Subcommittee on Native American Affairs, he was fuming. Right off the bat, he tossed aside the advice of his high-priced lobbyists. "I had a rather long and probably very boring speech drawn out, and I have decided not to read this speech," he told the subcommittee. "It was politically correct, it was something that was going to get me in no trouble whatsoever, but I just don't feel it is appropriate to go through it."

Instead, over the course of the hearing, Trump stunned the assembled lawmakers by unleashing the kind of fuming, racially charged tirade that would come to define him:

Trump: "If you look—if you look at some of the reservations that you have approved—you, sir, in your great wisdom, have approved—I will tell you right now, they don't look like Indians to me, and they don't look like Indians. Now maybe we say politically correct or not politically correct. They don't look like Indians to me, and they don't look like Indians to Indians, and a lot of people are laughing at it, and you are telling how tough it is, how rough it is, to get approved. Well, you go up to Connecticut, and you look. Now, they don't look like Indians to me, sir."

George Miller, a Democratic congressman from California and chairman of the House Committee on Natural Resources: "Thank God that is not the test of whether or not people have rights in this country or not, whether or not they pass your look test. . . . Mr. Trump, do you know in the history of this country where we have heard this discussion before: 'They don't look Jewish to me.' . . . 'They don't look Indian to me.' 'They don't look Italian to me.' And that was the test for whether people could go into business or not go into business."

Trump: "I want to find out—well, then, why are you approving—you are approving for Indian. Why don't you approve it for everybody then, sir? If your case is nondiscriminatory, why don't you approve for everybody? You are saying only Indians—wait a minute, sir. You are saying only Indians can have the reservations, only Indians can have the gaming. So why aren't you approving it for everybody? Why are you being discriminatory? Why is it that the Indians don't pay tax but everybody else does?"[53]

Before the hearing came to a close, another Democratic congressman, Neil Abercrombie of Hawaii, declared that "in my nineteen years on this committee, I don't know when I have heard more irresponsible testimony than I just heard."[54] Members of the Black Manafort team were equally appalled. At one point during Trump's rant, lobbyist Scott Pastrick, who was seated right behind the future president, stood up, walked out of the hearing room, and returned to the firm's office. "I was never more embarrassed in my life," he said in an interview.

Years later, when the St. Regis tribe of Mohawk Indians announced plans to build a casino in the Catskill Mountains,[55] Stone and Trump teamed up for another smear job. They set up a new organization, the New York Institute for Law and Society, to help them discredit their would-be competitors.[56] Stone commissioned private investigators to gather unflattering information about the Mohawks, and the institute placed ads on Catskill-area radio stations and in newspapers portraying the tribe's casino effort as a danger to the community.[57]

"The St. Regis Mohawk Indian record of criminal activity is well documented," read one ad. "Are these the new neighbors we want?"[58]

"Now the Mohawks want state approval of a $500 million casino . . . opening the door for organized crime,"[59] read another.

While the institute claimed it was funded by some twelve thousand "pro-family" supporters, Trump had secretly bankrolled just about the entire $1 million campaign.[60] Later, when New York governor George Pataki began an investigation,[61] Stone admitted that the institute was simply a front.

Investigator: You could hide Trump's actions?
Stone: Yes.
Investigator: From the public?
Stone: Yes.
Investigator: And you did that?
Stone: Yes.
Investigator: Over and over again?
Stone: Yes.

Stone added, "Nothing wrong with that, by the way."[62]

In the end, Trump and Stone agreed to pay a $250,000 fine—a state record—after officials discovered they'd failed to comply with New York's lobbying disclosure requirements.[63] As part of the settlement, Trump also pledged to run newspaper ads acknowledging that it was actually he who'd financed the institute's attacks on the Mohawks.[64] Paying such a large fine must have been infuriating for Trump, who kept extremely close tabs on his money. He once asked a Black Manafort lobbyist how much cash it would take to run for president.

"One hundred million dollars," the lobbyist responded.

"Ah, that's not worth it," Trump said.

Despite the work that the firm did for him, Trump often dragged his feet when it was time to pay his invoices. The partners occasionally had to travel up to New York and make their appeals in person. "He would always ask for a haircut," Black says.

Nevertheless, the firm remained on good terms with Trump. Around Christmas one year, a pair of Black Manafort lobbyists met Trump in New York to discuss the impact of the newly elected Congress on federal policies related to real estate. At the conclusion of the meeting, Trump tried to convince the lobbyists to remain in town for his Christmas bash, promising that there would be "a lot of talent" at the party.

As Black Manafort's corporate lobbying business exploded, the firm developed new ways to influence Washington. One of its most groundbreaking innovations was built right into its business model. Most lobbyists start their careers as junior aides in Congress or on political campaigns, working for either Republicans or Democrats. Due to the partisan divisions of Washington, these young aides develop contacts and clout within their own political party but rarely inside the opposing one. As a result, the relationships that such staffers bring with them when they leave public service for K Street remain tied to their partisan affiliations. Republican lobbyists use their contacts inside the GOP to try to persuade Republican officials; Democratic lobbyists handle the Democrats. Because Black Manafort's founders were Republicans, their influence in Washington remained mostly limited to Republican lawmakers and officials. Eventually, however, they realized that they could grow revenues even further if they had a way to reach Democratic members of Congress too. So, after Reagan's 1984 reelection, they hired a Democratic partner, former DNC finance chair Peter Kelly, and built out a team of Democratic lobbyists.[65] The firm, which was officially rechristened Black, Manafort, Stone & Kelly, became one of Washington's first bipartisan influence-peddling outfits.[66]

"Any lobbying requires access," Kelly says. "The difference is we would get it from both sides [of a political debate]."

Hiring Democrats elicited occasions of disharmony inside the firm, as the new employees didn't always mesh with the existing Republican operatives. Debbie Willhite joined Black Manafort a few years later, in 1993, after serving as a top strategist on Bill Clinton's presidential campaign. On her first day at the new job, she put on her nicest business suit, walked into the firm's Alexandria headquarters, and knocked on each partner's door to introduce herself. Stepping into Roger Stone's office, Willhite was shocked by the sign she found displayed on his desk. It read, "Hillary Clinton is a Cunt." (She complained to Black, and the sign was removed.)

Regardless of any such friction, the new Democratic lobbyists would immediately prove their value to the firm. As part of his second-term agenda, Reagan planned a sweeping overhaul of the US tax code. The goal was to lower taxes on businesses and individuals. Reagan hoped to pay for the tax cuts by closing off loopholes that had primarily benefited big corporations and their executives[67]—such as the notorious deductions for "three-martini lunches." Passing the legislation, though, would require Republicans to negotiate with Democrats, who had a majority in the House of Representatives. The political dynamics turned Dan Rostenkowski, the burly Democratic congressman from Chicago who chaired the House's tax writing panel—the Committee on Ways and Means—into the most important man on Capitol Hill. Lobbyists for all manner of corporate interests grew desperate to ensure that their clients received preferential tax treatment in the new legislation. But in order to do so, they needed access to Rostenkowski.

In this scramble to secure favors from Rostenkowski, the lobbyists at Black Manafort had a secret weapon. They'd recently hired a new partner: Jim Healey, who'd served as Rostenkowski's top aide for more than a decade before retiring from Capitol Hill at the start of Reagan's second term. Healey hadn't come cheap. After a protracted bidding war, the firm had agreed to pay him an annual salary of $400,000,[68] plus bonuses based on his success—an astounding compensation package for a first-year lobbyist in the mid-1980s. Yet the investment quickly paid off.

In November 1985 Rostenkowski and his staff had just about finished writing the bill and were preparing to bring it up for debate before the House Ways and Means Committee. Such committee sessions were free-wheeling legislative debates where any lawmaker could propose amendments to alter the bill. These committee votes could stretch for days as lawmakers bickered and negotiated over countless details: whether to approve a tax break sought by an industrial firm, for instance, or strip a tax credit enjoyed by a bank. It was during these chaotic committee sessions when the most consequential work of Congress often gets done—and when special interests have their best chance at convincing a lawmaker to insert a beneficial amendment into the legislation. It was also during these debates when lobbyists earn their fees.

A few days before the Ways and Means Committee was to begin voting on the tax bill, Healey received a call from his old boss.

"Take me to lunch," Rostenkowski said, according to Healey.

The request surprised Healey. When Congress was in session, Rosten-kowski normally ate lunch at his desk. With the votes on the tax bill just around the corner, he figured the congressman would have more important things to do than share a meal with a former aide. Still, Healey wasn't about to turn down the chairman.

"Where do you want to go to lunch?" Healey asked.

"Wherever it will do you the most good," Rostenkowski replied.

A few hours later, Healey drove over to Capitol Hill, picked up Ros-tenkowski, and escorted him into the Palm, the wood-paneled steakhouse that Washington insiders considered the place to see and be seen. Upon entering the crowded restaurant, Rostenkowski demanded a large table in the middle of the dining room. Over the next hour and a half, the roomful of lobbyists and consultants watched Rostenkowski, the powerful committee chairman, enjoy an intimate lunch with Healey, the rookie tax lobbyist, on one of the final days before Rostenkowski's committee would begin its critical work on the tax overhaul. Eventually Healey realized what was happening. As a way to thank his former aide for his years of dutiful service, Rostenkowski was promoting Healey's new career as a lobbyist by broadcasting to Washington just how close the two were. "The idea was: 'Holy moly, Healey is meeting with Rosty just before the tax bill starts,'" Healey recalled in an interview. The display proved beneficial. When Healey returned to his office, his phone was ringing with calls from corporate executives seeking his help on the tax bill.

By the time the legislative process was finished, the 1986 tax law had lowered the top tax rate for corporations from 46 percent to 34 percent and reduced the top rate for individuals from 50 percent to 28 percent.[69] For the corporations that had retained Black Manafort, the legislation came with additional goodies. Through his relationships with Rostenkowski and others on the tax committee, Healey inserted an investment tax refund provision into the bill that was worth $130 million to Bethlehem Steel. He negotiated a multiyear delay in new corporate taxes that saved Chrysler $58 million. He worked out a similar perk worth $38 million for Johnson & Johnson,[70] and he scored millions of dollars in tax incentives for Salomon Brothers to build a new Manhattan headquarters. Most of the provisions Healey helped slip in the bill didn't mention his clients by name but were written in a way that could benefit only them. In all, Healey scored tax breaks for all but one of his clients, saving the companies hundreds of millions of dollars in total.

Regardless of whether they were clients of Black Manafort, corporate leaders were delighted by what they were getting out of 1980s Washington. "A basic difference in this administration," an unnamed CEO told *U.S. News & World Report* magazine, "is that business is not viewed as an adversary the minute we walk in the door."[71] Another chief executive went even further. "I told a friend recently, 'I almost feel like I've died and gone to heaven.'"[72]

Inside the firm, the future was even brighter. Over the next several years, the Black Manafort founders would discover new ways to shape federal policy that went beyond the access-driven triumphs of their earliest days. By applying the skills they'd learned on the campaign trail to the stodgy work of lobbying, the partners wouldn't just get more done for their clients; they would propel K Street's transformation from a fraternity of clubby insiders to a twenty-first-century industry of cutting-edge tradecraft, interdisciplinary collaboration, and flood tides of money.

5

Summer 1986
The US Capitol Building

When Congress took up the Tax Reform Act of 1986—the same bill Jim Healey was shaping for the benefit of Black Manafort's clients—Tommy Boggs was retained by a slew of business interests. The legislation aimed to lower the top marginal rate by closing a number of tax loopholes. Boggs worked both sides of the issue, lobbying for a coalition of companies that wanted to eliminate special interest tax perks in order to lower the overall corporate tax rate—as well as dozens of firms seeking to protect their individual tax loopholes. According to a former Patton Boggs partner, during conference negotiations between House and Senate leaders over the final bill, a veteran Democratic lawmaker pulled aside Boggs.

Louisiana Senator Russell Long had been the chair of the US Senate Committee on Finance for the fifteen years prior to the 1980 election, when the conservative revolution handed control of the panel to Republicans. Though he was now a member of the minority party, Long remained an influential figure on the committee, and a good friend to Boggs. As the conference negotiations got under way, Long approached Boggs with a question.

"Hey, Tommy," the senator said. "What do you think about us taking all these [tax] deductions out?"

"I think it would be great," Boggs replied. "Because then I could spend the next twenty-five years trying to put them all back in."

By then, Tommy was earning more than $1 million a year,[1] and a *National Journal* survey of lawmakers and political insiders named him the city's top lobbyist.[2] Yet such accolades failed to capture the full scope of Boggs's stature in Washington. At age forty-six, he was more than the king of K Street; he was a campaign finance mastermind who'd transformed the role of corporate money in American politics. As he climbed the Washington hierarchy, he charted new ways to turn cash into political leverage, helping to kick-start a revolution in campaign fund-raising that forever changed the nature of our democracy. And none of it would have been possible without the lessons he'd learned years earlier—long before the 1986 tax reform effort—during the most humiliating chapter of his life.

Back in the late 1960s, only a few years after he'd joined Jim Patton at the law firm—and a full decade before his coup at the Federal Trade Commission—Tommy decided he didn't want to be a lobbyist after all, according to Burt Solomon's *The Washington Century*. What he really wanted to do, he realized, was to serve in Congress like his father. So, with the backing of the local Democratic establishment, he declared himself a candidate in the 1970 election for the congressional seat in the eighth district of Maryland.[3] This slice of suburban Washington stretched from the well-to-do enclaves of Montgomery County, where he and his parents lived, to the rural communities farther west. For Tommy, running for public office was a natural extension of the Boggs-Claiborne legacy. "Politics was in his blood," his wife, Barbara, recalled later. Plus, she added, Tommy's election to Congress would have made for an "interesting father-son combination."

Tommy viewed himself as the most liberal candidate in the race. He promised, for instance, to collect property taxes on the Chevy Chase Club, a wealthy golfing and social organization located in his own neighborhood. But while magnetic in person, Tommy was a lifeless politician—devoid of the public-speaking spark that made his father so compelling. Instead, the twenty-nine-year-old did what he could to project the image of an older, more distinguished statesman. He purchased black suits, and, according to some observers, he began mimicking John F. Kennedy's hand gestures during public appearances. Some even claimed that Tommy occasionally spoke to voters in a Boston accent. A bigger liability in the race was his father, who had not yet departed on his fateful fund-raising trip to Alaska. When articles about Hale's suspicious home improvement project—which triggered an FBI investigation—appeared on the front page of the *Washington Post*, Tommy was forced into a defensive crouch. "Voters in the Eighth District," he told the press, "are familiar with the differences between fathers and sons."

While distancing himself from his father in public, Tommy embraced the benefits of the Boggs family tree. Bess Abel, who'd served as social secretary to Lady Bird Johnson, threw a fund-raiser for Tommy, and Senator Ted Kennedy provided his endorsement. Sargent Shriver, the onetime brother-in-law of John F. Kennedy, opened his home for a campaign event even though he was in charge of one of the Democratic Party's national organizations and was therefore expected to remain neutral in all primary races. "I intend, of course, to live up to my commitment to Tom Boggs," Shriver said, "who is a personal friend and who has been helpful to me." After Maryland's Democratic governor, Marvin Mandel, pledged his support, Tommy went on to defeat his closest primary competitor by a comfortable margin.[4]

The general election was another matter. Boggs's opponent, Gilbert Gude, was a moderate Republican who'd earned voters' trust by supporting environmental regulations and opposing the Vietnam War. Yet despite the long odds of victory, Tommy was able to draw on the kind of top-tier political support that other rookie candidates couldn't dream of obtaining. Edmund Muskie, the senator from Maine who would soon become a leading presidential contender, starred in a television advertisement for the campaign. "Tom Boggs puts people first," Muskie assured viewers. The high-profile endorsements, however, weren't enough to shake the district's faith in its incumbent representative. Boggs lost the election by nearly 27 points.[5]

It was an embarrassing blow to Tommy's pride, and he never ran for office again. Still, the experience offered a powerful lesson. "I learned something very important: what it is for a politician to raise money."[6] This hunt for cash, he discovered, was a nonstop slog that consumed the bulk of a candidate's thoughts and schedule. "You have to get out of bed every day," Boggs said, "and go to coffee klatches and meet people and shake their hands and listen to them and tell them what you intend to do."[7] If a candidate couldn't scrape up enough money from this continuous cycle of fund-raising events and phone calls to wealthy acquaintances, he might, as Tommy discovered, have to reach into his own pocket. In the aftermath of his unsuccessful campaign, Tommy found himself $40,000 in debt.[8]

The firsthand look at the struggle of political fund-raising left a lasting impression on Tommy. When the race was over, and he turned his attention back to lobbying, he began looking for ways to use this insight to benefit his lobbying business. Eventually he found his opening.

The 1970s were a time of seismic changes in political campaigning. Traditional shoe-leather approaches to voter outreach—knocking on doors, posting yard signs, speaking to veterans groups—were giving way to newer techniques such as direct mail, modern polling, and radio and television advertising. Although more effective, these new tactics were also more expensive, and their widespread adoption precipitated a dramatic increase in the price of running for office. In 1960, for example, the total cost of all federal elections in the United States was $175 million. By 1980, that figure had surged nearly sevenfold to $1.2 billion.[9] As Tommy learned, television advertising was by far the biggest driver of this growth. He'd plowed three-quarters of his $100,000 campaign budget into the production and distribution of television ads, like the one featuring Senator Muskie.[10]

Meanwhile, just as the costs of political campaigns were skyrocketing, Congress overhauled the way candidates paid for them. Though corporations had long been barred from contributing directly to federal races, industry leaders were never content to watch elections from the sidelines. Massachusetts Democrat Tip O'Neill, who became Speaker of the House in 1977, told a fellow Democratic congressman about the creative hustle he'd used to pay for his elections in the years after he was first elected to Congress in 1952. According to the colleague, O'Neill would go to fund-raising events and busy himself playing cards—while corporate lobbyists and other political supporters would gather in another room and fill a sack with cash. When the evening was over, O'Neill would thank his hosts, grab the sack, and walk out of the house with thousands of dollars in reelection funds.[11]

US campaign laws were so porous before the 1970s that it is unclear whether O'Neill's fund-raising card trick even violated the law. Bribes from lobbyists had always been illegal, but lawmakers were permitted to accept cash donations to fund their campaigns. On Capitol Hill, some congressmen demanded payments from interest groups before agreeing to meet with them, and cash-filled envelopes passed freely from lobbyists to lawmakers. Veteran tax lobbyist J. D. Williams told the journalist T. R. Goldman the practice was so common that he once accidentally handed a cash envelope to a low-level congressman instead of a powerful commit-tee chairman.[12] Instead of an outraged rebuke, he received an appreciative phone call in return. "I knew you thought highly of me," the congressman told him.

The black-market fund-raising era came to an end with Watergate. Federal investigators discovered that many of the nefarious activities of Nixon's reelection campaign had been funded by companies, a violation of the 1907 law banning corporations from contributing money to candidates for Congress and the presidency. Watergate Special Counsel Archibald Cox indicted blue-chip firms such as Goodyear Tire and Rubber Company and American Airlines for their illegal political donations, and, all told, nearly two dozen businesses pleaded guilty to similar charges. The extent of the corruption in the democratic process stunned the public. "Although there had been sporadic federal investigations of corporate political practices in past elections," wrote the political scientist Herbert Alexander, "the picture that unfolded from 1973 to 1975 suggested illegal corporate giving on a scale unlike anything previously imagined."[13] In the wake of the scandal, liberal lawmakers and activists began searching for ways to fix America's broken campaign finance system.

One of the first major reforms of the post-Watergate period was the es-tablishment of clear rules for political action committees. In 1974 Congress passed a measure limiting the amount of money a PAC could contribute to an individual candidate for Congress or president to $5,000 apiece for the primary campaign and the general election, for a total of $10,000 per election cycle. Yet while it was intended to choke off the influence of special interests, the law had the opposite effect: it opened the door to what would become a river of spending on campaigns by corporate PACs, which were funded by donations from their employees. Prior to the reform, the law didn't make it entirely clear whether or not business executives had the legal authority to establish these fund-raising committees in the first place. But the new statute served as an explicit affirmation of corporations' right to form PACs, giving companies—for the first time since the Progressive Era—a legally sanctioned vehicle to make political contributions. It was a pivotal moment in the history of campaign finance. Suddenly business executives looking to curry favor with lawmakers didn't have to distribute secret envelopes of cash. They could simply set up PACs.[14]

Corporations and trade associations raced to adopt this new approach to political spending: from 1974 to 1980, the total number of business PACs in the United States ballooned from 89 to 1,888. It was here that Tommy saw his opportunity. He realized that by helping to ease the financial pressures that modern campaigning placed on lawmakers, he could make powerful friends on Capitol Hill—friends who would gladly take his call when he needed a hand. So, Tommy used the emerging PAC system to build one of Washington's most sophisticated political fund-raising machines. He organized his lobbying clients into a network of PACs, identified the most important congressmen for these businesses and trade groups to influence, and directed their PACs to deliver campaign checks to those lawmakers. Back at the firm's headquarters, his junior associates used a computer program to match cash-strapped congressmen with potential donors. On Capitol Hill, he rented a town house less than two blocks from the US Capitol Building and used it to host fund-raising receptions nearly every night of the week.[15] Though he enjoyed hobnobbing with congressmen and senators, every single dollar that Tommy funneled into a campaign had a string attached. "Attending fund-raising activities increases access," he explained. "If you expect a member of Congress to give you a few extra minutes, spend time raising money for him. Members keep track of contributions, the companies that contribute, and the lobbyists who help."[16]

The strategies that Tommy pioneered helped ignite a PAC-fueled eruption of corporate political spending without parallel in American history. During the 1975–76 campaign cycle, company and trade association PACs plowed a total of $6.8 million into congressional campaigns. A decade later, that figure had exploded by a factor of more than 10, to $82 million.[17] For members of Congress, this deluge of cash was nothing short of a godsend; finally, they had a sustainable way to finance their increasingly expensive reelection campaigns. But the windfall had another, more transformative impact on our political system: it reshaped the relationship between Congress and corporate lobbyists. While this development affected lawmakers on both sides of the aisle, it impacted one party more profoundly than the other.

After the 1980 election, Democrats in Washington awoke to a panic. Ronald Reagan's landslide victory was stunning enough, but the results of the congressional elections were downright terrifying. On top of winning the White House, Republicans had achieved a majority in the Senate and gained an alarming thirty seats in the House. For most of the prior fifty years, Democrats had maintained nearly uninterrupted control of both chambers of Congress. Now the GOP was one step away from ruling the entire city. And the only thing standing in their way was Speaker Tip O'Neill and his rickety twenty-five-seat Democratic majority in the House.

For Democratic leaders, the future looked even more troubling. Beyond the economic and social forces that had undermined liberal candidates on Election Day, the party had suffered from a key structural disadvantage. While Republicans had adapted to the modern fund-raising era, Democratic leaders had seen no reason to develop new ways to bring in cash. As a result, a vast financial disparity had opened up between the two parties. During the two years leading up to the 1980 election—a time when money was growing increasingly decisive to campaign outcomes— the Republicans' chief House fund-raising committee took in nearly $27 million, outperforming its Democratic counterpart by a factor of 13. In the gloomy months after the 1980 election, Speaker O'Neill and other Democratic leaders in the House grew desperate to raise more money.

The financial imbalance with Republican fund-raising committees, they came to believe, threatened to strip the party of its sole remaining toehold of power on Capitol Hill and permanently entrench the GOP's control of Washington. But how could House Democrats close this financial gap? Against a backdrop of fear and apprehension, the lawmakers made an unlikely decision, choosing an ambitious second-term congressman to be their new top fund-raiser. [18]

At not yet forty, Tony Coelho would be among the youngest ever to head the Democratic Congressional Campaign Committee (DCCC), the party's official campaign arm for House races. At the time of his appointment, Coelho was, in the words of the *Atlantic*, an "utterly anonymous"[19] lawmaker with no management experience. But during his five-year tenure at the DCCC, he would become the single most consequential figure ever to hold the post. He wouldn't just reengineer the DCCC's fund-raising apparatus and restore financial parity with Republicans, but also would alter the trajectory of the entire Democratic Party. Yet if things had turned out the way he'd hoped earlier in his life, Coelho never would have come to Washington in the first place.

It was eighteen years earlier, during the dark days following the assassination of John F. Kennedy, when Coelho found his original calling, according to *Honest Graft*, Brooks Jackson's 1990 book about Coelho. A Catholic himself, Coelho had always felt connected to the thirty-fifth president. He was inspired by Kennedy's lofty idealism—his belief that the government could use its power to improve the lives of ordinary folks, whether it was by dispatching Peace Corps volunteers to Ghana or sending financial aid to struggling farmers in Iowa. In the fall of 1963, as Lee Harvey Oswald was casing the Texas School Book Depository in anticipation of the arrival of Kennedy's motorcade, Coelho was a student at what is now Loyola Marymount, a Jesuit university in Los Angeles. When word of the shooting rippled across campus, Coelho walked to the chapel, gathered with his blank-faced classmates, and prayed that the president might survive.

The next several days were a fog. Coelho hardly ate, he didn't shave. He sat in his room and stared at the television. The national tragedy, it seemed, had taken away more than his political hero. Just one week earlier, Coelho had been a student body president excited to finish up college and head off to law school. Now he felt empty and rudderless. A legal career seemed frivolous. He didn't see the point in chasing a big salary. Other jobs, such as teaching, didn't appeal to him either. Eventually he realized he wanted to be like Kennedy. He wanted to help people. "What I really wanted to do was become a priest."[20]

The news stunned his family and friends. His parents, who were first-generation immigrants from the Azores islands of Portugal, urged him to reconsider. But Coelho's mind was set. He went on a religious retreat designed to measure his fitness for the priesthood, and it only furthered his commitment. Instead of a new car or a trip to Europe, he received Bibles and rosaries as graduation presents. Becoming a Catholic priest "burned with me," he said. "It became all-encompassing." Then, during a medical appointment in June 1964, his future changed once again: after years of unexplained headaches, blackouts, and convulsions, his doctor was finally able to diagnose his mysterious condition. Coelho, the doctor said, had epilepsy. And there was something else. Canon law, the doctor explained, barred epileptics from becoming Catholic priests because the Church considered them to be either "not quite in their right mind or possessed by the Evil One." Coelho could never join the clergy.[21]

It was a crushing development. "I was an outstanding senior at Loyola. God, I'd lived a full life," Coelho said. "All of the sudden somebody is saying that I'm handicapped, that I'm crippled, that I can't do certain things." California took away his driver's license, and his parents—who believed an Azorean superstition that epilepsy was God's punishment for a family's sins—refused to accept the diagnosis. "No son of ours has epilepsy," they told him. Disclosing his condition to prospective employers made it difficult to find work. Eventually he found a job as a liquor store cashier, but he quit after only two weeks. "I couldn't stand cashing Social Security checks for old ladies and then having them turn around and buy half-pints of liquor," he said. "I didn't want to be part of the downfall of these women."[22]

Without a job or a plan for his future, he returned to his empty fraternity house and collapsed into blackness. He felt abandoned by his family, rejected by his Church, and angry with God. He drank heavily and alone;

on the beach near his fraternity house; in a park while watching children play on a merry-go-round. One morning, Coelho woke up dirty and hung over, unable to recall what he'd done the night before. He saw no reason to go on. "There was no hope whatever for the future," he recalled. "And then I started thinking, the best way to resolve this, the easiest way to resolve this, was suicide."[23]

Around this time, Coelho had a conversation with his friend Father Ed Markey, a Jesuit priest.

"You're killing yourself," Father Markey told him.

"I know," Coelho replied.

"You've got to come out of it."[24]

The priest offered a way to pry Coelho from his depression. "I've got a job for you," he said. Through his work at Catholic Charities, Father Markey had become friendly with Bob Hope, the legendary stand-up comedian and TV star. As it turned out, Hope was looking to hire someone to help manage his affairs at his home in Palm Springs, California. Coelho jumped at the opportunity. "All of the sudden," he said, "I saw some light." He moved in with Hope's family and became a personal assistant to the celebrity funnyman—providing feedback on new material and accompanying Hope to TV studios. The excitement restored Coelho's spirit, and he developed a warm rapport with Hope. On their late-night drives home from the TV studio, they'd talk about Coelho's future; about how he'd still like to spend his life in service to others, even though he could never become a priest.

"If you're really serious about helping people," Hope said during one conversation, "why don't you go work for a member of Congress? You can satisfy your priestly needs and desires, you're working with people, you're helping people."[25]

The idea struck Coelho as a revelation. After all, it was 1964—the year that Lyndon Johnson kicked off his Great Society initiative. At the very moment that Hope and Coelho were cruising along the California freeway, President Johnson was using the muscle of the federal government to relieve poverty in Appalachia and prevent discrimination at schools in Mississippi. Suddenly it all made sense. Maybe Coelho wouldn't be able to deliver homilies at church or visit sick parishioners in the hospital. But through a career in politics, he believed he could help people in a different way—the way that Kennedy had. So, with the assistance of a politically connected uncle, he landed an internship in the Washington office of his local congressman, B. F. Sisk. At twenty-three years old, Coelho hopped in his Chevrolet jalopy, drove straight across the country, and arrived on Capitol Hill in the spring of 1965. "It was the beginning," he said, "of a whole new life."[26]

Coelho immediately impressed the congressman and his staff. He got to the office early, he remembered colleagues' birthdays and wedding anniversaries, and he tackled his assignments with competence and gusto. By 1970, the twenty-eight-year-old Coelho was the youngest chief of staff on Capitol Hill. During his thirteen years in Sisk's office, he worked behind the scenes to help the Democratic caucus realize a series of landmark achievements, including establishing a health insurance safety net for the poor, expanding voting rights for African Americans, improving safety standards at factories, and reducing pollution in the environment. Amid the excitement of his new career, Coelho grew less resentful of the Catholic Church. *This*, he now realized, was God's plan for him. "[I] absolutely fell in love with the work, the fact that you could really help out people, and you could change people's lives," Coelho reflected. "I could do much more in this job than I could as a priest."[27]

His position also gave him a street-level view of the corruption that marked the pre-reform era of political fund-raising. On Coelho's second day as chief of staff, as Brooks Jackson reports in *Honest Graft*, a textile lobbyist came by the office to ask for the congressman's help on a legislative matter. As the lobbyist got up to leave, he handed the young aide an envelope stuffed with $500 cash. Coelho was startled. "I didn't know whether it was for me or for my boss," he said. "But I knew what it was. I knew it was illegal." After discussing the incident with the congressman, Coelho decided to give back the money. He drafted a letter saying that it would be "inappropriate for us to accept a campaign contribution at this time," and he mailed it, along with a cashier's check for $500, to the textile lobbyist. Refusing to accept cash payments from special interests was so unusual in those days that, when the textile lobbyist received the letter, he tried to get Coelho fired.[28]

Coelho remained on the congressman's staff for another eight years, and the two became close. When Sisk was finally ready to retire, he urged his trusted chief of staff to run for his seat. Coelho won the election and was sworn in on January 15, 1979. After thirteen years as a Capitol Hill aide, there was no way he was going to spend his first term in office as an unknown backbencher, like most freshman House lawmakers did. Instead, Coelho began looking for a way to quickly move up the food chain.[29]

Despite the increasingly central role of money in politics, lawmakers often considered fund-raising the most loathsome part of their jobs. On top of the drudgery of calling donors and schlepping to breakfast meetings, there was a fundamental human fear. Congressmen hated being rejected, and they dreaded the possibility of being turned down by donors. Coelho, on the other hand, was a natural fund-raiser. Part of it was his engaging personality. "He's like a giant Saint Bernard," a colleague would later tell the *New Republic*. "Everybody loves him."[30] But the struggles in his past also proved helpful. Compared with the paralyzing depression he'd suffered back in the summer of 1964—when he considered taking his own life—getting rebuffed by a donor didn't seem so bad. So, in the run-up to the 1980 election, Coelho used his gifts as a fund-raiser to help influential Democrats keep their seats in Congress and make a name for himself inside the party. Reaching out to union leaders as well as corporate PAC managers, he hustled up $80,000 for House Majority Leader Jim Wright of Texas, and $100,000 for Representative James Corman, a twenty-year veteran from California. He even brought in $100,000 for President Carter's doomed reelection effort by organizing a campaign event in California. It was an impressive display—by a first-term lawmaker, no less. In the panic that followed the disastrous election of 1980, when Democrats were frantically searching for new ways to bring in money, Wright decided to take a chance. He nominated Coelho, the little-known political upstart, as the chief campaign fund-raiser for the entire House Democratic caucus.[31]

Republicans had established their fund-raising superiority following a dark period of their own. In the aftermath of Watergate, the party had collapsed into chaos. GOP officials struggled to recruit quality candidates, longtime donors withdrew their support, and voters defected to the opposition. In the election of 1974, which took place only three months after Richard Nixon resigned, Republicans suffered a historic forty-eight-seat loss in the House. But just when things seemed most bleak, party officials discovered a way to rebuild their caucus. By embracing the modern PAC system and investing in sophisticated tools to track down new donors, GOP leaders turned the National Republican Congressional Committee (NRCC)—their chief financial organ for House races—into a state-of-the-art fund-raising machine. NRCC operatives launched an advanced direct mail program that pulled data from a wide range of sources—voter registrations, conservative magazine subscriber lists—in order to target their fund-raising appeals to likely donors. At the same time, Guy Vander Jagt, the Michigan congressman who chaired the NRCC, led an aggressive, partywide effort to bring in contributions from corporate PACs. During speeches to business leaders, for example, he would share the story of Neil Staebler, a Democrat who'd lost his seat on the Federal Election Commission after siding with Republicans and voting in 1975 to support the right of companies to establish PACs. "This Democrat gave his political life to open the door for you," Vander Jagt would tell the crowd. "And if you don't have the gumption to walk through that open door, to take advantage of the change he gave you, you have no right to call yourself Americans." The dramatic flair paid off; the Republicans opened a titanic 13–1 financial advantage over the Democratic committee.[32]

By comparison, when Coelho first arrived at the Democratic Congressional Campaign Committee, he found an organization in crisis. The DCCC had no small donor division to try to raise $10 and $20 contributions from mom-and-pop supporters. Its direct mail database contained a pitiful thirteen thousand names, and it was $200,000 in debt. Before the shock of the 1980 election, the party's old-fashioned leaders had presided over congressional majorities for so long that they'd taken their power for granted. They simply hadn't considered fund-raising to be a critical element of political survival. The Democratic National Committee, for example, was still carrying debts from Hubert Humphrey's unsuccessful presidential run in 1968. For years, Democratic leaders had refused to build a modern campaign finance apparatus. During the late 1970s, when the Republican committee was using computer technology and installing its own television studio, the DCCC was a three-person outfit working at government-issued typewriters in a single room of a congressional office building. And that wasn't the worst of it. When Bill Sweeney became executive director of the DCCC in 1977, the House ethics committee was looking into an influence scheme that came to be known as Koreagate. He was so worried about potential problems resulting from the committee's tantalizing file cabinets stuffed with decades of records that he reportedly shredded thirty years' worth of documents.[33]

Upon taking charge, Coelho resolved to move the Democratic Party into the modern age. "What I wanted," he told a reporter, "was to make the DCCC like a business."[34] That meant forging new alliances and revisiting old ones. After pioneering the use of PACs back in the 1940s,[35] organized labor had become the financial ballast of the Democratic Party. By the time Coelho came to the DCCC, however, the labor movement had deteriorated considerably. Amid the collapse of the manufacturing industry, a renewed commitment on the part of business owners to prevent workers from organizing, and an influential campaign by corporate-funded scholars to delegitimize Big Labor, union membership had plummeted by one-third since its peak in the mid-1950s. Lower enrollment meant fewer funds for political contributions. In the 1976 election cycle, for the first time in modern American history, labor unions spent less on federal campaigns than corporations did.[36] From there, the trend lines sharpened. By the time Reagan was elected, a new corporate PAC was being formed, on average, every three days, and roughly two-thirds of this growing pool of cash was flowing to Republicans.[37] For Coelho, the future was clear: if he was going to revive the DCCC—and prevent Republicans from capturing the rest of Washington—he had to look beyond the party's old allies in organized labor. He had to make a new set of friends. So, in an effort to reach out to America's booming corporate sector, he organized the DCCC around a novel principle. "Special interest," he told a roomful of Realtors, "is not a nasty word."[38]

From Day One, Coelho scrambled to ingest every corporate PAC dollar he could find. He met with the major trade associations in Washington, and he hit the road—traveling as many as 150 days a year[39]—to visit with businesspeople in Texas, New York, Florida, and California. Using the party's most valuable commodity—control of the House—as leverage, he pressured business leaders to increase their contributions to Democrats the way a Mafia capo might shake down the owner of a neighborhood grocery store, as Brooks Jackson noted.[40] "We looked at the list of the [PACs] who were giving too much to the Republicans," committee aide Martin Franks told the New Republic. "And we basically gave them the come-to-Jesus message: 'We know who you are. You've been cavorting with the devil. But understand something here. We're in power. And I suggest you deal with us.'"[41] Inside the DCCC, staffers cold-called corporate PAC officials and pressed them to make PAC donations to various Democratic candidates. "We would try very, very hard to promote people who were more moderate," said Marta David, a senior Democratic aide. "We would go there with biographies and say, 'Well, look, he's owned a Pizza Hut.'" Coelho even organized fund-raising forums where Democratic candidates wore name tags and stood at booths, while corporate PAC managers circulated through the room and decided which candidates they would support with a campaign donation. To Washington operatives, these events were known as "cattle calls" or "meat markets."[42]

Another innovation of Coelho's, the "Speaker's Club," offered lobbyists and business leaders—for $5,000 a year for individuals or $15,000 for PACs—private meetings with Speaker O'Neill and other House leaders. Joining the club, according to a brochure, enabled wealthy corporate donors to "get the real story" of what was happening on Capitol Hill, through "exclusive" briefings. "Members of the Speaker's Club," the brochure said, "serve as trusted, informal advisors to Democratic members of Congress." Coelho was even more blunt when he was asked to describe the benefits of the club. "Access. Access," he told the journalist Elizabeth Drew. "We sell the opportunity to be heard."[43] Members also received white-glove treatment when they were in Washington. If there was anything these generous donors needed during their visits to the nation's capital—concert tickets, dinner reservations, face time with the chairman of the Commerce Committee—Coelho's team would see to it. If that wasn't enough, membership even came with a set of luggage tags that carried the Speaker's Club's emblem, "to distinguish you as a club member."[44]

Though it attracted little notice at the time, the growing role of money in politics precipitated structural changes at the heart of the Democratic Party. Coelho's first boss, Congressman Sisk, had been a tire salesman, a truck driver, a fruit picker, and a union organizer before his election.[45] But as the cost of running for office skyrocketed from $73,000 for the average House race in 1976 to almost $500,000 two decades later,[46] many candidates from working-class backgrounds were simply priced out of public office. At the same time, Coelho's overhaul of the DCCC accelerated an even more significant transformation: the political parties were deprioritizing voter mobilization efforts in order to devote more of their resources to fund-raising.[47] As a result, the Democratic Party grew less responsive to the needs of its poor and working-class voters, and, increasingly, it began to reflect the values of its more affluent donors.

Take the 1981 tax bill, for example. The legislation was intended to cut taxes on industry, but as it moved through Congress, an astonishing development occurred. Democrats in the House of Representatives, who in decades past had fought efforts to cut corporate taxes, were now adding provisions to make the legislation even more favorable to Big Business.[48] As David Vogel explains in *Fluctuating Fortunes*, his 1989 book about the political power of American industry, "Little more than a decade earlier, the automobile industry had found itself caught in a bidding war between the Nixon administration and the Democrats in the Senate. Each had tried to outdo the other in demonstrating its commitment to strict pollution control standards: the result was the 1970 Clean Air Act amendments. In 1981 a Republican president and a Democratic House also found themselves in a bidding war, this time to demonstrate their commitment to cut corporate taxes." In the end, the 1981 legislation was the most substantial tax cut in American history at the time, slashing corporate taxes by $151 billion over five years.[49]

In one particularly candid admission, Coelho explained to Brooks

Jackson how this sea of special interest money was impacting the Democratic process. "It does affect legislation," Coelho said. "You don't have the people feeling that they can be creative . . . because they've got to raise this fifty thousand, and they don't want to turn people [with money] off." He continued, "Take housing. Take anything you want. If you are spending all your time calling up different people that you're involved with, that are friends of yours, that you have to raise $50,000, you all of a sudden, in your mind, you're in effect saying, 'I'm not going to go out and develop this new housing bill that may get the Realtors or may get the builders or may get the unions upset. I've got to raise the fifty thousand; I've got to do that.'"

As Coelho put it, "I think that the process buys you out."[50]

As they sopped up this geyser of corporate political spending, Democratic lawmakers also grew more willing to accommodate—and, increasingly, support—the Reagan administration's sweeping deregulatory agenda. Indeed, the effort to get bureaucrats out of the private economy was by then both bipartisan and nonideological. In fact, it was the public interest advocate Ralph Nader who, just a few years earlier, had led the successful campaign to deregulate the airline and trucking industries. Nader approached the issue of deregulation from a different perspective than most pro-business lawmakers did. He argued that since Big Business had used its political clout to "capture" certain regulatory agencies—such as the Civil Aeronautics Board—consumers would be better served by reducing the government's authority in those industries. "Throughout the land people are repulsed by arrogant and unresponsive bureaucracies serving no useful public purpose, and they are looking to this Congress to get on with the national housecleaning job that is needed," Nader told lawmakers during a Senate subcommittee hearing on airline deregulation in 1975. "Can you think of a better place to start than the Civil Aeronautics Board?" Though intended as an act of consumer protection, Nader's deregulatory push served primarily to advance the idea that the federal government had no legitimate role in the US economy. In that sense, it was a gift to Big Business.[51]

In his crusade to close the fund-raising gap with Republicans, Coelho gave little apparent thought to the broader policy implications of his efforts.

As he later told a roomful of wealthy donors, "Don't let your ideology get in the way of your business judgment."[52] Nor did he seem bothered by the ethical messiness of openly selling political access to wealthy corporate executives. "I'm not going to let reformers scare me into thinking that I can't ask people for money," he told the *Los Angeles Times*. "I'm going to ask. I'm going to ask very passionately."[53] After all, as Brooks Jackson noted, Coelho had never been an ideologue. He hadn't stormed into Washington determined to eradicate corruption or stop an armed conflict. Quite the opposite. When he first arrived in Congressman Sisk's office, Coelho was, in the words of Jackson, "a lonely young man groping for structure in his life and an outlet for his extraordinary talent and energy."[54] Through his work in the Democratic caucus, he'd reclaimed the sense of identity he'd lost when his dream of becoming a Catholic priest ended. And when he was chosen to head the DCCC, he'd received a new divine mission: defeating the Republican Party. From his ends-justify-the-means perspective, Coelho viewed raising money from corporations as his chance to do for others what John F. Kennedy had done for him. "Unless you believe that the Democratic Party can really help people change their lives and provide some hope, you don't understand what I'm doing," he said. "You don't understand my drive, you don't understand why I want to change things. You don't understand why money is important."[55]

While Coelho was excoriated by watchdogs and ethics groups, he became something of a folk hero to business executives. "I'm one of the biggest contributors to the governor of Texas," said Thomas Gaubert, a venture capitalist from Dallas. "But can I get him on the telephone? Hell, no. Sometimes it takes a week. I call Tony at any hour of the day or night, and he gets back to me immediately. Some days he just calls to ask how I'm doing."[56] The result was a flood of corporate money into Coelho's DCCC. In his first two years as chairman, the committee more than doubled its fund-raising haul, and by the 1985–86 cycle, he had more than doubled it again, topping $12 million.[57] Even more importantly, Coelho managed to neutralize the GOP's advantage in the business sector. When he first took charge of the DCCC, corporate PACs were giving just one-third of their contributions to Democrats. Less than a decade later, thanks to Coelho's hustle and ingenuity, Democrats were winning nearly half of the donations from corporate PACs. "There was a touch of envy," said Guy Vander Jagt, the NRCC chairman and Coelho's chief GOP adversary. "As a fund-raiser, he was ten times more effective than I was."[58]

It was, by any measure, a monumental political achievement. Coelho's fund-raising surge helped Democrats win back twenty-six House seats in the 1982 congressional election, easing the party's fears of a Republican takeover. His Democratic colleagues were so thrilled that, in 1986, they elected him House majority whip, making Coelho the third-highest-ranking figure in the chamber. But Coelho's campaign finance coup had an even more profound effect: it made Democrats increasingly indebted to corporations and special interests. By the mid-1980s, Democratic House incumbents often received 50 percent or more of their reelection money from PACs, and they relied on donations from individual lobbyists and corporate executives for much of the rest. The flow of special interest cash was so prolific that some Democratic congressmen altogether abandoned the practice of raising money from the folks back home in their districts, preferring instead to hold big-dollar fund-raisers in Washington.[59] It was a development that the architects of our democracy never envisioned: the country's elected officials were becoming less beholden to their voters and more dependent on corporations and their agents in Washington. Few capitalized on this emerging dynamic more effectively than Tommy Boggs.

From the early 1980s through the late 1990s, Boggs helped finance the campaigns of more members of Congress than any other lobbyist in Washington.[60] The distinction made him a popular figure on Capitol Hill. Lanny Davis, a former Patton Boggs partner, recalls that shortly after he joined the firm as a young lobbyist just starting his career, he went to Tommy Boggs's office and asked for advice on how to succeed on K Street.

"I'm going to teach you the ropes of Washington," Boggs assured the rookie influence peddler. "One lesson is about the word *friend*. Everyone says they're your 'friend.' What does that mean? What is the definition of a 'friend' in Washington?"

After a moment, Boggs answered his own question. "The definition of a 'friend' in Washington is if they answer their phone."

To illustrate his point, Davis said, Tommy picked up his phone and dialed the Capitol Hill office of Russell Long, the powerful Louisiana senator who served as the chair of the Senate Finance Committee from 1966 to 1981. Minutes later, Russell was on the line, and Boggs explained to the senator that he was with his firm's newest lobbyist. "He wants to know the definition of a 'friend,'" the veteran lobbyist said.

Boggs then passed the receiver to Davis, who would go on to represent Donald Trump political fixer Michael Cohen. "You're talking to Russell Long," the senator said. "I don't pick up the phone for many people. I pick up the phone for Tommy."

Such powerful friends served as the engine of the lucrative feedback loop at the core of Boggs's business. Lawmakers who received donations from Boggs and his clients looked out for their political interests on Capitol Hill. This friendly treatment, in turn, helped Patton Boggs attract more clients, which allowed the firm to increase revenues, add staff, and support additional political fund-raising.

As the firm grew too big for the original office, Patton Boggs moved into the top two floors of a brand-new, ten-story building just east of Georgetown. Jim Patton lined the walls with works of modern art, the firm bought a fleet of luxury vehicles—a limousine, a Bentley, and three Rolls-Royces—and the partners jetted off to vacations in Saint Croix, Acapulco, and Barbados.[61] The success of Patton Boggs helped change the way Washington's legal community viewed the influence business. Back when Tommy was first starting out, the city's top-tier law firms looked down on lobbying as undignified. "If you wanted to be a member of the Metropolitan Club," said George Blow, a founder of Patton Boggs, "it was better if you were not a lobbyist."[62] As its influence-peddling revenue boomed, however, the same law firms that once condemned the practice were now opening lobbying offices of their own. Inside Patton Boggs, a hard-drinking culture developed. The firm held monthly, in-house happy hours, which became known as "third Thursdays," where the booze flowed freely. One female employee said she was fired after complaining of unwanted advances from male colleagues during one such event in the office. The employee filed a lawsuit against the company, which she later dropped.

It was during this period that Boggs assumed his full form. Each morning, he drove to the office in his tan-colored Rolls-Royce convertible; sometimes, on the way in, he'd take calls on his brick-sized car phone.[63] He'd light up a Cuban cigar in the morning—the first of as many as five he'd smoke a day. (One Patton Boggs partner recalls the time Boggs puffed a stogie while single-ski water-skiing in the Gulf of Mexico.) After a full day of client phone calls and meetings on Capitol Hill, Boggs and his partners reconvened in his office for stiff drinks and political gossip.[64] "Tommy is Big Time Charlie," a friend told *Vanity Fair* magazine. "Everything he does is too much. Too much food, too much expensive wine, too much of a belly. Everything is bursting out, bursting forth."[65]

Whenever he got the chance, Boggs slipped out of Washington to one of his two properties on the Eastern Shore of Maryland. In addition to his bayside farmhouse, he owned a hunting lodge called Tobacco Stick. It was here, on 425 acres of preserved marshlands, where Boggs hosted legendary duck hunting outings for committee chairmen and corporate executives. Following a morning hunt, the men would head back to the lodge's dining room, which could accommodate thirty-two guests, while Boggs prepared the ducks they'd bagged for dinner.[66] These boozy weekends were bonding experiences for Boggs and his powerful guests. Sometimes they attracted the wrong kind of attention.

In the early morning hours of Thanksgiving Day 1993, Boggs and a group of nearly two dozen guests—including Democratic congressman William Ford of Michigan—raised their shotguns over the Eastern Shore marshlands. Just after dawn, the men opened fire, unleashing a seven-hundred-shell fusillade at a sky full of birds for the next forty-five minutes. "It sounded like a war," said Vernon Ricker, a federal Fish and Wildlife Service agent. Dead ducks plunged from the air, injured birds flapped on the ground. The ambush was so lethal that Ricker, who'd been observing the events from a hidden location, jumped out and demanded that the men stop shooting. All told, Boggs and his guests slaughtered 182 ducks.[67]

Ricker and two officers from Maryland's Department of Natural Resources had staked out the property after obtaining evidence that the land had been baited with sorghum grain; doing so is a federal crime if it's used to lure wild ducks in order to kill them. When the agents inspected the dead birds, they found a single federally protected wild mallard duck among those pen raised for sport shooting.[68] Boggs took responsibility for the incident—an apparent effort to protect his influential friends—and paid a $4,000 fine for illegal hunting. "No one knew if they were killing wild ducks or preserve ducks," Ricker told the *Baltimore Sun* later. "They couldn't have. They never stopped firing long enough to see."[69] When details of the shooting appeared in the press, the outing was nothing more than a minor embarrassment for Congressman Ford.

The absence of political blowback reflected the changes taking place inside the Democratic Party. As business interests surpassed environmental advocates in the party's hierarchy of power, the illegal shooting of a federally protected duck[70] by a group of Democratic insiders was no longer much of a scandal. And yet, the Democratic Party's new allies on K Street still had much to learn from their adversaries in the consumer, labor, and environmental movements. Indeed, it was only by adopting the strategies and tools of liberal activists that corporate interests were able to achieve their objectives in Washington. And in this evolution of lobbying tactics, one liberal activist would prove particularly significant.

6

On a warm day in the nation's capital, an anxious Ted Kennedy lumbered up to a podium on the floor of the US Senate and thanked the presiding officer for giving him a few minutes to speak. In his dark suit and wavy silver hair, the ruddy-faced scion of a hallowed Democratic dynasty looked out at his fellow lawmakers and issued a frantic distress signal to his liberal compatriots. "Robert Bork's America," he began, "is a land in which women would be forced into back-alley abortions, Blacks would sit at segregated lunch counters, rogue police could break down citizens' doors in midnight raids, and schoolchildren could not be taught about evolution, writers and artists would be censored at the whim of government, and the doors of the federal courts would be shut on the fingers of millions of citizens for whom the judiciary is and is often the only protector of the individual rights that are the heart of our democracy."[1]

About forty-five minutes earlier,[2] President Reagan had realized the fears of Democrats throughout the country when he'd unveiled his nomination to fill a recently vacated Supreme Court seat. During his three decades as a lawyer and scholar, Robert Bork had emerged as the warrior-philosopher of the conservative legal movement. With his wispy beard and cranky disposition, the sixty-year-old federal appeals court judge had championed an uncompromising "originalist" view of the Constitution, insisting that society's leftward trajectory in previous decades had plunged the nation into a morass of permissiveness and crime.[3] While Kennedy's remarks distorted Bork's record,[4] Bork had criticized the 1973 *Roe v. Wade* decision legalizing abortion, objected to parts of the 1964 Civil Rights Act, pointed out flaws in a ruling that upheld affirmative action, and argued that pornography wasn't protected by the First Amendment.

For Senator Kennedy, though, the mathematical implications of Bork's selection were just as troubling as his views. Reagan had chosen Bork to re-place retiring Justice Lewis F. Powell Jr., the moderate justice appointed by President Nixon who—in the decades after he authored his famous memo to the US Chamber of Commerce—frequently cast the deciding vote on an otherwise evenly divided court. Over the prior fifteen years, Powell had sided with the court's four conservatives on criminal justice and eco-nomic matters. But when it came to the most contentious social issues of the day—abortion rights, affirmative action, the separation of church and state—Powell had joined with the four left-leaning justices to turn liberal priorities into settled law.[5] By replacing the centrist Powell with a rock-ribbed conservative like Bork, Reagan could alter the court's ideological balance for a generation. So it was against a backdrop of pending liberal doom that Kennedy came before his Senate colleagues and denounced the would-be justice in unusually bleak terms.

His dire tone captured the sense of panic that had engulfed liberal leaders in the wake of the nomination. After all, during almost six years in Washington, Reagan had already embedded conservative principles deep into the machinery for economic policy making. Now he was poised to enshrine a conservative majority on the nation's highest court. Worst of all, there didn't appear to be much liberals could do to stop him. Though Democrats held a majority in the Senate, it seemed unlikely that Kennedy would be able to rally enough votes to block Bork's nomination. At the time, the Senate viewed its role in the judicial confirmation process as sub-ordinate to the White House's; lawmakers held hearings on Supreme Court nominees but limited their questioning mostly to matters of professional competence and personal integrity.[6] Neither area would be a problem for Bork, who was considered by legal scholars to be among the most qualified Supreme Court nominees in history.[7] Indeed, if Kennedy was going to keep Bork off the bench, he'd need to do something big. And it was with this goal in mind that Kennedy stepped onto the Senate floor to deliver his apocalyptic address. "The damage that President Reagan will do through this nomination, if it is not rejected by the Senate," Kennedy told his fellow lawmakers, "could live on far beyond the end of his presidential term."[8]

After departing the floor, Kennedy launched a desperate—yet sophisticated—campaign to block Bork from the court. It was a long-shot effort, and it would succeed only if the senator could find the right people to help him run it. So, shortly after his speech, Kennedy reached out to an aggressive political operative who had just the skill set he needed.

Tony Podesta got the call from Kennedy in the years before he emerged as a K Street icon—the flashy lobbyist who welcomed lawmakers to his apartment in Venice, Italy, amassed an art collection of as many as 1,300 pieces, and built a $50 million business by pressing the political interests of Wall Street moguls, Silicon Valley hotshots, and pharmaceutical giants. At the time of Bork's nomination to the Supreme Court, Podesta was still making a name for himself as a progressive activist who used grit and ingenuity to combat the growing political clout of evangelical Christians. While his counterparts at Black Manafort were helping to elect conservative lawmakers who sought to expand the religious right's influence in Washington, Podesta was engaged in the opposite struggle, battling efforts by Christian activists to ban books, allow prayer in schools, and install right-wing judges on the federal bench. Upon speaking with Kennedy, the forty-four-year-old Podesta agreed to serve as a key tactician in one of the defining political battles of Reagan-era Washington.

Podesta's desire to keep Bork off the Supreme Court had more to do with his liberal values than his bank account. After all, his work as a political activist wasn't underwritten by seven-figure payouts from Fortune 500 conglomerates. But he was already honing the skills he'd bring to his future career. With his unique contribution to the effort, Podesta's role in the anti-Bork initiative would represent a significant milestone in his own professional ascent as well as the broader evolution of K Street. While Kennedy would pursue an old-fashioned "inside" strategy of personally imploring fellow senators to oppose Bork, Podesta and others were assigned the more complex task of whipping up opposition to the nominee among regular Americans. Such "outside" influence tactics—designed to activate ordinary citizens living hundreds of miles outside of the Beltway—had long been used by political activists, and the deployment of these tactics by lobbyists in the 1970s had helped corporations take power in Washington. But their potential had never been fully unleashed. Over the following months, as the anti-Bork effort gathered steam, Podesta would help show Beltway insiders that this "outside" influence approach was even more powerful than they'd recognized. And within a few years, thanks to the innovations of Podesta, Black Manafort, and others, these outside influence tactics would grow progressively cutting edge, effective, and essential. By the early years of the twenty-first century, the advanced tools of outside influence peddling had emerged as the cornerstone of the modern lobbying industry.

Tony Podesta had gotten hooked on liberal politics during his working-class childhood in 1940s-era Chicago. He was raised by Catholic parents of immigrant descent on the bottom floor of a two-story flat;[9] his aunt and cousins lived upstairs.[10] Tony's Italian American father, John Sr., never finished college. He supported the family through his job operating a cardboard-cutting machine in a factory that made advertising displays for bars and grocery stores.[11] While Tony's father was a sports junkie, his mother preferred Chicago's other obsession: politics. Mary Podesta, whose parents had emigrated from Greece, volunteered as a poll worker on Election Days.[12] On Saturday nights, she'd gather with Tony and his little brother, John Jr., to watch local political talk shows.[13] It wasn't until Tony enrolled at the nearby University of Illinois Chicago that he became active in politics himself: majoring in political science, landing the top post in the campus's chapter of the Young Democrats,[14] and serving as student body president. Podesta's running mate, Carol Moseley Braun, would go on to become the first Black woman to win a seat in the US Senate. Around this time, Podesta took a two-month trip to Japan with other politically active college students. Also on the trip was Dennis Hastert, who would later serve as GOP House Speaker.[15]

In 1964 Podesta traveled to Atlantic City, New Jersey, for the Democratic National Convention,[16] where he watched Lyndon Johnson accept his party's nomination. When the University of Illinois Chicago christened a new downtown campus, officials chose Podesta to participate in the ribbon-cutting ceremony, slotting the up-and-coming politico alongside Chicago's legendary Mayor Richard J. Daley and Illinois governor Otto Kerner Jr. "It was a big deal," Podesta recalled later. "A kid from the Thirty-Ninth Ward standing there with a governor and a mayor."[17]

Upon graduation, Podesta moved to Cambridge, Massachusetts, to pursue a PhD in political science at the Massachusetts Institute of Technology.[18] "I went there thinking I would be a professor," he would say. The tug of national politics, however, would soon lead him away from campus. After turning against President Johnson over his support for the Vietnam War, Podesta volunteered for the 1968 presidential campaign of Senator Eugene McCarthy of Minnesota,[19] the liberal Democrat who'd pledged to end the bloodshed. During that year's notorious Democratic National Convention in Chicago, where tensions between cops and antiwar protesters erupted into violence, Podesta was in the McCarthy campaign's suite, on the fifteenth floor of the Conrad Hilton Hotel, when police officers busted in, claiming that someone had been throwing things out of the window, and roughed up the staff. "A colleague had a billy club broken over his head," Podesta recalled.

After the convention, Podesta returned to MIT to resume his coursework, but his academic studies were soon upended by the fighting in Vietnam. When the federal government eliminated draft deferments for graduate students, Podesta received a letter from the Defense Department indicating that he would likely be drafted—and requiring him to report immediately for his physical examination. In a panic, Podesta reached out to his former undergraduate political science professor, who connected him with an administrator at Barat College, a small all-women's Catholic college outside of Chicago. The administrator, Mother Margaret Burke, agreed to give Podesta a faculty position, thereby enabling him to obtain a deferment from the draft. According to Podesta, Mother Burke even back-dated the employment contract—claiming he'd been hired months earlier than he actually was—so as to ensure that he wouldn't be drafted into the war. He remained at Barat for about a year and a half, until, at age twenty-six, he was too old to be drafted.

Before long, Podesta was right back on the campaign trail, serving as the senior strategist for Joseph Duffy, an ordained minister and antiwar activist who was running in 1970 to represent Connecticut in the US Senate.[20] As Duffy's underdog campaign electrified college students across the Northeast, Podesta was able to recruit a staff of some of the most promising young politicos of his generation, including Joe Lieberman, who went on to become a four-term senator from Connecticut; Larry Kudlow, a future director of the National Economic Council under President Trump; and an ambitious Yale Law student named Bill Clinton.

Podesta had first met Clinton about a year earlier at a gathering of young liberal activists in Martha's Vineyard, Massachusetts. In addition to their experiences on the Duffy campaign, Podesta would get to know the future president while working together on Project Purse Strings, a campaign designed to end the Vietnam War by pressuring Congress to cut off military funding. "He was charming and smart," Podesta said of the young Clinton. "A natural politician."

When Duffy lost his Senate campaign, Podesta moved to Washington and spent roughly six months working for Common Cause,[21] the pioneering watchdog group that, over the next few decades, would lead the outcry over the deluge of special interest money that was flowing into the political system. In 1972 he was hired as New England coordinator for the presidential effort of another antiwar Democrat, Maine Senator Edmund Muskie. The role made Podesta a firsthand witness to one of the more memorable episodes in American political history. On a snowy night that February, Muskie gathered with press and supporters outside of the headquarters of an ultraconservative newspaper in Manchester, New Hampshire. The candidate was furious at the *Manchester Union-Leader* for publishing an article that took a swipe at his wife. As Muskie laced into the paper, the presidential hopeful became so enraged that, at one point, he appeared to cry.[22]

Afterward, he climbed into a car with Podesta. "I shouldn't have broken down like that," Muskie told his young aide.

Muskie was right. In the days after the incident, as Muskie's tears became a national news story, the onetime Democratic front-runner watched his campaign falter.[23] Voters began to dismiss him as too weak to hold office.[24] Once Muskie dropped out of the race, Podesta joined the campaign of the party's eventual nominee, South Dakota Senator George McGovern, which, like the prior campaigns he'd worked for, ended in defeat.

It was around this time that Podesta—who left MIT without completing his PhD[25]—returned to Washington, DC, with his closest friend in liberal politics: his kid brother, John. The Podesta brothers had teamed up periodically over the years, working together on the Duffy and McGovern campaigns. But when both enrolled at Georgetown University's law school in 1973, their careers merged onto an identical track. "We lived together, and we had only one car, so we had to go to the same school," Tony Podesta joked. Each day, the two carpooled together to Georgetown's campus, where they served as editors of the prestigious law review. John was a notes editor; Tony edited articles. After graduating in 1976, they both became lawyers in Washington. Tony took a job with the US Attorney's Office for the District of Columbia, and John landed a position at the Department of Justice and later became a Democratic staffer for the Senate Judiciary Committee.[26]

The Podesta brothers had always been contrary in their physical appearances. Tony was a roly-poly figure partial to fine Italian wines and multicourse meals; John had a taut, wiry frame and an intense disposition and enjoyed long runs along the Potomac River.[27] In 1980 their ambitions diverged as well. While John continued to ascend the Democratic ranks as a Senate aide, Tony worked for the presidential campaign of Ted Kennedy before deciding to leave public service. In 1981 he joined a new interest group that was formed to address an emerging danger to the liberal establishment.

About a year earlier, acclaimed TV producer Norman Lear began developing what he hoped would be his latest smash hit. Lear had vaulted to Hollywood superstardom by creating a string of iconic sitcoms about 1970s America: *All in the Family, The Jeffersons, One Day at a Time.*[28] His latest endeavor would tackle a movement that was gathering steam at the start of the new decade. It was a comedy film about two New York City police officers who also worked as religious ministers,[29] and it would serve as a satire of the politically minded televangelists who were firing up the New Right. To research the project, Lear studied the TV shows of popular conservative preachers, consuming broadcast upon broadcast of Jerry Falwell's *Old-Time Gospel Hour*, Pat Robertson's *The 700 Club*, and other firebrands of the religious Right. The research, however, left him more alarmed than amused.

"It was the relentless political message that got to me," Lear said. "Hour after hour, they were telling people, 'You are a good Christian or a bad Christian, depending on your view of the Supreme Court, or capital punishment.'"[30] Lear saw the convergence of televangelism and conservative activism as an urgent threat to a sacred American value: freedom of thought. He tossed aside his movie script and went to work on a TV commercial depicting ordinary citizens who were fed up with TV preachers telling them which political views were godly and which were the devil's work. When Lear showed the commercial to a group of religious leaders, they told him it was good but insufficient. "One commercial isn't going to do it," they said. "You need an organization to keep this going."[31] So, Lear spent $300,000 to launch a new DC-based advocacy organization, People for the American Way.[32] He hired Tony Podesta as its first executive director.

Under Podesta's direction, People for the American Way—often referred to as PAW—would emerge as the liberal answer to the network of Christian conservative groups, such as Falwell's Moral Majority, that had proliferated in Reagan's Washington. By the early 1980s, the growing influence of conservative Christians was visible in the capital city and beyond. Organizations such as the Moral Majority were using "moral report cards" to evaluate lawmakers and spending millions of dollars to defeat candidates who backed abortion rights or the Equal Rights Amendment.[33] Outside of the nation's capital, some Christian activists took an even harder line. In 1981, following the wave of conservative victories in the presidential and congressional elections, the American Library Association recorded a spike in reports of local efforts to ban purportedly obscene books from public libraries.[34] Among the authors targeted were Arthur Miller, Kurt

Vonnegut, John Steinbeck, and J. D. Salinger.[35] The state of Texas went so far as to pull the Merriam-Webster dictionary from the public school system because it contained obscene words.[36] As Reverend George Zarris, the chairman of the Illinois chapter of the Moral Majority, put it, "If they have the books and feel like burning them, fine."[37]

At its inception, PAW had neither the financial muscle nor the insider sway to confront the religious Right head-on. So instead of pressuring lawmakers directly, Podesta pursued an outside influence strategy, using the mass media and Hollywood razzle-dazzle to bring public attention to what he viewed as the dangerous clout of evangelical political activists. At its DC headquarters, PAW staffers monitored the broadcasts of leading televangelists, like Falwell and Pat Robertson, and documented their most controversial remarks. PAW's team then highlighted these statements in radio reports, television interviews, and op-ed articles—often written under Podesta's byline—that were sent to 1,700 different newspapers across the country in the hopes that they might be published.[38] "We raise hell in the *Chicago Tribune* and on [PBS's] *MacNeil/Lehrer* [*Report*]," Podesta said of his approach. "We send material to three hundred talk radio shows. We're out there in the Edwardsville, Illinois, *Gazette*."[39] He continued, "If separation of church and state isn't going to sell in Edwardsville, Illinois, Washington is not going to save us."

PAW got A-list celebrities—actors Goldie Hawn and Carol Burnett, boxing champ Muhammad Ali—to appear in TV commercials touting the importance of freedom of thought.[40] In 1982 PAW debuted a thirty-minute TV documentary about the Christian Right, narrated by the actor Burt Lancaster; the film showed evangelical leaders burning books and making disparaging statements about gay people and Jews.[41] Podesta set up a legal defense fund for school boards in Alabama and Tennessee, which had been targeted by conservative activists for alleged offenses against Christian values.[42] In 1984 Hollywood producer Daniel Melnick pledged that he would contribute a share of the profits from *Footloose*—his recently released film about a high school student who challenges the dancing prohibition in his small town—to support PAW's efforts to combat book-banning initiatives and anti-dancing ordinances in communities across the country. "The very idea that anyone can ban reading and dancing," Podesta said, "is something that the American people should be thinking about."[43]

As a liberal activist, Podesta's approach to political influence—pressuring lawmakers in DC by generating buzz out in the states—was different from the way most corporate lobbyists went about their business at the time. "Lobbying in those days was mostly relationship driven," Podesta said, "and we were very outside driven." But his playbook was delivering results. As his efforts grabbed headlines, PAW was swamped by donors and supporters. Its budget tripled in three years, and, by the mid-1980s, it had nearly as many members—250,000—as the American Civil Liberties Union.[44] Increasingly, Podesta directed the group's attention to the courts, where conservative activists were proving remarkably effective at implementing their vision. As of November 1985, Reagan had appointed 221 of the 743 federal judges and appeals court judges in America, and he still had 77 vacancies left to fill. United Press International estimated that by the end of his second term, Reagan's appointees would represent half the entire federal judiciary.[45] The development rattled Podesta and his liberal allies, who feared that Reagan's conservative judges would invalidate the victories they'd achieved since the civil rights era. "I think the radical right acknowledges to itself that it cannot win legislatively and if they are going to undo the decisions of the last twenty years, they have to do it in the courts," said Ralph Neas, the executive director of the Leadership Conference on Civil Rights.[46] As a result, PAW set itself to sabotage Reagan's judicial selections.

In 1986 Podesta appealed to PAW's members around the country to oppose the nomination of US Attorney Jeff Sessions as a federal judge,[47] on account of allegations that the future US attorney general under President Donald Trump had shown racial prejudice while serving as the top federal prosecutor in Alabama. Though Sessions denied the claims,[48] PAW's supporters responded by inundating congressional staff with calls and letters[49] criticizing Sessions. In the face of mounting pressure, the GOP-led Senate Judiciary Committee turned down the nomination, making Sessions only the second would-be federal judge in nearly fifty years to lose a confirmation vote.[50] Next, PAW targeted Daniel Manion, the Midwestern lawyer whom Reagan had selected for a federal judgeship in Chicago. When the nomination was announced, Podesta assigned a PAW investigator named Ricki Seidman to dig into Manion's past. After traveling to Indiana, Seidman discovered that during his tenure in the state senate, Manion had introduced a bill allowing public schools to display the Ten Commandments. It was a significant revelation, since the Supreme Court had recently declared such legislation unconstitutional, and Podesta's team hustled to fashion the information into a political weapon. Back in Washington, PAW sent a dossier containing the findings of its investigation to Democratic members of the Senate Judiciary Committee, who used the information to interrogate the nominee. Podesta also launched a national advertising campaign to discredit Manion, enlisting the popular actor Lloyd Bridges to star in a TV commercial about the importance of unbiased judges, and taking out full-page ads in the *New York Times* and *USA Today* dismissing Manion as a "second-rate extremist." As Podesta put it, "We did everything we could think of." In the end, though, the effort came up just short. While PAW helped persuade five Republican senators to reject the nominee, Manion still managed to win the Senate's approval by a single vote.[51]

As a result of its brass-knuckled approach, PAW was despised by conservatives in Washington. "What they are is an uncivil organization," said Terry Eastland, a spokesman for Reagan's Department of Justice. "I think People for the American Way has helped lower the level of public discourse in this country."[52] But following its high-profile victories against the Moral Majority and the Reagan administration, PAW also became known as one of the most effective liberal groups in the capital city. And its scrappy executive director was hailed as a rising star. So, when Ted Kennedy needed a savvy operative for his crusade against Robert Bork, Tony Podesta was a natural recruit.

After excoriating the conservative judge from the floor of the US Senate, on July 1, 1987, Kennedy raced to block Bork from the court. He used his clout with Democratic leaders of the Senate Judiciary Committee to enact two critical changes to the upcoming confirmation hearings. One, committee leaders agreed to exercise their authority under the US Constitution to "advise and consent" on the president's judicial nominations more vigorously than they had in recent decades, expanding the scope of their inquiry to also include questions about Bork's judicial philosophy. And secondly, rather than holding the hearings right away, the Senate would postpone the proceedings until after the August recess—providing Kennedy additional time to execute his plan.[53]

That plan was two-pronged. In Washington, the senator and his allies worked up a list of lawmakers who were undecided on the nominee and dispatched anti-Bork senators to speak with each one.[54] Kennedy's aides then gave the wavering lawmakers thick dossiers of controversial Bork writings to review over the recess.[55] But in addition to this "inside" strategy of persuading senators directly, Kennedy also pursued an outside-influence strategy designed to drum up opposition among workaday Americans. The approach was born of experience. After four terms in the Senate, Kennedy understood that politicians were most willing to take an official action when their constituents were clamoring for them to do it. So, in order to pressure the undecided senators into opposing Bork, he began working to incite a national outcry against the conservative nominee. The result was the first modern campaign against a Supreme Court pick, a notorious conflict that established the rules of engagement for the bruising melees over judicial nominees that would consume Washington over the coming decades. For assistance with the campaign, Kennedy reached out to the enterprising liberal street fighter.[56]

Having worked on his unsuccessful presidential campaign back in 1980, Podesta was already a familiar face to Kennedy. Now that Podesta had developed into a maestro of "outside" political-influence tactics, the senator wanted his help in drumming up public opposition to Reagan's Supreme Court pick. It would be Podesta's job to connect Kennedy to civic leaders located far outside of Washington—pastors, mayors, union bosses—who might be willing to advocate against Bork in their local communities.[57]

Podesta played a key role in one part of a sweeping campaign that involved more than three hundred groups[58]—civil rights organizations, reproductive health advocates, public interest law firms, unions—as well as the Kennedy family's vast political network. That summer, Kennedy traveled to Chicago for a national meeting of grassroots organizations, where he implored the more than 1,200 assembled activists to mobilize against Bork.[59] He enlisted hundreds of men and women who'd once served on his or his brothers' staffs—in the White House, the Department of Justice, or the Senate—to write op-eds and speeches criticizing Reagan's pick. And he sent letters to every single Black elected official in the United States, some 6,200 in all.[60]

Podesta worked out of the senator's Boston office and, on occasion, at Kennedy's home. During the congressional recess in August 1987, he traveled to the storied Kennedy compound in Hyannis Port, Massachusetts—which had served as the de facto headquarters for JFK's 1960 presidential campaign—and helped arrange phone calls between Kennedy and more than one hundred Black political leaders from the South, including Atlanta mayor Andrew Young, New Orleans mayor Sidney Barthelemy, Mayor Richard Arrington of Birmingham, Alabama, and Mayor Johnny Ford of Tuskegee, Alabama.[61] "I dialed them up and gave [Kennedy] the phone," Podesta said, "and he made the sale."

These Southern figures were particularly important to the anti-Bork movement, since many of the senators who were undecided on the nominee hailed from the region. In his conversations with the Black leaders, Kennedy urged them to join his effort to oppose the conservative judge. "This guy's terrible," Kennedy explained, according to Podesta. "He'll roll back the clock on civil rights. He's a danger to the African American community. I need your help on this. I need you to call your senator."

For civil rights leaders like the Reverend Joseph Lowery, the message resonated. Kennedy had reached Lowery as the reverend was making final preparations for the annual convention of the Southern Christian Leadership Conference, the Atlanta-based civil rights organization that he co-founded with Martin Luther King Jr., according to Ethan Bronner's 1989 book *Battle for Justice*. The much-anticipated event would bring hundreds of Black preachers and civil rights advocates together at the Hyatt Hotel in New Orleans. Following his phone conversation with Kennedy, Lowery decided to devote a full day of the convention to strategizing against Bork. Over the coming weeks, the anti-Bork vehemence would spread from the SCLC convention hall to the pulpits of Black churches throughout the South. Some ministers harangued Reagan's nominee during services, others passed out pens and paper and instructed their congregants to write letters urging senators to vote against his confirmation. It was just as Podesta and Kennedy had hoped. The people were rising up against Bork, right here in the Lord's House.[62]

It wasn't long before this uproar reached back to Washington. When Kennedy returned to the floor of the US Senate, he ran into Senator J. Bennett Johnston, a white Democrat from Louisiana who had previously been undecided about Bork.

"What are you thinking, Bennett?" Kennedy asked his colleague, according to Podesta.

Johnston told Kennedy that he had been getting a lot of pressure from Black leaders in his state to vote against Bork, and, as a result, he'd decided to reject the Supreme Court nominee. "We're going to have to go with the brothers on this one," Bennett told Kennedy.

As the confirmation hearings approached, anti-Bork demonstrations sprouted up all over the country: 1,200 protesters staged a "Funeral for Justice" in Philadelphia, while nearly two dozen women's groups organized a press conference in DC.[63] Podesta's former colleagues at PAW broadcast a sixty-second television advertisement featuring actor Gregory Peck, which—like Kennedy's notorious Senate floor address—was criticized heavily for misconstruing Bork's views. Bork "defended poll taxes and literacy tests which kept many Americans from voting," Peck told the audience. "He opposed the civil rights law that ended 'whites only' signs at lunch counters. He doesn't believe the Constitution protects your right to privacy."[64] Bork's allies defended the embattled nominee by citing research concluding that as US solicitor general, Bork had sided with liberal causes over conservative ones just as often as Supreme Court Justice Thurgood Marshall had when he served as solicitor general under President Lyndon Johnson.[65] Such support, however, wasn't nearly enough to combat the torrent of allegations being leveled against him. Still, on the eve of the Capitol Hill proceedings, most Americans had no opinion about the conservative nominee.[66] That would change during the two weeks of televised hearings, when Bork's sour exchanges with members of the Senate Judiciary Committee alienated the public. "Bork came across on television as coldhearted and condescending," as the *Washington Post*'s TV critic put it. "Some viewers must have looked at Judge Bork and seen in him every haughty professor whose lectures they dreaded in college."[67] From the Senate dais, Kennedy could sense that victory was at hand. As he went about his questioning of Bork, Judiciary Committee Chairman Joe Biden passed him a series of notes written on Senate stationery. In these notes, Biden evaluated Bork's performance as if he were keeping score at a football game. Each time Bork stumbled, his point deficit increased.

"12–0," read Biden's first note to Kennedy.

"18–0," was the second.

"24–0."

Finally, when Kennedy was wrapping up, Biden wrote, "30–0 if [Bork] keeps on."[68]

In the face of Kennedy's outside pressure campaign and Bork's nightmare performance on Capitol Hill, lawmakers joined the public in turning against the would-be justice. In October 1987 fifty-eight senators— including Bennett Johnston—voted against Bork's nomination, while only forty-two voted to confirm him. It was the widest margin of defeat in the history of Supreme Court nominations.[69]

Conservatives were apoplectic over the anti-Bork offensive. Kennedy and his confederates had dumped the mud-slinging and half-truths of a political campaign into the typically decorous proceedings of the Senate Judiciary Committee. "This is a scary thing that's happening here," said Tom Korologos, who was working to help the White House during the confirmation process. "Gregory Peck advertisements on the radio, public opinion polls. . . . Is this how we operate now on Supreme Court nominations?"[70]

For Podesta, though, the Bork episode would serve as a springboard to a whole new career. Just one year after he helped torpedo the conservative Supreme Court nominee, Podesta departed the hardscrabble world of liberal activism for the comforts of DC's lobbying industry. Over the next three decades, as he established himself among the leading lights of K Street, Podesta would continue to ply the same outside influence tactics that he'd used in 1980s Washington. Only now, rather than deploying his playbook to advance the liberal cause, he would use it to shape federal policy to better suit corporate America.

1988
Alexandria, Virginia

As the Reagan era drew to a close, the partners at Black Manafort faced an unfamiliar tremor of uncertainty. The founders' close ties to the conservative president, of course, had been the animating force of their business. It was the friends they'd made during the Reagan revolution that had enabled this collection of cutthroats and rogues to reinvent themselves as the premier influence peddlers of 1980s Washington. Now, after seven years in office, Reagan was preparing to clear out of the White House. If the firm was to continue its success, Black Manafort would have to develop allies in a new administration.

Yet once again the firm had an edge. Unlike the other lobbying shops on K Street, Black Manafort also ran one of Washington's most sought-after political consulting outfits. This additional dimension allowed the firm to establish links to a full slate of Reagan's potential successors long before voters headed to the polls. During the 1988 presidential election campaign, Black Manafort's partners were the guiding hands behind nearly every candidate in the Republican primary field. Roger Stone served as a political consultant for Jack Kemp, a veteran congressman from New York, Charlie Black advised Bob Dole, and Lee Atwater helped run the campaign of the eventual winner, George H. W. Bush.[1] The firm was so deeply entrenched in the 1988 presidential process that at one point a congressional aide joked, "Why have primaries for the nomination? Why not have the candidates go over to Black, Manafort, and Stone and argue it out?"[2]

It wasn't just Republican candidates who flocked to the firm for help. After Black Manafort became bipartisan in the mid-1980s, its political consulting unit regularly found itself playing both sides of general elections.[3] During the 1986 congressional elections, Peter Kelly helped raise money for a slate of Democratic Senate candidates—including Patrick Leahy of Vermont, Bob Graham of Florida, and John Breaux of Louisiana—whose Republican opponents were being advised by Lee Atwater and Charlie Black.[4] Such conflicts of interest were a perfectly legal, if ethically dubious, feature of working at the firm, and the sheer size of its client roster led to uncomfortable workplace encounters. On one occasion, a Democratic candidate came into the office to meet with Kelly, and while the two were walking through the hallway, they ran into his Republican opponent, who, it turned out, was being advised by one of the firm's Republican partners. "Your opponent is in the office right there," Kelly explained to the Democrat, "so we're going to go to my office through here."

The partners' success as election strategists made them more potent as lobbyists. In Black Manafort's most notorious practice, the firm essentially combined its campaign consulting and government relations efforts into a so-called double-breasted[5] lobbying operation that increased its leverage over key members of Congress. The playbook was as simple as it was effective. When their work as campaign advisors succeeded in getting a candidate elected to Congress, the partners turned around and lobbied that same lawmaker on behalf of corporate and other interests. Many of the firm's former campaign clients—Senator Phil Gramm of Texas, Senator Arlen Specter of Pennsylvania, Senator Jesse Helms of North Carolina, and Senate Republican Leader Bob Dole of Kansas—became reliable allies to Black Manafort's lobbying clients.[6] Inside the office, staffers had a saying to describe how the firm used these two, legally distinct entities to gain access to lawmakers and influence their actions: "Elect 'em on the second floor, lobby 'em on the third floor."

Even more importantly, though, the partners' experiences running presidential campaigns enabled them to develop new approaches to lobbying that moved beyond the conventions of handshakes and smoke-filled rooms. Their innovations, which combined elements of old-fashioned access peddling with the cutting-edge tools of modern electioneering, would help transition K Street away from the inside influence tactics that marked the masters-of-the-universe era and toward the more advanced outside influence strategies that ideological activists, such as Tony Podesta, were already perfecting on behalf of liberal causes. This transformation—from inside lobbying to outside lobbying—would serve as a pivotal development in the evolution of the modern influence industry.

In 1984, for instance, Black Manafort was hired by Bethlehem Steel—the fading industrial giant—to secure the Reagan administration's help in a trade dispute. The problem, according to company executives, was that foreign firms were flooding the United States with cheap imported steel, making it impossible for Bethlehem to compete. (The company lost $1.5 billion in 1982.)[7] Bethlehem Steel's chairman called on President Reagan to level the playing field by blocking or taxing imported steel. The issue presented a conundrum for Reagan. As a free trader, he was ideologically opposed to shielding industries from market forces. But the appeal from Bethlehem Steel had arrived during a critical stretch of the 1984 presidential campaign, and if Reagan failed to deliver for the steel sector, he'd risk alienating the blue-collar workers whose votes he'd need at the ballot box.

Through their work on his campaigns and Lee Atwater's contacts in the White House political office, the Black Manafort partners had keen insight into the president's thinking. They understood that while Reagan aggressively championed conservative political theory, he left the details of how policies were implemented to his Cabinet secretaries. If the lobbyists could bring these trusted advisors around to their position, they realized, they could deliver a victory for Bethlehem Steel. As a first step, Black convinced Bethlehem Steel's executives to dial back their demands. Instead of insisting on strict import limits or tariffs on foreign steel, the company would ask the Reagan administration to call on foreign countries to voluntarily limit the amount of steel they were sending into the United States.

Since America was such a large consumer of steel, foreign governments were likely to submit to these voluntary limits in order to head off stricter import tariffs or restrictions down the road. Such voluntary agreements could reduce cheap imports while allowing Reagan to maintain his support of free trade. "By calling them 'voluntary,'" Black recalled later, "it was less offensive to Ronald Reagan and to the other countries."

Black also recognized that the request for trade protections would be viewed with more credibility if it came from those affected by the steel industry's decline, as opposed to smooth-talking lobbyists. So, he employed a strategy known as "grass tops" lobbying. Instead of making the pitch himself, he arranged for Bethlehem Steel's chairman and CEO, Donald Trautlein, to meet with top Reagan administration officials—including Commerce Secretary Malcolm Baldrige Jr. and US Trade Representative William Brock—and describe how cheap foreign imports had forced him to shutter factories, reduce salaries, and lay off workers. The firm also arranged for Lynn Williams, the international president of the United Steelworkers union, to meet with Labor Secretary Raymond Donovan and explain that imported steel had contributed to the loss of three hundred thousand jobs at his union.

The plan worked. About two months before the election, Reagan announced that he would negotiate voluntary steel import limits with foreign trading partners. The agreements weren't perfect, but they managed to reduce steel imports by about 30 percent.[8] Meanwhile, as a result of a confluence of forces—the ascent of global capitalism, the development of computer technology, and a burst of business activity that Republicans attributed to lower taxes and fewer regulations[9]—the US economy was rebounding in the 1980s. Amid this broader turnaround, the domestic steel industry roared back to life. Stock prices soared as Wall Street analysts recommended buying shares in steel companies. In March 1988 Bethlehem Steel reported its first annual profit since 1981, awarding bonuses averaging $2,000 apiece to more than twenty-four thousand employees.[10*]

---

*The turnaround would prove temporary. As the US economy continued to deindustrialize, Bethlehem Steel filed for bankruptcy in 2001.

As they continued to lean on their powerful friends in the administration, the partners at Black Manafort also learned to mobilize groups of everyday citizens. In 1989 the firm found itself in the middle of a heated debate over affordable housing. A bipartisan group of lawmakers was advancing legislation designed to increase the supply of low-cost mortgages to average Americans. The plan revolved around the Federal Housing Administration, a little-known entity that FDR established in 1934 in order to help people buy homes during the Great Depression. The FHA guaranteed banks' home loans for Americans who didn't have enough money to qualify for financing; at the time, mortgage applicants were often required to make down payments equal to as much as half the property's value. With the federal government protecting them against the risk of default, though, bankers were willing to give low-interest-rate mortgages to home buyers they would have otherwise turned down—thereby expanding home ownership throughout the country.

Over the following years, private companies began selling their own mortgage insurance products that, for some borrowers, were more attractive than the FHA program. Such private mortgage insurance policies, as they are called, enabled certain borrowers to buy homes with lower down payments and fewer up-front fees than the FHA typically requires. This soon became a profitable line of business, and, in order to prevent the government from outcompeting the private mortgage insurance industry, Congress restricted the FHA's authority. During the 1980s, the FHA was prohibited from insuring loans larger than $67,500 nationwide or about $100,000 in high-cost states such as California and New York.

By the end of the decade, though, real estate prices had increased substantially. As a result, the FHA was less able to help would-be home buyers—especially in high-cost states. Housing advocates argued that by raising its loan limits, the FHA could expand home ownership among working-class and middle-class Americans. In the fall of 1989, senators from California and New York introduced legislation to do just that. If enacted, the National Affordable Housing Act would have increased the FHA's caps considerably, allowing it to insure loans of up to 95 percent of a state's median home price.[11] At the time, that amounted to about $87,000 nationwide, or $165,000 in more expensive states.

The bill enjoyed widespread support among housing advocates and many members of Congress because it would help more people buy homes at little cost to the taxpayer. It sailed through the House and, after nearly forty senators endorsed the legislation, approval in the upper chamber appeared imminent. The effort, however, sparked fierce opposition from the private mortgage insurance industry. Companies that sold private-sector insurance for home loans, led by the mortgage insurance division of General Electric Co., had long viewed the FHA as their top competitor. After all, if more Americans obtain home loan insurance from the federal government, that leaves fewer customers for them. The Mortgage Insurance Companies of America, an industry trade group, estimated that the bill would cost the sector billions of dollars in profits. In order to make sure that the National Affordable Housing Act never became law, the trade association and G.E.'s mortgage insurance unit hired Black Manafort.[12]

As a first step, the partners leveraged their Rolodexes of former campaign consulting clients. They reached out to allies in the administration and made sure that neither President George H. W. Bush—a client of Atwater's—nor the new secretary of HUD, Jack Kemp—a client of Black's—would publicly announce their support for the legislation, according to a former mortgage industry lobbyist involved in the campaign. Still, there remained a problem of optics. To many Americans, the debate over the National Affordable Housing Act pitted a collection of selfless community advocates working to boost middle-class home ownership against a cartel of greedy corporations looking to pump up profits. To build support for their position, the lobbyists realized, the mortgage insurers needed a more sympathetic public face. In short order, the lobbyists established an alliance with a confrontational antipoverty group, National People's Action, which had achieved notoriety for its "hits"[13]—or surprise rallies at the offices or homes of its opponents. The activists opposed the legislation on different grounds than the mortgage insurers did: they considered the bill an unnecessary handout to people wealthy enough to obtain mortgages without the government's assistance. "There's no reason to increase [loan] limits to appease the rich," Gale Cincotta, the famed community activist who ran

National People's Action, said in a press release. "This proposal will increase foreclosures and losses to [the government], increase discrimination against lower-income borrowers, and all in the name of rich people that don't need help to afford a loan." In an effort to tank the FHA reform, the Republican lobbyists joined forces with the lefty activists, forming what the *Chicago Sun-Times* described as "American housing's odd couple of the decade."[14] By teaming up with the community activists, the lobbyists were able to accomplish what they might not have been able to on their own.

While Black Manafort worked connections in Congress and the administration, National People's Action carried out a grassroots lobbying effort, bringing hundreds of spirited activists to Washington for a series of 1960s-style protests. They staged a boisterous rally on Jack Kemp's front lawn and held a public demonstration outside of the FHA's headquarters, according to the former mortgage industry lobbyist. Cincotta led a crowd of protestors through the halls of Congress, the lobbyist said, where they urged senators not to expand the FHA's powers. To make the public aware of the community group's opposition, Cincotta issued press releases to the media and wrote letters to lawmakers. In the end, the alliance of Beltway lobbyists and rabble-rousing activists succeeded in torpedoing the National Affordable Housing Act. According to the former mortgage industry lobbyist, when the bill's author, California Democrat Senator Alan Cranston, walked off of the Senate floor after losing the vote, he told the assembled crowd: "Well, the private sector and the community folks just wanted it more than anyone else."

Though less widespread at the time, these so-called grassroots tactics would become increasingly central to corporate lobbying campaigns over the coming years. And while it may have strangled the dream of home ownership for middle-class Americans, tanking the National Affordable Housing Act helped pave the way for a booming decade in the mortgage insurance industry. In 1990, one year after the legislation was killed, the industry generated roughly $300 million in profits, according to a report by the think tank Urban Institute. By 1991, the figure reached $4 billion.[15]

As Black Manafort's profile expanded, its business practices started attracting the wrong kind of attention. Fred Wertheimer, the president of the watchdog group Common Cause, told *Time* magazine that the firm's two-pronged strategy—of lobbying the very lawmakers it helped to elect—was an "institutionalized conflict of interest."[16] The *New Republic* called Roger Stone a "state-of-the-art sleazeball."[17] Before long, the firm's penchant for controversy began sullying the reputations of its clients. During the 1988 presidential campaign, Democratic nominee Michael Dukakis made Black Manafort the focus of a political attack on his Republican rival, George H. W. Bush. The attack stemmed from the firm's efforts in the mid-1980s to help the Bahamian government repair its image after its prime minister's top lieutenants were linked to international drug trafficking. The work, for which Black Manafort earned an $800,000 payday, faced subsequent criticism on Capitol Hill.[18] A report by a Senate subcommittee concluded that the effort by American consultants to shape federal narcotics policies on the Bahamian government's behalf "raises troubling questions about conflicts of interest."[19]

When Charlie Black, Paul Manafort, and Roger Stone joined the Bush campaign as unpaid advisors partly to earn goodwill with the potential president, Dukakis used the Bahamian episode to impugn the loyalties of Bush's team. "In a Dukakis White House," he said at a news conference, "there will be no back door for foreign lobbyists. My staff will not have divided loyalties." He continued: "In a Dukakis White House, the staff will pledge allegiance to only one flag: Old Glory."[20] But while the firm itself was often mired in bad press, the bulk of Black Manafort's controversies derived from one source in particular.

For a man at the center of a widening national scandal, Paul Manafort appeared perfectly at ease. It was June 20, 1989, and the pricey lobbyist was seated before a bank of microphones in a crowded congressional hearing room. Wearing a crisp white shirt and a dark suit, he calmly explained to the assembled lawmakers and reporters that everything he'd done—and everything the firm had done—was aboveboard. At one point, when the subcommittee chairman asked him to speak a little slower so that the stenographer could log a full transcript, Manafort cracked wise.

"I'll just try to keep it up to your speed, Congressman," he said with a laugh.[21]

The events that put Manafort in the crosshairs of the high-profile congressional inquiry had begun three years earlier, when he was hired to help a private real estate firm obtain public funds for a redevelopment project. The company, CFM Development Corporation, was seeking tens of millions of dollars in federal grants and rent subsidies in order to renovate the Seabrook Apartments, a 326-unit low-income housing complex in Upper Deerfield Township, New Jersey.[22] At the time, federal funds for public housing projects were extremely limited; as part of the Reagan administration's effort to shrink government, officials had halted the construction of all new federally subsidized housing developments. About the only resource available was the Department of Housing and Urban Development's "moderate rehabilitation program," which offered financial assistance to developers who made improvements to federally backed apartments for the poor.[23]

This particular property, however, was a less than ideal fit for the program. The federal government had built the Seabrook Apartments during World War II as temporary housing for workers,[24] and it was subsequently used as an internment camp for Japanese Americans.[25] By the mid-1980s, the complex was teetering on the verge of collapse. Local authorities believed that any effort to renovate it would be a waste of taxpayers' money. As Upper Deerfield Township's mayor, Bruce Peterson, put it, "I think we would have preferred to see the majority of the units torn down, they were in such terrible shape."[26] Nevertheless, Manafort arranged for a lobbying colleague—and former HUD official—to work his contacts at the department and secure $43 million in public funds for the project,[27] which he himself had an ownership interest in.[28]

The property's residents, who included some elderly former internment camp prisoners,[29] were less enthusiastic. After the federal funds had arrived, the developers doubled the rental fees but failed to make meaningful improvements to living conditions. The neighborhood of one-story cinder block apartments had no paved roads or sidewalks.[30] A line of graffiti at the entrance to the complex read, "Welcome to the Jungle."[31] There were no refrigerators provided in the units, leaving one mother to feed her family with canned goods alone.[32] The poorly constructed roofs sagged during the rain;[33] the living room ceiling in one apartment collapsed entirely.[34] Repair workers used putty to cover up rotting wood, left plumbing exposed, and made the bathroom entrances so cramped that residents had to turn sideways in order to get in. "They have taken very small apartments and made them even smaller," one resident said. "They have turned it into a prison."[35]

Despite the complaints from residents, the project was a boon for Manafort. He and his colleagues earned a $326,000 fee[36] for securing generous federal subsidies for an apartment project in which he had an ownership interest. When a HUD audit revealed that tens of millions of dollars in housing-related perks had been routed to companies with high-powered GOP operatives working on retainers,[37] outraged lawmakers launched an investigation, and Manafort soon found himself at the witness table.

In the days before Manafort was scheduled to testify, the lobbyists at Black Manafort held a series of closed-door meetings to strategize about what he should tell the House Government Operations Subcommittee on Employment and Housing. During these meetings, Manafort was warned repeatedly against using the phrase "influence peddling" to describe the firm's work.[38] Yet when he took his place in the hearing room, the veteran political operator dismissed his colleagues' advice. "The technical term for what we do, and what law firms, associations, and professional groups do is lobbying," Manafort said. "For purposes of today, I will admit, that in a narrow sense, some people might term it influence peddling."[39]

Over the course of the hearing, lawmakers lambasted the lobbyists and government officials involved with the Seabrook Apartments project. "For some individuals," said Tom Lantos, a Democratic congressman from California, "obtaining these scarce rent subsidy funds was as easy as phoning in an order to Domino's for a pizza."[40]

Manafort, for his part, insisted that he was simply playing by the rules of Washington. "We worked within the system as it existed, so I don't think we did anything illegal or improper," he said.[41]

Despite all the firm's success, by the mid-1980s, Paul Manafort had lost interest in the stuffy work of corporate lobbying and federal electioneering. An adventure seeker by nature, he began exploring business opportunities in related fields. While his dalliance in real estate development would result in public embarrassment, Manafort would soon find the action he was looking for in the more intriguing, if shadowy, corner of the influence economy: foreign lobbying.

Although lobbying on behalf of overseas governments is perfectly legal, the practice has long been viewed with suspicion. In 1938, Franklin Roosevelt had signed the law that would come to regulate foreign lobbying, the Foreign Agents Registration Act, following revelations that a well-known New York City publicist, Ivy Lee, had used the cover of a German industrial syndicate to run a secret public relations campaign aimed at improving Americans' perceptions of the Third Reich.[42] At the time of Black Manafort's founding, most lobbyists in Washington refused to represent foreign clients, and those who did were considered dodgy. The Reagan revolution changed the incentive calculus, however, creating a booming new opportunity for political fixers willing to overlook the ethical messiness associated with appearing to be unpatriotic by representing overseas actors before their own government. While rewriting the blueprints for the country's economy, the Reagan White House had also revised the terms of the Cold War. As the *Atlantic* noted, the administration ramped up the effort to defeat the Soviet Union by backing anti-Communist insurgencies in Latin America, Africa, and Central Asia—a strategy designed to ensnare the Soviets in far-flung proxy wars that would exhaust Moscow's resources. As a result, hundreds of millions of dollars in weapons and military training became available to the mujahideen in Afghanistan, the contras in Nicaragua, and other rebel movements around the world. In order to access this windfall from the US government, these hardened guerrilla leaders would need a man in Washington—someone who could convince the White House and members of Congress to disregard their authoritarian excesses and bankroll their revolutions.[43] It was here that Manafort made his name in Washington.

Foreign work appealed to Manafort. Dictators paid even more handsomely than corporate CEOs did, and Manafort had never been one to pass up a good score. When George H. W. Bush won the presidential election, for instance, Manafort and his lobbying partners volunteered to help coordinate the inaugural celebration in Washington, according to the *Atlantic*. They arranged for a Rhode Island company to sell Bush-themed T-shirts and buttons at the parade. Once the day's festivities were over, one of the people who'd been out hawking the memorabilia arrived at the firm's offices with a bag of cash—an apparent commission on T-shirt and button sales that Manafort had secured for himself. "It was a Paul tax," an ex-colleague of Manafort's told the magazine. "This was classic: somebody else does the work, and he walks away with the bag of cash."[44] Advancing the interests of foreign autocrats was a far more lucrative racket, and before long, Manafort emerged as the go-to political fixer for problematic foreign regimes. During the 1980s, Manafort and his colleagues landed six- and seven-figure contracts with a slew of totalitarian governments: $1 million from Zaire,[45] $1 million from Nigeria, $500,000 from Kenya, $900,000 from the Philippines, $450,000 from Peru, and $250,000 from Somalia. At its peak, in 1990, foreign lobbying was generating $2.75 million in revenue a year for Black Manafort, up from $45,000 a year in 1984 when it first began representing foreign interests. "Black, Manafort, Stone, and Kelly lined up most of the dictators in the world we could find," Stone once bragged. "Dictators are in the eye of the beholder."[46]

In the competition to accumulate foreign clients, the firm had an edge over other lobbying shops. When Manafort's old mentor James Baker became President Bush's secretary of state, Baker began directing certain regimes in the developing world to hire Black Manafort to help them clean up their images in Washington, according to Kelly. No despot was too savage for the firm. At one point, Manafort asked a pair of staffers to travel to Somalia in order to finalize a $1 million contract with its president, Mohamed Siad Barre, whose military forces would murder an estimated fifty thousand unarmed civilians before the decade was through.

One staffer, Riva Levinson, expressed reservations about going into business with such a vicious figure, asking Manafort, "Are we sure we want this guy as a client?"

"We all know Barre is a bad guy," he replied. "We just have to make sure he's our bad guy."[47]

If it might grow his business, Manafort didn't think twice, even if it meant risking subordinates' lives. On their trip to finalize the contract with Siad Barre, Levinson and her colleague landed in the Somalia capital of Mogadishu just as a rebel army was closing in. They managed to escape the city before the fighting began, but only by bribing an airport employee.[48] Later, during a business trip to Angola, Levinson found herself in the middle of a street battle and had to dive under a military jeep to avoid the automatic gunfire.[49]

Not every foreign government got its money's worth. As one former Black Manafort lobbyist told a reporter, the firm attracted new clients with unrealistic promises—claiming, for example, that it could overhaul an authoritarian regime's image even if the authorities didn't improve their treatment of citizens. "At the end of a year or two, the clients figured out they were getting ripped off and would drop them, but they didn't care," the former lobbyist said. "They'd just sign up new clients. It was churn and burn."[50] But for some foreign clients, such as Angolan guerrilla leader Jonas Savimbi, Manafort was able to alter the course of history.

In 1975, after Angola won independence from Portugal, the southwestern African nation plunged into a chaotic civil war. One set of forces, the Popular Movement for the Liberation of Angola, adopted a Marxist ideology and drew the support of Cuban troops and Soviet weapons. An opposing set of forces was controlled by Savimbi and his National Union for the Total Independence of Angola, known as UNITA. With his strapping physique, scruffy beard, and bloodstained military fatigues, Savimbi was an ideologically flexible figure. Though he'd once been a Maoist,[51] Savimbi had since reinvented himself as a capitalist, and he was pressing the Reagan administration for military assistance in the form of antitank and antiaircraft missiles.[52] In many ways, Savimbi was just what the White House was looking for: a seasoned commando seeking to advance America's Cold War interests by crushing his Soviet-backed opponents. But there was a snag. During his years-long struggle for control of Angola, Savimbi had acted as a monstrous warlord, subjecting an impoverished country to a horrifying campaign of atrocities. His soldiers had murdered countless civilians and kidnapped tens of thousands of children—forcing boys to become warriors and girls to become sex slaves.[53] In one of many gruesome incidents, Savimbi's forces arrived in an Angolan town at night, roused the residents from their homes, and opened fire on the townspeople as they began to flee. One witness saw a wounded man's body being hacked to pieces by machete-wielding fighters.[54] Local hospitals filled up with children who'd lost limbs to UNITA's land-mines and women who'd been wounded by its soldiers.[55] Inside UNITA, Savimbi reportedly ordered suspected dissidents to be tortured and killed, and he burned alive civilians whom he accused of being witches. According to one account, an entire family of alleged witches was soaked in gasoline and set on fire at a public rally in a Southern Angolan town in 1983. When one of the accused witches tried to run away, Savimbi pulled out his hand-gun and fired at her.[56] If that wasn't bad enough, Savimbi's war was sustained through an alliance with South Africa's apartheid regime and by selling what came to be known as blood diamonds.[57]

While others saw a war criminal, Manafort spotted a business op-portunity. If he could improve Savimbi's public image and rally support for UNITA in Washington, he could secure federal funds for the Angolan guerrillas and land a big payday for himself. In the fall of 1985 he flew to Africa, traveling to an outpost near the Angolan border where he'd ar-ranged to meet the rebel leader. At the time, Savimbi was fighting off an intense attack from Cuban troops on a UNITA stronghold in southern An-gola. But he was so eager to meet the lobbyist from Washington that he left the battlefield and spent several days with Manafort. Within a week, Savimbi had signed a $600,000 contract with Manafort.[58] Returning to DC, Manafort began putting together a sophisticated political-influence plan that would blend traditional lobbying strategies with modern campaign tactics. The goal was to build support for UNITA by creating a coalition of right-wing Republicans, Democrats looking to get tough on Communism, and Cuban Americans who opposed Fidel Castro's regime.[59] The center-piece of this effort was a 1986 trip to the United States[60] designed to portray Savimbi not as a cynical and vicious warlord, but as a patriotic "Freedom Fighter" leading an underdog rebellion against Soviet expansion. Just as the Cuban revolutionary Ernesto "Che" Guevara[61] had come to symbolize the righteous struggle against colonial tyranny, Manafort would make Sa-vimbi the hero in the global fight against the dark forces of Communism.

The ten-day whirlwind tour of Washington and New York was me-ticulously choreographed by Manafort and his aides.[62] Savimbi traveled in a motorcade of stretch limousines, and he stayed in high-end hotels, such as the Waldorf-Astoria in New York City. Instead of his military fatigues, he arrived at appointments wearing a Nehru suit.[63] The makeover of the hardened guerrilla was guided by Manafort's belief that, in Washington, perception was reality. "If you want to be a president, you have to look like a president," said a former Black Manafort staffer who was involved with the Savimbi effort.

The lobbyists worked to project Savimbi as a cosmopolitan world leader by lining up discussions with high-profile media outlets, elite Washington think tanks, and top administration officials. Preparations had begun months earlier, when Manafort's team sent Savimbi detailed briefings on political developments in America and coached him on how to conduct himself during visits with influential figures in Washington.[64] Manafort arranged for Savimbi to meet with President Reagan in the Oval Office—even though the explosion of the space shuttle *Challenger*, which occurred two days before, had forced the president to cancel much of the day's schedule. Savimbi sat down with Secretary of State George P. Shultz, Defense Secretary Caspar W. Weinberger, Republican Senate Majority Leader Bob Dole, and Senate Foreign Relations Committee Chairman Richard Lugar, among others.[65] He scheduled interviews on CBS's *60 Minutes*, PBS's *MacNeil/Lehrer NewsHour*, and ABC News's *Nightline*. During a speech at the National Press Club in Washington, he framed his war in Angola as similar to America's fight for independence from England two centuries earlier. "I have been in the struggle for twenty-eight years now," he told the audience. "Fifteen years against Portuguese colonialism. Ten years now against Russian aggression. All that we want is for our people to have a say in the affairs of their own country."[66]

In visits to conservative think tanks and congressional offices, Savimbi—who'd earned a doctorate in political science and was fluent in at least six languages[67]—impressed audiences with his scholarly charisma. "If Jonas Savimbi were an American citizen," said the conservative activist Howard Phillips, "he would be the presidential candidate of the conservative movement."[68] While introducing Savimbi to attendees of the annual Conservative Political Action Conference (CPAC), the ardent neoconservative Jeane Kirkpatrick called the guerrilla leader a "linguist, philosopher, poet, politician, warrior . . . one of the few authentic heroes of our time."[69] Later, when Savimbi walked across the stage to accept an award from the American Conservative Union, the crowd broke into a chant.

"U-Ni-Ta!"

"U-Ni-Ta!"

"U-Ni-Ta!"[70]

During their trip, Savimbi and his delegation of Angolan commandos were awestruck by the nation's capital. As their motorcade passed through the National Mall, according to a former Black Manafort employee, a UNITA fighter pointed to the Washington Monument and declared: "One day, we will build one of these for Jonas Savimbi." Behind the scenes, though, the young staffers at Black Manafort had to scramble to keep the guerrillas out of trouble, according to former employees. At one point, a maid at a hotel in New York City found a live grenade in the room where one of Savimbi's commandos was staying. A quick-thinking Black Manafort lobbyist neutralized the crisis by reaching out to a contact in the New York City Police Department, who was able to safely—and quietly—dispose of the grenade. Other staffers managed to calm down the maid and keep the incident out of the news.

Over the course of the visit, Savimbi was occasionally confronted by protesters who were outraged by his alliance with South Africa's apartheid government,[71] and many Democrats in Congress rejected the idea of assisting UNITA's fighters. But Savimbi's political opponents were no match for his lobbyists. During the 1986 State of the Union address, President Reagan pledged his support for the "freedom fighters" in Angola.[72] Senate Republican Leader Bob Dole—a campaign client of Black's—introduced a congressional resolution backing the guerrilla movement. And shortly after Savimbi departed Washington, the United States began sending him roughly $15 million in covert military aid each year. When Reagan left the White House, federal dollars kept flowing. Before he'd even been sworn in, President Elect George H. W. Bush sent the guerrilla leader a letter vowing to continue the funding. As it turned out, the letter was written by a former Black Manafort lobbyist who'd since joined UNITA's public relations office.[73]

Over the years, the firm maintained support for UNITA in Congress by arranging for lawmakers to travel to Angola and meet Savimbi in person. In the late 1980s, when the partners were working to increase UNITA's clout with Democrats, Peter Kelly brought ex–Virginia governor—and future US senator—Chuck Robb to Savimbi's insurgent headquarters in the Angolan desert. The men took an eight-seat airplane into the active combat zone, flying just two hundred feet above the ground in order to avoid the Soviet-made radar systems. When the plane bounced to a stop on an airstrip, they were driven to a military encampment about a mile away. With artillery shells blasting overhead, they descended into a thirty-foot-deep bunker that had been fortified with sandbags. There they found Savimbi in his trademark fatigues. Over the next five hours,[74] the lobbyist, the politician, and the guerrilla leader sat together and talked. Robb, a former officer in the US Marines, was impressed by the worldly and charming commando. "He came away with a high regard for [Savimbi] as a human being, as a leader," Kelly says.

The Americans flew out just before daybreak. When their airplane landed at an airbase in neighboring Namibia, Robb turned to the lobbyist and joked, "I'd follow you anywhere." About a week later, according to Kelly, the plane they'd flown on was shot down by the Communist-backed forces.

Back in the United States, Robb emerged as a key ally of UNITA's. After winning a Senate seat in 1988, he became a member of the Senate Foreign Relations Committee, and he used his influence to continue support for the insurgent movement. With the help of Manafort and his colleagues, Savimbi secured some $250 million in secret federal funding for his war between 1986 and 1991, according to the organization Human Rights Watch; only the mujahideen in Afghanistan received more. Even Savimbi's enemies on the battlefield took notice. Manafort's work so impressed the regime that UNITA was fighting against—the Popular Movement for the Liberation of Angola—that it realized the best way to combat Savimbi was to hire a Washington lobbyist of its own.

Manafort's efforts on behalf of Savimbi reflected the broader evolution of the firm. No longer were the partners content to operate as old-fashioned access lobbyists—in the way that Tommy Boggs had worked liberal Washington during the prior decade—using their insider clout to directly influence Republican lawmakers and administration officials through phone calls or lunch meetings. Over the course of the 1980s, the partners adopted more advanced tactics, such as grassroots and grass tops lobbying, recruiting third-party allies—like community activists—to provide a sympathetic exterior for their influence-peddling efforts. Along the way, the partners at Black Manafort developed a whole new approach to political influence. By leveraging their prior experiences as election operatives, they began orchestrating elaborate lobbying campaigns that incorporated a full range of pressure tactics. The Savimbi effort, for example, involved public relations, image making, speech writing, research briefs, meetings with members of Congress and administration officials, visits to elite think tanks, and bringing lawmakers to Angola. "It was," according to a former Black Manafort lobbyist, "a hundred-point plan to gain acceptance for this guy's war in Angola." And as this new approach—the campaign model—gained favor on K Street, Washington's lobbying business accelerated its transformation from a clubby network of well-connected favor traders into a modern, diversified industry.

In Angola, the legacy of Black Manafort can be measured in human lives. It was in the firm's interest that the fighting continue as long as possible; if a peace accord were reached, Savimbi might not need his high-priced lobbyists. Critics have long argued that the firm's aggressive efforts to obtain federal funding for UNITA served to undercut the work of diplomats, who were desperately trying to bring the death and destruction to an end.[75] "Black Manafort played an important part in keeping the Angolan war going," said a former government official.[76] In 1996 the firm stopped representing UNITA—but that was only after Savimbi refused to accept the results of Angola's national election, violated the terms of a cease-fire agreement, and dragged the country back into bloodshed.

The conflict would continue for another six years, until February 2002, when images of Savimbi's bloodied corpse flashed across Angolan TV screens.[77] He had been killed in a shoot-out with government troops. All told, Savimbi's insurgency had lasted twenty-seven years. An estimated eight hundred thousand people perished in the fighting. Lifeless bodies were tossed into mass graves and buried in gardens.[78] Nearly four million Angolans were displaced from their homes.[79] One UN official called it "the worst war in the world."[80]

In the second year of George H. W. Bush's presidency, the partners at Black Manafort were confronting a tragedy of a different sort. On the morning of March 5, 1990, Lee Atwater arrived at a breakfast fund-raiser in a downtown Washington hotel. The RNC chairman was among the handful of GOP heavyweights who'd come out to speak in support of Phil Gramm, the Republican senator from Texas and longtime Black Manafort client. After Bob Dole had concluded his remarks, Atwater walked up to the podium and addressed the roomful of donors.

During his speech, Atwater took a practiced swipe at the man he'd smeared on the 1988 campaign trail; he told the crowd that in the infamous footage of Michael Dukakis riding a tank, the Democratic presidential nominee had resembled Rocky the Flying Squirrel. It was right about then that Atwater noticed his left foot begin to shake. The tremor blasted up his leg and gripped the left half of his torso. His head jerked back and forth, and he screamed in pain. As the audience looked on in stunned silence, Atwater collapsed.

"Somebody help me!" he said.[81]

Minutes later, the RNC chairman was lifted onto a stretcher and hustled into an ambulance. It was a short trip to George Washington University Hospital—the same building where, less than ten years earlier, President Ronald Reagan had been rushed to after he was shot by a would-be assassin. In the emergency room, Atwater's body began convulsing uncontrollably once again. Upon witnessing this second seizure, Dr. Burton Lee, who served as President George H. W. Bush's White House doctor and was a trained oncologist, pulled aside Atwater's wife.

"Your husband has a brain tumor," Dr. Lee said. "He's got about a year to live."

"How do you know?" Sally Atwater asked. "How can you say that?"

"It's just my business," Dr. Lee replied.[82]

Over the next thirteen months, as Atwater's condition deteriorated, a succession of political VIPs came to see the terminally ill operative. Among the well-wishers was Ron Brown, the Patton Boggs partner who was elected Democratic National Committee chairman in 1989. As they ascended to the top leadership posts of their respective party committees, Brown and Atwater—one a Patton Boggs lobbyist, the other an ex–Black Manafort political operative—illustrated just how central these two lobbying dynasties had become to the business of Washington. But until that point, Atwater's and Brown's relationship had been largely adversarial. As the heads of opposing political parties, they routinely attacked each other in the press, and, at one point, they nearly exchanged punches. In 1989, DNC and RNC staffers met on the Ellipse, just south of the White House, for their annual softball game. As the two teams shook hands following the DNC's 9–6 victory, Atwater lunged at Brown, and the two party chairmen had to be physically separated in order to prevent a fistfight. But after learning of Atwater's diagnosis, Brown offered his support. He visited Atwater in the hospital, and when Atwater was too sick to attend the birth of his third child, Brown sent the RNC chairman a stuffed donkey. "I just wanted to make sure that little Sally has a well-balanced upbringing," Brown said in a note. "Please make sure that this donkey stays by her side at all times (smile)."[83]

Meanwhile, as the cancer ate away at his mind and body, Atwater's thoughts occasionally drifted back to that heartbreaking afternoon in 1956, when he watched his three-year-old brother, Joe, suffer fatal burns from hot oil at his childhood home. In January 1991, following a surgery to extract dead tissue from his brain, Atwater was wheeled into the recovery room, where he cried out, "Joe, come home!"

Later, as the end approached, Atwater's mother flew up from South Carolina and began sleeping in his hospital room. At one point, Atwater asked about Joe.

"Mama, after Joe died, I remember you read a lot and tried to find meaning to all of that," Atwater said. "Did you ever find it?"

"No, I didn't," she replied.

"Mama, what was the real impact of Joe's death on me?" Atwater asked. His mother did not respond.

"Mama, wasn't Joe lucky?" Atwater said in a soft voice. "Wasn't Joe lucky?"[84]

By then, Atwater had spent months telling friends and reporters that he'd found God. During an event in Columbia organized to raise money for his treatment, Atwater described his "Jesus Christ" experience as "the greatest thing that has happened to me. . . . I hope every one of you tonight will find what I've found." He'd written "forgiveness letters" and made "forgiveness calls" to some of the people whom he'd harmed. Among those he contacted was his old friend Roger Stone.

"[Atwater] told me a number of really rotten things he had done to me that I never knew about," Stone recalled. "He just had to get them off his chest, and asked me to forgive him, and I did."[85]

While many of Atwater's supporters believed his spiritual awakening was sincere, others in Washington were suspicious. Perhaps the notorious operative was running one more operation, an eleventh-hour attempt to clean up his image as a race-baiting hatchet man. Even Stone didn't know what to make of it.

"Was the transformation real," he said, "or was it a desperate grasp? 'I'm gonna die, so just to be sure, get me a crucifix, a yarmulke, and a witch doctor!'"[86]

One of Atwater's former colleagues in the Reagan White House, Ed Rollins, reached his own conclusion on the matter. Prior to his death, Atwater had told Rollins that he'd been inspired by a copy of the Living Bible. Later, according to *Boogie Man: The Lee Atwater Story*, a 2008 documentary about Atwater, Rollins recounted the exchange to an RNC spokeswoman.

"I really, sincerely hope that [Atwater] found peace," he told the woman.

"Ed," she replied, according to Rollins, "when we were cleaning up his things afterward, the Bible was still wrapped in the cellophane and had never been taken out of the package."

For Rollins, the truth was clear. Even on his deathbed, Atwater was the same ruthless operative who'd arrived in Washington eleven years earlier. "He was spinning right to the end," Rollins said.[87]

8

On a summer evening in 1992, a black limousine navigated through the congested streets of New York City and rolled to a stop outside of a trendy Upper East Side nightclub. Next to the front door, a thick-shouldered bouncer in an Armani suit and a ponytail stood guard. Since its launch one year earlier, Tatou had become a buzzy destination for celebrities and bold-faced names. Pop singer Madonna was said to have been spotted partying there with a group of male models. Four months earlier, presidential hopeful Bill Clinton had climbed atop Tatou's stage to play the saxophone. But on this night, the biggest star in the restaurant was neither a music icon nor a presidential contender. When the door of the limousine swung open, it was a Washington lobbyist, Tommy Boggs, who stepped onto the curb, marched through the entrance, and captured the attention of the room.[1]

Inside the restaurant, a crowd of several hundred lawmakers, congressional aides, diplomats, and business executives sipped on cocktails and picked at finger food beneath a sweeping chandelier and a gilded balcony.[2] Patton Boggs had thrown the soiree to kick off a decisive week in American politics—and, indeed, for Tommy himself. The following morning, party leaders would gather three miles south, at Madison Square Garden, to bang the opening gavel on the 1992 Democratic National Convention, where the charismatic governor of Arkansas would formally accept the Democratic nomination to become the forty-second president of the United States. For the heads of the country's leading corporations, though, there was little to gain by walking the convention floor at the Garden. If they wanted to maintain their political clout in a Bill Clinton administration, they'd need to be here, under the dim lights of a chic Upper East Side restaurant, getting to know Tommy Boggs.

Despite the growing influence of conservatives in Washington, the 1980s had been a prosperous time for Tommy and his Democratic partners. The firm had amassed a 180-person staff, built a roster of 1,500 legal and lobbying clients, and christened new offices in Baltimore, Miami, and Moscow. By 1992, Patton Boggs was bringing in $50 million in annual revenue, the eighteenth most of any Washington law firm.[3] Now, after nearly twelve years of Republicans in the White House, Washington was on the precipice of historic change. And no lobbyist stood to benefit more handsomely than Tommy Boggs.

Boggs's ties to Clinton stretched back nearly three decades. In 1964 an eighteen-year-old Bill Clinton served with Tommy's cousin Charlie Boggs as copresidents of their freshman class at Georgetown University. When Hale Boggs was traveling home from Texas in the fall of 1972, a few weeks before his disappearance, Clinton—then a young aide to presidential hopeful George McGovern—gave him a ride to the airport, and the two stopped along the way for ice cream.[4] Early in Clinton's presidential campaign, Tommy pledged to help the Arkansas governor raise money.[5] Later, he supplied the future president with a network of political strategists; at least sixteen Patton Boggs lawyers joined the campaign. Over the coming years, their relationship would grow even stronger. Boggs would play hearts with Clinton aboard Air Force One and advise the embattled president during the Monica Lewinsky scandal that plagued his second term.[6] Despite the family history and shared colleagues, though, Boggs's friendship with Clinton was rooted in something more central to the business of Washington: money. Tommy was one of the campaign's top fund-raisers, a behind-the-scenes figure who helped bankroll Clinton's ascent from Little Rock to the doorstep of the White House. This early financial support was the sort of political arbitrage that many corporate lobbyists practice: investing in up-and-coming candidates early in their careers in the hopes that they'll be in a position to return the favor someday. In this case, Boggs's bet paid off big. Clinton was now poised to defeat incumbent George H. W. Bush in a victory that would give the veteran influence peddler—and his corporate clients—direct access to the leader of the free world at a time of seismic changes in the global economy.[7] It was for this reason that Tommy was mobbed by the businessmen and politicos who had crammed into Tatou that evening.

By the early 1990s, Boggs had used his mastery of the campaign finance system to get a family friend elected president, establish himself as one of the most powerful private citizens in Washington, and recalibrate the Democratic Party's priorities away from the factory floor and into the boardroom. "Some people pay to play," says a former Patton Boggs partner. "Tommy played to win." Despite it all, there was no time for the veteran lobbyist to bask in his achievements, as Washington was about to become consumed with the most consequential public policy battle in a generation—one that would pit the soaring ambitions of a new president against the growing influence of K Street.

In September 1993, less than fifteen months after the festivities at Tatou, Bill Clinton was standing atop the carved-wood rostrum in the House of Representatives chamber. When the applause died down and everyone took their seats, the still-boyish-looking commander in chief peered out at the lawmakers and Cabinet officials who'd turned out for the most anticipated speech of his young presidency. The address came at a pivotal point in the nation's history. Amid the conclusion of the Cold War, the dawning of the Internet age, and the emergence of a new globally connected economy, the republic had entered a transformational period, Clinton began. It was a time of great opportunity, but also one of unnerving discord. Rather than shrink from the upheaval of the twenty-first century, the president urged the assembled policy makers, as well as the tens of millions of Americans watching the address on television, to adapt to the new world.

"Our purpose in this dynamic age must be to change, to make change our friend and not our enemy," the president said. "To achieve that goal, we must face all our challenges with confidence, with faith, and with discipline, whether we're reducing the deficit, creating tomorrow's jobs and training our people to fill them, converting from a high-tech defense to a high-tech domestic economy, expanding trade, reinventing government, making our streets safer, or rewarding work over idleness. All these challenges require us to change."[8]

Yet it was for one change in particular that the president had brought Washington's dignitaries together at this joint session of Congress. Eight months earlier, in January 1993—just five days after his inauguration—Clinton had announced plans to create a health care system that provided coverage to all Americans. It would be a monumental political undertaking. Over the prior six decades, universal health care had emerged as the white whale of the liberal movement—an elusive, tantalizing chance to achieve the New Deal's final piece of unfinished business. Franklin Roosevelt himself had been forced to scrap his plans for a national health insurance program in the face of protest from industry leaders. In the decades to come, Presidents Harry Truman, Lyndon Johnson, and even Richard Nixon would chase similar ambitions, only to be blocked each time by Big Business. Still, the challenge proved irresistible to Clinton. As a matter of politics, enacting universal health care promised to endear a generation of middle-class voters to the Democratic Party. Moreover, an achievement of this magnitude would enshrine Clinton's legacy, alongside FDR and Lyndon Johnson, as one of the most accomplished liberal reformers in American history.

Despite the failures of his predecessors, Clinton had every reason to believe things would be different this time. By the early 1990s, the public had grown alarmed by the rising costs and uneven coverage of health care in America. As Clinton noted in his address, medical expenses were increasing at double the rate of inflation, and since health insurance was typically accessed through private employers, countless Americans were only a job loss away from losing their coverage. Nearly forty million citizens, meanwhile, didn't have health insurance at all.[9] As Clinton took office, roughly two out of three people expressed disapproval of the health care system. In Washington, the political landscape had turned favorable to reform. Clinton launched his effort amid the optimistic glow of a new administration, and his Democratic allies enjoyed comfortable majorities in both houses of Congress. Republicans, too, appeared willing to embrace new ideas. Just one year before Clinton's election, a universal health care bill in the Senate had gained the support of twenty-two Republicans. Indeed, in September 1993, when Clinton arrived at the House of Representatives chamber to officially unveil his vision for health care reform, public support for his plan topped 70 percent in certain polls.[10]

"For the first time in this century, leaders of both political parties have joined together around the principle of providing universal, comprehensive health care," Clinton told lawmakers. "It is a magic moment, and we must seize it."[11]

Beneath the surface, though, determined forces were gathering in opposition. In the years since the awakening of corporate power in the early 1970s, business interests had rearranged the traditional allegiances on Capitol Hill. Campaign contributions from corporate and trade association PACs—upon which Congress had become dependent—had made lawmakers from both parties increasingly sympathetic to corporate objectives. As a result, Republicans moved further to the right on matters of economic policy, and a growing block of business-friendly Democrats had emerged inside a caucus that had long been defined by union support. Likewise, the tactics of political influence had improved considerably. America's business leaders, who once responded to political threats as individual actors, now employed talented political strategists to mobilize broad coalitions of companies and trade groups. Lobbying itself had begun its evolution from a handshake business carried out by a handful of DC insiders into a sophisticated, nationwide industry that leveraged the new tools of political campaigning.

Faced with the prospect of the most far-reaching domestic reform since the New Deal, corporate interests deployed the full sweep of their resources to subvert the passage of Clinton's universal health care plan. They plowed nearly $70 million into efforts to block national health care—more than twice as much as what labor unions spent lobbying Congress to enact it. All told, the more than $100 million that special interests poured into the health care debate matched the total spending of Clinton's 1992 presidential campaign. As a report by the Center for Public Integrity put it, "Health care reform has become the most heavily lobbied legislative initiative in recent US history."[12] And amid this avalanche of corporate influence peddling, Washington's three great houses of lobbying would converge.

Like other major legislative efforts, Clinton's reform was actually a package of several distinct bills that were moving through Capitol Hill at the same time. Certain pieces of the legislation, however, were more critical than others. At the heart of Clinton's universal health care pledge was a central challenge: to expand coverage while minimizing costs. Most Americans at the time were dependent on medical care provided by their employers' health insurance plans. Under Clinton's proposal, all workers would be required to obtain health insurance, but their employers would pick up roughly 80 percent of premiums.[13] To make coverage more affordable to employers, Clinton's plan would create massive regional purchasing cooperatives—established by the government but operated by large insurance companies—that would use their negotiating power to obtain doctor and hospital services for previously uninsured Americans at lower costs. The vision offended the antigovernment precepts of conservatives in the House of Representatives who, under the guidance of New Right flamethrower Newt Gingrich of Georgia, were growing increasingly combative. Still, at the onset of the legislative process, House Republican leaders saw an opportunity to cut a deal with Clinton and craft a health care overhaul that both parties could support. But in order to communicate this willingness to compromise to the White House, House Republican leadership needed to find a discreet emissary. Someone who had close ties to the Clinton administration and the trust of senior GOP lawmakers. They called on Tony Podesta.

By then, Podesta had launched a new career on K Street. In 1987 he teamed up with his brother, John, secured office space in the basement of a Capitol Hill town house, and founded a lobbying firm called Podesta & Associates. Together, the Podesta brothers hustled to convert twenty years of Democratic contacts into customers and income. "Sometimes [Tony] had two phones going at once," said John Raffetto, an early employee.[14] During his first few years as a lobbyist, Podesta attempted to maintain his identity as a liberal activist; the new firm initially operated as a combination of corporate influence peddling and political advocacy. Early clients included many of Podesta's ideological allies from his days as a lefty rabble-rouser, including NARAL Pro-Choice America, the National Organization for Women, and Planned Parenthood. In 1990 the Podesta brothers helped organize an Earth Day rally that brought as many as 350,000 people to the National Mall for speeches by environmental leaders, appearances by celebrities such as actors Tom Cruise and Richard Gere, and performances by the Indigo Girls and rapper LL Cool J.[15] Over time, however, one side of the business became more attractive than the other. "It's hard to find nonprofit clients who pay you," Tony Podesta would recall. Liberal advocacy groups "always wanted some free advice," he said, while for-profit companies "were knocking on our door much more frequently." As the low-paying advocacy work declined, the firm's tally of lucrative corporate clients swelled. Soon the Podesta brothers were representing a range of business interests—the American Newspaper Publishers Association, the National Association of Broadcasters, the drug manufacturer Merck & Co.—before Congress and the federal government.

The family business got its big break in 1992, when Tony and John took roles in Bill Clinton's presidential campaign.[16] At the time, the governor and First Lady of Arkansas didn't have many contacts in Washington, other than Tommy Boggs. Tony and John, however, had known the Clintons for more than twenty years; the four of them had met during Reverend Joseph Duffy's Senate campaign in 1970. Upon Clinton's election, the new president welcomed the younger Podesta brother into his inner circle of advisers, hiring John as a senior White House aide. The day that John Podesta entered the White House, Tony Podesta became one of the best-connected lobbyists in Washington. During Clinton's first term, Podesta & Associates tripled its number of clients and increased its annual lobbying revenue to $1.6 million. Tony signed up Hollywood movie studios, major television networks, and the Pharmaceutical Research and Manufacturers of America.

Around the time that Clinton began urging congressional leaders to pass his health overhaul, Podesta received a phone call from Dennis Hastert, the Republican congressman from Illinois who'd been selected to lead the House GOP's Health Care Task Force. Though he hailed from the opposing party, Hastert was a longtime pal of Podesta's; the two shared Illinois roots, and they'd first met thirty years earlier during their two-month trip to Japan.[17] Now Hastert asked Podesta to contact the Clinton administration on his behalf and relay some ideas that House Republicans wanted to see in the legislation. Perhaps, Hastert explained, the two sides could work together to construct a health care overhaul that was more palatable to conservatives.

Podesta agreed to give his old friend a hand. He contacted a top aide to Hillary Clinton, Melanne Verveer, and laid out Hastert's proposals. The implication was that House Republicans were interested in making a deal. But the Clinton administration rebuffed the offer. After all, Democrats had strong majorities on Capitol Hill, a popular young president, and a public that was clamoring for reform. The administration, Podesta says, "thought they could do it alone."

With their hopes of a compromise dashed, the House GOP locked arms in obstruction. Every single Republican in the lower chamber agreed to oppose the health overhaul. Conservative lawmakers, however, weren't the only enemies of reform. Clinton's plan also represented a dangerous threat to the nation's small and midsized insurance companies. Many of these private insurance firms welcomed the idea of requiring more Americans to obtain health coverage, since it would mean additional business for them. But they were ardently opposed to other aspects of the bill. The legislation, for example, prohibited insurers from denying health plans to individuals with preexisting medical conditions—thereby banning the lucrative practice of selling coverage only to the healthiest Americans. At the same time, small and midsized insurance companies worried that the government-backed cooperatives would be able to offer health coverage at lower prices. "The new regulations would put them out of business," said

Chip Kahn, then a top executive at the Health Insurance Association of America.

Faced with this looming catastrophe, many of these companies looked to the lions of K Street for help. Patton Boggs went to work for the Health Insurance Association of America, as well as a handful of private insurance firms, while Black Manafort represented Phoenix Home Life Mutual Insurance Company, among others. When Clinton's reform effort got under way on Capitol Hill, the two firms established an informal lobbying alliance, meeting regularly to coordinate tactics and strategies. Despite their political differences, Charlie Black said he and Tommy Boggs were friends. A few years later, the two would become coinvestors in a politically themed restaurant in downtown Washington, the Caucus Room, along with about a dozen other corporate lobbyists. As a result, the strategy sessions on the health care bill were collegial and productive. Members of the two firms gathered around conference tables and hashed out which lobbyists were best suited to target specific lawmakers. "[We] divided up the list with Boggs," Black says.

One particularly significant assignment fell to Black himself. A top goal of the Boggs and Black Manafort lobbyists was to extend the wall of unified Republican opposition, which had begun in the House, into the Senate as well. This was no small task. Unlike the House of Representatives, where a culture of hard-line tribalism was taking hold, the upper chamber remained a less instinctively partisan institution. Many Republican senators still clung to the values of the party's more moderate establishment, viewing themselves as statesmen with a duty to stand above the fray of factional bickering. As the Republican Party's Senate leader, Bob Dole was the lobbyists' main target. The veteran lawmaker from Kansas had signaled his support for reforming the health care system in the past, and if he teamed up with Clinton to find a compromise that both parties could support, the legislation's passage in the Senate was all but assured. If, on the other hand, the lobbyists could prevent Dole and other Republican senators from working on a compromise package with the White House, they could deprive Clinton's reform of any GOP backing on Capitol Hill.

There was little question as to which member of the Patton Boggs and

Black Manafort alliance had the best chance of turning Dole against the health care effort. Charlie Black's ties to the senior senator from Kansas stretched back nearly two decades; after serving as the political director for Dole's unsuccessful vice presidential campaign in 1976,[18] Black helped guide the World War II veteran to reelection in the Senate. So even though Dole had recently cosponsored a GOP bill to achieve universal health coverage, after discussing the matter with Black, the senator cast aside his bipartisan credentials and joined his House colleagues in refusing to engage with Democrats in negotiations over Clinton's health overhaul. When Dole's Senate colleagues did the same, the entire congressional GOP became united in opposition to the legislation. If Clinton was going to get his health care reform package through Congress, he would have to do so with Democratic votes alone.

Thanks to lobbyists like Tommy Boggs, though, Clinton's Democratic allies weren't as reliable as they'd once been. In addition to his work with the Black Manafort team on behalf of small and midsized insurance companies, Boggs was also attacking the bill from a second angle. In an effort to reduce its overall price tag, Clinton's health care plan included a key legal reform. Malpractice litigation had long been linked to increased medical expenses. According to a 1991 Harvard study, malpractice insurance resulted in roughly $9 billion of additional health care costs annually, and the threat of litigation alone caused doctors to provide some $25 billion of unnecessary "defensive" treatments.[19] By reducing the number of frivolous malpractice lawsuits and astronomical jury awards, Clinton hoped to lower the costs of insuring all Americans. He planned to do this by capping the amount of money lawyers and patients could win from malpractice lawsuits. The provision, though, sparked outrage from a group of professionals who earned their livings by filing malpractice suits—trial lawyers—and their talented Democratic lobbyist.

Over the previous two decades, Boggs had used his command of the modern campaign finance system to turn the Association of Trial Lawyers of America (ATLA) into one of Washington's most formidable interest groups. Under his direction, ATLA's PAC doled out more than $5.5 million in campaign donations in the five years from 1989 to 1994; all told, lawyers contributed more money to congressional campaigns than any other occupational group at the time. Using this political clout, Boggs had successfully beaten back twenty years of attempts by lobbyists for doctors and hospitals to overhaul the malpractice system. But now that malpractice reform had become a part of Clinton's health care proposal, it would be tougher to defeat. At first, according to *Washington Monthly* magazine,[20] Boggs tried to entice the White House into dropping the malpractice provision. If Clinton and his advisors agreed to remove this one component from the bill, Boggs pledged that the trial lawyers would not only drop their opposition to the bill, but also they would join forces with the White House, put the full weight of their support behind health care reform, and help deliver a big victory for Clinton.[21] When the nice-guy act failed, Boggs adopted a more aggressive approach. The same man who provided the cash and staffers that Clinton had used to get to Washington was about to try to kill the president's signature legislative ambition.

Drawing on a lifetime of Capitol Hill instincts, Boggs used a mundane, procedural ploy to masterful effect. When Clinton's mammoth health care reform bill was introduced in Congress, its component parts were delegated to the various committees with jurisdiction over those specific issues. Initially, the bill's malpractice provisions were being handled by the House Ways and Means Committee, where Boggs's political influence was limited.

So, he convinced the chair to transfer responsibility for these provisions to the much friendlier turf of the House Judiciary Committee.[22] Boggs had spent years buttering up the Judiciary Committee for a moment like this. From 1989 to 1994, ATLA's PAC had contributed an average of $7,000 per election cycle to every Democrat on the panel. More importantly, committee chair Jack Brooks, a Democrat from Texas, was an old drinking buddy of Boggs's and a regular guest at his duck hunting lodge.[23] When Brooks became responsible for the bill, he did what he could to help out his lobbyist friend.

For those hoping to pass legislation on Capitol Hill, time is the enemy. Congress is organized into two-year sessions; all bills that are introduced in a given session must be approved before it ends—or they automatically die.

During this window, lawmakers must guide legislation through a maze of arcane procedures and tedious requirements: holding public hearings on the bill; winning approval from various committees and subcommittees; scheduling votes by the full House and Senate; merging the House and Senate versions of the legislation into a single bill; securing full approval of the combined legislation in both houses of Congress; and then, finally, sending it to the White House for the president's signature. That's a lot to accomplish in two years—and any number of things can go wrong along the way. During Clinton's first two years in office, more than thirteen thousand pieces of legislation were introduced; just a few hundred became law. It's for this reason that opponents of legislation often see gumming up the political process as their best chance of killing an undesirable bill. "Most of the time, you win by not having it happen," as Boggs once put it. It's "a lot easier to stop than it is to get."

When it came to the malpractice provisions of Clinton's health care bill, Boggs worked to stall the activity on Capitol Hill, thereby depriving the measures' proponents of precious time they'd need to enact the reform. In this effort, Congressman Brooks proved to be a valuable ally. Once the bill was sent to the Judiciary Committee for its review, the chairman simply sat on the bill. For months, Brooks refused to begin debate.[24]

When Brooks finally took up the bill in August 1994—after a six-month delay—Boggs's influence over the proceedings was clear. On the day of the committee's vote, as *Washington Monthly* reported, Boggs marched into the crowded hearing room and took a front-row seat that had been reserved specifically for him.[25] During the hearing, a group of Democratic lawmakers who'd taken ATLA's PAC contributions introduced a seemingly harmless amendment that limited lawyers' fees to 33 percent of malpractice judgments below $150,000 and 25 percent of judgments above $150,000. Slipped into the provision, however, was a controversial, far-reaching policy change: the text made clear that these new federal standards would override all existing state laws, even those—like California's—that had much tougher restrictions on lawyers' fees.[26] Though it attracted little notice in the committee that day, the provision promised to spark angry resistance if it ever reached the House floor. Lawmakers from states with tougher malpractice laws were sure to oppose the malpractice provision in the bill, and they'd likely even vote against the entire health care bill in order to make sure the malpractice changes never became law. And that, of course, was the whole point. The language had been inserted specifically to derail Clinton's malpractice overhaul. Such provisions are referred to as "poison pills" by lawmakers because, once inserted into a bill, they serve to kill the whole legislation. "It was a little time bomb," said lobbyist Elizabeth Richardson, "designed to detonate later and destroy all state tort reform."[27] Boggs's strategy worked exactly as planned. The House Judiciary Committee voted to approve the malpractice provision, but it never advanced to the full House.

With one provision neutered in the House Judiciary Committee, opponents of Clinton's health care initiative turned their attention to the House Commerce Committee. It was here that Capitol Hill's staunchest advocate for public health care was working to pass the central element of the entire reform effort: a provision mandating that all businesses provide coverage for their employees. Congressman John Dingell Jr., the six-foot-three, 260-pound chairman of the Commerce Committee, was known on Capitol Hill as "Big John." His support for national health care was inspired by his father, John Dingell Sr., who had been diagnosed with tuberculosis at the age of twenty and left to die. After an improbable recovery, John Sr. was elected to Congress in 1932 as a New Deal Democrat and went on to introduce one of the country's first bills to create a nationwide health care system. When John Sr. passed away in 1955, his son took his seat in Congress. Each year, the younger Dingell introduced a national health insurance bill numbered H.R. 16, after his Detroit-area congressional district.[28]

When the health reform legislation arrived in his committee in 1994, Dingell finally had the opportunity to realize his father's dream. To do so, he needed to secure the support of a majority of the forty-four lawmakers on the panel. Because the committee's seventeen Republicans had pledged to oppose the plan, it was essential that Dingell obtain the backing of all but four of his fellow Democrats.[29] Maintaining intraparty loyalty was trickier than it appeared. Health insurance lobbyists began deploying a dependable weapon—campaign contributions—to turn moderate

Democrats against the legislation. Among the lobbyists' top allies on the committee was Congressman Jim Cooper, a centrist Democrat from Tennessee who had endeared himself to health insurance executives by drafting an industry-backed health care bill.[30] Though he was already a friend of the insurers, securing Cooper's opposition to the reform would go a long way toward splitting Democratic support for the legislation in Dingell's committee.[31] As it happened, Cooper had recently declared himself a candidate for the Senate seat that had been vacated by Vice President Al Gore. For clever lobbyists, like Peter Kelly of Black Manafort, this upcoming campaign provided an opportunity to ensure that Cooper would do his part to sink the bill.

In March 1994, a few weeks before Dingell planned to call for a vote, Kelly helped organize a fund-raising event for Cooper at a private social club in Hartford, Connecticut. In addition to being Kelly's hometown, Hartford is a key hub for the insurance industry. A number of major health insurers are headquartered in the state, including Aetna Life and Casualty, the Travelers Corp., CIGNA, and Phoenix Home Life Mutual Insurance Company, which had hired Kelly to block the legislation. When Cooper arrived at the exclusive Hartford Club, he was greeted by some seventy insurance executives and their guests, each of whom had paid $250 or more to eat swordfish and sip white wine with the Tennessee congressman.[32] Returning to Washington, Cooper maintained his support for the insurance industry, becoming one of a growing number of Democrats in Dingell's committee to oppose the reform.

In addition to PAC contributions, business interests brought the tactics of modern electioneering to bear on their effort to kill universal health care. One of Patton Boggs's clients, the Health Insurance Association of America, led the way on this new approach. In the summer of 1993 the group hired one of the Republican Party's premier experts in public opinion polling, Bill McInturff, to help it achieve a more nuanced understanding of how citizens felt about health care reform. McInturff traveled the country to hear Americans' concerns firsthand, organizing intimate focus groups with small numbers of citizens in Saint Louis, Atlanta, Charlotte, North Carolina, and other cities. Through these listening sessions, McInturff discovered that many Americans didn't favor a radical reform of the health care system after all. Yes, changes were needed, but people generally liked their own health insurance plans. They did, however, have a more fundamental worry: Americans simply didn't trust the federal government to fix problems. "People wanted health care to pass, they wanted Clinton to get credit," McInturff said in *The System*, David Broder and Haynes Johnson's 1996 book. But "people don't believe the federal government can get anything done."

When he got back to Washington, McInturff shared his findings with the association's executives. He told them that the industry's best chance of defeating the bill was to weaponize the "very powerful wave" of public distrust of the government. McInturff coached the industry's lobbyists, media strategists, and consultants to change the way they talked about the issue. Instead of calling it "national health insurance," they should refer to Clinton's reform as "government health care" as a way to stoke the public's anxieties. "Just that word change," McInturff said, "made a powerful difference."[33]

Industry executives also made McInturff's findings the centerpiece of a pioneering national television advertising campaign. They hired an advertising firm and produced a thirty-second spot featuring "Harry" and "Louise," a workaday American couple discussing Clinton's plan around their kitchen table after their children had gone to bed. Following McInturff's advice, the ads—which aired beginning in the fall of 1993—were designed specifically to arouse citizens' fears.

"The government may force us to pick from a few health care plans designed by government bureaucrats," the announcer said in one ad.

Louise, sitting at the kitchen table, says: "Having choices we don't like is like no choice at all."

"They choose," Harry says.

"We lose," Louise says.

It was among the first times that a major American industry had used television advertising as a political-influence tactic—and it worked spectacularly. Senator Jay Rockefeller of West Virginia, a proponent of health care reform, called it "the single most destructive campaign I've seen in thirty years."[34] As the ads soured the public's views of the bill, business-friendly Democrats joined Republicans in opposing the legislation. The shift in momentum sent the White House and its allies into a panic. One DNC official went so far as to try to bully the actress, Louise Caire Clark, who portrayed Louise into disavowing the campaign. The official told the actress that if she didn't renounce what "Louise" had said in the ad during a public event at the White House, the Democratic Party's friends in Hollywood would blackball her from the entertainment business.[35]

In June 1994 Congressman Dingell announced that he didn't have the votes to move the bill through his committee. While he supported the bill, the "opponents of this legislation have great adroitness," Dingell told a reporter. He added: "I don't approve of their work product, but by God their mechanics have been great. They're spending huge money, and they've lobbied to beat hell."[36] A few months later, the Senate's Democratic majority leader announced that Clinton's effort to provide health coverage to all Americans was officially dead.

It was a landmark moment in the history of corporate power in Washington. By joining forces to help kill universal health care, Tommy Boggs and Black Manafort had ensured that American companies wouldn't be required to provide health coverage for their employees—delivering massive savings for businesses but leaving millions of citizens unguarded against the crushing financial burdens of serious illnesses. And the victory resonated far beyond health care. Business executives and trade associations had shown every politician in Washington that corporate power, when unified and motivated, was muscular enough to sink a popular legislative effort led by a well-liked president whose party controlled both houses of Congress.

The experience strengthened the GOP's ties to industry, but its impact on the Democratic Party was even more profound. For a new generation of Democratic leaders and party operatives, the defeat served as an indelible lesson. Corporate interests, they came to believe, had grown too strong to be confronted head-on. Passing legislation in the face of determined, united opposition from big businesses was simply no longer possible. Instead, if Democrats wanted a legacy of achievement, they needed to distance themselves from the party's New Deal tradition and step into the future of corporate capitalism.

Following the implosion of his national health insurance plan, President Bill Clinton pivoted to the right and embraced a decidedly pro-business agenda, realizing a full menu of corporate priorities: liberalizing trade agreements, balancing the budget by reducing government spending, and signing sweeping legislation to deregulate the economy. "Big bureaucracies and Washington solutions are not the real answers to today's challenges," Clinton said in his campaign platform during his 1996 reelection bid. "We need a smaller government."[37]

With Vice President Al Gore working to "reinvent government" into a smarter, more efficient enterprise, Clinton's new platform included slashing taxes for small businesses and jettisoning regulations on industry.[38] On the campaign trail, Clinton boasted about signing more than two hundred agreements to lower trade barriers—the most consequential of which was the 1994 North American Free Trade Agreement (NAFTA), which encouraged US manufacturers to move American jobs overseas. When it came to deregulation, the libertarian economist William Niskanen argued that Clinton's record was even more beneficial to industry than that of his Republican predecessor, President George H. W. Bush.[39] For example, Clinton embarked on a far-reaching effort to deregulate the nation's financial system, signing the Commodity Futures Modernization Act, which essentially blocked federal oversight of a set of complex financial instruments known as derivatives,[40] and enacting a partial repeal of the Glass-Steagall Act, a 1933 law that had prevented commercial banks from getting into the investment banking business.[41] Years later, both of these actions would be cited as causes of the 2008 financial crisis.[42] At the time, though, such corporate-friendly policy changes reflected the central evolution that was taking place among leading Democrats in Washington. Amid the sustained weakening of Democrats' once-formidable allies—private-sector unions, consumer advocates, public interest groups—the party had grown increasingly responsive to the CEOs and white-collar professionals who, more and more, were coming to represent its financial engine. These Clinton-era "New Democrats" were aligned with the earlier generation of

New Deal Democrats on social issues, such as abortion rights and school prayer. But unlike the party's earlier supporters, many New Democrats were themselves reaping the financial benefits of a less regulated and more globalized economy. As a result, they exuded a suspicion of government and a deference to markets that would have been unrecognizable to the urban party bosses of three decades earlier. And while it might have been a radical break from his party's ancestry, Clinton's administration came as a delight to some of the leading champions of the free market.

"He's a Democrat, but I do admire him," Barry Goldwater wrote in a 1995 letter to Newt Gingrich. "I think he's doing a good job."[43]

In addition to establishing the corporate lobby as the most powerful unelected force in Washington, the sinking of universal health care also served to accelerate a trend that had begun several years earlier—a development that would dramatically expand K Street's role in the economy. During the 1970s and early 1980s, business executives viewed Washington's lobbying industry as a means of advancing their political interests—a pool of operatives who could be called upon to block an undesirable bill or enact a beneficial one. But by the early 1990s, corporate America had come to see influence peddling as a tool to serve its commercial interests as well.[44]

The change was rooted in the new set of challenges facing corporate boardrooms. With the doing away of business regulations and international trade barriers, US firms were confronting increased competition at home and abroad. At the same time, the emerging "shareholder primacy" movement on Wall Street put new pressure on corporate executives to maintain steadily increasing stock prices or face revolts from large institutional investors. Any company whose stock price slumped too low risked becoming the target of a leveraged buyout by corporate raiders[45]—investors looking to snatch up shares on the cheap, take majority control of a business, and sack its executives. The result was a new generation of corporate executives, such as GE's "Neutron" Jack Welch, who were devoted to delivering strong quarterly growth at all costs,[46] whether that meant shuttering businesses, laying off staff, or exploring new revenue streams. Amid these ratcheted-up pressures, some advertising and public relations executives began to view the soaring revenues on K Street as a way to grow their own profits. During the early 1990s, the political-influence industry experienced a wave of acquisitions, as multinational advertising and PR conglomerates began snapping up lobbying firms.[47] Suddenly every influence-peddling outfit in Washington became a potential acquisition target. And among the most sought-after firms was Black Manafort.

Its partners, however, were divided over the merits of selling. Charlie Black believed it was time to merge with a larger corporation. In the years since they'd gone into business together, the men had evolved from cutthroat radicals to pillars of the Washington establishment. They were invited to state dinners at the White House and welcomed at private golf clubs. Moving forward, Black wanted to distance the firm from dodgy clients and shadowy practices and, according to former Black Manafort staffers, develop a reputation as a white-shoe enterprise. The best way to do that, Black argued, was to join forces with a large, well-respected partner such as Burson-Marsteller, whose parent company, the global public relations giant Young & Rubicam, was most interested in buying the lobbying firm. For their part, Paul Manafort and Roger Stone opposed the deal. They enjoyed the autonomy of owning their own firm, and they didn't want corporate managers meddling in their business. "Charlie Black really wanted to make sure the firm had a good, ethical reputation and do proper business," said one Black Manafort employee at the time. "Paul Manafort and Roger Stone wanted to make a lot of money." In the end, Black prevailed on his partners, and in January 1991 Young & Rubicam, the parent of Burson-Marsteller, purchased Black Manafort[48] for roughly $10 million plus incentives, an impressive sum at the time.

From the outside, the deal had little effect on the firm. As an independent subsidiary of Burson-Marsteller, Black Manafort kept its name, staff, and headquarters. After receiving an initial payout, the partners retained their roles and continued to run things largely as they had before. Inside the firm, though, the impact of the acquisition was clearly visible. Young & Rubicam didn't like the reputational risk associated with mixing campaign work and corporate lobbying, so the Black Manafort partners were required to do their campaign work on their own time. In addition, the new owners imposed on the lobbyists a set of stricter accounting require-ments designed to ensure that Black Manafort's revenue and expenses were reflected accurately in the financial statements of Young & Rubicam. This was a significant change. Now, for the first time, diligent corporate manag-ers would be examining the books of the freewheeling lobbying firm. And it wasn't long before these more exacting accounting policies would cause friction with Black Manafort's most ungovernable partner.

On account of his rule-breaking instincts and underhanded nature, Paul Manafort had long been a source of conflict within the firm. In 1992 his work on behalf of brutal dictators was featured in a scathing report from a watchdog group titled "The Torturers' Lobby."[49] And as he emerged as the public face of the shadowy industry, Manafort flouted the few ethi-cal standards that existed in the business. He once went to work for the Kashmiri American Council, a nonprofit organization designed to influ-ence American policy regarding Kashmir,[50] a mountainous region that both India and Pakistan have long laid claim to. Though Manafort said he didn't know it at the time, Yahoo! News in 2016 reported that the group was actually controlled by Pakistan's spy agency.[51] Regardless, according to the Indian government, when Manafort arrived in the region to produce a documentary for the council, he pretended to be a CNN reporter in order to secure on-camera interviews with government officials.[52] As a spokes-person for the Indian government put it, "The whole thing was obviously a blatant operation of producing television software with a deliberate and particularly anti-Indian slant by lobbyists hired by Pakistan for this very purpose."[53] On another occasion, Manafort struck a secret $900,000 deal to represent a front group for the corrupt Philippine dictator Ferdinand Marcos even though another partner at the firm, Peter Kelly, was run-ning an organization aimed at fostering democracy in that very country.[54] Kelly was outraged. The partners subsequently adopted a rule requiring Manafort to obtain the approval of Black and Kelly before signing up any new overseas clients.

Before long, such self-dealing inclinations stirred suspicions about Manafort's financial practices. As he jetted across the globe to seek out new customers, Manafort began spending long stretches of time away from the office, and the specifics of his overseas business dealings weren't entirely clear to his colleagues. Some staffers came to believe that he was fleecing his foreign clients to support his increasingly opulent lifestyle. Questions focused on the payments that Manafort billed as reimbursements for his business expenses, which, according to lobbying disclosure forms, had exploded from $21,000 to more than $300,000 over seven years. In 1992, for instance, Manafort charged the government of Kenya nearly $17,000 for stays at the Nairobi Safari Club and more than $100,000 for first-class travel, including several round-trip flights on the supersonic Concorde jet between New York and London. But those who worked for Manafort in Kenya didn't recall seeing much of him in the country. One staffer eventually complained to Black that Manafort was inflating the expenses that he billed to the impoverished African nation. "It was ridiculous that Kenya has to pay these expenses—Paul Manafort [was] not doing the work," said another Black Manafort employee who worked on the Kenya account. Even the legitimate expenses showed the decadent way of life that Manafort had grown accustomed to. He charged the government of the Philippines nearly $25,000 for work-related stays at the five-star Mandarin Oriental Hotel for himself and a colleague.

Over time, Manafort's lavish tastes and unscrupulous nature sparked rumors of alleged swindling on a spectacular scale. One tale held that Manafort had received a cache of blood diamonds as an off-the-books payment for his lobbying efforts on behalf of the Angolan warlord Jonas Savimbi. Another one claimed that he'd kept a suitcase stuffed with $10 million in cash belonging to the Ferdinand Marcos regime in the Philippines, even though he had pledged to hand over the money as an illegal contribution to Reagan's 1984 reelection campaign.[55] Though both stories remain apocryphal, their decades-long endurance in K Street's mythology, as the Atlantic's Franklin Foer pointed out, reveals the extent of the mistrust that Manafort engendered.

While the fees from foreign clients made Manafort the firm's biggest revenue producer, he increasingly came to be viewed as a risk to the business. His dealings with unsavory foreign governments tarnished Black Manafort's reputation with some of its clients and helped convince at least one key customer to cut ties with the firm. Salomon Brothers was among the first blue-chip corporations to hire the firm, and Manafort had been its primary point of contact. Though Manafort and his colleagues had succeeded in helping Salomon Brothers advance its agenda in Washington—securing a key tax break for a new headquarters in the 1986 tax bill, for instance—the Wall Street executives eventually grew uneasy about Manafort's relationships with repressive foreign dictators and the murky political culture in which he thrived. Not long before the 1984 election, a group of Salomon Brothers executives met with the Black Manafort team to discuss the Democratic primary. At one point, an executive asked about the prospects of Reverend Jesse Jackson, the Black activist and civil rights leader who'd surprised pundits with better-than-expected performances in several early primary contests. The lobbyists replied that Jackson had absolutely no chance of becoming president. The reason, they explained, was that Republicans had dug up a damaging allegation—that Jackson had secretly fathered a child out of wedlock—which party operatives planned to release publicly if Jackson's candidacy were ever to gain real traction. The exchange spooked the Salomon Brothers executives; they were disgusted to learn that the lobbyists they'd hired to protect their interests in Washington were trafficking in such unproven smut. When the contract's term expired, the Wall Street firm ended its relationship with Black Manafort. "We got very nervous about them," says a Salomon Brothers executive.

Following the acquisition of Black Manafort, the firm's new owners began more closely monitoring Manafort's business. At first, the scrutiny came in the form of the stricter accounting rules that Burson-Marsteller put in place. Manafort chafed at the new procedures. Irritated that he now had to get additional approval for his expense reports, he began feuding with the accounting department. Manafort directed much of his fury not at the Burson-Marsteller executives who created the policies but at the low-level accountant who enforced them. Fasseha Senbet was a well-liked staffer and something of a Black Manafort success story. An immigrant from Ethiopia, he began his career as a parking lot attendant at the firm's headquarters. Over the years, he became friendly with many Black Manafort employees; Roger Stone gave Senbet his old suits and let him drive his luxury vehicles.

When the partners learned that Senbet had been an accountant prior to immigrating to the United States, they hired him to fill an open position. Now, as the person tasked with administering the new financial documentation requirements, Senbet became the target of Manafort's grievances. On one occasion, Manafort approached Senbet at the end of the workday and asked him to approve reimbursements for tens of thousands of dollars in first-class air travel and high-end hotels. Under the new rules, Senbet was required to get a second partner to sign off. He took the report to Peter Kelly.

"Mr. Kelly, the only people here are you and Mr. Manafort," Senbet said, "and he wants to expense $70,000 in Concorde flights."

Kelly refused to approve such an exorbitant set of expenses. For the remainder of the evening, Senbet shuttled back and forth between the two partners' offices, trying to broker an agreement. At one point, an exhausted Senbet turned to Kelly. "In Africa, there is a saying," he said. "When there is a fight between two elephants, the only thing that gets hurt is the grass. And I am the grass."

Increasingly, Senbet found himself squeezed between the firm's cost-cutting managers and its big-spending lobbyist. The stress, according to former coworkers, was starting to wear on him. Colleagues joked that one day Senbet might tell his boss to go to hell, or simply quit. "Everybody thought he could snap at any minute," recalls one fellow employee.

Meanwhile, Burson-Marsteller was increasing the pressure on Black Manafort to bring in revenue in order to boost profits for its parent company. As a result, the lobbyists began seeking additional ways to extract cash from customers. According to one former Black Manafort lobbyist, some employees at the firm quietly added a 2 percent "service fee" to its clients' monthly bills. Other mysterious charges—a $600 phone call here, a $400 copying fee there—turned up on clients' invoices. "The whole thing was how to bill clients for things that didn't happen," says the former lobbyist. Black said he had no knowledge of these specific allegations and there was no firm-wide effort to bilk clients.

Despite the firm's triumph in the battle over health care reform, Black Manafort was falling short of the profits it had promised to deliver during negotiations over its acquisition, and the new owners were growing frustrated. In 1995 Tom Bell, the head of Burson-Marsteller's Washington operations, authorized a discreet review of Black Manafort's books to pinpoint the source of the deficit, according to people familiar with the internal investigation. "What they found," recalled Charlie Black, "did not inure to Paul's benefit."

The examination revealed that Paul Manafort was generating far less revenue than he'd promised from his foreign clients, and when Bell's team dug deeper, they discovered at least one reason why. On the desktop computers that the lobbyists had used, Burson-Marsteller found documents showing that Paul Manafort and Roger Stone had a secret side hustle. In addition to their work for the firm, the two were signing lobbying contracts with a number of clients that their partners and the firm's owners weren't aware of. According to people familiar with these deals, Manafort and Stone had been using the firm's expense account to recruit and service these non–Black Manafort clients. The misappropriated expenses would typically be charged to one of the foreign clients that Black Manafort represented, such as Kenya, Nigeria, or Jonas Savimbi's Angolan rebels.

The revelations enraged Tom Bell. On top of the secret business and over-the-top expenses, Paul Manafort had repeatedly failed to deliver a number of new clients that he'd promised to bring in. It dawned on Bell that Burson-Marsteller had been snookered into overpaying for Black Manafort. Bell called Stanton Anderson, the Washington lawyer who had represented Black Manafort in the sale.

"You sold me this turkey," Bell told Anderson. "You need to do something about it."

Anderson agreed to get to the bottom of the matter. He met Manafort for lunch and asked about the allegations. To his surprise, Manafort openly admitted what he'd done. Without a hint of remorse, he said he'd been lobbying for side clients and billing the firm for expenses related to this outside work.

"Yeah, I am doing that," Manafort said, "and I am going to continue doing that."

Anderson relayed the conversation to Bell, who decided to confront

Manafort. A few days later, in the spring of 1995, Bell drove to the Black Manafort offices in Alexandria. When he arrived in the first-floor lobby, he ran into one of the firm's Democratic lobbyists, Jim Healey. Bell, in a foul mood, barely responded to Healey's greeting. The two rode the elevator in silence. When they got to their floor, Bell stepped out, marched straight into Manafort's office, and closed the door. All Healey could hear was screaming.

Word spread quickly through the firm: Manafort and Stone were out. That afternoon, the remaining partners crowded into Manafort's office to page through the documents that had been discovered on his computer. "I can still remember Peter Kelly saying, 'What about this client? Have you ever heard of this client?'" said one former Black Manafort lobbyist who was in the room. The episode was humiliating for Charlie Black, who had vouched for Paul Manafort and Roger Stone in discussions with Burson-Marsteller executives. Despite their friendship of nearly two decades, Paul Manafort and Roger Stone had swindled him too. "Charlie Black was devastated by it," said a friend.

Even after Black Manafort broke apart, the partners didn't stray far from one another, at least at first. The original firm divided into two new lobbying shops headquartered in neighboring Alexandria offices. In March of 1996 both firms were shaken by a horrifying act of violence. At 6:43 on a Monday morning, police responded to reports of glass breaking and sounds of screaming at a condominium complex about four miles north of the old Black Manafort offices. Inside the condominium, officers found forty-year-old Fasseha Senbet, the Black Manafort bookkeeper, suffering from a self-inflicted gunshot wound that would prove fatal. Next to him, police discovered a handgun and the body of a fifty-two-year-old woman, Karen L. Mitsoff.[56]

Law enforcement determined quickly that Senbet had shot himself after murdering Mitsoff, his former live-in girlfriend who had grown fearful of him in her final months. About two weeks earlier, Senbet—reportedly upset that their romance had ended[57]—had broken into Mitsoff's apartment and threatened her with a gun. When she reported the incident to police,[58] Mitsoff gave a sworn statement: "He told me he had thought it through—and was going to kill me, and then himself. I talked him out of this . . . and then he left." Around this time, Mitsoff had been working to convince Senbet to see a therapist.[59] "Karen was at her wit's end with his threats to kill her," a friend told the local press. "But I think she still cared about him and didn't fully appreciate how dangerous he might be."[60] Police arrested Senbet after the first break-in, but he was released the next day.[61] Four days later, he killed Mitsoff. The gruesome murder of a beloved first-grade teacher horrified the Alexandria community. Outraged local leaders established a task force to find ways to improve Virginia's anti-stalking laws.[62]

For the lobbyists who'd worked with Senbet, the news was equally shocking. When the police arrived at the Alexandria office building, his former colleagues gathered in a conference room. They shed tears, consoled one another, and speculated about how this had happened. Everyone knew that Senbet had been under immense pressure to keep expenses in line with the new policies. But no one had seen him behave in a way that would indicate a potential for violence. One lobbyist wondered aloud if workplace stress had played a role in Senbet's actions.

The breakup of Black Manafort was an early warning about the self-destructive potential of this emerging new era on K Street—a period in which lobbying would come to be viewed as a vehicle for profit growth.[63] Yet the high-profile lobbying victories of the early 1990s—like the defeat of Clinton's health reform bill—would serve only to increase corporate America's faith in the value of influence peddling. As a result, in the years after Black Manafort came apart, a growing number of corporations came to regard lobbyists not just as tools of political influence, but as instruments of commerce.[64] Instead of simply fending off unfavorable laws or regulations, lobbyists would increasingly be called upon to use their Washington know-how to improve a firm's financial performance. That might mean helping a company grow revenue by obtaining government contracts, assisting a business to expand its market share by persuading antitrust regulators to approve a merger, or providing one firm with an edge over another by securing an advantageous rule. Put another way, the same influence peddlers who once spent their days shaping federal policies for the benefit of entire industries would now be more focused on assisting individual companies outcompete rival businesses.[65]

What began as a wave of acquisitions on K Street had evolved into a broad reimagining of the role of lobbyists in the corporate economy. And while it had already precipitated the unraveling of one of Washington's signature firms, it was only during the following decades that the full consequences of this development would become clear.

Part II

The Outside Game

2000–2015

9

Roughly six months after George W. Bush took office, an eager young law school student arrived at a nine-story, redbrick building overlooking the main boulevard of Washington's historic Georgetown neighborhood. He walked through the marble hallway, took the elevator up to the top floor, and stepped into the office's reception. Evan Morris had long dreamed of becoming a Washington power player. And today he would begin his career at one of the city's most illustrious lobbying firms, Patton Boggs LLP.

At twenty-four, Morris spoke with a trace of the leathery accent of his native New York City. He'd grown up in a comfortable, three-bedroom house in the Jamaica Estates section of Queens.[1] Each morning, his father took the train to Manhattan, where he worked as a personal injury lawyer, while his mother stayed home to raise Morris and his younger sister. As a boy, Morris was a die-hard New York Giants football fan. A poster of a Porsche sports car hung on his bedroom wall. Over time, other aspirations emerged.

In his early teens, Morris won a coveted admissions slot at Benjamin N. Cardozo High School, a four-thousand-student public school in Queens that *Newsweek* magazine would later call one of the country's best.[2] While there, he enrolled in the school's prestigious law and humanities program, earned a reputation as a diligent student, and developed an interest in politics. He landed an internship with Democratic congresswoman Nita Lowey, spending his after-school hours answering phone calls from constituents at her nearby district office, according to a former classmate. As editor of the high school newspaper, Evan scored an interview with New York City's recently elected mayor, Rudy Giuliani, which, according to what he later told friends, he turned into a front-page story. And in 1992 Arkansas governor Bill Clinton came by Morris's school to address students as part of a campaign swing during the presidential election.[3] But it was a subsequent brush with Clinton that would alter the trajectory of Morris's life.

Arriving at Union College, in Schenectady, New York, in 1995, Morris possessed a brash confidence that was unusual for a college freshman. Just a few weeks into his first term, he was selected editor in chief of the college paper, an impressive feat for someone so new to campus.[4] Several months later, he won an even more prestigious appointment: a three-month internship in the White House—the same program that, one year earlier, had introduced President Bill Clinton to a twenty-one-year-old recent college graduate, Monica Lewinsky. During his internship, Morris worked from a desk located just outside the office of one of the era's quintessential insiders.[5] Harold Ickes,[6] the son of an FDR confidant[7] who'd administered parts of the New Deal, was Clinton's chief political strategist.[8] In the spring of 1996, as the president prepared for his reelection campaign, Ickes's office served as the nerve center for the administration's agenda. Ickes's secretary patched through calls from Senator Ted Kennedy, civil rights leader Jesse Jackson, and political fixer Vernon Jordan. Senior campaign figures, such as James Carville, and top White House aides, including George Stephanopoulos, popped in to chat. Vice President Al Gore occasionally swung by for a word.

The experience of watching the White House's most influential advisors filtering in and out of Ickes's office left a lasting impression on Morris. Here he was, an ambitious, nineteen-year-old college student, sitting a few feet away from the epicenter of political decision-making for the free world. But while he desperately wanted to enter the room himself, he didn't have the standing. For the rest of his life, Morris would endeavor to break into this inner sanctum of political power. Returning to Union College for his sophomore year, classmates found him consumed by his goal of getting back to Washington in order to climb the ranks of the Democratic elite. He decided to major in political science, and he refused to smoke marijuana because he didn't want to derail his career in politics.

Friends started to notice other changes in Morris. Though his parents revered him and believed he was destined for greatness, Evan had always nursed fundamental insecurities. He was pudgy, tall, and unathletic. He wore awkward glasses that made him look dorky. His three months in the White House, however, seemed to offer the possibility of a new identity—a way to use his intellect and ambition to earn the respect of his peers. While still only a college student, he grew preoccupied with projecting the image of a DC insider. He told exaggerated stories about his time in Washington, claiming to friends that he'd played golf with President Clinton. He spent more of his time at the golf courses near campus, and he began smoking cigars.

After graduating from Union College with honors in 1999, Morris made his move to the nation's capital, enrolling at George Washington University Law School.[9] While it might lack the luster of the Ivy Leagues, GW Law's proximity to the seat of the federal government had made it something of a finishing school for members of Congress, agency officials, and federal judges. Alumni include FBI director J. Edgar Hoover[10] and former Senate majority leader Harry Reid.[11] Years earlier, Roger Stone was studying at George Washington University when he launched his own political ascent by volunteering for President Richard Nixon's 1972 reelection campaign.[12] Law school classmates recall Morris as a tireless student, studying up to sixty hours a week while eating pints of ice cream. In his determination to get to the top, he was willing to sabotage other students. Morris once intentionally unplugged a study partner's computer in order to erase his class notes.

For law students, the summer after their second year is perhaps more important than the school year itself. Summer internships, which are known as summer associate programs, provide the practical experience and professional connections that law students need to land full-time jobs upon graduation. These programs also allow future lawyers to test out the various areas of the legal profession—criminal defense versus contract law; civil rights versus bankruptcy—so that they can determine which field is most appealing. During his first year of law school, Morris applied for a summer program at the prestigious firm located only a few blocks away from GW's campus: Patton Boggs. It was an intense selection process. More than a thousand students from the country's leading law schools— Harvard, Yale, Stanford—submitted applications, and each candidate went through several rounds of interviews over the course of nearly a full year. Morris was among the thirteen students selected for Patton Boggs's 2001 summer class. While other applicants might have attended better schools or earned higher grades, Morris possessed a quality that the firm valued above all else: hunger.

Morris arrived at Patton Boggs during a period of transformational growth for the firm. From 1998[13] to 2003,[14] Patton Boggs's lobbying revenues doubled to $30 million, and the firm emerged as the largest player in the city's influence business. Its staff of 140 lobbyists was nearly twice the size of any of its competitors, and it serviced a distinguished roster of clients, including United Airlines, drugmaker Bristol-Myers Squibb Co., AOL Time Warner, the soda industry, the state of New York, and the largest association of trial lawyers.[15] *Roll Call*, an influential Capitol Hill newspaper, celebrated Tommy Boggs as the "King of K Street."[16]

In the office, the partners developed a culture of bravado that set it apart from other lobbying shops. Much like the buccaneers at Black Manafort, they viewed themselves as the cowboys of the influence business—more gutsy, tenacious, and enterprising than their rivals—and they prided themselves on partying as hard as they worked. The partners on the almost entirely male government relations staff had liquor cabinets in their offices. Each day, a female attendant pushed a drink cart through the hallway to see if anyone needed restocking. For the firm's monthly lunches, the partners gathered around noon for rounds of martinis before the first course arrived. They drank wine with their meals and then retired to another room for cognac and liquors.[17] When it came to business, the lobbyists were sharp elbowed and intense. New employees quickly learned the firm's unofficial motto, which encapsulated Patton Boggs's commitment to doing whatever it took to achieve political victories for their clients: "Wins over Sins."

The culture both attracted and developed lawyers who were comfortable bending the rules. Another member of Patton Boggs's 2001 summer class was a Georgetown University law student named Jeffrey Wertkin, who would go on to distinguish himself as a prosecutor in the Justice Department's Fraud Division. But in 2018 Wertkin was sentenced to more than two years in prison for stealing whistle-blower case files from the government and attempting to sell the top-secret information to the very corporations that law enforcement authorities were investigating.[18] When he was arrested in an FBI sting at a hotel in Cupertino, California, Wertkin, who was disguised in a wig and a fake mustache, told law enforcement, "My life is over."[19] During their summer together at Patton Boggs, Morris shared an office with Wertkin.

Morris's first day at Patton Boggs might have been his most consequential. When he arrived at the office, the manager of the summer associate program assigned each law student to the particular department where they would begin their internships. While most of his classmates were sent to offices in the firm's traditional law practices, Morris, by chance, was detailed to the lobbying division on the top floors of the firm's office. For an aspiring politico who was still unsure of his career path, it was a pivotal stroke of fate. Suddenly Morris found himself behind the curtain of Washington's often-inscrutable policy-making process. He was slapping backs with the giants of K Street, men who commanded six-figure fees to shape legislation on behalf of blue-chip companies and powerful foreign actors. He shared a bathroom and elevator with the godfather of the modern influence business, Tommy Boggs. And over the course of the summer, he got to taste the life of a Washington lobbyist. Partners took him to lunch at expensive restaurants, invited him golfing at exclusive country clubs, and welcomed him to dinner at their multimillion-dollar homes in the DC suburbs. There were glitzy all-staff cruises along the Potomac River. Each Friday, the associates knocked off work around noon and gathered at one of the upscale restaurants near the office. During these rollicking, booze-soaked lunches, their tables were cluttered with seafood towers, choice cuts of steak, bottles of rare wines, and glasses of aged scotch. The tabs, which typically exceeded $1,000, were picked up by the firm. After finishing lunch, the associates would head over to the strip of outdoor bars on the banks of the Potomac in Georgetown, where they knocked back martinis and watched the sun fade over the water.

During the week, though, the lobbyists put Morris to work. He was dispatched to Capitol Hill for congressional hearings, wrote up reports on committee proceedings for senior partners, and sat in on strategy sessions with Boggs and his team. The experience offered Morris a firsthand look at how corporate lobbyists turned the wheels of government. That summer, for instance, one of Patton Boggs's clients was in trouble. A few months before Morris started at the firm, Republican president George W. Bush had initiated a top-to-bottom review of America's armed forces, seeking to replace the Pentagon's armament of heavy, slow-moving artillery with lighter and more nimble weapons that would be better suited for twenty-first-century conflicts.[20]

"We are witnessing a revolution in the technology [of] war," Bush told an audience at Virginia's Naval Station Norfolk in early 2001. "Power is increasingly defined not by size, but by mobility and swiftness. . . . Our goal is to move beyond marginal improvements to harness new technologies that will support a new strategy." Among the items on the new president's chopping block was the Crusader, a forty-two-ton tank that could fire car-engine-sized missiles[21] at targets up to twenty-five miles away.[22] None of the Crusaders had been delivered yet, and critics argued that the gigantic tanks were outdated and too bulky for transport planes to carry.[23]

For United Defense LLC, the US defense contracting firm that manufactured the tanks, Bush's initiative represented an impending catastrophe.[24] In 1994 United Defense had struck an agreement to sell the US Army more than a thousand Crusaders for a whopping $11 billion.[25] The sudden loss of this revenue stream would be devastating to its balance sheet. In the wake of Bush's speech, United Defense's executives turned to the lobbyists they'd retained at Patton Boggs to save their lucrative tank program. By the time Morris arrived at the firm, the Crusader campaign was in full swing. The young law student assisted the lobbyists as they rallied their allies in Congress and the Pentagon to oppose efforts to scrap the program. The Crusader program's supporters in Congress, many of whom represented parts of the country where the weapon would be made, argued that the long-range artillery gun provided essential support to ground troops during war.[26] Morris drafted statements and one-page memos that were passed along to congressional offices on Capitol Hill, so that lawmakers could issue them under their own names. Patton Boggs succeeded in blocking official action for fifteen months—a delay that saved United Defense roughly a half billion dollars in revenue.

A year later, the lobbyists scored an even bigger victory. Though the Crusader program was technically killed in May 2002,[27] the Patton Boggs team helped persuade allies in Congress to insert a provision into a Pentagon funding bill for a fleet of "non-line-of-sight objective force cannons"—that was, in essence, the same Crusader tanks under a different name. For United Defense, the new deal was worth $2 billion. It was an impressive display of lobbying muscle; the Patton Boggs team had managed to undercut the ambitions of the president of the United States and deliver a key victory for its client. For Morris, the episode offered an important lesson in modern lobbying. It showed that a well-connected Washington operator could be just as important to a corporation's bottom line as its top salesman.

Though Patton Boggs's associates were supposed to rotate through various divisions in the firm over the course of their internships, Morris managed to remain in the firm's lobbying practice the entire time. By the end of his summer, his perspective of Washington had fundamentally changed. Five years earlier, during his internship at the White House, Morris had looked up to administration officials who worked to shape federal policy from inside the government. But after three months at Patton Boggs, he understood that political power had shifted away from the big marble buildings that he studied in his political science courses. Much of what happened in the capital city, he knew now, was determined by the well-paid men who didn't appear on the federal org chart. Morris had a new professional aspiration. He wanted to be a Washington lobbyist. In 2003, before graduating from law school, he eagerly accepted a full-time job at Patton Boggs as a junior associate in its lobbying department.[28]

The romance of Washington has long drawn talented young minds to the city. In the early 1960s America's best and brightest flocked to the nation's capital in order to take part in the magic of John F. Kennedy's "Camelot."[29] In the 1970s Harvard Law School grads were turning down lucrative careers at white-shoe firms in order to confront Big Business as members of "Nader's Raiders."[30] By the turn of the twenty-first century, however, the flood of corporate cash would create a new avenue for achievement in Washington.

When drafting the blueprints for America's federal center in 1791, the French architect Pierre L'Enfant outlined a four-mile-long stretch of road running east-west across the city, just two blocks up from the White House. It would be the widest boulevard in Washington, broad enough to accommodate the horse-drawn wagons that carried tobacco barrels and building materials from the shipyards along the Potomac River to the commercial center downtown. Over the following two centuries, as the growth of the federal government transformed Washington from a provincial backwater to a major world capital, the downtown corridor of this signature avenue, K Street, would emerge as the headquarters of DC's booming influence-peddling industry. By the early 2000s, hardworking twentysomethings could earn far more money on K Street than they could as congressional or agency staffers, and, thanks to the growing power of industry, corporate lobbyists were playing a greater role in the policy-making process. This aura of money and power pulled an increasing number of up-and-coming politicos, like Evan Morris, away from government service and into the influence business.

As Tommy Boggs put it, "Now what we do is in vogue."[31]

Morris began his lobbying career during a time of critical changes inside the influence business. In 2002, amid a public outcry over the corrosive effect of money in politics, President George W. Bush signed into law the first major campaign finance reform in nearly three decades.[32] The act, which was cosponsored by Arizona Republican Senator John McCain and Wisconsin Democratic Senator Russ Feingold, closed off a loophole in the existing restrictions on political spending. Following Watergate, Congress authorized limited PAC donations from corporations to political candidates, but it failed to completely shut off the flow of unlimited sums to the Republican and Democratic parties. Companies and labor unions were able to make large donations to certain accounts that could be used to cover expenses, such as paying the mortgages on their buildings, thereby freeing up other cash for political endeavors.

Though it had existed for many years prior, it wasn't until about 1992 that companies and labor unions began exploiting this loophole. Over the next decade, these so-called "soft money" contributions from US corporations and labor unions to the political parties ballooned by a factor of five, to about $300 million. In the 2000 presidential election, for instance, AT&T, Microsoft, and other corporations donated more than $1 million to both major parties. The development worked to reduce influence peddlers' role in the campaign finance process. Since the political parties were able to access so much cash directly from companies and labor unions, they became less reliant on lobbyists such as Tommy Boggs to help them secure funding. By the time President George W. Bush took office, however, many in Washington had concluded that these massive corporate donations created the appearance of corruption. The McCain-Feingold Act of 2002, which was passed mostly with Democratic votes, put an end to this practice. But while intended to reduce the influence of corporations and their lobbyists, the landmark legislation had the opposite effect.

By preventing the Democratic and Republican parties from accepting huge contributions from a relatively small number of special interest groups, the law forced politicians to handle more of the grueling work of fund-raising themselves. Cut off from this ocean of campaign cash, members of Congress had to schlep from one donor event to the next, trying to hustle up modest contributions—$500 here, $1,000 there—from as many people as possible. The dynamic created a new lever of influence for savvy insiders. Lobbyists began collecting stacks of checks from their networks of clients, colleagues, and friends for up to $2,000 per donor—the legal limit at the time. They then delivered the combined fund-raising hauls—often $100,000 or more—to the political candidates. This innovation, which

came to be known as "bundling," served to indebt lawmakers to the lobbyists who could gather large amounts of money for their campaigns.

In an interview with CNN,[33] Tommy Boggs said the McCain-Feingold
reforms had made K Street's role in the political fund-raising process "more
important, which is kind of ironic." Referring to the decade-long period,
from 1992 to 2002, when corporations flooded the political parties with
million-dollar contributions, Boggs said, "[T]he lobbyist's role was sort of
demoted because the levels of soft money were so high that members of
Congress picked up the phone and called the CEO of a company, as opposed to a Washington lobbyist." But after Congress banned corporations
from making large financial donations to political parties, as Boggs put it,
"[T]he lobbyist's role is up again." As a result of this development, firms like
Patton Boggs became indispensable sources of campaign cash for lawmakers, giving its lobbyists greater clout in making federal policy.

Morris recognized quickly that bundling political contributions was
his key to advancing at Patton Boggs. Just as Tommy Boggs had used the
campaign finance revolution of the 1970s to build his firm into a Washington powerhouse, Morris sought to leverage the new fund-raising laws
to further his career. Morris began working the Patton Boggs hallways,
going from one office to the next in order to hit up other young associates
for contributions of $500, $1,000, or $2,000 for various Democratic candi-
dates. For early career associates, such donations were considered financial
impositions, and the firm had a rule against senior lobbyists asking their
younger, less-well-paid colleagues for political contributions. As a junior
lobbyist himself, though, Morris figured the rule didn't apply to him. He
sometimes convinced his young colleagues to fork over checks by telling
them—falsely—that Tommy Boggs had personally asked him to donate
money. In other instances, Morris persuaded colleagues to make campaign
contributions by promising them VIP access to the Democratic Party's political convention, but the tickets never arrived. After he'd gathered up the
funds, Morris would meet Democratic lawmakers over dinner, where he'd
hand over the checks and, in return, enjoy the lawmakers' undivided attention as he explained the needs of the firm's corporate clients.

Morris was always on the hunt for new donors. "I flew home from a trip once and sat next to this advertising guy," he told a reporter. "We talked baseball, the Mets, growing up in New York. We emailed back and forth last baseball season. We spoke a lot more about [former Mets catcher] Mike Piazza moving to first than we did about politics. He ended up sending me a check for $500."[34] By 2004, Morris's cellphone was filled with some 6,843 political contacts,[35] whom he leaned on to build his influence in Washington. During the run-up to the 2004 presidential election, Morris bundled $100,000 in contributions for former Vermont governor Howard Dean. When Dean flamed out of the Democratic primaries, Morris shifted his support to the party's nominee, collecting $150,000 in checks for Massachusetts Senator John Kerry.[36] The generosity made Morris one of the Kerry campaign's "Vice Chairs," a title given to an elite cadre of supporters who bundled $100,000 or more for Kerry. Other Vice Chairs included Hollywood producer Jeffrey Katzenberg, Wall Street mogul Roger Altman, and Nevada Senator Harry Reid. Though Morris was new to Patton Boggs, he was one of two lobbyists at the firm to earn this distinction. In the summer of 2004 Morris's profile was bolstered further by the *New York Times*,[37] which featured him in an article about the hot, young fund-raisers who were bankrolling the next generation of pro-business Democrats. The story described an event that Morris organized at that year's Democratic National Convention in Boston. "On Thursday," the *Times* reported, "Mr. Morris summoned 10 politicians he considered rising stars to the Ritz-Carlton for a roundtable discussion." Guests included future Senator Cory Booker and Linda Sánchez, a thirty-five-year-old freshman congresswoman from California. Morris was also friendly with the recently elected San Francisco mayor and future governor of California, Gavin Newsom.

Thanks to the changes in the campaign finance laws, Morris was now raising more cash than some of America's largest corporations. In 2004 he brought in $400,000 for the Democratic Party[38]—a figure that exceeded the contribution totals for the PACs of some of the biggest sources of cash for the Democrats, such as Citigroup Inc., JPMorgan Chase & Co., and Comcast Corp. The young lobbyist recognized the significance of his achievement. "The guy who can aggregate a hundred thousand dollars," he explained to Ted Goldman, a lobbying reporter with the publication

Influence, "is now more powerful than the richest man."[39] By the 2004 election, bundlers like Morris were responsible for raising one-fifth of the total amount of money collected in the 2004 presidential campaign, a share that would swell to one-third during the 2008 presidential race.[40]

Inside Democratic circles, Morris was earning a reputation as a dependable source of cash that party officials could no longer obtain directly from corporations, unions, and wealthy individuals. The Democratic Senatorial Campaign Committee, which raises money for Democrats running for the Senate, started inviting Morris to its annual weekend retreat in Martha's Vineyard, where he played golf and mingled with Democratic leaders Tom Daschle, Chuck Schumer, Hillary Clinton, and others. These efforts increased Morris's standing at the firm. "When you have a record of raising money for members of Congress," a colleague recalled, "you become quite popular at Patton Boggs."

Tommy Boggs soon took notice. He began sending Morris to represent the firm at fund-raising events that he was too busy to attend. Eventually he made an even more flattering request: Boggs invited Morris to a weekend gathering at Tobacco Stick Lodge,[41] his duck hunting retreat on Maryland's Eastern Shore. These legendary drinking and shooting outings had become something of a rite of passage for Patton Boggs partners—a ritual that conferred entry into the firm's upper crust. It was extremely rare, however, for a lobbyist as junior as Morris to be invited. Not even Morris's direct supervisor had been asked to the lodge. Boggs had seen something in Morris. While he lacked the elite-Washington pedigree, Morris exuded the professional ambition and fund-raising savvy that a young Tommy Boggs had used to create his lobbying empire.

After the group had settled in at the lodge, Boggs took the firm's rising star out into the marshlands. When Boggs tossed him a shotgun, Morris caught it awkwardly. He fumbled with the weapon, trying to figure out how to hold it properly, according to a former colleague of Morris's. Boggs glanced skeptically at Morris. What the hell's wrong? he asked.

Sheepishly, Morris admitted that he'd never been hunting before. "This is the first time I've ever touched a gun," he said. "I'm from Long Island."

Boggs chuckled. He grabbed the shotgun from Morris and told him to go back inside the lodge to drink wine. That was fine by Morris. He hadn't traveled to the Chesapeake Bay to shoot ducks over the wetlands. He'd come to socialize with senior partners and soak up war stories about the lobbying business in the hopes that one day he might become a DC power broker himself.

Over the prior few decades, corporate interests had succeeded in rolling back federal authority over the banking, telecommunications, airline, and energy industries. The deregulatory fervor would spark a wave of corporate consolidation, which, in some cases, allowed a handful of massive conglomerates to gobble up smaller competitors and left consumers with fewer options to choose from. Yet even after business lobbyists succeeded in tanking Bill Clinton's reform, the health care industry remained tethered to Uncle Sam. Due in part to the rapidly expanding federal Medicare health care program for the elderly, government officials were playing an active role in the provision of medical services and the regulation of pharmaceutical drugs. Boggs had long viewed this development as a lucrative business opportunity. In the 1990s he'd assembled a phalanx of lawyers and ex–government officials and launched one of Washington's first health care lobbying practices. Boggs took a special interest in the division, devoting much of his time to recruiting new health care clients and devising ways to advance the industry's agenda in Washington.

Hoping to get more face time with Tommy Boggs, Morris angled his way into the health care practice, where he worked on behalf of pharmaceutical giants such as Pfizer Inc. and Bristol-Myers Squibb Co.[42] He was also assigned to one of the firm's most lucrative clients: the US subsidiary of Swiss-owned F. Hoffmann-La Roche Ltd., commonly known as Roche, which paid Patton Boggs $600,000 in 2002 alone.[43] Roche was one of the oldest and most successful health care companies and drug manufacturers in the world. But this secretive Swiss conglomerate also had a controversial past. And at the time that Morris began working for Roche, the company was still grappling with the fallout from an unusually personal uproar on Capitol Hill.

It was the morning of May 14, 2000—Mother's Day—and Congressman Bart Stupak and his wife, Laurie, were getting ready for church. The couple had spent the previous night in a hotel in Menominee, Michigan, so that their seventeen-year-old son, Bart Jr., could host a small party after his school's prom at their home, according to the *Washington Post*. Their older son, Ken, had remained at the house as a chaperone. Around nine in the morning, the phone in their hotel room rang. The couple raced home. By the time they arrived, the house was crowded with police officers and paramedics. Congressman Stupak stepped inside and walked toward the large room next to the kitchen. There, in a puddle of blood, he found the body of his namesake, Bart Jr., dead of a self-inflicted gunshot wound.[44]

Stupak was the first Democrat elected to represent his northern Michigan district in fourteen years. During his four terms in Washington, he'd legislated with the pro-business wing of the party. He was a pro-life Catholic who'd opposed Democratic-led efforts to restrict gun ownership.[45] It was Stupak's gun, purchased for home protection at Laurie's request, that Bart Jr. had used to kill himself. As Stupak built his career in politics, he'd remained a devoted father, coaching Bart Jr.'s Little League team and attending his football games. In the hours after the suicide, the Stupaks slipped into a fog of disbelief. Later that evening, after the congressman had finished cleaning the blood from the floor, he and Laurie sat down and clicked on the television. Bart Jr.'s death was the top story on the evening news.

"So this really isn't a bad dream?" Laurie asked.[46]

More than sixty of Stupak's fellow lawmakers traveled to Michigan to attend the funeral.[47] As the Stupaks wrestled with their grief, they experienced feelings of guilt. Why weren't they able to prevent their bright, beautiful son from taking his own life at age seventeen? What warning signs had they missed? By all accounts, Bart Jr. had been thriving—the president elect of his high school student council and a beloved member of the football team. In the weeks prior to his death, he'd registered to take the ACT test he'd need for his college applications, and he'd ordered his varsity letter jacket. For Mother's Day, he gave Laurie a long-stemmed rose along with a poem. On the evening of his suicide, he was grinning in photos with his prom date.[48] He'd never, to his parents' knowledge, suffered through bouts of depression. This was a happy, well-adjusted American teenager. How could this have happened?[49]

About four weeks after the tragedy, while Laurie was sorting through her son's possessions, she came across something that caught her attention. A package of Accutane, the prescription acne pills that Bart Jr.—along with twelve million others around the world—had been taking for five months prior to his death. Curious, she went to the computer and plugged "Accutane" into a search engine.[50] The results were alarming. Media reports—dozens of them—showed a possible link between Accutane and suicide. A few years earlier, the FDA had issued a warning about the potential psychological side effects of the medication, including the risk of suicide. Laurie printed out the materials and approached her husband.

"Look at this," she said.[51]

As a member of the congressional subcommittee that oversaw the FDA, Stupak was an expert on health care policy. The congressman zeroed in on the agency's February 1998 report, which found "isolated reports of depression, psychosis, and rarely suicidal thoughts and actions" associated with Accutane use.[52] The FDA report stated that the warnings would be included in the packaging of the medication. But when he retrieved the box that contained Bart Jr.'s medication, there was nothing about suicide. Stupak was furious. "If Laurie and I had any idea that Accutane could cause depression, suicide ideation, or suicide," he would later testify, Bart Jr. "never would have taken the drug."[53]

Determined to find out more, Stupak traveled to the FDA's headquarters in Rockville, Maryland, to dig through records.[54] With the help of his friend Tom Coburn, a Republican congressman and a former physician from Oklahoma, he obtained reams of scientific papers, reports from consumers, and FDA documents about the drug.[55] Though much of the information they found had already been made public by the FDA, the congressmen discovered that there had been a total of 147 cases of suicide or hospitalized depression potentially linked to Accutane stretching back to 1982.[56] They also tracked down a 1998 internal FDA memo in which the agency warned of a possible link between Accutane and suicide. It contained an ominous passage: "Given all the pieces of evidence available, it is difficult to avoid the conclusion that Accutane use . . . is associated with severe psychiatric disease in some patients."[57] On top of that, there was a cache of "adverse-reaction reports" showing that some of those who became depressed while using Accutane saw their symptoms dissipate when they stopped taking the drug, but then felt the darkness return once they went back on it.[58] The FDA considered that phenomenon particularly concerning.

As a result, in 1998 the agency formally advised physicians to monitor patients on Accutane for symptoms of depression. At the FDA's request, Roche added warnings about a possible connection between Accutane and suicide to the package inserts that it sent to health care professionals prescribing the drug, according to the *Washington Post*. The company followed up with letters alerting drug prescribers to this change. But Roche did not include the suicide warning in the product's packaging until May 2000—just one month after the Accutane prescription found by the Stupaks had been filled. Bart Jr.'s doctor, meanwhile, had never voiced concerns to the Stupaks about depression or suicide.[59]

In October 2000 the couple took their story to the press, blaming Accutane for their son's suicide during an emotional appearance on NBC's *Today* show. "If it can happen to our family," Stupak told viewers, "it certainly can happen to you."[60] With the public attention generated by the Stupaks, another 167 reports of suicides that were potentially linked to the drug soon surfaced, and an additional 37 cases were reported directly to the congressman's office.[61] What made these statistics all the more distressing was that, according to the FDA, they might represent just a fraction of the total caseload, because suicides are vastly underreported.[62]

Stupak was no longer simply a veteran congressman representing the Upper Peninsula of Michigan. He was a bereaved father on a crusade. In December 2002 he appeared before a congressional subcommittee for a hearing on the safety concerns related to Accutane. While he was enraged that federal regulators had failed to alert his family to the potential side effects, he directed his harshest rebuke at the pharmaceutical executives who manufactured the drug: Roche. The company "has continued to put profits before people. They have done everything possible to prevent the

American people from learning of the psychiatric injuries and deaths associated with Accutane," he testified. "We cannot allow the drug manufacturer and the FDA to continue to turn a blind eye to the lives lost, families devastated, and dreams dashed by an acne drug. The American people, our children, are not collateral damage in the scheme of corporate profits!"[63]

Through it all, Roche executives and FDA officials maintained that there was simply no ironclad proof that Accutane caused suicides; a court later dismissed Laurie Stupak's wrongful death suit against the company. Still, the congressional outcry over Roche's "miracle" acne treatment had come at a particularly inconvenient time, as the powerful drugmaker was already grappling with the fallout from failed innovations and other front-page scandals.

F. Hoffmann-La Roche Ltd. was founded in 1896 by a twenty-eight-year-old entrepreneur, Fritz Hoffmann-La Roche. The firm started out creating rudimentary medicines from a tiny factory along the Rhine River in Basel, Switzerland. Following a series of breakthrough products—a thyroid treatment, an orange-flavored cough syrup—the company expanded into the vitamin and nutrient business, and, by the 1940s, it had offices in three dozen countries, including the United States. Two decades later, a company scientist, Dr. Leo Sternbach, made a discovery that would drive the next generation of corporate growth: Valium, a combination sedative and anxiolytic used to treat ailments ranging from anxiety to muscle spasms. Valium was prescribed more than sixty-one million times in the United States in one year alone, becoming the world's first pharmaceutical product to eclipse $1 billion in sales.

Over the remainder of the century, Roche developed drugs that successfully treated leukemia, breast cancer, gastric ulcers, rheumatoid arthritis, melanoma, diabetes, insomnia, heart disease, and scores of other conditions. One of its treatments was included in a drug cocktail that reduced deaths from HIV/AIDS by more than half, saving thousands of lives. Its scientists earned three Nobel Prizes and developed an early test for the Covid-19 virus that was used more than two billion times during the deadly pandemic. More than thirty of the company's medicines are included in the World Health Organization's Model List of Essential Medicines. In

2002 Roche had about sixty-five thousand employees around the world and generated $17 billion in annual sales.

On its march to global dominance, however, the company was trailed by allegations of malfeasance. In 1976 a Roche-owned chemical plant in northern Italy exploded, spewing a cloud of toxic chemicals over the nearby town of Seveso. Residents fell sick, children developed skin lesions, and animals began dying. "One farmer saw his cat keel over," *Time* magazine reported, "and when he went to pick up the body, the tail fell off."[64] In 2010 *Time* declared it the eighth worst environmental disaster of all time. Roche said a contractor improperly stored the chemicals; after the explosion, the corporate giant properly disposed of the waste. In 1980 Hubert Flahault, the president of Roche's French subsidiary, was punished by a French court after tainted baby powder led to the deaths of more than thirty infants. Though Roche hadn't produced the powder, the company's chemicals were mistakenly added to it by a different firm. Following a two-month trial, Flahault was one of five executives from three different companies found guilty of involuntary homicide and injury.[65]

All the while, a much larger scandal was gathering beneath the surface. In 1973 Stanley Adams, a senior Roche executive who'd been snubbed for a promotion, slipped a stack of internal documents to European regulators. The documents showed that Roche executives were colluding with their competitors to increase the prices of the vitamins that they sold.[66] The regulators launched an investigation and initially fined the company about $500,000.[67] In Switzerland, however, the unauthorized disclosure of corporate information is a crime. Adams was arrested on industrial espionage charges and spent three months in solitary confinement. When his wife was told that he faced twenty years in prison, she committed suicide.[68]

Adams was released after six months.[69] He went on to publish a 1984 book[70]—later turned into a made-for-TV movie in Europe[71]—recounting his saga as a corporate whistle-blower and detailing his claims about price fixing at Roche. When similar allegations reached law enforcement officials on the other side of the Atlantic, the US Department of Justice exposed a criminal plot that was far more sinister than even Adams had imagined. As federal investigators would learn, executives at Roche and other vitamin

manufacturers had been gathering at secret meetings, held once a year during the 1990s, in order to create "budgets" that detailed how they would
manipulate prices in the fast-growing global vitamin market.[72] Virtually
every consumer in America was impacted, as the scheme pumped up
prices for the vitamins used most commonly to enrich human foods and
animal feeds, such as vitamins A, B_2, B_5, C, E, and beta-carotene.[73] It also
elevated prices for vitamin premixes that were added to breakfast cereals
and other processed foods.[74]

"On a daily basis for the past ten years, every American consumer paid
to eat and drink or use a product whose price was artificially inflated," US
Attorney General Janet Reno said at the time. "Day by day, consumers took
a hit in their wallet so that these coconspirators could reap hundreds of
millions of dollars in additional revenues."[75]

In May 1999 Roche was hit with what was then the largest criminal
fine in American history: $500 million.[76] "The vitamin cartel is the most
pervasive and harmful criminal antitrust conspiracy ever uncovered," Joel
Klein,[77] the head of the Justice Department's Antitrust Division, said during the announcement of Roche's guilty plea.[78] As the scope of the case
became clear, the publication *Corporate Crime Reporter* named Roche the
biggest "Corporate Criminal" of the decade.[79]

The scandal touched off a cascade of other problems at Roche. Vitamin
sales dropped, and executives eventually sold off the vitamin division,[80]
which had once been its engine of revenue growth. The move left Roche's
new vitamin-manufacturing plant in South Carolina sitting largely idle.
Meanwhile, sales of Valium and other previously high-flying drugs were
slipping as their patent protections expired, exposing them to new competition from cheaper alternatives. Company executives were desperate
to secure the next lineup of blockbuster drugs. But, one by one, Roche's
leading prospects flopped. In 1998 its highly anticipated new heart medication, Posicor, was pulled from the market at the FDA's request amid concerns that it triggered dangerous complications for patients taking other
medications. "Get off this drug and on to something else," the FDA's drug
chief, Murray Lumpkin, warned.[81] Sales of Roche's promising treatment
for Parkinson's disease, Tasmar, was halted in Europe and Canada after

several people taking it developed liver problems and died.[82] And sales of Roche's revolutionary weight-loss drug Xenical fell short of expectations thanks in part to a botched 1999 Super Bowl TV ad, which repulsed many Americans with its graphic description of potential side effects: "You may experience gas with oily discharge, increased bowel movements, an urgent need to have them and an inability to control them."[83] It was against this backdrop that, in May 2000, Bart Stupak Jr. killed himself, creating yet another public crisis for the embattled pharmaceutical giant.

To turn things around, Roche in 2001 installed George Abercrombie, a seasoned drug industry executive and former pharmacist, as the head of its US operations.[84] As a top priority, Abercrombie wanted to expand the firm's Washington presence and restore its sullied reputation. Politics had never been much of a concern for Roche. At the time, the company had only two lobbyists in its DC office, though, like many other large companies, it also retained outside lobbying firms that specialized in specific policy areas such as taxes or FDA regulation. The most prominent of Roche's outside lobbying firms was Patton Boggs. Roche had first hired Patton Boggs in the 1990s, and, by 2005, it was paying the firm $1.5 million a year—more than it paid any other lobbying shop. In the aftermath of Bart Stupak Jr.'s suicide, Patton Boggs helped Roche navigate the furor in Congress and the fallout at the FDA, which by then had mandated that all Accutane patients or their parents sign consent forms prior to taking the drug.[85] Roche also agreed to study Accutane's psychiatric effects.[86]

Through the political firestorm over Accutane, Roche executives had come to understand the critical role that lawmakers and agency officials play in the pharmaceutical industry. Abercrombie knew he could no longer afford to take Washington for granted; he needed to fortify his in-house lobbying team. It was around this time that Abercrombie got to know Evan Morris.

As a newcomer to Washington, Abercrombie was awestruck by the capital city. Morris impressed Abercrombie with his stories of hobnobbing with the Clintons and other Democratic luminaries, according to former employees of Roche. The young lobbyist promised to introduce Abercrombie to Hillary Clinton. Morris, in turn, was drawn to the money that Roche lavished on its executives; Roche once sent Morris to a meeting at its headquarters in Basel, Switzerland, aboard one of the company's corporate jets. After a Roche lobbyist left the company, Morris applied for the job. The young influence peddler insisted that he could do better than Roche's current lobbying team, but only if the company increased its Washington budget. In early 2005 Abercrombie offered Morris the position.

Morris was thrilled. But he worried that Boggs might see his departure, which came only about two years after his hiring, as an act of disloyalty. When the two met, however, Boggs was supportive, encouraging the up-and-comer to take the position. At twenty-seven, Morris had completed his education at Patton Boggs. It was time to strike out on his own.

When he arrived at Roche, the company was under pressure to find new sources of revenue, and Morris was eager to prove his worth. He quickly spotted an opportunity to do both. In early 2005 an outbreak of avian influenza in Asia led to dozens of deaths, mostly in China. A senior United Nations official predicted that if it spread to the rest of the world, millions could perish. As the story flashed across cable news channels, Americans began to worry. Michael Leavitt, the head of the Department of Health and Human Services under President George W. Bush, admitted that the US government was not prepared for an outbreak of the avian flu.[87]

Roche made the leading treatment for avian flu, a pill called Tamiflu. Sensing an opportunity, Morris hatched a plan to use the health scare to drum up new sales of Tamiflu for Roche. If he could persuade federal officials to create a stockpile of antiviral drugs for pandemics—and fill it with his company's product—it would be a windfall for Roche. Morris and his team went to work lobbying key members of Congress and the Bush administration directly. At the same time, using an approach that had been advanced by Black Manafort in the 1980s and Tony Podesta in the 1990s, he deployed a more sophisticated influence campaign that targeted the public. Though it could be difficult for corporations to get their pet issues covered by the mainstream press, the explosion of hyper-partisan, Internet-based media made it easier for companies to slip their propaganda into the news cycle. Morris paid consultants to dig up frightening accounts of the outbreak overseas and send them[88] to liberal or conservative web outlets that thrived on the sort of sensationalized news stories that activated readers' emotions. The goal was to stoke Americans' fears about avian flu in order to put public pressure on lawmakers, forcing them to act. Morris called this type of work, "black ops."

The fear-mongering paid off. In October 2005 thirty-two Democratic senators wrote a letter to President Bush expressing their "grave concerns that the nation is dangerously unprepared for the serious threat of avian influenza."[89] They urged the White House to stockpile avian flu treatments. Among the senators advocating this approach was a forty-four-year-old freshman senator from Illinois, Barack Obama. The following day, Obama, Hillary Clinton, and other Democratic senators introduced a bill to create a Strategic National Stockpile to prepare for a pandemic. Not long after it was introduced, Senator Joe Biden of Delaware lent his support to the measure.

As pressure mounted to stock up, Morris's team worked to ensure that Tamiflu would be selected to fill it. This was a complicated task. While the FDA had approved Tamiflu to prevent and fight the flu, neither this antiviral nor its competitors did much to address flu's more serious consequences, such as respiratory tract infections.

To convince the Bush administration that Tamiflu was the best treatment for avian flu, Morris and his team compiled a stack of research documents touting the drug's benefits. Among the studies was a February 2001 research paper led by Robert Welliver, a pediatric infectious disease researcher, and nine other doctors. They found that Tamiflu prevented the flu from spreading between family members living in the same household. There was also a 2003 paper by Laurent Kaiser, a Swiss university professor, and Frederick Hayden, a University of Virginia infectious disease researcher, and four others, which concluded that Tamiflu reduced dangerous respiratory problems related to the flu.[90] The studies became an important element of Morris's campaign. He and other Roche executives brought them to a high-stakes meeting with senior officials at the Department of Health and Human Services, where Morris, Abercrombie, and other Roche officials used the research to promote Tamiflu, according to a lobbyist who worked on the matter. And when Roche's chief medical director, Dominick Iacuzio, testified before Congress in May 2005, he pointed to the studies as evidence that Tamiflu prevented flu infections. As it turned out, though, several of the studies' coauthors had been paid by Roche in the past, an arrangement that undercut the objectivity of their findings. Had any policy makers known about the financial relationship between the drugmaker and the scientists, they might have been more skeptical about the studies and perhaps more likely to support a competing treatment from rival drug company GlaxoSmithKline. However, at no point during the process did Morris disclose that Roche had supported some of the researchers. To the lawmakers and administration officials, it seemed like independent science.

After Morris had obtained the letter from the thirty-two Democratic senators and circulated the studies, the Bush administration began the process of establishing the stockpile. At first, the White House planned to buy enough Tamiflu to treat about twelve million Americans. That would have been an impressive coup for the new hire, yet Morris set off to do even better. He learned that a World Health Organization official had once mentioned that countries should procure enough avian flu treatments to cover 25 percent of their populations; in the United States, that would mean eighty-one million people. Using his connections inside the Democratic Party, Morris and his team called the staff of key senators—including Barack Obama and Hillary Clinton—to advocate for a larger stockpile, while Roche's Republican lobbyists reached out to friends in the Bush administration. Eventually the government came around. Though a widespread outbreak never occurred in the United States, government officials grew so concerned about a future event that they took steps to guard against it. In October HHS Secretary Leavitt met privately with Obama and other key Democratic senators to tell them the White House wanted the stockpile to cover eighty-one million Americans.

Just before the agreement was finalized, however, there was another roadblock. Senator Chuck Schumer of New York argued that the government should contract with an American company to produce the flu treatments instead of a Swiss company like Roche. He also complained that

Tamiflu was too expensive, at $60 for a five-day course. Morris jumped in to save the deal, assuring Schumer's aides that although Roche was controlled by a foreign company, Tamiflu would be produced right here in the United States—mostly at the South Carolina manufacturing plant idled after the vitamin price-fixing scandal. And to address the concerns over costs, Roche promised to reduce the sales price for the US government below the sales price for any other country in the world. (In the end, though, this price break was minimal; Roche sold Tamiflu to Uncle Sam for $19.23 per unit and to its European customers for $19.24 per unit. A difference of one cent.) In any event, by the time Schumer was ready to meet face-to-face with Abercrombie, the disagreements had been ironed out.

The deal would result in more than $2 billion in Tamiflu sales to the federal government, states, and cities over the next few years. Overnight Morris became a company star.[91] He boasted to friends that, as a reward for his effort, Roche gave him a $1 million bonus, bought him a Porsche, and sent him and his wife on an expensive vacation. In December 2005, about a year after he was hired, executives put Evan Morris in charge of its entire lobbying operations and gave him the title of executive director of federal government affairs. Around this time, Morris directed employees to create a report specifying the amount of money that Roche spent on its Washington office—and how much revenue his team produced through sales to the government. In his first year at Roche, Morris calculated that his return on investment was an astounding 1,000 percent.

Morris's Tamiflu score reflected the new role that influence peddlers were playing in the American economy in the new millennium. In the late 1960s and early 1970s, industry lobbyists had been on the defensive, fighting a losing battle against the growth of government—overpowered by an alliance of better-organized opponents, including unions, environmentalists, and consumer groups. After business interests unified to beat back the public interest lobby, they went on offense, spending the 1980s and 1990s cutting taxes, liberalizing trade policies, gutting regulations, and crushing unions. By the onset of the twenty-first century, corporate America had put their Washington fixers to work on a different objective. Rather than pressing for policies that would benefit American industry as a whole, corporate lobbyists were increasingly competing with one another, seeking to change laws and regulations in a way that would help the companies that hired them and undercut their competitors.[92] Influence peddlers were spending more of their time assisting individual corporations to improve their financial performance—generating new revenue streams by securing government contracts, for instance, or expanding a firm's market share by helping it win regulatory approval for a merger. For many of America's biggest corporations, like the drugmaker Roche, the Washington office was no longer just a place to fight off proposed rules and pending legislation. It was an extension of their business operations.

Lobbying had become a profit center.[93]

10

In the early afternoon of a warm spring day, a congregation of upper-crust
Democrats began to gather outside a stone-and-stucco home in a wooded
neighborhood about ten miles west of the US Capitol. The residence was
perched on the banks of a 135-acre private basin, Lake Barcroft, where
neighbors liked to steer sailboats[1] against the afternoon breeze. When
the guests—who included House Minority Leader Nancy Pelosi, New
Mexico Governor Bill Richardson, and Vermont Senator Patrick Leahy[2]—
approached the entrance to the house, they discovered a spread of liba-
tions and delicacies that befitted the splendor of the occasion. A table of
sushi rolls that had been personally prepared by Kaz Okochi,[3] a popular
Japanese-born chef, was arranged along the circular driveway. Flutes of
champagne and glasses of pricey wines were available nearby. Another renowned local restaurateur, Roberto Donna, served as a caterer as well.[4]
Once they'd set aside their plates, the guests were free to enter the house
and wander into the basement, where, in a room with white walls and a
white floor, a museum-quality collection of modernist sculptures and pho-
tographic artworks was on display.

It was the union of a K Street power couple that had summoned the

Democratic ruling class out to this lakeside property in the Virginia suburbs. The groom, fifty-nine-year-old Tony Podesta, was by then a renowned political fixer.[5] During his nearly four decades in Democratic politics, he'd worked for a half dozen presidential candidates,[6] led Hollywood's battle against the religious Right, and built what would become the third-biggest lobbying empire in Washington;[7] at its peak, his firm would have more than a hundred clients and nearly $50 million in annual revenue. After about fifteen years as an influence peddler, Podesta had accumulated properties in Washington, Italy, and Australia, as well as a critically acclaimed art collection. But his most valuable asset was his illustrious last name.

Tony's brother, John Podesta, was a political heavyweight in his own right. The former chief of staff to President Bill Clinton and the future counselor to President Barack Obama, John was then in the process of building his new organization, the Center for American Progress, into the city's most exciting Democratic think tank. Few surnames in Washington commanded more respect. And on this day, the House of Podesta would enthrone a new member.

The wedding itself had taken place earlier in the day, at Tony's other house in northwest Washington. Unlike the star-studded reception, the ceremony had been an intimate affair. Only a handful of close family members had been present to witness John Buchanan, a former Alabama congressman and an ordained Baptist minister, join Tony with his new bride, Heather Miller. At thirty-three, Miller was an up-and-coming Beltway insider with a University of Virginia law degree[8] and a job as a Democratic aide on Capitol Hill. Though she was raised by two academics in the far less glamorous setting of Rochester, New York, she projected a highborn grace that impressed elite Washington. Arriving at Tony's northern Virginia home for the reception, the couple's postnuptial elation was evident. But so, too, was their twenty-six-year age gap. Tony, a plump, stocky, olive-skinned man, took heavy paces between his VIP guests and the buffet table. Heather, long and lithe, glided through the crowd in a whirl of air kisses and flattery. At most of the cocktail receptions and fund-raising dinners she attended, Heather's self-assured charisma had made her an object of attention. But at this event, it was her sartorial judgment that was turning heads. Heather had arrived at the glitzy reception in the same irreverent ensemble she'd worn to the altar: a red, silk wedding dress.[9]

This red wedding dress was a fitting piece of iconography for Tony and Heather Podesta's partnership. In the months after the ceremony, Heather would join her husband's line of work, adopt his celebrated last name, and go on to establish the country's most successful female-owned lobbying firm. Together, Tony and Heather would rocket to the apex of Washington society by flouting the conventions of their buttoned-down profession. Although most lobbyists preferred the anonymity of the shadows, the Podestas "strutted through smoke-filled rooms,"[10] as *Washingtonian* magazine put it, "like public ambassadors for their often vilified industry."[11] The two shared a distinctive aesthetic flair: Heather preferred vivid, attention-grabbing ensembles; Tony sported flashy ties and red Prada shoes.[12] "The Pope wears Prada," he once quipped to a reporter, "and so do I."[13] The couple jetted off to art festivals across the globe,[14] entertained lawmakers at their flat in Venice, Italy, and hosted high-dollar political fund-raisers at their homes in DC and Virginia. They steered rivers of cash to top-tier Democrats—Hillary Clinton, House Speaker Nancy Pelosi, Senate Leader Chuck Schumer—and wielded their influence to advance the political interests of some of the biggest companies in the world, such as Google, Wells Fargo & Co., Walmart Inc., and Boeing Co. Yet it was the pride that Tony and Heather seemed to take in their reviled profession that distinguished them from other DC operators. After Senator Barack Obama banned lobbyists from raising money for his presidential campaign in 2008, Tony and Heather arrived at the DNC convention in Denver wearing patches with an embroidered letter *L* on their lapels.[15] The badge represented the "scarlet letter for lobbyists,"[16] Heather explained to everyone who would listen.

Still, beneath the pomp and shimmer of their public personas, Tony and Heather Podesta would have an enduring impact on the lobbying industry, the Democratic Party, and the interplay between the government and the economy. During the early part of his career, when he was still a hardened liberal activist, Tony discovered how to persuade lawmakers to take official actions not by approaching them directly on Capitol Hill but by whipping up public pressure from their constituents back home in their districts. After becoming a lobbyist, he used this same playbook to benefit drug companies, oil giants, banks, and Big Tech firms. Along with the innovations of Black Manafort, Podesta's efforts helped hasten the development of a more advanced form of outside influence peddling that expanded the lobbying industry's reach beyond the capital city and into workaday communities all over the country. As much as any other innovation, it was the increased sophistication of outside lobbying tactics that would transform DC's lobbying industry from an exclusive club of backslapping insiders to a dynamic economy of twenty-first-century tactics.

Meanwhile, as they established themselves as K Street's most glamorous couple, Tony and Heather would turbocharge their political clout by sauntering through a loophole in Washington's latest ethics reforms. In response to a bombshell influence-peddling scandal, Congress in the mid-2000s banned one of K Street's most time-honored tactics: plying lawmakers with gifts in exchange for political favors. Though intended to prevent lobbyists from securing official perks through free steak dinners or complimentary golf outings, the legislation did nothing to address the far more consequential cycle of schmoozing and trading favors that took place at Washington-area fund-raisers. And it was here that Tony and Heather Podesta would enshrine their legacy.

By hosting splashy fund-raising soirees at their various properties in and around DC, the couple was able to endear themselves to top lawmakers in Washington and serve as a critical link between Big Business and the Democratic establishment—all without violating the restrictions of the new lobbying reforms. The lucrative pipeline of cash they steered to the capital city worked to expand the business community's influence with left-of-center politicians and to nurture a set of industry-friendly values inside the Democratic Party that was dramatically different from those of a generation earlier. Along the way, through their efforts on behalf of the Wall Street bankers and Silicon Valley hotshots who came to dominate the new economy, Tony and Heather emerged as the premier Democratic lobbyists of the post–Industrial Age.

•　•　•

It was during the 1990s that Tony—the once die-hard liberal advocate—earned his spurs as a corporate influence peddler. In 1993 his brother, John, left their lobbying firm for the Clinton White House, starting as staff secretary and working his way up to chief of staff.[17] John's professional ascent gave Tony Podesta a fraternal link to the administration and a powerful, if unspoken, selling point for his lobbying practice. When an executive at a potential client accidentally called him "John," Tony didn't correct him. In the evenings, Tony organized political events at his house, sometimes with the assistance of his mother, Mary Podesta, who had relocated to Washington in 1987 following the death of her husband. Attendees dined on pasta made with Mary's homemade pesto sauce while handing over campaign contributions to leading Democrats.[18] The fund-raisers could bring in as much as $50,000 a night.[19] Tony called it the "Pesto PAC."[20]

Before long, Podesta was generating so much cash that the King of K Street himself, Tommy Boggs, inquired about buying the business. Podesta got together with Boggs in his smokey West End office to discuss a possible deal. But nothing ever came of it. The two men, Podesta says, reflected two distinct eras of K Street. "Tommy was a giant," Podesta says. "I thought of myself as a kid." While Tommy worked Capitol Hill in a conservative business suit, Tony displayed a crackle of style that was unusual for the colorless federal city. Podesta arrived at Clinton's first inaugural festivities wearing red high-top shoes, a flashy tuxedo, and a red cummerbund with a matching bow tie. Their approaches to influence peddling were equally distinct. Although Tommy remained the quintessential inside operator, Podesta preferred the advanced outside tactics of the modern influence peddler.

Changes to the city's political topography had already begun to erode the effectiveness of traditional access lobbying. After the GOP took control of the House of Representatives during the "Republican Revolution" of 1994, House Speaker Newt Gingrich and the Clinton White House became locked in a political blood feud that left Washington bitterly polarized—a polarization that would only worsen over the coming decades. In this viciously partisan environment, activist groups were scouring the voting records, campaign finance reports, and personal financial data of their political opponents for ties to corporations or special interests. Lobbyists, long despised by the public, had come to be viewed as even more contemptible following Paul Manafort's well-publicized HUD scandal in the late 1980s. And now, any whiff of collusion between a lawmaker and a lobbyist would be turned into an attack ad or fed to the press. The poisonous atmosphere made it all the more dangerous for lawmakers to maintain close public relationships with lobbyists. As a result, members of Congress grew increasingly wary of taking official actions that could be viewed as favors to special interests. The development was a catastrophe for K Street. If lobbyists were going to achieve their objectives in Washington, they'd need to find new ways to pressure Congress.

Out of this crisis came innovation. By watching Ted Kennedy's effort to block Robert Bork from the Supreme Court, the Harry and Louise TV advertisements that helped to tank Clinton's health care reform, and other successful grassroots campaigns, lobbyists had learned that the most effective way to bring a lawmaker around to their position was through his or her constituents. With an election always just around the corner, members of Congress are uncomfortable taking any action that's not popular with the folks back home. Conversely, they are eager to support issues and causes that have—or appear to have—popular support among their constituents. Sharp lobbyists realized that if they could convince voters that a particular bill is in their best interest, their elected representatives would inevitably follow suit. To that end, corporations began spending less time trying to persuade individual members of Congress and more time targeting the people who sent them to Washington in the first place. They did this through public relations campaigns, grassroots efforts, and other strategies designed to whip up support or opposition to a particular issue in a lawmaker's home district.

When it came to this new approach to lobbying, Podesta proved particularly adept. It was, after all, precisely what he'd done during his years as a liberal activist. As the executive director of People for the American Way, he'd used media coverage and celebrity star power to foment public opposition to the religious Right. As a consultant to Ted Kennedy during the epic Supreme Court fight, he'd helped orchestrate the national outcry that crippled Robert Bork's nomination. Now, as a Washington lobbyist, he would operate from this same playbook. Only this time, he wouldn't be plying his outside influence tactics to further the liberal cause but to advance the interests of corporate America.

In 1994, for example, Podesta had been hired by the California Poultry Industry Federation to roll back federal guidelines permitting chicken to be labeled "fresh" even if it was frozen at a temperature above zero degrees Fahrenheit.[21] California companies blamed the rule for enabling corporate giants such as Tyson Foods Inc. to corner the state's poultry market. At first, Podesta and his team met with key members of Congress to discuss their complaints. But thanks to the lobbying clout of Tyson Foods and other chicken industry powerhouses, lawmakers had little interest in Podesta's appeals. "After a couple of meetings," Podesta says, "we realized that the standard approach was not going to be successful."

Instead, Podesta and his team cooked up a plan to pressure Congress from the outside. Podesta got celebrity chef Wolfgang Puck to come to Capitol Hill and cater a luncheon for members of Congress and their staffs. As the lawmakers enjoyed the barbecued chicken, Puck marched onto the balcony of the Rayburn House Office Building and bowled an eight-pound frozen chicken into a set of tenpins.[22]

"This debate over a frozen chicken and fresh chicken is crazy," Puck told a reporter. "When you can bowl with a frozen chicken, it's quite obvious it's not fresh."[23] Later, a Podesta employee in a chicken suit was dispatched to follow around Senate Minority Leader Bob Dole. "We did all kinds of guerrilla stuff," Podesta says. The efforts got such widespread media attention that Podesta's opposition in the debate, the National Poultry Federation, eventually asked him to stop his campaign. The two sides got together to negotiate, and, in a big win for Podesta's clients, they agreed to support revised federal guidelines stating that poultry could be labeled fresh only if it has never been chilled below twenty-six degrees.

Podesta brought this same flair for the dramatic to the debate over vitamin regulation, when he was retained by a coalition of dietary supplement manufacturers who were concerned about the FDA's growing interest in regulating vitamins as if they were pharmaceutical drugs.[24] The issue had emerged a few years before the price-fixing scandal at Roche. This more comprehensive regulatory framework would saddle the dietary supplement industry with additional costs and delays. To try to block any new regulations, his team produced a television ad in which a heavily armed SWAT team raided the home of Mel Gibson and arrested the Hollywood actor for possessing vitamin C. "If you don't want to lose your vitamins, make the FDA stop," Gibson told viewers. "Call the US Senate and tell them that you want to take your vitamins in peace. If enough of us do that, it'll work."[25]

He also pressured lawmakers by activating their constituents. Podesta's team obtained lists of vitamin customers and sent out thousands of letters suggesting that the FDA was threatening to put vitamin manufacturers out of business—a move that would rob consumers of their access to dietary supplements. Outraged customers confronted their representatives at town hall meetings. "All of the sudden," Podesta says, "these little old ladies are asking, 'Why are you going to take away my vitamins?'" He continued, "We wanted to give lots of members the impression that this was a grassroots movement. We created the illusion that there were lots of people all over the country that were really worked up about what the FDA was doing about dietary supplements." It worked just as Podesta had hoped. As the manufactured outcry gathered steam, FDA officials dropped their effort to regulate vitamins like pharmaceuticals.

Businesses that operate under strict federal oversight and intense public scrutiny are especially desperate for lobbying help, which is why the pharmaceutical industry has long been one of K Street's top customers. And it was on behalf of one such company that Podesta engineered his most ingenious campaign to date. In the mid-1990s Podesta was working for a South San Francisco–based firm that worried its innovative products would get marooned inside the federal bureaucracy. Founded in 1976 by a biochemist and a venture capitalist, Genentech Inc. was a pioneer in the new, cutting-edge class of medicines known as biotech drugs. While traditional pharmaceuticals are produced by mixing chemicals, biotech drugs are produced from living cells and proteins that are cultivated in labs. This advanced approach to drug manufacturing—so-called biologics—was quickly recognized as the future of the pharmaceutical industry. Though they can take longer to produce—up to fourteen years in some cases—they have the potential to deliver breakthrough results for patients with cancer and other life-threatening ailments. Biologics offer benefits to investors as well. Due to the tremendous amount of research required to produce them, biotech products are difficult to produce and therefore more profitable, since rival companies can't easily replicate them.

Genentech was among the most exciting players in the emerging bio-tech field; it was the first company to mass-produce human insulin for diabetes patients. And yet firms like Genentech represented only a sliver of the global drug market, which remained dominated by the powerhouses of the traditional pharmaceutical industry, such as Johnson & Johnson, Eli Lilly and Company, and Roche. Indeed, some of the most anticipated biotech treatments weren't even on the market yet because they were still being developed. Even once the drugs were perfected in the laboratory, it would be years before they would generate revenue because they would languish in the FDA's lengthy and onerous drug-approval process. Over time, Genentech's executives came to see the FDA's bureaucracy as a threat to the viability of their business. Emerging biotech companies had no rev-enue to sustain them through the years of waiting for regulatory approval. If they didn't find a way to speed up this process, Genentech's executives concluded, they risked being crushed by larger competitors.

Genentech had first hired Podesta in 1989 to help fend off attacks from the religious Right, which had targeted the company for using human DNA to develop drugs. But this latest assignment—convincing Congress to overhaul the FDA's protocols for approving new drugs—was a more elabo-rate task. Though he was exceptionally well wired on Capitol Hill and in the White House, Podesta understood that old-fashioned insider lobbying wouldn't be enough to motivate Washington to act on an issue as arcane as FDA reauthorization. Instead, he deployed an advanced set of tactics that were familiar to him.

Podesta recognized that calls to reform the FDA would be viewed more credibly if they came from those personally affected by the bureaucratic delays. So, as the first step in his plan, he sought to identify a sympathetic group of allies who could serve as the public face of Genentech's pressure campaign.[26] He found his messengers in the victims of the era's defining epidemic, HIV/AIDS, which by 1995 had become the leading cause of death for Americans aged twenty-five to forty-four, claiming an estimated fifty thousand lives in that year alone.[27] "AIDS guys were very effective because in those days," Podesta said, "if you got it, you died." Well educated and eloquent,[28] HIV/AIDS sufferers had been fuming for years over the glacial pace of approval for new drugs in America. While the FDA insisted on obtaining rock-solid proof that medications were safe and effective before permitting them to be sold, the activists called the agency's protocols unnecessarily rigid, especially when it came to experimental treatments for fatal diseases.[29] In 1988 some one thousand HIV/AIDS patients and their supporters thronged into the entrances of the FDA's headquarters in the Washington suburbs. "I'm here because the FDA is holding up drugs that are available and because people are dying," the HIV/AIDS activist John Thomas told the crowd, which waved signs and hollered in approval.[30] With hundreds of local cops and federal law enforcement officials looking on, the HIV/AIDS sufferers thundered their outrage at the federal regulators who, they argued, were callously denying them their last chance at survival.[31]

"Arrest Frank Young!" they chanted, referring to the FDA commissioner.

"Arrest Frank Young!"

"Arrest Frank Young!"[32]

As it happened, Genentech was just then working on treatments and a possible vaccine for HIV/AIDS, and its executives feared that these promising products would be delayed by the FDA's bureaucratic review process. So, Podesta decided to make the epidemic's desperately ill patients the centerpiece of his grassroots[33] lobbying campaign. "Expanding access to these drugs before the FDA's final approval was really important to AIDS patients and their brethren who were dying when there could be something on the shelf to help them," said Walter Moore, a former Genentech lobbyist. Podesta began pushing for legislation that would speed up FDA approval of drugs for serious and life-threatening conditions in cases where there were no treatments already on the market. Genentech's lobbyists pitched the idea as a win-win: HIV/AIDS and cancer patients would get speedier access to a potentially life-saving treatment, and Genentech could get its drugs on the market quicker.

Podesta understood that timing would be essential to the effort's success. He launched his operation during the 1996 campaign season, when lawmakers would be especially interested in keeping their constituents happy. Podesta arranged for groups of HIV/AIDS patients to meet with members of Congress all over the country. In these face-to-face discussions with their elected representatives, the patients expressed their indignation over the FDA. "Instead of simply testifying in hearings and meeting with staff in Washington, we took it to key players in their own backyards," Podesta explained. "We got patient groups organized, we got employees of medical device companies to meet with candidates on their home turf, we basically ran a grassroots political campaign."[34] In this way, Podesta said, Genentech was able to "convert what could have been seen as a deregulation scheme into a matter of patients' rights."[35]

Under pressure from HIV/AIDS patients as well as sufferers of other life-threatening diseases, House lawmakers began drafting a law to expedite the FDA's approval process for drugs designed to combat the most serious illnesses. As the legislation moved through Capitol Hill, Podesta shifted his focus back to Washington, where he used his clout to help steer the bill through the legislative process.[36] In addition to his brother, Tony Podesta had close relationships with other top White House officials, such as Greg Simon, who served as the chief domestic policy advisor to Vice President Al Gore. In his conversations with Simon, Podesta touted another benefit of the FDA reform legislation. Accelerating the drug-approval process, the lobbyist argued, would help consolidate the lumbering federal bureaucracy into a leaner, more nimble regulatory instrument that would allow American firms to better compete in an increasingly fast-paced and technology-driven global economy. During an earlier discussion with Senate aides, Podesta had spelled out this argument. "Either we were going to streamline the US government," he said, "or the most advanced health technology companies in the world were going to move all their jobs to Europe."[37]

The idea appealed to Simon and his White House colleagues. Ever since the collapse of Bill Clinton's health care bill in 1994—when the full power of the corporate lobby became clear—the administration had been picking fewer fights with Big Business and, increasingly, growing more supportive of its economic vision. Once Simon agreed to back FDA reform, Podesta served as the White House's "point person" during negotiations with business leaders over the bills' details. "Genentech was always at the meetings," Podesta said, "because I was the one who organized the meetings for the White House."[38] Finally, after months of bargaining and debates, Congress approved the bill unanimously, and on November 21, 1997, President Clinton signed the FDA Modernization Act.[39]

In remarks at the White House after signing the bill, President Clinton said the law reflected "the change, again, in the underlying nature of the society, moving from the industrial age to a technology, computer, information dominated age." The FDA reform, he continued, was a "model for what America has to do in area after area after area."[40]

The law's enactment strengthened Genentech's ties to the White House. The following year, Podesta arranged for Al Gore to appear at Genentech's headquarters outside of San Francisco when the vice president announced an extension of a federal research tax credit that provided tax incentives to biotech and other companies to invest in new products. "We held that event at Genentech to thank Gore for supporting us," Podesta explained.[41] A few months later, the Clinton administration appointed Genentech's head lobbyist, David Beier, to serve as Gore's top domestic policy advisor.[42] For Podesta, the passage of the FDA reform was equally significant. Orchestrating a multifront influence-peddling campaign that succeeded in modernizing a ninety-one-year-old federal agency served to ratify his conversion from hard-nosed liberal activist to high-powered corporate lobbyist. "I guess I'm maybe a little more economically conservative now, more fiscally responsible," Podesta told a reporter in the late 1990s. "I'm a little more libertarian in terms of what I think government can do."

In addition, the Genentech victory helped spark the next evolution of Podesta's career. Thanks in part to his efforts on behalf of this cutting-edge biotech innovator, he became convinced that the fast-growing technology industry, based largely in Silicon Valley, was on a collision course with Washington. In 1998 he rebranded his firm as podesta.com in order to appeal specifically to the tech industry. "This is our way of saying that we are ready for the millennium," he said.[43] He signed up a number of well-known tech clients—IBM, eBay Inc., Compaq Computer Corp., Qualcomm Technologies Inc., and WebTV Networks—and came to specialize in guiding computer and Internet firms through the tedium of federal policy making, while teaching crusty members of Congress about the emerging digital economy.[44] *Wired* magazine labeled him "among Washington's canniest and best-connected deal makers";[45] the *New York Times* anointed him one of the city's most influential people.[46]

By 2000, Podesta's firm had seventy clients and nearly $8 million in annual revenue, making it DC's eleventh largest lobbying operation. Even the Clinton White House was impressed. At one point, Ron Klain—then the chief of staff to Vice President Gore—approached Podesta about becoming Gore's deputy chief of staff. Though intrigued by the job initially, Podesta ultimately demurred because, as he explained later in an interview, he didn't want to walk away from his lobbying firm. Meanwhile, as his personal fortune swelled, Podesta became increasingly focused on what would become his signature passion.

Podesta first began collecting art as a volunteer on Ted Kennedy's 1980 presidential campaign.[47] Over the course of the race, Kennedy's team had developed an ingenious way to raise money and evade political spending restrictions. Using the senator's connections to famous artists, campaign officials convinced both Andy Warhol and Robert Rauschenberg to create limited-edition prints of the candidate and then donate them to his presidential effort. While the purchase price of these rare artworks would have far exceeded the limits on campaign contributions— $1,000 at the time—a loophole in federal election law enabled Kennedy's team to value the pieces at the cost of the canvases, paints, and other materials that the artists had used to make them. As a result of this technicality, Kennedy's campaign was able to accept this artwork as in-kind campaign donations worth a few hundred dollars apiece, and then turn around and sell them for thousands of dollars each. Later, when the campaign ran short on funds, it was forced to pay some of its staff with the donated art. Suddenly Podesta found himself with an assortment of these rare pieces by Warhol and Rauschenberg.[48]

Over the following two decades, Podesta would emerge as an internationally recognized collector of expensive modern art, filling his homes and offices with museum-quality paintings, sculptures, and photographs. By 2001, *Art & Antiques* magazine had added him to its list of the Top 100 Art Collectors.[49] "Some people spend a lot of money on golf," Podesta once said. "Like they play golf, I play art."[50]

Podesta seemed to have everything an ambitious DC operator could ask for: a thriving business, a celebrated stature, and a jet-set lifestyle. Still, something was missing.

His first marriage had ended acrimoniously in 1985. In court documents, obtained by *Washingtonian* magazine, Podesta's ex-wife alleged that when they split after five years together, he'd undervalued his income by about 50 percent, a move that reduced his child support obligations for the three children that the couple had adopted. Following more than four years of legal wrangling, Podesta agreed to a $265,000 settlement that released him from any further financial responsibilities related to the children, who, according to *Washingtonian*, were subsequently adopted by his former wife's new husband.[51] But by the turn of the twenty-first century, Podesta had been a bachelor for a decade and a half. He was ready to try again.

In 2001 Heather Miller was walking along a busy Washington street when she bumped into a friend. Miller's second marriage, she explained to her friend, had recently collapsed.[52] Heather had a tall, narrow build and distinctive white streaks in her long, dark hair. Despite the heartache of a second divorce, she wasn't willing to give up on love at age thirty-one. So, after some prodding from her friend, Miller agreed to be fixed up on a blind date. The friend, a former advisor to President Clinton named Dorothy Robyn, drew up a list of three eligible bachelors. Robyn eliminated the first two men on her list as overly wonky, but Heather agreed to go out with the third.[53] Later that fall, Miller had her first date with Tony Podesta. On their way to the opera, the two swung by Tony's home to retrieve his car, and, once inside, they walked by a few of the more eccentric pieces of his art collection. "I don't know why it is," Tony observed, "but I have artworks where the women have no heads."[54] The next day, Heather sent a thank-you note to Tony. She signed it, "Woman with a head."[55]

Following a swift courtship and a glamorous wedding, Heather at first continued using her maiden name, which she'd kept during each of her two prior marriages. Tony had warned her that becoming a Podesta could complicate her life; it would change the way she was perceived in Washington, making her an ally to some, an enemy to others. Eventually, though, Heather decided to take her husband's last name.[56] "That is so much cooler than being Heather Miller," she said. "I'm ready to be a Podesta."[57]

Around this time, Heather also joined her husband's profession. She departed Capitol Hill, where she'd most recently been an aide to Democratic congressman Robert Matsui of California, and became a lobbyist at a midsized law firm. From there, Tony and Heather emerged as K Street's most recognizable power couple, a dashing pair of regulars at the cocktail parties and charitable galas that animated elite Washington's social calendar. While pressing the interests of blue-chip corporations—Heather's clients would eventually include Boeing, HealthSouth Corp., and U.S. Steel; Tony had American Airlines Inc., Wells Fargo, and Walmart—the couple was soon donating more money to the Democratic Party and its candidates than any other lobbyists in Washington.[58] They hosted exclusive fund-raising events for the most influential Democrats in Washington, including Senate Leader Harry Reid, Senator Hillary Clinton, future House Speaker Nancy Pelosi, and future Senate leader Chuck Schumer. Their political events were as memorable as their wardrobes. To benefit the Pennsylvania Democratic Party during the 2004 presidential campaign, Heather organized a fund-raising dinner that featured Philadelphia cheesesteaks as the main course. "Just think," she said in the invitation, "you could be one more cheesesteak closer to a new president."[59]

Over the years, Tony and Heather amassed an extensive portfolio of real estate. It included, at various points, the $1.3 million waterfront home in Virginia where they were married, a $1.5 million town house near the US Capitol, a $3.2 million New York City condo, a $4 million home in DC's exclusive Kalorama neighborhood, a vacation property in Tasmania, as well as a home in Sydney with bracing views of the famous Harbour Bridge and Opera House. The couple's signature event, however, took place in the birthplace of Tony's paternal ancestors, at the flat they owned in Venice, Italy. "It's our weekend retreat," Heather boasted to a Capitol Hill newspaper. "Some people have a home in Dewey Beach [Delaware]—we have a home in Venice."[60] Every two years, over Columbus Day Weekend, they welcomed a small group of lawmakers, congressional aides, and top lobbying clients to their Venice home for the city's world-famous art show, the Art Biennale.[61] Guests have included Senator Ted Kennedy and Nancy Pelosi, as well as senior lobbyists for Home Depot, Walmart, and Wells Fargo. On one occasion, Janet Napolitano, the former Arizona governor and Obama Cabinet secretary, joined the Podestas in Venice after taking Tony and Heather on a private, after-hours tour of the Sistine Chapel, in Vatican City, which had been organized to celebrate Napolitano's birthday. During these visits, Tony often led the VIPs on behind-the-scenes tours of the Art Biennale, while Heather directed shopping excursions through the city's artisan shops and upscale boutiques. In the evenings, the couple usually rented out an acclaimed restaurant—one night it was Trattoria Antiche Carampane, another evening it might be the Michelin-starred Ristorante Ostello—where they treated their guests to Venetian fare and Tuscan wines. And, of course, whenever the Podestas were in Venice, they also made time to purchase some new pieces of art for themselves.

Tony and Heather had no children together.[62] Instead, they cherished avant-garde photographs and boundary-pushing sculptures. Through weekend sojourns to galleries and festivals in New York City, Europe, and South America,[63] the couple would eventually accumulate some 1,300 pieces of art,[64] which they held in a trust called the Tony and Heather Podesta Art Collection. As Tony put it, "Sometimes our life feels like an art travelogue."[65] They owned photographs by Andreas Gursky, as well as eight sculptures by Louise Bourgeois valued at an estimated $25 million.[66] "Tony's view of investment diversification is multiple artists,"[67] Heather once told a reporter.

The couple put some of their artwork on public display through loan arrangements with the Guggenheim, the Museum of Modern Art, the

National Gallery of Art, and other prestigious institutions.[68] But they also showcased the collection at the various properties they owned. Political dignitaries who arrived at one of the Podestas' homes for political events were occasionally jarred by the couple's edgy sensibility. When Hillary Clinton came over for a fund-raiser for her Senate campaign, she was greeted by an eight-foot-high photograph of a man lying on a bed with his penis exposed. The campaign's official photographer, according to the *Washington Post*, passed the evening with his back to the piece in order to ensure that he didn't snap a photo of Clinton standing next to the image.[69] "You've got to be pretty secure," Heather said of Tony, "to have an eight-foot-tall naked man in your living room in Washington, DC."[70]

At a different event, the Podestas' guests experienced an exhibition of performance art involving a naked woman. Still, it was in the guest restroom of the Podestas' Virginia home where visitors encountered the couple's modernist aesthetic in its most extreme form. Inside one particular toilet, Tony and Heather had set up a closed-circuit video camera that, as the *New York Times* put it, allowed "users to observe their bodily processes from a unique angle."[71] The bizarre contraption was, in fact, an installation by the Swiss video artist Pipilotti Rist. "Some people think it's a little weird," Tony once said about his taste in art. "But that's their problem."[72]

For Heather, this new life of hobnobbing with senators and jetting off to European art fairs was, at first, something of a culture shock. "There are times when I'm the daughter of an academic, in sneakers," Heather admitted. "I'm just that geek completely out of place."[73] But over time, she learned how to thrive in high-society Washington.

Meanwhile, at Podesta's lobbying firm, employees noticed a change in Tony as well. Heather's presence seemed to have a tender effect on their hot-tempered and demanding boss. "He's a yeller, he's a screamer—nasty emails 24-7," recalls a lobbyist who once worked for Podesta. "But with her, he was a complete freaking teddy bear. It was always better when she was around because he wasn't such a jerk to deal with."[74] The couple was so "schmoopy" with their affections that, according to a former employee of Tony's, it was uncomfortable being around them.[75] To everyone in Washington, it seemed that Tony and Heather Podesta were a K Street love story that would stand the test of time. "I'm the third husband, but this is the first time she's changed her name," Podesta once said. "That should tell you something."[76]

In the mid-2000s Washington's most notorious influence peddler contacted Podesta for assistance. After using cash, gifts, and favors to reach the peak of K Street success, Republican lobbyist Jack Abramoff now found himself at the center of a bribery and corruption scandal that was described by one former associate as "the Enron of Lobbying."[77] Over the course of the early 2000s, Abramoff had swindled Native American tribes out of more than $20 million,[78] operated a kickback scheme with a business partner, and, along with other lobbyists, bribed public officials with lavish gratuities, including seats in the luxury skyboxes[79] he leased at professional sports stadiums, World Series tickets, casino chips,[80] strip club visits,[81] and a golf vacation to Scotland.[82] Among other ways of buying off public officials, Abramoff had used a trendy sushi restaurant he owned[83] not far from the US Capitol to butter up lawmakers and their aides. Every night that Congress was in session, the bar at his Signatures restaurant was packed with Republican lawmakers and their modestly paid aides, who didn't make enough money to pay for the high-end cocktails the restaurant served. Members of Abramoff's lobbying team were always in attendance, looking after the lawmakers and aides and making sure they rarely picked up a tab. At last call, the lobbyists who remained would often decide among themselves which one of them would use their firm's credit card to cover the night's expenses.

In all, more than twenty lobbyists, aides, and public officials pleaded guilty or were convicted on federal charges related to the conspiracy. Republican congressman Bob Ney served seventeen months in prison. Tom DeLay, the former Republican House majority leader whose staff members had admitted to working with Abramoff to corrupt public officials, was not charged. But his ties to the disgraced lobbyist hurt his credibility, and he ultimately resigned from Congress. Hollywood turned the spectacle into a feature film, *Casino Jack*, starring Kevin Spacey as Abramoff, and workaday Americans were appalled by the incestuous dealings between Washington lobbyists and federal lawmakers. "The extent of Jack Abramoff's influence on our government is breathtaking," Chellie Pingree, then the president of the watchdog group Common Cause who later became a member of Congress, told the *Washington Post*. "The fact that he was an unscrupulous criminal who managed to work his way deep into many of Capitol Hill's most powerful offices is an indictment on our system as a whole."[84]

Amid a downpour of scathing news stories and law enforcement pressure, Abramoff approached Tony Podesta for help defending his reputation in Washington. Podesta initially seemed open to the idea, but members of his senior staff objected. Representing such a reviled figure, they argued, would irreparably damage the firm's brand. Before Podesta and his team could determine what to do, Abramoff made the decision for them. In January 2006 he pleaded guilty to federal charges of conspiracy, tax evasion, and aiding and abetting fraud.[85] He would go on to serve roughly three and a half years in prison.[86]

Though he never signed on as a Podesta client, Jack Abramoff would prove to be a critical figure in Tony and Heather's ascent. That's because the reforms that Washington enacted in the wake of the scandal served only to increase the value of the couple's preferred brand of influence peddling.

During the 2006 midterm elections, congressional Democrats used the Abramoff scandal as the linchpin of their campaign pitch, and the public's outrage over the GOP's "culture of corruption" helped hand Democrats control of the House of Representatives for the first time in twelve years. The newly elected House Speaker, Nancy Pelosi, made ethics reform her top priority, and Congress moved quickly to overhaul its rules for K Street. The Honest Leadership and Open Government Act of 2007 changed the way lobbyists went about their work in two fundamental ways.

First, it forced influence peddlers to disclose additional information about their lobbying activities and fund-raising efforts. The law, for example, required lobbyists such as Evan Morris to make public for the first time their campaign "bundling" efforts on behalf of political candidates.[87] It also mandated them to file twice as many disclosure reports about their contacts with lawmakers, and it called on Congress to create an online, searchable database so that the public could track lobbying activities more easily.[88] These measures brought an unwelcome ray of sunlight to an industry that thrives in darkness, and it increased the visibility of individual lobbyists at a time when the public was growing increasingly disdainful of the practice.

Second, the law banned lobbyists' preferred tool for currying favor with elected officials: paying for meals and drinks and distributing other gifts.[89] No longer could lobbyists hand out tickets to professional sporting events, golf junkets, or steak dinners in exchange for favors. "It is time to change the way business is done in the nation's capital," California Senator Dianne Feinstein told her colleagues on the Senate floor. "What is before us this morning is the single most sweeping congressional reform bill since Watergate."[90]

Among the central goals of the so-called gift ban was to eradicate the cozy social ties between K Street and Capitol Hill, which influence peddlers had long used to score sweetheart deals for their clients. But rather than uprooting this incestuous social culture, the new restrictions served only to relocate it. That's because the gift ban contained in the K Street reform legislation didn't apply to fund-raising events. So, while lobbyists could no longer try to curry favor with lawmakers by covering their tabs at steakhouses or by paying their greens fees at golf resorts, any corporate operative throwing a fund-raiser was free to ply members of Congress with expensive liquor and gourmet hors d'oeuvres while suggesting which way they should vote on an upcoming bill. One of the first people to identify this legal loophole was Abramoff himself. After finalizing his plea deal with prosecutors, the disgraced influence peddler told reporters that if he were to lobby under this new set of rules, he'd continue taking lawmakers to pricey golf clubs, playoff games, and sushi dinners. Only now he would make sure to hand each lawmaker a $1,000 campaign donation during the outing—turning what would otherwise have been an illegal "gift" into a perfectly permissible fund-raising expense. As Abramoff put it in his memoir: "Is corruption in Washington really ended by forbidding representatives from accepting free meals and, instead, permitting them to gorge to their heart's content, as long as it's at a fund-raising event— where they'll also pocket thousands of dollars in contributions? This is the kind of reform Congress proposes, passes, and then congratulates itself about?"[91]

As a result of the new law, political fund-raisers became legal sanctuaries where lobbyists could continue to socialize with lawmakers over food and drinks that they'd paid for themselves—precisely the type of activity that reformers had been hoping to eradicate. And during the post-Abramoff era, no one took fuller advantage of this loophole than Tony and Heather Podesta.

In 2006 the couple had paid $4 million for an eight-bedroom property located in D.C.'s Kalorama neighborhood,[92] the exclusive enclave where Ivanka Trump, Jeff Bezos, and even Obama himself would one day live. Tony and Heather then embarked on a two-year-long, multimillion-dollar renovation, partly to better accommodate the home for their art collection. To make sure it could hold a one-ton sculpture by Louise Bourgeois, the couple hired a structural engineer to reinforce the floor. When their four-hundred-pound installation of golden eggs couldn't fit through any of the home's doors, they removed a bay window in order to get the piece inside. Upon completion, the home came to serve as the headquarters of a fund-raising operation of cheeky flourish and breathtaking scale.

Every year, Tony and Heather hosted dozens of fund-raising events for top Democrats in Washington; some were large-scale cocktail gatherings, others were intimate dinners, but each was marked by the Podestas' unique sense of whimsy and pizazz. For an event for Washington Senator Patty Murray, they flew in chefs from Seattle who treated guests to the senator's home-state fare. For a February 2008 fund-raiser benefiting a pair of Democratic lawmakers in which gourmet hot dogs were to be served, the couple sent out invitations describing the event as the "Ultimate Sausage Party."[93] To honor the birthday of Vermont Senator Pat Leahy, the Podestas held a Ben & Jerry's–themed fund-raiser featuring ice cream flavors such as "Magic Brownies" and "Karamel Sutra." In an interview with Roll Call newspaper, Heather Podesta said the event would be "berry, berry extraordinary."[94]

While these fund-raising events enabled the Podestas to circumvent the federal gift ban and treat lawmakers to food and drinks they wouldn't have been able to otherwise, the most valuable thing they provided congressional Democrats was cold, hard cash. Tony and Heather might send out playful invitations, but they were dead serious about money. For a March 2009 fund-raiser benefiting the Democratic Congressional Campaign Committee, for instance, the couple asked guests to arrive with either a $5,000 individual donation or a PAC contribution of up to $30,000 to the Democratic Party. And it was through high-dollar events like these that Tony and Heather Podesta were able to, over the ten-year period beginning in 2008, donate more money to the Democratic Party and its candidates than any other lobbyists in the city.[95] This ocean of campaign cash was the source of the couple's power in Washington as well as the root of their impact on our democracy. The money that Tony and Heather funneled to Capitol Hill didn't just ensure that specific lawmakers would pick up the phone when they called; it worked to make the institution of Congress—year by year, fund-raiser by fund-raiser—more responsive to the Wall Street banks, drug conglomerates, and tech giants who were supplying the bulk of the campaign funds.

Tony and Heather Podesta's pride in their profession was on full display in 2008, when the Democratic universe converged on Denver to witness the coronation of a forty-seven-year-old senator as the party's presidential nominee. Barack Obama had framed much of his political movement as a repudiation of the likes of the Podestas. "I am in this race to tell the corporate lobbyists that their days of setting the agenda in Washington are over,"[96] he told a cheering crowd in 2007. "We're going to have to change the culture in Washington so that lobbyists and special interests aren't driving the process and your voices aren't being drowned out,"[97] he proclaimed during a 2008 debate.

As a candidate, Obama refused to accept donations from lobbyists or PACs,[98] and he pledged that, if elected, he would ban lobbyists from serving in his administration.[99] Nevertheless, when the husband-and-wife lobbying duo arrived at the seventy-six-thousand-seat Invesco Field at Mile High Stadium for the Democratic National Convention, they sashayed right through the increased scrutiny on their already loathed profession. Instead of slinking off to the sidelines, the Podestas swaggered straight for the limelight, hosting three events of their own and making appearances at countless others. And as they pranced from breakfast events to cocktail receptions, the K Street power couple thumbed their noses at Obama's anti-lobbyist ethos with a signature fashion accessory.

Tony and Heather spent the entire week in Denver sporting patches with the scarlet letter *L* on their lapels,[100] a not-so-subtle reference to the scarlet letter *A* that was branded onto an adulteress in Nathaniel Hawthorne's nineteenth-century novel.[101] "It's my little act of civil disobedience," Heather Podesta said. The emblems were made with great care; Heather hired a professional graphic designer to compose them[102] and selected the Gothic-style lettering only after scrapping about a dozen other options.[103]

But despite its playful flair, the protest sprang from a genuine irritation over Obama's treatment of lobbyists. "I feel a bit like a marked person," Heather said. "You can't volunteer, you can't give money, you can't even buy a twelve-dollar Obama T-shirt on the campaign's website," adding, "you don't want to be told that your time and money aren't wanted."[104] The husband-and-wife team weren't the only influence peddlers to nurse feelings of persecution. The stickers were so in demand at the convention that Heather quickly exhausted her supply of one hundred.[105] In a sense, the Podestas' scarlet letter *L*s had come to serve as a symbol of resistance for a K Street establishment that was, once again, facing the prospect of reform. "I can't tell you how many people want them," Heather said of the stickers. "They are the hottest commodity in town."

Even senior lawmakers joined in on the fun.[106] At one point, during a breakfast event at a Denver hotel, Vermont Senator Patrick Leahy gathered with Tony and Heather Podesta and quipped, "Get a picture of me with these two scarlet letter *L*s."[107]

11

Beneath a cold sun and a bracing wind, Barack Obama placed his hand on a Bible once owned by Abraham Lincoln, nodded to Supreme Court Chief Justice John Roberts, and recited the Oath of Office. After the US Army's Third Infantry Division had fired off its twenty-one-gun salute and the Marine Corps band had finished playing "Hail to the Chief," the lanky new president glided up to the podium on the West Front of the US Capitol and looked out at the crowd. An estimated 1.8 million people had bundled into knit hats and winter coats in order to witness the inauguration of America's first black commander in chief. It was believed to be the largest gathering to ever assemble in Washington.

Yet despite the roars of the spectators and the historic significance of the ceremony, Obama was taking charge of the government during a time of great peril. A coast-to-coast mortgage crisis was ejecting nearly four million people from their homes and a pernicious recession was putting millions of Americans out of work. During his nearly twenty-minute address, Obama used stirring language to insist that the country would get through its current calamity with the same spirit of resiliency that had pulled prior generations of Americans past the great struggles of their days. "We remain the most

prosperous, powerful nation on Earth," Obama said. "But our time of standing pat, of protecting narrow interests and putting off unpleasant decisions—
that time has surely passed. Starting today, we must pick ourselves up, dust
ourselves off, and begin again the work of remaking America."[1]

Even under the shadow of hardship, Obama's inaugural address captured the soaring optimism that had consumed the Left in the afterglow
of the 2008 election. Following eight years of Republican George W. Bush's
administration, the Democratic Party now had a popular leader in the
White House, control of both houses of Congress, and a mandate to pursue
the sorts of broad structural reforms that had long bedeviled liberal policy
makers. First and foremost was overhauling the US health care system,
which, at the time of Obama's election, 73 percent of Americans considered either to have major problems or be in crisis,[2] an increase from 69 percent in September 1994, the month Bill Clinton's health care reform effort
officially perished.[3] Though Democratic presidents from FDR to Clinton
had failed in their efforts to create a national health insurance program,
Obama believed that a less radical expansion of the health care safety net
could extend coverage to tens of millions of Americans while lowering the
costs of treatment for all. "So let there be no doubt," Obama told a joint
session of Congress a month after his inauguration, "health care reform
cannot wait, it must not wait, and it will not wait another year."[4]

As he electrified liberal Washington, Obama's call to revamp the health
care system was sending K Street into a panic. Lobbyists for the pharmaceutical and health insurance industries began racing to shield corporate
profits from the reach of reform. For one hotshot young influence peddler,
the scramble to sabotage Obama's health care plan was particularly intense.
But when his underground tactics were exposed in the press, he would find
himself facing the resentment of lawmakers, the outrage of his superiors,
and the potential collapse of his new life as a Washington power broker.

After his Tamiflu win in 2005, Evan Morris was the undisputed crown
prince of Roche's Washington office, and he relished the power that he could
now wield over his subordinates. When he wanted the large corner office
that was still being occupied by Roche's former lobbying director, Mike

Eging—who had been moved to another position—Morris complained to George Abercrombie and watched Eging pack his things and clear out. "Evan was very concerned about his image in Washington," recalls a former colleague. As a manager, Morris was just as ruthless. One former Roche lobbyist says that Morris seemed to take pleasure in ruining her weekends by calling her into his office on Friday afternoons and assigning her work that had to be done by Monday morning. Another Roche lobbyist recalls slipping out to the gym at five o'clock one evening for a quick workout to clear her mind. After exercising, she retrieved her phone from the locker room and discovered a dozen voicemails and emails from Morris. The next day, Morris sent an all-staff memo announcing a new rule: from now on, if he emailed or called between the hours of eight in the morning and eight at night, employees were required to respond within twenty minutes. The intensity burned out most staffers; within a year, every member of Roche's lobbying office who had been there when he started had left. The pressure was particularly withering on Eging. In May 2006 he was rushed to the hospital on account of what he believed was a heart attack. He soon left the company. To replace the departing staffers, Morris hired dozens of lobbyists and consultants from various K Street firms. Each of these nearly one hundred influence peddlers, who were contracted through outside firms, owed their roles to Morris. So, they were fiercely loyal to him.

Morris's newly inflated sense of self was visible to all. He often started his day with a round of golf at one of the several Washington-area country clubs where he held memberships. Though these exclusive clubs prohibited members from using their phones on the course, Morris flouted the rules, taking calls and firing off emails between swings. At the office, he sometimes conducted meetings with a 7-iron golf club over his shoulder and an unlit cigar clenched between his teeth—a signature habit of Tommy Boggs's. On many afternoons, he left the office early and walked over to the W. Curtis Draper Tobacconist, a cigar shop located across the street from the White House, to puff expensive stogies during phone calls with fellow lobbyists or political contacts.

In his first year at Roche, Morris tried to land the chairmanship of the DNC's Business Council, a network of lobbyists, lawyers, and insiders charged with soliciting donations for the Democratic Party from corporate lobbyists, business executives, and industry PACs. Though it was a volunteer role, it offered a prestigious title and an opportunity for Morris to boost his standing in Democratic circles. The position was typically filled by a seasoned Washington lobbyist with decades of experience in Democratic politics. To win the post, Morris would have to prove that he could bring in hefty contributions from special interests for the Democratic Party. One day that summer, Morris took a cab to Capitol Hill, walked into the DNC's headquarters, and entered the office of Lindsay Lewis, the fund-raising director for the organization's chairman, Howard Dean. According to Lewis's 2014 book *Political Mercenaries*, Morris extended a fistful of checks, declaring to Lewis that it totaled $75,000 in donations for the party.[5]

"No one else can raise this kind of money," Evan boasted, waving the checks in the air, Lewis recalled. "You have to make me chair."

Lewis had reservations about Morris. Along with other DNC officials, he considered the young lobbyist too arrogant and immature for the role. We're not going to give you the job, Lewis flatly told Morris.

Morris's face turned red. Looking Lewis dead in the eye, he ripped up the campaign checks, tossed the scraps toward the trash can, and stormed out of the building.[6]

Morris's former colleagues noticed that after his promotion, their old friend had begun to change. Roche was still a Patton Boggs client, so Morris continued working regularly with the veteran lobbyists who were once his superiors. Only now, it was Morris—the cocksure twentysomething—giving the orders. While Morris maintained his reverence for Tommy Boggs, his relationship with senior members of the firm's health care team soured. Over time, it seemed, Morris came to believe that his former superiors still considered him the rookie summer associate they'd send off to handle their mundane tasks. To set them straight, Morris slashed Patton Boggs's annual lobbying fee from $1.5 million to $320,000. When he still didn't receive the deference he felt he deserved, Morris fired Patton Boggs and passed its duties along to one of the other K Street shops he had on contract. Morris gleefully boasted to friends about what he'd done to his old firm. "He wanted to be feared," says a friend. "He enjoyed it being known that he was willing to fire Patton Boggs. He wanted to show that he was in charge."

In 2008 Morris was named one of the top forty-five drug industry executives under the age of forty-five by *Pharmaceutical Executive* magazine.[7] As his career took off, he began to enjoy the fruits of his early success. He paid $1.725 million for a 5,800-square-foot home in Belle Haven, Virginia, a few miles outside of Washington. He told people he spent another $1 million on renovations, transforming it into a five-bedroom, seven-bath showpiece. He spared no expense, plowing $10,000 into light fixtures, he told neighbors. He bought a barn in Texas, knocked it down, and used the wood to install a custom three-thousand-bottle wine cellar. He added a walk-in cigar sitting room and a built-in ventilation system. The house had surround sound in every room and an intricate security system, even though the neighborhood had minimal crime. Morris's wife, Tracy, quit her job as a public school teacher to care for the couple's two children. In February 2008 he accompanied Roche's CEO on the firm's corporate jet to Glendale, Arizona, for Super Bowl XLII, where he watched his beloved New York Giants upset the previously undefeated New England Patriots from a luxury box alongside Arizona's governor, Janet Napolitano. He traded in his purple Mazda Miata for a Porsche 911 convertible.

Morris took delight in his sudden prosperity. He told his landscaper that he made more than $500,000 a year, and he liked to show off pictures of his new Porsche. "Roche is going to make me a very rich man," he told a colleague. His fixation on wealth unsettled some of his coworkers. One colleague from Switzerland recalls traveling to Washington to meet with Morris. During their discussions, he spoke about all the money he was making at Roche and what he planned to do with it. When she returned to her office in Switzerland, she pulled aside her boss and made an ominous prediction. "One day," she said, "I am going to open the paper, and there is going to be a huge story about Evan, and it's going to be very embarrassing for Roche."

A few years after his promotion, Morris faced a serious threat to his standing. In 2009, Roche's executives in Switzerland moved to complete plans to acquire a 100 percent stake in the innovative biotechnology firm that Tony Podesta had been working for during his successful campaign to speed up Washington's drug approval process.[8] Genentech was a leader in a cutting-edge class of biologic drugs, which were considered to be the future of the industry. Roche had previously controlled 56 percent of Genentech; now it would own the remaining 44 percent as well.[9] The $47 billion deal[10] made Roche a dominant player in both traditional drugs and biologics, but it also triggered uncomfortable changes within the company. Roche's US pharmaceutical operations would be rebranded under the Genentech name,[11] and its American drug headquarters would move from New Jersey to South San Francisco.[12] More important for Morris, the two companies would have to merge their Washington lobbying teams into a single unit. That raised a big question: Who would run the new, combined Washington office?

While Morris desperately wanted the job, so too did a top lobbyist from the Genentech side. Heidi Wagner was a whip-smart lawyer and former staffer to a pair of Republican congressmen. In an industry ruled by men, she had scrapped her way to the top by using her mastery of the arcane details of health care law and regulation. A group of Roche and Genentech executives was assigned to an informal search committee, which would interview the two candidates and conduct its own research to determine who should lead the Washington office. Initially, Morris and Wagner had agreed not to interfere in the search committee's work. But when Morris suspected that Wagner was maneuvering for the job, he launched a lobbying campaign to win the panel's support. For this effort, Morris enlisted the help of the army of lobbyists and consultants on his payroll, and he deployed tactics similar to those he'd used to shape federal policy.

Since the targets of this campaign were other company executives, as opposed to public officials, Morris was not limited by the anti-bribery rules that applied to lobbying government officials. One way to butter up the selection committee, Morris realized, was to get the executives tickets to the White House Easter Egg Roll. The annual springtime event, hosted by the president and First Lady, brings administration officials and other DC elites to the South Lawn of the White House, where they watch their children play games and get their pictures taken with the president and the

Easter bunny. It's a sought-after gathering; invitations are notoriously hard to obtain. Morris, though, had an inside source: Hunter Biden, the son of Vice President Joe Biden. The younger Biden was an active supporter of a nonprofit called the Artists and Athletes Alliance, which offers a platform for Hollywood stars, musicians, and professional athletes to weigh in on public policy matters. Its advisory board has included TV stars Kelsey Grammer and Jason Alexander, as well as LA Dodgers pitcher Clayton Kershaw.[13] Hunter Biden helped raise money for the organization by lending his name to it and attending several events.[14] In an effort to curry favor with the vice president's son, Morris had directed as much as $50,000 a year from Roche to the nonprofit.

This wasn't purely an act of generosity. Morris parlayed the donations for perks for himself, including a private tour of the White House and a behind-the-scenes visit to the Bureau of Printing and Engraving, where Morris watched as freshly minted bills spun off a massive printing press. When Obama was first inaugurated in 2009, Morris used his donations to score a ticket to a star-studded bash at Café Milano, where he partied alongside Hunter Biden, Jennifer Lopez, Marc Anthony, Tobey Maguire, and Queen Noor of Jordan. In the spring of 2009, as part of his effort to land the top job of Genentech's restructured lobbying office, Morris used the connection to secure a handful of tickets to the White House Easter Egg Roll, which he distributed to members of the search committee. The gifts allowed Morris to garner goodwill with the committee members while also demonstrating his political connections.

As he cozied up to the search committee, Morris was also plotting to sabotage his rival for the job. A consultant on Morris's payroll began digging into Heidi Wagner's past, searching for embarrassing personal or financial information that could be used to discredit her. After he failed to uncover anything salacious, he circulated a false rumor, whispering to DC reporters that he'd unearthed an "incident report" from the Transportation Security Administration involving Wagner. The report, the consultant claimed, documented an episode in which Wagner had lost her cool at an airport checkpoint and threatened a TSA agent. In reality, the report didn't exist, and the incident never took place.

Morris, meanwhile, was working yet another angle. In brainstorming sessions with lobbyists working for him, he realized that he held one key strategic advantage over Wagner. The 2008 election put a Democrat in the White House and expanded the party's majorities in the House and Senate. Yet the lobbying offices of most major drug companies were still run mostly by Republicans. These GOP lobbyists, like Wagner, had been hired to open doors in Washington at a time when President George W. Bush was in the White House and Republicans held majorities in Congress. Morris and his team began promoting the idea that Democratic lobbyists were better suited to advocate for the pharmaceutical industry because they had access to the lawmakers and White House officials then in power. To deliver this message to his company's top executives, Morris used the media. He arranged for friends in the influence business to contact a *Politico* reporter and suggest he write a story about the battle for control of Genentech's Washington office. Morris's allies in congressional offices, meanwhile, provided the writer with anonymous quotes supporting Morris for the top job.

On May 7 *Politico* published the story, headlined: "Will Roche Get a Republican Leader?"[15] It reported that some Democrats on Capitol Hill were "dumbfounded"[16] that Roche would consider installing a Republican as the head of its Washington office. "It'd be a strategic blunder, not only for Roche but for the pharmaceutical industry to continue to pander to Republicans,"[17] one Democratic staffer told *Politico*. It was "absurd, at a time when we have the Congress and the White House, that any company in this town would consider hiring a Republican to head their shop,"[18] said another. The ploy worked. Less than two weeks later, Morris was named the top lobbyist of Genentech's combined Washington office.[19] His title was vice president of government affairs, making him, at age twenty-eight, the second youngest vice president in the company's 120-year history.

For her part, Wagner left the firm.

For Morris, there was little time to rejoice, as he quickly became consumed with the era's defining legislative battle. Though the country remained mired in the Great Recession, Obama in 2009 pressed forward with a sweeping plan to overhaul the nation's health care system. The president's goal was to expand health care coverage to millions of Americans, but his plan also contained a lesser-known element of critical significance to the pharmaceutical industry. In order to bring down health care costs, Obama and Democratic leaders in Congress wanted to cut prescription drug prices. One way to do that, they concluded, was through the federal government's rules for incentivizing the development of biologic drugs.

Though essential to the nation's prosperity, the creation of new drugs is an expensive, tedious process requiring legions of scientists and marked by years of dead ends. The vast majority of new prospective treatments fail before reaching the market. In the 1980s the federal government created an incentive structure to encourage firms to invest the millions of dollars it takes to invent new pharmaceutical drugs. Under the rules, once a pharmaceutical firm wins regulatory approval for a new drug, the government provides it with what is essentially a legal monopoly on the product for five years. During this "exclusivity period," the manufacturer can sell the drug without any competition, allowing it to charge higher prices, pump up profits, and recoup its investment. It is only after this period ends that other companies can begin selling knock-off versions, driving down the drug's price. The rules seek to strike a balance between the need to provide pharmaceutical companies with enough financial incentives to invest in new drugs and the desire to keep prices low for consumers by allowing competitors to sell generic versions of the same drug.

While the exclusivity period of five years was already set for traditional pharmaceutical drugs, no time frame had been determined yet for the more advanced biologic drugs, such as those made by Genentech. Biologics soon became the drug industry's fastest growing sector, producing treatments for everything from anemia to breast cancer. By 2009, the top six prescription drugs that the government distributed to seniors via its Medicare program were all biologics.[20] By requiring biotech companies to share the "ingredients" of individual biotech drugs with generic drug manufacturers after a relatively short exclusivity period, Obama and key Democrats saw a golden opportunity to slash prescription drug costs for all Americans. Obama proposed a seven-year exclusivity period for biologic drugs,[21] which, according to the White House, would save $9 billion in drug costs over a decade by allowing knock-off versions onto the marketplace sooner.[22] On Capitol Hill, the price-cutting effort was led by Congressman Henry Waxman, a liberal Democrat from California who'd been arguing for years that the government should use its power to drive down pharmaceutical costs. Now, as the chairman of the House Committee on Energy and Commerce, where much of the health care bill would be approved, he would finally get his chance. Waxman sought an exclusivity period for biologic drugs that was even shorter than Obama's timetable: five years.[23]

For the biotech industry, Waxman's proposal was a nightmare. Such a short monopoly window would eat into the profits of firms like Genentech. Morris and his fellow drug industry lobbyists sprang into action, launching a furious effort to block the five-year exclusivity period and establish a longer, twelve-year timetable[24] by arguing that the longer period was essential to ensuring the companies had enough incentives to invest in developing new drugs and entice investors. While the pharmaceutical companies had made sure to ply most committee members with generous campaign contributions, the industry's most helpful accomplice was Democratic Representative Anna Eshoo, whose Northern California district bordered on Genentech's headquarters outside of San Francisco. Eshoo, who'd received tens of thousands of dollars in campaign contributions from Genentech over the years, introduced a proposal that called for the twelve-year exclusivity period[25] championed by the biotechnology industry. During a meeting between the two Democratic lawmakers, Eshoo assured Waxman that they'd work together to iron out the differences in their competing proposals. As Waxman recalled in an interview, Eshoo told him, "Don't worry, we'll find a compromise."

The issue came to a head at a committee vote in late July 2009. As the two sides arrived at the hearing room in the Rayburn House Office Building for the critical showdown, Waxman appeared to have the advantage. President Obama had publicly opposed the twelve-year exclusivity period, arguing that the lengthy time frame "means you're keeping important drugs off the market and driving up those costs further."[26] And Democrats, many of whom had promised to cut drug prices on the campaign trail, had majorities in both houses of Congress. But in an unexpected show of political muscle, Genentech and the drug industry—armed with one of the biggest campaign-funding operations in Washington—rallied the bulk of the committee members against Waxman's measure and behind Eshoo's.

As Waxman recognized the direction that the vote was heading in, he pulled Eshoo aside and reminded her about her promise to cut a deal on the measure. "Why should I compromise? I have the votes," Eshoo said, according to Waxman.

To spare himself the embarrassment of losing a vote in his own committee, Waxman shifted gears and attempted to concede. He called for a voice vote—a parliamentary maneuver that doesn't require a precise tally of all votes.[27]

But Eshoo blocked the move, demanding that each lawmaker record his or her vote publicly.[28] The lobbyists wanted to trumpet every detail of their humiliating drubbing of the chairman as an expression of the industry's strength—and as warning to other lawmakers about what happens when you get crossways with the pharmaceutical lobby.

"You've won," Waxman said, hoping to avoid a recorded vote. "Do you want a roll call vote?"

"I would like one," she said,[29] twisting the dagger into Waxman's back.

In the end, forty-seven committee members—including many Democrats—voted in favor of the industry's preferred twelve-year exclusivity period, with just eleven lawmakers voting with Waxman. Morris and his fellow lobbyists hadn't simply crushed the effort to reduce drug prices, they'd turned the chairman into a cautionary tale.

Eshoo, for her part, says she wasn't trying to embarrass the chairman. "I always ask for a vote," she said. "A recorded vote is always determinative—it shows the level of support."

Later that year, when Obama's health care bill was signed into law, Morris and his fellow drug lobbyists would toast the official adoption of their twelve-year exclusion period. It was an extraordinary feat. At a time when Democrats controlled all of Washington and policy makers were fixated on finding ways to lower prescription drug prices, Morris and his allies would manage to extend—by *seven years* over traditional drugs—the monopoly period for the pharmaceuticals of tomorrow. While Obama would succeed in expanding health care access to millions of Americans, the forty-fourth president—like many before him—would fail to arrest the rising prices of prescription drugs. Waxman would later come to view the biologics episode as one of the worst defeats of his forty-year career. Around the time that the committee voted to adopt the twelve-year exclusion period, he had told reporters that "by passing this amendment, we're not only missing a historic opportunity to bend the cost curve, we're guaranteeing higher drug costs for the foreseeable future."[30]

Eshoo went on to win the Legislator of the Year award from the Biotechnology Industry Organization.[31]

Morris's victory on the exclusivity issue, however, was overshadowed quickly by an embarrassment of his own making. In the fall of 2009, as the health care bill moved to the full House of Representatives, where it would pass on a mostly party-line vote, Morris wanted to make sure the twelve-year exclusivity would remain in the legislation. The Senate still needed to take up its own version of the bill, and, even after it was signed into law, the health care overhaul would face years of legal challenges. So, in the days before the final House vote, he engineered an effort to get as many lawmakers as possible to issue public statements supporting the Genentech-backed provisions. Morris ordered his lobbying team to draw up remarks and talking points—one version for Republicans; a different version for Democrats—and distribute them to congressional offices.[32] The Genentech lobbyists then asked their friends in Congress to go to the floor of the US House and ask the clerk to enter at least portions of these statements into the official written account of the day's proceedings, called the *Congressional Record*, under their own names. The goal was to make it appear as though these specific provisions enjoyed broad bipartisan support, even though the health care law as a whole was divisive.

All told, forty-two members of the House[33]—some of whom had received campaign contributions from Genentech—made use of its talking points, including by putting the remarks written by Morris's lobbyists into the *Congressional Record* as if the words were their own. The result was a compilation of nearly identical public statements:

Blaine Luetkemeyer, a Republican congressman from Missouri: "One of the reasons I have long supported the US biotechnology industry is that it is a homegrown success story that has been an engine of job creation in this country. Unfortunately, many of the largest companies that would seek to enter the biotechnology market have made their money by outsourcing their research to foreign countries like India."[34]

Joe Wilson, a Republican congressman from South Carolina: "One of the reasons I have long supported the US biotechnology industry is that it is a homegrown success story that has been an engine of job creation in this country. Unfortunately, many of the largest companies that would seek to enter the biotechnology market have made their money by outsourcing their research to foreign countries like India."[35]

Yvette Clarke, a Democratic congresswoman from New York: "I see this bill as an exciting opportunity to create the kind of jobs we so desperately need in this country, while at the same time improving the lives of all Americans."[36]

Donald Payne, a Democratic congressman from New Jersey: "I see this bill as an exciting opportunity to create the kind of jobs we so desperately need in this country, while at the same time improving the lives of *all* Americans."[37]

It was a masterstroke of corporate influence peddling—until, suddenly, it blew up in Morris's face. In November 2009, not long before the full House passed the health care bill, a *New York Times*[38] reporter published an article exposing Genentech's lobbying team as the hidden hand behind the industry-friendly statements issued by more than three dozen members of Congress. In the story, titled "In House, Many Spoke with One Voice: Lobbyists," journalist Robert Pear reported: "It is unusual for so many revisions and extensions to match up word for word. It is even more unusual to find clear evidence that the statements originated with lobbyists."[39] Noting the involvement of twenty Democrats and twenty-two Republicans, the reporter described Morris's effort as "an unusual bipartisan coup for lobbyists."[40] After being contacted for comment by the reporter, one lawmaker, Bill Pascrell of New Jersey, expressed his "regret that the language was the same."[41] For his part, Morris made some of his only on-the-record remarks to the press during his years with Genentech, telling the *Times* that there "was no connection between the contributions and the statements."[42]

Though corporate lobbyists regularly try to persuade lawmakers to regurgitate their propaganda, those efforts don't typically achieve such widespread success, and they're nearly always kept hidden from public view. As a result, the *New York Times*'s revelations triggered a crisis for Morris. He was inundated with angry phone calls from members of Congress and their aides. His boss, George Abercrombie, was seething. As the pressure intensified, Morris became obsessed with figuring out how the media had uncovered his ploy. Initially, he fumed at his outside consultants for being so careless. Later, he grew convinced that someone from his own office had leaked the story to the *Times* in order to undermine him. Just a few years after he'd dazzled his superiors with his Tamiflu feat, the aggressive young lobbyist was imploding. Paranoid, angry, and embarrassed, Morris began to worry about losing his job. He grew desperate to find a way to redeem himself with his company's top executives before it was too late.

12

While things were falling apart for Morris, another Washington insider was on his way up. By the early years of the Obama era, Jim Courtovich had established himself as the beloved host of the cocktail party circuit. Twice a year, he opened his $2 million town house in DC's tony Kalorama neighborhood, not far from Tony and Heather Podesta's home, for his famous "Gaucho" parties.[1] In keeping with the theme of the events, which he named after the unruly horsemen of the pampas,[2] Courtovich stocked his kitchen with wine from Spain and beef from Argentina. He dressed the wait staff in custom-made aprons, and stationed valets in front of his house. The buffet table was arranged with great care; on one occasion it was decorated with candles and roses, and over the course of the evenings, he laid out indulgent spreads of cuisines, including Weisswurst with stone-ground mustard and cabbage, pecan-crusted lamb chops, beef tenderloin, lobster mac and cheese, and, for dessert, frozen custard sandwiches and salted caramel oatmeal cookies, according to a writeup in *Politico*'s Playbook.

These parties—which the *Washington Post* declared were "legendary"[3]—attracted red-carpet crowds of political and media celebrities. One might bump into senior Obama administration officials, including White House

Chief of Staff Rahm Emanuel[4] or onetime White House Chief Strategist David Axelrod.[5] Top advisors to Joe Biden, then the vice president, were mingling with the crowd. There were also leading Republican figures, such as superlawyer Ben Ginsberg[6] and former President George W. Bush administration spokesman Gordon Johndroe.[7] At every turn, guests spotted prominent journalists, like NBC's *Today* show host Savannah Guthrie,[8] CBS's *Face the Nation* host Bob Schieffer,[9] or Jeff Zeleny,[10] the *New York Times* political reporter and future chief national correspondent for CNN, who also happened to be Courtovich's live-in partner.

"Gotta be a Jim Courtovich party," *Politico* once wrote, "one of the few Washington occasions that brings together so many Ds and Rs, along with press corps galore."[11]

Courtovich said the Gaucho party tradition began one Sunday in the 2000s, when he met the ambassador of Argentina for brunch in Georgetown, and he ended up bringing a good portion of the consular office back to his house for a barbecue. Courtovich invited other friends and, before long, some seventy-five people were crammed into his property. Within a few years, the guest list would swell to more than four hundred. "It's all about how many people you can invite without turning the backyard into Grand Central Station," Courtovich once said.[12]

Courtovich told guests that hosting the Gaucho parties and other social gatherings cost him hundreds of thousands of dollars a year. While other Beltway operators went to great lengths to keep their social lives quiet, Courtovich trumpeted his extravagant events, promoting them on Twitter, Facebook, and Instagram, and welcoming gossip columnists, who namechecked his attendees in their party coverage. In many ways, Courtovich himself was the parties' main attraction. Then in his midforties, he was tall and trim, with a gray, receding hairline that he kept closely cropped. He wore custom-fitted suits from his tailor in London—cuff links, pocket squares—and $2,000 shoes. As a host he was charming and courteous: a bon vivant, a connoisseur of fine food and drink, and a master at small talk, sharing stories about his Middle East travels, checking on the needs of party guests.[13] He was anointed by *Politico* as one of Washington's "scenemakers,"[14] and *Washington Life* magazine named him one of twelve "Uber

Connectors" in DC.[15] As these Gaucho parties developed into a ritual of elite-Washington life, Courtovich adopted a symbol for the event: a bull. Guests might find an ice sculpture of a bull[16] at the entrance to his house, or a bull made out of wire on the bar.[17] Images of bulls were printed onto cocktail napkins[18] and featured on the flag hanging from the front of his house.[19] For one spring barbecue, Courtovich commissioned a sculpture that seemed to encapsulate his standing in Washington: a nine-foot-tall bull, made out of topiary trees, with large testicles.[20]

As he cracked jokes with network TV anchors and served pork shoulder to Obama and Biden aides, Courtovich took the form of a distinctly Washington archetype: the self-assured insider who uses charm, intellect, and powerful friends to effortlessly navigate the city's political, media, and corporate establishments—and have a good time along the way. Still, there was always an air of mystery about Courtovich. While he seemed to know everyone who was worth knowing in Washington, his own biography and business interests were harder to determine. His houseful of guests knew him as a high-end media strategist who worked to get favorable press for blue-chip corporations and foreign governments. Yet it was not always clear who he worked for or what he did in return for the fees that could reach up to $150,000 a month. A profile of Courtovich on the website Racked said he "could be accurately dubbed a real-life Olivia Pope," the political fixer and star of the ABC television show Scandal. "Although his company's policy is to keep clients' identity a secret," the article reported, "Courtovich confirms he represents many in the fashion, retail, pharmaceuticals, finance, defense, and telecommunication industry."[21]

Courtovich was a new kind of influence peddler, whose buzzy social events provided a unique advantage in the post-Abramoff era. While lobbyists were no longer permitted to pay for the steak dinners, golf outings, and baseball games that they'd once relied upon to build personal relationships with public officials, Courtovich could continue to butter up the congressional aides, lawmakers, and White House staffers who turned out for his Gaucho parties. That's because Courtovich's gatherings were considered "widely attended events" and therefore exempted from the post-Abramoff reforms. What's more, instead of seeking favors directly from

Congress and the administration, Courtovich usually sought to influence policy through the Washington press corps—one component of a practice that came to be known as "shadow lobbying."

Even less was understood about his life prior to arriving in the capital city, before he emerged as the man who topped off the drinks of the country's most powerful decision-makers. He told his party guests that he grew up in an old moneyed family outside of Boston, where his father was a wealthy businessman. To some, Courtovich was a Washington version of Jay Gatsby, the inscrutable young millionaire from F. Scott Fitzgerald's classic novel who threw lavish parties for hundreds of guests without revealing much about himself. "He is Jim Gatsby," says one longtime acquaintance. "Nobody knows where he came from."

It was this dapper, smooth-talking insider whom Evan Morris turned to for help when the *New York Times* exposé threatened his professional ascent.

Morris had first met Courtovich years earlier, shortly after taking his job at Roche. At the time, Morris was looking for a way to improve the company's reputation in Washington, which had been sullied by the vitamin price-fixing scandal and the suicide of Congressman Bart Stupak's son. Morris worried that Roche's poor standing with lawmakers and the Bush administration would make it more difficult for him to advance the drug manufacturer's political interests. Most pressing, Morris needed to make sure the Bush administration had the confidence that Roche was up to the task of producing the millions of Tamiflu pills it had ordered. For assistance with his brand-polishing project, Morris reached out to several consulting firms around the city, and he eventually came upon a charismatic image maker at a top political-advertising company who was trying to make a name for himself in an emerging corner of the influence business.

By then, Courtovich was already a veteran political operative. He began his career in politics some five hundred miles north of the capital city, in his home state of New Hampshire. During the late 1980s, Courtovich landed a job in the state office of a Republican congressman from New Hampshire, Bob Smith. From the start, Courtovich exuded a sense of aristocratic refinement. He explained to colleagues that his businessman father had made generous donations to GOP candidates throughout the state, according to people who once worked with him. He spoke wistfully about the family vacations he'd taken as a child, and he intimated that he was old friends with a number of celebrated politicians and business executives. A former colleague recalls Courtovich asking to be dropped off after work in front of a stately mansion with elegant marble columns. Later, when Congressman Smith launched a campaign for Senate, he put Courtovich in charge of the fund-raising efforts. Courtovich spent his days calling affluent supporters and organizing events for high-end donors. His colleagues remarked on how well he seemed to fit in with the country-club set.

As a boy in the beach town of Hampton, New Hampshire, Courtovich learned the importance of outward appearances. He lived in a simple, three-bedroom, two-and-a-half-bath house a few hundred yards from a public campground that filled with beachgoers each summer. Neighbors parked their boats on their front lawns during the winter. Though Courtovich was raised in a modest home, his father, George Courtovich, was fanatical about its appearance. He kept the lawn tight and the shrubs trimmed. "The house was meticulous," recalled one neighbor. "Everything was neat; everything was just the way it was supposed to be." On fall weekends, George would climb onto the top of his house with a leaf blower to clean the roof. After returning from work, he regularly scrubbed the driveway with a long-handled sweeping brush before hosing it down with water. Once, when a horse belonging to another home owner got loose and left hoof prints on his driveway, George stormed over to the neighbor's home and exploded at him. He then returned to his house to scrub and reseal the driveway, stewing the whole time. "He was a freak about the house and a freak about the driveway," one neighbor said.

Over time, people on the block came to fear George's temper and did whatever they could to avoid setting him off. "George Courtovich was always a very angry man, always," said a neighbor. "I think he was angry about life."

George was the son of a Greek immigrant who'd worked for General

Electric in Boston and liked to host lavish meals for his extended family. George's only sibling, Dr. Claire Van Ummersen, was a family success story. She distinguished herself in the intensely competitive field of academia, serving as the chancellor of the University System of New Hampshire, a regent for the Department of Higher Education in Massachusetts, and as president of Cleveland State University. George never achieved such acclaim. He co-owned a small factory that produced graphite casings for nuclear submarines. It was an unglamorous career that nonetheless provided a secure—if not quite bountiful—life for his wife and two children. "They grew up middle class," Van Ummersen said in an interview before she died.[22] "No one ever talked about taking off on a couple-of-week cruise. They didn't have the funding to do that kind of thing."

To the neighbors, Courtovich's childhood seemed to lack an element of parental tenderness. On weekends, according to one nearby resident, Courtovich and his brother were sent outside for hours. The boys were raised "in a home that we wouldn't necessarily want to have," said one neighbor. "It was not wonderful."

By junior high school, Courtovich, then known as Jimmy, was attracting attention from bullies. Unlike his popular and athletic older brother, Courtovich didn't play sports, serving instead as the equipment manager for the soccer team. He was taunted, picked on, and beaten up. At school, he was called by a derisive nickname, "Courto-bitch." One afternoon, a neighborhood boy chased Courtovich from the bus stop and pushed him over a wall, according to the boy. The next morning, the boy's father stopped by the Courtovich home to apologize for his son's behavior. George Courtovich, who was in the middle of shaving at the time, screamed at the boy's father so violently that shaving cream splashed onto the front door.

Courtovich's mistreatment continued at Winnacunnet High School, a large public school that mixed well-to-do students from gated communities located closer to Portsmouth, New Hampshire, with blue-collar teens whose parents worked at the nearby nuclear power plant. Courtovich existed between those two worlds; he was neither raised at the country club nor enrolled in the school's vocational programs. But according to a former classmate, Courtovich's name-brand attire—Lacoste shirts, Nike sneakers—expressed a measure of financial comfort that stoked resentment among his more hardscrabble peers. "Because Jim wears an alligator shirt to high school and my family can't afford a Lacoste shirt, then they must be rich," the classmate explained. "It was unfortunate, but his family was targeted for being a little bit better off than the average resident."

Courtovich's home was vandalized; rotten eggs were splattered against his house, toilet paper was unspooled into the trees. The mischief occurred so frequently that Courtovich's brother, George, resolved to try putting a stop to it. One evening, George stayed up late to keep watch. When he spotted a group of boys approaching the house, George—who was older and bigger than his brother—jumped out to confront them.

"What are you doing here?" he demanded.

Frightened and embarrassed, the boys admitted they'd come to vandalize the house. But they pleaded with George not to call the police. "We know Jimmy," one of them explained.

George marched the boys to the front porch and went inside the house to wake up his younger brother. When a groggy Courtovich emerged, he confirmed to his sibling that the would-be vandals were indeed his classmates. "I always kind of felt sorry for the way his family was treated," said one of the mischief makers who was turned away that night.

Courtovich denies being the victim of bullying. In a text message, he claimed that because his father's company was a major regional employer, "No one would fuck with me."

Courtovich blossomed into a charming and intelligent teenager. "He seemed much more interested in flirting with girls in class and buttering up teachers," said a classmate. "My mother loved Jim," recalled another. While he worked as the student manager for his high school's sports team, it was his fascination with national politics that distinguished him from other students. Each Election Day, Courtovich would arrive at school wearing a campaign-style straw hat. "A lot of kids I don't remember," said Bob Devantery, who taught Courtovich's government class, "but I definitely remember Jim because he was interested in politics."

Like his father, Courtovich cared deeply about appearances. Despite his family's middle-of-the-road station, he presented himself as the descendant of privilege. During his senior year, he was voted the "Preppi-est" student by his classmates, according to a copy of Winnacunnet High School's 1983 yearbook.

When it came time for college, Courtovich enrolled at the University of New Hampshire, the crown jewel of the state's public school system. But after only a few months, he dropped out and transferred to Plymouth State College, a small public college that, during his senior year, ranked eighth on *Playboy* magazine's list of party schools.[23] Arriving on campus, Courtovich joined a fraternity, developed a reputation as a gregarious attention seeker, and took his first steps toward a career in politics. He attended meetings of the College Republicans, served as president of the student body, and worked as the campus coordinator for the 1986 reelection campaign of New Hampshire Senator Warren Rudman, a moderate Republican. Upon graduation, Courtovich worked for Bob Dole's 1988 presidential campaign in New Hampshire, before landing a job with Congressman Bob Smith.

After Smith won election to the Senate in 1990, Courtovich moved to DC to join his Capitol Hill staff, where his upscale tastes set him apart from the other up-and-coming politicos. He was impeccably dressed in crisp shirts, suits, and polished shoes. "He was already projecting a sense of refinement," said a fellow congressional aide who knew Courtovich when he first arrived in Washington. "He never set foot outside the door without everything being just right." He preferred expensive restaurants, and he knew how to read a wine menu. Outgoing and charismatic, he quickly developed a large circle of friends in politics and media—and he always seemed to be the most interesting person in the room. "He is a public relations guy, and his number one client is him," one friend recalled. Courtovich began hosting dinner parties for friends and political contacts at his apartment. "The people who attended his parties were people who he had collected along the way," recalled one dinner guest. "For Jim, being able to have a party and have a lot of people show up who are influential is a really big deal." To his male friends, he boasted eagerly of his sexual exploits. When he brought a date back to his group home, he hung her bra on the outside of his door to display his conquest.

While building out his social network, Courtovich was drawn to the trappings of status and power. In 1992 he went to work in New Hampshire for Steve Merrill, a Republican who was running for governor. At one point during the campaign, Courtovich was dispatched to the office of New Hampshire's sitting Republican governor, Judd Gregg. While there, Courtovich pulled aside one of Gregg's young aides and tried to convince him to join the Merrill campaign.

"How much money do you make?" Courtovich asked.

The young aide replied that he was an unpaid volunteer.

Courtovich reached into his jacket, pulled out a bulky cell phone, and brandished the novel device for the young aide. "If you come to work on the governor's race," Courtovich said, "I will get you a cell phone."

Years later, the young political aide still recalled the incident vividly. Courtovich "had a chip on his shoulder from growing up," he recalled. "I think he was embarrassed by that because he wanted to be part of the elite money crowd."

Around this time, Courtovich's supervisors were growing frustrated with him. He was increasingly distracted and unreliable and, according to John Stabile, the manager of the Merrill campaign, he began disappearing from work for days at a time. The complaints came to a head during a campaign appearance at a Fourth of July parade in the small town of Hollis, New Hampshire. Courtovich had been assigned to drive Merrill in the backseat of a 1935 Ford convertible while the candidate waved at voters along the parade route. But according to Stabile, Courtovich failed to properly handle the vehicle's maintenance, so that after only a few blocks along the parade route, steam began rising from under the hood. The vehicle sputtered and stalled out. Amid the gasps and snickers from the crowd, Courtovich and the humiliated candidate were forced to get out and push the overheated convertible to the side of the road.

The campaign manager was furious. "We looked like rookies," Stabile recalled.

Courtovich was promptly fired. "I was already sick of him anyway," Stabile said. The dismissal touched off a difficult stretch for the ambitious young operative. When Merrill won the race and moved into the governor's mansion, he didn't offer Courtovich a position in his adminis-tration. Courtovich enrolled in graduate school at the University of New Hampshire, only to drop out a short while later. At about that time, Cour-tovich appeared on a nationally syndicated daytime TV program, *The Jenny Jones Show*. It was an episode in which several mothers selected dates for their daughters, and Courtovich appeared as an eligible bachelor. After the show was recorded, the young men and women who appeared in the episode went out for dinner and drinks together. According to one of the women who attended the outing, Courtovich drank so much alcohol that he passed out at the dinner table and had to be sent back to the hotel in a cab, while the rest of the group carried on partying.

In May 1995 Courtovich's life was rocked by tragedy, when his only brother, George, died unexpectedly.[24] George, thirty-three, was married with a young daughter. At the time of his passing, he still lived in New Hampshire, a few miles from where the Courtovich boys had grown up. The circumstances of George's death are unclear. Courtovich told col-leagues that his brother had suffered a heart attack after returning home from playing tennis, drinking a few beers, and taking some painkillers for his injured knee. The family's neighbors in Hampton offered other expla-nations. Some said George committed suicide, while others believed he died of a drug overdose.

During the funeral service at St. Michael Church in Exeter, New Hampshire, Courtovich delivered a moving tribute to his big brother—the man who'd stood up for him against the neighborhood bullies. "Today we have come to say good-bye to my brother, my best friend. . . . George, we love you." Courtovich, who by then had returned to Washington as a Sen-ate aide, had the eulogy inserted into the *Congressional Record*.

That summer, Courtovich's career got a boost when he joined the presidential campaign of Phil Gramm, the Republican senator from Texas. In many ways, the effort was doomed from the start. President Bill Clin-ton was running for reelection in 1996, and popular incumbent presidents rarely lose. Even within the Republican Party, Gramm—a conservative insurgent—was considered a long shot to defeat GOP front-runner Bob Dole, who was then the Senate majority leader. Still, the campaign offered the twenty-nine-year-old Courtovich a chance to learn from some of the party's top strategic minds. Jim's new boss was none other than Charlie Black. As Phil Gramm's chief campaign strategist, Black understood that the senator faced an unlikely path to victory, and so he implemented a Hail Mary strategy: raise as much money as possible; use the cash to bombard the country's first primary state, New Hampshire, with pro-Gramm television advertisements; and—hopefully—generate enough attention to establish Gramm as the conservative alternative to Bob Dole. Black hired Courtovich to manage Gramm's campaign in New Hampshire.

The first elements of the plan came together just as Black had hoped. By January 1996, the official start of the presidential primary season, Gramm had raised roughly $20 million, matching the Republican front-runner. It was a staggering sum at the time—six times what Bill Clinton had raised at the same point four years earlier. "Thanks to you," Gramm told donors at a Dallas fund-raising dinner, "I have the most reliable friend you can have in American politics—and that's ready money."[25] Black plowed a good deal of the cash into a massive television advertising campaign[26] designed to boost Gramm's popularity in New Hampshire.

For that job, Black turned to the political advertising business that had split off from Black Manafort years earlier. By 1996, that firm, National Media Inc., was being run partly by his colleague, Alex Castellanos. Much of Gramm's fund-raising haul passed through National Media and Castellanos, who purchased the airtime for Gramm's TV spots and, in exchange, took a 10 percent to 15 percent cut of all advertising spending. Media buying, as the business is known, is an obscure but highly lucrative offshoot of the political consulting industry. The arrangement ensured that each ad that Castellanos aired for the campaign put money into his own pocket. Castellanos continued to saturate New Hampshire with television advertisements, even though it became evident that the approach might actually be hurting Gramm's chances. According to an internal memorandum that was obtained by the *New York Times*, the New Hampshire voters who watched a sample campaign ad weren't all that impressed with Gramm. "Thank God for the mute button," one voter remarked.[27]

While the Gramm campaign struggled to gain traction, Courtovich emerged as a memorable press agent. In a state of "parkas and boots," as one journalist put it, Courtovich operated in a "crisp white dress shirt buttoned at the cuffs."[28] More importantly, he was always ready with a witty quote. When word leaked that Pat Buchanan, one of Gramm's rivals for the conservative vote, was considering naming a Democrat as his running mate, Courtovich told a reporter: "The USS *Contradiction* is about to run aground."[29] He also worked to discredit Steve Forbes, the multimillionaire publishing mogul who was running for the GOP nomination, by labeling him an out-of-touch elitist. Courtovich once said of the Forbes campaign: "Grassroots for them is a good golf course."[30] In remarks to the *Washington Post*, Courtovich went even further, declaring that "the toughest challenge Steve Forbes ever had to face was when he was a sperm swimming upstream to the egg."[31]

Courtovich's skills as a spinmeister even earned him a cameo in *Losers: The Road to Everyplace but the White House*, Michael Lewis's book about the 1996 presidential campaign. "Like most of the professional political people who landed jobs with the heavily financed candidates," Lewis observed, "Courtovich is consumed by strategy. Whatever beliefs or principles or character traits distinguish his boss from his rivals mean far less to him than the trick of winning. Strategy is the soul of modern politics."[32] In the end, the campaign flopped. Gramm finished a distant fifth in the Iowa caucuses, and a few days before the polls opened in New Hampshire, he dropped out of the race. Nevertheless, the experience of the Gramm campaign—with its massive fund-raising operation and free-spending media strategy—proved to be a turning point for Courtovich. Gramm's campaign sent roughly a hundred times more money to his television-advertising firm, National Media, than it paid Courtovich for his work, according to FEC reports. Returning to Washington, he followed Black and Castellanos into the lucrative world of corporate consulting.

Courtovich took a job with Black as a corporate consultant at Burson-Marsteller, the public relations conglomerate whose parent company had purchased Black, Manafort & Stone. Then, a few years later, Jim was hired to work with Alex Castellanos at National Media. When it first formed, the firm had focused on creating and placing advertisements for political campaigns. But by the mid-1990s, it had branched into the increasingly profitable business of issue advocacy, or producing advertisements on behalf of corporate interests that were used to influence voters' opinions on specific policy matters. National Media built a large business by creating these television and radio advertisements for Washington trade groups and Fortune 500 companies. "The bottom line is that members of the business community have to define themselves—before others do," Courtovich said in a National Media pitch to potential clients.

It was on account of this expertise that Morris approached Courtovich and National Media for help overhauling Roche's image in Washington. In 2005 the two men reached an agreement. In exchange for a $25,000 fee, Courtovich began a rebranding campaign for Roche, developing advertisements designed to project an image of strength and dependability for the 109-year-old company. Courtovich aired radio spots on DC stations and placed print ads in Capitol Hill newspapers, targeting directly the members of Congress and agency officials who had authority over Roche and its pharmaceutical products.

It was the first business deal in what would become a decade-long partnership between the young drug lobbyist and the suave media strategist. Over the next ten years, Morris would pay tens of millions of dollars in fees to Courtovich and the firms where he worked for his help in executing Morris's agenda in Washington. Along the way, the two men would discover a shared interest in rare wines, a preference for exclusive restaurants, and, above all, a ferocious desire to get rich in the nation's capital. In a sense, the team of Morris and Courtovich represented a union of two great houses of Washington lobbying. Morris came from the Tommy Boggs dynasty, while Courtovich, through his work with Charlie Black, was a descendant of the Black, Manafort & Stone bloodline. But while Tommy Boggs and Black Manafort had defined earlier Washington epochs, this new partnership was uniquely suited for the modern influence industry. As they climbed the ranks of the K Street elite, Morris and Courtovich plied cutting-edge tactics, pressed the interests of one of the era's most powerful drug conglomerates, and encountered all the temptations that accompany success in the modern influence business in Washington—where hundreds of millions of dollars flow to consultants, media strategists, and other political insiders with minimal disclosure to the public, the government, and even the companies paying the bills.

In 2010, while Morris was still reeling from the *New York Times* exposé, he saw his chance to get back on top. It would involve turning a crisis into an opportunity.

The trouble was that one of Genentech's most profitable products had come under threat from FDA regulators. Avastin is a biologic medicine that, when used in combination with chemotherapy, had been used successfully to treat an array of cancers, including tumors found in the lungs, kidney, cervix, colon, and ovaries. It was also extraordinarily expensive: a full course ran up to $90,000 per patient depending on the type of cancer—a price tag that helped generate $6 billion in revenue for Genentech and Roche worldwide in 2009. Genentech came to believe that Avastin should be marketed to treat an additional disease: breast cancer. Though there were already many drugs on the market to treat breast cancer, an initial drug trial showed that adding Avastin to chemotherapy extended the time patients lived without their cancer getting worse by nearly six months. As a result, in 2008 Genentech was able to take advantage of an accelerated FDA approval process allowing urgently needed drugs to be approved temporarily while the manufacturer completed the additional studies needed for full approval. This accelerated approval pathway, which enabled Genentech to market Avastin as a breast cancer treatment for the time being, had become law in 1997 with the help of Democratic power broker and Genentech lobbyist Tony Podesta. However, when additional drug trials found that Avastin stopped breast cancer from advancing by only two or three months—not six—regulators concluded that there was not enough evidence to demonstrate that its benefits outweighed its risks, which included heart attack, high blood pressure, and bleeding. The FDA moved to rescind its approval of the drug for breast cancer treatment, a decision that could have cost Genentech as much as $1 billion a year in lost sales.

For Morris, the administration's actions represented an opportunity to regain the favor of Roche's top executives. He had little chance of persuading the regulators to reverse course, since the scientific debate was apparently settled. But anything he could do to delay the agency's decision could be worth hundreds of millions of dollars for Genentech, because the company could keep marketing the drug while the FDA deliberated. Morris drew up a plan to throw sand in the gears of the drug safety agency. After having been humiliated in the public fallout from his efforts regarding Obama's health care proposal, Morris was determined to keep his work a secret this time. So, he teamed up with Courtovich, and together they carried out the kind of covert campaign that he'd used in his Tamiflu score.

A centerpiece of the strategy was to turn cancer patients and doctors into the public faces of Genentech's effort to protect its profits. Cancer sufferers and medical professionals are far more sympathetic than multinational drug conglomerates or Washington influence peddlers. And the personal testimonies of those impacted by the disease would go a long way toward pressuring the FDA. To that end, Courtovich formed a credible-sounding advocacy group, the Patient Care Action Network, to build a database of breast cancer patients, doctors, and nurses who'd had positive experiences with Avastin. Courtovich launched a Patient Care Action Network website, started an online petition, and established a toll-free number to help recruit supporters. When callers dialed the number, they were patched through to a "call center" where "operators" told them how they could write letters in support of Avastin to the FDA's commissioners; the operators even provided the callers with prewritten letters and the commissioners' addresses. In addition, the operators helped callers identify their representatives in Washington, and they encouraged them to call or write to their members of Congress and share their favorable experiences with Avastin. In reality, the call center was a bank of phones that Courtovich had installed in his DC office, and the operators were the Washington lobbyists and consultants hired by Genentech. Courtovich and Morris told their staffs to scrap their weekend plans in order to man the phones.

Through his online petition, Courtovich succeeded in gathering the names of some 3,500 cancer patients and medical professionals. He and his staff then began contacting respondents individually in order to collect their firsthand accounts of how Avastin had helped.

292 | The Wolves of K Street

A breast cancer survivor: "I wouldn't be able to sign this petition if it
     wasn't for the success of Avastin. . . . If it ain't broke, don't fix it!"
An oncology nurse: "*Please* don't remove a drug from the market that
     has provided great benefit to our patients."
Another cancer survivor: "Please, please do not take this option away
     from women. . . . We have so few options. A woman should have a
     right to choose if Avastin works. . . . How horrid to take it away!"

To determine if their efforts were working, Morris and Courtovich
turned to one of the city's leading public opinion research firms, Target-
Point Consulting, to conduct focus groups with congressional staff and
opinion leaders in DC. The results showed there was little awareness
inside the Beltway of either Avastin or the FDA's actions regarding the
drug. So, Morris and Courtovich set themselves to crafting a compelling message for their campaign, something that could break through the
noise in Washington. They found inspiration in a recent legislative battle.
One year earlier, conservative activists had worked to discredit President
Obama's health care reform by claiming that the law would create "death
panels"[33] of government bureaucrats who were empowered to determine
which Americans would receive medical treatment and which ones would
not. Though no such body was ever envisioned, the hysterical warnings
about death panels from right-wing rabble-rousers, such as former Alaska
governor Sarah Palin,[34] succeeded in galvanizing Republican opposition
to the bill. In this disingenuous political attack on an effort to provide
health care to millions of Americans, Courtovich and Morris discovered
their rallying cry.

In internal documents that outlined their messaging plan, Courtovich
framed the FDA's efforts to ensure that Avastin was a safe and effective
breast cancer treatment as a "first step toward death panels." He and other
Genentech consultants peddled the Avastin-death-panel story to right-
wing media outlets, and, before long, the issue exploded as the smoking
gun that conservative activists had been seeking. "Your first death panel is
here,"[35] Glenn Beck, the right-wing media provocateur, told his Fox News
audience regarding the FDA's review of Avastin. To stress the urgency of

the issue, Courtovich also connected conservative media outlets with the breast cancer survivors whom he'd identified through his Patient Care Action Network. Some of the women were quoted in articles about the FDA's impending decision. Other breast cancer survivors recorded their own videos touting Avastin's effectiveness, which they posted on YouTube.

In one such video, a thirty-eight-year-old single mother from Mississippi and her son told a heartwarming story of her health battle, crediting Avastin with helping her overcome stage 4 breast cancer. Morris paid YouTube to promote this video and others like it in order to bring more public attention to the effort. As the death-panel message gathered steam in the conservative media, Morris worked to secure allies on Capitol Hill.

One lawmaker seemed particularly primed for recruitment. David Vitter, a Republican senator from Louisiana who was then running for reelection, had only recently emerged from a star turn in the tabloids. Three years earlier, Senator Vitter's phone number was found in the records of Deborah Jeane Palfrey, the so-called DC Madam who was later accused of running a high-end escort service in Washington[36] and convicted of crimes related to the business. After *Hustler*, the pornographic magazine, discovered the senator's link to the prostitution ring,[37] Vitter, a self-proclaimed religious conservative, acknowledged that he'd committed a "sin."[38] Later, at a press conference, he stood next to his wife and apologized for his behavior.[39] The scandal had served to align Vitter's interests with Morris's. By fighting for breast cancer patients in their struggle against the FDA's supposed death panels, Vitter had an opportunity to regain the trust of women voters in his state.

After Morris landed a meeting at Vitter's office, the senator became Avastin's leading champion on Capitol Hill. He wrote to the FDA and demanded meetings with top agency officials so that he could urge them to keep Avastin on the market as a breast cancer treatment. In his public remarks on the issue, he made dark allusions to death panels. "I shudder at the thought of a government panel assigning a value to a day of a person's life," Vitter said in a news release in the summer of 2010. "It is sickening to think that care would be withheld from a patient simply because their life is not deemed valuable enough. I fear this is the beginning of a slippery slope leading to more and more rationing under the government takeover of health care that is being forced on the American people."[40]

Morris's Democratic allies pitched in as well. He was a longtime financial backer of Representative Debbie Wasserman Schultz, a high-ranking Democrat who'd once been treated for breast cancer. During his Avastin effort, Morris directed Genentech's PAC to make a $5,000 contribution—the most allowed by law per election—to the Florida congresswoman's political account. A few months later, Wasserman Schultz announced that she supported the continued use of Avastin as a breast cancer treatment. "As a breast cancer survivor," she said in a press release, "I know how important it is that women have every possible cancer-fighting tool at their disposal."

Together, Morris and Courtovich had managed to transform the profit-seeking instincts of a gigantic drug conglomerate into an emotional debate over life and death—a dispute that involved breast cancer sufferers, claims of death panels, and public appeals from lawmakers in both political parties and in both houses of Congress. It was just the kind of political mess that FDA officials, who pride themselves on making decisions based on scientific evidence alone, seek to avoid. The FDA's initial move against Avastin came in July 2010, when an independent panel of medical experts voted 12–1 to recommend stripping the drug of its approval to treat breast cancer.[41] But in the face of an outcry from patients and pressure from Congress—much of which had been ginned up by Morris and Courtovich—the agency continued to deliberate the issue for more than a year. When the FDA held a two-day hearing on the matter in the summer of 2011, Morris and his allies quietly helped stage a demonstration of Avastin users right outside of its headquarters. Among the participants was Terry Kalley, whose wife was using Avastin in her fight against cancer. "What right does the FDA have to make a decision that should be left to a woman and her doctor?" the resident of Troy, Michigan, said from the microphone. "What will they take away next?"[42]

Morris's secret effort helped delay the final FDA decision until November 2011, when the agency finally revoked Avastin's approval as a breast cancer treatment. It had been nearly a year and a half since the FDA took its first steps on the matter. During this lengthy delay, countless breast cancer patients had been charged up to $90,000 for a year's worth of treatments in the false hope that it might aid their chemotherapy treatments and extend their lives more significantly. But while the drug did little for breast cancer sufferers, the "black ops" campaign was enormously beneficial to Genentech. By slowing down the FDA, Morris and Courtovich boasted that they'd saved the drug conglomerate $1 billion in sales that would have been lost otherwise. "We bought them one year of sales," said one lobbyist who worked with Morris and Courtovich on the campaign. Genentech paid Courtovich more than $500,000 for his role in the effort.

The Avastin campaign had been a massive, complex undertaking. Morris and Courtovich had enlisted the help of dozens of lobbyists and consultants. They'd conducted focus groups, created a new organization, made political contributions, manipulated the press, met with lawmakers, and delivered targeted ads over social media—all to create the false impression of a groundswell of public support for an expensive, and ultimately unproven, breast cancer treatment. Yet nearly the entire lobbying effort was carried out in secret. By employing a new approach to political influencing that had been gaining favor over the previous few years, Morris and Courtovich were able to keep their Avastin campaign hidden from reporters, consumers, and the FDA officials they were seeking to sway. The new approach was called shadow lobbying.

This more advanced form of lobbying gained favor in the wake of Washington's last great lobbying and corruption scandal. The unintended consequences of the post-Abramoff reform effort, as it turned out, extended beyond the DC fund-raising circuit. When the new legislation banned lobbyists from handing out gifts to lawmakers, mandated more disclosures on lobbying activities, and drew additional public scorn to an already reviled profession, K Street did something no one expected. It went underground.

In the first decade under the new rules, more than 3,200 lobbyists—over a fifth of the entire industry—stopped reporting any efforts to influence Congress or the administration. These influence peddlers hadn't retired from the profession; they'd simply stopped registering as "lobbyists"—a term that carried an undesirable stigma—and started calling themselves "consultants" or "strategists." They still worked to influence policy but made sure their activities fell outside the strict definition of lobbying. For example, federal law requires anyone who spends more than 20 percent of their time directly influencing a public official to register as a lobbyist.[43] To avoid hitting the critical threshold, influence peddlers began installing time-tracking software on their computers, according to *Politico*, or asking colleagues to make lobbying calls on their behalf.[44] There was even a cottage industry of lawyers who monitored the time spent by influence peddlers to make sure they devoted less than 20 percent of their hours on lobbying work in order to avoid triggering the law's threshold for filing lobbying disclosure reports. The post-Abramoff reforms didn't reduce lobbyists' clout but simply pushed the industry deeper underground.[45]

The reforms also accelerated the shift in lobbying strategies from traditional insider approaches to the more advanced outside pressure tactics—public relations campaigns, grassroots efforts, new media ploys—intended to shape public opinion among the lawmakers' constituents back home in their districts. This evolution from inside to outside strategies would have a transformative effect on the business of Washington. Since it takes more resources to reach an entire voter block than it does a single lawmaker, the political-influence industry experienced a period of rapid expansion. Instead of simply buttonholing a member of Congress, lobbying firms were now regularly collaborating with a broad spectrum of industries, including public relations strategists, social media gurus, political consultants, pollsters, and experts in data analytics. And as new businesses sprouted up on K Street, the flow of money and man power directed toward political influence exploded. While the number of registered lobbyists was on the decline, the broader advocacy industry in Washington swelled by nearly 25 percent to 115,000 people from 2002 to 2016, according to a report by the Stephen S. Fuller Institute for Research on the Washington Region's Economic Future at George Mason University.

For influence peddlers, this approach offered another benefit. While efforts to lobby Congress directly must be reported publicly, there's no requirement to disclose activities designed to influence their constituents. As such, these indirect lobbying campaigns could be conducted under cover of darkness. The 2007 ethics reforms served only to reinforce this shift in tactics. When the ban on gift giving further limited the ability of lobbyists to influence lawmakers directly, K Street firms directed even more of their resources toward trying to achieve their policy objectives by shaping the opinions of voters. At the height of Evan Morris's work with Jim Courtovich, Genentech's advocacy budget had ballooned to $50 million, yet only $5 million was spent on traditional lobbying activities.[46] The remaining $45 million was for public affairs, grassroots, polling, data analytics, and other tactics that fell outside the technical definition of lobbying. And on account of the gaps in the regulation of K Street, none of this $45 million shadow lobbying budget had to be disclosed to the public.

It was here that the modern influence industry was born. To build his firm in the 1970s, Tommy Boggs had used his personal connections to directly persuade lawmakers to back the interests of his corporate clients. In the 1980s Black Manafort brought the tools they'd developed as campaign consultants to the business of lobbying. During the 1990s and 2000s, Tony Podesta was using his experience as a liberal activist to further advance the science of outside influence peddling. Now, in the wake of the post-Abramoff reforms, Morris and Courtovich were blazing a trail in the new world of shadow lobbying, where DC-based operators carry out the secret, sophisticated campaigns that target voters far beyond the Beltway, foment seemingly organic public outcries, and pressure lawmakers into taking actions that benefit their corporate clients. It was this very script that Morris had used for his Tamiflu coup, and that he and Courtovich had followed in their Avastin campaign.

The success of Morris's Avastin campaign helped him regain the faith of George Abercrombie and Genentech's other executives. As his compensation package grew to more than $1 million a year, Morris adopted the lifestyle of the Patton Boggs partners he'd looked up to back when he was a twentysomething law school student. He kept more than a thousand fine cigars—costing up to $50 apiece—in a half dozen humidors in Genentech's office. He purchased a collection of Rolex, Omega, and Cartier watches worth as much as $100,000 each. He owned three Porsches, and he joined eight exclusive country clubs in various parts of the country, including the Olympic Club in San Francisco and Liberty National Golf Club, a private club outside of Manhattan that costs $500,000 to join. At his home in the northern Virginia suburbs, Morris hosted intimate dinner parties for friends, lawmakers, and Capitol Hill aides. Sometimes he hired well-known chefs, including the founder of the New York hotspot Momofuku, to cook for his guests.

For his frequent visits to Genentech's headquarters, Morris bought a $1.365 million condo on Mission Street in downtown San Francisco.[47] The 645-foot, blue-and-gray glass skyscraper was, at the time, the tallest residential building on the West Coast. Morris's neighbors included Hall of Fame NFL quarterback Joe Montana, National Basketball Association All-Star and Most Valuable Player Kevin Durant, San Francisco Giants baseball star Hunter Pence, and billionaire investor Thomas Perkins, whose venture capital fund helped launch Amazon.com Inc., Google, and Genentech. In 2011, less than a decade after the embarrassing hunting adventure with Tommy Boggs, Morris paid $3.1 million in cash for a waterfront Georgian estate and guest cottage on Maryland's Eastern Shore, not far from Boggs's duck hunting retreat. The 7,800-square-foot home featured six bedrooms, eight baths, a pool, a hot tub, and a pair of Sea-Doo watercrafts. Morris renovated most of the house, adding an outdoor kitchen and expensive marble countertops. He called it "the house that Tamiflu bought."[48] A year later, he acquired a $300,000, custom-made, thirty-foot mahogany speedboat. The all-wood Hacker-Craft vessel had a Corvette engine with 415 horsepower. Only a few dozen of the handcrafted boats were made each year. Other owners included Hollywood stars, Middle Eastern sultans, Russian oligarchs, and corporate leaders. Morris docked his boat at his private pier next to his Sea-Doos. He christened it "Mulligan."[49] To learn how to dock the boat, he bought a second motorboat to practice.

Morris's stature in Washington was also on the rise. He landed a seat on the board of directors of the James Beard Foundation after routing a $150,000 donation from Genentech to the prestigious culinary arts organization. To try to get himself on the board of the charitable foundation for PGA golfers, he began making annual donations of $100,000 from Genentech to the organization. The corporate money also served as Morris's entree into the Clinton political network, which he'd long craved to join. He convinced the Biotechnology Industry Organization, a trade group that represented Genentech and other leading drug manufacturers, to pay Bill Clinton a total of $325,000 for a speech before an audience of pharmaceutical executives and a second appearance at the trade association's annual convention. After Hillary Clinton had stepped down as secretary of state, Morris arranged for the trade group to pay the future Democratic presidential nominee $335,000 for a speech at its conference in San Diego. In addition, Morris directed as much as $275,000 in donations from Genentech and the Roche Family Foundation to the Bill, Hillary & Chelsea Clinton Foundation.

As he emerged as a generous source of funds for the Clintons, Morris was finally able to realize his dream of playing golf with the former president. He would later regale his colleagues with a story about the round, explaining that at one point Clinton had ducked behind a tree just off the course to relieve himself, prompting Morris to playfully chastise the former commander in chief for urinating in public. "I am the president," Clinton responded. "I can piss anywhere I want." On another occasion, Morris was running a golf event to raise money for Democratic congressman Bill Pascrell at the Bayonne Golf Club in New Jersey when he bumped into Clinton, who was there to play his own round. After donors finished playing, Morris invited them into the clubhouse to shake hands and snap pictures with Clinton. Morris took great pride in his access to the ex-president. On the wall of his office, Morris prominently displayed a framed photograph of himself and Clinton on the golf course.

Though he'd supported Hillary Clinton during the 2008 Democratic primaries, once the election was over, Morris used his financial resources to ingratiate himself with Barack Obama and Joe Biden. He arranged for a $750,000 donation from Genentech to help fund the celebration surrounding the second-term inauguration. Morris and his wife were invited to an exclusive White House reception hosted by Barack and Michelle Obama before the public inaugural festivities began. He scored prime seats in front of the White House for the inaugural parade down Pennsylvania Avenue. Morris, who watched the swearing-in ceremony at a bar with other lobbyists, gave the passes to his wife and her friend, and they snapped up-close pictures of the president getting out of his limousine and walking the final stretch of the parade route. The following year, Morris was invited to an intimate White House concert with performers Aretha Franklin, Patti LaBelle, Ariana Grande, and Melissa Etheridge.[50] About two hundred people attended, including the president, First Lady Michelle Obama, her mother, and several Cabinet secretaries. Morris and his wife sat in the front row.

The partnership with Morris was profitable to Courtovich as well. The lucrative fees that Courtovich received from Genentech helped him cultivate the mystique of a dashing and powerful insider. Just days after signing his first business deal with Morris in 2005, Courtovich bought the $2 million house in Kalorama where he hosted his legendary Gaucho parties. After neighbors complained about the noise from the parties, Courtovich moved into a more opulent residence, paying $3.8 million for a 3,700-square-foot house near the vice president's residence at the US Naval Observatory. He then spent $500,000[51] to transform the five-bedroom, five-bath property into an ideal party pad. He added a second kitchen with a twelve-foot walnut-and-marble island, and he created a separate charcuterie room for curing meats, complete with a deli slicer and meat locker.[52] He told friends that he bought the deli slicer for $3,000 online late one night, after overindulging in wine.

He ripped out the existing pool and installed a new one with sprinklers, he built a locker room stocked with spare swimming suits for his guests, and he acquired an industrial ice maker. The renovated home was featured in the *Wall Street Journal*'s prestigious real estate section, Mansion. "I really wanted to create a casual and usable space for entertaining," he told the newspaper, "because there's a lot of formality in Washington."[53] Above an entryway, Courtovich displayed a five-foot-long wooden sculpture of a blue fish. He called the house "Le Poisson Bleu."

As his roster of clients expanded beyond Genentech—to include Boeing, major Wall Street firms, the kingdom of Saudi Arabia, and Russia's largest bank—Courtovich became a regular in the first-class cabins of international flights, and he hobnobbed with wealthy elites in Europe and the Middle East. He dined with Princess Beatrice of York in London, and he sat in the owner's box for the annual FC Barcelona v Real Madrid soccer match in Spain. Once, he spent $50,000 on a spur-of-the-moment shopping trip in London, he told a reporter. In Washington, as he moved to the top of the social pecking order, he maintained a standing reservation at BLT Steak, a go-to power lunch spot for the city's ruling class. When Courtovich arrived, the maître d' welcomed him by name, and a server delivered the first of his midday drinks, a $25 glass of Elizabeth Spencer Cabernet. He boasted to others that he was one of the restaurant's top customers nationwide. He often held boozy staff meetings over lunch at the steakhouse that sometimes devolved into boisterous sessions as the wine flowed. At one, Courtovich took offense to the tie worn by a subordinate and snipped it off with a pair of scissors, drawing snickers from others in the restaurant. Courtovich had an employee record a video of the event, which he posted on social media for all to see.

Courtovich became a fixture at the annual White House Correspondents' Dinner, the glitzy gathering of White House officials, media celebrities, and Hollywood stars. He cohosted an exclusive brunch on the weekend of the event at the Georgetown mansion once owned by the late *Washington Post* publisher Katharine Graham. Likewise, he became a familiar face at the summertime picnic that Joe Biden hosted for members of the media at the vice president's residence, where Biden handed out Super Soakers to the children of his guests for the annual water gun fight. Courtovich even attended a formal state dinner at the White House hosted by President Obama for the prime minister of Singapore.[54]

With business on the upswing, Courtovich struck out on his own. Though he maintained a partnership with National Media, he launched his own consulting firm in the late 2000s, Sphere Consulting LLC, and moved into a prestigious office a few blocks from the White House. It was the same office that Vice President Elect Al Gore had used during the interim period after the 1992 election and before his swearing-in. Courtovich's company, Sphere Consulting, aimed to cash in on a lucrative niche in the influence business created by the recent lobbying reforms and the explosion of corporate money in Washington. In roughly a decade at National Media Inc., Courtovich had encouraged companies to run advertisements in the Washington media market as a way to get their lobbying pitches in front of members of Congress and their staffs. "This is not the time for America's business leaders to sit back and wait for the storm to blow over," Courtovich said in a National Media press release projecting that interest groups would spend as much as $50 million on ads featuring unflattering portrayals of corporate America. "Companies who fail to take an active approach and distinguish themselves and their good practices risk being tarred by the same advertising brush," he added.[55]

For many years, corporations hoping to reach policy makers through advertisements relied almost exclusively on the *Washington Post*, spending $50,000 and up for full-page ads[56] in the city's biggest daily newspaper. That changed during the 2000s, when the flood of new political spending transformed DC's media industry. The boom in so-called issue ads prompted a set of once-sleepy Capitol Hill newsletters—like *Roll Call*, *The Hill*, *National Journal*, and *Congressional Quarterly*—to begin growing their newsrooms and expanding their coverage of Capitol Hill in order to attract more lobbying advertisements. *Roll Call* and *The Hill* increased their publication schedules and reinvented themselves as daily newspapers. *National Journal* and *Congressional Quarterly* launched twice-daily editions. Before long, these upstart publications became required reading for lawmakers, congressional aides, and political insiders—providing corporate lobbyists with a handful of new outlets in which to place ads targeting policy makers. These insurgent publications were also more cost-effective. Compared with the *Washington Post*, a four-color, two-page spread in *Roll Call* was a steal at about $12,000 a pop. By "making *Roll Call* a must-read on Capitol Hill and unleashing far more reporting firepower on previously unaccountable dark corners of the Washington power game," wrote former *Roll Call* editor Susan Glasser, the publication "had scores of companies and lobbying groups eager to buy what was now branded 'issue advocacy' advertising."[57]

In this changing media environment, Courtovich pursued a new opportunity. He cultivated relationships with a coterie of influential reporters who were widely read on Capitol Hill—and then signed up US corporations that could benefit from their coverage. Put another way, Courtovich used his clout with friendly reporters to try to entice them to write articles that helped advance his clients' objectives in Washington. In describing his strategy to a group of foreign businessmen, Courtovich offered a blunt assessment: "We're controlling what is being said."

Among the companies that saw the value of Courtovich's approach was Goldman Sachs Group Inc. In 2009, when the US Senate launched a highly publicized probe into the causes of the financial crisis,[58] Goldman Sachs faced an onslaught of congressional criticism and an aggressive effort to curb executive pay.[59] As they worked to fend off the attacks, Goldman executives realized they had a problem. Despite the firm's close relationships with reporters on Wall Street, it had few ties to the Capitol Hill press corps—the journalists whose coverage would be most influential among lawmakers themselves. "We needed someone with a Washington perspective who knew the reporters," recalled a Goldman executive who helped hire Courtovich. "Who is writing about us? What are they saying? Not the beat reporters for the *Wall Street Journal*—we knew them—but who was writing about the policy that would impact us." Goldman agreed to pay Courtovich $35,000 a month to help "put into context what was going on in the policy-related media in Washington," the Goldman executive said, and then "selectively advocated the reporters we wanted to engage." This could involve feeding information to Washington reporters that would either benefit Goldman Sachs or undermine the lawmakers taking aim at the company.

At the same time, Courtovich told people he was spending hundreds of thousands of dollars on flashy cocktail parties and intimate dinners for Washington reporters, cable news producers, federal policy makers, and corporate lobbyists. For Courtovich, these parties weren't just social events, they were the source of his power in Washington. Through his live-in partner, CNN correspondent Jeff Zeleny, Courtovich got to know some of the most influential figures in the political press corps, and he made sure to invite them to his parties. This allowed Courtovich to create a network of contacts in the upper reaches of the media that he could turn to when he was trying to garner positive news coverage for a corporation or foreign government.

Courtovich focused on White House and congressional reporters for the *New York Times*, *Washington Post*, and *Wall Street Journal*, as well as producers at CNN, Fox, and the broadcast networks. In return, the reporters got access to exclusive social events, where they rubbed elbows with senior administration officials and congressional aides, while lapping up gossip and news tips from Courtovich and his guests. "We have invested significantly in relationships with individual reporters," he said later in a written pitch for prospective business. "These personal relationships allow us to get a fair hearing for our clients with reporters who value straight talk rather than public relations spin." In a business pitch he made to Wall Street firms at a time when they were fighting efforts to restrain executive pay, Courtovich said he could get friendly articles published by a "host of reliable journalists known to Sphere" at the *New York Times*, *Financial Times*, and Bloomberg. Just as importantly, hosting hot-ticket parties for Washington's A-list was the perfect way for Courtovich to advertise his services. As he clinked glasses with cable-TV reporters and gossiped with Obama aides, he seemed like just the type of insider that a Fortune 500 company or a foreign government should hire when they needed help getting what they wanted out of Washington. And, sure enough, some of them did.

In 2009, for example, Courtovich was hired by a Saudi Arabian investment fund to discredit a business rival. The massive investment fund, known as Ahmad Hamad Al Gosaibi & Brothers Co., was embroiled in an international financial scandal. At issue was whether Courtovich's Saudi client, or a business rival, was at fault for billions of dollars in investment losses.[60] As part of the effort, Courtovich launched an influence-peddling campaign designed to convince the US public and officials in Washington that his client's adversary was to blame.

Courtovich began by assisting a reporter he knew at the *Wall Street Journal* write a front-page story that included an unflattering portrayal of the rival.[61] Next, he set off to convince government officials in Washington to launch an investigation into his client's rival, reaching out to several congressional aides whom he'd cultivated at his social events. One of them, a top aide to New York Republican representative Peter King, agreed to send a letter from the congressman to US Attorney General Eric Holder alleging that the business rival had laundered billions of dollars through US banks. The letter cited allegations about the matter that were first published in the *Wall Street Journal*, which Courtovich himself had helped arrange. Then, in September 2010, Courtovich persuaded Congressman King to allow his client's lawyer, Eric Lewis, to testify at a US House Committee on Financial Services hearing on the matter. "The fraud and money laundering that I wish to address involves the sluicing of approximately one trillion dollars," Lewis said at the hearing. He added that it "was masterminded by a Saudi named Maan al-Sanea"—the business rival of Courtovich's client.

After the hearing, Congressman King wrote a second letter to the Justice Department about the matter, and Courtovich followed up with one of his own. In his letter, Courtovich cited the congressional testimony and the letters from the congressman as evidence that the matter should be a priority for the Department of Justice. "Last September, the House Financial Services Committee heard testimony about the startling mechanics of the scheme, and Chairman Peter King of the House Homeland Security Committee has twice requested that the Department of Justice investigate the matter," he wrote. What Courtovich failed to mention was that he himself had helped orchestrate the letters as well as the congressional testimony. Nor did Courtovich register his lobbying work on behalf of the Saudi investment fund with the Justice Department, as required by the law. Courtovich, who was paid $7.7 million for the work, never faced charges.

Meantime, as Evan Morris continued to deliver lobbying victories, George Abercrombie gave him the autonomy to run the Washington office largely as he pleased. With this increased authority, Morris worked both to expand the size of Genentech's political-influence operation and to increase his control over it. He had consolidated a half dozen previously independent divisions, such as the office responsible for lobbying state capitals, into a single advocacy unit that reported directly to him, and he personally determined which lawmakers would receive contributions from the corporation's PAC, which doled out some $500,000 annually. He fired many of Genentech's existing lobbyists, including Tony Podesta, and he expanded the number of outside lobbyists to more than a hundred, up from less than two dozen the year before he joined the company. He hired scores of additional K Street operators for help with media campaigns, grassroots activism, public opinion research, and other influence efforts. The arrangement put Morris in control of an entire lobbying economy. As Genentech's advocacy budget ballooned to about $50 million a year, Morris exercised broad discretion over how each dollar was spent. And because he kept such tight control over the cash flow, it was difficult for any of his colleagues to get the full picture of the office's finances.

At the same time, Morris was developing a reputation for excessive spending. He regularly got together with Courtovich and other lobbyists for what he called "drunk lunches," where business was casually discussed over a half dozen bottles of wine; afterward, Morris passed out generous tips to maître d's and servers. One lobbyist recalls Morris ordering a $2,000 bottle of wine during a weekday lunch; once they'd finished it, the sommelier opened another bottle for free. At a company retreat in Northern California, Morris told a young female employee that if she jumped in the pool with her clothes on, he would give her $1,000 in cash. Morris had a practice of having the wine he ordered for Genentech's political events delivered directly to his home. According to one of his former assistants, Morris once ordered $10,000 worth of wine for an office retreat held at his Eastern Shore home but ended up serving only a handful of bottles during the event. Afterward, the staff couldn't find the unused bottles.

There was other bizarre behavior. One morning, Morris's secretary received a call from his wife. Tracy Morris explained that her husband had left the house early, and she couldn't locate him. The secretary, who hadn't seen Morris, either, checked his calendar; there were no appointments listed. The secretary assured Tracy that she'd call as soon as she saw him. A few hours later, however, a red-faced Morris stormed into Roche's offices and confronted the secretary.

"Why did you tell my wife that I wasn't in the office?" he demanded. "If my wife calls, and I am not around, tell her that I'm in a meeting."

The secretary apologized, promising never to make the same mistake again. Curious, she asked where Morris had been. He explained that he had put in a few hours of work in the office early that morning before heading over to the gym. After his workout and shower, he'd sat down in a comfortable chair in the locker room and drifted off to sleep. The story sounded fishy. When Morris left, the secretary checked the office's keycard history. There was no record of Morris entering the office that day before he'd confronted her.

Over time, colleagues and rival lobbyists began whispering about Morris's lifestyle. When asked how he could afford memberships at eight different private golf clubs, Morris offered different explanations. To some, he said he'd received the memberships from Bill and Hillary Clinton's foundation as payment for having organized fund-raising events at the clubs. To others, he said it was Genentech that had given him the memberships. He told a college friend he was given a membership at New Jersey's Liberty National Golf Club after getting the state's governor and senators to resolve a water issue at the club, and he claimed he'd received a membership to a San Francisco–area club as a favor after he'd secured help from California lawmakers with a similar issue there. Accounts of how he acquired other possessions conflicted as well. He told his wife that he'd obtained his custom-made mahogany speedboat by purchasing all fifty thousand available tickets at a charity auction.[62] He claimed to others that he'd bought the boat from a person who'd ordered it but ultimately didn't have the necessary funds to complete the purchase. He explained to his family that Genentech had provided him with the condo in San Francisco so that he'd have someplace to stay when he traveled to company headquarters. To colleagues at Genentech, it was a gift from his father-in-law, who was a physician for an NBA team.

He sought favors from the outside lobbyists and consultants whom he paid through Genentech's advocacy budget. One lobbyist says Morris asked him to cover the rental fees for a beach house on Bald Head Island, North Carolina, where Morris planned to take a summer vacation with his family. On another occasion, during a round of golf with a different lobbyist at the Belle Haven Country Club, in northern Virginia, Morris proposed an unusual deal. He said he would increase the amount of money that Genentech paid the lobbyist if, in exchange, the lobbyist would purchase a membership for one of Morris's colleagues to a prestigious golf club. Morris described the membership as a way for him to reward the colleague for his hard work, and the unusual financial arrangement was necessary, he explained, because Genentech had refused to pay for the membership directly. The lobbyist balked at the offer. About a month later, Morris fired him.

Inside Genentech's Washington office, Morris's handling of the budget had long been the subject of questions. Shortly after he took over the lobbying division, a group of veteran employees grew so alarmed by how freely he was spending the company's money that they filed a complaint with Genentech's human resources department. A team of human resources staffers traveled to Washington to conduct an internal investigation, and the employees detailed the exorbitant lunch tabs and missing bottles of wine. One secretary told the Genentech lawyers that Morris had instructed her to create phony expense reports so that he could get reimbursed for meals and other outlays that he had never actually incurred. "We spilled our guts," the employee recalls. But after the investigators left, the employees never heard about the inquiry again. Around this time, Morris purchased memberships at a Washington-area country club for every member of his staff.

Of all the questions about Morris's leadership, none was more puzzling than his partnership with Courtovich. Though Morris directed a considerable portion of Genentech's Washington budget to Courtovich's firms—funneling more than $3 million in contracts to him in 2012 alone—other consultants often struggled to figure out what work Courtovich was doing to earn his fees. Courtovich occasionally dialed in to the weekly calls with Genentech's advocacy team, but he rarely spoke. Eventually the business contracts between the two men began to attract scrutiny. One former Genentech contracting officer recalls reviewing a $450,000 agreement between Morris and Courtovich. The wording of the contract was unusually vague; instead of detailing the specific tasks that Courtovich would be required to perform, the document simply stated that Genentech was to hire Courtovich for the broad purpose of "media consulting." Realizing that the imprecise language would raise red flags with the company's lawyers, the contracting officer called Morris and asked him for a more detailed explanation of the required work. Morris referred questions to Courtovich.

But when Courtovich got on the phone, he said it was Morris who had the information. Unable to obtain the details, the officer submitted the contract to Genentech's internal contracting system, where, as predicted, it was rejected because it lacked specificity. Morris was able to get the contract approved by calling officials in Genentech's headquarters and personally vouching for the expense. Still, the experience made the contracting officer so uncomfortable that she called Genentech's legal department in San Francisco and expressed her concerns. Nothing ever came of it.

The partnership had also aroused suspicion among Courtovich's ex-colleagues at National Media. Though Courtovich had since left for his own consulting firm, he continued to rely on the accounting department at his former firm to process bills and payments. National Media's managers became uneasy about the Genentech contracts and unusual payments to Morris. The odd financial arrangement between Morris and Courtovich worked like this: After Courtovich had signed a contract to perform media or consulting work for Morris, Genentech sent payments to one of Courtovich's companies—usually National Media or Sphere Consulting. Then, once Courtovich had obtained the funds, which were typically in the six- to seven-figure range, he often asked National Media's accountants to send a portion of the money right back to Morris, or other entities, as reimbursements for expenses that Morris had incurred during the course of the work. As a result, hundreds of thousands of dollars were regularly flowing between bank accounts controlled by the two men. Over time, National Media and its chief accountant, Jon Ferrell, grew uncomfortable with what he saw as the loose business arrangement and the flow of money to Morris.

As a by-the-book CPA with three decades of experience, Ferrell simply didn't understand the need for Courtovich and Morris to be passing such exorbitant sums of money back and forth to each other in this manner. And after years of grudgingly processing the reimbursement checks, Ferrell eventually had enough and demanded a change: National Media would stop all personal reimbursements to Evan Morris. He told Courtovich and Morris that Genentech would have to pay its vendors directly. The final straw came in 2012. In March Courtovich and Morris agreed to a $2 million[63] consulting contract between National Media and Genentech that was to be paid in three installments. A few weeks later, in early April, Genentech made a $750,000 payment to National Media. One of Courtovich's employees asked Ferrell to prepare a $303,048.95 reimbursement check for a business called the Hacker Boat Company.

The request puzzled Ferrell. The Hacker Boat Company was a prestigious manufacturer of luxury boats. The company, which was located on Lake George in upstate New York, produced expensive, custom-crafted mahogany motorboats for a high-net-worth customer base of movie stars, Wall Street traders, and foreign royals. Courtovich's employee told Ferrell that the check was to pay the costs of a political event Morris organized for the Democratic Attorneys General Association, which was held at the boat maker's headquarters. The invoice submitted to Ferrell by Courtovich's team was fuzzy on details, lacking an address, phone number, date, and tax identification number. If National Media were ever audited by the IRS, the documents would never pass muster. Ferrell rejected the payment request, telling Courtovich's assistant that he'd need to provide more information about the expense. When Courtovich failed to supply the additional details in a timely manner, Ferrell grew frustrated and decided to investigate the matter himself. He searched online for a phone number, called the Hacker Boat Company and asked to speak to someone who could get the missing information. A company representative said he would call back.

Before anyone from the company returned the call, Evan Morris sent over a new invoice that included the information required to meet standard accounting requirements. The document, dated April 2, 2012, was entitled "Invoice for Democratic Attorney General Event." It was printed on a single sheet of paper that also carried the Hacker logo. The invoice stated that the two-day fund-raising event included a kick-off networking session, an all-day policy briefing by the staff of the Democratic Attorneys General Association, an afternoon of wine tasting, and a lunch provided by Genentech. According to the invoice, the payment to the Hacker Boat Company covered the costs of renting showrooms, storage facilities, and conference rooms at Hacker's lakeside headquarters. The funds would also cover meals for the conference's 150 attendees, as well as the fees for the water taxis that shuttled guests between their hotel and the conference. Though Ferrell remained uncomfortable, he processed the payment request and drew a check on National Media's bank account for $303,048.95 to the Hacker Boat Company.[64] But he refused to involve National Media or himself any further in the dealings of Morris and Courtovich. The unusual business practices of the two, Ferrell told National Media executives, was simply too odd. If the IRS ever examined the transactions closely, his CPA license could be in jeopardy.

It was the last payment involving Genentech that National Media ever issued. National Media stopped working for Genentech, making the drug manufacturer the only client it had ever fired. Neither Genentech nor Morris ever contacted National Media again.

13

Spring 2011
Federal Trade Commission headquarters, Washington, DC

One afternoon in the spring of 2011, the five top officials at the Federal Trade Commission gathered at the agency's DC headquarters for a meeting of such sensitivity that it wasn't listed on its public agenda. The FTC's three Democratic and two Republican commissioners wore business attire as they took their places in the rounded, wood-paneled hearing room. Beside them, a coterie of agency lawyers, government economists, and other stern-faced officials settled into chairs. Located a few blocks from the US Capitol, the sturdy limestone and granite building was intended to project a stable and robust federal government during the upheaval of the Great Depression; FDR had laid the cornerstone himself in 1937.[1] On either side of the building are matching limestone sculptures depicting shirtless, muscle-bound men, each restraining an angry workhorse. The sculptures—called *Man Controlling Trade*—are thought to symbolize the agency's mission to shield consumers from the abuses of corporate capitalists.[2] It had been a long time, though, since the agency had lived up to its New Deal–era mandate.

After crossing paths with Tommy Boggs during the children's TV advertising debate of the late 1970s, when it was derided as "The National Nanny" by the *Washington Post*, the FTC had grown increasingly accommodating to corporate empire building. By the turn of the twenty-first century, it was green-lighting some of the largest corporate mergers in American history, including the $81 billion merger of Exxon and Mobil, the $90 million merger of pharmaceutical firms Pfizer and Warner-Lambert, and the $165 billion merger of America Online and Time Warner.

Inside the agency, however, some rank-and-file bureaucrats nursed a cautious optimism that the recent election of Barack Obama—with his soaring calls to eradicate the influence of special interests in government—would revive the FTC's tradition of tough-minded regulation. And when they discovered the subject of the meeting that day at the agency's headquarters, these staffers grew even more hopeful. Unlike the general public, some FTC employees were permitted to attend the gathering. So, with a buzz of intrigue and anticipation, the staffers filed into the hearing room, found seats in the observation benches, and watched the FTC commissioners begin the proceedings.

It was the alleged actions of an iconic technology firm that had brought the federal regulators together that day. Many months earlier, the FTC had begun receiving complaints that Google, the Internet search engine giant based in Mountain View, California, had been illegally using its market power to bludgeon rivals, smother competition, and harm consumers.

Internet competitors, such as Yelp Inc. and Tripadvisor Inc., had accused Google of stealing its content by copying information from their online reviews, while Amazon.com claimed that the company generated search results that unfairly steered users to Google-owned products and services. The meeting was convened so that the FTC's five commissioners could consider authorizing a formal antitrust investigation into Google's business practices, a decision that could very well lead to an antitrust lawsuit against the company. Bringing an antitrust case against Google would send an unmistakable signal that Washington's long-dormant consumer protection bureaucracy was rumbling back to life and that the FTC—reinvigorated by the "hope and change" of a dynamic new administration—was willing to confront the corporate malefactors of the digital economy.

For Larry Page and Sergey Brin, the former Stanford University PhD classmates who'd founded Google more than a decade earlier, the FTC's actions represented an existential crisis. If the agency pursued a formal antitrust lawsuit, a judge could force Google to unwind acquisitions—such as its purchases of YouTube or the online advertising firm DoubleClick—or even dismantle the entire company. Such actions could trigger chaos at a business that handled about two-thirds of all web searches in the United States, generated nearly $30 billion in annual revenue, and had a phalanx of powerful investors to please. Yet the danger posed by the FTC's commissioners extended well beyond Google's ledger sheet. From the time they founded Google, Page and Brin had presented Google as the antithesis of the soulless corporate blobs that had consumed much of the economic skyscape. Google provided its staff with free meals—bacon and waffles for breakfast, seared diver scallops for lunch—whipped up by the former chef for the Grateful Dead. Engineers brought their dogs to work and rode red, blue, green, and yellow bikes[3] across the company's twenty-six-acre, tree-lined campus, known as the "Googleplex." Brin sometimes arrived at meetings on Rollerblades, and both founders took pride in Google's high-minded corporate motto, "Don't be evil." As the company stated in its 2004 prospectus to the Securities and Exchange Commission, "We believe strongly that in the long term, we will be better served—as shareholders and in all other ways—by a company that does good things for the world even if we forgo some short-term gains."[4] A federal antitrust case against Google wouldn't just threaten the company's shareholders—it would imperil the enlightened mythology of a Silicon Valley fairy tale.

During the 2011 meeting at the FTC, the commissioners recognized the magnitude of the decision before them. At one point in the discussion, a commissioner raised a question. "Even if we can find a violation here and defend it on appeal, what's the remedy?" he asked. "Are we talking about breaking Google up?"

Splitting up Google would mean requiring it to break into a series of smaller firms, each one focused solely on its distinct line of business, such as Internet search, video sharing, mobile phones, or cloud computing, among others. These smaller, legally separate companies would have less power to harm rivals in the marketplace and fewer financial incentives to favor Google-owned products in web searches.

Jon Leibowitz, the agency's chairman, pressed for an investigation, expressing confidence that the commission would find evidence that Google had engaged in anticompetitive practices. After the meeting, the agency's leaders held a confidential vote to authorize the FTC's investigators to subpoena internal documents from Google—the first step in what was shaping up to be one of the biggest antitrust investigations of the twenty-first century. FTC investigators hoped to find emails or other documentation showing that top Google executives had knowingly used the web giant's size and strength to harm competitors or consumers.

Word of the probe quickly reached Google's executives in California and its top outside lobbyist in Washington, Tony Podesta. Over the previous six years, Podesta had played a key behind-the-scenes role in helping Google's idealistic, politically naïve leaders construct one of the most ruthless influence-peddling machines in Washington. He'd urged executives to learn from the mistakes that its rival, Microsoft Corp., had made during its clash with federal regulators in the late 1990s, when an arrogant Bill Gates had sneered at the government's authority. Podesta redirected Google's political-influence strategy away from earnest, policy-minded dialogues and toward a more cold-blooded application of state-of-the-art tactics. Under the guidance of Podesta and others, Google's DC team managed to integrate all four elements of modern influence peddling—inside lobbying, outside pressure, political fund-raising, and academic research—into a single operation. It was a triumph of profit seeking and corporate ambition that wowed even veteran K Street operatives. Upon learning the outcome of the FTC's vote, Podesta and the rest of Google's DC team now set themselves to killing the potentially historic antitrust case. Together, they launched an influence campaign that would test not only Podesta's standing as the signature Democratic fixer of the Obama era, but also the ability of a sophisticated, multipronged lobbying effort to outmuscle the federal government's newly rejuvenated consumer protection agency.

Long before the FTC started looking into Google, Podesta had established himself as Silicon Valley's Man in Washington. Through his work for Genentech in the 1990s,[5] he'd come to believe that increased government intervention in the tech sector was only a matter of time. "As [tech firms] got bigger and bigger and bigger, Washington began to look at them," Podesta recalled. "Their competitors went to Washington and said, 'This ten-thousand-pound gorilla is eating our lunch—and it's bad for competition." Podesta also recognized that lawmakers and tech executives held starkly opposing views of one another. "For a lot of politicians, high tech is basically just a photo-op," Podesta told a reporter.[6] "You tell some Valley guy, 'We're gonna meet with the head of the Office of Information and Regulat[ory] Affairs at the Office of Management and Budget,' and he thinks, 'Oh, nobody important.'" Unlike other operators on K Street, Podesta was bilingual; he could chat about legislative riders with members of Congress and discuss digital innovation with dotcom entrepreneurs. "I'm not so much of a tech 'guy,'" Podesta said. "What I really am is a translator."[7] In 1998 Wired magazine called him the "ideal matchmaker for any high-tech company needing to do business on Capitol Hill, in the White House, or wherever regulation, trade, and government contracts are on the table."[8]

Among the most enduring lessons that influence peddlers learned during this period came through watching the political missteps made by a technology powerhouse based outside of Seattle. In 1975 a nineteen-year-old Harvard dropout named Bill Gates joined with his pal Paul Allen to found Microsoft,[9] a garage-space start-up that developed software for the upstart business of personal computing. By the 1990s, Microsoft was the biggest software company in the world, and its flagship operating system, Windows, was installed in more than eight out of ten personal computers. But as revenues swelled, other Silicon Valley firms began complaining that Microsoft was using its market dominance to illegally steamroll smaller competitors. In the 1990s the FTC began investigating claims that Microsoft had intentionally designed its widely used Windows operating system so that it would favor other Microsoft software at the expense of its competitors. Later, the Department of Justice picked up the probe, turning its attention to allegations that Microsoft was using licensing agreements with computer manufacturers to block rival software from reaching consumers.[10] Neither effort amounted to much. The FTC deadlocked on the question of whether or not to bring formal antitrust charges,[11] and the Justice

Department reached a settlement with Microsoft requiring the company to make a few modest changes.[12] As it turned out, though, these scrapes were merely a preview of a much farther-reaching showdown.

In May 1998 the Justice Department and attorneys general in twenty states filed two massive antitrust complaints against Microsoft, alleging that the firm was acting as an illegal monopoly in the software industry.[13] Specifically, prosecutors charged that rather than engage in open competition, Microsoft had violated the century-old Sherman Antitrust Act by forcing the manufacturers of personal computers to install a Microsoft-made web browser, Internet Explorer, on all computers that ran its Windows operating system.[14] Prosecutors claimed that this arrangement illegally squeezed Netscape's Navigator and other competing Internet browsers out of the market.[15]

This was a thermonuclear event. If the Justice Department and state attorneys general prevailed, they could force the breakup of Microsoft. CNN called the lawsuits "one of the biggest antitrust assaults of the century," adding that the case "reviv[ed] images of trust-busting fervor against industrial titans like Standard Oil, AT&T, and International Business Machines."[16] *BusinessWeek* claimed the allegations "paint a picture of a modern day robber baron."[17] The head of the Justice Department's Antitrust Division, Joel Klein, condemned "the barrage of illegal, anticompetitive practices that Microsoft uses to destroy its rivals and to avoid competition on the merits."[18] And in an indication of the government's commitment to winning the case, the Justice Department hired the hotshot litigator who'd defended IBM against federal antitrust charges roughly two decades earlier, David Boies, to lead the prosecution. "We're in for a full-fledged firefight now," Richard Blumenthal, attorney general of Connecticut, told the *New York Times*.[19]

For many observers, the Microsoft case was a classic example of a corporate King Kong abusing its power. But on K Street, a different perspective emerged. Lobbyists and other Beltway insiders argued that Microsoft's most significant mistakes had less to do with business practices than with political strategy. In their view, Microsoft wasn't a software monopoly that had been sanctioned for smothering competition. It was a cavalier upstart that had been punished because it failed to manage Washington properly.

Even as it exploded into the world's biggest software developer,[20] Microsoft had refused to make much of an investment in the nation's capital. During the early 1990s—a time when Microsoft knew federal and state antitrust regulators were increasing their scrutiny of the firm—it didn't even have a physical lobbying office in Washington. Jack Krumholtz, the lobbyist who led Microsoft's tiny DC lobbying operation, worked from Microsoft's government-contracting office in suburban Maryland or a Starbucks coffee shop; he conducted business from the front seats of his Jeep Cherokee. Over time, other K Street influence peddlers began referring to Microsoft's lobbying operation as "Jack in his Jeep."

The company's refusal to prioritize Washington reflected the perspectives of many Silicon Valley chieftains that there was nothing to be gained—and much to lose—by engaging with out-of-touch lawmakers and rule-following bureaucrats. Like the railroad tycoons and automobile executives of prior eras, the pioneers of the technology business just wanted the government to leave them alone. Microsoft founder Bill Gates took this view a step further. While he emerged as America's wealthiest person and became a cult hero to a generation of techies, he developed a particularly low regard for politicians and regulators. During the FTC's investigation of Microsoft in the early 1990s, Gates openly derided the agency's authority. He joked to a *BusinessWeek* reporter that "the worst that could come of this is I could fall down the steps of the FTC building, hit my head, and kill myself."[21] In a 1995 meeting with executives at the computer processing chip manufacturer Intel, Gates likewise dismissed the Justice Department's efforts. "This antitrust thing will blow over," he said. "We haven't changed our business practices at all."[22] But it was his behavior during the Justice Department's 1998 antitrust case that would prove most damaging.

In August 1998 Bill Gates was deposed by government prosecutors at Microsoft's headquarters in Redmond, Washington. Over three days of questioning in a company boardroom, the software magnate was by turns haughty, combative, slippery, and aloof. During fits of squirms and evasion, Gates claimed repeatedly not to recall[23] events at issue in the lawsuit, and he haggled over the meanings of words such as *we*, *compete*,[24] and *concerned*.[25] Stephen Houck, one of the Justice Department's top prosecutors in the case, told a reporter that "there's an exchange between [Gates] and David [Boies] on the second day, where David showed him an email which came from billg@microsoft, which was his handle. David said something like, 'Did you write this?' He said no. So David asked, 'Where'd this come from?' Gates said, 'A computer.'"[26] At trial, prosecutors played portions of Gates's deposition on a video monitor. The billionaire's responses during the questioning were so absurd that, at one point, while the video was playing in court, Judge Thomas Penfield Jackson burst out laughing.[27] Later, the judge told an interviewer that Gates had a "Napoleonic concept of himself and his company, an arrogance that derives from power and unalloyed success."[28]

With things in the courtroom not going so well, the software giant turned to its less than formidable Washington operation—"Jack in his Jeep"—to try to soften the government's resolve. But the bumbling escapades of Microsoft's lobbyists only worsened the company's predicament. Early in the fall of 1998, a few months after Gates's deposition, a company-controlled PAC quietly made a $25,000 campaign contribution to the opponent of Bill Lockyer, the Democratic attorney general of California who had been among the twenty state prosecutors to file the antitrust charges. The Microsoft-backed candidate, Republican Dave Stirling, had criticized the state's lawsuit against Microsoft. The effort to unseat a legal adversary backfired on Microsoft; Lockyer won the race and discovered the company's involvement in his opponent's campaign. "They've never been involved in California politics before this lawsuit," an aide to Lockyer told the *Wall Street Journal*, "and the way they got into it was pretty awkward."[29] After failing to get the state attorney general voted out of office, Microsoft began working to deprive the Justice Department's Antitrust Division of the resources it needed to prosecute cases. Microsoft's lobbyists pressured congressional appropriators to cut about $10 million in funding from the Antitrust Division's budget, or roughly 9 percent of its total budget. Once again, word of the machinations leaked to the media, and the *Washington Post* published a front-page story exposing the company's apparent plan for retribution.[30] Yet these were minor embarrassments compared to what came next.

In June 1999, as the trial entered its final month, a set of full-page advertisements supporting Microsoft in the antitrust case appeared in the *Washington Post* and *New York Times*. The ads contained a statement signed by 240 academic experts arguing that the case should be decided in Microsoft's favor. Inside the courtroom, the ads made waves, prompting prosecutors to address the issues raised by the academics during the trial. But the source of funding for the ads became the subject of curiosity. The ads stated that they were paid for by a little-known California-based organization called the Independent Institute. David Theroux, the head of the think tank, insisted the campaign hadn't been financed by Microsoft. "We're independent," he told the *New York Times*.[31]

But lobbyists for a Microsoft competitor, Oracle Corporation, weren't buying it. Oracle's Washington team hired a private investigator to comb through the trash bins outside of the institute's headquarters in Oakland, California—a practice that Oracle's operatives referred to as "garbology." While sifting through the trash, the investigator made a startling discovery. He found receipts—now soiled and stinking—proving that Microsoft not only had financed the newspaper ads but also had reimbursed Theroux and an associate $5,966 for round-trip, first-class flights from San Francisco to Washington, DC, to speak at a news conference criticizing the government's antitrust case. In all, Microsoft had provided reimbursements totaling $153,868.67 to the organization that produced the pro-Microsoft ads.[32] The Independent Institute, as it turned out, wasn't so independent after all.

The subsequent story on the front page of the *New York Times*— "'Unbiased' Ads for Microsoft Came at a Price"[33]—was humiliating for Gates and his associates. For a time, Microsoft officials attempted to fight back in the media, criticizing Oracle for the dumpster-diving tactics.[34] But Oracle CEO Larry Ellison had the last laugh. Speaking at a press conference, he offered to send a bag of his household trash to Gates's office at Microsoft.[35]

In April 2000, after a months-long trial, Judge Jackson ruled that Microsoft had indeed broken antitrust laws. And later, in an unusually harsh punishment, he ordered the software giant be split up. One year later, though, Microsoft got a last-minute reprieve when a panel of appellate judges scrapped the breakup order while affirming that the company had violated federal antimonopoly law. With Microsoft's fate still unclear, the 2000 election of Republican George W. Bush shifted the political environment in the company's favor. When the new president took office, the Justice Department adopted a more hands-off approach to antitrust issues, and in November 2001 the two sides reached a settlement agreement. Though not nearly as draconian as the original decision, the settlement would nonetheless subject Microsoft to increased federal scrutiny for several years. By the time the consent decree expired, in 2011, Microsoft had been scuffling with federal antitrust regulators for twenty-one years—more than half of its entire life span.[36] That's twenty-one years of additional legal expenses. Twenty-one years of diverting executives' attention away from the business. Twenty-one years of maligning Microsoft's brand name. While the software dynamo may have narrowly escaped being broken apart, its clash with federal authorities had created a two-decade-long encumbrance.

On K Street, Microsoft's conduct surrounding the antitrust probe was viewed as political malpractice. In the years before the case, Microsoft had failed to build out a robust DC office that could cultivate allies on Capitol Hill and de-escalate conflict with regulators. As the legal proceedings got under way, Gates's deposition conveyed his disregard for Washington's authority so clearly that it encouraged the government—and, ultimately, the judge—to come down hard on his company. And during "Jack in his Jeep's" bungled attempts to influence the outcome of the case, Microsoft managed to harden the resolve of the prosecutors and turn itself into a front-page laughingstock. For a generation of corporate lobbyists, the Microsoft case offered a seminal lesson in government relations: a company like Microsoft might very well be smarter than Congress or more innovative than the bureaucracy, but at the end of the day, the federal government still has broad power over its business. Firms that didn't demonstrate sufficient deference to lawmakers and regulators were far more likely to incur their wrath. So, for a fast-growing company that hopes to become a multinational powerhouse, engaging with Washington is as essential as advertising to customers.

Tony Podesta was among the first to learn this lesson. As he developed into the go-to political fixer for Silicon Valley's technologists, he urged them not to neglect Washington the way Bill Gates had done. "They don't understand," Podesta said of tech firms, that "it's in their interest to pay attention"[37] to Washington.

Another tech industry operative put it more bluntly: "You can fight city hall, or you can co-opt city hall. And it's a hell of a lot easier to co-opt city hall."

In 2005, with the Microsoft case still reverberating on K Street, Podesta was hired by another game-changing tech firm, Google. It was a critical period for the Silicon Valley phenom. Google had handled 141 billion web searches that year alone,[38] and by converting the user data it collected into targeted search advertisements that it sold to other businesses, its revenue blasted from $86 million in 2001 to $6.1 billion in 2005.[39] After the company went public in 2004, Google's booming stock price turned roughly a thousand of its employees—including its former in-house masseuse—into millionaires.[40] Merriam-Webster added the term *google* to its English language dictionaries.[41] The company remained guided by its original mission statement: "to organize the world's information and make it universally accessible and useful." But amid its extraordinary growth, founders Larry Page and Sergey Brin looked for additional ways to achieve this goal, widening Google's ambition beyond its flagship search engine and pursuing a series of new ventures. The company launched Google News in 2002, and it later announced its desire to create a digital repository of every book ever published.[42] Then, in 2006, Google paid $1.65 billion to acquire YouTube,[43] outbidding rival Microsoft and media mogul Rupert Murdoch for the popular video-sharing platform.

Google's encroachment onto this new turf—news, books, video—petrified the incumbent leaders of those industries, many of whom had been watching their balance sheets weaken since the dawn of the Internet age. "There has never been a company whose influence extended so far over the media landscape and which had the ability to disrupt so many existing business models," the *New Yorker* said of Google.[44] "And its competitors share a vague worry that Google is more or less out to rule the world." These business rivals, which included a lineup of multinational conglomerates with sophisticated Washington operations, dispatched battalions of lobbyists to undermine Page and Brin's efforts. But the influence peddlers of competing firms weren't Google's only threat in the nation's capital. As Google grew in size, it became a bigger target for antitrust enforcers. According to former Intel CEO Andy Grove, the alarm over Google might have been even more widespread than the concerns that surrounded Microsoft in the 1990s. That's because while Microsoft's empire was limited to the computer software business, "Google's power is shaping what's happening to other industries," Grove told the *New Yorker*.[45] To protect itself from jittery competitors and federal regulators, Google needed a Washington operation that was every bit as powerful as its algorithms.

When Google began its lobbying efforts in 2003, company officials were determined not to repeat what they saw as Bill Gates's mistakes. One of Google's earliest lobbyists, Leo Giacometto, told executives explicitly, "You don't want to screw up like Microsoft did." Nevertheless, when Alan Davidson came aboard as the company's first full-time Washington employee in 2005, Google's government relations team was as poorly resourced as "Jack in his Jeep." At the time, the web giant had an annual lobbying budget of just $260,000, and its DC operation was headquartered in a small office where employees shared a receptionist, fax machine, and office supplies with other interest groups, including the Washington representatives of Kurdistan.

Despite being Google's top official in Washington, Alan Davidson lacked the profile of hardened corporate lobbyists. He had a background in engineering, a math and computer science degree from MIT, and an ambition to extend Google's "Don't be evil" mantra into the realm of federal politics. Under Davidson, the office functioned more like a university department than an influence-peddling enterprise. Google officials called Davidson their "tech evangelist," and he spent much of his time preaching to politicians and government officials about the wonders of the Internet. Before long, though, Davidson realized that he could benefit from the guidance of an experienced Beltway operative, and in 2005 he hired Tony Podesta to be his DC "consigliere."

Arriving at the company as its highest-paid outside lobbyist, Podesta was underwhelmed by Davidson's team. "He was naïve to the ways of

Washington," Podesta recalled. Davidson believed that new laws and regulations were worked out through good-faith debates and that the best way to influence lawmakers was with a sound argument. "They saw DC as, if you could explain what we do, then everyone will be on our side, and Alan could explain it better than anyone," Podesta says. "But it wasn't enough." Podesta helped persuade Davidson to invest more resources in Washington, but the firm's executives resisted at first. It wasn't until Google squared off with a seasoned corporate lobbying machine that the company recognized the flaws in its approach.

In late 2005, the incoming chairman of AT&T Inc., Ed Whitacre, made a series of remarks that would come to be known as the "shot heard around the web." Large phone and cable companies such as AT&T, Verizon Communications Inc., and Comcast Corp. had been spending billions of dollars to build out the broadband networks that carry Internet traffic to and from consumers. In an interview with *BusinessWeek*, Whitacre argued that AT&T and other phone and cable companies should be paid for allowing companies like Google to use their broadband networks. "How do you think they're going to get to customers?" Whitacre said.[46] "Through a broadband pipe. Cable companies have them. We have them. Now, what they would like to do is use my pipes free, but I ain't going to let them do that because we have spent this capital, and we have to have a return on it. So, there's going to have to be some mechanism for these people who use these pipes to pay for the portion they're using."

Inside companies like Google, Whitacre's comments sparked panic. The owners of popular websites and digital platforms feared that AT&T and other Internet service providers would begin demanding exorbitant tariffs in exchange for broadband access. More worrisome still was the threat that if these online destinations refused to pay up, the broadband companies would throttle down their web speeds or redirect traffic to competing search engines and video-streaming sites, many of which were owned by AT&T, Comcast, and other telecommunications companies themselves. As the issue became the subject of heated debate in Washington, Google's lobbying team began advocating for "net neutrality":[47] the principle that the corporate owners of the Internet's "pipes" should treat all web traffic fairly. Davidson and his colleagues wanted Congress and the Federal Communications Commission to create an open Internet policy that prevented AT&T and other telecommunications giants from favoring certain websites at the expense of others. Charging fees for the use of high-speed Internet lines, Google's lobbyists argued, would kill off start-ups and strangle innovation. At the start of the effort, Davidson tried to bring Congress and the administration around to its position through substantive policy conversations with key officials. But when Google's lobbyists and executives traveled to Capitol Hill, they found that these well-reasoned appeals did little to move members of Congress who had been expertly cultivated by AT&T's lobbyists.

At the time of Whitacre's comments, AT&T's army of more than three hundred lobbyists represented the biggest corporate influence-peddling operation in America. The $23 million that it had plowed into lobbying in 2005 was three times greater than the total amount spent by the entire Internet industry. And AT&T had spent the past several decades buttering up lawmakers with generous campaign donations in order to ensure that the telecommunications giant would get a friendly hearing during policy disputes. When the fight over net neutrality got under way, these investments paid off. After hiring pollsters to determine which messages would resonate best with lawmakers, AT&T ran advertisements in print publications on Capitol Hill claiming that Google wanted to block innovation and establish a monopoly. The company also sought to capitalize on Washington's increasingly partisan nature. AT&T's operatives circulated a news article showing that 98 percent of the political contributions made by Google's employees in the most recent election went to Democratic candidates and allied groups. In the 2004 presidential campaign, for example, Google employees donated a total of $250,000 to Democrat John Kerry and the Democratic National Committee and just $2,250 to George W. Bush and the Republican Party. The bulk of Google's lobbyists, AT&T's opposition researchers learned, were Democrats as well.

"We portrayed those guys as adjuncts of the Democratic Party," said Jim Ciccone, who ran AT&T's Washington office at the time. "We made the argument that their supporters wanted the government to take over the networks we'd built and nationalize them. We viewed that as a Socialist concept—and so did Republicans." At a time when Republicans controlled Congress and the White House, AT&T used these Democratic Party ties to discredit Google on Capitol Hill. Some went so far as to claim that if "George W. Bush" was typed into Google's search engine, the first result was "miserable loser."

AT&T's smear campaign succeeded in turning many Republicans on Capitol Hill against Google. "There was a real fury among the GOP side," recalled one of the few Republican lobbyists then working for the company. "Google was perceived as the opposition." At first, Google executives didn't appreciate the extent of the damage that AT&T's lobbyists had inflicted. That changed when Tony Podesta and a Republican lobbyist for Google brokered a series of secret, after-hours discussions between Davidson and senior Republican aides in Congress. Some of the Republican staffers were so afraid of being spotted with Google officials that they met in obscure dive bars, where they wouldn't bump into other GOP aides. During these "listening sessions," as Davidson called them, the staffers made it clear to Google's representatives that the Internet search giant was viewed as an enemy of the GOP. Estranged from the party in power, overmatched by a more muscular corporate lobbying adversary, and unable to gain traction for net neutrality policies, Davidson concluded that his team simply didn't have the wherewithal to achieve its objectives. Google's Washington office, he realized, would need a strategic overhaul to build better relationships with both parties.

Davidson jetted off to Google's headquarters in Mountain View to press for more resources and lobbyists, carrying with him the news article reporting that 98 percent of the company's campaign donations went to Republicans. But while Davidson's appeals were less than successful, Google's executives proved receptive to the advice of his "consigliere." Thanks to the guidance of Podesta and others, Google's government relations operation began to transform from a group of idealistic policy wonks into a team of trained killers.

Among Google's first priorities was to make friends on Capitol Hill, especially with the Republican lawmakers who'd frozen them out. "We always argued for a bigger, bipartisan presence," Podesta recalled. At the urging of Podesta, Google in 2006 created a political action committee, NetPAC, that for the first time allowed it to bankroll the campaigns of members of Congress. Though NetPAC was initially funded mostly by executives in Mountain View, California—Brin, Page, and CEO Eric Schmidt each kicked in $5,000 to provide the initial funding—its spending was controlled largely by the firm's lobbyists in Washington. In its first year, NetPAC provided roughly $30,000 in campaign donations, which it directed primarily to Republicans, such as House Majority Leader John Boehner of Ohio. As part of this effort to develop allies on the right, Podesta—who had by then added Republicans to his originally all-Democratic firm—dispatched the best-connected GOP lobbyists at podesta.com to assist Google. One such lobbyist, Dan Mattoon, was a lifelong friend and former top aide to Republican House Speaker Dennis Hastert, who was himself an old pal of Podesta's. Mattoon escorted Davidson and a delegation of Google officials around Capitol Hill, introducing them to Republican lawmakers who served on the committees responsible for crafting Internet policy. Another firm lobbyist, Josh Hastert, had even closer ties to the Republican leadership: he was the eldest son of the House Speaker. Podesta put Josh to work connecting Google executives to key GOP members of Congress. From there, Davidson further strengthened Google's credibility with the Republican Party by hiring one of President George W. Bush's top White House advisors and two former GOP senators, Connie Mack of Florida and Dan Coats of Indiana, who, like scores of other Washington lawmakers, had gone into lobbying after retiring from Congress.

While assembling the component parts of an effective inside-game strategy, Podesta agitated quietly for more changes at Google's Washington office. In private discussions with colleagues, he complained that the DC team was a bunch of "nerds"—comfortable with nuances of complex issues but lacking the stature and savvy to bend legislation in Google's direction. "It's not about policy," Podesta told his colleagues often, "it's about communications." Top Google executives would come to share in these concerns. From 2006 to 2008, Google's lobbying spending more than tripled to $2.8 million, and its Washington team swelled to include fifty-three lobbyists as well as dozens of media strategists, grassroots operatives, and public relations agents. Among the new hires was Pablo Chavez, a seasoned political operative and top aide to Republican Senator John McCain, who in 2009 took charge of the lobbying office. The enterprise moved into a prestigious office building on New York Avenue, a few blocks from the White House. At first, Google's DC team occupied a single floor of the building. But as new employees began flooding in, it expanded onto a second floor. Before long, Google's lobbying division grew so big that it needed a third floor as well. Eventually they bought a whole new building for the division a few blocks from the Capitol.

This initial period of growth was marked by the sloppiness and foul-ups of a typical start-up. Congressional aides struggled to get their calls returned by Google's lobbyists. Emails went ignored. Compounding the disorganization were the vast differences in the way business was conducted in Silicon Valley versus Washington. "They were these snooty, Harvard-educated policy experts who wore blue jeans instead of suits," a Google lobbyist said of the firm's influence-peddling team. Jim Ciccone, the head of AT&T's government relations department, said Google's original Washington team was "infected with hubris. They thought they were the smartest people in the world and they were dealing with troglodytes."

The deficiencies in the lobbying operation became especially clear in June 2006, when Sergey Brin decided to swing by Capitol Hill to try to drum up support for Google's position on net neutrality. The trip was hastily arranged[48] and poorly executed.[49] Since Brin alerted the DC team to his visit only the night before he arrived, Google's lobbyists were unable to secure meetings for him with certain key senators.[50] "I don't care if you are the Queen of England," said a Google lobbyist involved with the trip, "you don't call at the last second for a meeting." Though the lobbyists ultimately succeeded in scheduling a few appointments with lawmakers, including a first-term Democratic senator named Barack Obama, Brin failed to get any face time with Ted Stevens, the Alaska Republican whose chairmanship of the Senate Commerce Committee made him the upper chamber's most influential figure on net neutrality issues. Moreover, the Google cofounder showed up on Capitol Hill wearing silver mesh sneakers, jeans, and a black

T-shirt[51]—an outfit that signaled a Bill Gates–level of contempt for Washington's authority. "We are doing the best we can," Brin told the *Washington Post*.[52] "I think we are putting in a pretty good effort, but we don't have, you know, thirty or a hundred years, or however long [telecommunications companies] have been lobbying Congress."[53]

But the company's executives didn't seem to be learning from their mistakes. During another trip to Washington, Sergey Brin and Chief Executive Eric Schmidt showed up unannounced at the office of Senator Dianne Feinstein, where they were told that the senator had no availability in her schedule. A top aide to Feinstein, who was escorting another CEO out of the senator's office, recognized the Google executives and arranged for a quick chat. Members of Congress found their visits to Google's California headquarters just as disorderly. Once, when a group of lawmakers traveled to the Googleplex to test-drive prototypes of the company's self-driving cars, the engineers who had the car keys were nowhere to be found. The test-drives were canceled, and the lawmakers were sent home.

Despite such stumbles, Google's investment in Washington slowly started to pay off. With a push from two of Tony Podesta's allies in Congress—California Democratic Representative Anna Eshoo and Zoe Lofgren[54]—Google executives won a sweetheart deal from the National Aeronautics and Space Administration that allowed the Internet search giant's executives to keep a fleet of luxury business jets at a NASA-run airstrip just three miles from its Googleplex headquarters. Google's top executives were authorized to park a Boeing 767, a Boeing 757, several Gulfstream V jets, and a pair of helicopters owned by its executives at the joint civil-military Moffett Federal Airfield, which is also located in Mountain View. The company was even permitted to fuel up the jets with heavily discounted fuel from the Pentagon. In exchange, Google agreed to loan one of its planes to NASA officials to conduct scientific missions. Years later, internal investigators at NASA raised questions about the arrangement; they determined that NASA had used the plane only roughly two hundred times over a five-year period, while Google executives, including Brin, Page, and Schmidt frequently visited the airstrip for flights to Washington and New York, as well as vacation destinations such as Hawaii, the

Caribbean, and the island of Tahiti. The NASA investigators concluded that the arrangement regarding discounted fuel, which saved the internet search giant millions of dollars over the years, was improper.

More significantly, Google's DC office succeeded in securing regulatory approval for a historic acquisition spree that turned the Silicon Valley darling into a bona fide corporate empire. From 2005 to 2007, Google purchased nearly three dozen firms, including the video game advertising technology company Adscape Media for $23 million,[55] part of Internet map developer Endoxon for $28 million,[56] and the mobile operating system Android for $50 million.[57] These and other deals extended Google's reach far beyond the media industry and into a range of cutting-edge sectors: from web-based phone calling and word processing,[58] to 3-D modeling[59] and videoconferencing.[60]

When each acquisition was announced, Podesta and his staff marched up to Capitol Hill, sat down with the staff of key lawmakers, and explained why that particular deal didn't present any antitrust concerns. The goal, Podesta said, was to snuff out potential objections before they took root. "You win these fights largely by how they get characterized in the early days," Podesta says. "We made [the acquisitions] sound like they were in a parallel line of business rather than additive to their dominance in search." As a result, Podesta says, "We managed to sail through a lot [of acquisitions] without a lot of investigation from regulators."

The merger boom served to intensify the fears of business rivals and antitrust authorities, creating a whole new set of challenges for the company. And with the arrival of a forty-seven-year-old president who pledged to uproot the influence of K Street, Google's lobbying team would be forced to deploy an even more sophisticated array of tactics to achieve its objectives in Washington.

14

A few hours after Barack Obama was sworn in as America's forty-fourth presi-dent, an invite-only crowd of Hollywood stars and Washington lawmakers crammed into Washington's Andrew W. Mellon Auditorium. Actors Glenn Close, Jessica Alba, and Ben Affleck mingled with Democratic leaders such as New York Senator Chuck Schumer and Massachusetts Senator John Kerry[1] inside the seven-story Classical Revival building where, in 1949, President Harry S. Truman and his European counterparts gathered to establish the North Atlantic Treaty Organization. The events team at Google, which was throwing the A-list bash, had decorated the auditorium with a modernist flair in order to capture the forward-looking ethos of the digitally hip president. Campaign buzzwords—*Opportunity*, *Renewal*—were projected onto the ceiling. Glowing cubes were arranged around the dance floor. The winning submissions of a Google-sponsored children's essay contest about the future were posted for the guests to review. And the entire space was bathed in an all-white color scheme meant to signify the fresh start of the Obama administration.[2]

But the lavish celebration did more than just welcome a new commander in chief to Washington. It also served as a coming-out party for

Google's DC operation—the first public display of an unusually cozy re-lationship between the Obama team and the powerful digital conglomer-ate. As the *Los Angeles Times* put it, "Another inauguration took place in Washington this week—Google Inc. officially became a political power player."[3]

Google and Barack Obama had been allies well before his 2008 victory. As a younger member of the Senate, Obama was one of the first senators to recognize the Internet's potential to revolutionize how societies func-tion. He also understood that Google and other tech firms were capable of reshaping the entire economy and introducing new competition to once-stodgy industries. That's why, as a junior senator from Illinois, Obama had been one of the few lawmakers to endorse Google's net neutrality proposal, and during Sergey Brin's disastrous first lobbying trip to Capitol Hill, Obama was among the handful of senators who made time to receive him.[4] In 2007 Obama traveled to Google's Mountain View headquarters and un-veiled an industry-friendly tech policy platform[5] to a standing-room-only crowd of programmers and engineers. "I will take a backseat to no one in my commitment to network neutrality,"[6] he told the audience. After Obama launched his presidential campaign, Google employees donated a total of $800,000 to the effort—a sum greater than the amount Obama raised from employees of all but two other companies. Such support extended beyond the generosity of its employees. Google's engineers had developed many of the digital tools that Obama's famously tech-savvy campaign staff used to identify supporters and raise cash. The company's CEO, Eric Schmidt, endorsed Obama publicly and later hit the campaign trail with the soon-to-be president. On a warm November night in 2008, Schmidt was among the jubilant patrons at the campaign's victory party in Chicago.

In the months leading up to its glitzy inaugural celebration at the Mel-lon Auditorium, Google became deeply enmeshed in the incoming admin-istration. Four Google officials served on Obama's transition team, and the White House appointed Eric Schmidt to the President's Council of Advisors on Science and Technology as well as an advisory board tasked with devel-oping a plan to pull the economy out of the 2008 recession. Over the course of Obama's White House tenure, scores of Google employees left Silicon

Valley for DC. Megan Smith, a Google vice president, became Obama's chief technology advisor. Andrew McLaughlin, a public policy chief, was hired as his deputy chief technology officer. Not every role was so glamorous. When the administration's healthcare.gov website stalled out amid the crush of Americans signing up for Obamacare in the fall of 2013, a swat team of Google engineers was brought in to iron out the glitches. And, of course, Google had one of Washington's best-connected lobbyists.

Tony Podesta didn't start out as an Obama insider. Prior to 2008, in fact, he had few discernible ties to the incoming president. Like the bulk of the Democratic establishment, Podesta had backed Hillary Clinton over Obama during the 2008 presidential election, and he hadn't donated to Obama's 2004 campaign for the Senate (though his wife, Heather Podesta, had). Obama, for his part, had framed his presidential bid as a repudiation of the likes of Tony Podesta; on the campaign trail, he fulminated against the "lobbyists who kill good ideas and good plans with secret meetings and campaign checks."[7] Yet when Obama won the Democratic nomination, Podesta was able to create the impression that he was a close associate of Obama's top aides—and then, eventually, he became one.

This feat of political contortionism involved strategic calculation and a prestigious last name. The appointment of Tony's brother, John Podesta, as a chair of the Obama-Biden transition team,[8] endowed Tony with the aura of high-level access. From there, Tony advanced the notion that he was close to the new administration by reminding corporate clients and Beltway operatives that Obama and his senior advisors had their roots in his hometown of Chicago. The splashy party that Tony and Heather hosted on Inauguration Day helped polish his Obama bonafides, and a high-profile act of philanthropy worked to enshrine his reputation as a trusted confidant to the new White House. On January 9, 2009, the Smithsonian Institution announced that Tony and Heather Podesta had provided the funds for the museum system to acquire Shepard Fairey's iconic portrait of Barack Obama, *Hope*.[9] The K Street power couple had been admirers of Fairey's work for years; they owned a number of his other pieces. Now, through their gift, the throngs of spectators who arrived in Washington for Obama's swearing-in ceremony would be able to see the original image on the walls of the National Portrait Gallery. The donation made national headlines. "It seemed like a historic moment for the country," Tony told the *Washington Post*, "and a chance to do something for art and Democrats."[10] For the veteran influence peddler, though, this public act of generosity also served a business purpose, advertising his seemingly unique connection to Obama's political movement. "This donation does," as *Politico* reported, "leave little doubt about which lobbyist has good friends in the White House."[11]

Over time, Podesta turned this perception into reality. He visited the White House on behalf of lobbying clients on more than fifty occasions during Obama's first term, and he was invited regularly to social events at 1600 Pennsylvania Avenue. He attended a White House celebration of Greek Independence Day. He mingled with dignitaries at an East Room reception hosted by First Lady Michelle Obama that benefited the Foundation for Art and Preservation in Embassies. And when President Obama served salmon and salt-cured ahi tuna for the leaders of five Nordic nations at a formal state dinner, Podesta was there in his tuxedo, rubbing shoulders with pop singer Demi Lovato, actor Will Ferrell, and former *Late Night* host David Letterman.[12]

Such high-level access turbocharged Podesta's business. From 2007 to 2010, the firm's roster of lobbying clients jumped from 80 to 141. As annual revenue exploded from $11 million to nearly $30 million, the firm— which was renamed the Podesta Group—catapulted up the K Street food chain, climbing from the twentieth largest lobbying firm in Washington to the third. To handle the onslaught of new business, Podesta lured in staffers from congressional offices by offering salaries of roughly $320,000 a year, or about twice the annual pay of top members of Congress. Before long, Podesta had doubled the number of lobbyists on staff to fifty, and the firm had moved into an elegant office building in downtown Washington, paying $200,000 a month for two floors of office space connected by a spiral marble staircase. Podesta earned more than $2 million a year in salary and drew as much as $10 million in annual commissions and bonuses that he awarded to himself. *GQ* magazine anointed him as one of the "50 Most Powerful People in DC."[13] Things were so good that, according to a former Podesta Group lobbyist, the firm fired one of business mogul Elon

Musk's companies as a client because Musk demanded too much of the staff's time.

Podesta used his clout in Obama's Washington to benefit an array of blue-chip clients. On behalf of Warren Buffett's NetJets, he pushed Congress to allow partial owners of corporate jets to deduct the costs of flights from their taxes. For Oracle, he lobbied the Obama administration to let more high-skilled foreign workers into the domestic labor market. Working on behalf of Hertz, Dollar Rent A Car and a rental-car industry trade association, Podesta helped win Senate approval of a measure that limited consumers' ability to sue rental car companies if they were injured in an accident. Though the legislation was opposed by a powerful Democratic ally—trial lawyers—Podesta made a personal appeal to Senator Hillary Clinton to prevent her from voting against the bill. "He just asked her if she'd stand down, and she did," said Dan Mattoon, a lobbyist who managed the effort for Podesta. When the legislation passed without opposition in the Senate, the firm received an $800,000 bonus from his clients.

Podesta's K Street success put him in conflict with the liberal ideals of his past—as well as his own brother. When Democrats in Congress began crafting a policy to limit carbon emissions from oil and gas companies, Podesta saw his next opportunity for growth. "This is going to be one of the front-burner issues for Washington as far as one can reasonably look forward," he told a reporter.[14] Podesta was so aggressive in his recruitment of energy firms that by 2009, when Obama began pushing for climate change legislation, his lobbying firm was representing nine different clients with vested interests in weakening federal climate change measures, including British energy concern BP, Sunoco, and a coalition of large coal companies. "He would never leave money on the table," said Mattoon, the Podesta Group lobbyist. For much of the time Podesta was working to advance the interests of oil and gas firms, his brother John was working in the White House, where limiting greenhouse gas emissions was a priority. Such internal family conflicts were of little concern to Tony. "If John thinks the opposite of what I think, that's okay," Tony once told reporters. "We're still having dinner on Wednesday."[15]

In the aftermath of the 2008 housing crisis, Podesta assisted a number of financial institutions in managing the political fallout. He helped block a congressional effort to subject the credit-rating agencies, such as his client Standard & Poor's, to beefed-up regulations. He aided Wall Street investment funds like Fortress Investment Group in dodging new Treasury Department rules on mortgage bonds. When Wells Fargo faced allegations that it had discriminated against Black home buyers, Podesta recruited the heads of major civil rights organizations—including the NAACP, the Leadership Conference on Civil Rights, and the Urban League—to sit on a new, informal civil rights council that would meet quarterly with the CEO of the banking conglomerate and offer advice on issues involving minorities. The claims of discrimination ultimately subsided.

As he shaped federal policies on behalf of Big Business, Tony belittled the White House's efforts to reduce the power of influence peddlers, dismissing Obama's criticism as "part of his shtick." After the president announced strict new conflict-of-interest rules that included a ban on registered lobbyists working in his administration, Tony told a reporter the president "doesn't really mean it," and he recalled the time when Podesta's mother served Obama pasta at a fund-raiser at the lobbyist's home. Obama "seemed very happy to come to our house then," Podesta said.[16] In order to satisfy the new ethics rules, Tony joked that he was "taking my brother out of my will."[17] And in an interview with the New York Times, he expressed K Street's long-standing view of the futility of lobbying reform. "Whatever they're gonna do, they'll do," Podesta said. "They can ban lobbyists from having driver's licenses. We'll all get cars and drivers."[18]

Tony's wife, Heather Podesta, was at the same time building a considerable lobbying footprint of her own. She'd signed up blue-chip clients such as Eli Lilly & Co., Prudential Financial Inc., and Marathon Oil Corp. and become, according to the Washington Post, "an It Girl in a new generation of young, highly connected, built-for-the-Obama-era lobbyists."[19] As their business empires grew, Tony and Heather emerged as fixtures of Obama-era high society. Tony had a regular table at Tosca, an Italian restaurant in downtown DC that was popular with lobbyists and lawmakers. The walls of Tosca's dining room were sometimes adorned with artwork from Podesta's personal collection, which the couple had loaned to the restaurant.

He also became a part-owner of Centrolina, an Italian restaurant in a new billion-dollar development frequented by government insiders, politicians, and corporate chieftains. In addition to their $4 million mansion in DC's tony Kalorama neighborhood, Tony and Heather paid $3.2 million for a flat on Fifth Avenue in New York. To celebrate his sixty-fifth birthday, Tony threw himself a party at Washington's National Museum of Women in the Arts. Members of Congress, Obama administration aides, and scores of other VIPs turned out for the soiree, dubbed, "A Red Shoe Affair."

Podesta wasn't Google's only influence peddler to enjoy extraordinary access to the administration's key decision-makers. A top in-house Google lobbyist, Johanna Shelton, visited with Obama's aides at the White House a total of sixty times during the president's first four years in office—triple the total number of White House visits made by the entire lobbying department at Comcast, which was itself a well-connected firm. Given the number of ex-employees in the administration and the white-glove treatment afforded to its lobbyists, it could be difficult to tell where the White House ended and Google began. When the White House was considering rules for self-driving vehicles, an Obama technology advisor reached out directly to Google. "I'm pulling some more folks together this week to move to our next phase of consideration on self-driving cars," wrote the White House advisor R. David Edelman in an email to several Google employees. "Perhaps we might schedule a conference call in the next couple of weeks to touch base on the conversations you've been having, and what you see as top priorities for the likes of us government-types?"[20]

Despite its friends in the White House and its growing roster of influence peddlers, Google would soon experience the limits of traditional inside-game lobbying. In May 2011 the Internet search giant faced a serious threat to its business when senators introduced a measure titled Preventing Real Online Threats to Economic Creativity and Theft of Intellectual Property Act, acronymed PROTECT IP Act, or PIPA. The bill was designed to eradicate the online black market for pirated media and counterfeit goods by providing federal law enforcement authorities with new powers to crack down on such illicit transactions. Soon after, House lawmakers introduced companion legislation—the Stop Online Piracy Act, or SOPA—targeting Americans who use the Internet to illegally download or share music, movies, and other copyright-protected content. Among other things, the bills took dead aim at platforms such as Twitter, Facebook, and Google's YouTube by making them accountable for copyright infringement claims on materials posted by their users—a step that would expose ordinary Internet users as well as popular web firms to harsh legal liabilities.

The antipiracy effort enjoyed enthusiastic backing from a range of entrenched corporate interests that had suffered steep losses from online bootlegging, such as the Motion Picture Association of America, the Recording Industry Association of America, the Pharmaceutical Research and Manufacturers of America, HarperCollins Publishers Worldwide, NBCUniversal, and the National Football League. Inside Washington's special interest establishment, SOPA and PIPA were so popular that they managed to unite the city's bitterest rivals—the US Chamber of Commerce and the AFL-CIO labor union federation—in support of the effort. This broad coalition of politically connected corporations and trade associations plowed an astounding $90 million into lobbying on behalf of the bills, and by the summer of 2011, passage seemed all but assured. More than a third of all US senators had endorsed the PIPA bill, and the House version quickly garnered about thirty cosponsors. "Everybody thought there was no blocking the bill," recalled Aaron Cooper, an aide to Vermont Senator Patrick Leahy, who drafted the PIPA bill.

The bills' opponents had far fewer resources. They included a collection of politically unsophisticated web platforms—including Facebook, Twitter, eBay, and Tumblr—which, like Google, feared that stronger copyright infringement protections would make it harder to survive, as well as a collection of nonprofits who worried that the vague language in the legislation would restrict free speech and smother innovation. Hoping to persuade Congress to scrap the bills, Google and the other web platforms initially pursued a traditional inside-game strategy, dispatching lobbyists to Capitol Hill to make their case directly to lawmakers. By then, Google possessed considerable lobbying muscle; it had retained 125 different lobbyists and spent more than $11 million on lobbying activity that year alone.

Yet during their conversations with lawmakers, lobbyists for Google and its allies were unable to generate any support. "I was going to the Judiciary Committee, getting killed," one of them recalled to a reporter.[21] Against such well-financed and influential opponents, the futility of this inside-game approach soon became clear; if Google and its compatriots were going to turn back the antipiracy bills, they'd need to find another way.

It was around this time that one of Google's Washington strategists suggested an alternative strategy: the outside game. As a senior member of Google's Washington office, Adam Kovacevich, then thirty-four, had spent the past four years building out the firm's capacity for the more innovative lobbying tactics that were gaining favor on K Street. The Harvard University graduate had cut his teeth in political communications during stints on Capitol Hill and during the 2004 presidential campaign. At Google, he cultivated allies among customers, Internet users, and nonprofit groups who would be willing to go to bat for Google during future policy disputes. In its scramble to establish these alliances, Google began making donations to all manner of influential DC institutions, even those pushing agendas that clashed with Brin and Page's liberal worldviews. For instance, Google's founders were so concerned about climate change that they offered employees a $5,000 subsidy for buying fuel-efficient cars.[22] Yet in Washington, Google became among the largest contributors to the annual fund-raising dinner for the Competitive Enterprise Institute, a libertarian think tank and a prolific climate change denier. Another Google-backed group, the American Conservative Union, sponsored the annual CPAC conference that sustained the appeal of far-right heroes from Sarah Palin to Donald Trump. Still, in return for Google's generous donations, these right-wing organizations were willing to write letters on the company's behalf to Republican lawmakers during legislative debates.

Other outside-game efforts were more complex. As part of its "Get America's Businesses Online" program, Google employees traveled to various states around the country to hold seminars in which they helped create websites for local small businesses at no charge. The events were typically held at rented spaces in convention centers or libraries; inside, teams of computer programmers wearing Google T-shirts filled out rows

of workstations outfitted with computers and wired with high-speed Internet connections. The workshops were hugely popular, with hundreds
of small business owners clamoring to claim their free websites. But despite the clear benefit to these local entrepreneurs, Google's Get America's
Businesses Online program was less an act of philanthropy than a tool of
political influence.

Though they took place far outside of the Beltway, the location of each
event was selected carefully in order to advance the firm's agenda in Washington. For example, Google hosted a workshop in Iowa because it wanted
to gain favor with Iowa Republican Senator Chuck Grassley, the top Republican on the Senate Judiciary Committee. Likewise, it organized an event
in Minnesota in order to butter up Democratic Senator Amy Klobuchar, a
senior member of the Judiciary Committee's antitrust subcommittee. Both
Grassley and Klobuchar had broad purview over Google's business, and
each had expressed skepticism about the company's rapid expansion. So,
Google's DC team was thrilled when, during a Judiciary Committee hearing called to draw attention to the company's swelling size and power, both
senators spoke favorably of the Get America's Businesses Online program.

Google's Washington office viewed the senators' comments as a key
affirmation of its outside influence strategy. "I thought, 'Holy shit! These
events are working!'" said one Google lobbyist. Accordingly, when Google's
traditional lobbying efforts ran aground during the debate over antipiracy
legislation, Kovacevich decided to shift tactics. "We could see that the inside game was not working," he recalled. So, Kovacevich told his colleagues,
"Let's rally our users."

Adopting a strategy that Black Manafort and Tony Podesta had helped
pioneer years earlier, Kovacevich turned Google's opposition to the antipiracy legislation from a DC-focused lobbying push into a coast-to-coast
political-influence effort with all the bells and whistles of a presidential
campaign. Google brought in veteran political strategists, pollsters, and advertising firms. It set up the kind of "war room" that Bill Clinton's campaign
had made famous during the 1992 race; it even installed Robert Boorstin—
the political strategist who'd managed Clinton's war room—as the leader
of the operation. Twenty-four hours a day, Google's war room pulsed with

election-night intensity, as teams of young, tech-wise operatives worked in shifts to monitor news coverage, ensure that Google's perspective was included in all critical articles, and scour the Internet for potential allies.

Like any well-financed presidential bid, the Google team hired pollsters and focus groups to craft messaging for their effort. The campaign slogan they settled on—"Don't Kill the Internet"—vastly oversimplified the impact of the bill but succeeded in stirring apprehension among web users. To further stoke these fears, Google produced a series of newspaper advertisements depicting an enraged King Kong towering over the US Capitol while clutching a computer screen in its giant palm. "Attack of the Internet Killers," the advertisement read. "Jobs, innovation and investment, Internet security, and the next great Internet idea will all meet their doom if these monster bills survive." Antipiracy legislation, it claimed, would snuff out the web industry's growth.

Google and its allies did all they could to disseminate their message in the home districts of lawmakers facing tight reelection contests, who are more likely to bend to public pressure from voters. One nonprofit group supported by Google funded a massive phone call campaign targeting voters in these districts. In some cases, the approach worked too well. Not long after the calls started coming into Palm Springs, California, one irate constituent contacted the office of his congresswoman, Mary Bono, and threatened to kill the Republican lawmaker if she voted for the bill. Another target of the bill's opponents was Lamar Smith, the Republican congressman who authored the House legislation. Smith represented an Austin, Texas–area community with a burgeoning tech industry. So, one of Google's allies, the nonprofit group Fight for the Future, erected giant billboards in Austin to draw Smith's attention. Using the same red, white, and blue colors that appeared on the Texas flag, the billboards pulled from the state's famous motto in order to warn readers, "Don't Mess with the Internet."

All the while, Google was dispatching operatives to Austin to recruit business and civic leaders who could pressure Smith into dropping the antipiracy cause. One such recruit, Lanham Napier, was the founder of a data storage company and a friend of Congressman Smith's son. After

Google lawyers explained to him how the legislation would harm his business, Napier traveled to Washington with a delegation of Austin-area tech executives to personally express his concerns about the bill. Though opposition to the antipiracy effort was led by progressive tech companies and lefty Internet advocates, Google also worked hard to cultivate allies among the Far Right. The search giant hired Republican consultants to persuade leaders of the burgeoning right-wing Tea Party movement to oppose the legislation, arguing that it represented a dangerous incursion of the federal government into the free market. At the annual conference of the Conservative Political Action Committee, tech advocates handed out flyers with the exaggerated claim that the bill would give the Obama administration new powers to shut down websites.[23]

Ever so slowly, cracks began to emerge in the once rock-solid support for the antipiracy measures. After discussions with Tony Podesta, House Democratic Leader Nancy Pelosi announced that she had concerns about the legislation. When Congressman Smith brought the bill up for debate in the Judiciary Committee in mid-December, a handful of lawmakers who opposed the legislation used procedural tactics to postpone the panel's vote until after the holiday recess. During the delay, additional members of Congress turned against the legislation. Republican Senator Mike Lee of Utah said that he was rescinding his prior endorsement of the bill, and on January 14 Obama's White House issued a statement in which it declined to support the legislation due in part to worries that it could create cybersecurity risks by changing the Internet's architecture.[24]

Despite these defectors, the legislation still had a clear path through Congress. Senate Majority Leader Harry Reid had promised to hold a vote on the bill when the chamber reconvened after the recess. If Google and its allies were going to derail the antipiracy effort, they had only a couple of weeks to figure out how to do so.

There was one last option to consider. Over the past several months, tech advocates had been pleading with Google to participate in an upcoming protest in which websites, Internet portals, and social media platforms would either go dark or replace their typical content with critical information about the bills. Organizers hoped that this daylong protest would trigger enough outrage from Internet users to convince Congress to drop the legislation. Never before had Google used its platform to oppose legislation, and its executives worried about potential damage to the company's brand. But despite some initial hesitation, Google agreed to pitch in.

The decision proved to be a tipping point. Once Google came on board, other large web platforms followed suit, and on January 18, 2012, this collection of tech firms and nonprofit groups pulled off the mother of all outside influence campaigns. When users logged on to the web that day, they discovered, to their great frustration, that many of the sites they'd come to rely upon—Wikipedia, Reddit, Craigslist[25]—were either blacked out or displayed text outlining the detrimental impacts of the bills. Google, for its part, inserted a black censorship bar over its multicolored logo and posted a tool that enabled users to contact their elected representatives. "Tell Congress: Please don't censor the web!"[26] a message on Google's homepage read. With some 115,000 websites[27] taking part, the protest achieved a staggering reach; tens of millions of people visited Wikipedia's blacked-out website,[28] 4.5 million users signed a Google petition opposing the legislation,[29] and more than 2.4 million people took to Twitter to express their views on the bills.[30] "We must stop [these bills] to keep the web open & free,"[31] the reality-show star Kim Kardashian wrote in a tweet to her ten million followers.

As millions of ordinary Americans became foot soldiers in the campaign to kill the bills, congressional offices were swamped with angry messages from constituents. One irate Internet user called her senator's office and demanded directions to the closest McDonald's restaurant.

"I'm sorry, ma'am," a confused Senate aide responded. "How would I know where your nearest McDonald's is?"

"If you hadn't shut down the Internet, I could find it myself," the caller said. "So now I need you to tell me."

Similar exchanges were taking place all over Capitol Hill, as millions of Americans called or emailed their congressional representatives to demand the defeat of the bills, according to adversaries. Meanwhile, tech advocates and lobbyists were fanning out across the House and Senate to discuss the legislation with lawmakers. "The whole time in these meetings, you heard

344 | The Wolves of K Street

in the background the phones ringing constantly," said Erik Stallman, one of the tech advocates, "and you really thought that this is working. It was extraordinary."

With bracing speed, the public outcry began to dismantle the legislation's support. During a meeting with fellow House Republicans, Oklahoma congressman Tom Cole barked, "If this bill is so good, why don't I have two thousand constituents calling and saying how good it is? Because I have two thousand people calling me and saying how bad it is." Sensing the shift in momentum, Rick Lane, a lobbyist for Rupert Murdoch's News Corp, raced to Capitol Hill to urge the bill's proponents to remain firm. He was greeted by a frazzled congressional aide who told him that his office was being overrun by calls from the bill's opponents. "The calls are coming in a thousand to one," the aide told him, "and you are the one." An aide to one lawmaker, Democrat Mike Doyle of Pennsylvania, contacted Google's lobbying office with a simple plea: "Can you tell people to stop calling our office?"

By the end of the day, lawmakers were abandoning the legislation in droves. Over the course of a twenty-four-hour span, the number of House lawmakers endorsing SOPA dropped from eighty to sixty-five, while the number opposing it rocketed from thirty-one to more than a hundred. On January 20, 2012—two days after the protest—Senator Harry Reid canceled the Senate vote on PIPA, and Congressman Lamar Smith called off the committee debate on SOPA. The legislation was officially dead.

The abrupt demise of the antipiracy measures astonished the political-influence industry. Former Senator Chris Dodd, who advocated for the bills as the head of the Motion Picture Association of America, said he couldn't recall seeing "an effort that was moving with this degree of support change this dramatically."[32] In one sense, the episode was a triumph of modern outside-game strategy—a high-stakes demonstration of how a state-of-the-art effort to shape public opinion could vanquish a nearly $100 million campaign rooted in old-fashioned insider lobbying. More broadly, though, the defeat of SOPA and PIPA revealed a fundamental shift in the balance of power on K Street. Despite being dramatically outspent, Google and other whiz kids of Silicon Valley had managed to outmuscle the traditional pillars of DC's corporate lobbying establishment, including Hollywood movie studios, the pharmaceutical industry, and the US Chamber of Commerce. When the dust of the antipiracy debate finally settled, it became clear that a new age of corporate influence had dawned on the capital city. Google and its allies were no longer an assortment of popular websites and social media platforms. They were "Big Tech."

As former Google lobbyist Josh Ackil said, "Tech had a loaded gun and was pointing it around. People were scared of us." In subsequent years, lawmakers checked in with Google's lobbying team before introducing any legislation that might impact the company. "They would come to us and say, 'Is this bill okay? I don't want to get PIPA'd,'" recalled one former Google official.

While most of Washington was only then waking up to the immense power of Big Tech, officials at one federal agency were already well into an investigation of whether Google had grown too big and too dominant. Early in 2011, staff at the Federal Trade Commission had quietly launched an informal probe to determine if the Internet search giant was violating federal antitrust laws. A central question was whether or not Google was illegally using its dominance in the web-search business to steer Internet users to products and services that Google owned, at the expense of competing companies. At the confidential meeting at the agency's headquarters that spring, the FTC's five commissioners had voted to initiate a full-blown investigation into the company's business practices. The FTC set off to gather documents, interview witnesses, and follow leads in an effort to find out if there was enough evidence to bring formal antitrust charges against Google—a step that would trigger the most consequential clash between Silicon Valley and Washington since the Microsoft drama nearly fifteen years earlier. The FTC's chairman, Jon Leibowitz, had been the top Democratic lawyer for the Senate's antitrust subcommittee during the Microsoft battle, and at the outset of the Google probe, he recognized the possibility for a career-defining case of his own. Yet in order to bring a blockbuster lawsuit, Leibowitz and his colleagues would have to do more than uncover evidence of illegal activity; they'd have to withstand the pressure organized by Google's DC office. Because at the same time that the agency was carrying out its probe, an entire ecosystem of Google lobbyists, media strategists, and political operatives was toiling just as assiduously to make sure that the work of the FTC's investigators never saw the light of day. "It was an all-hands-on-deck kind of fight," Podesta recalled.

Unbeknownst to the FTC, Google's executives had already learned of the probe's existence and had begun working to derail it. At first, the web giant's officials didn't think there was much they could do to stop the federal agency. Inside Google's DC office, however, a key operative was pressing for a more aggressive approach. That spring, Adam Kovacevich drafted a detailed memo to company executives in Washington laying out a multifaceted campaign with the express goal of sapping the FTC's resolve. Google, he wrote, should treat the antitrust investigation "like a presidential primary" rather than a "papal conclave."

Among the campaign's central components was an innovative plan to mobilize a set of Washington figures who aren't typically thought of as corporate influence peddlers. By recruiting university professors, antitrust attorneys, and former FTC officials to advocate for Google in the press, the Internet search giant was able to apply a gloss of credibility to the agenda of its lobbyists. Inside Google's Washington office, this initiative was given a code name: Project Eagle.

The targets of Project Eagle were the agency officials who would ultimately decide whether or not to bring an antitrust case against Google: FTC chairman Leibowitz and his four fellow commissioners. Shaping the views of the commissioners, however, was tricky business. As an independent agency, the FTC was specifically designed to shield its leaders from political pressure. Commissioners are nominated by the White House and confirmed by the Senate, and they can't be fired by the president during their seven-year terms. But Kovacevich understood that the FTC's commissioners are political players, and they prefer to take actions that have the support of members of Congress, former colleagues in the legal community, and respected antitrust scholars. As such, the objective of "Project Eagle" was to gin up criticism of the FTC's treatment of Google among the very people the commissioners look to for support. By generating

disapproval from such policy experts, Google's operatives hoped to persuade the FTC's leadership to drop the antitrust probe.

In the months before the FTC had even voted to open a formal investigation, Google's operatives began assembling a roster of antitrust experts
who were willing to push back against the FTC's investigation in the press.
The company's vast financial resources helped lubricate the recruitment
process, as the bulk of the Project Eagle thought leaders—a network that
would eventually include about fifty—had previously received payments
from Google or benefited from the company's largess, either directly or
indirectly.

For example, in June 2011, as Google was planning to publicly announce that it was under investigation, its operatives reached out to Project
Eagle experts to see if they'd be willing to help the company. Among the
most enthusiastic participants in this PR push was David Balto, a former
antitrust lawyer at the FTC and the Department of Justice. On June 23, the
day before Google planned to announce the investigation, Google officials
spoke with Balto on the phone. The following day, Balto rebuked the FTC's
inquiry in several ways. He told Reuters that "the complaints presented
to the FTC are from disgruntled advertisers, not consumers,"[33] and he remarked to the *Los Angeles Times* that "any alleged power by Google is much
more evanescent than the concrete power that Microsoft possessed."[34] In his
interview with the *LA Times*, Balto even deployed a phrase—"competition
is literally a click away"—that was nearly identical to the slogan cooked up
by Google's messaging team, "Competition Is Just a Click Away." In addition, a white paper that Balto had written defending Google against claims
that it was abusing its market power—titled, "Internet Search Competition:
Where's the Beef?"[35]—was posted online in the early morning of the day of
the announcement. This coordinated timing allowed the company's media
strategists to direct journalists to the Google-friendly research as soon as
the news broke of the FTC's investigation. Both the white paper and the
media interviews created the impression that Balto was an independent
antitrust expert with no affiliation to Google. But that wasn't exactly the
case: he worked for an organization that received funding from Google,
the Center for American Progress, and he had previously received funding

from Google for a research paper. The operatives in charge of Project Eagle referred to Balto as "our leading liberal voice."

Other Project Eagle experts also pitched into this PR campaign. Following discussions with Google's Washington office, Geoffrey A. Manne, a former University of Chicago Law School lecturer and the founder of the Google-backed International Center for Law & Economics, published an op-ed in the news outlet Main Justice asserting that the FTC's antitrust probe into Google was an exercise in "political aggrandizement."[36] Manne wrote that FTC chair Jon Leibowitz "appears more interested in using Google as a tool in his and [FTC Commissioner J. Thomas] Rosch's efforts to expand the FTC's footprint."[37] Google's operatives also spoke by phone with Adam Thierer, a senior research fellow at another think tank funded by the company, the Mercatus Center at George Mason University. Less than a week after the FTC's antitrust investigation into Google was made public, Thierer wrote an opinion piece for Forbes.com in which he lamented, "[T]he prospect of Uncle Sam as Search Czar raises the more problematic specter of heavy-handed regulation of cyberspace and the fast-evolving Digital Economy in general."[38] In neither case did Manne or Thierer disclose Google's financial support for the organizations where they worked; think tanks and academic institutions don't always require such disclosures.

All told, over more than two years, the dozens of antitrust experts affiliated with Project Eagle churned out more than seventy-five op-eds, many of them targeted at specific lawmakers or FTC commissioners. One pro-Google opinion piece was placed in a small community newspaper in Cedar Rapids, Iowa, the *Gazette*,[39] in order to catch the attention of the state's Republican senator, Chuck Grassley, an influential player on antitrust issues. A piece by David Balto ran on a website that focuses on political news in Wisconsin, wispolitics.com,[40] in the hopes that it would reach Wisconsin's Herb Kohl, a senior Democrat on the Senate antitrust panel. Google also benefited from an article by conservative former federal judge Robert Bork,[41] then a consultant to Google, that was intended to harden the opposition of the FTC's two Republican commissioners against bringing a case. The financial relationships between Google and some of the authors were transactional. Former FTC chairman James Miller III was given a Google contract worth between $10,000 and $15,000 to take part in the Project Eagle effort and perform some additional consulting work, according to a person familiar with the arrangement. As part of his contract, Miller authored opinion articles and provided general advice on antitrust matters. Miller published six pro-Google opinion pieces in the *Wall Street Journal*, the *National Review*, *The Hill*, and the *Washington Examiner*. "Former FTC commissioners love to be paid," said one Google operative involved in this effort. Unlike some of his Project Eagle compatriots, Miller disclosed his ties to Google in his articles.

Among Google's fundamental objectives, Kovacevich said later, was to erode the faith of Leibowitz and his fellow FTC commissioners in the viability of an antitrust case. "We knew that Leibowitz wanted to make Google the next Microsoft," Kovacevich recalled. "So, we needed to show him that the FTC's legal theories were flawed." He continued, "Our whole strategy was sowing doubt inside the FTC that this was a winnable case in court." As part of this effort, Google's DC operatives deployed another component of Project Eagle: a $2 million program that funded and promoted academic research at prestigious universities to help substantiate Google's legal views. Kovacevich had hired a Princeton University academic, Deven Desai, to run the operation for Google's Washington office. Starting in 2009, the company helped finance hundreds of research papers at institutions such as Harvard University and the University of California at Berkeley; most—though not all—of this work was supportive of Google's political objectives. According to thousands of pages of emails obtained by the *Wall Street Journal*,[42] Google funded professors whose papers, for instance, declared that the company didn't use its market dominance to improperly steer users to Google's commercial sites or its advertisers and that it hadn't unfairly quashed competitors.

"Hi, Dan," Kovacevich wrote in an April 2011 email seeking to recruit a University of Michigan professor. "I head up our public affairs and policy work on competition issues and would love the chance to chat with you."

Google's support for such scholarship came in the form of grants from its academic-research division—ranging between $5,000 and $400,000 per project—or through financial contributions to think tanks. But the professors don't always reveal Google's backing in their research. University of Illinois law professor Paul Heald, for instance, sent an email to Google in which he pitched an idea for a research project on copyrights. Though he received $18,830 from Google, the 2012 paper neglected to name his financial backer. "Oh, wow. No, I didn't. That's really bad," he told a *Journal* reporter, Jack Nicas, who'd asked him about the matter. "That's purely oversight."[43]

Behind the scenes, Google's lobbying office took an active role in the production and dissemination of this academic work. In certain years, Google officials in Washington compiled wish lists of academic papers that included working titles, abstracts, and budgets for each proposed paper— then they searched for willing authors, according to consultants who worked for Google on the initiative.[44] "We said, 'What might be good to have in the environment?'" recalled one person involved in the effort. "Then we went to find the academics who could do that." As the projects neared their conclusions, some of the researchers shared their work with Google's operatives before publication and allowed company officials to edit unpublished drafts. "It's in really great shape!" a Google lawyer wrote in an email to a University of Utah law professor who was writing a paper that supported Google's position on US patent laws. "Would be good to discuss a couple of things briefly . . . that are somewhat related."[45] When the work was published, Google promoted the research papers to government officials and sometimes paid travel expenses for professors to meet with congressional aides and administration officials, according to the former lobbyist.

As the FTC's regulators began scrutinizing Google, the company used its academic-research initiative to deflect antitrust accusations. During the years that the agency was conducting its investigation, Google helped bankroll three dozen academic papers focusing on antitrust matters, many of which supported Google's viewpoint. Google helped fund a paper co-written by Geoffrey A. Manne and George Mason University law professor Joshua Wright, "Google and the Limits of Antitrust: The Case Against the Case Against Google."[46] The paper was funded in part by a grant from the International Center for Law & Economics, which, in turn, received funding from Google. David Balto, the former FTC official who defended the company in the press, wrote a paper titled "Using Antitrust Enforcement Prudently in High-Tech Markets: The Flaws of a Potential Antitrust Case Against Google."[47] Balto's paper was commissioned by the same Google-funded center that helped finance the study by Manne and Wright.

Though the authors acknowledged Google's support in the papers themselves, the company wasn't always transparent about its hand in the research. In September 2011 Google CEO Eric Schmidt appeared at a tense hearing before the Senate Judiciary Committee's antitrust subcommittee, and in his written testimony following his appearance, he cited one of Balto's papers.[48] "As David Balto, the former policy director of the Federal Trade Commission recently observed: 'Google has consistently led the industry in innovations and has played an important role in the evolution of search,'" Schmidt wrote to the committee.[49] The CEO neglected to tell the senators that his own company had helped finance this work.

Google's influence-peddling campaign was exactly the sort of zealous corporate advocacy that Lewis Powell had called for some thirty-eight years earlier, when he urged a beleaguered business community to "press vigorously in all political arenas for support of the enterprise system." But until Google began its crusade to tank the FTC's antitrust case, few American corporations had realized Powell's vision quite so fully.

On top of these more advanced outside-game strategies, Google was using old-fashioned brute force to encumber the work of the commission staff. In July 2011, just a week after revealing the existence of the probe, Google leaked to the media that it had retained twelve additional lobbying firms in a hiring spree that was, in part, a show of force designed to intimidate the FTC's leadership. The development spiked Google's lobbying spending from $5 million in 2010 to $11.5 million in 2011, increasing the total number of lobbyists on the web giant's payroll from 57 to 125. Among the new lobbyists it engaged was Charlie Black, the former Black Manafort founder whose connections to Senate Republicans were unrivaled. Meanwhile, Google's legal team, led by Wilson Sonsini, based in Palo Alto, California, was frustrating the FTC's investigators. As part of its antitrust inquiry, agency officials had issued subpoenas demanding that Google turn over reams of internal communications and other documents. But when the subpoenaed files arrived at the FTC, the agency's staff was surprised by how few documents were included. One FTC official involved with the probe believed Google's lawyers shielded many emails from the subpoena's reach through "super aggressive" assertions of legal privilege, saying, "They held back millions of documents." The official continued: "The staff was deeply suspicious but couldn't do anything about it" because the FTC's leaders were unwilling to engage in an additional struggle with Google's tenacious legal team.

Other efforts were more personal in nature. When a senior antitrust investigator working on the Google probe departed the FTC for a top job in Microsoft's Washington office in early 2012, officials at the Internet search giant alleged that he would share confidential information from the agency with its competitors. Google operatives worked to plant stories in the media suggesting a sinister motive behind Microsoft's hiring of ex-FTC attorney Randall Long. A story in Reuters, for instance, said that Long had access to "thousands" of confidential documents related to FTC investigations into Google,[50] implying that he might relay that information to his new employer. Then, once word of Long's hiring by Microsoft appeared in the press, a group called Americans for Limited Government wrote a letter to the FTC's inspector general demanding an investigation into the matter. Though the agency didn't accuse Long of wrongdoing, the episode infuriated FTC Chairman Jon Leibowitz because he viewed it as an effort by Google to intimidate his antitrust investigators by showing them that the company was capable of targeting them—personally—even after they'd left the government. Leibowitz confronted a top Google lawyer in his FTC office.

"That was so out of line it was disgraceful," the FTC chairman told the Google attorney. "You need to apologize."

"We shouldn't have done it," the Google lawyer admitted. "We are learning as we go along."

Despite Google's elaborate pressure campaign, the staff of the FTC's Bureau of Competition, which has purview over antitrust matters, did exactly what

Google most feared. In the summer of 2012, they formally recommended that the commissioners move forward with antitrust charges against the web giant.[51] Following its roughly two-year investigation, the FTC staff submitted a 160-page report to the agency's leadership concluding that Google's "conduct has resulted—and will result—in real harm to consumers and to innovation in the online search and advertising markets."[52] The staff advised the agency to take Google to court over three alleged violations of antitrust law. The staff alleged that Google had copied content from rival websites such as Yelp, TripAdvisor, and Amazon, and when these competitors asked it to stop pilfering their content, Google threatened to remove them from its search engine. "It is clear that Google's threat was intended to produce, and *did* produce, the desired effect," the report said, "which was to coerce Yelp and TripAdvisor into backing down."[53] Through such actions, according to the report, Google was able to send the message that it would "use its monopoly power over search to extract the fruits of its rivals' innovations."[54] The FTC's staff also alleged that Google had violated antitrust laws by manipulating the results of its dominant search engine to steer users to its own products and by restricting websites that published its search results from working with rivals like Yahoo! and Microsoft's Bing. With this recommendation from the FTC's staff, formal antitrust charges against Google seemed likely. The only thing standing in the way of the case was the approval of the FTC's commissioners, who nearly always follow the lead of their staff. Washington's long-slumbering consumer protection bureaucracy, it appeared, was indeed ready to roar back to life.

Inside Google, word of the report touched off an eleventh-hour scramble to persuade the FTC's leadership to reject the staff's recommendations. The company's Project Eagle–affiliated experts moved into overdrive, pumping out pro-Google op-eds at an accelerated clip. On October 25, 2012, Ryan Radia, of the Competitive Enterprise Institute, posted an opinion piece on CNET titled "Google Is Many Things—but Not an Illegal Monopoly."[55] The following year, Google became the biggest donor to the Competitive Enterprise Institute's annual gala. A week after Radia's article was published, Ed Black, the president of the Computer & Communications Industry Association, of which Google is a member, published an op-ed in the right-wing

Daily Caller concluding that when it came to proving harm to consumers, "FTC's case against Google is practically nonexistent."[56]

Meanwhile, Google's lobbyists and top executives were huddling with senior officials at the White House and the FTC. In the days after Barack Obama secured his reelection victory in November 2012, Google's top in-house lawyer, David Drummond, flew to Washington to meet face-to-face with FTC Chairman Jon Leibowitz. Afterward, the two had a follow-up phone conversation. "Am traveling back home but had a quick question," Drummond emailed Leibowitz on Friday, November 9. "Do you have five minutes to chat over the weekend?" The following week, Google lobbyist Johanna Shelton and a top Google antitrust lawyer went to the White House to meet with Obama's senior technology advisor. Around this time, Google's lead outside attorney, a former top FTC official named Susan Creighton, sent an eight-page letter to Chairman Leibowitz poking holes in the government's case. The letter cited research from Harvard Law School professor Einer Elhauge and Boston University professor Michael Salinger, each of whom received funding from Google. Creighton did not disclose the Google funding in her letter.

All the while, Tony Podesta and other Google lobbyists were busy rallying the company's backers on Capitol Hill. Following news leaks suggesting that the FTC was considering suing Google under the FTC Act if it couldn't make a case under the more restrictive Sherman Antitrust Act, Podesta helped persuade lawmakers to sign a letter from Congress to the FTC trashing the move. "Such a massive expansion of FTC jurisdiction would be unwarranted, unwise, and likely have negative implications for our nation's economy," read the November 2012 letter, which was signed by two of Podesta's friends in Congress, Representatives Zoe Lofgren and Anna Eshoo, the biotech industry champion whom Podesta had first met years earlier when they both worked as aides on Ted Kennedy's 1980 presidential campaign. Podesta then helped persuade one of his best contacts in the Senate, Democrat Dianne Feinstein, to draft her own letter to the FTC's leaders. "I hope that, out of fairness to the company, any investigation can be wrapped up and resolved one way or another in a reasonable time, and that the leaks will stop," Feinstein wrote.

Since much of the effort involved the sort of shadow lobbying tactics that did not require public disclosure, few at the agency understood the full extent of Google's influence campaign. This cloak of secrecy made it even more effective. The continual flow of pro-Google op-eds, Google-funded research, and letters from Google-friendly lawmakers succeeded in creating what one senior FTC official described as a "surround sound" effect: everywhere that FTC officials turned, they saw respected policy experts or lawmakers denouncing the agency's investigation. "These papers keep landing in your in-box," said the senior FTC official. "You'd be sitting at your desk and—*bam!*—here comes a letter from Zoe Lofgren or Anna Eshoo saying that an enforcement action would not be a great thing. And then an economist like Geoff Manne or Josh Wright publishes a paper and—*bam!*—that would land in your in-box." Gradually, this tide of criticism seemed to soften the resolve of the agency's leaders. "You could tell there was a change in the FTC's attitude toward the case," recalled one official. "It didn't feel right compared to every other investigation we had worked on, particularly toward the end."

Still, for the FTC staffers, some of whom were idealistic, young political appointees eager to bring antitrust charges, there was one more card to play. For more than six months, the agency's investigators had been pressing for a formal interview with Google founder Larry Page. Such on-the-record questioning provided a final opportunity for the FTC's staff to obtain evidence of alleged anticompetitive actions by Google. But the Google founder never seemed to be available. Page had originally been scheduled to give a deposition from his Mountain View office almost a half year earlier, on June 1, 2012. But when a team of FTC lawyers arrived in California for the proceedings, Google's lawyers said that Page was ill and not able to speak. A new date was set for later that month in Washington. Yet this interview was also called off after Google's lawyers again said Page was sick. Months went by, and Google's lawyer still claimed that Page was too sick to answer questions from the FTC lawyers.

In mid-October the head of the FTC's Bureau of Competition sent a terse email to one of Page's lawyers. "I see the reports that Mr. Page has begun speaking at public events," she wrote in an email. "Can he be in

Washington for a day at the end of next week?" Once again, the Google lawyer responded that Page's voice was "still quite hoarse and raspy" and that he was "not presently able to conduct a deposition."

The agency finally scheduled a deposition with Page at FTC headquarters for late November, and the Google founder boarded one of his firm's luxury business jets and flew to Washington for the occasion. But although Page gave his long-awaited deposition on November 27, the investigation's momentum had by then been critically undermined by Google's pressure campaign. Google's executives had also grown tired of the FTC's investigation; they wanted the agency to either sue the company or move on. At a high-stakes meeting, Google executives Page and Eric Schmidt told the FTC chairman that they were prepared to defend the company in court. In order to file an antitrust lawsuit, however, Chairman Leibowitz needed a majority vote from the agency's five commissioners—but only he and one other commissioner were willing to vote in favor of bringing a case against Google.

Leibowitz had no choice but to back down. On November 28, the day after Page's deposition, a top Leibowitz aide emailed FTC staff with the news: "We're going to start our settlement discussions with Google," he wrote.

Shortly before Christmas, the FTC informed Google that it wanted to resolve the matter without bringing antitrust charges. Google lawyer David Drummond and FTC chair Jon Leibowitz got to work on a settlement agreement, and, within a few days, they were nearing a deal. As they were wrapping up, holiday travel plans disrupted their discussions. Leibowitz had flown to Costa Rica with his wife and children; Drummond was vacationing in Hawaii. "Cell phone service is generally good," Leibowitz wrote to Drummond a few days before Christmas. "Feel free to call any time."

"Just tried you," Drummond responded. "Am in much more pedestrian Hawaii. . . . Am on my cell so any time works for me too."

"I'll wait until it's at least 9:00 AM on the Big Island (and various smaller ones)," Leibowitz responded the following morning.

Eventually, after several days of missed calls, the FTC chairman and the Google lawyer managed to hammer out a final agreement. The settlement was an unambiguous victory for the Internet search giant. In exchange for the FTC dropping its antitrust investigation, Google promised to make a few minor, voluntary changes to its business practices—none of which addressed the issues flagged as anticompetitive by some of its critics inside the agency. FTC staff shared copies of the proposed settlement over email and allowed Google lawyers to make changes.

By New Year's Eve 2012, everything appeared to be set. Then Google's lawyers made an unusual demand.

At the last minute, the web giant's attorneys refused to sign the settlement agreement unless the FTC allowed Google to read the agency's public statement on the settlement before it was released. "[H]aving an understanding of the substance of the Commission statement is of the utmost importance to Google," a Google lawyer wrote in an email to two senior Leibowitz aides. The web firm's lawyers worried that Leibowitz would publicly accuse Google of abusing competitors. "If you accuse us of breaking the law," a Google official would later recall telling the FTC, "then we are going to court."

The Leibowitz aides rejected the request, refusing to share any further information until Google agreed to sign the settlement. Suddenly the two sides were at an impasse.

That evening, one of the FTC lawyers alerted Leibowitz to the snag. "We never wrote Google a blank check promising to make them happy about our messaging," wrote Christopher Renner, a senior counselor to the FTC chairman. Leibowitz received the email while celebrating New Year's Eve at a small dinner party held at a vacation home in the Blue Ridge Mountains of Virginia. The property was owned by Ron Klain, a longtime aide to then Vice President Joe Biden who would later serve as President Biden's first White House chief of staff. Leibowitz excused himself from the dinner party and retreated to one of Klain's bedrooms, where he typed out a frustrated email to his staff.

Google has "not honored their commitment (and really you can add 'yet again')," he wrote. "From the Commission's perspective, we are done. Please tell Google we no longer have a deal." He continued: "I propose that everyone enjoy their New Year's and someone figure out how to do a conference call tomorrow afternoon to discuss. You also need to make sure that all the Commission offices are aware of this startling, disturbing development very shortly."

A minute later, Leibowitz emailed the FTC's two other Democratic commissioners with the news. "At this point, I am done: I just want to end negotiations and bring a case on Wednesday." Leibowitz ended his email by writing: "I need to have a few drinks before I can think clearly."

Before rejoining the New Year's Eve dinner party, Leibowitz called an aide and asked him to relay his threat to attorney David Drummond.

The next morning, Leibowitz loaded his family and luggage in his car for the three-hour drive back to Washington. As he connected by cell phone with Drummond, Leibowitz told his two teenage daughters—both of whom were in the car—not to listen in on his conversation.

"The deal is off," Leibowitz told him as his car cruised down the highway. "We will go to court."

Shortly thereafter, Drummond backed down. By noon that day, the FTC had received a signed settlement agreement from Google. Despite the eleventh-hour chaos, it was now official. Google had escaped from the FTC's antitrust lawsuit.

Later that day, Drummond sent a final email to Leibowitz: "Happy new year to you," the Google lawyer wrote.

"Aloha," the commissioner replied.

A few days later, on January 3, the FTC announced the settlement. In his public remarks, Leibowitz did not criticize Google.

Following his unsuccessful effort to bring a lawsuit against Google, Leibowitz announced his retirement from the FTC. To replace him, Obama tapped Edith Ramirez, the sole Democratic commissioner who declined to move forward with the antitrust case.

15

On the second Sunday of the month, Tommy Boggs pulled into the parking lot of FedExField, the eighty-thousand-seat football stadium located about ten miles east of the US Capitol, and hobbled up to the luxury skyboxes. It was a day of optimism for the people of Washington. Though the city's NFL football team had posted a humiliating last-place finish the prior year, on this afternoon of the first home game of the new season there was a feeling among the spectators that better days were ahead. As the fabled lobbyist settled into his VIP suite, Boggs absorbed the auspicious atmosphere. It was a bright, pleasant day; sixty-seven degrees at kickoff. The crowd erupted in cheers when Washington took a 21–0 lead in the second quarter. Inside the skybox, Boggs sipped a drink and chatted with family and friends, including his wife of fifty-four years, Barbara; the youngest of his three sons, Douglas; and a handful of the current and former lobbying colleagues who had remained loyal to him throughout the unpleasantness of the past few years. Down on the field, the local NFL team would defeat the visiting Jacksonville Jaguars by a score of 41–10, much to the delight of Boggs and the rest of the die-hard Washington fans in attendance. With the sun shining and the home team winning, the mood inside the VIP suite began to evoke the triumphant morale of Boggs's earlier years—back when the gregarious master of political influence used to go duck hunting with members of Congress and play cards on Air Force One. But these days, it seemed, no one was calling the King of K Street for advice anymore.

When the game ended, Boggs lumbered back to his car. It was a few days before his seventy-fourth birthday, and his unsteady frame creaked and groaned when he moved. Decades of second helpings and stiff drinks had ballooned Boggs's waistline, and on account of an old back injury, he now needed a cane to walk. The deterioration wasn't limited to Boggs's body. While his mental faculties remained sharp, his spirit seemed to have wilted. The man whose Cajun-spiced charisma once mesmerized heads of state and captains of industry now appeared, to those around him, sullen and withdrawn. Reaching his vehicle, Boggs and his wife drove back into Washington, where they met friends for dinner at a sushi restaurant before returning to their home in nearby Chevy Chase, Maryland. Barbara went to bed. But Tommy stayed up. His schedule, in recent months, had grown more accommodating of late nights and lazy mornings. On tomorrow's day planner, there were no critical meetings about the direction of the lobbying firm, no last-minute negotiations with Senate leadership. Instead, Boggs poured himself a drink, sat down on the couch, and clicked on the TV.

Tuning to PBS, Boggs found a documentary on the presidency of Franklin Delano Roosevelt. It was a fitting telecast for him to watch, especially this evening, because of how crucial the thirty-second president had been to the Boggs family legacy. After all, it was FDR's political coalition that had sent the family's patriarch, Hale Boggs, to Washington nearly three-quarters of a century earlier. And it was the economic philosophy that FDR had helped enshrine in the city—of a muscular federal government that could shield consumers from the excesses of capitalism—that Tommy Boggs had done so much to discredit as he turned himself into the premier Democratic lobbyist of his generation. At some point, Boggs drifted off.

The television was still on the next morning, when Boggs's wife found him. His body was slumped over on the couch. At first, Barbara thought he was still sleeping. But he never woke up.

Over the following days, the Democratic Party's ruling class would conduct all the rituals and traditions that attend the loss of political giants in Washington. Boggs's obituaries appeared in the *Washington Post* and the *New York Times*. Senate Democratic Leader Harry Reid announced his death on the Senate floor[1] and proclaimed him "an institution in this city." House Democratic Leader Nancy Pelosi delivered a eulogy at his funeral. Over at the Palm, the downtown DC power-lunch spot favored by corporate lobbyists, the staff arranged to have Boggs's preferred midday location, table 30, covered with a black tablecloth.[2] Friends, lobbyists, and lawmakers issued reverential statements to the press. "Washington is a much better place," Senator Patrick Leahy told *Politico*,[3] "because of Tommy Boggs passing through here."

Though the family declined to conduct an autopsy, Boggs's sister, the TV journalist Cokie Roberts, told the media that the lobbyist had died of an apparent heart attack.[4] It was a reasonable conclusion: four years earlier, Boggs had been airlifted from a cruise ship for emergency coronary bypass surgery. But to the friends and family who'd remained close to him at the end, there was another factor to consider. The painful conflict that had consumed his firm over the past several years—with all the backstabbing, the bitterness, and ultimately the loss—had left a once towering figure isolated and bereft. For this reason, some of Boggs's friends thought there was another explanation for his passing. Perhaps Washington's legendary master of influence hadn't died of a blocked artery but, rather, a broken spirit.

The trouble at Patton Boggs began to surface at the conclusion of what had been a blockbuster period for the illustrious lobbying firm. Boggs and his colleagues opened the twenty-first century with a series of lucrative victories. In 2003 the firm helped secure passage of the Medicare Prescription Drug, Improvement, and Modernization Act, which permitted Medicare to purchase prescription drugs as part of its health insurance coverage for seniors but expressly prohibited the government from trying to lower its costs by negotiating bulk discounts from the pharmaceutical industry. By authorizing Medicare to buy massive quantities of drugs at full price, the new law boosted sales for Patton Boggs's pharmaceutical clients, such as

Roche Group, while keeping drug costs elevated for older Americans. On behalf of Walmart, Patton Boggs's lobbyists pressed Washington to water down consumer protection regulations and enact a free trade agreement with Caribbean nations that served to undermine America's manufacturing workers. For Wall Street banks, the firm undercut federal efforts to provide lower-cost home loans to Americans through the government-controlled mortgage-finance giants Fannie Mae and Freddie Mac. For Exxon Mobil Corp., it helped reduce the financial penalties that the oil and gas giant incurred after a massive 1989 spill by the Exxon *Valdez* oil tanker in Alaska.[5] For trial lawyers, Boggs blocked a bill providing legal liability protections to the US manufacturers of asbestos products—a measure that would have robbed plaintiffs' lawyers of a lucrative source of fees. The legislation was backed by the GOP, and Republican Senate leaders believed they had just enough votes to secure its passage when they'd obtained the support of a key Democratic lawmaker, Senator Daniel Inouye of Hawaii. But at the last minute, Boggs tracked down Inouye at his wife's bedside in a Washington-area cancer ward and pressed the senator to skip the vote. When the measure came up for consideration on Capitol Hill, Inouye was nowhere to be found. The bill failed by a single vote. A month later, Inouye's wife died.

These and other achievements helped propel annual revenue at Patton Boggs—already the biggest lobbying firm in the city—from nearly $20 million to $42 million over the first seven years of the decade. In 2008, though, things took a sudden turn.

As a historic mortgage crisis devolved into the most pernicious economic recession since the 1930s, many corporations reduced their spending on Washington lobbyists as part of broader efforts to preserve cash. While this retrenchment stung the entire influence industry, it was particularly painful for Patton Boggs. In a single year, the firm lost around a hundred clients, or roughly a quarter of its roster, and watched its lobbying revenue plateau. Among the clients who departed were the private-jet industry, Royal Caribbean Cruise Lines, and Delta Air Lines Inc. Facing comparable declines, other K Street shops moved to shore up their balance sheets by slashing expenses and laying off staff. There was a case to be made for similar belt-tightening at Patton Boggs. The firm had spent the prior two decades carrying out an ambitious expansion effort, turning what had once been a homespun partnership into the sort of multinational conglomerate that its lobbyists represented in Washington. Patton Boggs opened offices in seven US cities[6] in order to serve regional companies and lobby state governments. The firm also opened offices in two Mideast countries[7] whose interests it represented in Washington. It more than tripled the number of attorneys at the firm, to 550, and it ballooned its payroll by hiring hundreds of additional highly paid staffers.[8] What's more, because the firm's profits were divided up and distributed to partners at the end of each year, Patton Boggs didn't have much in the way of savings to weather a financial downturn. Yet despite its considerable overhead, meager reserves, and the revenue slump from the Great Recession, Patton Boggs declined to pursue the type of budget cuts that its peers had undertaken. It adopted a stay-the-course strategy that reflected the instincts of its chairman.

Tommy Boggs's stewardship during the economic crisis displayed both his loyalty as a boss and his deficiencies as a financial manager. Though he'd spent much of his career as the firm's top executive, he remained far more adept at striking deals with senators than analyzing ledger sheets. Moreover, Tommy simply didn't have the stomach for the kind of cold-blooded, dollars-and-cents decisions that business leaders are forced to make during tough times. By that point, he'd spent nearly a half century at Patton Boggs; he viewed the firm as his home and his colleagues as more than employees. "It was a little bit like a family," said longtime partner Don Morehead. Laying off fellow lobbyists, in Boggs's view, wasn't a path through a recession, it was an act of betrayal. So rather than making significant cuts to the budget, Boggs told his partners that the firm would survive the contraction by hunkering down. "We'll get through it," he assured them.

Even before the Great Recession, Patton Boggs had faced an increasingly competitive environment on K Street, with new trade groups, boutique lobbying shops, and corporate government relations offices sprouting up year after year.[9] Still, Boggs had reason to be optimistic that the company could withstand the contraction. While the firm's lobbying income might be plateauing, Patton Boggs's overall revenue remained stable thanks to a small number of extremely profitable legal clients. One was a group of Americans who had sued the government of Libya for its role in the 1988 terrorist bombing of Pan Am Flight 103 over Lockerbie, Scotland. In 2008, when Libya began making payments on a $1.5 billion settlement,[10] Patton Boggs received a $12 million fee that flipped what was expected to be an annual loss into a profitable year. Over the next several years, a second terrorism-related case provided an additional stream of eight-figure annual fees. In return for defending New York City against a raft of lawsuits filed by firefighters and police officers following the attacks of September 11, 2001,[11] Patton Boggs raked in legal fees of more than $40 million in 2010 and $20 million in 2011. But while these windfall payments managed to sustain the firm through the Great Recession, they did nothing to address the structural pressures impacting its lobbying business: growing competition, stagnating revenues, expensive salaries, and elevated overhead. "The money," said John Jonas, then a member of the firm's executive committee, "allowed Patton Boggs to paper over its problems." Furthermore, as the September 11–related lawsuits wound down, the flow of hefty fees began to dry up. If Boggs was going to keep his beloved firm afloat, he'd need to identify a new source of revenue—and fast.

It was during this period of uncertainty that one of the firm's rainmakers offered Boggs a financial lifeline. As the head of Patton Boggs's office in Newark, New Jersey, attorney James Tyrrell Jr. had developed an expertise in the kind of complex, high-stakes litigation that generated massive fees. Nicknamed "the Devil's advocate" and "the master of disaster,"[12] Tyrrell was the lawyer who'd secured the multimillion-dollar payouts in the September 11–related lawsuits. Now Tyrrell had identified another promising case. In 1993 a group of thirty thousand subsistence farmers and indigenous people in Ecuador filed class-action lawsuits accusing an American oil company, Texaco Inc., of being responsible for the drilling-related pollution that, according to the Ecuadorians, had led to elevated rates of birth defects and cancer among the local population.[13] After a federal judge tossed the case for procedural reasons in 2001, the plaintiffs' attorneys refiled the case in Ecuador against the oil giant Chevron Corp., which had since purchased Texaco.[14] As the litigation proceeded through the courts, Steven

Donziger, the American litigator serving as lead attorney for the Ecuadorians, approached a hedge fund in New York, Burford Capital, about helping it cover some of his legal costs in exchange for a portion of what the lawyer hoped would be a multibillion-dollar judgment.[15] The hedge fund, in turn, contacted Tyrrell to see if his team would join the venture as well. The hedge fund's executives offered a 25 percent cut of their contingency fee to Patton Boggs if the firm agreed to use its legal muscle to ensure that the Ecuadorians obtained all of the money they'd be entitled to if they won the lawsuit.[16] The payout to Patton Boggs, according to former partners, could be an astronomical $500 million—a sum that would instantly cure its financial afflictions. Each of the firm's roughly one hundred equity partners stood to make millions off the case; Boggs would rake in $40 million himself. For a chance at that kind of jackpot, the firm's partners lined up to approve Tyrrell's new client.

At first, the lawsuit seemed poised to play out just as Tyrrell had promised. In early 2011 an Ecuadorian court ruled that Chevron was liable for pollution-related damages totaling some $9 billion—a figure that swelled to more than $18 billion when the oil giant refused to apologize and make payment.[17] But then the case collapsed into a legal quagmire. Chevron filed a federal lawsuit in New York accusing the American lawyer and the Ecuadorian plaintiffs of running "an extortionate scheme"[18] involving manufactured scientific reports, ghostwritten legal filings, and other machinations.[19] The allegations spilled over onto Patton Boggs, which was identified in Chevron's legal complaint as a nonparty coconspirator in the alleged misdeeds.[20] Next, according to *Politico Magazine*, the hedge fund pointed the finger at Tyrrell, claiming that Patton Boggs had furnished it with "false and misleading advice"[21] about legal proceedings and prospects for success. If that wasn't enough, a federal judge gave Chevron the green light to file legal claims against Patton Boggs for attempting to cover up alleged wrongdoing on the part of the lead plaintiffs' lawyer.[22]

For Boggs and his partners, it was a maddening turn of events. The case that once promised to resolve the firm's fiscal conundrum had deteriorated into yet another albatross—draining its resources and tarnishing its reputation. Though Tommy Boggs continued to insist that the financial pressures would blow over and the firm would locate new revenue else-where, the implosion of the Chevron case would mark a turning point for Washington's largest lobbying firm. It discredited the firm's leadership in the eyes of many employees, fueling a growing sense of distrust among the partners. As this discontent spread, some lawyers and lobbyists began rais-ing a once-unthinkable question: Is it time for Tommy Boggs to go?

Beginning years before the collapse of the Chevron case, a coterie of primarily younger Patton Boggs partners had been whispering to one an-other their concerns about the direction of the firm. Chief among them was Ed Newberry, a Republican lobbyist in his forties who'd won the respect of his colleagues by generating consistently high revenues. Originally from New York, Newberry had first arrived in Washington in 1980 in order to play shortstop for the baseball team at George Mason University in nearby Fairfax, Virginia. Upon graduation, he went on to work as an aide on the House Appropriations Committee and earned a degree from Georgetown Law School. Over the course of his two decades at Patton Boggs, however, Newberry grew disturbed by what he viewed as financial rot at the core of the firm. The average Patton Boggs partner cost $240,000 in overhead expenses each year; Boggs himself had three secretaries. Yet a considerable number of these highly paid attorneys weren't bringing in enough income to justify their salaries. One-third of the hundred equity partners at Patton Boggs had billed less than three hundred hours of legal work in all of 2010, the equivalent of less than two months' work. Half of the equity partners put in fewer than the 1,800 hours of legal work expected of them each year. In 2011, when he was named the firm's managing partner, Newberry was finally able to dive into Patton Boggs's financial statements in detail. What he found was even more alarming than he'd imagined. Amid the down-ward pressure on revenues, the firm's inflated overhead and unproductive attorneys—"deadwood" as he called it—had put the business into what he believed was a death spiral.

Three weeks into the job, the firm's chief financial officer told New-berry that the firm didn't have enough money to pay partners their share of the profits from the prior year, an amount that typically made up one-third of their total compensation. In order to make the payments, Newberry took a loan from the firm's bank, Citigroup. As part of the financing arrangement, Newberry agreed to let a team of Citigroup consultants study the firm's finances. In their "Citi Restructuring Plan," the consultants determined that rising expenses and declining productivity were eroding profits. They found that Patton Boggs partners performed about half as much legal work each year as those at other Washington firms. Without meaningful reductions in payroll and expenses, Newberry believed, Patton Boggs would go bankrupt.

Though Newberry was a generation younger—he was the firm's youngest equity partner when he joined the management team—and from an opposing political party, he considered Tommy Boggs a mentor. "Tom was like a father to me," Newberry recalled years later in an interview. "And I was like a son to him." Back in 2011, Newberry recognized that questioning Boggs's leadership would be seen as treason. Still, in Newberry's view, the only way to save the firm was to defy the legendary lobbyist. "I'm the captain of the *Titanic*, and I can see the iceberg," he said. "I'm calling the home office, and they are saying, 'Stay the course.'" So, during a 2011 meeting of the board's executive committee, Newberry offered a motion to cut the salaries of lawyers whom he considered overpaid. Boggs brushed aside Newberry's concerns; he and his many allies on the executive committee voted overwhelmingly to scuttle the proposal. Yet even in defeat, Newberry's motion would prove significant. What had begun as hushed grumbling by a small collection of junior lobbyists was becoming the sort of threat that Boggs hadn't faced in his more than forty years at Patton Boggs: an open revolt against his authority.

In the spring of 2012 Newberry arranged for a Wells Fargo business consultant to provide a presentation on the state of the business to a gathering of the firm's partners at a Chesapeake Bay resort. The outlook was dire. The consultant said the firm would need to cut roughly seventy-five partners in order stay afloat. Newberry also hired Peter Zeughauser, a management consultant who specializes in the business of law firms, to conduct a thorough review of Patton Boggs's books. After spending several weeks at the firm's Washington office, poring over internal financial documents and interviewing about fifty partners, Zeughauser reached a similar conclusion: years of mismanagement had left the business so financially unsound as to require draconian steps such as layoffs and steep budget cuts. In September 2012 Zeughauser attended a meeting of the board's executive committee to present his analysis to Boggs and other partners. But just a few minutes into the presentation, Tommy Boggs cut him off and announced it was time for lunch. As Zeughauser looked around in confusion, Boggs turned to the consultant and leveled an icy glare. "You can leave," Boggs told him. "You are not welcome back after lunch."

Not long after, at another executive committee meeting, Newberry made a motion to lay off a few dozen lawyers. Boggs objected, arguing such dismissals would damage the firm's morale, and a majority of the executive committee sided with Boggs. Nevertheless, Boggs offered a compromise to Newberry and his supporters. He suggested that the firm create formal performance standards for lobbyists and lawyers and encourage those who didn't measure up to leave by the end of the year. Though it was only a minor concession, Boggs's willingness to yield any ground at all was notable. It reflected a gradual shift in the internal politics at his namesake lobbying firm.

Over time, the continued deterioration of Patton Boggs's finances forced even Tommy Boggs's boardroom allies to confront the fiscal crisis they'd long ignored. At the end of 2012, the firm fell short of its budget projections. Total annual revenues—income from the law and lobbying practices combined—had dropped 6.5 percent[23] from the prior year to about $318 million.[24] Amid the financial strain, some lobbyists and lawyers began to wonder silently if Boggs was still capable of effectively managing the firm.

Board members had been contemplating a post-Boggs future since before the 2008 recession. In the mid-2000s the firm's executive committee had secretly flown to a hotel in Colorado Springs, where—without Boggs's presence—they held meetings about succession plans but ultimately failed to settle on a strategy. By the time the financial trouble hit, a few years later, Boggs was in his seventies and hobbled by a litany of health concerns. A back problem stemming from an old high school football injury left him with nagging pain. He grew increasingly sedentary, adding more and more weight to his already obese frame. He sold his Tobacco Stick hunting preserve. Friends and colleagues encouraged Boggs to exercise, but he hated going to the gym. He hired a diet coach but ignored advice to cut down on red meat and booze. "Tom never saw a piece of meat he didn't like," recalled Stuart Pape, a former managing partner at the firm. When a doctor recommended surgery for his ailing back, he refused the procedure rather than deal with the drudgery of rehab. Instead, he relied on a cane to walk and traveled by car as much as possible—even to one of his favorite lunch spots, Ristorante La Perla, the Italian restaurant located directly across the street from the Patton Boggs office.

According to colleagues, Boggs began self-medicating with alcohol and the painkillers he'd been prescribed for his back pain. He usually poured his first cocktail around noon. One partner recalled driving Boggs to Richmond for a speech, and on the way home, Boggs asked the partner to pull over at a gas station rest stop. Boggs shuffled inside and returned with a six-pack of beer, which he polished off in the car during the roughly three-hour drive home. As his diet and exercise habits worsened, his health issues grew more severe. In 2010 Boggs traveled to Vancouver, British Columbia, for the annual convention of his biggest client, the association of trial lawyers, and then joined his wife and two of his grandchildren for a cruise along the Alaskan coastline. A few days into the trip, Boggs's breathing became strained, and he asked the onboard medical staff for help. The ship's physician detected an urgent heart issue, and Boggs was immediately airlifted to a hospital. As a crowd of tourists looked on, Boggs was hoisted onto a medevac chopper and flown to a remote landing strip in the Alaskan landscape—the same unforgiving panorama where, some four decades earlier, his father had disappeared. He was then loaded onto a private plane for the several-hour flight to the closest major hospital, in Seattle. After several days, Boggs was stable enough to fly back to Washington, where he underwent a successful heart bypass surgery. When he returned to the office, though, Boggs still seemed a bit shaky. He began offloading more of his work to other partners.

Meanwhile, the firm's finances were continuing to deteriorate. In early 2013 Newberry learned that revenues from the firm's September 11 terrorism cases were going to collapse from a projected $20 million to just $2 million for the year. Moments later, his phone rang. It was another lawyer explaining that a big case handled by the firm's Texas office had settled before going to court. That meant another $6 million that the firm had been expecting was gone. Over the course of a few minutes, Patton Boggs lost $24 million in expected revenue.

The sudden decline in income further weakened Boggs's standing among the partners, while Newberry's influence only grew. Newberry attempted to implement layoffs on his own, firing eighteen lawyers whom he considered part of the deadwood. One of these lawyers earned a $500,000 annual salary but had billed roughly one day's legal work for the entire year. Another provided less than one week of legal work for $1 million in pay. Still, the move outraged Boggs, who contended that Newberry lacked the authority to dismiss employees himself. When the matter came before the executive committee, Boggs was able to soften Newberry's directive by providing the offending attorneys until the end of the year to find other jobs. A few months later, Newberry pressed for steeper cuts, calling on the executive committee to dismiss 130 legal associates and staff. Once again, Boggs objected, arguing that the move would poison the firm's culture. Newberry fired back: "If you don't do this to the culture, there won't be a culture because there won't be a firm." After several contentious meetings, the committee voted to approve a round of layoffs but scaled down the reduction to half of what Newberry had recommended.

Later that month, the ax fell. Patton Boggs announced that it was letting go sixty-five[25] employees from its Washington, Newark, Denver, and Dallas offices.[26] Among those laid off were secretaries, paralegals, and some of the cafeteria workers who had spent the prior two decades serving meals to well-heeled lawyers and corporate lobbyists. On top of this effort to "right-size"[27] the firm's payroll, Newberry also won approval for additional cost-cutting measures. He negotiated a lower monthly lease payment for the firm's Georgetown headquarters and relocated the IT, accounting, and human resources departments to cheaper office space in Virginia. Meanwhile, in a scramble to raise cash, Patton Boggs began filing small-dollar lawsuits against former clients who'd skipped out on legal bills.

These maneuvers, however, served only to signal to employees the extent of the firm's troubles, precipitating an exodus of staff. Over the course of a few months, more than thirty lawyers and lobbyists bolted from Patton Boggs to competitors.[28] Among those to jump ship was veteran partner Jonathan Yarowsky, who took with him much of the business for one of Tommy Boggs's most lucrative and longest-running clients, the trial lawyers association, when he departed for rival law firm Wilmer Hale.[29] Patton Boggs's chief financial officer quit rather than sort through the financial chaos.

To K Street and beyond, the departures offered a grim indication of Patton Boggs's financial health, and it wasn't long before the firm's bankers grew nervous. In the summer of 2013, Citigroup demanded that Patton Boggs put up collateral to secure its $26 million line of credit. When Newberry refused, he was forced to find a new bank. He quickly hustled together a new line of credit from a consortium of banks including Wells Fargo, PNC Financial Services Group, and Capital One Financial. But a few months later, Patton Boggs made an accounting error that put it $2 million over its credit limit and, technically, in default.

To keep the credit line open, Newberry agreed to additional restrictions on company expenses, forcing him to go looking for more cuts. He took aim at the Newark and New York offices—the money-losing bureaus controlled by partner James Tyrrell. Newberry laid off ten of Tyrrell's lawyers in Newark, and he won approval from the executive committee to give Tyrrell permission to talk to other firms about moving his team elsewhere. Still, the situation had grown so desperate that Newberry had come to believe that there were only two remaining options to avoid bankruptcy. Patton Boggs would need to either sell itself or merge with another firm.

For Tommy Boggs, such a deal was unimaginable. Despite the ongoing turmoil, Patton Boggs remained the biggest lobbying firm in the nation's capital. Surrendering its independence to an outside company would represent a humiliating demise for a Washington institution—and a sad final chapter for Boggs's own legacy. In discussions with Newberry and other partners, Boggs expressed heated objections to a merger. However, given the firm's financial condition and his own diminishing clout, Boggs reluctantly authorized Newberry to explore all options. In late 2013 Newberry approached a Dallas-based law firm,[30] Locke Lord, about a potential merger. Though he considered it an inferior firm, Newberry was growing impatient. Eventually Tommy and a group of Patton Boggs partners flew to Dallas to meet with Locke Lord's senior partners. But during the talks, Boggs and his colleagues felt they weren't being treated with adequate respect, and Boggs ended the discussions. As the merger talks faltered, the pressure on management intensified. Patton Boggs's total revenues fell by 12 percent in 2013,[31] as lobbying fees dropped by roughly 15 percent.

In the nearly three years since Newberry first challenged his leadership, Boggs had seen senior partners defect to competing firms, watched longtime allies throw their support behind his boardroom rival, and witnessed his own influence wane at the company he helped build. His bitterness was most apparent during meetings of Patton Boggs's executive committee, which had turned increasingly hostile as Newberry gained clout. "I don't care what you think," Boggs hissed at a colleague during one session. "You have never contributed anything to this firm." It was against this acrimonious backdrop that the executive committee gathered in early 2014 to consider another round of cuts. Once again, Newberry targeted Tyrrell's unit, recommending cutting the pay of a group of lawyers, some of whom were on Tyrrell's team. Newberry put the issue before the executive committee, which would make the decision.

While the committee typically gathered in the firm's large conference room on the ground floor, for this meeting Boggs invited the partners into his corner office overlooking Georgetown's main boulevard. Adorned throughout the room was the memory of Boggs's father. On one wall hung a glass-enclosed case displaying the dozens of pens that President Lyndon Baines Johnson had used to sign into law the central elements of the Great Society programs, legislation that Hale Boggs had helped usher through Congress as House leader. Above the door, there was a framed panoramic photograph of a glacier in Alaska—the severe, desolate terrain where Hale Boggs's plane was last seen before it vanished in 1972. When the partners entered the room, the air thickened with cigar smoke and absorbed the stench of liquor. Some of the lawyers crammed into seats around Boggs's oval conference table; others poured cocktails from a bar inside the credenza.

As the proceedings got under way, Newberry described the problems with James Tyrrell's Newark and New York offices as a straightforward matter of economics; the firm simply could no longer afford to cover the monthly losses. For Boggs, the issue was more complex. It was, after all, the millions of dollars in fees from Tyrrell's September 11–related lawsuits that had helped carry Patton Boggs through the economic downturn. Cutting his team's pay was an act of naked disloyalty. Besides, Boggs continued, the firm was in urgent need of the massive legal fees that Tyrrell could bring in.

It was the same argument that committee members had been hearing from Boggs for years. Boggs's "greatest asset was also his greatest liability: loyalty to people," recalled Joe Brand, a partner who started at the firm the same time as Boggs. "The firm had a lot of deadwood, and he didn't do anything to fix that." Until then, committee members had given him the benefit of the doubt and acquiesced to his appeals. But now, with the firm on the brink of bankruptcy, Boggs's steadfast refusal to consider cutting expenses at an office that was losing millions of dollars seemed increasingly out of touch. So as the meeting dragged on, and Boggs continued to insist on supporting Tyrrell, some of his colleagues grew frustrated.

"Do we really have to go over this again!?!" snapped partner Norman Antin when Boggs rehashed his defense of Tyrrell.

Stunned, Boggs stared down at the table.

"There's no reason to be disagreeable," said another partner, "especially when you are being disagreeable with Tom."

"I will talk any way I want to talk," Antin snorted, as he gathered his papers and departed the office.

The exchange shocked many in the room; never before had Boggs been treated with such open contempt. For a growing number of partners, it seemed, Boggs was no longer the King of K Street. He was a feeble old man unwilling to accept reality.

Boggs lost the executive committee's vote.

Afterward, James Tyrrell—who'd been present for the entire meeting— asked to speak with Boggs privately outside the room. When the two came back, Boggs approached Newberry and explained that he would exercise his right to appeal the committee's decision by calling for a vote by all of the firm's partners.

"We don't agree with this," Boggs said, "and we want a vote on this by the partners."

The next day, Newberry and Tyrrell stood before more than one hundred Patton Boggs lawyers and made their arguments for and against Tyrrell's team. From a front-row seat in a ground-floor conference room, Boggs looked out at the scores of partners whom he'd helped hire over the years. His impact on the firm was visible to everyone in attendance. Just a few steps down the hallway were three other conference rooms, each named in honor of the storied lobbyist; Boggs A, Boggs B, and Boggs C.

Once Newberry and Tyrrell had addressed the gathering, Boggs took the floor. He made a final emotional plea on behalf of Tyrrell, urging his colleagues to reject Newberry's motion. When Boggs had finished, the matter was brought to a vote. An overwhelming majority turned against Boggs, moving to slash the pay of the lawyers on Tyrrell's team.

A month later, in February, Patton Boggs told the *Washington Post* that it would shutter the Newark office entirely.[32] The decision to close Tyrrell's office signaled a decisive shift in the firm's power structure; it might be Tommy Boggs's name on the building, but Ed Newberry was now calling the shots. Around this same time, in early 2014, the chairman of a Cleveland-based law firm arrived in Washington to meet with Patton Boggs's leadership. Jim Maiwurm of Squire Sanders had reached out to Newberry a few months earlier about the possibility of combining their two firms, explaining in a letter that a deal would benefit both sides. The leaders of each firm went to great lengths to keep their discussions secret, arranging to meet in a private room at an Italian restaurant in downtown DC. Maiwurm and Boggs staggered their arrival times so as not to attract attention, while Newberry slipped in through the kitchen. It was "like a John Grisham novel," a partner later recalled. Over Tuscan fare, Maiwurm touted the upsides of a merger. Squire Sanders was four times larger,[33] but Patton Boggs had a desirable reputation. Joining the two firms would create a distinguished legal powerhouse with offices in more than twenty countries.[34]

Then a new threat emerged. The firm's bankers told Newberry that they'd grown so doubtful about Patton Boggs's well-being that they wouldn't renew its $20 million line of credit—a move that would push the firm into insolvency unless it could find a new lender or come up with the millions of dollars required to repay the loan. A bankruptcy filing would cast suspicion on the firm's financial viability and might prompt Squire Sanders to walk away from the merger. Patton Boggs's management contacted bankruptcy lawyers and scrambled to find money. "We were hours from collapse," recalled former partner John Jonas. "Checks were not getting paid; we were calling clients to ask them to accelerate payments." Newberry raced to find yet another bank, and eventually a DC-area lender, Eagle-Bank, agreed to extend a line of credit. But the following day, the bank changed its mind; now it demanded collateral for the loan. After a flurry of negotiations, Newberry and Boggs agreed to put up $3.5 million of their own money as collateral and fork over their shares of the monthly partnership payments that made up a big part of their annual compensation.

Newberry hustled to get the merger completed before the firm's finances collapsed. After Squire Sanders's leaders expressed concerns over the potential liability related to the Chevron lawsuit, Patton Boggs agreed to pay the oil giant $15 million[35] to settle the dispute and issued a statement saying it "regrets its involvement"[36] in the matter. When Patton Boggs partners sensed Squire Sanders was getting cold feet, they leaked stories to the press suggesting that other firms were also vying to merge with Patton Boggs.[37] The ploy worked just as they'd hoped, triggering a sense of urgency on the part of Squire Sanders. Finally, in May 2014, the two sides signed a formal merger agreement.[38] Under the terms of the deal, Tyrrell did not join the new firm.

The transaction made the new company, Squire Patton Boggs, one of the largest law and lobbying firms in the world, with approximately 1,600 lawyers,[39] including 280 in Washington alone.[40] After the Patton Boggs board voted to affirm the merger, Newberry placed a phone call to Tommy Boggs, his mentor turned adversary. "Tom, you started this little law firm that had a hundred thirty lawyers when I joined in 1991," Newberry said. "Now today, with this merger, your name is on the door of forty-seven offices in twenty-two countries. That is something you should be proud of."

Indeed, to the public, Boggs portrayed the deal as a triumph, declaring in a statement that Patton Boggs had "evolved into an industry game-changer," and boasting that "[t]hrough our combination with Squire Sanders, we are doing it again."[41] Other K Street operators heaped praise on Boggs. "He's a brilliant guy who invented what a lot of us do,"[42] Tony Podesta told the *Post* in an article about the merger.

Beneath the public spin, though, Boggs was profoundly wounded. The merger had come at a staggering cost to his self-regard. Fifty-two years after its founding, his namesake lobbying firm had been stripped of its independence. More emasculating still, the terms of the transaction had put Boggs out to pasture. Once the deal was complete, Boggs was handed the ceremonial title of chairman emeritus and forced to give up his seat on the board. While three years of boardroom battles had gradually chipped away at his clout, the merger agreement had ratified his impotence.

Many of Boggs's longtime colleagues viewed the merger as the end of their lobbying empire. Minutes after Patton Boggs's board signed off on the deal, John Jonas and the firm's lucrative health care lobbying practice decamped for rival Akin Gump.[43] Days later, the election-law division bolted as well.[44] While campaign lawyers don't generate as much income as health care lobbyists do, the election-law team was a prestigious unit. It included Benjamin Ginsberg, a top lawyer for George W. Bush's presidential campaigns, and Don McGahn, who went on to serve as chief White House counsel for President Donald Trump.[45] Then came even more dispiriting news. In July 2014 newly released lobbying disclosure reports showed that for the first time in eleven years, Patton Boggs was on pace to lose its place as Washington's top revenue-producing lobbying firm.[46] It was a bitter milestone for an iconic Washington business. Tommy Boggs's beloved firm was being displaced as the King of K Street.

With his colleagues departing, his legacy crumbling, and his influence vanishing, Boggs spent the months after the merger following the routine of the influential lobbyist he'd once been. He smoked cigars in his eighth-floor corner office, and around noon most days he made the short drive to one of his favorite restaurants, like the Palm or Ristorante La Perla. He still took occasional trips to Capitol Hill, but by then his health ailments were so severe that it was physically painful to walk across the marble floors of Congress. Though he remained deeply resentful about the merger, according to colleagues, he consoled himself with the belief that the transaction had helped preserve the jobs of hundreds of Patton Boggs lawyers and lobbyists. So, he was apoplectic when, a few months after the merger, Newberry and Maiwurm fired another three dozen partners, most of whom were former Patton Boggs employees. Boggs confronted Newberry and urged him to change his mind. But under the terms of the merger agreement, Boggs no longer had any say over layoffs or management decisions. He had been removed from the chain of command.

This, as it turned out, was his final indignity. A few weeks later, on September 14, 2014, Boggs gathered with family members and business associates at a skybox in FedExField for Washington's home opener. In the days after his passing, former colleagues, clients, friends, and family assembled at memorial services and downtown bars to say their good-byes and reflect on his memory. There was plenty to recollect: the duck hunting trips, the conference negotiations, the boozy partners' lunches, and the discord that had gripped Patton Boggs during his final years, when the prideful power broker had to watch his influence evaporate at the firm he helped build. And while the newspapers might say it was a heart attack, in the eyes of some of Boggs's contemporaries, it was the emotional trauma from the firm's final chapter that precipitated his passing. The strain and grief of losing control of Patton Boggs, some had come to believe, had simply been too much.

"I think the stress of all that is probably what led to his death," said former Senator Trent Lott, the onetime Republican Senate majority leader who became a Patton Boggs lobbyist in 2010. "That was his baby; he created it. He was the spirit of the firm. When it struggled and started taking on water, he was not able to take action to fix it. There was no question that it was very stressful for him."

16

On a warm summer day, Evan Morris decided to sneak out of the office early.
He exited Genentech's sleek eleven-story building located one block from
the White House, hopped into one of his two brand-new Porsche 911s,
and made the forty-five-minute drive to his favorite club: the Robert Trent
Jones Golf Club in Gainesville, Virginia. When Morris arrived, employees
were preparing the grounds for a nationally televised PGA golf tournament hosted by Tiger Woods that would take place in just three weeks.
With the help of a generous donation from Genentech, Morris had landed
a coveted spot in a charity tournament scheduled for the day before the
professionals teed off. He was slated to play with Erik Compton,[1] a professional golfer who had relied on a Genentech drug to keep his body from
rejecting a transplanted heart.

After pulling into the parking lot, Morris retrieved his clubs and
headed to the first tee with his favorite caddie, Tony. Since the club allows
only a few hundred members, there was never a wait for a tee time. A few
hours into his round of golf, his cell phone buzzed. It was Genentech's top
lawyer, Frederick Kentz, with an ominous message. He was flying in from
San Francisco and demanded to see Morris first thing the next morning.

The two would meet not at Genentech's Washington office, but at the law offices of Gibson, Dunn & Crutcher, a powerful white-collar firm whose clients include Apple Inc. and Facebook Inc. founder Mark Zuckerberg, as well as Chevron in the Ecuadorian case that had caused such havoc for Tommy Boggs. Kentz ordered Morris to clear his schedule for the day.[2] But he offered no details.

The call troubled Morris. He contacted a lawyer, and he texted a friend to cancel their plans to play golf the following morning. "General Counsel is on a plane," Morris wrote. "Yeah, it's not something I did, but probably something big and bad." The more he thought about the meeting, the more frustrated he became. He shouted and swung a club violently in the air as he worked his phone.

Over the previous few days, friends and colleagues had been growing concerned about Morris. He seemed distracted and aloof. Earlier that week, one of Morris's executive assistants inquired about him.

"Are you okay?" she asked.

"I just have a lot going on," Morris replied. The roof on his Eastern Shore vacation home had collapsed, he explained, and he was growing impatient with the pace of the repairs.

"You need to get some sleep," she said. "You look tired."

While Morris was still on the golf course, a second executive assistant of his, Shannon Cottrell-Steward, received a similar message from Genentech's top lawyer. Cottrell-Steward had worked closely with Morris for years. She managed most aspects of his professional life, including his schedule and meal reservations. Although she was an administrative employee, Morris sometimes asked her to sign her name to certain contracts with vendors, contractors, and lobbyists. In an email, Kentz had told Cottrell-Steward to block time in her schedule the following day to meet with the company's attorneys. Once again, the lawyer declined to say what the meeting was about. The message puzzled Cottrell-Steward. She was attending a lunchtime baby shower for one of Genentech's female lobbyists when she received the email. She read it aloud to the half dozen women at the luncheon, and then forwarded it to Morris.

Following his round at the Robert Trent Jones Golf Club, Morris drove back to his office in Washington, where he continued to stew. At one point, he met with a lobbyist on his team and read her the text of Kentz's email to Cottrell-Steward. He then peppered her with questions about what Kentz might want to discuss. When Cottrell-Steward returned to the office from the baby shower, she huddled with one of Morris's other secretaries.

"Girl, something is going on," Cottrell-Steward whispered. "Evan got a call from someone in compliance. Rick [Kentz] is coming to the office and wants to see him."

"Oh my God," the other secretary responded. "This is it."

It was a bad time for such distress. That evening, July 8, Morris was hosting a fund-raiser at the $2 million home he shared with his wife, Tracy, and their two young children, to benefit a Democratic candidate running for the Virginia State Senate. Among their guests would be Terry McAuliffe, the governor of Virginia.[3] McAuliffe was also the former chairman of the Democratic Party and the kingpin of Bill and Hillary Clinton's political-finance empire.

During the fund-raiser, Morris seemed preoccupied. His face had an unusual, reddish complexion, and at times he was sweating. The following day's meeting was on his mind. He told some friends it was no big deal; the lawyers probably just wanted to discuss an upcoming corporate acquisition. But he admitted to others that it was eating at him.[4] He appealed to close friends for their thoughts on what it could all be about.

In the weeks before the event, Morris had begun wondering if it was time to depart the high-stakes intensity of Washington politics. He'd recently told colleagues that he might be done with lobbying for good, and he even had an exit plan: raise enough money for Democrats and Hillary Clinton's 2016 presidential campaign to land a job as a US ambassador, perhaps to Switzerland, where Roche had its world headquarters.[5] Tracy had brought up the possibility of leaving DC in the past. Now, for the first time, Morris was telling people at the party that he might be willing to do so.

As the evening drew to a close, Morris joined McAuliffe and a handful of local politicians on the back patio to smoke cigars and taste wine from Morris's personal collection. They opened a bottle of Pétrus,[6] the rare

French vintage that can cost more than $10,000 a bottle. It was Morris's favorite. He told the governor that he wanted to host a fund-raising event for Hillary Clinton's 2016 presidential campaign at his home. McAuliffe liked the idea. As the governor left, he told Morris that his assistant would be in touch to find some dates that might work for Clinton.

The next morning, Morris drove his Porsche into the city for the much-anticipated meeting. He walked into the third-floor conference room at the law office of Gibson Dunn in downtown Washington. To his surprise, he was greeted not by Genentech's lawyer but by Michael Bopp, a partner at Gibson Dunn who specializes in investigations and crisis management, and by Maureen Stewart, a tenacious young lawyer at the firm. Bopp invited Morris to take a seat at the conference table, beside a stack of files and documents. He explained why Morris had been summoned.

A few weeks earlier, Genentech had received an anonymous letter that warned of unusual financial expenditures by Morris.[7] As a result, Genentech had asked Bopp's law firm to conduct an internal investigation, and, after beginning to comb through financial documents and emails, the lawyers had become puzzled by some odd transactions. Though they did not tell Morris at the time, Bopp and his colleagues were curious as to why Morris had paid more than $20 million in Genentech funds to three different firms that were each linked to the same person, Jim Courtovich. Morris's reasons for making these payments was of particular interest to the lawyers because they hadn't been able to determine what, if any, work Courtovich or the consulting firms had done in exchange for the funds.

During the meeting, Bopp explained that the investigation was not yet completed, and he hoped Morris could help him make sense of the unexplained flow of funds. The lawyers then opened up the manila folders and began asking about specific contracts and transactions that Morris had authorized. At first, Morris responded confidently to the inquiries. But after a few minutes, his demeanor changed. Morris stood up, said he wasn't feeling well, and asked for a bathroom break. Rather than heading to the restroom, though, he fled the building.[8]

Kentz, the Genentech lawyer who had flown in from San Francisco, had planned to meet with Morris in person to tell him that he was being suspended from his job while the company looked into the matter. However, the lobbyist left before he had the opportunity, so Kentz delivered the news over the phone.

Morris got in his white Porsche and drove toward the Robert Trent Jones Golf Club.[9] When he arrived, he reserved three rooms in the club's cottages, where guests could stay the night. But then he canceled all but one.[10] He headed onto the course and teed off by himself. Afterward, he showered and put on a blue blazer with the club's insignia. He ordered a steak at the clubhouse. When he finished his meal, he announced he was buying a round of drinks for everyone in the dining room.[11] Around four o'clock, he asked to see a wine list and ordered a $1,500 bottle of his favorite wine, Pétrus. He told the wait staff that he had work to do, and, with the July sun still aloft in the sky, he walked to the fire pit a few hundred yards down a hill from the clubhouse. The fire pit was stacked with wood and encircled by white Adirondack chairs.[12] It was a secluded spot, and Morris was alone. He took a seat in an Adirondack chair, lit up a cigar, and poured himself a glass of wine.

By then, Morris's wife, Tracy, was beginning to panic.[13] Her husband had been acting strangely all day. Despite all of his angst in the run-up to the meeting, Morris wasn't providing her any details about the confrontation. His responses to her text messages were curt.

"Not going to end well," he wrote at one point.

Later, after he'd slipped away from the lawyers, Morris suggested in some of his text messages to his wife that he was still in the meeting with the attorneys in DC. "Not sure this will be resolved today," he texted. "Will be ongoing for a bit. Likely will be here late."

When Tracy called, he didn't pick up. She texted him, but he replied with short, ambiguous answers.

"Lots of little shit—no big items."

"May be the fall guy. I'm ok with it."

"They are going to put me on paid leave. Will call you when I can."

Then Morris stopped responding.

Growing desperate, Tracy began contacting Morris's colleagues and friends. "I haven't seen Evan all day," she said in a voicemail to one of his executive assistants. "Do you know where he is?"

A friend of Morris's raced to Genentech's office to look for him. The owner of the cigar shop located across from the White House, which Morris frequented, drove to the couple's home in Virginia to offer his help. Family friends searched the parking garage for Morris's Porsche.[14] It was not there. Eventually one of Morris's friends gave Tracy an idea. He suggested that she go online to check her husband's debit and credit card activity;[15] any recent transactions could provide clues as to his whereabouts.

When Tracy logged on to his accounts, one purchase stood out. At 2:26 p.m., Morris had used his credit card at a store called Loudoun Guns Inc.[16] to buy a .357 Smith & Wesson revolver and a box of ammunition.

The revelation alarmed Tracy. She frantically called and texted her husband. He didn't answer. She left a pleading voice mail, insisting that everything would be okay. She sent him photos of their two young children.[17] When Morris still didn't respond, Tracy contacted the police[18] and filed a missing persons report. A police officer arrived at the Morris home.

Another friend of the family called the Robert Trent Jones Golf Club. Tracy knew her husband often sought refuge at his beloved club, occasionally even staying overnight at one of the private cottages. But the club's staff understood how closely Morris guarded his privacy. When reached about Morris's whereabouts, the club's staff was no help.

At the fire pit, Morris appeared to be enjoying the peace and quiet of a summer evening. Around 5 p.m., a club employee arrived at the fire pit in a golf cart to do some maintenance. The two exchanged pleasantries. Morris said he was wiped out and wanted to relax.[19]

Back in Washington, Kentz sent an email to the Washington staff informing them that Morris had been placed on unpaid leave. The government affairs division, he wrote, would report to Kentz in San Francisco for the time being. Kentz did not explain the reasons for relieving Morris of his duties.

Beside the fire pit, Morris was descending into hopelessness. He sent a text message to his wife containing contact information for the couple's accountant, insurance agent, and financial planner. At 6:02 p.m., he sent her another text. "I want to be done with this shit." It was the last message he wrote.

Morris pulled out the box containing the Smith & Wesson .357 revolver and opened it. Pushing aside the safety manual and the registration card, Morris gripped the silver revolver by its black handle. He then retrieved the package of .357 shells and slid six bullets into the chamber of the revolver. He tore a brown piece of paper from the Smith & Wesson packaging.[20]

In blue ink, he scrawled an instruction on a brown piece of paper. He placed the note on his lap. "Do Not Resuscitate," it read.[21]

Morris hadn't touched a gun since his duck hunting trip with Tommy Boggs nearly a decade earlier, when he fumbled with the rifle in the scrublands of Maryland's Eastern Shore. Back then, Morris was willing to do whatever it took to become a K Street legend himself. In the years since, he'd achieved the wealth, status, and influence he'd longed for. But now, he was alone at an exclusive golf club, drinking a bottle of expensive wine, and clutching a revolver.

At about seventy-thirty, Morris aimed the gun at the unlit fire pit and squeezed off a test shot.[22] He then put the muzzle of the gun into his mouth.[23] At around ten o'clock, the clubhouse server returned to check on Morris and found the body.[24]

Part III

The Reckoning

2015–Present

17

On a damp, gray morning, thousands of outraged protestors descended on the nation's capital. Wearing "Not My President" hats and waving placards that read "Resistance," they marched through the streets near the White House while blaring horns, blowing whistles, and shouting chants. "No Trump! No KKK! No Fascist USA!" Although most of the Inauguration Day demonstrators were peaceful, the crowds also contained elements of extremism. At certain points, left-wing radicals dressed in all-black smashed storefront windows and toppled newspaper boxes. A half dozen police suffered minor injuries from the rocks and other items that had been hurled into the air. Outside of the *Washington Post*'s headquarters, a stretch limousine went up in flames.[1]

It was an ominous backdrop for the day's central event. At noon sharp, Donald Trump stood on a platform on the West Front of the US Capitol, placed his hand on a pair of Bibles, and recited the oath of office. America's forty-fifth president then walked up to the podium, flashed a thumbs-up to his supporters, and delivered a grim address. Our great nation, he declared, had devolved into a wasteland of urban poverty, decaying factories, inept schools, drugs, gangs, and crime. This "American carnage," as he put it, was the result of decades of self-serving policy making, in which the needs of ordinary citizens had been subsumed by the interests of Beltway elites. "For too long," Trump told the spectators, "a small group in our nation's capital has reaped the rewards of government, while the people have borne the cost. Washington flourished, but the people did not share in its wealth. Politicians prospered, but the jobs left and the factories closed. The Establishment protected itself, but not the citizens of our country. Their victories have not been your victories. Their triumphs have not been your triumphs, and while they celebrated in our nation's capital, there was little to celebrate for struggling families all across our land."

"That all changes," Trump pledged, "starting right here and right now."[2]

Neither the day's dark rhetoric nor its bursts of violence, however, were able to keep Washington's most illustrious Democratic lobbyist from marking the occasion. As Trump assumed control of much of the federal government, Tony Podesta was following the proceedings from inside the historic Willard InterContinental Hotel, where he and his lobbying partners were hosting an invite-only inauguration party for the very elites the new president was decrying. Podesta had gathered corporate lobbyists and foreign dignitaries in a mezzanine-level room overlooking the parade route. The location of the hotel, just across the street from the White House, offered sweeping views of the angry protestors, the elated Trump enthusiasts, and the president and First Lady as they made their way down Pennsylvania Avenue to the White House. Inside the room, inaugural buttons and containers of Podesta Group–branded lip balm were available as party favors for the journalists, corporate executives, lawmakers, and political operatives who arrived. The hotel's wait staff served truffled grilled cheese sandwiches and tomato soup shooters, while bartenders passed out glasses of champagne and encouraged guests to try the event's signature cocktail: a hot apple cider and brandy dubbed the Trump Toddy.[3] Attendees included the actor Jon Voight, German Ambassador Peter Wittig, onetime Bush administration spokesman Geoff Morrell, and GOP Representatives Mike Gallagher of Wisconsin and John Moolenaar of Michigan.[4] At the center of it all was Tony Podesta—smiling and laughing, shaking hands and exchanging hugs, greeting old friends and making new ones. Over the course of the afternoon, the veteran lobbyist worked the room like it was any other Inauguration Day. As if things had turned out exactly as planned.

Behind his façade of breezy confidence, Podesta was deeply troubled by the events transpiring in Washington. "It was horrible," he recalled later. "I worry about the future of our country." But the earthquake of Trump's election hadn't just offended his liberal sensibilities, it had delivered a serious blow to the firm—precipitating an outflow of clients and revenue, making him the target of political attacks from the combative new president, and intensifying the financial pressures that had been accumulating quietly over the past few years. In truth, though, the most perilous threat to Podesta's empire had originated long before Trump's victory.

Back in 2012, Podesta had partnered in a foreign lobbying venture with a founding member of one of Washington's other renowned lobbying dynasties: Paul Manafort.[5] At first, their work on behalf of an obscure Ukrainian nonprofit attracted little attention. But within a few years, as Manafort made his improbable ascent from swashbuckling foreign operative to chairman of Trump's presidential campaign, the press began digging into the partnership.[6] And in the months following Trump's inauguration, Podesta and Manafort's Ukrainian lobbying campaign would become a focus of a high-profile federal investigation, trigger the most consequential influence-peddling scandal in a generation, and destroy the careers of two K Street magnates.

For the rest of Washington's influence-peddling industry, the impact of Trump's election was equally momentous. As Beltway operatives scrambled to figure out how to shape the decisions of this new, anti-Washington president, they were forced to create a whole new lobbying playbook, blending a set of old-fashioned access-driven tactics—which had grown increasingly obsolete over the prior decades—with the cutting-edge tools of the digital age. Suddenly lobbying firms were doing everything from hiring the few people in DC with personal connections to Trump to targeting the specific coordinates of his Mar-a-Lago residence with social media advertisements. Among lobbyists, it came to be known as the "audience of one" strategy.[7]

But for the K Street ruling class, that wasn't the worst of it. Trump's arrival in the White House would signal the unraveling of the pro-business consensus that had guided Washington policy makers for most of the prior four decades. Fueled by "Drain the Swamp" intensity and anti–Big Business populism, the Make America Great Again movement represented a fiery backlash against the Republican Party's traditional alliance with Washington's corporate lobbying establishment. At the same time, Trump's rise to power occurred just as a growing number of Democrats were calling for the breakup of Wall Street banks and Silicon Valley behemoths. As this hostility to industry permeated both parties, K Street would confront its most unfavorable political environment since before the corporate revolution of the 1970s.

None of this looming danger, of course, was apparent to anyone who saw Podesta at the Willard Hotel on Inauguration Day. After nearly three decades in the influence-peddling business, he understood the importance of projecting vitality during periods of distress. Now more than ever, it was essential to signal to Washington that, despite everything going on inside the firm, it was business as usual at the Podesta Group. As he mingled with guests, Podesta, according to former employees, did his best to convince everyone in the room that while the election might not have gone his way, the firm was nonetheless well positioned to thrive in Republican-controlled Washington.

It was an impressive performance. Yet even Podesta himself couldn't have known how bad things would get, or how quickly it would all unravel. Indeed, not a single person in Washington could have imagined that in less than a year, the city's third largest lobbying firm—a $50 million enterprise—would simply collapse. [8]

The business arrangement that would prove so disastrous for Podesta and Manafort had begun nearly five years earlier, under a perfectly conventional set of circumstances. In April 2012 Paul Manafort's top deputy, Rick Gates, arrived at the Podesta Group's[9] spacious, tenth-floor conference room—decorated with art from Podesta's collection—and greeted an audience of influence peddlers. Tony Podesta and about eight of his colleagues were in attendance. Also present were Vin Weber, the former GOP congressman turned high-powered lobbyist, and a handful of operatives from Weber's firm, Mercury Public Affairs. After exchanging pleasantries, Gates laid out the details of the joint lobbying venture he'd come to discuss. Manafort and Gates were spearheading an effort to generate political support for the government of Ukraine among key figures in Washington, and they wanted to hire a team of DC-based political strategists to help. Each of the firms would be paid roughly $500,000 a year.

By the time of the meeting, Paul Manafort had become the top political consultant to the pro-Russian president of Ukraine, Viktor Yanukovych. Manafort was, according to the *New York Times*, "as well known in Ukrainian political circles as Karl Rove or James Carville in America."[10] He played tennis with the president, relaxed in the hot tub of the 350-acre presidential estate,[11] and raked in astronomical consulting fees from the oligarchs of the country's eastern region. It was the culmination of more than fifteen years of traveling the world as an independent consultant, working with clients who were every bit as shady as the warlords who'd made his former lobbying colleagues uncomfortable.

Following his ouster from Black Manafort in 1995, when the firm's new owners discovered a pattern of misused funds, Paul Manafort had left the nation's capital in an attempt to satisfy a hunger for adventure, status and wealth that had grown even more rapacious since the glory days of Reagan-era Washington. While still at the firm, Manafort had become increasingly taken with a Lebanese arms dealer, Abdul Rahman Al Assir, who'd served as an intermediary to some of his overseas clients.[12] Al Assir hailed from a universe of carefree decadence that even K Street titans couldn't penetrate. His onetime brother-in-law, Adnan Khashoggi, was an illustrious Saudi Arabian arms dealer whose $4 billion fortune (in the 1980s) featured[13] a $30 million Manhattan apartment, a nearly 200,000-acre ranch in Kenya, a 282-foot yacht, a $40 million private jet that *Time* magazine called a "flying 21st century Las Vegas disco," and a traveling entourage that included a barber, a masseur, a chiropractor, and a valet.[14] As an emissary of Khashoggi's, Al Assir enjoyed a similarly indulgent lifestyle. "The miracle of Al Assir," according to *Sourakia*, a London magazine written for an Arabic-speaking audience, "is that he will have lunch with [Spanish King] Don Juan Carlos, dinner with [Moroccan King] Hassan II, and breakfast the next day with [Spanish Prime Minister] Felipe González."[15]

When their business dealings blossomed into a personal friendship, Al Assir asked Manafort to be the godfather of his child, and their two families began spending vacations together in the South of France.[16] Manafort's peek inside this higher stratosphere of wealth had a profound impact on him, says John Donaldson, a former associate and longtime family friend. Al Assir "showed him the difference between five hundred thousand dollars and five million dollars," Donaldson recalled, "and Paul really liked it."

Over time, Al Assir became something of a role model. Manafort started dressing like the worldly arms dealer—wearing suede loafers with no socks, for instance—and gallivanting around the globe in search of the sort of windfall business deals[17] that could vault him into this upper echelon of extravagance. The transactions that Manafort gravitated toward often contained elements of glamor, intrigue, danger, and corruption. In the early 1990s, for instance, Manafort and Al Assir helped broker the sale of an advanced fleet of French-made submarines to Pakistan, in a controversial deal that would become mired in allegations of kickbacks and was connected to a 2002 car bombing in Karachi that left eleven members of the French navy dead.[18] Neither Manafort nor Al Assir was implicated in the attack. In 2001 Manafort and others created a movie production company, Manhattan Pictures International, with a film producer named Julius Nasso, who was shortly thereafter sentenced to more than a year in jail after he hired mob enforcers to try to extort cash from action movie star Steven Seagal.[19] In 2002 Manafort and Al Assir helped convince a Portuguese private bank to make an investment worth fifty-seven million euros in a biometrics firm located in Puerto Rico. When the deal went bust, the bank imploded, but Manafort still managed to walk away with a $1.5 million profit by unloading his shares before their value plummeted.[20]

By 2004, Manafort's pursuit of plunder and kicks had brought him to Ukraine,[21] the resource-rich, politically chaotic former Soviet republic situated along the fault lines of a high-stakes diplomatic struggle. The bulk of the Russian-speaking minority in Eastern Ukraine wanted closer ties to the Kremlin; most other citizens preferred to ally with the West. Manafort initially came to Kiev to help a pair of wealthy foreigners safeguard their business interests from the ongoing political upheaval.[22] One of these men eventually connected him to the country's most powerful oligarch, a coal-and-steel magnate named Rinat Akhmetov. Before long, the American political consultant and the Ukrainian oligarch would join forces on a political revival.

When he began working in Ukraine, Manafort found a country subsumed in the sort of electoral corruption, industrial racketeering, and geopolitical gamesmanship in which he'd long thrived. The year he arrived, Ukraine's highest judicial body had invalidated the results of its presidential election in the climax of a volatile campaign season marked by massive fraud,[23] a poisoned opposition candidate, and a wave of street protests that would come to be known as the Orange Revolution. The uprising, which culminated in the election of a pro-Western president named Viktor Yushchenko, was a crushing setback for the business tycoons in the country's eastern region, many of whom were eager to see Ukraine realign with Russia. From the ashes of defeat, these oligarchs began searching for a path back to power.

Rinat Akhmetov, for his part, was more concerned about his vast business empire, according to Rick Gates, a then-thirtysomething operative who got his start as a Black Manafort intern, arrived in Ukraine in the mid-2000s, and eventually became Manafort's right-hand man.[24] Though Akhmetov was not closely aligned with the Kremlin himself, he was interested in bankrolling politicians who could win key elections in Ukraine and, in return, provide him with protection from prosecution and access to future business deals, says Dr. Taras Kuzio, a political science professor at the National University of Kiev Mohyla Academy. Eventually, Dr. Kuzio says, Akhmetov came to view the oligarchs as his best bet for achieving his objectives. But while he was willing to invest some of his fortune into their political comeback, the endeavor could only succeed if the right person was leading it. So, according to Gates, Akhmetov put the oligarchs in touch with a veteran political-image maker who might be able to help. "Rinat Akhmetov," Gates says, "was the primary conduit that initially introduced Paul into Ukrainian politics."

After representing a guerrilla leader in Angola, a murderous despot in Zaire, and a corrupt dictator in the Philippines, Manafort's work in Ukraine had a familiar quality. The Party of Regions, whose image he was tasked with rehabilitating, was backed by the Kremlin and linked to the criminal underworld. In a 2006 cable, an official at the US embassy in Ukraine called the party "a haven for mobsters";[25] some of its financial benefactors were reportedly implicated[26] in the kidnapping and murder of Ukrainian reporter Georgy Gongadze, whose decapitated body was dumped in the woods outside of Kiev. The party's leading politician, Viktor Yanukovych, was, in the words of an American consultant who did business in Ukraine, a "kleptocratic goon."[27] An orphan from a hardscrabble mining town in the country's East, Yanukovych was convicted of robbery and assault before becoming the country's prime minister in 2002, making him Ukraine's second-highest elected official. During the 2004 presidential election, he was suspected of being involved in the dioxin poisoning of his pro-Western rival, Yushchenko.[28] When the Ukrainian Supreme Court concluded that Yanukovych's apparent victory in the election had been achieved only through menace and fraud, the outcome was reversed, and Viktor Yushchenko was sworn in instead.

In the wake of Yanukovych's humiliating loss, Manafort was tasked with performing what the US embassy in Kiev described as an "extreme makeover" of the Party of Regions. Specifically, according to the 2006 cable, which was later made public by WikiLeaks, the veteran K Street operator was charged with creating the image "of a legitimate political party"[29] for a coterie of oligarchs and thugs. It was no simple chore. Yanukovych was a dour, unsmiling man—"he looked liked a bouncer at a discotheque," Dr. Kuzio said—and the party's ties to illicit cartels weren't exactly a secret. But for Manafort, the assignment was more than an opportunity to exercise his genius for image making. It was a chance for a monster payday. After all, one of the Party of Regions' primary patrons, according to Rick Gates and Dr. Kuzio, was none other than Rinat Akhmetov, who was believed to be the richest person in the country.[30]*

---

*Though a team of federal prosecutors and investigators[31] assigned by the Special Counsel's Office concluded in a November 2018 report that Akhmetov "had a long association with the Party of Regions,"[32] a press secretary for him, Anna Terekhova, said Akhmetov "never provided any financial support" to the Party of Regions.

According to Gates, when Manafort learned that a different business partner was prepared to accept a $45,000-a-month contract for the work in Ukraine, Manafort returned to the Party of Regions and complained that the payment was too low. He managed to renegotiate a new deal for a much higher fee: about $3 million for roughly nine months of work.

In exchange for his unusually steep fees, according to Gates, Manafort brought the wonders of American-style electioneering to his new clients in Ukraine, hiring a cavalcade of US-based pollsters, media specialists, advance staffers, and other operatives. Much of what Manafort's team did was rudimentary by Western standards—holding a convention, establishing a party platform—but novel in this eastern European nation. Manafort required Yanukovych's allies to put on makeup and rented Hugo Boss suits when they went on Ukrainian TV. Afterward, the suits were returned to campaign headquarters.[33] Still, even with all these tactics, the Party of Regions' political standard-bearer, Viktor Yanukovych, presented a challenge for Manafort. Yanukovych's rough past and austere demeanor didn't exactly endear him to voters, and the corruption associated with his 2004 presidential campaign had made him a deeply unpopular figure. "People avoided him," Philip Griffin, who worked for Manafort in Ukraine, told the *Atlantic*. "He was radioactive."[34] Nevertheless, Manafort believed he could improve the public's perception of the former prime minister and resurrect his career. He polished Yanukovych's image with a tight haircut, tailored suits, clean shirts, and sharp ties.[35] He coached him to wave to voters, project empathy to audiences—"I feel your pain," he began saying—and conduct breezy small talk with ordinary citizens.[36] With the help of his Washington-based consultants, Manafort even staged political events where Yanukovych could shake hands and kiss babies. "He literally trained the guy to smile," Gates said.

Not all of Manafort's strategies were aimed at the heartstrings. While his party platform might have made gauzy allusions to a future Ukraine serving as a "bridge" between Russia and the West, Manafort was also stoking discord among neighbors.[37] At Manafort's behest, for instance, Yanukovych rebuked NATO.[38] And when polling indicated that he could benefit by inflaming the country's long-standing ethnic tensions,

Manafort suggested that Yanukovych advance dubious claims that government officials had abused Ukraine's Russian-speaking minorities.[39] According to the *New York Times*, internal materials related to Manafort's campaign criticized the current government's less friendly posture toward the Kremlin, dismissed the Orange Revolution as a "coup," and called attention to the polarizing debate over whether Russian should be a second national language.[40] In many ways, says Dr. Kuzio, it was the same divisive playbook that Manafort and his pals had used on behalf of Republican candidates in 1970s and 1980s America. "Manafort [brought] the 'Southern Strategy' to Ukraine," Dr. Kuzio said. "And that's what began to split the country up."

This playbook of flashing big smiles while stoking cultural resentments would prove exceptionally effective. In the ugly aftermath of the 2004 presidential election, Yanukovych's approval rating had flopped to around 13 percent, according to Gates. But under Manafort's guidance, Yanukovych was able to reclaim the prime minister's office in 2006. Four years later, Manafort helped Yanukovych secure the presidency of Ukraine, powered by votes from the country's more pro-Russian eastern region. After the victory, Manafort helped arrange a congratulatory phone call from President Barack Obama. Manafort also sent an email praising his team of political operatives, who'd helped engineer the triumph. "Everyone from Yanukovych to [his campaign aide Vladimir] Demeko know that but for the efforts of this team, there will be no celebration," Manafort wrote. "I spent five hours with Yanukovych on election night, and he made the point continuously to thank the team. This is not something that he has done much in the past. This time, he definitely gets it."[41]

The success at the ballot box led to bigger financial scores. Manafort steered a river of consulting fees—funded primarily by pro-Russian oligarchs—into his own pockets by continuing to work as a political advisor to the new Ukrainian president, who gave his talented American advisor 24-7 access to his executive office.[42] "Paul would ask for a big sum," as one of Manafort's associates put it, and once Yanukovych signed off on the payment, the Ukrainian president's top deputy "would go to the other oligarchs and ask them to kick in. 'Hey, you need to pay a million.' They would complain, but Yanukovych asked, so they would give."[43] It was the jackpot Manafort had been searching for—a nearly decadelong arrangement that generated more than $60 million of revenue.[44] After inking his first deal to represent the Party of Regions in 2004, Manafort had purchased a 1,500-square-foot condominium on the forty-third floor of Manhattan's Trump Tower; within a few years, his real estate holdings grew to include a $2 million house outside of Washington, a $3 million loft in SoHo, a $3 million brownstone in Brooklyn, and a $13 million estate in the Hamptons on Long Island.[45] During his time in Ukraine, Manafort spent nearly $1.4 million on bespoke suits and other clothing, $934,350 on ornate rugs, $623,910 on antiques, and $334,000 over two years at a high-end menswear and jewelry store in Beverly Hills.[46] Among the items Manafort purchased from Alan Couture, an upscale men's retailer in Manhattan where he was a top-five customer, was a $15,000 ostrich-skin jacket and $9,500 matching vest.[47]

Like many of Manafort's foreign escapades, his work in Ukraine carried an air of danger. After a meeting with a group of Ukrainian businessmen and politicians, Manafort told his deputy Rick Gates that one of the men in the room had used a car bomb in an unsuccessful attempt to murder another person in the meeting years earlier in a dispute over assets. Later, according to Gates, Manafort discovered that his movements were being tracked by intelligence officials loyal to one of Yanukovych's political rivals. He began keeping a low profile, staying in hotels rather than getting an apartment, driving a small car, and eschewing the sort of private security detail that he believed would draw attention. Despite these risks, the deluge of money that was flowing into Ukraine's elections made the country a leading importer of American political gurus. Obama's pollster Joel Benenson, ex–Bernie Sanders strategist Tad Devine, onetime John McCain aide Steve Schmidt, and former Mitt Romney pollster Neil Newhouse were among the stampede of high-end American campaign consultants cashing in on the market.[48] Many of the American political consultants worked for pro-Western politicians.

At one point, Gates was in a restaurant in Ukraine when he spotted an old friend who'd recently arrived for a payday.

"You're never going to believe who I bumped into," Gates said to Manafort.

It was Roger Stone.

Manafort burst out laughing.

While Manafort was living it up in Kiev, policy makers in Washington were viewing the political developments in Ukraine with growing concern. Yanukovych's election had sparked rebukes from members of Congress and Obama administration officials who were alarmed by the new president's ties to Putin. Some lawmakers introduced measures criticizing Yanukovych and his pro-Russian Party of Regions. The rancor intensified in late 2011, when Yanukovych's regime imprisoned his main political rival, the pro-Western Yulia Tymoshenko,[49] whom he had defeated by a mere 3.5 percent in the election. Amid the criticism of his most lucrative client, Manafort launched a political-influence campaign aimed at, among other things, improving the Party of Regions' image and securing new allies for its leaders in the American capital.

Gates helped Manafort find the right group of DC lobbyists for the job. For assistance influencing key Republican lawmakers, he selected Vin Weber and his colleagues at Mercury Public Affairs. For help with congressional Democrats and the Obama administration, Gates chose Tony Podesta. He made the latter decision, Gates said, because of Podesta's "personal relationships" with important Democrats as well as his past experience working for foreign clients.

In April 2012 Gates traveled to Washington to meet with the two firms[50] and outline the scope of the work. The conversation included one important detail: Gates said the lobbyists wouldn't be working on behalf of the Yanukovych regime. Their official client would be the European Centre for a Modern Ukraine, a nonprofit entity that he said was unaffiliated with the Ukrainian government.

The meeting spooked some of the assembled lobbyists. Once it ended, three Podesta Group employees marched into the office of Kimberley

Fritts, the firm's CEO, to express their concerns. Listening to the pitch, the Podesta Group lobbyists had grown suspicious that the European Centre was actually a front for Yanukovych. "There was no mystery that this was connected to the Party of Regions and the government was commissioning it," said one Podesta employee who attended the meeting. The lobbyists told Fritts they didn't want to help advance the Kremlin's interests in Ukraine. What's more, they simply didn't trust the man who was bringing them the business. "People at the firm were wary of taking Ukraine specifically because it was referred to them by Manafort," recalled one Podesta Group lobbyist. Manafort and Gates, the lobbyist said, were "considered shady and untrustworthy."

Fritts heard out the lobbyists' concerns. "You don't have to work on it," she told them. "But Tony Podesta is taking the money."

Kimberley Fritts would soon have her own doubts about the European Centre. As the lobbying contract was being finalized, she set about compiling the necessary paperwork to register the project with the Department of Justice, as required by the Foreign Agents Registration Act (FARA), a 1938 law that obligates influence peddlers to publicly disclose their lobbying and public relations activities on behalf of foreign countries.[51] But when Fritts tried to learn more about the European Centre, she was stumped.

"I have done a pretty extensive web search and cannot find an address, phone number, or website for the Centre," Fritts wrote to Gates, in one of the many emails that were obtained by federal prosecutors during the Robert Mueller investigation into Russia's interference in the 2016 presidential election and are being reported publicly here for the first time. During an email exchange on April 5, 2012, Fritts asked Gates for information about the financial backers funding the nonprofit.

Gates responded with a link to a bare-bones website for the European Centre. He did not provide the names of any funders. "As for [financial] backing for the center pls talk with Tony as he can explain the system," Gates wrote to Fritts. "I do not think you were in the mtg when this was discussed."

Fritts emailed Podesta. "I honestly am not trying to be difficult but the website isn't live—it's a demo site; it has no contact information," she wrote. "Separately, I was in the room when he talked about members of the board of regents and industrialists being the funders, but there was no more specificity than that. Assume you have had no further intel there."

Podesta said he planned to meet with Gates in a few days; he promised to obtain the information Fritts was requesting.

A week later, Gates coughed up an address for the European Centre, but he still failed to produce any information about its financial backers, information Fritts needed to complete the FARA registration. Under the law, lobbyists must file such registration forms with the Justice Department within ten days of agreeing to work for a foreign principal. As the deadline approached, Fritts grew impatient. She spoke by phone with Gates, but, once again, he was unable to provide the details she needed. Frustrated, she emailed Podesta. "I posed the question [to Gates] again about listing others," Fritts wrote, "and was told that he doesn't even know who all of the individuals are behind the effort."

Fritts then contacted Mike Burns, a lawyer at the Podesta Group. Like Fritts, Burns was beginning to suspect that the Ukraine Centre was not the independent nonprofit that Gates claimed it was. "Foreign people/groups must fund the thing," Burns wrote to Fritts.

Around this time, Gates sent Fritts a written description of the Centre and its backers, which Fritts considered too vague. "We really need to address the funding issue for the FARA disclosure," she wrote to Gates on April 18. "I worry that your language," she continued, "raises more questions than it answers."

A few days later, Gates agreed to draft a new description: "The [Ukraine Centre] does not receive funding from any foreign governments or foreign political parties but through foreign principals." When an attorney for Vin Weber's firm, Mercury, reviewed the statement and concluded it was legally sufficient, the Podesta Group's executives agreed to put aside their concerns. "Well, if their outside counsel doesn't care, maybe we are reading too much into it," Fritts wrote to Burns. Besides, she added, "Tony is signing this form, that is for sure."

As the Podesta Group was finalizing the paperwork, however, officials at Mercury Public Affairs introduced a complication. They now said that they actually didn't need to register the Ukrainian project with the Department of Justice after all. With this, the mystery of who controlled the Ukraine Centre moved from a question of ethics to a matter of law.

Federal law requires all influence peddlers to record their lobbying activities with the government. But the type of registration varies depending on the nature of the client. Lobbyists representing overseas interests typically have to register under FARA; those representing US entities must comply with a different law, the 1995 Lobbying Disclosure Act, commonly referred to as the LDA. Washington's influence peddlers prefer not to register their work under FARA unless it's absolutely necessary, because FARA's requirements are far more stringent than the LDA's. FARA mandates that influence peddlers make public a great deal of information about their activities, including details about each conversation with US government officials. It also compels them to register as foreign agents with the Justice Department. Due to the sense of unseemliness associated with representing overseas interests before one's own government, filing a FARA registration can damage a lobbyist's reputation.

While the Podesta Group's executives had already concluded that they'd have to register the Ukrainian project under FARA, Mercury's top outside counsel, Ken Gross of the firm Skadden Arps, said that he'd found a way to sidestep the undesirable disclosure requirements. The European Centre—per Gates's assurances to the lawyer—was neither a foreign government nor a foreign political party, so it technically didn't fall under FARA. Mercury and Gates embraced this apparent loophole. But the Podesta Group's leadership remained skeptical.

In a lengthy email exchange, senior officials at the Podesta Group debated what they viewed as the central issue: Who was funding the European Centre? Was the group controlled by Ukrainian president Viktor Yanukovych? Did it exist for the primary benefit of the government of Ukraine? If the answer to any of these questions was yes, then the lobbying firms would be required to register as foreign lobbyists under FARA. It was a tedious but critical distinction. Failure to properly disclose overseas lobbying is a federal crime, punishable by up to five years in prison.

"I still don't know where the actual money is coming from," wrote John Anderson, a firm principal, in a group email to Podesta and other senior colleagues.

"So actually if we were asked by the [Justice Department] about the filing, our response would be 'Rick Gates told us they're not funded or controlled by the government,'" wrote Steve Rademaker, the head of the firm's foreign lobbying division. "To which they would likely respond, 'Who's Rick Gates?'" In other words, the Podesta lobbyists couldn't simply absolve themselves of wrongdoing by blaming Gates for providing inaccurate information.

"I guess my broader point is that we've never actually had any contact with this client," Rademaker continued. "Our contact has been with Rick Gates, who so far as I know works either for the government or the ruling party, but not for the Center. For this reason, it would be nice to have some more facts before we assert to the [Justice Department] that we're working for something other than the government."

"This email made me lol—who is rick gates," Fritts responded. "This whole thing is a mess."

"My understanding of this is that we can't be making a mistake if we file under FARA," John Anderson wrote, "but we could make a mistake if we file under LDA."

"The fact that [Gates] has been unable to give us any details in response to Kimberley Fritts' question makes me wonder if the real reason is that they're not independent of the government," Rademaker wrote.

Podesta was convinced.

"Seems FARA to me," Podesta wrote to the group. "Anyone disagree?"

No one did. The Podesta Group's executives set off to register the project under the foreign lobbying rules. Mercury had resolved to file under the domestic lobbying regime.

But there was a problem. The two firms realized that their lobbying disclosure forms for the Ukraine project should be consistent. Registering the same client under two different laws—FARA for Podesta Group, LDA for Mercury—would raise red flags with the Justice Department. Burns, the

Podesta lawyer, reached out to Mercury's lawyers to try to persuade them to file under FARA.

"We're operating with little to no information about the funding situation," Burns told the Mercury lawyers on an April 30 phone call, according to emails and notes of the call obtained by federal prosecutors. With the little they had to go on, it was impossible to know whether or not the lobbying work was intended to benefit Yanukovych or his ruling party.

"I didn't convert them," Burns wrote to Fritts after the call. "But I did get third-party affirmation that we are operating in the dark and that we need further information. And Mercury's agreed to pursue it."

"They can pursue it all they want but the issue is that Gates will provide no info on funding," Fritts responded. "I mean, hello, we have been asking for this since April 2."

Mercury's lawyers pressed Gates for the information. In a phone call in early May, Gates provided a verbal guarantee that the Ukraine Centre was neither funded nor controlled by Ukrainian government officials. It was enough to satisfy Mercury's legal team. "We are going to follow Ken Gross's advice and file as LDA," a Mercury attorney told the Podesta Group in an email. Gross says his legal guidance was based on the information he received from Gates, which, at the time, he believed to be true.

Podesta and his colleagues continued to harbor doubts. The firm's compliance lawyer pulled up articles on European websites stating that the Centre was a puppet for Yanukovych. "If I can find all this on a quick google search, so can DOJ (or the press)," Burns wrote in a May 3 email. "We should FARA for Ukraine because the ties between [the Centre] and the Party of Regions in Ukraine are too close to ignore."

The various snags and holdups began to irritate Podesta. Since the veteran Democratic lobbyist was already registered as a foreign agent, he wasn't bothered by the prospect of making additional FARA disclosures on the Ukrainian project. But all the unanswered questions were delaying the payment of his lobbying fee. "Tony just wanted the money," recalled one Podesta Group lobbyist, "and the registration process was blocking the money."

Eventually Podesta called Gates and asked for a written, signed declaration that the European Centre was unaffiliated with the Ukraine government. The Podesta team thought a written statement from their client could help shield them from criminal liability if it turned out that the Centre was, in fact, a front for the government. If Gates could deliver such an affirmation, Podesta would agree to register the Centre under the less stringent domestic lobbying law. Several days later, when Podesta still hadn't received the signed declaration, he sent a testy message to Gates. "No contract no money no registration LDA," read the subject line on the May 8 email. "This is a problem," Podesta wrote.

Shortly thereafter, Gates sent over the promised statement as well as signed copies of the lobbying contracts with the Podesta Group and Mercury.

"Are we set?" Podesta wrote in an email after receiving the documents.

Within days, the two firms had filed their LDA registration documents. The LDA form asks if any foreign entity "directly or indirectly, in whole or in major part, plans, supervises, controls, directs, finances, or subsidizes activities of the client." Both firms checked the box for "No."

But warnings about the true nature of the European Centre continued to emerge. At one point, a Podesta Group lobbyist contacted an aide to New Jersey Senator Robert Menendez, a high-ranking Democrat on the Senate Foreign Relations Committee, in the hopes of arranging a meeting to discuss the Ukrainian client. The aide turned him down. "Sorry," the aide wrote in an email. "This current government is really not so good." The aide also sent over a blog post reporting that "the Party of Regions has launched and is financing the European Centre for a Modern Ukraine." The top aide to Committee Chairman John Kerry called a Podesta Group lobbyist to express his concerns that the Centre was tied to pro-Russian forces in Ukraine.

"I just don't get how this is possible under LDA. Can you explain?" Andrew Kauders, the Podesta Group lobbyist in charge of the Ukraine account, wrote in a May 18 email to colleagues after Gates asked the firm to organize meetings for Ukraine's minister of foreign affairs with lawmakers and Obama administration officials.

"I am surprised as well," wrote Burns, the Podesta Group lawyer. Burns emailed a Podesta assistant, Kevin Griffis. "Kevin, have you or Tony heard any explanation about how it's possible that this third-party group is setting up fly-ins for the minister and other gov't officials without the gov't directing or supervising them?"

"No," Griffis replied, "and I can't see how it passes the smell test."

Fritts, the Podesta Group's CEO, responded with exasperation. "I'm not getting involved," she said in an email to her colleagues. "I have done battle enough over FARA/LDA etc."

Podesta didn't appear to be concerned. He began working to satisfy Gates's request. "Can you work on 2 dems?" he wrote to one of his lobbyists. "Also alert country director + NATO planner."

But Kauders was still nervous. On May 21 he contacted Gates to discuss his worries about the legality of setting up meetings between US government officials and members of the Yanukovych regime. According to emails, Kauders told Gates that his requests "appear to trigger FARA registration requirements." That same day, Kauders received a call from a Mercury lobbyist, Ed Kutler, who "seemed surprised that these types of requests could be limited to an LDA registration," as Kauders put it in an email to colleagues. During their discussion, both lobbyists agreed that the two firms should change their registrations from LDA to FARA.

Kauders emailed Vin Weber to explain that the Podesta Group "can no longer pursue these meetings without registering under FARA." He added that Gates "seemed comfortable with us proceeding, given that there will likely be additional meeting requests coming our way."

"We'll consult with Ken Gross," Weber responded, referring to the firm's outside counsel, "but will probably follow your lead."

Kauders contacted Podesta to explain that he and Kutler had agreed that both firms needed to change lobbying registration from LDA to FARA.

"Good work," Podesta replied.

At long last, the matter appeared to be settled. Within a few days, the Podesta Group had completed its FARA paperwork, and Tony Podesta had signed the form. "Just need to date and file," Burns wrote in an email. Yet before they could submit the FARA documents to the Justice Department, the Mercury team raised still another objection.

Podesta reported to his colleagues that Vin Weber had a personal reason for not wanting to register under FARA: he had been moonlighting as a
foreign policy advisor to the 2012 presidential campaign of former Republican governor Mitt Romney. According to emails sent between Podesta
Group employees, Podesta told them that Weber worried that registering
as a foreign agent under FARA could embarrass Romney and jeopardize
his own standing in the campaign. "Vin is reluctant to FARA for Ukraine
until further this summer/fall due to his position on the Romney campaign," Fritts wrote in a June 19 email to colleagues.

For advice, Podesta turned to Steve Rademaker, the firm's top foreign
lobbyist, who was also an advisor to the Romney campaign. Rademaker
said that, as a practice, he didn't tell the Romney campaign about new foreign clients "unless I thought the registration might be controversial, in
which case I would want to give them a heads-up." Rademaker noted that
he "would definitely put Ukraine in the controversial category, so I don't
fault Vin for feeling he would need to run this one past the campaign and
worrying that they might have a problem with it." It was possible, Rademaker noted, that political rivals could weaponize Weber's overseas clients
as a way of "accusing Romney of being beholden to foreign interests."

As a favor to Weber, Podesta agreed to follow the legal advice of Mercury's lawyer and disregard the repeated warnings of his staff. Both firms
would maintain their registration of their Ukrainian client under the less-
transparent requirements of the LDA. The FARA filing that Tony Podesta
had signed would remain in a file cabinet in the office of his firm's lawyer
for years instead of being submitted to the Department of Justice. It was
a big mistake. Years later, Gates would plead guilty to federal charges related to the Ukraine lobbying venture; among his admissions was that he
lied to Mercury's lawyer Ken Gross about the behind-the-scenes role that
Ukraine's president had played in the influence-peddling scheme.[52]

Podesta's willingness to ignore his staff's concerns underscores the
profit-seeking calculus that pervades the foreign lobbying industry. The
red flags raised about the Ukrainian Centre weren't treated as evidence
that this shadowy organization might be detrimental to Ukrainian citizens
or American foreign policy. Rather, they were seen as minor annoyances

getting in the way of a big payday. And with such a lucrative contract on the line, Tony Podesta was able to set aside the weighty questions of whether representing a mysterious outfit in a volatile part of the world risked doing real harm to real people. Instead, he focused his attention on a mundane clerical matter: Which is the correct form to file?

During the two years of their influence-peddling campaign for the European Centre for a Modern Ukraine, lobbyists at Podesta Group and Mercury did all they could to advance the interests of their client. Thanks to their allies in Congress and their knowledge of how to gum up the parliamentary process on Capitol Hill, they managed to delay the White House and the State Department from endorsing sanctions on Ukraine for nearly two years and to kill several embarrassing resolutions in Congress that would have condemned the Yanukovych administration. "I used to call them the dynamic duo," Gates said of the two firms. Though Manafort remained mostly behind the scenes, Gates was a more visible presence, often working from a laptop in a small conference room at the Podesta Group's headquarters.

In the late summer of 2012 Manafort directed Gates to check in with Podesta about the possibility of getting the Ukrainian president on the phone with Vice President Joe Biden, who was set to be formally nominated as the party's vice presidential candidate at the Democratic National Convention in Charlotte, North Carolina. "I am thinking of recommending a call from VY to Biden to congratulate Biden on his nomination," Manafort wrote to Gates in a late-August email that has never before been public. "Pls check with Tony as to his opinion on this," Manafort wrote. Gates forwarded Manafort's email to Podesta. "Ideally, this would happen after the DNC," Gates wrote to Podesta. "Let me know your thoughts on this matter and, specifically, if you see any reason not to do it." Podesta liked the idea. "Only downside is [if] biden presses him personally on politics of criminal prosecutions" of his political opponents, Podesta responded. "I would say worth the risk."

There were repeated indications of Yanukovych's involvement in the lobbying effort. "I need that info ASAP before Paul's meeting with the President later today," Gates wrote in an email to the lobbyists. In another, he wrote: "Paul met with the big guy yesterday." For their services, the Podesta Group was paid not by the European Centre for a Modern Ukraine but through mysterious offshore bank accounts. However, since the Ukrainian lobbying venture wasn't attracting any scrutiny from federal officials or the American press, there was little reason for Podesta to fear that his dealings with Paul Manafort would ensnare him in a scandal. That was good news for Podesta, since, at the same time that he was working with Manafort in Ukraine, he was enduring a personal crisis at home.

18

Though it had long served as a totem to their splashy love story, Tony and Heather Podesta's art collection would emerge as a source of marital strife. For Tony, acquiring new paintings and sculptures was, as he once put it, a "form of addiction."[1] As he traveled the world snatching up expensive pieces, the couple's collection swelled to more than 1,300 items. To manage the volume, the Podestas converted their home into something of an art gallery. By removing walls, they created an open interior space where visitors could study pieces from their provocative collection, which included several multimillion-dollar sculptures by the French American artist Louise Bourgeois[2] that were about the size of Tony's Mini Cooper convertible. To house excess pieces, they rented a large, climate-controlled storage facility. The couple organized private exhibits in their home and regularly loaned pieces to prestigious art museums.

Over time, though, Heather began complaining to friends that her husband was spending too much time and money on art. She confronted Tony about what she viewed as his problematic habit, and he agreed to slow down. So, when she discovered that Tony had gone behind her back and discreetly purchased a new piece for more than $1 million, Heather was furious. The tension over Tony's art purchases fueled discord in the relationship, and, before long, the two were sleeping in separate beds. In late 2012, as he was working with Paul Manafort on Ukraine, Tony and Heather split up. The couple sold the home they owned in Sydney, and, in early 2013, Heather began removing her possessions from their Kalorama mansion.

News of the separation appeared in DC's gossip pages,[3] and the couple began talking to a marriage mediator about how to divvy up their assets. Still, Tony Podesta remained optimistic that their time apart would prove brief. He agreed to help Heather purchase a $3.8 million property in the same Kalorama neighborhood where they'd lived for several years.[4] In March 2013 he provided roughly a half million dollars toward the down payment[5] on a five-thousand-square-foot Beaux Arts mansion and carriage house. The property, which was owned by both Podestas, had seven bathrooms and eight bedrooms, each with its own fireplace.[6] But while Heather moved in by herself, she wasn't exactly alone. She'd already begun dating a fifty-two-year-old movie director, Stephen Kessler, whose credits include *Vegas Vacation*, a 1997 comedy featuring Chevy Chase.[7]

Despite his stated desire to reunite with his wife, Tony was pursuing other romantic partners, too. On one occasion, he sought late-night companionship from an employee of his own firm. A few months into the separation, Tony invited a younger, female employee of the Podesta Group to lunch to discuss a job offer she had received from another company. During the meal, Tony shifted the conversation to personal issues, asking about her recent divorce and sharing intimate details about his problems with Heather, according to the former Podesta Group employee. When the employee mentioned she was traveling to New York City for a bachelorette party, Podesta said he also would be there to assist a client with meetings at the United Nations.

Early Friday evening, when the employee was on the train to New York, she received a text message from Podesta.

"Where do we meet?" he asked.

The employee responded that her train was late, and she wouldn't be there in time to see him. She met up with her friend for dinner and the bachelorette party.

Around eleven o'clock, Podesta texted again.

"Where are u," he wrote.

"Just finished dinner," the employee responded. "we are debating where to grab a drink. We r in south midtown/murray hill. Where r u"

"Home if u want to come over," Podesta wrote. "170 fifth avenue. Apt 6"

"Prob staying in this area," the employee wrote back. "but you welcome to meet us."

Podesta wrote back: "Come next weekend."

The employee tried to ignore the implications of the text exchange with her boss. But the next morning, she woke up concerned, according to the former Podesta Group employee. While on an Amtrak train back to Washington, she sent an email to managers at the Podesta Group to report the incident.

The event marked a turning point for the employee's tenure at the firm. Over the following weeks, she attempted to resume a professional working relationship with Podesta. But, according to the former Podesta Group employee, the boss stopped talking to her. She felt increasingly isolated at the office, and she grew uncomfortable at the job she'd once enjoyed. She could no longer see a future at the firm. Not long after the late-night email exchange, the employee accepted a buyout and left the Podesta Group.

Podesta denies these allegations: "I socialized occasionally with male and female employees," he says, "but I never had an inappropriate relationship with her or anyone else. I liked her, but there was never any romance in it. I didn't push her out of the firm."

Still, Tony wasn't prepared for Heather to move on. One day, he spotted a snapshot of Heather and her new boyfriend in a magazine, and he soon learned that the two had appeared together at DC events.[8] Tony became enraged; he believed Heather had deliberately kept him in the dark about her Hollywood beau in order to sucker him out of his $500,000 down payment. "He felt hurt," said a person close to Tony. "He still cared about her."[9] In April 2014 Tony and Heather had a heated argument at their marriage mediator's office. That night, Tony and Heather traded angry emails for hours. The following morning, Heather was served with divorce papers.[10]

The ensuing divorce battle, Podesta versus Podesta, was a spectacle of wounded feelings, legal maneuvering, and tabloid intrigue. According to allegations contained in court documents, the lobbying industry's most glamorous husband-and-wife duo had become consumed by petty recriminations. As their fairy tale fell apart, Tony changed the locks on the couple's marital home in Kalorama, while Heather changed the locks at the Venice flat.[11] Tony blocked Heather's access to the couple's art database and began donating works from their collection to museums without her approval. In return, Heather filed for an injunction preventing Tony from unilaterally disbursing the artwork. She forced the cancelation of an exhibit at the Australian embassy by revoking her approval to lend pieces from their collection. At one point, Heather received permission from Tony to come into the marital home with a videographer to document an inventory of their belongings. But according to Tony's legal filings, upon entering the house, Heather proceeded up the stairs, "only to leave the videographer downstairs, lock herself in Mr. Podesta's bedroom, and rummage through the safe and his suitcase."[12]

Since Tony and Heather had no children together, most of their bickering revolved around the division of financial assets. Heather asked the judge for a fifty-fifty split of the art collection, real estate, retirement funds, and jewelry.[13] She also demanded half ownership of Tony's lobbying firm and full possession of the $4 million Kalorama home where the couple had once lived.[14] Tony objected, accusing Heather of trying to embarrass him by subpoenaing his employees. He claimed that Heather had wasted hundreds of thousands of dollars on "couture clothing, valuable jewelry, luxury cars, and travel to visit her paramour."

At the core of Tony and Heather's dispute, though, was a struggle for ownership of what had been their most valuable possession: the Podesta brand. In his complaint for divorce, Tony's lawyer argued that Heather's success in the influence business was derived from the veteran lobbyist's last name. When the two first met, the lawyer wrote, Heather had been a thirty-three-year-old attorney at a trade association, with a $55,000 annual salary and no assets to speak of. It was only after their wedding that Heather emerged as a K Street big shot. "Ms. Podesta's career has risen meteorically since the parties' marriage, with Mr. Podesta's assistance and connections," Tony's lawyer wrote. Specifically, according to his court filings, Tony "taught" Heather about the lobbying industry, shared "the knowledge he had gathered through decades of experience," and introduced her "to important political, social, and business contacts." Heather, Tony's lawyer wrote, "has used Mr. Podesta's name and reputation to advance her own business and interests." To drive home this point, the lawyer noted that Heather "adopted the Podesta name when the parties married. She had not taken the name of either of her two prior husbands."[15]

For her part, Heather's lawyer contended that she'd changed her name to Podesta "as a loving commitment" to her new husband.[16] The lawyer insisted that Heather and Tony played equally important roles in their only-in-Washington partnership. "As a married couple who both lobbied, they strategically cultivated their public image, and worked to build the 'Heather and Tony Podesta' brand for the success of their shared enterprise," Heather's attorney said. "Both parties, as a result of their joint marital efforts, experienced an unprecedented earnings surge that neither of them experienced before the marriage."[17]

When the two sides met in court for their first hearing, the Podesta name remained a subject of disagreement. Heather's lawyer referred to his client as "Ms. Podesta," while Tony's attorney made a point of using her maiden name, calling her "Ms. Miller Podesta."[18] In the end, neither party was forced to relinquish their stake in the brand. Rather than endure further embarrassment by taking the case to a public trial, they resolved their dispute with an out-of-court settlement.[19] The agreement, which was finalized by the court in July 2014, entitled both Tony and Heather to full ownership of their respective lobbying firms—as well as the famous last name.[20] As soon as the paperwork was signed, the feuding Superlobbyists worked to repair their images by heaping praise on each other. "In politics, the art world, and life, there is only one Tony Podesta,"[21] Heather gushed in a statement sent to the media. In a magnanimous press release of his own, Tony said, "It was a great joy to share my life with Heather Podesta."[22]

Though the divorce was finally over, the battle had taken a visible toll on Tony. As his relationship with Heather soured, Podesta had added pounds to his already meaty torso. His posture seemed hunched over. He flew several times a year to a fitness camp at Rancho La Puerta, a high-end resort in Mexico that cost more than $5,000 a week. At the office, employees found him increasingly irritable and hot-tempered. Podesta was already a notoriously demanding and needy boss. He required his secretaries to sort through his email, print out the ones he should read, and take dictation of his responses. Emails and written documents—sometimes even dirty dishes—were to be placed in the in-box on his desk without disturbing him, while those he put in his out-box were to be immediately removed. If a secretary spoke too slowly, he'd interrupt and demand she stop wasting his time. When flying, an aisle seat was an absolute must, and if a secretary neglected to enter his frequent-flier details into his itinerary, he would erupt. Over the years, his various secretaries had compiled a thirty-seven-page manual detailing the specific requirements of serving him, which they quietly passed down to new members of his administrative staff. The entries show the painstaking steps his secretaries took to properly organize his life and avoid his wrath:

- If he is typing all caps in his emails, he has somehow accidentally turned on the caps lock on his keyboard. Go into his office and turn it off for him.
- Meals are the most important part of the day to Tony. Dinners are typically reserved for friends or very elite people, whereas lunches and breakfasts are sometimes people he "doesn't care about."
- Tony cannot say no when people ask him for meetings. . . . A common situation is him telling you that someone is not important and then telling that same person he is "happy to meet with them and my scheduler will get it on the calendar." It will be your responsibility to find a creative way to push the meeting or schedule it on a slow day.
- Tony is pretty up to date on technology, but sometimes he'll accidentally do something to his phone or computer and insist it is broken. . . . More often than not, he has accidentally turned his ringer off, switched on sleep mode or is looking at the bottom of his in-box for his emails.

- Tony does not like to do more than one "BS" meeting per day.
- When he travels internationally, you may have to include a photo of the electrical outlet so he knows which converter to pack.
- Tony loves wine. He receives wine magazines and emails from different wine websites. I do my best to block these emails and keep the magazines from him, as he has way too much wine already.
- Tony will also rip out movies and tell you to add them to the list. Search his contacts for "Movies" and add the movie he has circled to the notes section. They are listed in alphabetical order. You should include: The name of the movie, the year it was made, the director, the source and the date of the clipping, and add the number of stars should there be any.

During Podesta's breakup with Heather, former employees said, he became more volatile. At one staff meeting, he dressed down a senior lobbyist in front of two dozen colleagues, prompting the employee to quit. On another occasion, a secretary sent documents to Podesta's house through a courier service. Later, when the secretary ran into Podesta in the hallway, he said she wasted money and should have driven the papers to his house. When he considered a memo from a senior lobbyist deficient, he crumpled it up and asked an intern to bring it into the lobbyist's office and throw it at her. After a young aide cooked a meal for an event at Podesta's home, Podesta emailed his staff with curt review: "Chicken incinerated."

The impact of the divorce on Tony's bank account was more significant still. In order to retain control of his lobbying firm and the art collection, he had to relinquish much of everything else. Under the terms of the divorce agreement, Tony gave up homes in Washington and Manhattan, and surrendered nearly $5 million in retirement savings. He was also required to make payments to Heather of a whopping $200,000 every three months for five years.[23] To help absorb his expenses, Tony turned to his art. On the day the divorce was finalized, he obtained a loan from Citibank using some of his art as collateral.[24] It was one of a number of loans that Podesta had secured against his art and real estate. He had refinanced his Kalorama mansion with a short-term, interest-only mortgage, and he had a separate

$10 million line of credit from Citibank for his lobbying firm. In the aftermath of his breakup with Heather, Tony Podesta suddenly found himself millions of dollars in debt.

As the divorce began to strain his finances, Podesta took a scalpel to his firm's budget. Business travel was curtailed, expense reports were scrutinized more rigorously, and starting salaries plateaued. Lobbyists accustomed to receiving bonuses of $100,000 or more saw their annual payouts slashed to around $25,000. Friends got the nickel-and-dime treatment as well; Podesta began charging them to stay at his Venice flat. For years, he had covered the travel expenses of the companions he brought on overseas trips. But after the divorce, he started asking his guests to reimburse him for the fees he incurred when he used his airline miles to book their tickets. "There was a feeling among some of my colleagues that Tony had to tighten his belt to pay for the divorce," said one Podesta Group lobbyist. When it was used to benefit himself, though, Tony was less meticulous about the company's spending. He was known to add unnecessary business meetings to his overseas leisure trips so the firm would pick up the tab for his vacations. He got his firm to pay him $360,000 to rent pieces of art from his collection to display at the office. The Podesta Group covered half of the salary of his personal art curator, and he once billed his firm more than $300,000 in shipping and handling fees for artwork that he'd purchased. After an Internal Revenue Service audit, the federal government found that the firm didn't pay enough tax for handling the art.[25] The Podesta Group was required to pay more than $60,000 in back taxes and fees to resolve the matter, according to internal documents.

Over time, Podesta grew so averse to spending his own cash that, according to a former Podesta Group lobbyist, he once asked for a receipt after buying a newspaper at New York's Penn Station so he could get reimbursed for the expense. Eventually staff members set up an internal control system to prevent the boss from being refunded for nonwork expenses. "Tony likes to get reimbursed for everything," according to the instruction manual compiled by his secretaries. "It is up to you and your best judgment as to what gets reimbursed." But even that didn't always force Podesta to reach into his own pocket. On one occasion, when the firm's accountant denied Podesta's request to cover the costs of his then-girlfriend's international flight, the lobbyist sent the woman an invoice rather than pay the airfare himself.

As these monetary stresses were gathering, Podesta's employees offered him a financial lifeline. In early 2014, not long before the divorce was finalized, senior Podesta Group lobbyists approached him about purchasing a portion of the business.[26] Tony initially seemed open to the idea,[27] which would have given top staffers equity stakes in the firm in exchange for providing Podesta with a much-needed infusion of cash. Over a three-hour dinner at a favorite Italian restaurant, Casa Luca, Podesta and about a dozen senior lobbyists talked over the possibility. The employees estimated the Podesta Group was worth about $50 million; Podesta said it was worth more. At the conclusion of the evening, Podesta suggested they convene again with lawyers to dig into the details. A second meeting was scheduled for three weeks later. On the appointed day, the firm's managers took their seats in a Podesta Group conference room, which they had reserved for five hours. Tony never showed.[28] He was simply unwilling, it seemed, to relinquish control of his namesake lobbying firm.

Instead, Podesta sought to boost the firm's revenue by widening its base of clients to include companies and organizations that—for one reason or another—would have been considered too objectionable to work for in the past. At a staff meeting after the divorce, Podesta urged his team to sign up new customers in less-than-reputable industries, such as gun manufacturing, tobacco production, and liquor distilling.[29] They were leaving money on the table, Podesta insisted, by refusing to work for these firms. The meeting rankled some employees. One of the firm's lobbyists stormed out of the conference room and immediately wrote a letter of resignation. Alcohol and cigarettes, he explained to colleagues, had ruined the lives of several family members. A few months later, the lobbyist left the firm, taking with him a set of clients that cost the Podesta Group roughly $2 million in annual revenue.[30] Other lobbyists followed suit, draining more income from the coffers.

Amid this push to increase profits, Podesta took on new lobbying clients whose interests conflicted with those of existing clients. The firm represented the defense-contracting colossus Boeing Co., as well as its chief rival, Lockheed Martin Corp. Despite Podesta's long history of working for Google, the firm ramped up work for rival tech giant Oracle Corp. at a time when the companies were engaged in a long-running feud over Oracle's claims that Google had stolen its software for mobile phones. Once, Podesta maintained clients with opposing stakes in a major weapons deal: In 2016 Lockheed Martin needed approval from the Pentagon to sell eight F-16 fighter jets to Pakistan for nearly $700 million. The arms sale was strongly opposed by Pakistan's leading adversary, the government of India, which was also a client of the Podesta Group. The Pentagon permitted the sale, and the firm collected a nice payday that year from both sides in the dispute, earning $550,000 from Lockheed Martin and $700,000 from India. In spite of all the money he was making at the firm, he also operated a side business. In 2015 he signed on as a consultant to the US unit of Pirelli, the Italian tire maker, even though his lobbying firm lobbied for a competing tire manufacturer, Michelin. Podesta kept his work for Pirelli a secret from both Michelin and his employees.[31]

Podesta was even willing to cross his most important political patrons. In 2015 he agreed to represent Raffaello Follieri, a flamboyant Italian con man sentenced to four and a half years in federal prison after swindling an investment fund run partly by Bill Clinton.[32] Follieri had described himself as the chief financial officer of the Vatican.[33] He met regularly with the Pope,[34] he claimed, and he said he could use his Vatican connections to obtain Church-owned land at steep discounts for the fund, which had been set up by billionaire investor and prolific Clinton financier Ron Burkle.[35] By the time he was through, Follieri had bilked the fund out of more than $1 million.[36]

In 2008 Follieri was indicted on federal fraud charges[37]—a major embarrassment for the Clintons. Details of Bill Clinton's ties to the financial huckster surfaced just as Hillary Clinton was campaigning for the Democratic presidential nomination against Barack Obama, who offered voters a clean break from the cycle of scandals that consumed Washington the last time a Clinton was president. The revelations of Follieri's deceit reminded voters that another Clinton presidency would come with baggage. Yet none of this was enough to stop Podesta—whose ties to the Clintons were the launchpad for his lobbying career—from helping Follieri attempt to bounce back from his criminal past. In 2015 the admitted fraudster paid Podesta roughly 250,000 euros to help him in Washington. Podesta helped Follieri clean up his image as the convicted felon sought a pardon from President Obama and floated the idea of Follieri writing a book about his life. Since Podesta never publicly disclosed his work for Follieri, no one in the Clinton political network was aware of his betrayal. While the pardon never materialized, Follieri later tapped Podesta to serve as chairman of his Italian investment fund, FHolding Ltd.[38]

As much as anything else, though, Podesta's hunt for more revenue would lead him into the murky business that Paul Manafort had revolutionized back in the 1980s—foreign influence peddling—where Beltway operators could earn staggering fees by advancing the interests of overseas governments or political parties. Not all foreign clients were shady or nefarious; during the 1970s, for instance, Tommy Boggs worked for Central American sugar producers and Korean fishing interests. Still, the practice has long carried an unsavory stigma. "There is an inherent suspicion that advancing foreign interests is antithetical to US interests," said David Laufman, a former top official in the Justice Department's FARA division. On top of that, requiring overseas lobbyists to register as "foreign agents," Laufman says, "makes it sound like you are a spy." As a result, many large US companies refused to hire lobbyists who also worked for questionable foreign entities. And most reputable members of the K Street establishment avoided the practice altogether.

Foreign lobbying, however, did offer one key advantage over domestic influence peddling: money. To account for the reputational damage associated with the work, overseas governments generally paid higher lobbying fees than corporations. Following the revelation that most of the jetliner hijackers in the September 11 terrorist attacks hailed from Saudi Arabia, for example, the oil-rich kingdom spent more than $100 million to influence Washington policy makers over the next decade—a floodtide of cash that far exceeded the lobbying outlays of most large US firms. This nexus of risks and rewards attracted a particular type of Washington player: someone willing to trade his or her good name for a lucrative payday.

The international work appealed to Podesta's worldly sensibilities, and he'd dabbled in it over the years; in early 2012, for instance, he teamed up with Manafort for the Ukrainian lobbying venture.[39] "Tony loved the travel," said a Podesta Group lobbyist who worked with him on overseas accounts. "He loved embassy parties and hanging out with ambassadors." Podesta wasn't much bothered by the reputational risks associated with working for distasteful foreign governments or political leaders. Once, during a meeting to discuss the possibility of representing an overseas dictator who'd been accused of genocide, Podesta became frustrated when his lobbying team refused to sign up the despot. "Haven't you ever made a mistake?!?" he snapped.

In the aftermath of his divorce, Podesta turned his overseas practice into a linchpin of the firm. Back in 2010, when Tony and Heather were still together, the Podesta Group's foreign business was tiny, with the $1.8 million in fees earned from overseas clients that year accounting for only about 5 percent of the firm's annual revenue. But by 2015, the first full year after his divorce was final, the Podesta Group had nearly tripled its overseas business to $5 million,[40] and the international share of the firm's total revenue had grown to nearly 20 percent. About one-quarter of its roughly forty lobbyists were registered to work for foreign clients.

Podesta wasn't terribly discerning about the foreign clients he signed up, and, before long, his firm was representing a full slate of brutal regimes that had been credibly accused of human rights violations. The government of Azerbaijan paid the Podesta Group $50,000 a month[41] partly to help its corrupt president, Ilham Aliyev, avoid punishment by the US government for throwing his domestic critics in jail. Saudi Arabia retained the firm for $1.7 million a year to assist it in deflecting criticism of what Yahoo! News described as its "hard-line domestic suppression of political dissidents, with draconian punishments such as the sentence—by beheading—recently given to a twenty-year-old Shiite political prisoner."[42] And for a $240,000 annual fee, the government of South Sudan secured the firm's help in shielding it from the tough sanctions that watchdog groups were demanding in response to human rights abuses in the war-torn African nation. These atrocities, according to the Center for Public Integrity,[43] which cited a United Nations report, included raping and murdering civilians, and forcing child soldiers to wage war.

From the outside, Podesta's strategy of shaving expenses and scooping up shady clients seemed to make economic sense. By the end of 2015, the Podesta Group was the fourth largest lobbying enterprise in Washington, just one spot behind Tommy Boggs's former company, Squire Patton Boggs.[44] Podesta himself was earning roughly $2 million in annual salary while taking home millions more in commissions.[45] Beneath the surface, though, Podesta's financial position was more rickety than it appeared. Though loaded up with divorce-related expenses, he continued to spend freely on fine wines, exclusive restaurants, overseas travel, and, of course, art—a lavish lifestyle that, more and more, he was financing with borrowed money. And despite the massive size of the firm, its balance sheet was showing signs of trouble. The Podesta Group's 2015 lobbying revenue had fallen 20 percent from 2010[46] amid a general decline in the lobbying industry, and its foreign business wasn't growing fast enough to compensate for the decline. Podesta's overstretched, over-leveraged bank account might have enabled him to maintain his glitzy persona, but it left him with little financial cushion to fall back on if something went wrong. Still, at the conclusion of the Obama years, the veteran political fixer had every reason to believe that money wasn't going to be an issue for him much longer.

As Hillary Clinton emerged as the odds-on favorite to win the presidential election, 2016 was shaping up to be a historic year for the Podesta Group. Following the death of Tommy Boggs, Tony Podesta was more closely connected to the Clinton political machine than any lobbyist in the city. He possessed a decades-long relationship with the ex-president and First Lady, and his brother, John, was the chair of Hillary's campaign and in line for a senior post in her White House. Over the course of the race, Tony Podesta did everything he could to ensure that Hillary would defeat her Republican rival. He hosted a fund-raiser for her at his Kalorama mansion that raked in tens of thousands of dollars for her campaign. Guests gathered on his backyard patio and munched on pizza that had been prepared on his outdoor brick oven grill by James Alefantis, the coowner of Comet Ping Pong, a Washington pizza parlor that was popular with young families and college students. Later, Tony recruited his brother John—who'd spent the campaign season living in one of Tony's multimillion-dollar New York apartments—to headline a second fund-raising event that was billed as a "campaign briefing and brunch" for donors. In all, Tony Podesta helped raise $900,000 for Clinton's campaign and the Democratic Party. This cash was an investment as much as it was a contribution. After all, the election of America's first female president would make the Podesta Group the most powerful lobbying firm in the city.

Expectations of Hillary's victory had already begun to boost revenue at the firm. In the months leading up to Election Day, the Podesta Group welcomed an influx of new clients, as corporations and foreign governments came to view a Hillary Clinton White House as inevitable and Podesta as their best vehicle for influencing it. The firm signed up Airbnb Inc., the embassy of Vietnam, and Saudi Aramco, the world's largest oil conglomerate. Podesta also agreed to represent the US arm of Russia's largest state-owned bank, Sberbank, partly to assist in its effort to wriggle free from US sanctions. But just as momentum seemed to be shifting in Podesta's direction, the political trade winds turned against him.

As the presidential race got into full swing, Washington's pro-business consensus emerged as a central campaign issue, with candidates from both parties fulminating over the corporate-friendly framework that had guided federal policy over the prior four decades. The outrage was most intense on the Right, where the billionaire real estate mogul Donald Trump seethed at "the special interests, the lobbyists, and the corrupt corporate media that have rigged the system against everyday Americans."[47] While lambasting Wall Street—"the hedge fund guys are getting away with murder"[48]—he championed a brand of economic nationalism that was heretical to corporate executives and Republican elites. Trump blasted the loose immigration policies that had furnished entire sectors of the economy with low-wage labor. He castigated American firms that moved jobs overseas as a means of reducing their expenses, and he raged against international trade agreements that prioritized corporate profits over American workers. Trump saved some of his harshest invective for China, a booming source of cheap materials and manufacturing that American companies were desperate to access. China, he insisted, was an "economic enemy, because they have taken advantage of us like nobody in history. . . . It's the greatest theft in the history of the world what they've done to the United States. They've taken our jobs."[49]

Anticorporate populism was gaining traction with Democrats as well. Vermont Senator Bernie Sanders's longtime opposition to free trade helped power his surprisingly strong showing in the Democratic primaries. In October 2015, when the Obama administration announced that it had struck a twelve-nation trade deal known as the Trans-Pacific Partnership, Sanders blasted the accord. Making it easier to import foreign goods, Sanders and other TPP critics believed, would only encourage US manufacturing firms to relocate jobs overseas. "It is time for the rest of us to stop letting multinational corporations rig the system to pad their profits at our expense," he fumed. Sanders's chief Democratic rival, however, was less well suited for this anticorporate zeitgeist. Thanks in part to her decades-long association with DC's corporate lobbying establishment, Hillary Clinton was the preferred candidate of most business executives, and nearly everyone on K Street assumed that she would win. Wall Street investors, who are historically among the largest sources of campaign cash for both Republicans and Democrats, gave four times as much money to Clinton as they did to Trump. Employees of Bank of America Corp., for example, contributed more than $500,000 to Clinton and just $75,000 to Trump. But against this rising tide of populism, Clinton struggled to prove that she wasn't beholden to Washington's special interests. In October 2015 she followed Sanders's lead and announced that she too opposed the Trans-Pacific Partnership.[50] It wasn't enough. Throughout the campaign, Trump's allies continued to portray Clinton as an emblem of the Washington swamp. And before long, they saw a golden opportunity to tie the Democratic front-runner to a high-profile lobbyist.

In April 2016 the International Consortium of Investigative Journalists began publishing details from a secret trove of eleven and a half million documents that had been obtained from one of the world's largest offshore law firms, the Panama-based Mossack Fonseca. While many of these files, which came to be known as the "Panama Papers,"[51] exposed the network of shell companies and legal loopholes that the global elite use to hide their wealth from tax authorities, the documents also revealed that Tony Podesta had begun lobbying for the state-owned Russian bank Sberbank. In short order, the disclosure became a cudgel with which to bludgeon Trump's Democratic opponent. "It should be noted that Tony Podesta is a big-money bundler for the Hillary Clinton presidential campaign, while his brother John is the chairman of that campaign, the chief architect of her plans to take the White House this November," John R. Schindler wrote in an op-ed published in the *New York Observer*—the media outlet then owned by Jared Kushner, Donald Trump's son-in-law and a campaign advisor. Schindler called Tony Podesta a lobbyist "for Vladimir Putin's personal bank of choice, an arm of his Kremlin and its intelligence service."[52] For his part, Trump used his massive social media following to highlight Podesta's work for the Russian bank. "Was the brother of John Podesta paid big money to get the sanctions on Russia lifted?" he asked in a Tweet. "Did Hillary know?"[53]

Word of Podesta's dealings with the pro-Putin bank spooked the lobbying firm's own lender. For many years prior, Podesta Group had depended on SunTrust Banks for a line of credit, a large purchasing card, and several foreign bank accounts. But in July 2016 a SunTrust executive sent a letter to the Podesta Group's CEO, Kimberley Fritts, explaining that on account of "increased risk," the bank would stop doing business with it.

"The compliance department of SunTrust is running scared of reputational damage" related to the lobbying firm's work with the pro-Putin bank, said the Podesta Group's chief financial officer, Scott Chesson, in an email after speaking with the bank's officials. For many inside the firm, SunTrust's actions were a clear indication that in his rush to increase revenue, Podesta had overlooked the risks associated with representing controversial overseas entities. "Tony thinks these types of clients have no repercussions on the firm; this should really provide evidence that we have to take the clients we bring on seriously," Fritts said in an exasperated email to Chesson.

"My thoughts exactly," he replied.

Podesta, though, wasn't alarmed. He simply moved the firm's accounts over to Chain Bridge Bank, a McLean, Virginia–based bank owned by a former Illinois Republican senator that did lots of business with political candidates and lobbying firms. It wasn't until a few months later that Podesta came to appreciate the damage that a dubious foreign client could do to a landmark Washington institution.

19

After returning from the commercial break, Chuck Todd, the host of NBC's *Meet the Press*, introduced his next guest to the audience of his venerable Sunday morning program. "Joining me now from Southampton, New York, is the chairman of the Trump campaign—the head coach, if you will—Paul Manafort," he said. "Mr. Manafort, welcome back to the show, sir."[1]

It was early summer in the nation's capital, one month before the Republican National Convention, and four years after Manafort had launched his joint lobbying venture with Tony Podesta. For Manafort, the former hotshot of 1980s Washington, time had certainly left its mark. Through their TV screens that morning, viewers encountered a sixty-seven-year-old man with a fleshy face and a droop beneath his eyes. His hairline, which was dark brown during the Black, Manafort & Stone era, was now frosted with silver, and he was carrying additional weight in his torso and hips. Yet in his crisp dark suit and precisely coiffed hair, Manafort radiated the same polished, self-assured charisma that he'd used to conquer the capital city a generation earlier. With the artistry he'd developed during a lifetime of machinations, he succeeded in turning each of Todd's questions into an attack on his boss's Democratic opponent.

In response to a query about England's plans to leave the EU, Manafort replied: "This election, in 2016, where Donald Trump is the only change agent, is set up perfectly on those same themes, because Hillary Clinton is the epitome of the establishment. She's been in power for twenty-five years."[2]

Manafort was an unlikely vessel for Donald Trump's revolt against the Beltway establishment and the global elite. After enriching himself as a DC influence peddler, Manafort had spent the second half of his career in the shadowy business of foreign political consulting. As he guided his Kremlin-aligned clients to power in a volatile Ukraine, Manafort amassed the sort of fortune that's typically associated with French monarchs or Wall Street kingpins.[3] At the time of his *Meet the Press* appearance, he owned three Land Rovers, a $21,000 watch from an appointment-only menswear boutique on Rodeo Drive in Beverly Hills, and an $18,500 python-skin jacket. Among his roughly half dozen different properties was a 2.4-acre Hamptons estate with a ten-bedroom house, a putting green, a waterfall, a tennis court, a pool, a basketball court, and a display of flowers arranged into the shape of the letter *M*.[4] But for this inveterate political hustler, the Make America Great Again movement wasn't an expression of populist rage. It was a vehicle out of a crisis.

Despite the aura of confidence and prosperity that he projected on *Meet the Press* that morning, the truth was that Manafort's life was in a state of implosion. Roughly two years earlier, around the time that his principal client, Ukrainian President Viktor Yanukovych, was ousted from power in a popular uprising, Manafort's finances had begun to unravel.[5] Business dried up, unpaid bills mounted.[6] A Russian oligarch was hassling him about a missing $19 million investment.[7] As the cash crunch intensified, Manafort experienced a more personal calamity. His wife of twenty-seven years, Kathy, discovered that he'd been keeping a mistress[8] and threatened to leave him. Manafort ended up in a rehabilitation facility for sex addiction in Arizona, where he sobbed nearly every day.[9] At one point, things got so dark that he suggested taking his own life. "My dad," Manafort's daughter Andrea said in a June 2015 text, "is in the middle of a massive emotional breakdown."[10]

While Manafort was at his lowest point, Trump's White House bid became the lobbyist's path to redemption. As it happened, the real estate mogul was just then searching for an experienced fixer to help him navigate a potential floor fight at the upcoming GOP Convention. With the help of an old lobbying partner, Roger Stone, Manafort was able to talk his way onto Trump's team,[11] and when the campaign's manager was fired in June 2016, Manafort got the top post. It was an astonishing turn of events. One year earlier, Manafort had been blubbering into the phone at a sex-addiction clinic and expressing thoughts of suicide.[12] Now he was hashing out strategy with Ivanka Trump and Jared Kushner and appearing on prestigious Sunday-morning political shows. Over the next several months, as he navigated Trump through the treacherous RNC nominating process,[13] Manafort would help elect a right-wing populist whose antiestablishment fury would dismantle the very pro-business policy consensus that Manafort had spent the first half of his career working to erect.

Yet even then, as he flashed his cocksure smile at the *Meet the Press* viewers, Manafort was already looking beyond the 2016 election, plotting an even bigger score. Joining the Trump campaign, after all, was only the first step in Manafort's master plan to reclaim his standing in Washington, get the creditors off his back, and accrue even more influence than he'd wielded during the heyday of Black Manafort. "He was going to do what he had done before," says Rick Gates, the former Manafort deputy, "but on a much grander scale."

Manafort's Ukrainian gravy train began to stall out[14] about the time that a wave of civil unrest engulfed the capital city of Kiev. In late 2013 President Yanukovych—the Kremlin-aligned leader whom Manafort had steered to office—rejected an agreement that would have strengthened Ukraine's ties to the European Union in favor of aligning the country more closely with Russia. The development sparked widespread protests in Kiev; angry citizens poured into the city's Independence Square.[15] When Yanukovych tried to quell the unrest through force, dozens of unarmed demonstrators were shot and killed; the country appeared on the brink of civil war. In February 2014 Yanukovych fled Kiev with the assistance of the Kremlin, as Putin has said;[16] the ousted Ukrainian president eventually landed in Russia.[17] In his absence, Ukraine's parliament accused Yanukovych of "mass killings of civilians" and voted to remove him from office.[18]

As the situation in Kiev deteriorated, and false rumors circulated about Yanukovych having been captured or shot, the American consultants retreated to Washington, where Manafort slipped into a haze of disbelief. "He was," Gates says, "just desperately upset."

According to Gates, Manafort had been urging Yanukovych to sign the European Union accord, and he considered the agreement's rejection to be a personal betrayal. Beyond that, when the protestors took to the streets, Manafort had expected Yanukovych to reach out for advice, Gates says. But the call never came. Instead, once Yanukovych slipped away to Russia, he cut Manafort out of his circle of advisors. According to Gates, Manafort thought Yanukovych must have blamed his American strategist for the political upheaval that led to his ouster. The excommunication was tough on Manafort's self-image. "You spent ten years of your life building this," Gates says, "and then all of a sudden everything flips on a dime." It was even more punishing on Manafort's business. His work in Ukraine had grown so lucrative that he'd neglected to develop clients elsewhere; almost all of his revenue was tied to this single country.[19] And amid the turmoil in Kiev, Manafort's income was drying up.[20] "All of the oligarchs who were funding the party and therefore funding Paul are now in their own scramble," Gates says, "trying to get out of the country."

But even before Yanukovych's ouster, Manafort had fallen behind on payments to the Podesta Group and Mercury for their work in the Ukrainian lobbying venture. In December 2013 Tony Podesta complained to Gates about the missing fees. "Any updates on bank wires," Podesta wrote in an email. "We are pushing 5 months in arrears." A few weeks later, when Podesta's unpaid invoices reached $200,000, he forbade his staff from working on the project. In early 2014 the lobbyists received dubious letters from "Loyal Bank" in the West Indies regarding the late payments. In the unsigned letter, the bank's chairman apologized for the "difficulties you may have faced in having outward and inward wire transfers transacted through our bank in the last few weeks" and promised to promptly resolve the matter. Lawyers for the lobbying firms described the letters as "very questionable." Though the firms did receive some payments over the following months, they were still owed money. By April 2014, Podesta had seen enough. He dropped Manafort as a client and, shortly thereafter, the European Centre for a Modern Ukraine shut down.

After Yanukovych fled Ukraine, Manafort struggled to find new clients. He managed to secure a $6 million contract to represent a slate of former Party of Regions candidates, but in the end, he received only a fraction of the promised payment. By 2015, Manafort's cash-flow bonanza in eastern Europe had completely evaporated, touching off an acute financial crunch.[21] Manafort's lavish lifestyle had come with staggering monthly bills—in certain years, he paid more than $200,000 for landscaping on the Hamptons estate alone—and it didn't take long for debts to mount. There were other sources of fiscal pressure too. Lawyers representing Oleg Vladimirovich Deripaska, the billionaire Russian oligarch who first sent Manafort to Kiev, were after him about the missing $19 million that Manafort had invested on his behalf in a Ukrainian telecommunications company in 2007. Deripaska later asked for the return of his investment funds, as the global financial crisis was wrecking his balance sheet. When Manafort failed to repay him, Deripaska filed a lawsuit in 2018.[22] A Manafort spokesman told the *Washington Post* that "we are surprised by the filing," adding that he believed that the issue had been "addressed and resolved years ago."[23] The case has been on hold since the federal government placed sanctions on Russia's government and industry, including Deripaska's company.

As the squeeze on Manafort's bank account intensified, the man whose annual clothing budget regularly exceeded $210,000 began scrambling to save cash. "He is suddenly extremely cheap," his daughter Andrea remarked in a 2015 text message, which was contained in the years' worth of her texts that were obtained by hackers and posted online. While making plans for a prewedding reception for Andrea and her fiancé, Manafort had refused to pay for drink mixers or ice, recommending instead a cut-rate event with paper plates and hot dogs.[24] "Hot dogs. Can we just discuss how gross that is," Manafort's other daughter, Jessica, wrote in a text exchange with her sister, Andrea. "This isn't a fucking grill out," Andrea replied.

As these financial troubles escalated, Manafort faced a crisis on the home front. A few months after his break with Yanukovych, his daughters discovered that he was carrying on an elaborate affair. Manafort had set up his paramour, who was more than three decades younger than he, with a Manhattan apartment, a Hamptons beach house, and access to an American Express card.[25] "He was fucking his mistress when Grandma was in surgery," Andrea wrote in a text. In the spring of 2015 Manafort's wife, Kathy, confronted him about the affair. He broke down, begged forgiveness, and checked into the same Arizona clinic where, according to a text from one of Manafort's daughters, the actor Michael Douglas had been treated for sex addiction. While at the clinic, Manafort's only contact with the outside world came during the fifteen minutes of phone time he was allotted per day.[26] "I guess he sobs. Like a lot," Andrea texted a friend. Over time, his daughters grew concerned he might harm himself. "He is acting like he is going to end his life," Jessica texted Andrea. "He is writing a letter to mom and then he said he will be gone forever," Andrea replied.

While Manafort was coming unglued at the Arizona treatment center, a celebrity client of his former lobbying firm was gliding down an escalator at Trump Tower on his way to the press conference where he would announce his White House bid. It was Manafort's dream to get back into American politics, Gates says. But such a return had always seemed impossible. In the two decades since he last worked on a US presidential campaign—Bob Dole's ill-fated 1996 venture—Manafort's ties to flashy arms dealers and vicious foreign tyrants had made him too much of a liability for any mainstream candidate. During the 2008 presidential race, according to Gates, one of Manafort's well-connected friends had urged the top brass of John McCain's campaign to bring him aboard, but to no avail. Trump was different. As an outcast of the Republican establishment, he didn't have many experienced Washington operatives in his orbit. And thanks in part to all the scandal and bad press in his own past, he was more willing to overlook a few problems on the resumes of the people he hired.

Manafort shared some loose affiliations with Trump. In addition to his ex-firm's lobbying work on behalf of the New York mogul in the 1980s and 1990s, Manafort and his wife had squired Trump around the 1996 Republican National Convention, in San Diego. At one point, as Kathy led Trump through the pomp and excitement of the convention floor, she heard Trump speaking to himself.

"This is what I want," he said. "This is what I want."[27]

In the years after Manafort purchased his Trump Tower apartment, he would occasionally exchange friendly small talk with the real estate billionaire when they bumped into each other in the building.[28] There were also some mutual friends. Manafort's old lobbying partner Roger Stone had been a political advisor to Trump when his casino business was a lobbying client of Black Manafort. The billionaire private equity founder Tom Barrack had been close with both men for many years.[29]

By early 2016, Manafort was taking the first steps of his improbable comeback. With his finances in shambles, his personal life in chaos, and his emotional state so despondent that he was hinting at suicide, he would use the New York playboy-turned-right-wing-firebrand as his vehicle out of the darkness. After his four weeks in rehab, Manafort reached out to his buddy Tom Barrack. "I really need to get to" Trump, he said, according to what Barrack told the *Washington Post*.[30]

Manafort set himself to securing a role in the famously antiestablishment campaign. With Barrack acting as an intermediary, he delivered a five-page pitch to Trump in February 2016 in which he recast his exile from Republican politics as a selling point.[31] "I have had no client relationships dealing with Washington since around 2005. I have avoided the political establishment in Washington since 2005," Manafort wrote. "I will not bring Washington baggage." To accentuate this message, Manafort referred to Karl Rove, the ex–George W. Bush strategist who'd emerged as a vocal Trump critic, as "my blood enemy in politics" stretching back to the College Republicans in the 1960s. Manafort also alluded to lobbying work he'd done for Trump in the past, and he mentioned his place in Trump Tower.[32]

The pitch landed on Trump's desk during a period of the campaign when Manafort's talents seemed particularly valuable. Though Trump had secured key primary victories in New Hampshire and South Carolina, political operatives from the GOP's establishment wing were plotting to torpedo his candidacy by engineering a delegate revolt at the upcoming Republican National Convention in Cleveland. Manafort, of course, had helped arm-twist Gerald Ford to victory during the GOP's last contested convention, in 1976. "You've got to bring Manafort on," Roger Stone told Trump in a phone call. "He knows how to deal with delegate selection. He understands what the rules are. He's got experience in the national campaigns; you need him to come in and be the delegate coordinator, convention coordinator."[33]

For the famously tightfisted Trump, there was another benefit to retaining Manafort. "I am not looking for a paid job," Manafort explained in his memo. Such an unpaid role, Manafort believed, would make it more likely that Trump would see him as a peer, as opposed to a subordinate.[34] But the veteran Washington insider also understood that if Trump won the election, his ties to the new president would enable him to earn far more money as a K Street influence peddler than he could ever make as a campaign staffer.

At first, Trump was suspicious of Manafort's offer to forgo a paycheck. "Everybody wants something," Trump said to Manafort in the days after hiring him.

"Maybe in the future I'll want something," Manafort responded, "but right now I just want to get you elected."[35]

Trump welcomed Manafort to the team in March 2016, and, right away, he was impressed. Trump liked Manafort's political experience as well as his polished presence; he mentioned to aides that his freshly tanned new advisor appeared many years younger than his age.[36] (Manafort was sixty-six when he joined the campaign.) "Dad and Trump are literally living in the same building," Manafort's daughter Andrea wrote in a text to her sister, Jessica, "and mom says they go up and down all day long hanging and plotting together." Trump often bragged about how much value he was getting out of his unpaid strategist.[37] Though a convention-floor coup never materialized, Trump soon found a more important role for the operative. In June 2016, when the campaign appeared to be in jeopardy amid declining poll numbers, anemic fund-raising, and growing doubts about Trump's temperament, the billionaire real estate mogul fired his hotheaded campaign manager, Corey Lewandowski. The move made Manafort, who'd been promoted to chief strategist a month earlier, the operation's top official.[38] "I think it's time now for a different kind of a campaign,"[39] Trump said of the leadership change.

Manafort's daughters were thrilled by the news. "Im not a trump supporter but I am still proud of dad," Andrea texted her sister. "He is so happy," Jessica replied. "I told him this is what happens when you straighten out your life." Once word of Manafort's new job became public, a friend reached out to Andrea with a reference to her father's past. "sadly [Charlie] black went elsewhere," the friend texted, "but with [Roger] stone and Manafort w Trump, all we need is the ghost of Lee Atwater and the whole dirty tricks team is back!!! This is awesome."

In many ways, however, Trump was advancing the opposite agenda of the one that Manafort and the "dirty tricks team" had helped enshrine in Washington. As a member of Reagan's 1980 presidential campaign, Manafort worked to promote the free-market ideology of America's corporate establishment. During his years on K Street, he and his partners helped bend federal policy to the desires of Wall Street kingpins and multinational conglomerates. Now Trump was thundering his way to the top of the Republican primary field by railing against corporate-friendly trade and immigration policies and excoriating individual firms for moving jobs overseas. In July 2015, for instance, when he learned that the automaker Ford Motor Co. planned to move some of its manufacturing activities out of the United States,[40] an outraged Trump took to Twitter and promised to stop it as president.[41] A month later, Trump said he would boycott Oreo cookies[42] after Mondeléz International Inc., the maker of the world-famous treat, said it was transferring some production to Mexico.[43] Following his victory in the New Hampshire primary, Trump blasted a US-based air-conditioner company, Carrier Global Corp., for its plans to do the same.[44] "It's disgraceful that our politicians allow them to get away with it," he said several months later, during a speech at the Economic Club of New York. "It really is."[45]

Trump's appeals proved popular with the rural and blue-collar voters who'd been left behind by the prior four decades of federal policy making, when Washington raced to globalize the economy without regard for the millions of workers who had neither the skills nor experience to succeed in the new economy. Lacking the shelter of strong unions and assertive federal regulators—protections that had been gradually whittled away by Tommy Boggs, Black Manafort, Tony Podesta, and other Big Business lobbyists—these workers were unguarded against the free market's destructive potential. So, unlike their onetime allies in C-suites and boardrooms, many working-class Americans began to view corporate capitalism not as a pathway to prosperity, but as an instrument of industrial collapse, stagnant wages, poor social mobility, and structural hopelessness. Some thirty-five years earlier, many of these workers had joined Ronald Reagan's revolt against the federal bureaucracy. Now they would power Donald Trump's crusade against the corporate elite.

While Trump's economic nationalism was anathema to the free-market conservatives Manafort had spent much of his life putting in office, Manafort wasn't one to let ideological purity get in the way of his ambitions. And his primary objective, according to his longtime deputy Rick Gates, was to get Trump elected so that he could use his clout with the new White House to escape his deep financial hole. "He was immediately thinking about how to monetize this," says Gates, who went to work as a top lieutenant to Manafort on the Trump campaign. Manafort planned to get Trump elected and then get back into the influence-peddling business, representing high-paying foreign clients before an administration he'd helped bring to power.

While other campaign staffers were angling to secure West Wing desks in the event of a Trump victory, Manafort's eyes remained fixed on the influence business. At one point during the campaign, according to Gates, Trump approached Manafort with a question. "Hey, if we actually win this thing, what Cabinet position do you want? I'll give you anything that you want." Manafort responded that he had no interest in joining the administration. It was precisely the same calculus that Manafort had made back in 1980, when he and his three pals had converted their ties to the Reagan revolution into the era's signature influence-peddling enterprise. Only this time, in Trump's unlikely rise, Manafort saw an opening to parlay his MAGA connections into the sort of lobbying empire that would make Black Manafort look like a charity. "He knew better than anyone how much financial compensation you could get on the international side," Gates says.

As soon as he joined the Trump campaign, in fact, Manafort began looking for ways to use his newfound political influence to settle his old debts. He emailed news articles about his role in the Trump campaign to a former associate in Ukraine, Konstantin Kilimnik. "How do we use to get whole?" Manafort asked. "Has OVD operation seen?" referring to Oleg Vladimirovich Deripaska, whose lawyers had been hounding Manafort about his missing $19 million investment. Kilimnik was hopeful, suggesting in one reply that Manafort's and Deripaska's teams "will get back to the original relationship."[46]

Though such windfall payouts would only materialize if Trump won the election, Manafort was confident he could deliver. He saw in Trump the same potential that he'd identified in his former Ukrainian client, Viktor Yanukovych. According to Gates, Manafort considered Trump "a blank piece of paper" whom he could craft into a more polished and disciplined candidate capable of appealing to a broader array of voters, just as he'd done for Yanukovych six years earlier. "Paul thought Trump was the ideal candidate for him," Gates says. "He said, 'If I get this guy scripted on a message—the right message—he's a shoo-in.'"

There was, however, a fundamental problem in the plan. Manafort discovered quickly that Trump was not nearly as coachable as his Ukrainian client. The former reality-show star fumed when Manafort spoke on his behalf during media appearances. "The only person that speaks for Donald Trump is Donald Trump," the future president told Gates. When a leaked audio recording captured Manafort telling a private audience of RNC officials that Trump had merely been playing a "part" on the campaign trail and that he was currently in the process of "evolving" into a more conventional candidate,[47] Trump was apoplectic. "That was the first time that he blasted Paul as an underling, not as a peer," Gates says.

Despite the growing tension, Manafort's relationship with Trump didn't fully rupture until August 2016, when Manafort's prior work in Ukraine became the subject of a series of unflattering new articles. The

New York Times delivered the first serious blow, revealing the existence of handwritten ledgers in Kiev indicating that nearly $13 million in off-the-books cash payments from the pro-Putin Party of Regions had been earmarked for Manafort.[48] The disclosures were especially damaging to Trump in light of his repeated insistence that he wasn't beholden to outside interests. Manafort released a public statement denying the most salacious claims, but he generally followed the old Washington adage that campaign staffers should never willingly draw press attention away from the candidate and toward themselves. This muted response displeased the future president. As a veteran of New York City real estate battles and tabloid grudge matches, Trump expected his campaign's top strategist to rebuff the allegations more aggressively. Manafort's refusal to engage in a public slugfest over the negative press was, in Trump's eyes, an indication of weakness. "You could be guilty or you could be innocent, but you've got to fight," Gates recalls Trump saying. "Why isn't Paul fighting this?"

Days later, Trump's top strategist faced an even more damaging revelation: this time about the 2012 joint venture with Tony Podesta and Vin Weber. "AP Sources: Manafort Tied to Undisclosed Foreign Lobbying," read the headline from the Associated Press.[49] The story revealed that, by using the European Centre for a Modern Ukraine as a pass-through, Manafort had "helped a pro-Russian governing party in Ukraine secretly route at least $2.2 million in payments to" the Podesta Group and Mercury Public Affairs, doing so "in a way that effectively obscured the foreign political party's efforts to influence US policy." Such surreptitious foreign lobbying, the article suggested, might violate the Foreign Agents Registration Act—just as Podesta's employees had warned. In fact, some of the firm's own staffers helped expose the truth about the campaign. When an AP reporter reached out to the Podesta Group lobbyists who had refused to work on the Ukraine matter, he found sources who were willing to corroborate the story.

From there, Manafort's demise came swiftly. Trump's family members withdrew their support,[50] and internal adversaries rooted for his dismissal. Trump sidelined Manafort by appointing a new campaign manager, Kellyanne Conway, and chief executive, Steve Bannon.[51] Five days after the media frenzy began, Manafort surrendered. "This morning Paul Manafort offered, and I accepted, his resignation from the campaign," Trump said on August 19. "I am very appreciative for his great work in helping to get us where we are today, and in particular his work guiding us through the delegate and convention process. Paul is a true professional, and I wish him the greatest success."[52]

For Manafort, the development shattered everything. Ousted and scandal tarred, he would never be able to build the lobbying juggernaut he'd envisioned, the one that would make Black Manafort look like a charity. His K Street fortune would vanish before it had even come to him. Just months after his big promotion, Manafort was right back where he'd been during his stint in rehab: mired in financial uncertainty, suffering from professional humiliation. And while his former client would go on to a stunning victory in November's presidential election, Manafort's circumstances were about to get even worse.

20

November 9, 2016
Washington, DC

On the morning after Election Day, as DC's political establishment was still absorbing the shock of Trump's victory, one veteran Republican operative was already hard at work. Jim Courtovich had never before been a champion of MAGA rage. As a lifelong Beltway insider, he was the embodiment of the entrenched special interests whom Trump had made the central villain of his campaign. During the Republican primary, Courtovich had been a financial supporter of one of Trump's main rivals, Jeb Bush, the former governor of Florida and a favorite of the Republican elite. In the general election, he hadn't bothered to vote at all. Yet not long after the sun rose on November 9, 2016, Courtovich sent an email to clients and reporters in which the career influence peddler—whose clients included Goldman Sachs, Boeing, and the kingdom of Saudi Arabia—expressed praise for a populist firebrand whose political appeal was rooted in the public's contempt for Washington and its lobbyists. "Donald J. Trump will bring an unprecedented level of change to the nation's capital," Courtovich wrote. "In pledging to 'drain the swamp,' he has promised to oust the old model of doing business through cronyism and back-room deals."[1]

Courtovich then went online and made a $2,700 donation—the

maximum amount allowed by law—to Trump's November election, even though the billionaire real estate mogul had already been voted into office. That same day, he tweeted his thoughts on the political tsunami that had just slammed into the city. "Day after the election in DC. Broken dreams and newly minted stars," Courtovich wrote. "In with the [new] and out with the old. As always."

It was an adage that perfectly encapsulated the level of chaos inside Washington's political-influence business, where the jolt of Trump's victory had touched off the most dramatic reshuffling of K Street's pecking order since the conservative revolution of 1980. Suddenly every wheeler-dealer in the city was racing to position his or her business for success with the new administration: hustling to make friends in Trump's orbit, portraying themselves as longtime backers of the MAGA movement, and creating new strategies for getting what they wanted out of the president elect. DC's entire lobbying industry, it seemed, was reinventing itself overnight.

The reinvention of Jim Courtovich, however, had begun years earlier. Following the death of Evan Morris and the evaporation of lucrative contracts from Genentech, Courtovich had been forced to develop new sources of revenue. Using his famous charm and resilient ambition, he'd managed to locate another business partner, secure a fresh source of capital, and open a brand-new firm, SGR Government Relations and Lobbying. Now, as the FBI continued looking into his decadelong financial relationship with Morris, Courtovich would commence another professional makeover: presenting himself as an ally of Donald Trump. "Sphere Consulting's unparalleled stable of relationships and unique business model," he wrote in his November 9 email to clients and journalists, "has been built for this day."[2]

It was a cunning gambit. And, for a time, it seemed to be working.

Courtovich's transition from a consultant affiliated with Evan Morris to one focused on Donald Trump had begun before the death of his business partner, when contracts from Genentech began drying up. The regular flow of funds had halted around the time that Courtovich learned the IRS was auditing his firm.

In October 2014 Courtovich met with IRS officials[3] to discuss the audit. On the morning of the meeting, Courtovich and Morris kept in touch via text.

"Heading to their office now," Courtovich texted Morris.

"For what?" Morris replied.

"Here now, waiting to go over the numbers and get the total," Courtovich texted, "work out payment plan."

"Got it. Give me [a] call when you are done," Morris responded.

Courtovich would ultimately reach an agreement with the IRS to pay a large amount of money to cover back taxes. When the meeting was over, he expressed relief.

"Well, glad that is done. . . . case closed," Courtovich wrote in a text to Morris.[4]

"Was told by the supervisor that they would not put us on the watch list,"[5] Courtovich continued. "Had to write a 20% payment to start repayment. Anyway, we need a fun lunch."[6]

The relief wouldn't last long. A few months later, on February 25, 2015, Courtovich received an urgent email from his accountant, Kimberly Clark. "I don't mean to alarm you, but this is very concerning," she wrote. The IRS, it turned out, had frozen about $4 million in the bank account of Courtovich's firm due to "unresolved timeline of repayment,"[7] according to an email the accountant wrote to Courtovich.

Courtovich forwarded the email to Morris. "Well speak of the devil," Courtovich wrote. "[I]t looks like they want the repayment schedule sped up a bit." The next day, Morris signed a new contract for Genentech to pay Courtovich's firm $750,000 for consulting services, according to a copy of the document.[8] It would be the final deal of their decadelong partnership.

The tens of millions of dollars in contracts that Morris had steered his way since 2005 was a major share of Courtovich's business. With this income disappearing, Courtovich searched for ways to generate new revenue. In late 2014 he reached out to a former associate about a new business idea.

A few years back, Courtovich had worked with Simon Charlton on a lobbying campaign on behalf of a wealthy Saudi Arabian investment fund.

Like Courtovich, Charlton was a dapper, charismatic figure who appreci-
ated life's amenities. The two had dined together in London and Dubai,
and Charlton had begun dating the prominent journalist who lived a few
houses down from Courtovich in Washington, Jan Crawford of CBS News.
In 2014 Courtovich and Charlton cohosted a lavish summertime soiree
at Courtovich's $3.8 million DC home, Le Poisson Bleu. Journalists, ad-
ministration aides, and Capitol Hill staffers partied in a backyard gazebo
that had been decorated with fresh-cut yellow, pink, and red roses. A uni-
formed wait staff served Argentinian beef, steamed mussels, and French
wine to a guest list of more than a hundred. Following dinner, a French pop
band called the Gypsy Queens treated the crowd to a raucous late-night
performance. Maureen Dowd, the *New York Times* columnist, danced with
the band.

That December, around the time the IRS was seeking back taxes,
Courtovich suggested to Charlton that they team up to start a new lobbying firm. Over the next several months, as the two men discussed the
details of the project, Courtovich told Charlton how much money it would
take to launch the firm: $4 million—a figure that precisely matched the
amount of money the IRS had frozen in his bank account.[9] Charlton, who
had no knowledge of Courtovich's tax issues, agreed to become his silent
partner in the new lobbying firm.

Returning to Dubai, Charlton pitched the idea to members of the Al
Gosaibi family, and the Saudi Arabian investors agreed to underwrite the
business. In March 2015 Courtovich and Charlton drafted a business agreement outlining the terms of the new company, SGR LLC, Government Relations and Lobbying. Charlton provided $4 million in seed money from
the Saudi investors to get the business off the ground. Courtovich would
handle the firm's day-to-day operations: securing clients and working to
advance their political objectives. Each would own roughly 50 percent of
the company.

According to the contract, the $4 million in financing from the Saudi
investors was to be divided in half. Roughly $2 million would be used as
start-up money for the new business. The other half would buy a critical
tool for Courtovich's brand of influence peddling: a DC property near the

US Capitol where he could hobnob with lawmakers and entertain reporters. That same month, Courtovich used the Saudi funds to make an all-
cash, $1.65 million purchase of a town house on Capitol Hill[10] that he then
went about turning into an ideal party pad, renovating the kitchen to give it
more space to prepare food and serve cocktails to guests. The house would
be used almost exclusively for parties. Since it was located in a residential
neighborhood, Courtovich told friends that he paid a person to take out
the garbage cans on trash collection day, so that it appeared as if someone
lived there full-time.

Several months later, on July 9, 2015, Evan Morris's body was discovered at
the Robert Trent Jones Golf Club.

In accordance with Jewish custom, Morris's funeral service was held
quickly after his death. On Sunday, July 12, hundreds of mourners packed
into a northern Virginia synagogue. The crowd represented the full arc of
Morris's life: old high school friends, college buddies, former Patton Boggs
colleagues, Genentech lobbyists, and even members of the Prince William
County Sheriff's Department, which had responded to his suicide. Jim
Courtovich did not attend. On the morning after Morris's death, he'd flown
to London on business. In his stead was his partner, Jeff Zeleny, by then an
on-air political correspondent at CNN.

Amid the grief, the funeral carried an odd sense of mystery. Many
there didn't know how Morris had died. When the rabbi told mourners
that Morris had died by suicide, gasps rippled through the congregation.

Andrew Lazerow, a Washington lawyer and friend of Morris's, was
among those who eulogized the deceased lobbyist. During his remarks,
Lazerow recounted the great fun he'd had with Morris on various lavish
adventures, such as a trip to Disney World with their families when they
stayed at the Four Seasons. Some of Tracy's friends began to wonder how
Morris had paid for the lavish vacation. One Capitol Hill staffer who attended the funeral had recently gone to a dinner party at the Morris home
that was catered by celebrity chef David Chang. The celebration, Morris
had claimed, was in honor of his fortieth birthday. During the funeral,
though, the staffer learned that Morris was thirty-eight when he died. At a

reception following the service, one of Morris's former assistants from San Francisco introduced himself to members of Morris's Washington staff. The DC-based employees were caught off guard. Morris had told them that his San Francisco assistant had died under an astonishing set of circumstances; after passing away in his apartment, his body had been eaten by his dog. Yet here the assistant was, alive.

Over the course of the reception, Tracy listened as her husband's high school and college friends recalled extraordinary tales that Morris had told about himself and others over the years. From a young age, the old friends explained to Tracy, Morris had a reputation for manipulating the truth. He embellished facts about events that happened, and he created elaborate narratives about things that never did. Now, as they discussed Morris's history of fabrication with his widow, some of Morris's high school and college classmates began wrestling with guilt. If they had done more to address Morris's lies and embellishments years ago, they wondered, would their old friend still be alive today?

In the days following the funeral, Tracy grew increasingly uneasy. Her father had been a successful physician, even serving as a doctor for an NBA team. Yet after a lifetime of work, he didn't possess the wealth that Morris had accumulated in his decade with Genentech. Hoping to sort out the truth, Tracy and her friends contacted some of Morris's former colleagues and pals in Washington, including Matt Krimm, the owner of W. Curtis Draper Tobacconist, the shop where Morris liked to take phone calls and puff stogies on weekday afternoons. Morris had told colleagues that in addition to his lobbying work for Genentech, he had ownership interests in at least two DC restaurants. One was a swanky wine bar near the well-to-do Chevy Chase section of Washington, which Morris said he and Krimm owned together. But Krimm said Morris wasn't an owner; he merely made recommendations for the wine list. Morris had also fabricated his claim of being a coowner of Marcel's, the elegant French-Belgian establishment in downtown DC. The revelations raised a deeper question: If Morris didn't have these outside sources of income, how was he able to sustain his lavish spending?

Tracy and her loved ones weren't alone in their suspicions. Soon after

Morris's death, a team of attorneys and investigators from Genentech's law firm—Gibson, Dunn & Crutcher—arrived at the pharmaceutical company's Washington headquarters. On the day of the tragedy, Morris had bolted out of Gibson Dunn's offices when the firm's attorneys began questioning him about the unusual financial transactions that they'd uncovered. With Genentech's employees still reeling from the shock, investigators hired by the company entered Morris's office to search for additional information.

Inside the room, the attorneys and investigators found the walls lined with framed snapshots of a grinning Morris shaking hands with various Democratic luminaries, including Bill Clinton, the man who'd inspired him to pursue a career in Washington nearly two decades earlier. Moving through the office, the team took a detailed inventory of Morris's belongings, collecting his computer and documents from his desk. One of the Gibson Dunn attorneys noticed a peculiar image on the office wall. It was a glossy photo of Morris's longtime business partner, Jim Courtovich, smiling in his shirtsleeves and tie. The picture had appeared in *Politico*, alongside an article that celebrated Courtovich as one of Washington's most accomplished "scenemakers."[11]

But unlike the other photographs in Morris's office, this one lacked a framed display. Instead, it had been cut out of the publication, attached to a dartboard, and impaled with a dart—right through Courtovich's forehead.[12]

Over the following weeks, the Gibson Dunn attorneys conducted an exhaustive investigation of Morris's corporate spending. They sifted through bank records, internal financial documents, business contracts, and data from Morris's cell phone and iPad. They eventually discovered that, during the years that Morris controlled the budget for Genentech's Washington operations, he'd steered roughly $25 million in contracts to three firms that Courtovich either worked at or controlled: National Media, Sphere Consulting, and Kearsarge Global Advisors. Despite the large sums of money involved, the contracts were unusually vague. Oftentimes, the written agreements didn't contain clear objectives for the work the firms were required to do in exchange for six-figure fees. One contract simply called for "competitive intelligence gathering" and "weekly monitoring of media."

Another paid hundreds of thousands of dollars for "media monitoring," a task Courtovich accomplished in part by setting up a Google alert for news articles that mentioned Genentech by name and then emailing the relevant stories to Morris.

The Gibson Dunn lawyers hoped that Courtovich could help them make sense of this flow of money. But during two in-person meetings, they found him pleasant but unhelpful, according to a person familiar with the interviews. He deflected questions about his work for Genentech with ambiguous responses. In the first meeting, he insisted that he had never sent any money to Morris.

After the interview, the Gibson Dunn investigators discovered a clue: when they looked into Evan Morris's personal bank accounts, they found a balance of $11 million—including $10 million in deposits drawn on checks from Courtovich himself or his firms. A closer look showed a pattern: not long after Genentech began paying out on one of the contracts negotiated between Morris and Courtovich, Morris would receive a check from Courtovich or one of his companies.

When the Gibson Dunn lawyers called Courtovich in for a second interview, he changed his story. This time he said he had an unusual financial arrangement with Morris that began when the pair first started working together in 2005. According to what Courtovich said, Genentech wanted Morris, its new young lobbyist, to develop a reputation as a DC heavyweight by making large donations to Washington think tanks, charities, and social events. According to Courtovich's claims, Genentech's leadership believed that these donations would be most beneficial to Morris if they appeared to come from the lobbyist's own bank account—as opposed to Genentech's corporate budget. So, according to Courtovich's story, the company's top brass authorized Morris to use his personal checks to fund company events, charities, and political causes. Courtovich would then reimburse Morris for the expenses using funds that he'd received from Genentech as a result of contracts arranged by Morris. Courtovich insisted that he sent reimbursement funds to Morris only after receiving written invoices that documented the expenses. Then Courtovich clammed up, refusing to talk further.

The lawyers didn't need any more convincing. They contacted law enforcement officials in San Francisco and told them that an employee had embezzled millions of dollars from Genentech. The following month, agents from the Washington office of the Federal Bureau of Investigation formally launched an investigation into corporate fraud. According to FBI documents, the bureau issued subpoenas, interviewed dozens of people, conducted surveillance, and seized computers, documents, and emails. In October four members of the Gibson Dunn legal team met in Washington with officials from the FBI and the Justice Department, according to an FBI report, to "provide a presentation of findings related to a potential kickback scheme between EVAN MORRIS and [name redacted]." People familiar with the investigation say the redacted name was Jim Courtovich. The lawyers handed over a three-hundred-page bound and tabbed report containing the results of their investigation, which they considered to be evidence of a federal crime.

By then, Genentech had initiated the process of recovering some of Morris's signature possessions, which, the company concluded, had been purchased with funds he'd stolen from his employer. For example, Genentech lawyers filed documents in San Francisco's superior court showing that Morris had bought his $1.365 million Mission Street condo, as well as a $57,000 GMC Yukon, using money from Genentech that had been laundered through an unidentified "Party B." In meticulous detail, the Genentech lawyers provided the court with more than two dozen canceled checks and bank transfers showing Morris had directed roughly $4 million in Genentech contracts to bank accounts controlled by "Party B" in the years before the purchase. During that same period, "Party B" sent roughly $3 million to Morris's personal bank accounts, the documents revealed. "On that basis," Genentech's lawyers stated, Morris had "purchased the GMC Yukon and the property using the Genentech Inc. funds." The court agreed and awarded the San Francisco condo and the SUV to Genentech.

Back in Washington, workers had entered Morris's office and taken out humidors filled with pricey cigars. Genentech had seized his custom-made Hacker-Craft boat, transported it to a marina in Baltimore, and put it up for sale. When refrigerated trucks rolled up to the Morris home in Belle

Haven, a team of movers got out and retrieved more than five thousand bottles of rare wines from the basement and packed them into shipping crates. Later, another set of workers came to the house and loaded Morris's two Porsches onto large trucks. Morris had purchased the sports cars shortly before his death, and they were among his most prized possessions. In his childhood bedroom in Queens, New York, a young Morris had hung a poster of a Porsche on the wall. Now, as Tracy looked on, the transport vehicles rumbled off with the flashy sports cars.

Almost no one in Washington had any idea that Courtovich was under FBI scrutiny for his potential involvement in Morris's crimes. On September 9, 2015—as the bureau was ramping up its investigation—Courtovich hosted an A-list crowd of journalists and policy makers for the grand opening bash at what he called his firm's new "Hill House." Republican congressman from California Ed Royce, ABC News political director Rick Klein, and reporters and television producers from the *Washington Post*, *New York Times*, CNN, and *Politico* were among those who turned out. Inside, waiters dressed in white outfits handed out champagne flutes filled with $100-a-bottle Veuve Clicquot. There was a Five Guys pop-up shop, where guests could enjoy burgers and fries from the popular chain. For party favors, attendees received T-shirts that read "Keep Calm and Hire Sphere."[13]

As the journalists, lawmakers, and congressional staffers partied late into the night, they had no idea that Courtovich's swanky new Hill House had been purchased with funds from wealthy Saudi investors for the express purpose of influencing his guests. During the party, a snapshot was taken of Congressman Royce—chair of the powerful House Foreign Affairs Committee—chatting with a Reuters reporter and the Washington bureau chief of the *Financial Times*. Courtovich put the image in a brochure that he used to attract new clients to the firm.[14] The sales materials trumpeted Courtovich's "unmatched contacts" with reporters at major media organizations. "We have invested significantly in relationships with individual reporters at these entities,"[15] Courtovich wrote in a letter to the government of Qatar. "These personal relationships allow us to get a fair hearing for our clients with reporters who value straight talk over public relations spin."

The sales materials added that the Hill House is an "excellent venue to drive policy events, media opportunities," and to "elevate"[16] a client's brand. Through the snapshot of the congressman socializing with journalists and the marketing language in the brochure, the pitch to would-be clients was clear: if you want help from reporters or lawmakers in the nation's capital, hire Jim Courtovich.

The pitch resonated with corporations and foreign governments facing problems in Washington. Courtovich signed up the Detroit-based home-mortgage giant Quicken Loans just as it was being sued by the Department of Justice over allegations of improper lending practices. (Quicken Loans later paid $32.5 million to resolve the claims; it did not admit wrongdoing.) In October Courtovich's new firm agreed to represent the former owners of a private bank in the tiny European nation of Andorra, Banca Privada d'Andorra, which had gone out of business after the US Treasury Department accused it of laundering money for Chinese officials, Venezuelan government leaders, and Russian mobs. In September 2016 Courtovich's firm inked a $45,000-a-month deal with the kingdom of Saudi Arabia to try and defeat a bill that would have permitted victims of terrorism to file lawsuits against the countries that harbored their attackers.[17] The effort put Courtovich on the opposing side of families who'd lost loved ones in the September 11 attacks. Courtovich's contract shows that he was hired specifically by Saud al-Qahtani, a top foreign policy and media advisor to the crown prince of Saudi Arabia, Mohammed bin Salman, and a figure who would later oversee the murder of *Washington Post* journalist Jamal Khashoggi. Courtovich wasn't the only Washington operative retained to help lobby against the bill—Qahtani also hired Tony Podesta. As part of his effort to block the legislation, Courtovich met with his former party guest Congressman Ed Royce, although the lawmaker wasn't persuaded, and the bill passed Congress.[18]

Then, in November 2016, an unexpected new business opportunity arrived in Washington.

About six weeks after Election Day, Donald Trump arrived at the Trump International Golf Club in West Palm Beach, Florida, for a round of golf with PGA superstar Tiger Woods.[19] After completing eighteen holes, Trump walked into the clubhouse and basked in the glow of his improbable election victory—shaking hands, trading smiles, and exchanging warm greetings with everyone who approached. But when Stanton Anderson came up and introduced himself, the soon-to-be president turned cold.

Anderson wasn't just another well-to-do golfer; he was a senior advisor at the US Chamber of Commerce, the more than hundred-year-old trade group that serves as corporate America's top advocate in Washington. Headquartered directly across the street from the White House, the Chamber of Commerce represents the interests of roughly 80 percent of Fortune 100 companies. From 1998 to 2016, it spent $1.5 billion on lobbying—three times more than any other interest group. As part of its mission to support a business-friendly commercial environment, it pushes for lower taxes, fewer regulations, increased international trade, and immigration policies that give US firms access to foreign workers.

Over the course of the 2016 campaign, the Chamber of Commerce's longtime president and CEO, Thomas Donohue, came to see Trump's attacks on corporate-friendly trade and immigration policies as a serious threat to American industry. Unlike other corporate leaders, who preferred to avoid direct confrontation, Donohue was willing to punch back. Donohue told a Bloomberg TV reporter that Trump had "very little idea about what trade really is," and the Chamber of Commerce tweeted that Trump's trade plan would result in "higher prices, fewer jobs, and a weaker economy."[20]

The criticism infuriated the Republican front-runner. At a campaign rally in Bangor, Maine, Trump declared that the Chamber of Commerce was "controlled totally by various groups of people that don't care about you whatsoever."[21] Still, most business leaders remained unconcerned about Trump because they were certain he'd lose to Hillary Clinton. And even after his unexpected win, many corporate advocates, such as Stanton Anderson, held out hope that Trump's populist fury was simply campaign-trail theatrics. Once he settled into the White House, they hoped, Trump would moderate his anticorporate rhetoric and adopt trade and immigration postures that were more in line with the priorities of Big Business.

So, when he spotted the president elect at the golf club, Anderson saw an opportunity to ease the conflict between corporate America's top advocacy group and the incoming commander in chief. Anderson walked up to Trump, explained his role at the Chamber of Commerce, and extended his hand.

Trump refused the handshake. "You guys did everything to stop me," the president elect scowled, his face reddening. "I haven't forgotten."

The exchange reflected the increasingly contentious relationship between the corporate establishment and the incoming president. In the weeks after his election, Trump escalated his attacks on Big Business. In December 2016 he drove drug company stocks lower by pledging to "bring down drug prices,"[22] and he threatened to cancel the purchase of a new Air Force One aircraft from Boeing due to what he claimed were cost overruns. The following month, he blasted Toyota Motor Corp. for its plans to construct a new facility in Mexico that would manufacture cars for sale in the United States. "NO WAY!" Trump wrote in a tweet. "Build plant in U.S. or pay big border tax."[23]

Such anticorporate wrath triggered panic on K Street, which simply wasn't equipped for Trump's takeover of Washington. In the run-up to the 2016 election, according to an article in *Washingtonian* magazine, corporate and special interests had staffed up with Democratic lobbyists and consultants—like Tony Podesta—in preparation for what they believed would be a Hillary Clinton administration. Now, in the wake of Trump's victory, they were desperate to hire Republicans. But there was a problem: Washington's stable of GOP influencers didn't have many friends in Trump's administration.[24] A large number of Republican operatives—who would have thrived under a traditional Republican president such as Jeb Bush—had been vocal critics of Trump. Among those critics was Charlie Black, the veteran GOP lobbyist who, along with his former partners Paul Manafort and Roger Stone, had helped introduce Donald Trump to Washington more than two decades earlier. In 2000, however, Black dropped his celebrity client after growing tired of having to beg the billionaire real estate mogul to pay his lobbying bills. When Trump reemerged as a force in national politics, Black refused to endorse him, working instead for former

Ohio governor John Kasich. Though Black had volunteered for nearly every GOP nominee over the prior thirty years, when Trump secured the nomination, he declined to assist his campaign. "I didn't think Trump would be a good nominee and a good president," Black recalled later.

Most other Republican influence peddlers followed Black's lead. As a result, Trump's antiestablishment campaign was run, by and large, without the typical cast of insiders who were already familiar to the city's lobbyists. "You can almost look at it like this," said one GOP consultant. "There's Republicans, and there's Democrats. And then you almost have to go and find the third-party people, which is Trump people."

Just as Reagan's victory had opened the door for Black, Manafort & Stone in the 1980s, Trump's election minted a new class of K Street power brokers. All of a sudden anyone connected to Trump—or who could plausibly claim to be—could refashion themselves as a high-priced Washington influencer. Many Trump campaign aides were lured away to lobbying firms, while others—like his former campaign manager Corey Lewandowski[25]—launched their own consulting outfits. Corporations and lobbying firms, which were frantically trying to gain access to the new president, shelled out extraordinary sums of money to the president's associates in the hopes of getting Trump's ear. Squire Patton Boggs announced a "strategic alliance" with the president's former personal attorney, Michael Cohen, entitling him to a $500,000 retainer plus a cut of the revenues generated by any clients he lured to the firm. Cohen also secured a separate deal with AT&T, earning $600,000 to, among other things, advise the company on its proposed merger with Time Warner,[26] an $85 billion deal requiring approval from regulators in Washington, many of whom would be nominated by Trump.

Ties to Trump became so valuable that one lobbyist, Michael Esposito, grew his firm's revenue about sixfold—to nearly $6 million in 2019—simply by boasting about his "strong personal and professional relationship with President Trump." As it turned out, Esposito was a former Democrat with no meaningful connections to the new president or his family. When the *Washington Post*'s Beth Reinhardt and Jonathan O'Connell revealed this deception, the FBI raided Esposito's K Street office as part of a fraud investigation.[27] In the end, though, Esposito didn't face charges. "There was a Wild West quality to the lobbying industry during the early days of the new administration," says GOP lobbyist Matthew Johnson of the Klein/Johnson Group.

Changes to the way policy was created in Trump's Washington were more significant still. Prior to Trump's arrival, officials throughout the federal bureaucracy were involved in major policy decisions. But when the billionaire real estate mogul assumed the White House, he took personal charge of policy decisions that had previously been left to Cabinet secretaries, federal agencies or congressional committees—all of which were in Republican control during his first two years in office. Trump's preferred tool for bypassing Washington's policy-making apparatus was the executive order, which enabled the president to enact policy without having to wait for the House and Senate to produce legislation. He used executive orders to advance the MAGA agenda throughout the bureaucracy: expanding US energy production, reinforcing the Mexican border, undermining the Obama health care law, and rolling back clear-air regulations. All told, Trump issued more executive orders—220—than any president had signed during a four-year term since Jimmy Carter.

"It's two different worlds," says Eric Bovim, a veteran public affairs strategist. "Under President Obama, the government was a finely tuned instrument, all the parts working together to produce a single note. You needed to work with everybody to calibrate the sound." In the Trump era, Bovim continued, it was more like a "one-man band; the president in a never-ending guitar solo on the White House lawn, overpowering all the other instruments."[28]

This change forced K Street to rip up its existing playbook and develop a new influence-peddling strategy for the Trump era. Rather than trying to reach the whole of Washington, lobbyists and consultants began deploying every tool in their arsenal—from traditional media plays to advanced digital tactics—to try and shape the thinking of one man. Inside DC's influence business, the approach became known as the "audience of one" strategy.[29]

Lobbyists ran print ads designed to catch Trump's attention in the *New York Times*, the *New York Daily News*, the *New York Post*, and the *Wall Street Journal*—Big Apple newspapers that they believed Trump was reading. They also took advantage of the peculiar way that certain news articles reached the new president in order to try and advance their clients' agendas. For most of 2017, members of the White House communications team put together packets of flattering news stories about Trump and delivered them to the Oval Office each morning and afternoon. This pro-Trump story folder, which the president nearly always read, offered K Street operatives an opening. One GOP consultant said he would regularly plant articles favorable to his corporate clients on a right-wing website, Breitbart News, and then send the articles to a White House pal who would insert them into the folder. "If you have a friend in there that can get something on the Resolute desk," the operative said, "it doesn't really matter what the source is anymore."[30]

Lobbyists also used new technology to try and shape the president's thinking. Through a digital technique called geofencing, influence peddlers sent ads directly to Trump using his then-favorite social media platform—Twitter—as well as Facebook and YouTube. When the commander in chief was in Washington, they sent their ads to IP addresses that covered the White House and the Trump International Hotel where he and his aides visited often. If Trump headed to his golf club in New Jersey, they beamed the ads to IP addresses there. When he went to Mar-a-Lago, they sent them to his club in Florida. K Street consultants also geofenced the Kalorama home of Jared Kushner and Ivanka Trump with digital ads in an effort to shape their views. Some firms targeted DC's power restaurants, such as Central Michel Richard, in case a top White House aide popped in for lunch.[31]

The cornerstone of the audience-of-one strategy, though, was Trump's addiction to television. After the election, consultants began buying commercial time during *Fox & Friends,* the conservative morning show that the president was known to watch religiously. But how did they get a seventy-two-year-old man with little interest in policy to watch a commercial on ethanol subsidies? Well, the influencers decided, find old footage of

Trump discussing the issue on the campaign and make him the star of the commercial. "The president's favorite topic is himself," said a Republican consultant. "What better way to get him interested in a message than by providing him with the thing that he's most obsessed with?"[32]

Corporate lobbyists ran similar spots during any show they suspected the President might be watching, whether that meant the shows he likes (Sean Hannity on Fox News) or those he hate-watches (*Morning Joe* on MSNBC, *Saturday Night Live* on NBC). Even Democrats got into the act. Tony Podesta helped produce a round of television ads for a Saudi Arabian interest that was trying to persuade Trump to end America's warm diplomatic relationship with Qatar. To ensure that Trump—an avid golfer—saw these anti-Qatar advertisements, Podesta's team aired the spots during the British Open golf championship in July 2017.[33]

The uncertainty created by the Trump presidency—as well as the questions surrounding the effectiveness of these latest influence-peddling tactics—led to additional lobbying spending. Overall, lobbying spending increased 9 percent, to $3.5 billion, from 2016 to 2018. In the end, despite the many millions of dollars that K Street spent to cook up this newfangled playbook, the best way to influence Trump turned out to be the most straightforward. Lobbyists with connections to Trump's family members or key aides had the most success in persuading the president to take actions that benefited their clients. But business leaders with the clout to deal directly with Trump, like Fox News founder Rupert Murdoch, fared best of all. According to *Vanity Fair*, Murdoch personally urged the forty-fifth president to open up additional federal lands to fracking, a move that would increase the value of Murdoch's fossil-fuel holdings. Sure enough, Trump went on to issue proclamations that allowed fracking on more than ten million acres of federal land. At the same time, Murdoch pushed Trump to use the government's authority to crack down on Google and Facebook for diverting eyeballs and advertising dollars from his various media concerns. Over the following years, officials installed by Trump at the FTC as well as his Department of Justice launched antitrust investigations into Google, Facebook and other tech firms.[34]

In that sense, the Trump era represented a brief reversal of the nearly four-decade-long trend that had come to define the modern influence industry. With Trump in the Oval Office, K Street operators deprioritized the sophisticated "outside game" tactics that they'd used to reach targets far outside of the White House in favor of a traditional, access-driven approach. The president who promised to "drain the swamp" had in fact precipitated the lobbying industry's return to the secret deals in smoke-filled rooms of 1930s-era Washington.

The era's biggest winner was Brian Ballard, a Florida lobbyist who parlayed his existing relationship with the new president into a K Street fortune. As soon as Trump won the election, Ballard—who'd begun lobbying for Trump's business interests in Florida years earlier[35] and went on to raise millions for his presidential campaign—opened an office in Washington,[36] disseminated word of his close ties to Trump, and signed up federal lobbying clients like Amazon, the US sugar industry, and the government of Qatar. During Trump's four years in office, Ballard and his small team earned about $100 million by representing more than 120 corporations and foreign countries. Instead of the complex, grassroots-and-media campaigns that defined the pre-Trump years, much of Ballard's work involved one-on-one conversations with the president or his top advisors. When a private prison firm, the GEO Group Inc., wanted to overturn a federal cap on the number of inmates that a private prison company could manage, it hired Ballard. After Ballard talked to a few Trump officials on the company's behalf, the cap was eliminated and the GEO Group's business with the government nearly doubled, to $900 million.

Courtovich was among the few Washington influence-peddlers with links to Trump's inner circle. In the final stretch of the 2016 campaign, he'd begun working for a leading figure in Trump's political movement. Michael Flynn was a retired three-star US Army general who—through the assistance of Paul Manafort[37]—became a top national security advisor to the Trump campaign. Flynn's outspoken distaste for Hillary Clinton made him popular with MAGA diehards. While he was delivering an address at the 2016 Republican National Convention, in Cleveland, the crowd broke into an anti-Hillary chant.

"Lock her up!"

"Lock her up!"

From the podium, Flynn nodded his head and voiced his approval. "Damn right—exactly right," he said. "If I did a tenth—a tenth—of what she did, I would be in jail today."[38]

Flynn's role in the Trump campaign helped attract new business to his consulting firm, Flynn Intel Group. Among the clients to seek his assistance was Inovo, a Dutch company controlled by Turkish American businessman Kamil Ekim Alptekin, who had ties to top figures in the Turkish government. In August 2016 Alptekin's company agreed to pay Flynn's firm more than $500,000 to, among other things, investigate a chief political rival of Turkey's repressive president, Recep Tayyip Erdoğan. The rival, Fethullah Gülen, was a Turkish imam then living in Pennsylvania who'd been accused by the Turkish president of engineering a coup attempt earlier that summer[39]—a claim that remains unproven.

As part of the effort, Flynn's company hired Courtovich's firm to try and persuade the United States to extradite Gülen. On November 8, 2016—Election Day—Courtovich's firm used its contacts in the media to publish an opinion article written by Flynn in *The Hill*, a Capitol Hill newspaper.[40] In the piece, Flynn attacked Gülen, accusing the cleric of "running a scam," writing, "Gülen portrays himself as a moderate, but he is in fact a radical Islamist." Flynn continued, "He has publicly boasted about his 'soldiers' waiting for his orders to do whatever he directs them to do. If he were in reality a moderate, he would not be in exile, nor would he excite the animus of Recep Tayyip Erdoğan and his government."[41] Gülen has denied involvement in the coup, and he was never extradited.

At no point in the op-ed did Flynn acknowledge that his criticism of Gülen came as he was being paid a half million dollars to orchestrate an influence-peddling campaign to benefit the president of Turkey. Nor did Flynn register as a foreign agent with the Department of Justice, as the Foreign Agents Registration Act requires. Though it went unnoticed at the time, Flynn's failure to make such disclosures would eventually prove calamitous.

Following Trump's election, Courtovich worked to burnish his connections to the incoming Trump White House. In mid-November he hosted a postelection party at his "Hill House" featuring his "world famous lasa-gna" and a vodka-and-pineapple cocktail known as a "Stoli Doli." Besides the regular crowd of reporters and operatives, guests included a slate of Trump-connected figures, such as Nick Owens, a behind-the-scenes oper-ator in Trump's presidential campaign; Patrick Fleming, an aide to Trump's future Secretary of State, Mike Pompeo; and Bijan Kian, who was Michael Flynn's business partner. Courtovich set off to parlay these Trump contacts into clients and revenue.

By touting his relationship with Flynn, who would soon become Trump's national security advisor, Courtovich landed a $50,000-a-year contract with a subsidiary of Sberbank, Russia's largest state-owned bank. Sberbank, which had parted ways with Tony Podesta a few months earlier, was seeking to persuade the Trump administration to remove the sanc-tions that the United States had imposed on it following Russia's 2014 inva-sion of Crimea. According to a former bank official, Sberbank decided to hire Courtovich in January 2017 after the GOP influence peddler made "all these promises, like he has unparalleled access to the Trump administra-tion." The following month, Courtovich secured a $1.8 million annual deal with Ethiopia after pledging to use his clout in Trump's Washington to kill a congressional resolution condemning the East African government for alleged human-rights abuses. At one point, according to former Trump campaign aide Nick Owens, Courtovich even proposed to the president of Albania that, in exchange for a $1 million fee, he could arrange for him to appear in a photograph with Donald Trump, which would provide him with the appearance of support from the new American president. Though nothing ever came of the proposal, fellow lobbyists were floored by Cour-tovich's audacity. "He was selling his access to Trump," another influence peddler said.

With a growing roster of overseas clients and an existing customer base that included large US corporations like Boeing, Goldman Sachs, and Quicken Loans, Courtovich was thriving once again. As Trump assumed control of the federal government, Courtovich was radiating the confi-dence that had made him the toast of Washington's insider establishment. In January 2017 he got together for dinner with Ed Royce, the chairman of the Foreign Relations Committee, at BLT Steak in downtown Washington. That same month, Courtovich appeared on a Sirius XM satellite radio show, where he described his signature way of advancing the interests of the corporations and foreign governments he represented in Washington. Hosting dinner parties with government officials, Courtovich explained, allows him to "have a conversation and actually get some points across," he told the program's host, Julie Mason, an old pal. "We do a lot of events to bring people together," he continued, "at least we can do it over a good meal."

Mason, a longtime Washington reporter, agreed: "Half of the people I know are from your parties."

It was a remarkable achievement. Over the prior two years, Courtovich had watched millions of dollars' worth of business from his most lucrative client—Genentech—stop completely. He'd lost his former business partner to suicide. And he'd come under the suspicion of white-shoe attorneys as well as federal law enforcement officials over his potential involvement in what Genentech officials believed had been a multimillion-dollar kickback scheme. Yet at the dawn of the Trump era, he had a billionaire financial backer in Saudi Arabia, a $1.6 million party house on Capitol Hill, and an influence-peddling firm that was scooping up new clients in an uncertain business environment. What's more, Courtovich seemed to have emerged unscathed from the Genentech scandal. Law enforcement officials hadn't charged him with any crimes, and the existence of the FBI probes into the financial transactions had remained a closely guarded secret. Nearly all of Washington was in the dark about the alleged kickback scheme.

But for this dashing Republican operative, life was about to get complicated.

21

When Paul Manafort opened his bedroom door around six o'clock in the morn-ing and saw more than a dozen armed agents in flak jackets, he was actually a bit relieved to discover that it was only the FBI executing a "no-knock" search warrant on behalf of the Special Counsel's Office.[1]

In the eleven months since his departure from the Trump campaign, Manafort's life had grown increasingly unpleasant. His prior work for Kremlin-aligned interests in Ukraine had become a focal point of Robert Mueller's investigation into Putin's possible influence in the presidential election—especially since the man in charge of Manafort's office in Kiev, Konstantin Kilimnik,[2] was, according to a 2021 statement from the US Treasury Department, a "known Russian Intelligence Services agent" who had received internal Trump campaign polling information from Manafort during the 2016 race and passed it along to Russian intelligence officials.[3] Gates insists that Kilimnik was not a Russian spy, and he argues that Manafort only gave the polling data to Kilimnik so he would forward it to a handful of Ukrainian oligarchs who still owed Manafort more than $2 million for political consulting work he'd previously conducted. According to Gates, Manafort believed that showing the oligarchs that he had enough clout in the Trump campaign to obtain the polling data would make them more likely to pay up. In any event, protecting himself from Mueller's prosecutors was an expensive proposition. Manafort's legal bills had reached nearly $1 million.[4] His business had cratered and, given the allegations now swirling around him, it was impossible to secure new clients. Most nights, Manafort could get only a couple of hours of sleep on account of the stress.[5] And over time, he'd become paranoid about the rumors he'd heard of powerful Russian figures out to get him.[6]

The sense of relief he felt upon seeing federal agents in his home, guns drawn, would quickly vanish. Over the next thirteen hours, Manafort looked on as teams of FBI agents went room by room, searching every computer and sock drawer. By the time it was over, the feds had carted off materials related to Manafort's business dealings stretching back over two decades, including computers, cameras, hard drives, and binders of documents.[7] The early morning raid represented a dramatic escalation of the Special Counsel's efforts to secure evidence and testimony as part of its probe. In the weeks after the FBI search, as his friends inside the Trump administration stopped taking his calls,[8] Manafort began to feel like his life was spinning out of control.[9]

By then, however, Manafort wasn't the only K Street heavyweight feeling the squeeze of Mueller's prosecutors. When the AP roughly a year earlier exposed the covert lobbying campaign on behalf of the European Centre for a Modern Ukraine—which is to say, on behalf of Viktor Yanukovych—the news organization had suggested that Manafort, Podesta, and Weber might all have broken the law by failing to register as foreign agents under FARA.[10] Before long, the Special Counsel's Office obtained authority to expand the scope of its probe into Russian interference beyond the 2016 campaign to include the joint lobbying venture in Ukraine. The developments cast a shadow of suspicion over Podesta, spooking the firm's existing clients and making it more difficult to attract new ones. Podesta was forced to retain high-priced defense attorneys for himself and his employees; failure to disclose overseas lobbying was punishable by up to five years in prison. Law enforcement officials looking into the matter showed up on the doorsteps of more than a dozen current and former Podesta Group employees, including the staffers who had first objected to working for the Ukrainian client as well as the young employee Podesta had texted during the New York bachelorette party.

But for the illustrious Democratic lobbyist, the Mueller investigation was just one of the crises that had emerged since the summer of 2016, when the details of his partnership with Paul Manafort had burst into public view.

In October 2016, just a few weeks before Election Day, WikiLeaks had released the first of thousands of emails that had been hacked from the account of Tony's brother, John Podesta, who was then overseeing Hillary Clinton's presidential campaign. The emails contained correspondence between John Podesta and top Clinton campaign officials discussing election strategy. They also included mundane discussions between Tony and John regarding dinner plans and messages showing that John was friendly with James Alefantis, the owner of the DC pizza restaurant Comet Ping Pong, who had catered fund-raisers for Hillary Clinton in Tony's backyard.[11] In the fever swamps of far-right websites, these exchanges became evidence of a sweeping plot in which Democratic elites were operating a satanic child-sex trafficking ring out of the basement of Comet Ping Pong. As the "Pizzagate" delusions gained traction online, conspiracy theorists used police sketches to claim that Tony and John were involved in the 2007 kidnapping of Madeleine McCann, the three-year-old British girl who disappeared during a family trip to Portugal. Tony began receiving emails from conspiracy theorists asking him to pick them up a cheese pizza— a coded term for child pornography. Angry callers insisted he was going to hell; others just breathed heavily into the receiver. The harassment was directed at John as well. Though he usually ignored the calls, John's wife, Mary Podesta, would occasionally answer the phone and try to reason with the Pizzagate fanatics, according to a person who visited John and Mary Podesta's house during this time.

The ugliness of Pizzagate, coupled with the allegations of illegal lobbying activity, unnerved many of the Podesta Group's corporate clients, who preferred to stay clear of such publicity. Yet Tony operated as if the whole mess would soon blow over. A Clinton victory would turbocharge the firm's revenue and liberate him from his postdivorce financial squeeze. As Election Day approached, Podesta betrayed no sign of being worried about the outcome of the race. For most of the month, he wasn't even in Washington. Over Columbus Day weekend, he departed on his annual expedition to Venice, along with a delegation of corporate clients. During the following weeks, he jetted off to New York City, San Francisco, New Orleans and Italy. On Election Day, Podesta flew back from Italy to New York, where he had tickets for Clinton's Election Night victory party. But ultimately, he decided to skip the event.

Clinton's unexpected loss was a serious setback for the firm. Overnight, Podesta's close ties to the former First Lady had become worthless on K Street, and clients of all sorts began terminating their contracts. Among those who immediately departed the Podesta Group were the drugmaker Amgen Inc., the health insurer Blue Cross Blue Shield, and the Biotechnology Industry Organization, a trade association that included Podesta's onetime marquee client, Genentech. Less than two months after the election, Google—the once-naïve tech start-up that Podesta helped mold into a political colossus—decided that it too was cutting ties with the firm, ending their ten-year partnership. The outflow of clients triggered acute financial stress. In an internal report, top executives predicted that the Podesta Group's revenue would plunge by about 20 percent, or $10 million,[12] in 2017. For a company that was already mired in an earnings slump, a criminal investigation, and the misguided leadership of its founder, there would be no postelection boom to turn things around.

Amid the crashing revenue projections, Podesta's financial position continued to deteriorate. He took out another short-term, interest-only loan on his Kalorama mansion, and he sold his $4 million Park Avenue apartment. At the firm, he instituted a hiring freeze and began slashing expenses. Year-end bonuses were canceled. Commissions were cut in half. Yet even then, as the fiscal noose was tightening, Podesta was unable to control his own spending. When employees returned to the office after the holidays, they were greeted by a new, eighty-five-piece art installation called "Shifting Degrees of Certainty,"[13] a duplicate of a piece on display at New York's Museum of Modern Art.

As a show of confidence, Podesta decided to move forward with the firm's Inauguration Day party. But once the guests had cleared out of the Willard InterContinental Hotel, the pressures continued to mount. That spring, the Podesta Group filed documents with the Justice Department admitting for the first time that it had submitted improper disclosure statements for the Ukrainian lobbying campaign. Meanwhile, federal prosecutors sent subpoenas to the Podesta Group and several of its lobbyists demanding records relating to the firm's lobbying work for Paul Manafort and Ukraine. Rumors began to spread that Podesta's indictment was imminent. Lobbyists bolted to other firms. More clients fled.

Around this time, Tony's ex-wife, Heather Podesta, made a decision that showed just how radioactive the Podesta brand had become in Washington. She changed the name of her lobbying firm from the eponymous Heather Podesta + Partners to the more abstract Invariant.[14] It was a remarkable decision. Just three years earlier, Tony and Heather had waged a bitter legal struggle over who was responsible for building their famous K Street brand. Now, in the wake of the foreign lobbying scandal, Hillary Clinton's election loss, the Pizzagate chaos, and the Mueller inquiry, she was distancing herself from it. The Podesta name, Heather told friends, was bad for business.

Tony Podesta's effort to bring in new revenue only added to the turmoil. Over the summer, the firm's employees were dumbfounded to learn that, despite the ongoing criminal investigation into whether his Ukraine lobbying effort violated FARA, Podesta had signed up yet another dubious overseas outfit. In June, the Podesta Group agreed to represent the Saudi American Public Relation Affairs Committee, a group created to generate support for the kingdom of Saudi Arabia. At first, Podesta didn't disclose his work for the Saudi group to the Justice Department, as is required for clients that are financed or controlled by foreign regimes. News reports soon circulated raising questions about a potential link between his new Saudi client and the kingdom of Saudi Arabia. When an audit conducted by an outside law firm identified some red flags among the firm's clients, the Podesta Group stopped working for some of these organizations and registered as a foreign agent for the Saudi Arabian client. By then, however, employees were getting fed up with their boss's reckless behavior. The firm's chief financial officer, Scott Chesson, soon quit.

Amid the chaos, senior staffers reached back out with their offer to purchase a stake in the firm. In early August 2017 more than a dozen lobbyists and executives met Podesta for a private dinner at Casa Luca, the same Italian restaurant in downtown DC where they'd gathered during their failed negotiations three years earlier. The employees now valued the firm at $40 million—$10 million less than last time. Still, it amounted to a last-minute reprieve for Podesta, a way to escape his quickly unraveling circumstances with millions of dollars in his pocket. Podesta said he'd consider it.[15] And over the course of the evening, he apologized for the pain he had caused the firm and his employees.[16] It was the first time he had admitted any fault.

But there would be no deal. After the dinner, Podesta departed on vacation. For most of the remainder of the summer—with clients fleeing, revenue plunging, and federal investigators circling—the veteran political fixer was 3,600 miles away from Washington, in the French beach town of Saint-Pierre-Quiberon.[17]

Later that fall, Manafort got the bad news. On October 28, 2017, his attorney informed him that the Special Counsel's Office was going to indict him.[18] Manafort made arrangements to return from his home in Florida, where he was then staying, to Washington, DC, so he could surrender to the authorities. Around eight thirty the following morning, Manafort and his wife arrived at the Palm Beach International Airport. They sat down in a restaurant directly across from their gate, eating breakfast as they waited for the plane to board. Eventually the couple was approached by an FBI agent who had been tracking their movements through the airport.

"Mr. Manafort," the FBI agent said. "We don't know what you're trying to do but you have to board your plane, and it's leaving in twenty-five minutes."

"I know," Manafort replied, "the gate is two minutes away."

"No, you are in the wrong area," the FBI agent said. "You have to return to the main terminal and go through a long security line."

Amid the intensity of the morning, Manafort had misread his ticket.

He sprinted for the correct gate, his wife and a pair of FBI agents trailing him. He dashed through the concourse, got permission to cut the security line, and reached the gate just in time to make the flight.[19]

The next day, October 30, a federal marshal picked up Manafort from FBI headquarters near the National Mall and drove him to a detention center in Southeast Washington. Along with his top lieutenant, Rick Gates, Manafort was booked on a twelve-count indictment in federal court in DC containing charges of failure to register as a foreign agent for Ukraine, conspiracy against the United States, conspiracy to launder money, failure to report foreign bank accounts, and lying to federal authorities.[20] Less than four months later, prosecutors would file an additional thirty-two-count indictment against Manafort and Gates in the federal court of the Eastern District of Virginia, charging the two with bank and tax fraud.[21] Among other things, prosecutors alleged that Manafort had received roughly $75 million for his work in Ukraine and, with the assistance of Gates and a series of offshore accounts, had hidden roughly $30 million of it from the IRS in order to finance his opulent lifestyle.

After posting a $10 million bond,[22] Manafort was released on home confinement pending separate trials in Washington and Virginia on the criminal charges. He recognized that if he was convicted, he would end up right back in federal custody. If that happened, the sixty-eight-year-old wheeler-dealer might never see the outside of a prison again.

At Tony Podesta's firm, word of Manafort's indictment arrived with similar gravity. "The press concluded," Podesta later said, "that we were going to be indicted together." Over the prior few days, these rumors triggered a flood of frantic phone calls from clients, who were anxious to know what the heck was going on.[23] Employees wondered if Tony Podesta would be arrested. An official at Chain Bridge Bank, the firm's new lender, called to check in.[24] The landlord stopped by to see if the Podesta Group would make its November rent payment.

Podesta raced to protect the firm. For much of the week, he hunkered down and worked the phones—reassuring anxious clients, calming jittery employees, and trying to allay the concerns of his creditors. By then, the exodus of lobbyists and staff had hollowed out the office, which was marked by empty hallways and vacant desks. The marble staircase in the center of the office now led to a mostly deserted second floor.

On the afternoon of Saturday, October 28, Podesta stepped away from the panic to attend a surprise seventieth birthday party for Hillary Clinton.[25] Despite his brother's role on the campaign—and the great benefit that a Clinton victory would have provided his own firm—Podesta says he was unimpressed by Hillary's performance during the race. "Her whole campaign was about women; she never evinced any concern about men," Podesta said in an interview. "She was preachy screechy, and she seemed unapproachable." Podesta says he even predicted to at least one company that Clinton would lose to Trump. "I didn't tell my brother that," he says.

Arriving at the surprise party, Podesta waited awkwardly in a lengthy receiving line to pay his respects to the former Democratic presidential nominee. His foot was in a cast after a hiking accident. Other party guests came by to offer condolences for his troubles. After a cold handshake from Hillary Clinton, Podesta hobbled back to his Kalorama mansion and met with the Podesta Group's CEO, Kimberley Fritts, who was spearheading an eleventh-hour effort on the part of the firm's senior executives to purchase a portion of the business. For several hours, Fritts and a team of attorneys pressed Podesta to allow the employees to acquire a stake in the company. Once again, Podesta refused to relinquish control. Fritts departed without an agreement.

On the day of Manafort's indictment, news camera operators gathered outside of Podesta's $4 million Kalorama home, ready to capture footage of the Democratic lobbyist's arrest. But while no perp walk took place— neither Podesta nor his firm ended up being charged—Mueller's actions would prove punishing nonetheless. In the indictments, the Special Counsel alleged that the Podesta Group, identified as "Company B," had helped Manafort and Gates carry out their illegal influence-peddling campaign on behalf of the pro-Russian front group.[26] Podesta denied wrongdoing and wasn't arrested, but his firm was now publicly tied to the unfolding scandal. For the once-exalted lobbyist, there was little choice. At about ten in the morning—around the time Paul Manafort was being booked by law enforcement—Podesta called a staff meeting. In emotional remarks to the several dozen employees who remained, he announced he was stepping back from his namesake firm.[27]

At the same time, Donald Trump was pouring gasoline on the fire. "The biggest story yesterday, the one that has the Dems in a dither, is Podesta running from his firm," Trump said in a Tweet posted the day after the indictments were unsealed.[28] From there, the unraveling accelerated. Blue-chip corporate clients—Oracle, Walmart, Wells Fargo—canceled their lobbying contracts. Employees called rival lobbying firms to see if they were hiring. The landlord stopped by again. Officials with Chain Bridge Bank, the firm's new lender, came in for a meeting to discuss the bank's concerns about its line of credit.

That night, as the firm scrambled to address the emergency, Podesta headed to a birthday party for former Mississippi governor Haley Barbour, who was then a top Republican lobbyist. When Podesta arrived, Barbour gave him a hug.[29]

While Podesta was at the birthday party, he received an email from Don Cognetta, the firm's new chief financial officer. The CFO told Podesta that Chain Bridge Bank had demanded that Podesta come up with $655,000 in cash or collateral within twenty-four hours or the bank would cut off the firm. "If we don't have collateral pledged prior to 5 pm tomorrow, we will be in default," Cognetta wrote. "They will collect as they see fit, and we will not be able to meet our rent, your art payments, ad campaigns, and most importantly payroll."[30]

With clients fleeing, legal bills mounting and a $200,000 rental payment due the next day, the Podesta Group was perilously low on cash. It couldn't survive without the bank's help. Cognetta recommended using Podesta's personal line of credit to secure the loan. Another senior member of the firm's management suggested that Podesta use his art collection as collateral.

"How do you want to proceed?" the CFO asked Podesta.

Podesta refused to put up his art or own money to keep the firm alive. Instead, he sought to cut expenses by firing staff. "Need list of next 5 layoffs,"[31] he wrote in an email to Cognetta and Fritts, the CEO. "Whose salaries can we reduce." Podesta also asked Fritts to use her personal credit cards to pay down some of the firm's debt.

In the end, Podesta ignored the bank's deadline and left town. The following afternoon, with his firm teetering on the edge of collapse, Podesta boarded a plane for an art show in Turin, Italy.[32]

But there was no escaping the crisis. Days later, on Friday, November 3, the Podesta Group's managing principal sent an urgent message. In an email with the subject line "Winding Firm Down," Podesta was informed that their new CFO, Don Cognetta, had quit as well.[33] There was an even more pressing development with Chain Bridge Bank. "My understanding is that the bank has frozen the firm's funds," the managing principal wrote. "This means we have no way to pay employees."

The lender's decision to pull the firm's credit triggered a whole new problem for Podesta. Under US labor laws, businesses must inform their employees when they lack sufficient funds to cover payroll. "If we do not alert employees immediately that we have no way to pay them for their work, the firm is committing fraud,[34] according to our labor and employment attorney," the managing principal wrote. "It's therefore imperative that we provide notice to employees as soon as possible that the firm has no ability to compensate them and that it is effectively closing immediately." The managing principal concluded her email by stating: "Please advise."

"Can someone talk to the bank," Podesta replied. "What's our cash position? Don has created this situation," he wrote, referring to the CFO who quit that day. "We should try to find a way out."

"Tony, I think you're the best person to talk with the bank," the managing principal responded, "as you're the sole owner of the company and the only person who can make decisions as to path forward."

"Happy to speak to whomever," Podesta wrote. "Never got the financial information I requested. What cash position are we in. Payables. Receivables." He named two lobbyists who should be fired immediately. "Paul Cristina go today," he wrote.

"It sounds like we have $240k in cash," the managing principal wrote. "At this point, there's no money to meet payroll on the 15th, so you should plan to have staff meeting on Monday to alert the staff." Such an announcement, the managing principal continued, "would help [avoid] any lawsuits moving forward, and of course, it's the right thing to do."

Late that evening, Podesta finally reached David Evinger, the chief credit officer at Chain Bridge Bank. Following their phone conversation, Podesta emailed his staff with an update. The bank had agreed to cover the firm's November rent payment, Podesta wrote back, but it would provide little else in the way of credit. Podesta pushed his colleagues for information about what other sources of cash the firm might be able to access. "Is Saudi in? What else is shaky? Can receivables be put in new bank? Been asking for a plan and got zero from don."

During these exchanges, Podesta reiterated his refusal to put up his art collection as collateral for more loans—even though obtaining additional credit was about the only way for the firm to survive. "not going into personal bankruptcy for don," he wrote,[35] referring again to the recently departed CFO.

Cognetta, who was at the firm for just two months before quitting, said in an email he disputes "any implication that I was responsible for the firm's downfall."

Over the next several days, as things were falling apart in Washington, Podesta remained in Italy. He wanted to stay for the art show. Yet he continued to worry about the pieces from his own art collection that were still at the firm. He told another employee that he needed to get his art out of the firm's headquarters so it could not be seized by creditors. He sent instructions for his personal art curator to make arrangements with the landlord to have his art carefully packed and removed. On Wednesday, November 8, a team of professional movers arrived at the Podesta Group's offices and began carrying away the artwork.[36] Some of the pieces were too large to fit inside the elevator, so the movers placed them on top of the elevator instead. At one point, the elevator broke down.

With the company's founder away, it was up to Fritts—the executive who had tried so desperately to warn her boss about the Ukrainian Centre—to break the bad news to her colleagues.[37] That same day, she gathered the staff in a conference room and laid out the details. All employees would be terminated the following week. Annual bonuses and commissions were being canceled. Employees would lose their health insurance coverage at the end of the year.[38] And since the company had so little cash in the bank and no access to credit, their final paychecks would be for one cent.

A pair of junior employees were dispatched to a nearby liquor store. For the rest of the afternoon, as the movers carted away Podesta's beloved artwork, the Podesta Group's soon-to-be-ex-staffers sipped beer and wine from plastic cups, trying to absorb the shock of the news.

By then, Podesta had left Italy for New York City. He was in the Big Apple to attend the rollout of a fashion calendar published by Pirelli,[39] an Italian tire maker who Tony had been working for on the side. The two-day bash was capped by a black-tie dinner attended by fashion model Naomi Campbell, rapper and fashion designer Sean "P. Diddy" Combs, and other celebrities.[40]

In mid-November, around the time that employees received their final, one-cent paychecks, Podesta paid $365,000 to break the firm's lease. By the end of the month, the Podesta Group was out of business. For a man who once controlled a $50 million lobbying empire, it was a crushing turn of events. "My whole world is crumbling," Podesta told a friend.

In a final act, Podesta gave himself an advance on his lobbying commissions[41] and filed expense forms seeking reimbursement for his most recent trip to Venice. His employees—incensed by his audacity—refused to approve the disbursement.

22

Once the judge called a recess to prepare her decision, Paul Manafort turned to the front row of the courtroom gallery and locked eyes with his wife. In the three years since she'd learned of his infidelity, Kathy had reconciled with her husband. Throughout the entirety of his legal ordeal, she had been an unflappable source of support. But when he glanced back at Kathy that morning, Manafort could see in his wife's face an unfamiliar element of fear. It was as if she sensed, just as he did, that things wouldn't turn out the way they'd expected. For a moment, Manafort wanted to cry.[1]

It had been seven and a half months since Manafort's indictment on federal charges of money laundering, tax fraud, failing to file foreign-lobbying disclosures, lying to law enforcement officials, and conspiracy. For nearly all of that time, he'd been living in home confinement. The circumstances weren't ideal. But the arrangement, secured against a $10 million bond, allowed him to have lunch with his wife and wake up in his own bed as he prepared for his two separate trials. In early June, however, the Office of Special Counsel had filed a brand-new indictment. This time, prosecutors accused Manafort of attempting to persuade two possible witnesses in the Ukrainian lobbying case to provide false testimony. It was these allegations of witness tampering that brought Manafort back to court that morning.

Upon returning from her chambers, Judge Amy Berman Jackson got right to it. Manafort's alleged actions were so troubling, she said, that she could no longer permit him to remain in home confinement. She revoked his bail and ordered him jailed pending his trials. "You have abused the trust placed in you six months ago," the judge said.[2]

The ruling was far harsher than Manafort's legal team had anticipated, and it slammed into Manafort with concussive force. The color drained from his face.[3] He felt numb[4] and sick to his stomach.[5] A federal marshal led him out of the courtroom and into a nearby cell block, where Manafort turned over his valuables and his belt and tie[6]—and fixated on the awful stories he'd heard about the conditions inside DC's jails.[7] "You've got to put me in a safe environment," Manafort told his lawyer during a brief meeting in the cell block. "I can't be put into the DC prison system."[8]

As it turned out, Manafort's destination was outside of the city. After several hours alone in a holding cell, the handcuffed-and-shackled Beltway operative was loaded into a van, driven about ninety miles south to Warsaw, Virginia, and processed into Northern Neck Regional Jail.[9] During the ride, another inmate in the van, who'd been arrested for illegal gun possession and drug distribution charges, asked what he was in for.

"For something I didn't do," Manafort responded. "I was set up."

"We all set up by the man!" the inmate remarked.[10]

The sentiment resonated with the newly incarcerated political consultant. Manafort viewed himself as the righteous victim of a despotic, politically motivated Special Counsel who—in partnership with the mainstream media—was determined to take down Donald Trump by any means necessary. Robert Mueller's team of prosecutors, Manafort fumed, were so bent on destroying the forty-fifth president that they'd arranged to have him thrown in jail in the hopes that it would pressure him into flipping on Trump. None of the charges Manafort faced had anything to do with Russia's influence in the 2016 election. And besides, Manafort insisted he'd never seen anything to suggest that Trump had colluded with Vladimir Putin or his allies during the campaign.

When the van arrived at the Northern Neck Regional Jail, an official led Manafort away from the other inmates and explained that on account of his notoriety, life inside the facility would be a bit different for him. For one thing, Manafort wouldn't go through the traditional booking process, meaning no mug shot would appear in the press. Instead of a jumpsuit, he was issued a T-shirt, boxers, and gym shorts.[11] "Prison is tough," one official told him, "but we will make it a little better for you."[12]

Not all of these special conditions were welcome. The official told Manafort that, due to concerns for his safety, he would not be permitted to interact with any other inmates. He would serve his time in solitary confinement—alone in a windowless concrete room with a single bed, a shower, a sink, a toilet, and a ten-inch television.[13] To Manafort, the austere living arrangement was simply a pressure tactic—another way for Andrew Weissmann, the federal prosecutor handling his case, to try to force him into turning against Trump. "Weissmann wasn't interested in my safety," Manafort wrote in his memoir, titled *Political Prisoner*. "He was only interested in making my life so miserable that I would gladly offer to cooperate to get out of that hellhole."[14]

For Manafort, resisting the Special Counsel's pressure had a strategic benefit. If he refused to assist Robert Mueller's team in its investigation of Trump, Manafort could prove his loyalty to the president and earn himself a White House pardon in the event that he was convicted of the charges he faced. Still, he wouldn't even need a pardon if he could beat the indictment in the courtroom. Manafort had a law degree from Georgetown University, and over the next few days, he managed to refashion the Northern Neck Regional Jail into his personal law office. By agreement with the warden, he obtained access to a computer and a flash drive inside his cell, which enabled him to review the hundreds of legal documents that prosecutors had filed in his case at any time, day or night. Since there was no power outlet in his cell, he arranged to have a thirty-foot extension cord connect his computer to a hallway socket—a privilege no previous Northern Neck Regional Jail inmate had ever secured, Manafort was told.[15]

Manafort was permitted to leave his cell only to attend meetings with his legal team, and the isolation had a dulling effect on his mind. In an effort to prepare for his trials and keep his faculties sharp, Manafort scheduled visits with his lawyer or his paralegal every day—going so far as to hire a former FBI agent to meet with him at the jail on occasions when the others couldn't make it.[16] As prison life goes, it was a comfortable setup. Instead of his cramped and hot cell, Manafort visited with his legal team in the jail's spacious education room, where two functioning air conditioning units kept things nice and cool.[17] At first, prison officials limited the length of these meetings. But eventually, rather than taking the time to clear all of the hallways between Manafort's cell and the education room—which was required to prevent the high-profile inmate from coming in contact with other inmates—jail officials allowed Manafort to remain in his makeshift office for as long as he pleased.[18]

The routine helped the days pass quickly. So even though Manafort was soon transferred to a less accommodating jail in Alexandria, Virginia,[19] before long it was July 2018, and jury selection was under way in his financial fraud trial in the US District Court for the Eastern District of Virginia. Rather than hiring a jury consultant, Manafort assigned the role to himself.[20] He reviewed the questionnaires that each of the forty potential jurors had filled out, using his experience analyzing political data to identify men and women who he believed would be most likely to see things his way.[21] Manafort was encouraged by the result. The twelve-person jury that was ultimately impaneled was educated enough to understand complex tax law, and many of them lived outside of Virginia's inner suburbs—where anti-Trump sentiment was most intense.[22] As the trial got started, Manafort was guardedly confident. He believed he had a fair judge and an open-minded jury.[23]

Things didn't turn out as he'd hoped. On August 21, 2018, the jury found Manafort guilty of eight counts of tax fraud, bank fraud, and a related charge. As he headed back to jail, Manafort was furious at his longtime deputy, Rick Gates, who had buckled under the pressure from Robert Mueller's prosecutors and agreed to a plea deal. Gates provided critical testimony against his former boss. But for Manafort, there was at least one piece of encouraging news. Shortly after the verdict, President Trump—who was apoplectic over the recent revelation that his former personal attorney, Michael Cohen, had agreed to cooperate with the Mueller probe—showered appreciation on his former campaign manager. "I feel very badly for Paul Manafort and his wonderful family," Trump said on Twitter. "'Justice' took a twelve-year-old tax case, among other things, applied tremendous pressure on him, and, unlike Michael Cohen, he refused to 'break'—make up stories in order to get a deal. Such respect for a brave man!"[24] Manafort did indeed seem to be in line for a presidential pardon.

The next month, just two days before he was to stand trial in the Ukraine lobbying case, Manafort pleaded guilty to two counts of conspiracy. While it was a relief to have both cases behind him, his combined prison sentence ultimately totaled more than seven years. Still, in each of the five different facilities he served time in, Manafort did what he could to make life more bearable. At the Alexandria Detention Center in Virginia, he used a transistor radio to listen to Washington Nationals baseball games and nod along to the talk shows of right-wing pundits such as Rush Limbaugh, Mark Levin, and Dan Bongino.[25] When he was transferred to Manhattan to face related charges in New York State, Manafort's buddies who worked in the jail's kitchen procured for him hard-to-find items like vegetables and ice cream sandwiches.[26] (The charges were ultimately tossed out.) As soon as he arrived at Pennsylvania's Loretto Federal Correctional Institution, in August 2019, Manafort was approached by a friendly inmate named Ralph.

"You're Italian, right?"

"Yeah," Manafort replied.

"Well, you don't have anything to worry about. We got your back," said Ralph, speaking on behalf of a group of fellow Italian inmates.[27]

Ralph and his Italian pals weren't hardened mafiosos and, in any event, Loretto was not a violent place. Over time, Manafort developed a schedule: devouring books by Walter Isaacson, watching *Fox and Friends* in the TV room and, every now and then, placing bets on college basketball games through the prison's bookie. When an episode of CNBC's *American Greed* featuring Manafort's case appeared on the prison's TV, the once-flashy campaign consultant became something of a celebrity with the younger inmates, who began turning to him for business advice.[28]

On the other side of the prison's walls, Manafort's former boss was continuing to bulldoze the once sacrosanct alliance between Big Business and the Republican Party. Six months before Manafort was imprisoned, Trump enraged the corporate establishment by imposing tariffs on a host of imported goods and materials, including solar panels, washing machines, steel, and aluminum. The subsequent 25 percent tariff that Trump placed[29] on billions of dollars' worth of Chinese imports prompted Beijing to slap reciprocal tariffs on US goods. The stock market plunged 700 points—nearly 3 percent—over fears of a prolonged trade war, as hundreds of business executives signed letters urging the president to drop the tariffs. Next, Trump rankled the pharmaceutical industry by proposing a new rule requiring drug companies to disclose the price of drugs in their TV advertisements.[30] Yet it was for the technology industry that this groundswell of anticorporate populism would prove most consequential.

In April 2018 Trump signed a law permitting law enforcement authorities and victims to sue websites that promote or facilitate sex trafficking, carving out an exemption to Internet platforms' legal immunity for material that third parties post on their sites.[31] The legislative effort had faced intense opposition from Google and other tech industry lobbyists, who worried that creating this one exception might embolden lawmakers to strip away other liability protections safeguarding web platforms from lawsuits. But the lobbyists were no match for the vigorous backlash against the technology industry sweeping through Washington. Democrats fumed over allegations that Russia had used Google and Facebook to boost Trump in the 2016 election, Republicans blasted Silicon Valley for what they claimed was censorship of conservative voices, and key figures in both parties decried the sheer size and power of Big Tech. Against these forces, Google's lobbyists were unable to block the bill's enactment—a crushing defeat for the Internet search giant that had spent more than a decade erecting one of the most powerful influence-peddling operations in Washington. It was a stark reminder that, despite the multimillion-dollar budgets and fancy new tools, even the most talented lobbyists are limited in what they can do for a company whose brand has become toxic in Washington.

In the months after Trump signed the anti–sex trafficking bill, a growing chorus of Republicans and Democrats began calling for even more aggressive intervention into Big Tech; some went so far as to suggest that the giants of Silicon Valley should be broken apart. Amid the increased scrutiny on its industry and the declining influence of its Washington operation, Google fired about one-third of its lobbying firms in 2019 as part of a top-to-bottom revamp of its Washington office.[32] Among those it let go was the lobbying shop run by Charlie Black. Google might still be the dominant player in the internet search market, but it was no longer the top dog on K Street.

Meanwhile, corporate lobbyists were having trouble making sense of Trump's economic philosophy, which was erratic and unpredictable. In some areas, the billionaire real estate mogul delighted CEOs by governing as an ordinary country club Republican. Trump weakened banking regulations that had been established following the 2008 financial crisis and loosened environmental protection requirements for the construction of oil pipelines, highways, bridges, and other infrastructure projects. For business executives, though, the biggest score was the 2017 law that enshrined the largest overhaul of the federal tax system since the Reagan era—slashing the corporate tax rate from 35 percent to 21 percent.[33]

But the most enduring element of Trump's economic legacy was the wedge he drove between America's corporate elite and the Republican Party's growing base of white, working-class voters. Some four decades earlier, political operatives like Charlie Black, Paul Manafort, Roger Stone and Lee Atwater had helped turn these voters into the foot soldiers of the GOP's campaign to remove government from the commercial sector, empower corporate actors in the market, and globalize the economy. Now, through the influence of Trump—and the collapse of once-thriving manufacturing communities—these same voters had come to see Big Business as every bit as menacing as Big Government. Referencing the February 2023 crash of a Norfolk Southern Corp. train in East Palestine, Ohio, that led to the release of toxins into the water, air, and soil,[34] Ohio Republican Senator J. D. Vance said, "if you go to East Palestine, and you talk to people, yeah, they're very skeptical of the EPA—but they really hate Norfolk Southern."[35]

This revolt on the right occurred just as progressive insurgents, like

New York congresswoman Alexandria Ocasio-Cortez, were expressing outrage over the country's spectacular levels of economic inequality and spearheading an anticorporate uprising on the Left. CEOs grew alarmed by this bipartisan upsurge of populist animosity toward Big Business. In Washington, corporate advocates did what they could to stem the tide. In August 2019 the Business Roundtable—the organization of blue-chip CEOs that helped power the corporate political revolution in the 1970s— took the extraordinary step of declaring that the primary purpose of a corporation was no longer to maximize shareholder value, but rather to foster "an economy that serves all Americans."[36] Such pronouncements did little to quell the unrest.

After nearly two years in prison, Manafort caught an unexpected break. Due to the Covid pandemic and his underlying medical conditions—high blood pressure, liver disease[37]—the Federal Bureau of Prisons had approved his request for a release to home confinement.[38] Though he wasn't a free man, Manafort would be allowed to serve the remaining roughly four years of his sentence in his Alexandria, Virginia, apartment. At a quarter to six in the morning on May 13, 2020, a corrections officer arrived at Manafort's cell and escorted the seventy-one-year-old political operative toward the gate.[39]

Loretto, a complex of low-slung buildings enclosed by spiral razor wire fencing, is located in a part of rural Pennsylvania where the MAGA movement enjoyed enthusiastic support. So as Manafort made his way down the long hallway, he received a heartfelt sendoff from the prison staff. Several guards wished him luck.[40] Others helped carry his bags. At one point, a corrections officer pulled him aside.

"I hope Trump pardons you right away," the officer whispered.[41]

23

It was around eleven o'clock at night when a pair of local cops pulled up to a $2.4 million beach house with a charming back porch, handsome palm trees, and an outdoor swimming pool. Deputy Christopher Hampton of the Charleston County Sheriff's Office and Officer Carlos Hernandez of the Sullivan's Island Police Department had arrived in response to a noise complaint. When they got out of their squad cars, both officers could hear loud voices and music playing at a high volume inside the house[1]—an unusual late-night racket for this sleepy community.

As Deputy Hampton approached the property, the front door opened, and a fifty-four-year-old man emerged. It was the home's owner, Jim Courtovich. But the Courtovich that police encountered that night wasn't the charming and gracious cocktail party host who'd captivated elite Washington. Rather, according to a police report that Deputy Hampton later filed on the incident, it was an angry and drunk man.

As soon as he opened the front door, Courtovich unleashed a "loud boisterous profanity-laced rant"[2] about the chief of the Sullivan's Island Police Department, according to the incident report. Deputy Hampton tried to explain why the police had been called out, but Courtovich just "continued with his rant." Deputy Hampton asked Courtovich to turn down the music, and, eventually, someone inside the house complied with the request. The officer then explained that if the police received another noise complaint, they'd have to issue a citation. With that, the cops began to depart. But as they walked to their vehicles, Courtovich remained on his front porch, "yelling profanities toward Officer Hernandez and the Sullivan's Island Chief of Police."[3]

Even after the cops left, Courtovich couldn't let it go. Less than a half hour later, he contacted the police department and asked to speak with a supervisor. Since Deputy Hampton and Officer Hernandez were the only cops working on Sullivan's Island that night, the two returned to Courtovich's home and knocked on his front door.[4] Courtovich recognized the two officers from their prior visit, and he wasn't happy about it.

"I wanted a supervisor," Courtovich told them, as he slammed the door shut.[5]

At that point, according to the incident report, the two cops started to leave. But Courtovich quickly reappeared on the front porch and resumed shouting profanities. Deputy Hampton told Courtovich to knock it off. If Courtovich didn't stop screaming and cussing, the police officer warned, he'd be arrested for disorderly conduct.

"Fuck you," Courtovich shouted in response, according to the incident report.[6]

And that was it. Deputy Hampton told Courtovich that he was under arrest, put him in handcuffs, and drove him to the Charleston County Detention Center.[7] At a quarter after one in the morning, Courtovich was booked on a misdemeanor charge of public disorderly conduct.[8]

It was a dark time in the life of Jim Courtovich. Despite the flourish of good fortune he experienced in the opening days of the Trump era, the following two years had brought one disaster after the next. In February 2017 the FBI's probe into allegations of financial wrongdoing at Genentech became a front-page news story. Not long after, Courtovich's business dealings with Donald Trump's disgraced former National Security Advisor, Michael Flynn, led to his entanglement in Robert Mueller's sweeping inquiry into the 2016 election. Amid the stench of concurrent scandals,

Courtovich's reputation imploded. Clients cut ties with his firm and legal bills piled up. Friends began avoiding him at DC cocktail parties. Fellow Beltway insiders gossiped about how he now looked thin, tired, and old. Those who asked Courtovich about his well-being received an angry lament about the unfairness of life.

As things were falling apart in Washington, Courtovich began spending more time at his handsome beach retreat in Sullivan's Island, South Carolina. But here too, there was trouble. The house parties Courtovich threw fueled conflict with neighbors, who complained about the noise. Courtovich once got into a heated dispute with a retiree who lived nearby. During their argument, the neighbor said Courtovich threatened to slit his wife's throat. When the neighbor said he might take legal action, Courtovich boasted that he had powerful Washington and New York law firms on retainer and would crush any lawsuit. Before long, nearby home owners began taking their complaints to the Sullivan's Island's Police Department, which led to a series of ugly interactions between Courtovich and the cops. By the summer of 2020—after years of mounting pressure—the dashing, gregarious figure who once filled the cocktail glasses of Washington's elite was, according to police records, in a state of drunken belligerence more than five hundred miles from the nation's capital: screaming profanities at a pair of local police officers, slamming his front door in the cops' faces, and sleeping it off in the local jail.[9]

It was the ghost of his longtime business partner that precipitated Courtovich's collapse.

In the fall of 2016 an investigative reporter for the Wall Street Journal began looking into the death of Evan Morris. The reporter, Brody Mullins—who is also one of the authors of this book—had found it curious that there was so little in the news about the dramatic suicide of one of Washington's premier drug industry lobbyists. Mullins made some preliminary phone calls to a few pharmaceutical lobbyists, and he soon learned that Morris had worked closely with Jim Courtovich.

By then, Mullins had covered Washington's political-influence industry for nearly two decades. He was familiar with Courtovich's reputation as the host of splashy social functions for political power brokers and media celebrities. Mullins had even attended one of these events himself. When Mullins reached out to him about Morris, Courtovich refused to speak on the record. Over the next several months, Mullins contacted dozens of other lobbyists and consultants who had worked with Morris over the years. Like Courtovich, these influence peddlers declined to be interviewed by name. Nevertheless, through not-for-attribution conversations with Morris's former associates, Mullins picked up the rumors that had long circulated about the upstart Genentech lobbyist.

Morris, the influence peddlers claimed, had always seemed to be living beyond his means. Even with his lucrative salary—nearly $1 million, including bonus and stock options—Morris's associates couldn't understand how he was able to afford the sports cars, the golf memberships, the wine collection, and the various properties. There was reason to believe that Morris hadn't been truthful about how he was financing his glitzy lifestyle. For example, he'd told friends different stories to explain how he paid for his golf memberships, one of which—the Robert Trent Jones Golf Club—cost about $150,000 to join. In one version, Morris covered the fees by holding fundraising events at the golf courses for the Bill, Hillary, and Chelsea Clinton Foundation. But he told other people that he received the memberships as rewards from Genentech. Likewise, Morris gave contradicting accounts of how he'd obtained his $300,000 mahogany speedboat. He told some people that he won it in a charity auction after buying all fifty thousand raffle tickets. To others, he claimed he'd purchased it from someone who had ordered the boat but who went bankrupt before it was delivered.

One influence peddler told the *Journal* that Morris's associates had whispered about the possibility that the Genentech lobbyist had accumulated his luxury items through illicit activity. "The talk was kickbacks," the influence peddler said.

As he pursued the story, Mullins learned that he wasn't the only one looking into Evan Morris. When the reporter discovered that Morris owned a $300,000 mahogany speedboat, Mullins contacted Hacker Boat Company, one of the few American companies that makes luxury wooden speedboats. Hacker Boat is a tiny company in Upstate New York that sells only a handful of custom-made boats each year. So few people work in its office that when Mullins called, the company's president and chief executive, George Babcock, answered the phone.

After identifying himself as a reporter for the *Wall Street Journal*, Mullins began asking a set of initial questions about the company and its products. Babcock cut him off.

"What is this really about?" Babcock asked.

Mullins explained that he was looking into the sale of a thirty-foot boat that Hacker had sold to a Washington lobbyist in 2012.

It was then that Babcock offered a striking piece of information. Several months back, Babcock said, he'd been contacted by FBI agents who were seeking details about the same sale.

For Mullins, the existence of the FBI probe was a major revelation; it suggested that Morris may indeed have been involved in something nefarious prior to his death. The more reporting Mullins did, the more deception he uncovered. For example, when Mullins looked into the two different explanations that Morris had given friends about how he'd paid for his golf memberships, the reporter found that neither was true. A spokesman for the Clinton Foundation said the organization had never covered golf membership fees for Morris, and a spokesman for Genentech said the firm had never given him golf memberships as a bonus—or for any other reason. At the same time, Mullins was beginning to find holes in Courtovich's professional resume. Courtovich's company biography stated that he "oversaw communications efforts" for the 1998 merger of automakers Daimler-Benz and Chrysler as well as the 2009 merger of drug manufacturers Roche and Genentech. As Mullins discovered, neither assertion was wholly accurate. Courtovich did, of course, have business contracts with Genentech. But a Genentech spokesman told Mullins that Courtovich played no role in Roche's 2010 purchase of Genentech. Similarly, while Courtovich had worked on the Daimler-Benz account after being hired by Charlie Black at Burson-Marsteller, Courtovich's work on the matter ended before the $36 billion merger was even announced. "The name James Courtovich is not familiar to us," a spokeswoman for Daimler North America Corp. told the *Journal*. In addition, Mullins learned that during Morris's 2009 campaign to secure the top lobbying job at Genentech, it was Courtovich who had spread the lies about Morris's chief rival, Heidi Wagner, having berated a TSA official at an airport security checkpoint. When Courtovich and his lawyer told Mullins about a meeting during which they claimed Morris's bosses instructed Courtovich to reimburse the young lobbyist for personal expenditures, Mullins called the half dozen executives Courtovich said were in attendance. Each said there was no such meeting.

Still, it wasn't until he examined documents related to Morris and Courtovich's transactions that Mullins found apparent evidence of serious wrongdoing. For instance, Mullins found documents showing that in late 2012 Morris had hired Courtovich's firm, Sphere Consulting, for $880,000 to do policy work with think tanks. Genentech paid Sphere in two equal installments: $440,000 on November 1, 2012, and $440,000 on December 1, 2012. No one at Genentech could determine what Courtovich had done in exchange for the money, according to people familiar with the contract. Nine days after the final payment was received, according to the records Mullins reviewed, Courtovich's firm sent $448,986.22 to Morris's personal bank account.[10] An attorney for Courtovich and his firm, Eric Lewis, told Mullins that the payment was to reimburse Morris for the personal funds the lobbyist claimed to have put toward an event with a DC-based conservative think tank, the American Enterprise Institute. Lewis provided Mullins with an AEI invoice for the $448,986.22 that Morris had given Courtovich's firm.

But a spokeswoman for AEI said the invoice was fake.[11]

In another case, Mullins obtained documents showing that in early 2012 Genentech had paid National Media, where Courtovich was working at the time, $2 million for public affairs and strategic consulting.[12] After National Media received the final payment, according to documents and interviews, Courtovich asked the firm to issue a $303,048.95 reimbursement check to the Hacker Boat Co. This was the request that had so unsettled National Media's chief accountant, Jon Ferrell. The accountant continued to puzzle over the request even after Courtovich submitted a one-page invoice—bearing Hacker Boat Company's logo—indicating that the reimbursement was related to the costs of renting facilities at Hacker's lakeside headquarters for a political event with the Democratic Attorneys General Association. In the end, Ferrell put aside his suspicions and authorized the $303,048.95 reimbursement payment. But the accountant refused to involve himself in any further transactions between Morris and Courtovich. Not long afterward, National Media parted ways with Courtovich.

Sifting through the details of this transaction, Mullins turned up indications of likely corporate embezzlement. Spokespeople for the Democratic Attorneys General Association, as well as the Hacker Boat Co., said no such event ever took place. And when Mullins asked Hacker for the cost of Morris's boat, the company confirmed that it was equal to the exact payment that Courtovich arranged: $303,048.95.[13]*

On February 13, 2017, the *Wall Street Journal* published Mullins's 3,800-word investigation into Evan Morris's career in Washington, titled "The Rise and Fall of a K Street Renegade."[14] The story revealed for the first time that the FBI suspected Morris of embezzling "millions of dollars from his company over a decade in a kickback scheme involving Washington consultants he did business with." In the article, a spokesman for Genentech admitted that their onetime star lobbyist had been involved in illicit financial dealings. Morris "created schemes to misappropriate company funds for personal gain and deliberately concealed his actions." Courtovich's lawyer insisted the veteran media consultant had done nothing wrong. The attorney, Eric Lewis, told the *Journal* that neither Courtovich nor his firms had ever willingly conspired in Morris's crimes. Rather, the attorney said, Courtovich had been duped by his late business partner's scheming. "Sphere is shocked and dismayed that Sphere's client provided fake documents that defrauded not only his company but Sphere as well," Lewis told the newspaper. "At no time," Lewis continued, "did the Sphere team (or anyone else to our knowledge) have any reason to believe that any of these payments were anything other than what they were on their face: bona fide reimbursements."[15]

Despite the protests of innocence, the *Wall Street Journal* investigation triggered the collapse of Courtovich's standing in Washington.

*The Hacker Boat Company has never been accused of wrongdoing.

Clients—such as Goldman Sachs—cut ties. Members of Sphere's already-small staff bolted for other jobs. Public officials distanced themselves. Friends avoided him at Washington social functions. Eventually weeds began to grow around the Capitol Hill party house. Courtovich's marquee event, the semiannual Gaucho barbecue, would never be held again.

Courtovich's troubles extended beyond his work for Genentech. As the FBI was examining his secret payments to Morris, an entirely different set of law enforcement officials demanded he turn over documents related to another client. This second team of federal authorities was investigating Michael Flynn, the retired army general turned pro-Trump rabble-rouser who resigned as National Security Advisor on February 13, 2017—the same day that the *Wall Street Journal* story was published. Flynn had stepped down under pressure after only twenty-four days on the job, following revelations that he'd misled Vice President Mike Pence and senior Trump administration officials about his possibly illegal communications with a top Russian diplomat. These law enforcement officials, however, weren't inquiring about Russia. They wanted to know more about Courtovich's efforts to help Flynn's consulting firm promote the interests of the government of Turkey.

Though both Flynn and Courtovich had filed lobbying-disclosure documents asserting that their work was not for Turkey's government, US authorities had come to suspect that—much like how Paul Manafort and Tony Podesta's lobbying campaign was actually on behalf of the president of Ukraine—the efforts by Flynn and Courtovich were secretly directed by the president of Turkey. Failing to properly disclose who is really behind such lobbying activities—as Manafort and Podesta had learned—could land a lobbyist in prison.

Under pressure from federal investigators, Flynn submitted documents to the Department of Justice in March 2017 in which he belatedly admitted that Turkish government officials were the principal beneficiary of the lobbying effort. Courtovich's firm did the same, blaming its erroneous initial filing on incorrect information provided by Flynn's company. But the paperwork failed to resolve the matter. In April, Courtovich's firm received a subpoena from prosecutors in the Eastern District of Virginia who demanded the company turn over documents and emails related to its work for Michael Flynn's consulting firm. A short while later, the Flynn probe was absorbed into Robert Mueller's far-reaching examination of possible Russian influence in the 2016 election. Suddenly Washington's beloved cocktail party host was entangled in two separate federal investigations.

Meanwhile, in a quiet beach town on the South Carolina coast, Courtovich was getting crossways with another set of law enforcement officials. A few minutes after noon on September 4, 2017, Sergeant Darren Botticelli, of the Sullivan's Island Police Department, pulled his squad car up to Courtovich's property. The officer was responding to a report that a vehicle near the home had been left idling with its lights on for about an hour.[16] Arriving at the address, he spotted what appeared to be the car in question: a dark SUV with its lights on, parked in a driveway behind the house. Botticelli walked toward the SUV to get a better look. While cutting across the property, he ran into Courtovich, who was hosting a Labor Day party.

Courtovich asked why Botticelli was on his property.[17]

Just then, one of Courtovich's guests stepped in and told the officer that the car left running was hers, according to an incident report filed by Botticelli.[18] The woman apologized to the officer for making him come all this way to check up on her vehicle. With that, the matter appeared to be resolved. Botticelli went to call the police station so he could tell his colleagues that everything was fine. But before he could do so, according to the incident report, Courtovich erupted. "He then yelled at me to get off his property," Botticelli said in the report.[19]

Botticelli complied with Courtovich's demand and walked back toward his squad car. Courtovich pursued him. "The owner came off his property and approach[ed] me on Middle Street," Botticelli said in his report. "The owner became belligerent again. The owner got in my personal space and this officer gave him a verbal command asking the owner to step back."[20] Only then did Courtovich retreat.

The episode did not end there. Later that evening, Botticelli received a call from police dispatch relaying that Courtovich had requested to speak with a supervisor at the Sullivan's Island Police Department. There were only a handful of officers on the force and, as it happened, Botticelli was the supervisor that night. So along with another officer, Botticelli drove back to Courtovich's house.[21]

When the two officers arrived, Courtovich was intoxicated, according to the incident report.[22] Courtovich began complaining to Botticelli about his interaction with law enforcement earlier that day, without realizing that Botticelli was the officer he'd confronted. The second police officer tried to explain why police had been summoned to his property earlier, but Courtovich wouldn't relent. "The owner was still belligerent toward officers," Botticelli said in his incident report, adding that Courtovich was "using profanity words and cursing."[23]

As the confrontation escalated, Botticelli told Courtovich that the officers were recording the incident with their body cameras, and the second officer warned Courtovich that if he continued cursing and screaming, he'd be charged with disorderly conduct. Finally, Courtovich backed off.[24]

The next few months brought good news for Courtovich. In late September 2017 the Department of Justice scrapped its Genentech investigation without bringing any charges.[25] The decision followed a two-year FBI probe involving grand-jury subpoenas, search warrants, surveillance, and interviews with dozens of lobbyists, consultants, and others. From the start, FBI agents had faced two critical challenges in gathering sufficient evidence to substantiate a criminal complaint. First, the only person who knew everything that had gone on at Genentech—Evan Morris—was dead. Secondly, the same high-priced Washington law firm that was representing Courtovich and his consulting firm in the probe—Lewis Baach—was also representing many of the firm's employees. This arrangement, which is sometimes used as a legal defense tactic, served to hinder the FBI's investigation, because it made it harder for law enforcement officials to cut deals with Courtovich's employees that would have allowed them to talk to law enforcement officials in exchange for immunity. With key witnesses either deceased or unwilling to be helpful, federal prosecutors felt it wasn't possible to prove beyond a reasonable doubt that Courtovich hadn't simply been duped into sending secret payments to the Genentech lobbyist, as he'd claimed.

Two months later, Courtovich was boosted by another law enforcement development. On December 1, several days before Courtovich was scheduled to testify in front of a grand jury, Michael Flynn pleaded guilty to several charges, including lying about his contacts with the Russian ambassador.[26] In making his admission, Flynn also acknowledged that he'd lied in his FARA registration when he stated that officials in the Turkish government were not behind the lobbying effort. The agreement brought Courtovich's dealings with Robert Mueller's office to an end. After securing Flynn's guilty plea, the Special Counsel's office had no further interest in the Republican media strategist. With that, the pair of federal investigations that had encumbered Courtovich's life over the prior two years were over. No charges would be filed against him.

As the legal clouds began to clear, Courtovich was free to focus more of his attention on his influence-peddling business. In the coming years, he would help the governments of Morocco and Qatar, as well as a presidential candidate in El Salvador, polish their images in Washington.[27] On occasion, he and Jeff Zeleny turned up at exclusive DC social functions, like the invite-only brunch that then–*Politico* owner Robert Allbritton hosted at his Georgetown mansion following the White House Correspondents' Association's annual dinner. Still, Courtovich would never recover the clout he'd possessed prior to Morris's death, when Washington's star reporters and senior policy makers crammed into his backyard for French wines and Argentine beef. Instead, amid a swirl of financial debts, civil lawsuits, and run-ins with the cops, Courtovich's downward trajectory would only continue.

In early 2018 Courtovich lost his biggest client, the government of Ethiopia. In FARA reports to the Department of Justice, Courtovich claimed that he'd contacted dozens of American government officials as part of his work for Ethiopia. But when a reporter reached several of those same American officials, many said they'd never had any interactions with Courtovich on this issue. In March the law firm that represented Courtovich and his consulting firm in the Genentech and Flynn investigations sued Courtovich and his firm for $572,801.87 of allegedly unpaid legal bills.[28] Lewis Baach claimed that Courtovich and his firm hadn't paid it in nearly two years. Though Lewis Baach's attorneys insisted they'd attempted to resolve the matter out of court—offering to arrange a payment plan or reduce the balance if Courtovich agreed to settle the debt immediately— it was only after the embarrassing lawsuit became public that Courtovich began making payments, and the law firm dropped its suit.

The following month, Simon Charlton and the Saudi Arabian investors who'd bankrolled Courtovich's foreign-lobbying business sued Courtovich for breach of contract and fraud.[29] In the three years since lending Courtovich money to launch the foreign-lobbying business, the Saudis said, Courtovich hadn't made a single payment on the $4 million loan, and he'd refused to provide his business partners with any financial statements. More significantly, although the terms of the contract explicitly forbade him from doing so, in September 2015 Courtovich had used the Saudi-financed "Hill House" as collateral to secure a $1.3 million mortgage in his own name, according to the complaint. A few weeks later, Courtovich and Jeff Zeleny made an $800,000 down payment to purchase their beach house in Sullivan's Island, according to property records.

Documents Courtovich turned over to the court as part of the lawsuit showed he diverted some of the Saudis' investment to pay taxes to the IRS and cover other bills, according to people familiar with the case. Other unpaid bills were piling up as well. The landlord of his downtown office space filed a lawsuit claiming Courtovich owed more than $200,000 in rent, taxes, and fees. His landscaping company sued him for allegedly failing to pay about $25,000 worth of lawn mowing, flower pruning, and other yard work.[30] His credit card company sued him for failing to pay a $75,000 past-due balance.

Meanwhile, in the upscale beach community of Sullivan's Island, South Carolina, Courtovich's behavior was increasingly problematic. At about seven in the evening on September 2, 2019, Courtovich was leaving the Obstinate Daughter,[31] a local restaurant and bar where he was a regular. After getting behind the wheel of a dark-colored golf cart, he began backing out of a parking lot. According to a police incident report, Courtovich backed the golf cart out at a high rate of speed, crossed both lanes of traffic, and slammed into a parked vehicle. He then fled the scene in his golf cart.[32]

Witnesses told police that "there was a lot of commotion from various bystanders who were also present at the time of the accident, attempting to shout to the male driver to tell him to stop and that he had struck a vehicle," according to the incident report. "However, the driver did not stop and proceeded down Middle Street."[33]

After receiving reports of a hit-and-run incident, members of the Sullivan's Island Police Department were able to identify Courtovich as the driver of the golf cart from witnesses who wrote down the license plate of the golf cart and from a surveillance camera across the street at the Sullivan's Island Town Hall. They issued arrest warrants against Courtovich for reckless driving, leaving the scene of an accident, and driving under a suspended license.[34] Courtovich fought the charges for two years before agreeing to pay fines to settle the matters.

Washington's once-renowned party host had become a small-town nuisance.

24

By the time he got the good news, Paul Manafort had been out of prison for seven and a half months. Upon his departure from the Loretto Federal Correctional Institution in May 2020, Trump's disgraced former campaign chairman returned not to the chic $3.2 million condominium in historic Old Town Alexandria, but to a modest three-bedroom rental in a less exclusive part of the city. Manafort's entanglement with Robert Mueller had been pricey, costing him about $5 million in attorney's fees[1] and forcing him to relinquish—through government seizures or private sales—more than $22 million in real estate, including the Trump Tower pad, the Hamptons estate, the SoHo loft, the Brooklyn town house, and the Virginia condominium. His new apartment in Alexandria, Virginia, was roughly half the size[2] of the luxury condo he'd once owned there. But for a man who was still serving time on nine felony counts, it would have to do.

As he settled back into the Washington area, Manafort continued to seethe over the courtroom betrayal of his former business associate, Rick Gates, and he harbored feelings of bitterness toward the many friends who'd turned their backs on him while he was in prison. Still, he remained hopeful that, with the help of a presidential pardon, he could reclaim his freedom and refurbish his reputation. When Trump's reelection effort got under way, Manafort reconnected with his friends in the president's orbit. Despite the terms of his home confinement—the ankle monitor, the regular check-ins with his case manager—he began "indirectly" advising Trump's team during the 2020 campaign.[3]

Around the time that Trump lost the election and began spreading false claims of widespread voter fraud, Manafort dispatched his lawyer, Kevin Downing, to raise the issue of clemency with Trump's lawyers.[4] It was brimming with irony; one of the most famous lobbyists in the world would now have to rely on others to lobby on his behalf.

On December 23, 2020, Manafort learned that he had received a presidential pardon. The ecstatic Beltway operative fixed himself a double Bombay martini and placed a call to his old lobbying partner, Roger Stone,[5] who had been pardoned that same day for his conviction of lying to Congress, witness tampering, and other charges related to the Mueller investigation. Nearly four decades earlier, Manafort and Stone had helped a young real estate playboy get what he wanted out of Washington. Now, Trump had done the same for them.

The following day, Christmas Eve, was Manafort's first full day of freedom. At about 6 p.m., he received a call from a number he didn't recognize. It was the White House switchboard. "Paul Manafort," an operator said, "the president would like to speak to you."

Moments later, Trump was on the line. "I've been wanting to do this for a long time," the president began.[6]

During their conversation, the two discussed the 2016 election, Manafort's experiences over the past two years, and the president's plans to spend the winter in Florida. As they wrapped up, Trump expressed his gratitude for the way Manafort had conducted himself over the course of the Mueller investigation. Someone of lesser character, Trump said, would have cracked.

"You are a man," the president told his former campaign chairman. "You are a real man."[7]

25

When the mob of Trump supporters busted through the police barricades, crashed into the US Capitol, and violently attempted to overturn the results of the election, Tony Podesta was only a few miles away, watching news coverage of the melee from the safe remove of his $4 million home. The 9,200-square-foot property, located two houses down from Barack and Michelle Obama's residence, had witnessed the sun rise and fall on Podesta's influence-peddling empire. Just a few years earlier, it was frequently crammed with artists, journalists, and political bigwigs who walked through his front door, admired his avant-garde artwork, and forked over generous campaign checks. But after getting mixed up with Paul Manafort and Robert Mueller, Podesta had become a pariah to the same Democratic lawmakers he'd done so much to empower. The crowds of political hotshots vanished, and the home fell silent. "I don't do much in Washington anymore," Podesta later admitted. "I just live here."

It was a painful time for the once-mighty lobbyist. In the three years leading up to the January 6 attacks, he'd cycled through feelings of anger, resentment, and isolation. He was incensed with the Special Counsel's lead prosecutor, Andrew Weissmann, whom he insisted was the source of the damaging media leaks about his involvement in Mueller's probe—leaks that, according to Podesta, served to scare off clients and drive the firm out of business. And he was bitter with his fellow Democrats who'd turned their backs on him the moment he was touched by scandal. When associates of the top two Democrats in Congress at the time, Chuck Schumer and Nancy Pelosi, asked Podesta not to attend upcoming fund-raising events, the lobbyist was appalled. "Nancy, who came to my mother's funeral," Podesta recalled in an interview, "said I shouldn't be seen with her."

Although prosecutors had wrapped up their inquiry in 2019 without bringing charges against him, Vin Weber, or anyone at their firms, Podesta couldn't escape the suspicion. At one point, he attended a wedding where he met a woman whom he would later marry. When another wedding guest saw the woman talking to Podesta, the guest pulled her aside.

"Be careful of him," the wedding guest advised. "He was investigated by Mueller."

Meanwhile, without the income from his lobbying firm to cover his soaring legal bills, Podesta's bank account continued to drain. The best way to keep himself afloat, he eventually concluded, was to liquidate his most cherished possessions. Podesta converted his $2.6 million DC penthouse into an appointment-only showroom and, according to the *New York Times*,[1] began selling off pieces of his art collection. Though the proceeds were considerable—one Louise Bourgeois sculpture fetched $5.6 million—the market was fickle. And when the Covid pandemic struck, the art buyers disappeared, and Podesta's new business cratered. Podesta sold off the DC condo as well as another property in New York City. But he also put his knowledge of the Washington bureaucracy to work, securing a nearly $43,000 loan from the Paycheck Protection Program, a federal initiative designed to help restaurants and other small businesses survive the pandemic.[2] The funds, Podesta told the *Times*, went primarily toward salaries for himself, his art curator, and a third employee.[3]

As if things weren't bad enough, Podesta soon lost access to his email accounts when Chinese Internet scammers hacked into one of his website domains and used it in a phishing scheme.[4] "It's not been an easy time," he told the *Times*.[5]

Still, for the down-and-out influence peddler, January 6 was a particularly harrowing day. Watching the mayhem unfold on the news, Podesta
didn't just see Trump supporters beating cops and waving confederate
flags, he saw Washington as he knew it perish before his eyes. "Biparti-
sanship was largely pronounced dead on that day," he says. "We're sort of
divided into two countries sitting together."

Podesta gave little apparent thought, however, to the role that Washington's great lobbying dynasties had played in the rise of political extremism and the destabilization of our democracy. Back in the 1970s, Tommy
Boggs had used his insider access to undercut the once-sweeping influence
of unions, environmental advocates, and consumer groups while bringing corporations to power in the nation's capital. Throughout the 1980s
and early 1990s, the operatives at Black, Manafort & Stone deployed their
experience as campaign consultants and their credibility inside the conservative movement to give rise to Fox News, introduce Donald Trump to
Washington, and help reorient federal policy around a set of free-market
ideals. During the late 1990s and the 2000s, Podesta used his talents for
campaign finance to ensure that this CEO-friendly economic vision—of
weak regulations on industry, low taxes on billionaires and businesses, and
minimal trade barriers for large multinational corporations—was embedded inside the Democratic Party as well.

Together, members of these three lobbying houses helped to tilt the
playing field against ordinary Americans in all sorts of ways. Through their
efforts on behalf of Big Business, they kept drug prices elevated, blocked
universal health insurance, made it tougher for lower-middle-class families to access safe mortgages, and prevented the United States from taking
aggressive action to combat climate change, among others. Along the way,
these three influence-peddling dynasties helped bring about a fundamental transformation in the priorities of Washington—bequeathing a legacy
that was far more destructive than any individual feat of lobbying. For
much of the twentieth century, a ruling class of New Deal liberals had used
the federal government as an instrument to protect consumers from the
excesses of capitalism and to moderately redistribute wealth downward.[6]
But beginning in the late 1970s—and thanks to the influence of corporate

lobbyists—lawmakers and administration officials in both political parties began pursuing a principal tenet of the conservative revolution: reducing government authority and maximizing economic efficiency. In the absence of sufficiently strong countervailing forces such as organized labor or public interest groups, which had been unable to regain strength in the face of industry opposition, this pro-business policy consensus would serve as the ballast of economic policy making in Washington for roughly forty years. And it would work, alongside other factors such as technological innovation and globalization, to widen the gap between the rich and the poor to levels not seen since the 1920s.[7]

The result was an economy that enabled highly educated workers in certain fields to flourish, but was often punishing for the more than 62 percent of Americans without a college degree.[8] A political system that could respond to the desires of wealthy elites, but was dangerously disconnected from the needs of most citizens.[9] And a society subsumed in the sort of economic inequality[10] that fuels political polarization, breaks down social cohesion, and broadens the appeal of political extremists—ideal conditions, that is, for someone like Trump to ascend.

Yet it was the rise of Trump that finally shattered Washington's pro-business policy consensus. Indeed, turning the Republican Party against the corporate establishment may prove to be the most enduring element of his economic legacy. In the years after he departed the White House, Trump's animus to Big Business has become an increasingly central feature of the modern-day GOP, as right-wing lawmakers level attacks on commercial interests and pursue the type of anticorporate government activism that would have been unthinkable for conservative leaders of earlier generations. During the course of the Biden administration, nearly 40 House Republicans joined with more than 200 of their Democratic colleagues in voting to enact legislation giving federal antitrust regulators more resources to block corporate mergers deemed harmful to consumers. Republican Senator Josh Hawley of Missouri teamed up with liberal Senator Elizabeth Warren to introduce a bill requiring the federal government to claw back compensation of executives at failed banks.[11] GOP Senator Chuck Grassley wrote a bill to give federal regulators additional tools to combat monopolies in the meat and poultry industries.[12] Florida Senator Marco Rubio backed a unionization drive at an Amazon plant,[13] and Ohio Senator J. D. Vance issued support for the Davis Bacon Act requiring construction workers to be paid union-scale wages for public works projects. Outside of the nation's capital, Florida governor Ron DeSantis feuded with Walt Disney Inc. after its CEO opposed a Florida law banning discussion of gender identity and sexual orientation in some public-school classes.[14] And in Texas, the Republican comptroller blocked the state from doing most forms of business with financial firms including BlackRock, Goldman Sachs, and JPMorgan—accusing Wall Street banks of spurning investments in the oil and gas sector as part of an effort to combat climate change.[15] "We are at a tipping point," says Kyle Plotkin, a political advisor to Senator Hawley. "In the past, Republican-elected officials wouldn't come near these issues with a ten-foot pole. But now many are embracing it because their constituents are demanding it."

Tennessee Senator Marsha Blackburn put it differently in a statement to the *Wall Street Journal*. "Gone are the days," she said, "that Republicans are going to sit on the sidelines as big behemoths take advantage of the American people."

The GOP's split from Big Business was driven by an array of social, political, and economic forces. For one thing, many Republican voters began blaming corporate friendly policies—like free trade and liberalized immigration—for the loss of manufacturing jobs and the decay of once-thriving rural communities. In addition, CEOs have come under intense pressure from employees, shareholders, and customers to stake out progressive social positions in order to align their firms with the younger, wealthier, and college-educated Americans whom they consider essential to future profitability. Such political activism, as corporations like Walt Disney have learned, stokes the fury of right-wing culture warriors, led by Donald Trump. At the same time, there was a third factor behind the Republican Party's rupture from the corporate establishment: campaign finance.

During the four decades following the corporate political revolution of the 1970s, Republican lawmakers came to depend on industry PACs for a substantial portion of their reelection funds. In recent years, though, they've grown considerably less reliant on this once-essential source of cash. In the 2016 election, for instance, 128 House Republicans received more than 40 percent of their campaign funds from corporate PACs. But during the 2022 election, according to the *Wall Street Journal*, just forty-two did. Overall, corporate PAC contributions to Republican congressional candidates fell 27 percent, to $189 million, from 2016 to 2022.[16] Instead, GOP lawmakers are obtaining a growing share of their campaign funds from small-dollar donations from ordinary citizens. While such independence from the corporate PAC system empowers Republicans to oppose Big Business, it makes them more reliant on a pool of individual, small-dollar donors that, according to a 2016 paper by Brigham Young University associate professor Michael Barber, tend to favor ideologically extreme candidates.[17] The same trend is playing out on the left as well. Many Democratic lawmakers—along with a handful of Republicans—now refuse to accept any funds from corporate PACs. Democratic candidates, as a whole, are obtaining a shrinking share of their election funds from Big Business. As a result, members of Congress from both political parties have less incentive to reflexively support pro-business legislation.

In addition, a high-profile legal development has worked to further dilute corporate America's role in the campaign finance ecosystem. In its 2010 decision in the case of *Citizens United vs. The Federal Election Commission*, the Supreme Court overturned federal restrictions on companies and labor unions using internal funds to call for the election or defeat of candidates for Congress or the White House. Though companies are still prohibited from donating directly to candidates, they are now free to make unlimited donations to political groups that could run advertisements for or against federal candidates. Watchdog groups and good-government activists decried the ruling. They argued that, by enabling Big Business to funnel even greater sums to campaign groups, US corporations would further expand their influence in Washington. In practice, however, the decision has had the opposite effect.

While some large oil companies—like Chevron and Occidental Petroleum Corp.—have taken advantage of the ruling to pump money into

Republican campaign groups, most publicly traded companies have declined to make such donations. Doing so, they reasoned, could upset their shareholders, employees, and customers, who include Democrats and Republicans alike. Instead, a different group—politically active millionaires and billionaires—has responded to the decision by flooding the campaign finance system with massive donations. Figures such as the petrochemical magnate Charles Koch and libertarian venture capitalist Peter Thiel. Seventeen of the top twenty donors to the GOP's Senate Leadership Fund in 2022, for example, were conservative billionaires or small privately held companies. In contrast, corporate America's marquee advocacy group, the US Chamber of Commerce, ranked number twenty on the list of top donors. On the Democratic side, the contrast was even more stark. No publicly traded company ranked among the top twenty donors to the election of Senate Democrats.

Rather than widening the influence of Big Business in Washington, the Citizens United decision has diminished the role of corporations in the campaign finance system—all while elevating another set of financial benefactors, activist billionaires, whose political agendas are often more extreme than the corporate establishment.

These developments have erected new obstacles on K Street. As business interests grow alarmed by the groundswell of anticorporate populism in Washington, influence peddlers are confronting the most hostile political environment in a generation. In the fall of 2022, the Conservative Political Action Conference urged Republican lawmakers to promise to stop meeting with lobbyists for companies that have expressed support for progressive causes like abortion and LGBTQ rights.[18] At a private bank-industry conference in January 2023, Republican House Speaker Kevin McCarthy—an outspoken critic of so-called woke capitalism—interrupted Jamie Dimon when the JPMorgan Chase CEO began opining about politics. "Why don't you just focus on running your bank," McCarthy barked. By late 2022, the two most powerful Republicans in the House of Representatives, Kevin McCarthy and Steve Scalise, no longer permitted officials from the US Chamber of Commerce to visit their offices.[19] The banishment came after the country's largest business lobbying organization reversed a

502 | The Wolves of K Street

tradition of supporting mostly Republican candidates for Congress and instead endorsed two dozen vulnerable Democratic lawmakers in the 2020 election. "The Chamber left the party a long time ago," McCarthy told Breitbart News in 2022. "I just assume they have as much influence in the future as they do now—none."[20]

Such rebukes stand in sharp contrast to the deference with which previous Republican leaders treated corporations. Less than ten years earlier, then–Republican House Speaker John Boehner held a weekly lunch in the US Capitol with business executives and industry lobbyists where, as a group, they traded information and plotted out ways to enact pro-business policies.

But while the collapse of the pro-business policy consensus brings to an end a four-decade period in which commercial interests exercised extraordinary influence over our democracy, it does not represent the death knell for corporate power in Washington. The Big Business lobby retains an enormous financial advantage over its political adversaries; in 2022 the fifteen top-spending corporations and trade associations plowed a total of $415 million into lobbying. It's certainly true that the GOP's break with Big Business, as well as the rise of corporate animus inside the Democratic Party, have scrambled corporate America's influence-peddling playbook. Yet the same structural imbalance that brought Big Business to power in the late 1970s—a thriving corporate sector versus a weak coalition of unions, environmental advocates, and consumer groups—remains equally present today.

What would it take for that to change? Ironically, the political realignments of the Trump years have offered new hope for reinvigorating what was once America's marquee "countervailing" force, organized labor. While the anticorporate backlash has created areas of agreement among progressive Democrats and populist Republicans on key economic matters, the blood feuds of the culture wars will likely prevent these two sides from establishing a durable working coalition on their own. Labor unions, however, could provide a vehicle for these rival groups to join forces and advocate for their shared interests. Organized labor is in an extraordinarily weak position; only 10 percent of American workers belonged to unions in 2022, an all-time low.[21] Still, that same year, public approval of unions hit a fifty-seven-year high,[22] with 71 percent of Americans expressing a favorable view, a figure that slipped slightly, to 67 percent, in 2023. Though Trump was by no means a pro-union president, approval of unions among Republicans increased from 26 percent in 2011 to 47 percent in 2023.[23] With an improved perception among its voters, as well as an eagerness on the part of its lawmakers to project solidarity with blue collar workers, it is possible the party of Lincoln will bring to an end—or at least de-escalate— its forever war against organized labor. That alone won't resurrect union power, but it could be a first step in restoring the political clout that organized labor enjoyed in the 1960s and early 1970s, when it had the size and strength to offset the influence of Big Business in Washington.

Regardless of whether it leads to a revival of union power or not, the ungluing of the pro-business consensus has already ushered in a period of change and uncertainty for Washington's lobbying industry. Yet adapting to change is nothing new for corporate influence peddlers. Indeed, the history of K Street is one of continued evolution and persistent ingenuity. When old-fashioned shoe leather lobbying became less effective, operatives pioneered new tools to influence lawmakers through their constituents back home in their districts. When lawmakers banned corporations from sending six-figure checks to political parties, lobbyists discovered how to collect bundles of $1,000 and $2,000 checks and deliver them to members of Congress. When Washington enacted new lobbying disclosure requirements in the wake of the Jack Abramoff scandals, many DC insiders simply deregistered as lobbyists and became "shadow lobbyists." No matter what new obstacles have emerged, K Street has always managed to invent new ways to exercise its power over Washington.

Our current moment is no different. The unwinding of the pro-business consensus won't doom Washington lobbyists. It will simply force them to innovate once again: to develop new alliances, tools, and tactics to advance their agenda in a changing capital city. It will also, of course, require new people. A new set of power brokers and lobbying dynasties to define a new era. New fortunes to be made, new rules to be broken. New stories to be told.

Epilogue

Tommy Boggs was buried at the Congressional Cemetery in Washington, DC,[1] a small burial ground on the banks of the Anacostia River, about two miles from the US Capitol. He rests alongside a stone memorial to his late father, the former House majority leader Hale Boggs. Each year on the anniversary of his death, dozens of former colleagues gather at the Palm to share drinks and memories.

In March 2023 **Paul Manafort** agreed to fork over more than $3 million to settle a DOJ civil lawsuit alleging that he didn't report more than twenty overseas bank accounts that he'd possessed while working in Ukraine years earlier.[2] Manafort's lawyer, Jeffrey Neiman, told Axios that while his client could have fought the government in court, he preferred to put his entanglement with Special Counsel Robert Mueller behind him. "Paul has moved on," the lawyer said.[3]

One year earlier, CNN obtained footage from a team of Danish filmmakers, who were working on a documentary about **Roger Stone**, which showed that the former lobbyist and longtime Trump advisor was talking about discrediting the results of the 2020 election even before the votes were tabulated.[4] "Fuck the voting, let's get right to the violence," Stone said at one point.[5] The footage was turned over to the House committee that investigated the January 6th attack on the US Capitol.

The third member of the old Black, Manafort & Stone team, **Charlie Black**, recently stepped down as chairman of the lobbying enterprise he formed in the 1990s, following the breakup of the original partnership. Black's firm, most recently called Prime Policy Group, represented a range of corporate clients, including AT&T and FedEx. In 2010 Black was elected to the Hall of Fame of the American Association of Political Consultants. Unlike his ex-partners, Black remains sharply critical of Trump. "He tried to overthrow the government," Black said. One of Black's former lobbying partners, Howard S. Liebengood, was the father of a US Capitol police officer who responded to the Capitol on January 6. Three days after the attack, his son, Officer Howie C. Liebengood, committed suicide.

In late 2021, about four years after the collapse of his firm, **Tony Podesta** returned to the lobbying business, earning $1 million by helping a controversial Chinese company, Huawei Technologies,[6] build inroads with the Biden administration despite its suspected ties to the Chinese government. Podesta's other recent lobbying clients include a Bulgarian oil-and-gas firm and the government of Libya. In May 2022 the National Gallery of Art named Tony Podesta one of its biggest all-time benefactors, carving his name into one of the gallery's marble walls. Roughly a year later, Podesta was married for a third time. Only one member of Congress—California Representative Anna Eshoo—attended the ceremony. In early 2024, Podesta sold his Kalorama home for $8.2 million.

After **Evan Morris**'s death, Morris's wife, Tracy, and Evan Morris's estate reached a settlement agreement with Genentech for money the company believed was stolen. Settlements were also reached with the IRS and Commonwealth of Virginia, which claimed they were owed taxes on some of Morris's illegal income. No one was charged with any crimes related to his embezzlement.

Tracy Morris sold the couple's Virginia home for $1.4 million and moved away from Washington with her children. She resumed her teaching career and recently purchased a modest home near her parents. She doesn't want the public to know where she lives.

Jim Courtovich remains an influence peddler in Washington. His most lucrative client, the government of Qatar, increased its contract with Courtovich's firm to $55,000 per month in June 2022. For a time, FARA reports he filed showed that he regularly contacted the reporters who attended his parties to promote Qatar's interests. But in 2022, he stopped filing the required foreign-agent disclosure reports, even as, according to his social media accounts, he continued to advance the interests of Qatar. But his business is not what it once was; one recent employee said that there was so little work to do that he eventually quit. Courtovich's onetime Saudi investors continue to pursue a lawsuit against him for the $4 million they say that he swindled from them in early 2015. Courtovich has disputed the claims. Recently, he turned his Capitol Hill town house into a rental property and sold the Sullivan's Island beach house.

When asked for his response to the facts and allegations contained in this book, Courtovich responded with a series of emails and text messages, including:

"You're a fucking moron who lives in shitsville."

"Im coming after you full guns and that's why I live where I do and why you live where you do. And that's why I've never worked in a cubicle or taken the metro."

"We are going to the mattress and like everything in my life I will win."

After serving forty-five days in prison as part of the reduced sentence he received in exchange for cooperating in the Mueller investigation, **Rick Gates** launched a new consulting company, Tungsten LLC, to help companies navigate Washington.[7] In October 2020 Gates told *Politico* that his firm had two clients but he refused to name them.[8] He's also an adjunct professor at Regent University, in Virginia Beach, Virginia, where he's taught classes on political communications and political campaigns. He no longer speaks with Paul Manafort.

Heather Podesta now runs the fifth largest lobbying firm in Washington. The $38 million in lobbying revenue that her firm, Invariant, earned in 2022 was more than the lobbying fees reported by either Tommy Boggs's old firm, Squire Patton Boggs, her former husband's firm, or the firm run by Charlie Black. In the years after her 2014 divorce from Tony Podesta, her firm has represented more than two hundred corporate clients, including Apple, Home Depot and Elon Musk's SpaceX. In 2017 she paid $7.7 million for a sprawling mountain lodge in Santa Monica whose visitors over the decades included Walt Disney and Clark Gable.[9] Last fall, she married her Hollywood boyfriend.

Vin Weber remains a partner at Mercury Public Affairs in Washington, DC. He was not charged with any crimes in relation to his work with Paul Manafort and Tony Podesta for the government of Ukraine. He remains a respected figure in the Republican Party.

Tony Coelho went on to become one of the main sponsors of the Americans with Disabilities Act, the landmark legislation that President George H. W. Bush signed in 1990. Following his departure from Capitol Hill, Coelho worked for an investment fund on Wall Street. He served as chairman of the Epilepsy Foundation and in 2020 was a vice-chair of the Democratic National Convention that nominated President Joe Biden.

Ed Newberry is now the global managing partner of the renamed Squire Patton Boggs, taking over when Jim Maiwurm retired not long after the merger. Many of the firm's lobbyists still work out of the old Patton Boggs office near Georgetown. In keeping with his wishes, Boggs's office has not been touched since he died.

Jeff Zeleny, who has never been accused of wrongdoing, remains a senior national correspondent for CNN. He and Jim Courtovich are no longer dating.

Amid the collapse of the Podesta Group, **Kimberley Fritts** left the firm and started a new lobbying shop, Cogent Strategies, bringing with her a number of senior Podesta Group lobbyists and clients.[10] Today Cogent is among Washington's most influential woman-owned lobbying enterprises.

In March 2019, more than fifty years after he first made his name as a consumer activist, **Ralph Nader**'s twenty-four-year-old grandniece was killed when a Boeing 737 Max jet crashed after taking off from the Ethiopian capital of Addis Ababa.[11] The incident followed a similar disaster less than five months earlier, when another Boeing 737 Max jet crashed near Indonesia.[12] All told, 346 people died. In the wake of the tragedies, Nader urged key figures in Washington to increase federal oversight of airplane safety.[13] Though he lacks the political clout that he exercised in the 1960s and 1970s, during the heyday of the consumer movement, Nader's ongoing efforts to address the outsized sway of corporations on our democracy serve as a reminder of a bygone era. A time when Washington's most influential advocates used their power on behalf of everyday Americans.

Acknowledgments

From Both Authors

It took an entire universe of sources, editors, fact-checkers, and loved ones to get this book out into the world. We are grateful to every one of them.

Our original editor at Simon & Schuster, Priscilla Painton, saw what this book could be long before we did. She gave us the time and space to do it right—so much time, in fact, that she was promoted to editor-in-chief long before we turned in the manuscript! Though Priscilla, thankfully, continued to advise us throughout the project, her promotion provided us the great pleasure of working with an additional Simon & Schuster editor, Megan Hogan—a brilliant thinker, elegant writer, and absolute delight of a human. Their talents and care are imprinted on every page.

Throughout the project, we felt the warm support of Simon & Schuster CEO Jonathan Karp, who joined our original pitch meeting and was making tweaks to the front cover right up to the last minute. Our agent, Richard Pine of InkWell Management, guided us through the daunting process of selling our first book proposal, and he remained at our side until the final comma was in place. We are indebted to both.

When it comes to the story itself, Michael Podhorzer first showed us the glass display case containing the several dozen pens that President Johnson used during the 1960s to sign much of the Great Society legislation. This revelation opened our eyes to what had been possible in Washington before corporate interests took power and, in many ways, set us off on our reporting journey.

We are indebted to the many lobbyists, lawyers, and insiders who generously shared their time to get the story right, including Tony Podesta, Charlie Black, Doug Boggs, Ed Newberry, Peter Kelly, and John Donaldson, as well as the scores of current and former employees of the companies and lobbying firms we write about.

From there, we were aided by the generosity of other journalists and scholars, who provided their published works as source material and offered their time to assist our research. Burt Solomon gave us unpublished transcripts of interviews with Tommy Boggs, which he'd conducted while writing *The Washington Century.* Rick Perlstein sent us early drafts of his book *Reaganland.* Lee Drutman, the author of *The Business of America Is Lobbying,* met us for lunch to discuss his research. Kim Phillips-Fein, the author of *Invisible Hands,* responded to questions over email. Franklin Foer, who wrote the 2018 article "Paul Manafort, American Hustler" for the *Atlantic,* provided helpful thoughts.

Other books that were foundational to our research include: David Vogel's *Fluctuating Fortunes;* Thomas Edsall's *The New Politics of Inequality;* John B. Judis's *The Paradox of American Democracy;* Benjamin C. Waterhouse's *Lobbying America;* John Brady's *Bad Boy;* Brooks Jackson's *Honest Graft;* Jacob Hacker and Paul Pierson's *Winner-Take-All Politics;* and David Broder and Haynes Johnson's *The System.* We can only hope that one day, some other first-time author might turn to this book for help in understanding a complex subject, the way we have looked to theirs.

Our raw manuscript only became publishable through the skill and attention of fact-checkers Justine Makieli and Aishvarya Kavi, attorney Carolyn Levin, copyeditor Phil Bashe, proofreader Ben Lubitz, and the terrific folks in Simon & Schuster's design department. We're also grateful to the *Wall Street Journal* and *Washingtonian* magazine, which provided the support and flexibility necessary to complete this project.

Most of all, though, we'd like to thank our family. Our younger brother, John, is the pride and joy of the Mullins clan. His wife, Gillian, is the sister we never had. Their children—Keaveny, Reid, and Quinn—are fabulous nieces, nephews, and cousins. Gillian's family—Barbara, Mike, Doug, his wife, Sara, and their daughter, Lila—is an extension of our own. We felt your support each and every day.

Last but not least, Mom and Dad. You are our inspiration, our role models, and our best friends. Though it doesn't begin to repay all you've done for us, this book is dedicated to you.

We love you.

From Luke

I've had the good fortune of learning from a number of talented editors over the years; I'm particularly grateful to Alan Kline, James Bock, Jim Pethokoukis, Garrett Graff, Denise Willis, Kristen Hinman, Michael Schaffer, Sherri Dalphonse, Patrick Hruby, and Bill O'Sullivan. But my most influential teacher has always been my older brother.

When I was still trying to figure out what to do with my life, Brody made me want to be a reporter. He's since become my best editor and my biggest cheerleader. Teaming up with you on this book, Brody, has been the time of my life. I can't thank you enough, and I love you.

I wouldn't be here today if it weren't for Dr. Katherine A. Thornton, Mary Cox, and the wonderful staff at Sibley Memorial Hospital and the Sidney Kimmel Comprehensive Cancer Center at Johns Hopkins. I'm also indebted to everyone who has looked after my health in the years since, especially Dr. Christian Meyer, Dr. Steven A. Burka, and Carole Palmer.

I'm grateful to my wife's parents, Ethel and Pat Lennon, who allowed us to live in their home in Lewes, Delaware, for two years during the Covid pandemic. Ethel, Pat, and the rest of the Grenache Court gang made us feel right at home as we chipped away at this book.

I'd like to thank our wonderful son, Sean, who communicates joy more effectively than any writer ever could. I am so proud of you, bud. I'm also incredibly grateful for the many folks that have done so much to help Sean— and his parents—over the past few years, including: Taylor Scantling, Lane Thimmesch, Catherine Gaddis, Tykia Owens, Bersabeh Miliard, Alexis Seidner, Octavia Carpenter, Janae Jones, Keisha Knight, Masi Preston, Rachel Riback, Stephanie Yoo, Coleen Bennett, Destany Moore, Hanh Twitchell, Masha Tulush, Alice Mohrman, Kaitlynn Wagner, Juliana Bonilla, Corinne Zmoos, and Jane Mikkelson. Your efforts mean everything to us.

Finally, this book simply would not have been possible without the enduring support of my extraordinary wife. Christina, you are the best mother on the planet and the love of my life. Thanks for all the kindness, patience, strength, and encouragement you've provided over the past ten years. I couldn't do it without you. I love you.

From Brody

This book is a culmination of more than twenty years covering the ways businesses play the game of political influence. There are a lot of people who helped make that happen, such as Paul Warren, who gave me my first job at *Communications Daily,* and Lou Peck, who let me cover Capitol Hill for the first time for *Congress Daily.* Jim VandeHei and John Bresnahan inspired me to move to *Roll Call,* where I worked alongside amazing reporters like Ben Pershing, Paul Kane, Chris Cillizza, Mark Preston, Tory Newmyer, Anna Palmer, Erin Billings, and many others.

The money in politics reporting of Glenn Simpson and John Wilke drew me to the *Wall Street Journal,* where I was hired by the world's best bureau chief, Jerry Seib, who produced great journalists and good people. At the *Journal,* I worked for fantastic editors, such as John Harwood, Nik Deogun, Jake Schlesinger, David Wessel, Jeanne Cummings, Aaron Zitner, Matthew Rose, Jay Sapsford, and John Corrigan. I also want to thank several New York editors, including the indomitable investigative editor (and bridezilla) Mike Siconolfi, Sam Enriquez, Mike Allen, Dan Kelly, and Mitch Pacelle. Each helped craft stories at the *Journal* that became the seeds for this book. Paul Beckett and Matt Murray have my gratitude for blessing this project.

During my time at the *Journal,* I have had the pleasure to work with some of the best reporters in political journalism, including Michael Phillips, Rebecca Ballhaus, Patrick O'Connor, Susan Davis, Neil King, Ted Mann, Julie Bykowicz, Mary Jacoby, Tom Catan, Elizabeth Williamson, Chris Cooper, Chris Conkey, Sara Murray, Evan Perez, Damian Paletta, Kara Scannell, Devlin Barrett, Aruna Viswanatha, Jake Sherman, Susan Pulliam, Adam Entous, Julian Barnes, John McKinnon, Janet Adamy, T. W.

Farnam, Danny Yadron, Jim Oberman, Tom McGinty, Josh Mitchell, James Grimaldi, Joe Palazzolo, Chad Day, and John West. Each has taught me in different ways and contributed to this book. I thank you all.

My career is largely owed to the hundreds of lobbyists, lawyers, campaign finance experts, executives, union officials, media consultants, government officials, and other Washington insiders who have trusted me enough to share their stories, insights, and anecdotes. I would name you all—but I don't want to get you in trouble.

This book is dedicated to our parents, Mary and Jim. But we could not have succeeded without the support, love, and encouragement from other family members.

I wrote several early outlines and drafts from my father-in-law's beach house on the Jersey Shore during the Covid pandemic. I want to thank Big Dave for his indulgence and patience (as well as our late night-strategy sessions that regularly resulted in too many cocktails). Thank you to Joe, Audrey, and Vivie LeStrange for their support, as well as my mother-in-law, Patti, who has endured endless fact-checking calls since moving in with us in Washington.

My children—Nola, Navy, and Bobby—sat patiently (and quietly) through scores of boring phone interviews that I conducted from the kitchen table or driver's seat while shuffling them to or from school, sports practices, and playdates. Nola: You are the best first child I could ever have and my shining light. You have taught me to be empathetic, caring, and do the right thing. Navy: You taught me to be tough, to stand up for I want—and never back down. Bobby: You make me smile like you will never know. My wife, Lauren, has endured seven years' worth of repeated stories about the people in this book. Lauren: You are the love of my life, my support—and my best friend. I hope I have made you all proud.

Finally, I want to thank another member of my family: my brother Luke. Without Luke's help, this book would have been a shadow of itself. Through his wizardry, Luke transformed what would have been a drab history of lobbying into a vibrant narrative full of colorful characters. He is a brilliant writer with an unmatched eye for narrative storytelling. I could not have asked for a better partner (or brother)—and I will always be thankful (and blessed) for the time we spent together. I love you, Luke.

Notes

This book is based on interviews with hundreds of people with direct knowledge of the events depicted as well as thousands of pages of public records, including court filings, divorce filings, policy reports, lobbying disclosure reports, foreign agent disclosures, newspaper accounts, and high school yearbooks. All living individuals named in this book have been contacted and asked for their comments or responses. None of the companies named were implicated in any wrongdoing.

Prologue

1. "Police Report Supplement Regarding Death of Evan Morris," Federal Bureau of Investigation, Washington Field Office.
2. Ibid.
3. "Our Story," Robert Trent Jones Golf Club online, https://www.rtjgc.com/history.
4. Dave Anderson, "Robert Trent Jones Sr., Golf Course Architect Who Made Mark on U.S. Open, Is Dead at 93," *New York Times* online, June 16, 2000, https://www .nytimes.com/2000/06/16/sports/robert-trent-jones-sr-golf-course-architect-who -made-mark-us-open-dead-93.html.
5. Herbert Warren Wind, "A First Look: The World's Most Exclusive Golf Course," *Sports Illustrated* online, January 24, 1955, https://vault.si.com/vault/1955/01/24/a -first-look-worlds-most-exclusive-golf-course.
6. "History: More Than 25 Years of Competition and Excitement," Presidents Cup online, https://www.presidentscup.com/history.
7. Kate Bennett, "Obama Joins Private Golf Club in Virginia," CNN online, last modified May 15, 2017, https://www.cnn.com/2017/05/15/politics/obama-robert-trent -jones-golf-club/index.html.
8. Brody Mullins, "The Rise and Fall of a K Street Renegade," *Wall Street Journal* online, February 13, 2017, https://www.wsj.com/articles/the-rise-and-fall-of-a-k-street-ren egade-1487001918.
9. "Police Report Supplement Regarding Death," Federal Bureau of Investigation, Washington Field Office.

10. Ibid.
11. Brody Mullins, "Rise and Fall of a K Street Renegade."
12. Brody Mullins, "When the Party's Over: Washington's Premier Social Connector Fades from View," *Wall Street Journal* online, January 2, 2020, https://www.wsj.com/articles/when-the-partys-over-washingtons-premier-social-connector-fades-from-view-11577997343.

Introduction
1. Robert C. Byrd, "Lobbyists" (transcript of speech delivered to the US Senate, September 28, 1987, United States Senate online, last modified 1989, https://www.senate.gov/legislative/common/briefing/Byrd_History_Lobbying.htm).
2. Ibid.
3. "Historical Highlights: The Crédit Mobilier Scandal," United States House of Representatives, History, Art & Archives online, accessed March 15, 2023, https://history.house.gov/HistoricalHighlight/Detail/35789.
4. John B. Judis, *The Paradox of American Democracy: Elites, Special Interests, and the Betrayal of Public Trust* (New York: Routledge, 2001), 38.
5. Lee Drutman, *The Business of America Is Lobbying: How Corporations Became Politicized and Politics Became More Corporate* (Oxford: Oxford University Press, 2015), 49.
6. Ibid., 50.
7. Ibid., 55.
8. Ibid.; Jacob Hacker and Paul Pierson, *Winner-Take-All Politics: How Washington Made the Rich Richer—and Turned Its Back on the Middle Class* (New York: Simon & Schuster, 2010), 90–91.
9. Hacker and Pierson, *Winner-Take-All Politics*, 90–91.
10. "Federalist Papers: Primary Documents in American History," Library of Congress online, accessed October 17, 2023, https://guides.loc.gov/federalist-papers/full-text.
11. "A History of Lobbying in the U.S.," OpenSecrets online, last modified July 2014, https://www.opensecrets.org/resources/learn/lobbying_timeline.php.
12. Hacker and Pierson, *Winner-Take-All Politics*, 41–72.
13. Timothy Noah, *The Great Divergence: America's Growing Inequality Crisis and What We Can Do About It* (New York: Bloomsbury Press, 2012), 122.
14. Hacker and Pierson, *Winner-Take-All Politics*, 41–136.
15. Franklin Foer, "Paul Manafort, American Hustler," *Atlantic* online, March 2018, https://www.theatlantic.com/magazine/archive/2018/03/paul-manafort-american-hustler/550925; "Lobbying Data Summary," OpenSecrets online, accessed March 16, 2023, https://www.opensecrets.org/federal-lobbying.
16. Gerhard Peters, "Federal Budget Receipts and Outlays: Coolidge–Biden," American Presidency Project, last updated May 28, 2021, https://www.presidency.ucsb.edu/statistics/data/federal-budget-receipts-and-outlays.

17. Drutman, *Business of America Is Lobbying*, 14.

18. Hacker and Pierson, *Winner-Take-All Politics*, 41–136.

19. Martin Gilens and Benjamin I. Page, "Testing Theories of American Politics: Elites, Interest Groups, and Average Citizens," *Perspectives on Politics* 12, no. 3 (September 2014): 564–81, https://doi.org/10.1017/S1537592714001595.

20. Drutman, *Business of America Is Lobbying*, 26–28.

21. Thomas Byrne Edsall, *The New Politics of Inequality* (New York: W. W. Norton, 1984), 202–3.

22. Ibid.

23. David Vogel, *Fluctuating Fortunes: The Political Power of Business in America* (New York: Basic Books, 1989), 287.

24. Drutman, *Business of America Is Lobbying*, 9.

25. Ibid., 49.

26. Kim Phillips-Fein, "The Long Unraveling of the Republican Party," *Atlantic* online, September 6, 2022, https://www.theatlantic.com/magazine/archive/2022/10/republican-party-extremist-history-hemmer-continetti-milbank-books/671248.

27. Hacker and Pierson, *Winner-Take-All Politics*, 41–72.

28. "Income Inequality, USA, 1820–2021," World Inequality Database online, accessed March 16, 2023, https://wid.world/country/usa.

29. House Select Committee on Economic Disparity and Fairness in Growth, *Bridging the Divide: Building an Economy That Works for All* (Washington, DC: US Government Publishing Office, December 12, 2022, https://www.govinfo.gov/content/pkg/CRPT-117hrpt619/pdf/CRPT-117hrpt619.pdf).

30. Nik Popli, "Income Inequality in America Hasn't Risen in a Decade. It May Not Feel Like It," *Time* online, October 5, 2022, https://time.com/6220111/income-inequality-us-2/.

31. Alana Semuels, "American Inequality Is (Finally) Lessening," *Time* online, March 31, 2023, https://time.com/6267552/falling-american-inequality/.

32. Reid Epstein, "As Faith Flags in U.S. Government, Many Voters Want to Upend the System," *New York Times*, July 13, 2022; David Leonhardt, "A Crisis Coming," *New York Times*, September 17, 2022.

33. Judis, *Paradox of American Democracy*, 11.

Chapter 1

1. Burt Solomon, *The Washington Century: Three Families and the Shaping of the Nation's Capital* (New York: Harper Perennial, 2005), 244.

2. Alessandra Stanley, "C. Wyatt Dickerson, Businessman and Man About Washington, Is Dead at 92," *New York Times* online, December 3, 2016, https://www.nytimes.com/2016/12/03/us/c-wyatt-dickerson-dead.html?searchResultPosition=5.

3. Ibid.

4. Ibid.

5. Solomon, *Washington Century*, 383.

6. Ibid., 244.

7. Lindy Boggs and Katherine Hatch, *Washington Through a Purple Veil: Memoirs of a Southern Woman* (New York: Harcourt Brace, 1994), 246–47.

8. Solomon, *Washington Century*, 129.

9. Boggs and Hatch, *Washington Through a Purple Veil*, 183–84.

10. Ibid., 246–47.

11. Ibid.

12. Ibid., 247.

13. Ibid., 250–51.

14. Ibid., 247–48.

15. Richard Norton Smith, *An Ordinary Man: The Surprising Life and Historic Presidency of Gerald R. Ford* (New York: Harper, 2023).

16. Boggs and Hatch, *Washington Through a Purple Veil*, 248.

17. Solomon, *Washington Century*, 245.

18. Ibid., 39–40.

19. Ibid., 88; Boggs and Hatch, *Washington Through a Purple Veil*, 103.

20. Joseph C. Goulden, *The Money Lawyers: The No-Holds-Barred World of Today's Richest and Most Powerful Lawyers* (New York: Truman Talley Books, 2006), 64–65.

21. Philip Shabecoff, "Big Business on the Offensive," *New York Times* online, December 9, 1979, https://www.nytimes.com/1979/12/09/archives/big-business-on-the-offensive.html.

22. Burt Solomon graciously shared interview notes and tape recordings with the authors, including many transcripts of his interviews with Barbara Boggs, Tommy Boggs, and others that the authors have used in this book.

23. Solomon, *Washington Century*, 36–41; Boggs and Hatch, *Washington Through a Purple Veil*, vii, 43.

24. Boggs and Hatch, *Washington Through a Purple Veil*, 43.

25. Solomon, *Washington Century*, 37–38.

26. Roger H. Davidson, Susan Hammond, and Raymond Smock, eds., *Masters of the House: Congressional Leadership over Two Centuries* (New York: Routledge, 1998), 224.

27. Solomon, *Washington Century*, 37.

28. Ibid., 40.

29. Boggs and Hatch, *Washington Through a Purple Veil*, 51–52.

30. Solomon, *Washington Century*, 41.

31. Boggs and Hatch, *Washington Through a Purple Veil*, 72.

32. Solomon, *Washington Century*, 41.

33. Ibid., 35–36.

34. Ibid.

35. William E. Leuchtenburg, "Franklin D. Roosevelt: The American Franchise," University

of Virginia Miller Center online, https://millercenter.org/president/fdroosevelt/the-american-franchise.

36. Boggs and Hatch, *Washington Through a Purple Veil*, 78.

37. Ibid., 74.

38. Solomon, *Washington Century*, 110.

39. Ibid., 87.

40. Ibid., 48.

41. Rosemary James and Philip Moreton, "The Majority Leader: A Short History of a Controversial Man," *New Orleans*, July 1971, as published in the *Congressional Record: Proceedings and Debates of the 92nd Congress, First Session*, 117, pt. 23, *August 5, 1971, to September 8, 1971*, 30,834.

42. Boggs and Hatch, *Washington Through a Purple Veil*, 139–41.

43. Solomon, *Washington Century*, 81.

44. Ibid., 117–19.

45. Ibid., 119.

46. Stephanie Mansfield, "A Boggs Political Dynasty," *Washington Post* online, May 21, 1982, https://www.washingtonpost.com/archive/lifestyle/1982/05/21/a-boggs-political-dynasty/8cb97666-0beb-4eef-a1ea-9ad78d26a717.

47. Boggs and Hatch, *Washington Through a Purple Veil*, 166.

48. Solomon, *Washington Century*, 141.

49. Ibid.

50. Hale Boggs, recorded interview by Charles T. Morrissey, May 10, 1964, 33, John F. Kennedy Library Oral History Program.

51. Solomon, *Washington Century*, 143.

52. Ibid., 117.

53. Goulden, *Money Lawyers*, 65.

54. Ibid.

55. Ibid., 66; Solomon, *Washington Century*, 168–69.

56. Solomon, *Washington Century*, 169.

57. Ibid.

58. Goulden, *Money Lawyers*, 66.

59. David McKean, *Tommy the Cork: Washington's Ultimate Insider from Roosevelt to Reagan* (Hanover, NH: Steerforth Press, 2003), 70.

60. Ibid., 147.

61. Douglas Frantz and Dean McKean, *Friends in High Places: The Rise and Fall of Clark Clifford* (New York: Little, Brown, 1995), 42–43, 62.

62. Ibid., 9, 214.

63. Ibid., 165–73.

64. Joseph C. Goulden, *The Superlawyers* (New York: Weybright and Talley, 1971), 71.

65. Lee Drutman, *The Business of America Is Lobbying: How Corporations Became Politicized and Politics Became More Corporate* (Oxford: Oxford University Press, 2015), 51.

66. David Vogel, *Fluctuating Fortunes: The Political Power of Business in America* (New York: Basic Books, 1989), 34.

67. Ibid., 33.

68. Drutman, *Business of America Is Lobbying*, 53–54.

69. Vogel, *Fluctuating Fortunes*, 7.

70. Drutman, *Business of America Is Lobbying*, 50–51.

71. Vogel, *Fluctuating Fortunes*, 96.

72. Ibid.

73. Kim Phillips-Fein, *Invisible Hands: The Businessmen's Crusade Against the New Deal* (New York: W. W. Norton, 2009), xi.

74. Mark Mizruchi, *The Fracturing of the American Corporate Elite* (Cambridge, MA: Harvard University Press, 2013), 94–96.

75. Ibid., 98.

76. Ibid., 94.

77. Phillips-Fein, *Invisible Hands*, xi.

78. Vogel, *Fluctuating Fortunes*, 24–25.

79. Ibid.

80. Ibid.

81. Ibid., 25.

82. Mizruchi, *Fracturing of the American Corporate Elite*, 76.

83. Vogel, *Fluctuating Fortunes*, 25.

84. Benjamin C. Waterhouse, *Lobbying America: The Politics of Business from Nixon to NAFTA* (Princeton, NJ: Princeton University Press, 2014), 18–20.

85. Mizruchi, *Fracturing of the American Corporate Elite*, 81–110; Waterhouse, *Lobbying America*, 18–20.

86. Waterhouse, *Lobbying America*, 18–20.

87. Ibid.

88. Vogel, *Fluctuating Fortunes*, 25.

89. John B. Judis, *The Paradox of American Democracy: Elites, Special Interests, and the Betrayal of Public Trust* (New York: Routledge, 2001), 83.

90. Thomas Whiteside, *The Investigation of Ralph Nader: General Motors vs. One Determined Man* (New York: Pocket Books, 1972), 3–30.

91. United States Senate Subcommittee on Executive Reorganization of the Committee of Government Operations, 89th Congress, July 1965, Washington: US Government Printing Office, 1966, 780.

92. Vogel, *Fluctuating Fortunes*, 43–44.

93. Whiteside, *Investigation of Ralph Nader*, 3–30.

94. Ibid.

95. Ibid.

96. Ibid.

97. Ibid.

98. Ibid.
99. Ibid.
100. Ibid.
101. Ibid.
102. Vogel, *Fluctuating Fortunes*, 45.
103. Ibid., 46.
104. Ibid.
105. Ibid., 44.
106. Drutman, *Business of America Is Lobbying*, 56.
107. Vogel, *Fluctuating Fortunes*, 13, 38.
108. Ibid., 55.
109. Ibid.
110. Drutman, *Business of America Is Lobbying*, 55; Vogel, *Fluctuating Fortunes*, 146.
111. Vogel, *Fluctuating Fortunes*, 59–61.
112. Ibid., 146.
113. Ibid., 94.
114. Davidson, Hammond, and Smock, *Masters of the House*, 237.
115. Ibid.
116. Solomon, *Washington Century*, 169–71.
117. Carl Bernstein, "King of the Hill," *Vanity Fair* online, March 1998, https://archive.vanityfair.com/article/1998/3/king-of-the-hill.
118. Solomon, *Washington Century*, 208–10.
119. Vogel, *Fluctuating Fortunes*, 194.
120. Ibid., 8.
121. Ibid., 8, 146.
122. Ibid., 54.
123. Ibid., 55.
124. Ibid., 55–56.
125. Ibid., 57.
126. Ibid., 55–56.
127. Ibid., 56–57.
128. Phillips-Fein, *Invisible Hands*, 151.
129. Steven V. Roberts, "Bank of America Big Coast Target," *New York Times* online, May 16, 1971, https://www.nytimes.com/1971/05/16/archives/bank-of-america-big-coast-target-for-bombers-and-critics-its-a.html.
130. Phillips-Fein, *Invisible Hands*, 151–52.
131. Taylor Haggerty, "Forty Years Ago, a Mob of Students Stormed the Bank of America Building," *Daily Nexus* (University of California, Santa Barbara) online, February 25, 2010, https://dailynexus.com/2010-02-25/forty-years-ago-a-mob-of-students-stormed-the-bank-of-america-building/.
132. Drutman, *Business of America Is Lobbying*, 56; Vogel, *Fluctuating Fortunes*, 120–26.

133. Vogel, *Fluctuating Fortunes*, 56–57.

134. Thomas Ferguson and Joel Rogers, *Right Turn: The Decline of the Democrats and the Future of American Politics* (New York: Hill and Wang, 1986), 81.

135. Vogel, *Fluctuating Fortunes*, 123–24.

136. Ibid., 145.

137. Ibid.

138. Ibid.

139. Ibid.

140. Solomon, *Washington Century*, 215–17.

141. Ibid., 202–4.

142. Ibid.

143. Ibid., 215.

144. Ibid., 215–16.

145. Ibid., 216–17.

146. Ibid., 219–20.

147. Ibid., 221.

148. Ibid., 219–26.

149. Ibid., 221–23.

150. Ibid., 225–26.

151. Ibid., 226.

152. *Congressional Record: Proceedings and Debates of the 92nd Congress, Second Session*, 118, pt. 28, *October 16, 1972, to October 18, 1972*, 37,160.

153. Boggs and Hatch, *Washington Through a Purple Veil*, 251–56.

154. Ibid., 251–54; Solomon, *Washington Century*, 244–45.

155. Boggs and Hatch, *Washington Through a Purple Veil*, 256.

156. Isabel Goyer, "1972 Cessna 310C Alaska Disappearance of Hale Boggs and Nick Begich," *Plane & Pilot* online, August 18, 2022, https://www.planeandpilotmag.com/news/pilot-talk/1972-cessna-310c-alaska-disappearance/.

157. Boggs and Hatch, *Washington Through a Purple Veil*, 259.

158. Goulden, *Money Lawyers*, 81.

159. Solomon, *Washington Century*, 234.

Chapter 2

1. Kim Phillips-Fein, *Invisible Hands: The Businessmen's Crusade Against the New Deal* (New York: W. W. Norton, 2009), 156–60.

2. Ibid., 157.

3. Ibid.

4. Karl A. Lamb, *The People, Maybe: Seeking Democracy in America* (Belmont, CA: Wadsworth, 1971), 34.

5. Benjamin C. Waterhouse, *Lobbying America: The Politics of Business from Nixon to NAFTA* (Princeton, NJ: Princeton University Press, 2014), 58.

6. Lewis F. Powell Jr. to Eugene B. Sydnor Jr., memorandum, "Attack on American Free Enterprise System," August 23, 1971, Washington and Lee University School of Law Scholarly Commons online, Lewis F. Powell Jr. Papers, https://scholarlycommons .law.wlu.edu/powellmemo/1.

7. Phillips-Fein, *Invisible Hands*, 162–63.

8. Waterhouse, *Lobbying America*, 60.

9. Ibid., 59–61.

10. Ibid., 60–61.

11. David Vogel, *Fluctuating Fortunes: The Political Power of Business in America* (New York: Basic Books, 1989), 220.

12. Ibid., 220–21.

13. Phillips-Fein, *Invisible Hands*, 169.

14. Ibid., 169–73.

15. Vogel, *Fluctuating Fortunes*, 224.

16. Phillips-Fein, *Invisible Hands*, 162.

17. Vogel, *Fluctuating Fortunes*, 222.

18. Ibid., 221.

19. Ibid.

20. Waterhouse, *Lobbying America*, 60.

21. Ibid., 28; Phillips-Fein, *Invisible Hands*, 187.

22. Ibid.

23. Vogel, *Fluctuating Fortunes*, 207.

24. Waterhouse, *Lobbying America*, 61.

25. Ibid.

26. Vogel, *Fluctuating Fortunes*, 10–11.

27. Waterhouse, *Lobbying America*, 60.

28. Lee Drutman, *The Business of America Is Lobbying: How Corporations Became Politicized and Politics Became More Corporate* (Oxford: Oxford University Press, 2015), 57–58.

29. Ibid., 58.

30. Vogel, *Fluctuating Fortunes*, 194.

31. John B. Judis, *The Paradox of American Democracy: Elites, Special Interests, and the Betrayal of Public Trust* (New York: Routledge, 2001), 121.

32. Vogel, *Fluctuating Fortunes*, 194.

33. Joseph C. Goulden, *The Money Lawyers: The No-Holds-Barred World of Today's Richest and Most Powerful Lawyers* (New York: Truman Talley Books, 2006), 90.

34. Rick Perlstein, *Reaganland: America's Right Turn 1976–1980* (New York: Simon & Schuster, 2020), 202.

35. Emily Langar, "Michael Pertschuk, Unyielding Consumer Watchdog, Dies at 89," *Washington Post*, November 18, 2022.

36. Perlstein, *Reaganland*, 202.

37. Kirk Victor, "FTC at 100: Michael Pertschuk's Turbulent Years as FTC Chairman," *FTCWatch* online, January 15, 2015, https://www.mlexwatch.com/articles/1725 /print?section=ftcwatch.

38. Larry Kramer, "FTC Is Becoming the Consumer's Aggressive Crusader," *Washington Post* online, January 2, 1979, https://www.washingtonpost.com/archive/politics/1979/01/02 /ftc-is-becoming-the-consumers-aggressive-crusader/6b2d7c4c-055f-4571-aabd -30915b266433/.

39. Victor, "FTC at 100: Michael Pertschuk."

40. Ibid.

41. Perlstein, *Reaganland*, 245.

42. Ibid., 248.

43. Ibid., 248–49.

44. Ibid., 248.

45. Burt Solomon, *The Washington Century: Three Families and the Shaping of the Nation's Capital* (New York: Harper Perennial, 2005), 293–94.

46. Editorial Board, "The FTC as National Nanny," *Washington Post* online, March 1, 1978, https://www.washingtonpost.com/archive/politics/1978/03/01/the-ftc-as-na tional-nanny/69f778f5-8407-4df0-b0e9-7f1f8e826b3b.

47. Michael Pertschuk, "Stoning the National Nanny: Congress and the FTC in the Late 70's" (lecture before the School of Business Administration of the University of California, Berkeley, California, November 11, 1981, https://www.ftc.gov/news-events /news/speeches/stoning-national-nanny-congress-ftc-late-70s).

48. Ibid.

49. Solomon, *Washington Century*, 293.

50. Vogel, *Fluctuating Fortunes*, 203.

51. Solomon, *Washington Century*, 293.

52. Philip Shabecoff, "Big Business on the Offensive," *New York Times* online, December 9, 1979, https://www.nytimes.com/1979/12/09/archives/big-business-on-the-offensive.html.

53. Solomon, *Washington Century*, 294.

54. Victor, "FTC at 100: Michael Pertschuk."

55. Ibid.

56. Ibid.

57. Kirstin Downey and Kirk Victor, "FTC at 100: Reagan Revolution Transforms FTC in the 1980s," *FTCWatch* online, February 13, 2015, https://www.mlexwatch.com/ar ticles/1788/print?section=ftcwatch.

58. Perlstein, *Reaganland*, 773.

59. Vogel, *Fluctuating Fortunes*, 168.

60. Ibid., 197.

61. Ibid., 149–52.

62. Ibid., 160.

63. Ibid., 181–90.

64. Ibid., 176.

65. Ibid., 159.

Chapter 3

1. John Brady, *Bad Boy: The Life and Politics of Lee Atwater* (Reading, MA: Addison Wesley, 1997), xv–xix.

2. Ibid.

3. Ibid.

4. Gary Karr, "Atwater Remembered at Hometown Funeral," Associated Press online, April 2, 1991, https://apnews.com/article/c8b720b30c41e91541d53db4361b787f.

5. Thomas B. Edsall, "GOP Battler Lee Atwater Dies at 40," *Washington Post* online, March 30, 1991, https://www.washingtonpost.com/archive/politics/1991/03/30/gop-battler-lee-atwater-dies-at-40/97a948b0-2403-46d7-b5c6-bd1981afeec9.

6. George Gates, "The Sultan of Spin, and a Life of His Own Invention," *Buffalo News*, March 2, 1997.

7. Edsall, "GOP Battler Lee Atwater Dies."

8. Tom Turnipseed, "What Lee Atwater Learned," *Washington Post* online, April 16, 1991, https://www.washingtonpost.com/archive/opinions/1991/04/16/what-lee-atwater-learned/317f6237-0a2e-4ae9-880f-890ef4cc3310.

9. Brady, *Bad Boy*, 82–85.

10. "George Bush and Willie Horton," Opinion, *New York Times*, November 4, 1988, https://www.nytimes.com/1988/11/04/opinion/george-bush-and-willie-horton.html.

11. Edsall, "GOP Battler Lee Atwater Dies."

12. Ibid.

13. Thomas B. Edsall, "Atwater Is Elected Chief of RNC, Outlines Goals," *Washington Post* online, January 19, 1989, https://www.washingtonpost.com/archive/politics/1989/01/19/atwater-is-elected-chief-of-rnc-outlines-goals/bd5a6e22-7195-4da0-b70d-f868c6b1c0f2.

14. Karr, "Atwater Remembered."

15. Brady, *Bad Boy*, 268–69.

16. Ibid., 283.

17. Ibid., 284–87.

18. Ibid., 284, 299, 317.

19. Ibid., 319.

20. Ibid., 273.

21. Ibid., 318.

22. Ibid., 152.

23. Robin Toner, "Washington at Work; The New Spokesman for the Republicans: A Tough Player in a Rough Arena," *New York Times* online, July 31, 1990, https://www.nytimes.com/1990/07/31/us/washington-work-new-spokesman-for-republicans-tough-player-rough-arena.html.

24. Ibid.

25. Brady, *Bad Boy*, xvi, 279, 291.

26. Lee Bandy, Knight-Ridder Newspapers, "GOP 'Bad Boy' Atwater Says He's Found Jesus," *Chicago Tribune*, November 3, 1990.

27. Ibid.

28. Brady, *Bad Boy*, 279, 296.

29. Ibid., 287–89.

30. Associated Press, "Gravely Ill, Atwater Offers Apology," *New York Times* online, January 13, 1991, https://www.nytimes.com/1991/01/13/us/gravely-ill-atwater-offers-apology.html.

31. Brady, *Bad Boy*, xi.

32. Ibid., 321.

33. Ibid.

34. Monica Langley, "Black, Manafort & Stone Cuts Controversial Path Between Campaign Consulting and Lobbying," *Wall Street Journal*, December 23, 1985.

35. Ibid.

36. Franklin Foer, "Paul Manafort, American Hustler," *Atlantic* online, March 2018, https://www.theatlantic.com/magazine/archive/2018/03/paul-manafort-american-hustler/550925.

37. Ibid.

38. Evan Thomas, "The Slickest Shop in Town," *Time* online, March 3, 1986, https://content.time.com/time/subscriber/article/0,33009,960803,00.html.

39. Foer, "Paul Manafort."

40. Clark Porteous, "Battle Begins for Leadership in GOP Meeting," *Memphis Press-Scimitar*, June 8, 1977.

41. Foer, "Paul Manafort."

42. *The MacNeil/Lehrer Report*, "Young Republicans," aired June 8, 1977, available at the American Archive of Public Broadcasting, http://americanarchive.org/catalog/cpb-aacip-507-0z70v8b41f.

43. Foer, "Paul Manafort."

44. Ibid.

45. "About: Past Chairmen," Young Republicans National Federation online, accessed March 26, 2023, https://www.yrnf.com/about.

46. Brian Whitson, "U.S. Secretary of Defense Robert M. Gates ('65) to Address William and Mary Graduates During Commencement Exercises May 20, 2007," news release, April 30, 2007, College of William and Mary online, https://www.wm.edu/news/stories/2007/u.s.-secretary-of-defense-robert-m.-gates-65-to-address-william-and-mary-graduates-during-commencement-exercises-may-20,-2007.php.

47. Foer, "Paul Manafort."

48. Ibid.

49. Ibid.

50. Ibid.

51. Porteous, "Battle Begins for Leadership in GOP Meeting."

52. Les Seago, "Roger Stone Elected President of Young Republicans," Associated Press, June 10, 1977.

53. Foer, "Paul Manafort."

54. Paul Manafort, *Political Prisoner: Persecuted, Prosecuted, but Not Silenced* (New York: Skyhorse, 2022), 15–16.

55. Ibid.,16.

56. Foer, "Paul Manafort."

57. "Former New Britain Mayor Paul Manafort Dies," *Hartford (CT) Courant* online, January 25, 2013, https://www.courant.com/2013/01/25/former-new-britain-mayor-paul-manafort-dies.

58. "Connecticut City Weighs Changing Manafort Street Name," Associated Press online, September 26, 2018, https://apnews.com/article/1a98be7e479743e1adde24ab63541d14.

59. Manafort, *Political Prisoner*, 17.

60. Ibid., 18.

61. Christopher Keating and Don Stacom, "Manafort's 40-Year Journey to the Trump Campaign," *Hartford (CT) Courant*, October 31, 2017.

62. Foer, "Paul Manafort."

63. Theodore A. Driscoll and Tom Barnes, "Paul Manafort Tied to Perjury," *Hartford (CT) Courant*, July 12, 1981.

64. Foer, "Paul Manafort"; Driscoll and Barnes, "Paul Manafort Tied to Perjury."

65. Driscoll and Barnes, "Paul Manafort Tied to Perjury."

66. Foer, "Paul Manafort"; Driscoll and Barnes, "Paul Manafort Tied to Perjury."

67. Michael Knight, "Conn. Jai Alai Appears and The Scandal Disappears," *New York Times*, May 23, 1976.

68. Lyn Bixby, "For State's Top Prosecutor, Jai Alai Case Stirs Up Memories," *Hartford (CT) Courant*, August 3, 1996.

69. Foer, "Paul Manafort"; Driscoll and Barnes, "Paul Manafort Tied to Perjury."

70. Foer, "Paul Manafort."

71. Driscoll and Barnes, "Paul Manafort Tied to Perjury."

72. Foer, "Paul Manafort"; Driscoll and Barnes, "Paul Manafort Tied to Perjury."

73. Driscoll and Barnes, "Paul Manafort Tied to Perjury."

74. "Joseph 'Pippi' Guerriero, Gambler," obituary, *Hartford (CT) Courant* online, April 9, 1993, https://www.courant.com/1993/04/09/joseph-pippi-guerriero-gambler.

75. Foer, "Paul Manafort."

76. Ibid.

77. Driscoll and Barnes, "Paul Manafort Tied to Perjury."

78. United Press International online, "A Seven-Year Probe into Political Corruption Called a 'Dark . . . ,'" June 23, 1984, https://www.upi.com/Archives/1984/06/23/A-seven-year-probe-into-political-corruption-called-a-dark/1044456811200.

79. Foer, "Paul Manafort."

80. Christopher Keating, "New Britain's Paul Manafort Working to Put Trump in White House," *Hartford (CT) Courant* online, June 12, 2016, https://www.courant .com/2016/06/12/new-britains-paul-manafort-working-to-put-trump-in-white -house.

81. Manafort, *Political Prisoner*, 18–19.

82. Keating, "New Britain's Paul Manafort Working."

83. Manafort, *Political Prisoner,* 19–20.

84. Manuel Roig-Franzia, "The Swamp Builders: How Stone and Manafort Helped Create the Mess Trump Promised to Clean Up," *Washington Post* online, November 29, 2018, https://www.washingtonpost.com/graphics/2018/politics/paul-manafort-roger-stone.

85. David Segal, "Mover, Shaker, and Cranky Caller?: A GOP Consultant Who Doesn't Mince Words Has Some Explaining to Do," *Washington Post*, August 25, 2007; Matt Labash, "Roger Stone: Political Animal," *Weekly Standard*, November 5, 2007.

86. Labash, "Roger Stone: Political Animal."

87. Lee Edwards, The Conservative Revolution: The Movement That Remade America (New York: Free Press, 1999), 90.

88. Barry Goldwater, *The Conscience of a Conservative* (1960; repr. Washington, DC: Regnery, 1990), 24.

89. Thomas B. Edsall, "Partners in Political PR Firm Typify Republican New Breed," *Washington Post* online, April 7, 1985, https://www.washingtonpost.com/archive /politics/1985/04/07/partners-in-political-pr-firm-typify-republican-new -breed/8d0b8c04-fabc-43ae-887b-25c7e8af0ec0.

90. Stephanie Mansfield, "The Rise and Gall of Roger Stone," *Washington Post* online, June 16, 1986, https://www.washingtonpost.com/archive/lifestyle/1986/06/16/the -rise-and-gall-of-roger-stone/d8ce308b-7055-4666-860e-378833f46e17.

91. Kim Phillips-Fein, *Invisible Hands: The Businessmen's Crusade Against the New Deal* (New York: W. W. Norton, 2009), 119.

92. Ibid., 119–20, 126–27, 129–39.

93. Mansfield, "Rise and Gall of Roger Stone."

94. Edwards, *The Conservative Revolution*, 13.

95. Lee Edwards, "The Origins of the Modern American Conservative Movement," The Heritage Foundation, transcript of a lecture, November 21, 2003, https://www.heri tage.org/political-process/report/the-origins-the-modern-american-conservative -movement.

96. Mansfield, "Rise and Gall of Roger Stone."

97. Labash, "Roger Stone: Political Animal."

98. Mansfield, "Rise and Gall of Roger Stone."

99. Ibid.

100. Ibid.

101. Labash, "Roger Stone: Political Animal."

102. Ibid.
103. US Congress, Senate, Select Committee on Presidential Campaign Activities, *The Final Report of the Select Committee on Presidential Campaign Activities*, 93rd Cong., 2d sess., 1974, 197–98.
104. Ibid., 198.
105. Ibid., 192–95.
106. Ibid., 195–96.
107. Ibid., 192–93.
108. Roig-Franzia, "Swamp Builders."
109. Labash, "Roger Stone: Political Animal."
110. Ibid.
111. Phillips-Fein, *Invisible Hands*, 187.
112. Mansfield, "Rise and Gall of Roger Stone."
113. Office of President Ronald Reagan, "Nomination of Paul J. Manafort, Jr., to Be a Member of the Board of Directors of the Overseas Private Investment Corporation," news release, May 13, 1981, available at the American Presidency Project, https://www.presidency.ucsb.edu/documents/nomination-paul-j-manafort-jr-be-member-the-board-directors-the-overseas-private.
114. Foer, "Paul Manafort."
115. Peter Baker and Susan Glasser, *The Man Who Ran Washington: The Life and Times of James A. Baker III* (New York: Doubleday, 2020), 77; Foer, "Paul Manafort"; Ken Silverstein, "Paul Manafort, RIP: My First Hand, Very Personal and Painful Ordeal," August 19, 2016, https://washingtonbabylon.com/735-2.
116. David Vogel, *Fluctuating Fortunes: The Political Power of Business in America* (New York: Basic Books, 1989), 228.
117. Ibid., 229.
118. Ibid., 228–29.
119. Rick Perlstein, *The Invisible Bridge: The Fall of Nixon and the Rise of Reagan* (New York: Simon & Schuster, 2014), 415.
120. Vogel, *Fluctuating Fortunes*, 234.
121. Ibid.
122. Ibid., 228–29, 231–34.
123. Ibid., 234.
124. Rick Perlstein, *Reaganland: America's Right Turn 1976–1980* (New York: Simon & Schuster, 2020), 325.
125. Thomas Byrne Edsall, *The New Politics of Inequality* (New York: W. W. Norton, 1984), 73–74.
126. Ibid., 74–75.
127. Brady, *Bad Boy*, 69–70.
128. Ibid., 66–71.
129. Ibid.

130. Edsall, "Partners in Political PR Firm."
131. Brady, *Bad Boy*, 70.
132. Ibid.
133. Edsall, "Partners in Political PR Firm."
134. Brady, *Bad Boy*, 66–71; Edsall, "Partners in Political PR Firm."
135. Brady, *Bad Boy*, 1–10.
136. Ibid., 10.
137. David Remnick, "Why Is Lee Atwater So Hungry? A Political Animal Observed," *Esquire*, December 1, 1986.
138. Brady, *Bad Boy*, 23–24.
139. Edsall, "Partners in Political PR Firm."
140. Brady, *Bad Boy*, 31–32.
141. Ibid., 33.
142. Edsall, "Partners in Political PR Firm."
143. Ibid.
144. Edsall, "GOP Battler Lee Atwater Dies."
145. Rick Perlstein, "Exclusive: Lee Atwater's Infamous 1981 Interview on the Southern Strategy," *Nation* online, November 13, 2012, https://www.thenation.com/article/archive/exclusive-lee-atwaters-infamous-1981-interview-southern-strategy.
146. Toner, "New Spokesman for the Republicans."
147. Edsall, "Partners in Political PR Firm."
148. Toner, "New Spokesman for the Republicans."
149. Ibid.
150. Ibid.
151. Ibid.
152. Ibid.
153. Edsall, "Partners in Political PR Firm."
154. Langley, "Black, Manafort & Stone."
155. Edsall, "Partners in Political PR Firm."
156. David S. Broder, "Jesse Helms, White Racist," *Washington Post* online, August 29, 2001, https://www.washingtonpost.com/wp-dyn/content/article/2008/07/06/AR2008070602321.html.
157. Edsall, *New Politics of Inequality*, 74–75.
158. Vogel, *Fluctuating Fortunes*, 241.
159. Thomas B. Edsall, "Profit and Presidential Politics," *Washington Post* online, August 12, 1989, https://www.washingtonpost.com/archive/politics/1989/08/12/profit-and-presidential-politics/a2107972-c10d-4960-b9da-660d0d57182a/.
160. Perlstein, *Reaganland*, 37–38; Edsall, "Profit and Presidential Politics."
161. Donald T. Critchlow, *The Conservative Ascendancy: How the Republican Right Rose to Power in Modern America* (Lawrence: University Press of Kansas, 2011), 128.
162. Myra MacPherson, "The New Right Brigade," *Washington Post* online, August 10,

1980, https://www.washingtonpost.com/archive/lifestyle/1980/08/10/the-new-right-brigade/24c8ed98-3af7-4385-9c0e-f973bea20612.

163. Perlstein, *Reaganland*, 32.

164. Ibid., 32–33.

165. Ibid.

166. Ibid., 233.

167. Perlstein, *Reaganland*, 387.

168. Ibid., 388.

169. Ibid., 387.

170. "The Crist Switch: Top 10 Political Defections," *Time* online, accessed April 1, 2023. https://content.time.com/time/specials/packages/article/0,28804,1894529_1894528_1894518,00.html; Wallace Turner, "Reagan Cuts $503 Million from the Budget Passed by California Legislature," *New York Times* online, July 4, 1971, https://www.nytimes.com/1971/07/04/archives/reagan-cuts-503million-from-the-budget-passed-by-california.html.

171. Jacob Weisberg, "The Road to Reagandom," Slate, last modified January 8, 2016, https://slate.com/news-and-politics/2016/01/ronald-reagans-conservative-conversion-as-spokesman-for-general-electric-during-the-1950s.html.

172. Ronald Reagan, "Remarks to State Chairpersons of the National White House Conference on Small Business," Old Executive Office Building, Washington, DC, August 15, 1986, https://www.reaganlibrary.gov/archives/speech/remarks-state-chairpersons-national-white-house-conference-small-business.

173. Ike Flores, "Young Republicans Elect Pro-Reagan Chairman," Associated Press, 1977.

174. Foer, "Paul Manafort."

175. James Harding, *Alpha Dogs: The Americans Who Turned Political Spin into a Global Business* (New York: Farrar, Straus and Giroux, 2008), 200.

176. Foer, "Paul Manafort."

177. Ibid.

178. Flores, "Young Republicans Elect Pro-Reagan Chairman."

179. Foer, "Paul Manafort."

180. Flores, "Young Republicans Elect Pro-Reagan Chairman."

181. Foer, "Paul Manafort."

182. Ibid.

183. Flores, "Young Republicans Elect Pro-Reagan Chairman."

184. Tom Raum, "Ronald Reagan Declares His Candidacy for President," Associated Press, November 13, 1979.

185. Ibid.

186. Ronald Reagan, "Remarks Announcing Candidacy for the Republican Presidential Nomination," November 13, 1979, available at the American Presidency Project, https://www.presidency.ucsb.edu/node/255827.

187. Raum, "Ronald Reagan Declares His Candidacy for President."

188. Roig-Franzia, "Swamp Builders."

189. Vogel, *Fluctuating Fortunes*, 240–42.

190. Ibid., 240–41.

191. Ibid., 241–42; United States Senate, "Party Division," n.d., accessed April 3, 2023, https://www.senate.gov/history/partydiv.htm; United States House of Representatives History, Art and Archives Office, "Party Government Since 1857," n.d., accessed April 3, 2023, https://history.house.gov/Institution/Presidents-Coinciding/Party-Government.

192. Edsall, "Partners in Political PR Firm."

193. Vogel, *Fluctuating Fortunes*, 274.

194. Ibid.

195. Ibid.

196. Ibid.

197. Ibid., 272–74.

198. Jim Geraghty, "In *The Art of the Deal*, Trump Shows His Soft Side," *National Review*, September 24, 2015, https://www.nationalreview.com/2015/09/donald-trump-the-art-of-the-deal-review.

199. Vogel, *Fluctuating Fortunes*, 274–75.

200. Ibid., 242.

201. Ibid.

202. Ibid.

203. Ibid., 246.

204. Sidney Blumenthal, *The Rise of the Counter-Establishment: The Conservative Ascent to Political Power* (New York: Union Square Press, 2008), 76.

Chapter 4

1. Thomas B. Edsall, "Partners in Political PR Firm Typify Republican New Breed," *Washington Post* online, April 7, 1985, https://www.washingtonpost.com/archive/politics/1985/04/07/partners-in-political-pr-firm-typify-republican-new-breed/8d0b8c04-fabc-43ae-887b-25c7e8af0ec0.

2. Franklin Foer, "The Quiet American," Slate, last modified April 28, 2016, https://slate.com/news-and-politics/2016/04/paul-manafort-isnt-a-gop-retread-hes-made-a-career-of-reinventing-tyrants-and-despots.html.

3. Manuel Roig-Franzia, "The Swamp Builders: How Stone and Manafort Helped Create the Mess Trump Promised to Clean Up," *Washington Post* online, November 29, 2018, https://www.washingtonpost.com/graphics/2018/politics/paul-manafort-roger-stone.

4. Franklin Foer, "Paul Manafort, American Hustler," *Atlantic* online, March 2018, https://www.theatlantic.com/magazine/archive/2018/03/paul-manafort-american-hustler/550925.

5. Ibid.

6. Foer, "Quiet American."

7. John Brady, *Bad Boy: The Life and Politics of Lee Atwater* (Reading, MA: Addison Wesley, 1997), 138–39.

8. Roig-Franzia, "Swamp Builders."

9. Adam Clymer, "The Advisers Branch Out," *New York Times* online, August 11, 1985, https://www.nytimes.com/1985/08/11/business/the-advisers-branch-out.html.

10. "Tosco Uses Oil Unit as Loan Collateral," *New York Times* online, October 8, 1981, https://www.nytimes.com/1981/10/08/business/tosco-uses-oil-unit-as-loan-collateral.html.

11. Jane Mayer, "Australia's Murdoch Is Getting His Kicks in U.S. Political Races—His Big Papers Back Reagan, and *New York Post* Takes Steady Aim at Ms. Ferraro," *Wall Street Journal*, November 2, 1984.

12. Jerry Knight, "Mark Fowler Plans to Resign as FCC Chairman in Spring," *Washington Post* online, January 17, 1987, https://www.washingtonpost.com/archive/politics/1987/01/17/mark-fowler-plans-to-resign-as-fcc-chairman-in-spring/0e0131e4-fe53-49c3-9f2f-917f0c74af3b/

13. Ibid.

14. "News Corp" (timeline), *Hollywood Reporter* online, November 14, 2005, https://web.archive.org/web/20061208130444/http://www.hollywoodreporter.com/hr/search/article_display.jsp?vnu_content_id=1001479107.

15. Thomas Byrne Edsall, *The New Politics of Inequality* (New York: W. W. Norton, 1984), 202–3.

16. Ibid., 202–4.

17. David Vogel, *Fluctuating Fortunes: The Political Power of Business in America* (New York: Basic Books, 1989), 248–49.

18. Ibid., 249.

19. Ibid.

20. Ibid.

21. Ibid., 250.

22. Ibid., 248–50.

23. Ibid., 270.

24. Ibid.

25. Edsall, "Partners in Political PR Firm."

26. Evan Thomas, "The Slickest Shop in Town," *Time* online, March 3, 1986, https://content.time.com/time/subscriber/article/0,33009,960803,00.html.

27. Foer, "Quiet American."

28. Stephanie Mansfield, "The Rise and Gall of Roger Stone," *Washington Post* online, June 16, 1986, https://www.washingtonpost.com/archive/lifestyle/1986/06/16/the-rise-and-gall-of-roger-stone/d8ce308b-7055-4666-860e-378833f46e17.

29. Edsall, "Partners in Political PR Firm."

30. Foer, "Paul Manafort."

31. Ibid.

32. Ibid.

33. Roig-Franzia, "Swamp Builders."

34. Jacob Weisberg, "How Trump Adviser Roger Stone Became Washington's Sleaziest Political Operator" (reprint of the December 9, 1985, article in the *New Republic*), Slate, last modified August 3, 2016, https://slate.com/news-and-politics/2016/08 /jacob-weisbergs-classic-new-republic-profile-of-trump-adviser-roger-stone.html.

35. Roig-Franzia, "Swamp Builders."

36. Foer, "Paul Manafort."

37. Ibid.

38. Ibid.

39. Silverstein, "Paul Manafort, RIP: My First Hand, Very Personal and Painful Ordeal."

40. Brady, *Bad Boy*, 138–39.

41. Mansfield, "Rise and Gall of Roger Stone."

42. Roig-Franzia, "Swamp Builders"; Foer, "Paul Manafort."

43. Roger Stone, interviewed by Charlie Rose, *Charlie Rose*, "Republican Strategist Roger Stone Discusses Donald Trump and Changes in the GOP," July 20, 2016, https://char lierose.com/videos/28482.

44. Dylan Byers, "The Return of Roger Stone," CNN online, April 19, 2016, https://www .cnn.com/2016/04/19/politics/roger-stone-donald-trump/index.html.

45. Paul Manafort, *Political Prisoner: Persecuted, Prosecuted, but Not Silenced* (New York: Skyhorse, 2022), 27.

46. Caitlin Byrd, "To the Archives! Donald Trump and His Mega-Yacht Sailed into Charleston," *Post and Courier* (Charleston, SC) online, September 14, 2020, https:// www.postandcourier.com/news/to-the-archives-donald-trump-and-his-mega -yacht-sailed-into-charleston/article_76a4d3ce-9704-11e6-a9be-4390f9d1a13e.html.

47. Roig-Franzia, "Swamp Builders."

48. Foer, "Paul Manafort."

49. Randall Rothenberg, "The Media Business: Advertising; Shuttle Hires Consultants from Politics," *New York Times* online, January 23, 1990, https://www.nytimes .com/1990/01/23/business/the-media-business-advertising-shuttle-hires-consul tants-from-politics.html.

50. Randall K. Q. Akee, Katherine A. Spilde, and Jonathan B. Taylor, "The Indian Gaming Regulatory Act and Its Effects on American Indian Economic Development," *Journal of Economic Perspectives* 29, no. 3 (Summer 2015): 185–208, https://pubs.aeaweb.org /doi/pdfplus/10.1257/jep.29.3.185.

51. Wayne King, "Trump, in a Federal Lawsuit, Seeks to Block Indian Casinos," *New York Times*, May 4, 1993.

52. Ibid.

53. *Hearing of the Subcommittee on Native American Affairs of the Committee on Natural Resources*, US House, 103rd Cong., 1st sess. (October 5, 1993), Serial No. 103-17, Part V.

54. Ibid.

55. Joseph Tanfani, "Trump Secretly Funded Campaign Vs. Indian Casino," *Press of Atlantic City (NJ)*, July 3, 2016.

56. Foer, "Quiet American."

57. Tanfani, "Trump Secretly Funded Campaign."

58. Foer, "Quiet American."

59. Tanfani, "Trump Secretly Funded Campaign."

60. Ibid.

61. Foer, "Quiet American."

62. Tanfani, "Trump Secretly Funded Campaign."

63. Charles V. Bagli, "Trump and Others Accept Fines for Ads in Opposition to Casinos," *New York Times* online, October 6, 2000, https://www.nytimes.com/2000/10/06/nyregion/trump-and-others-accept-fines-for-ads-in-opposition-to-casinos.html.

64. Foer, "Quiet American."

65. Thomas B. Edsall, "Profit and Presidential Politics," *Washington Post* online, August 12, 1989, https://www.washingtonpost.com/archive/politics/1989/08/12/profit-and-presidential-politics/a2107972-c10d-4960-b9da-660d0d57182a/.

66. Roig-Franzia, "Swamp Builders."

67. Vogel, *Fluctuating Fortunes*, 279–89.

68. Edsall, "Profit and Presidential Politics."

69. Patrick J. Wilkie, James C. Young, and Sarah E. Nutter, "Corporate Business Activity Before and After the Tax Reform Act of 1986," *SOI Bulletin: A Quarterly Statistics of Income Report* (Washington, DC: US Department of the Treasury, Internal Revenue Service, pub. 1136, Winter 1995–96), 32–45, https://www.irs.gov/pub/irs-soi/96rpwinbul.pdf.

70. Edsall, "Profit and Presidential Politics."

71. Vogel, *Fluctuating Fortunes*, 251.

72. Ibid.

Chapter 5

1. Burt Solomon, *The Washington Century: Three Families and the Shaping of the Nation's Capital* (New York: Harper Perennial, 2005), 310.

2. Ibid.

3. Ibid., 210.

4. Ibid., 210–12.

5. Ibid., 212.

6. Joseph C. Goulden, *The Money Lawyers: The No-Holds-Barred World of Today's Richest and Most Powerful Lawyers* (New York: Truman Talley Books, 2006), 79.

7. Ibid.

8. Solomon, *Washington Century*, 212.

9. US Senate, Committee on Rules and Administration, "Campaign Finance Reform Proposals of 1983," 98th Cong., 1st sess., on the Federal Election Campaign Act of

1971, as Amended, and on Various Measures to Amend the Act, January 26, 27, May 17, and September 29, 1983, 495.

10. Solomon, *Washington Century*, 212.

11. Brooks Jackson, *Honest Graft* (Washington, DC: Farragut, 1990), 58.

12. T. R. Goldman, "Mastering Deals over 2 Ounces of Tanqueray," *Influence*, July 7, 2004.

13. David Vogel, *Fluctuating Fortunes: The Political Power of Business in America* (New York: Basic Books, 1989), 115–17.

14. Ibid., 118–20.

15. Solomon, *Washington Century*, 312.

16. Goulden, *Money Lawyers*, 85–86.

17. Vogel, *Fluctuating Fortunes*, 207.

18. Jackson, *Honest Graft*, 51–54.

19. Gregg Easterbrook, "The Business of Politics," *Atlantic* 258, no. 4 (October 1986): 28–38, https://www.theatlantic.com/past/docs/politics/polibig/eastbusi.htm.

20. Jackson, *Honest Graft*, 22.

21. Ibid., 22–23.

22. Ibid., 23–24.

23. Ibid., 24.

24. Ibid., 27.

25. Ibid., 24–28.

26. Ibid., 28.

27. Ibid., 28, 31–32, 36.

28. Ibid., 29–31.

29. Ibid., 45.

30. Ruth Shalit, "The Undertaker: Tony Coelho and the Death of the Democrats," *New Republic* online, January 2, 1995, https://newrepublic.com/article/72322/the-undertaker.

31. Jackson, *Honest Graft*, 47–52.

32. Ibid., 53–54, 74.

33. Ibid., 54, 58–59, 75.

34. Easterbrook, "Business of Politics," 28–38.

35. Rick Perlstein, *Reaganland: America's Right Turn 1976–1980* (New York: Simon & Schuster, 2020), 37.

36. Vogel, *Fluctuating Fortunes*, 207.

37. Jackson, *Honest Graft*, 69–70.

38. Ibid., 292.

39. Easterbrook, "Business of Politics," 28–38.

40. Jackson, *Honest Graft*, 78–79.

41. Shalit, "Undertaker."

42. Jackson, *Honest Graft*, 69.

43. Morton Mintz, "When Money Talks, Politicians Listen," *Washington Post* online, September 4, 1983, https://www.washingtonpost.com/archive/entertainment

/books/1983/09/04/when-money-talks-politicians-listen/7f1b9b1c-b9d4-4c2a-9475-53f2311d05ac/.

44. Jackson, *Honest Graft*, 98–99.
45. Ibid., 33.
46. Joseph E. Cantor, "Congressional Campaign Spending: 1976–1996," Congressional Research Service, August 19, 1997, https://www.everycrsreport.com/files/1997081 9_97-793_da76d4049c9ac2262ad4b35023c6e91f3d9beab2.pdf.
47. Thomas Byrne Edsall, *The New Politics of Inequality* (New York: W. W. Norton, 1984), 20.
48. Vogel, *Fluctuating Fortunes*, 244–45.
49. Ibid.
50. Jackson, *Honest Graft*, 108–9.
51. Vogel, *Fluctuating Fortunes*, 170, 237.
52. Shalit, "Undertaker."
53. Ibid.
54. Jackson, *Honest Graft*, 38.
55. Ibid., 19, 38.
56. Easterbrook, "Business of Politics," 28–38.
57. "Democratic Congressional Campaign Committee Inc.: Financial Summary," Federal Election Commission, n.d., accessed April 18, 2023, https://www.fec.gov/data/committee/C00000935/?cycle=1986.
58. Shalit, "Undertaker."
59. Jackson, *Honest Graft*, 89–90.
60. Carl Bernstein, "King of the Hill," *Vanity Fair* online, March 1998, https://archive.vanityfair.com/article/1998/3/king-of-the-hill.
61. Solomon, *Washington Century*, 309–10.
62. Ibid., 209.
63. Ibid., 310.
64. Ibid., 233.
65. Bernstein, "King of the Hill."
66. Ibid.
67. William Thompson, "Hunt Bags 182 Ducks, but 1 Is Costly," *Baltimore Sun*, January 4, 1994, 1B.
68. Ibid.
69. Ibid.
70. Ibid.

Chapter 6

1. Ethan Bronner, *Battle for Justice: How the Bork Nomination Shook America* (New York: Union Square Press, 2007), 98.
2. Ethan Bronner, "Kennedy Tells How He Roused Opposition," *Boston Globe*, October 11, 1987, 1.

3. Bronner, *Battle for Justice*, 94.

4. Ibid., 99.

5. Al Kamen, "Justice Powell Resigns, Was Supreme Court's Pivotal Vote," *Washington Post* online, June 27, 1987, https://www.washingtonpost.com/wp-srv/national/long term/supcourt/stories/powell062787.htm.

6. Bronner, *Battle for Justice*, 99.

7. Ilya Shapiro, "Commentary: The Original Sin of Robert Bork," Cato Institute online, September 9, 2020, https://www.cato.org/commentary/original-sin-robert-bork.

8. Bronner, *Battle for Justice*, 99.

9. Kenneth Vogel, "Russia Scandal Befalls Two Brothers: John and Tony Podesta," *New York Times* online, November 10, 2017, https://www.nytimes.com/2017/11/10/us /politics/john-tony-podesta-mueller-russia-investigation.html.

10. Carol Felsenthal, "How the Podesta Brothers Rose from the 39th Ward to the White House," *Chicago* online, December 19, 2013, https://www.chicagomag.com/Chi cago-Magazine/Felsenthal-Files/December-2013/How-the-Podesta-Brothers-Rose -From-the-39th-Ward-to-the-White-House/.

11. Brody Mullins and Julie Bykowicz, "How Tony Podesta, a Washington Power Broker, Lost It All," *Wall Street Journal* online, April 18, 2018, https://www.wsj.com/articles /how-tony-podesta-a-washington-power-broker-lost-it-all-1524065781.

12. Felsenthal, "How the Podesta Brothers Rose."

13. Ibid.

14. Ibid.

15. Ibid.

16. Ibid.

17. Ibid.

18. Ibid.

19. Ibid.

20. Sam Roberts, "Joseph D. Duffey, 88, Dies," *New York Times* online, March 3, 2021, https://www.nytimes.com/2021/03/03/us/politics/joseph-duffey-dead.html.

21. Don Nicoll, "Interview with Anthony 'Tony' Podesta," transcript, September 16–18, 2002, available at Yumpu, https://www.yumpu.com/en/document/read/10686676 /interview-with-anthony-tony-podesta-by-don-nicoll-bates-college.

22. Robert Mitchell, "The Democrat Who Cried (Maybe) in New Hampshire and Lost the Presidential Nomination," *Washington Post* online, February 9, 2020, https:// www.washingtonpost.com/history/2020/02/09/new-hampshire-ed-muskie-tears -primary/.

23. Larry Sabato, "Edmund Muskie's New Hampshire 'Cry'—1972," *Washington Post* on-line, 1998, https://www.washingtonpost.com/wp-srv/politics/special/clinton/frenzy /muskie.htm.

24. R. W. Apple Jr., Edmund S. Muskie, 81, Dies; Maine Senator and a Power on the National Scene," *New York Times* online, March 27, 1996, https://www.nytimes

.com/1996/03/27/us/edmund-s-muskie-81-dies-maine-senator-and-a-power-on
-the-national-scene.html.

25. Felsenthal, "How the Podesta Brothers Rose."

26. Vogel, "Russia Scandal Befalls Two Brothers."

27. Caleb Daniloff, "A Running Conversation with John Podesta," *Runner's World* online, May 1, 2014, https://www.runnersworld.com/runners-stories/a20852230/a-running -conversation-with-john-podesta/.

28. Robert A. Jones, "Norman Lear's PAW Takes a Swipe at the New Right," *Christian Science Monitor* online, July 23, 1981, https://www.csmonitor.com/1981/0723/072366.html.

29. Robert A. Jones, "High-Tech Tactics; People for 'Atheists' or Crusader?," *Christian Science Monitor*, November 29, 1996.

30. Ibid.

31. Ibid.

32. Associated Press, June 25, 1981.

33. Jones, "Norman Lear's PAW Takes a Swipe."

34. Colin Campbell, "Book Banning in America," *New York Times*, December 20, 1981, sec. 7, 1.

35. Jones, "Norman Lear's PAW Takes a Swipe."

36. Paul S. Boyer, *Purity in Print: Book Censorship in America from the Gilded Age to the Computer Age* (Madison: University of Wisconsin Press, 2002), 325.

37. Fred M. Hechinger, "The Essence of Censorship in the Schools," About Education, *New York Times* online, October 27, 1981, https://www.nytimes.com/1981/10/27/sci ence/about-education.html.

38. Jones, "High-Tech Tactics."

39. Howard Kurtz, "Norman Lear's Crusade Widens," *Washington Post* online, February 3, 1986, https://www.washingtonpost.com/archive/politics/1986/02/03/norman -lears-crusade-widens/72fb9dde-1d34-423c-9956-b25f3deba10c/.

40. Jones, "Norman Lear's PAW Takes a Swipe."

41. "TV's Latest Listing: Archie Vs. Jerry," *Newsweek*, October 18, 1982.

42. Jones, "High-Tech Tactics."

43. Associated Press, March 15, 1984.

44. Jones, "High-Tech Tactics."

45. Judi Hasson, "Reagan Leaving Judicial Mark: Reagan Appointments Changing the Face of Federal Judiciary for Decades to Come," United Press International online, November 3, 1985, https://www.upi.com/Archives/1985/11/03/Reagan-leaving-ju dicial-markNEWLNReagan-appointments-changing-the-face-of-federal-judiciary -for-decades-to-come/3200499842000/.

46. Ibid.

47. Marylouise Oates, "Tending the Grass Roots of 'People For,'" *Los Angeles Times* online, June 11, 1986, https://www.latimes.com/archives/la-xpm-1986-06-11-vw-10594 -story.html.

48. "What Jeff Sessions Has Said About Race and Civil Rights," ABC News online, November 18, 2016, https://abcnews.go.com/Politics/jeff-sessions-race-civil-rights/story?id=43633501.

49. Oates, "Tending the Grass Roots."

50. Michelle Ye Hee Lee, "The Facts About the Voter Fraud Case That Sank Jeff Sessions's Bid for a Judgeship," *Washington Post* online, November 28, 2016, https://www.washingtonpost.com/news/fact-checker/wp/2016/11/28/the-facts-about-the-voter-fraud-case-that-sunk-jeff-sessionss-bid-for-a-judgeship/.

51. Philip Shenon, "Praise and Pillory for a Liberal Lobby Group," *New York Times*, August 6, 1986, A16.

52. Ibid.

53. Bronner, "Kennedy Tells How," 1.

54. Ibid.

55. Ibid.

56. Ibid.

57. Ibid.

58. Sonja Bolle, review of *The People Rising: The Campaign Against the Bork Nomination*, by Michael Pertschuk and Wendy Schaetzel, *Los Angeles Times* online, December 10, 1989, https://www.latimes.com/archives/la-xpm-1989-12-10-bk-427-story.html.

59. Mitchell Locin, "Push Nation to Left, Progressives Urged," *Chicago Tribune*, August 3, 1987, 5.

60. Bronner, "Kennedy Tells How," 1.

61. Ibid.

62. Ibid.

63. Bolle, review of *The People Rising*.

64. Stuart Taylor, "Ads Against Bork Still Hotly Disputed," *New York Times* online, October 24, 1987, https://www.nytimes.com/1987/10/21/us/ads-against-bork-still-hotly-disputed.html.

65. Jeffrey A. Segal, "Amicus Curiae Briefs by the Solicitor General During the Warren and Burger Courts: A Research Note," *Western Political Quarterly* 41, no. 1 (1988): 135, https://doi.org/10.2307/448461.

66. Robin Toner, "Poll Finds Most Undecided on Bork," *New York Times* online, September 15, 1987, https://www.nytimes.com/1987/09/15/us/poll-finds-most-undecided-on-bork.html.

67. Tom Shales, "The Bork Turnoff," *Washington Post* online, October 9, 1987, https://www.washingtonpost.com/archive/lifestyle/1987/10/09/the-bork-turnoff/5342ccb1-404c-4540-92af-7f5a4b6b9b82/.

68. Bronner, "Kennedy Tells How," 1.

69. Linda Greenhouse, "Bork's Nomination Is Rejected, 58–42; Reagan 'Saddened,'" *New York Times* online, October 24, 1987, https://www.nytimes.com/1987/10/24/politics/borks-nomination-is-rejected-5842-reagan-saddened.html.

70. David Lauter and Ronald Ostrow, "Backers Blame Bork Defeat on Lobbying by Foes," *Los Angeles Times*, October 7, 1987, 19.

Chapter 7

1. Franklin Foer, "Paul Manafort, American Hustler," *Atlantic* online, March 2018, https://www.theatlantic.com/magazine/archive/2018/03/paul-manafort-american -hustler/550925.

2. Evan Thomas, "The Slickest Shop in Town," *Time* online, March 3, 1986, https://content.time.com/time/subscriber/article/0,33009,960803,00.html.

3. Foer, "Paul Manafort."

4. Thomas, "Slickest Shop in Town."

5. Foer, "Paul Manafort."

6. Ibid.

7. Warren Brown, "Fading Muscle," *Washington Post* online, April 23, 1983, https://www.washingtonpost.com/archive/business/1983/04/24/fading-muscle/33274650 -0033-4acb-812b-e70590f244d6/.

8. Stuart Auerbach, "Steel Imports to Be Cut 30%, White House Announces," *Washington Post*, December 20, 1984.

9. Martin Anderson, "The Ten Causes of the Reagan Boom: 1982–1997," Hoover Institution online, last modified October 1, 1997, https://www.hoover.org/research/ten -causes-reagan-boom-1982-1997.

10. Frederick H. Lowe, "Bethlehem Steel Workers Receiving $2,000 Bonuses," *Chicago Sun-Times*, March 5, 1988.

11. Kenneth R. Harney, "Study May Short-Circuit FHA Maximum," *Chicago Sun-Times*, May 12, 1989.

12. Robert Trigaux, "Mortgage Insurers Fight FHA Growth with Heavy Hitters," *American Banker* 154, no. 170 (August 31, 1989).

13. H. Jane Lehman, "Chicago-Based Coalition Proves a 'Hit' in D.C.," *Chicago Tribune*, April 21, 1991.

14. Kenneth R. Harney, "Groups Form Unique Alliance to Back HOME Saving Plan," *Chicago Sun-Times*, July 14, 1989.

15. David Vogel, *Fluctuating Fortunes: The Political Power of Business in America* (New York: Basic Books, 1989), 251.

16. Thomas, "Slickest Shop in Town."

17. Jacob Weisberg, "How Trump Adviser Roger Stone Became Washington's Sleaziest Political Operator" (reprint of the December 9, 1985, article in the *New Republic*), Slate, last modified August 3, 2016, https://slate.com/news-and-politics/2016/08 /jacob-weisbergs-classic-new-republic-profile-of-trump-adviser-roger-stone.html.

18. Stephen Engelberg, "Concern That Aided Bahamas Has Officials Advising Bush," *New York Times* online, September 8, 1988, https://www.nytimes.com/1988/09/08 /us/concern-that-aided-bahamas-has-officials-advising-bush.html.

19. *Drugs, Law Enforcement and Foreign Policy: A Report by the Subcommittee on Terrorism, Narcotics and International Operations of the Committee on Foreign Relations*, US Senate, 100th Cong., 2d sess. (December 1988), https://nsarchive2.gwu.edu/NSAEBB/NSAEBB113/north06.pdf.

20. Robin Toner, "Dukakis Assails Bush on Advisers' Ties to Bahamian Leaders," *New York Times*, September 11, 1988, 30.

21. C-SPAN, Clip from the Moderate Rehabilitation Housing Program Hearing, House Government Operations Subcommittee on Employment and Housing, June 21, 1989, 0:13 to 00:39, https://www.c-span.org/video/?c4688661/user-clip-manafort-influence-peddling-full.

22. Philip Shenon, "Bush Consultant Peddled Influence at H.U.D., He Says," *New York Times* online, June 21, 1989, https://www.nytimes.com/1989/06/21/us/bush-consultant-peddled-influence-at-hud-he-says.html.

23. William Kleinknecht, *The Man Who Sold the World: Ronald Reagan and the Betrayal of Main Street America* (New York: Nation Books, 2009), 189–90.

24. William J. Eaton, "GOP Consultant Admits Using Influence to Obtain Hud Grant but Defends Action," *Los Angeles Times* online, June 21, 1989, https://www.latimes.com/archives/la-xpm-1989-06-21-mn-2408-story.html.

25. Shenon, "Bush Consultant Peddled Influence."

26. Kleinknecht, *Man Who Sold the World*, 190.

27. Eaton, "GOP Consultant Admits Using Influence."

28. Kleinknecht, *Man Who Sold the World*, 189–90; Shenon, "Bush Consultant Peddled Influence."

29. Peter Kerr, "Housing Renovation Raises Ill Will," *New York Times* online, May 22, 1989, https://www.nytimes.com/1989/05/22/us/housing-renovation-raises-ill-will.html.

30. Kleinknecht, *Man Who Sold the World*, 189–90.

31. Kerr, "Housing Renovation Raises Ill Will."

32. Kleinknecht, *Man Who Sold the World*, 190.

33. Kerr, "Housing Renovation Raises Ill Will."

34. Kleinknecht, *Man Who Sold the World*, 189–90.

35. Kerr, "Housing Renovation Raises Ill Will."

36. Shenon, "Bush Consultant Peddled Influence."

37. Ibid.

38. Manuel Roig-Franzia, "The Swamp Builders: How Stone and Manafort Helped Create the Mess Trump Promised to Clean Up," *Washington Post* online, November 29, 2018, https://www.washingtonpost.com/graphics/2018/politics/paul-manafort-roger-stone.

39. C-SPAN, Moderate Rehabilitation Housing Program Hearing, House Government Operations Subcommittee on Employment and Housing, June 21, 1989, 00:07:15 to 00:07:19, 04:01:57 to 04:02:04, https://www.c-span.org/video/?8094-1/moderate-rehabilitation-housing-program.

40. Shenon, "Bush Consultant Peddled Influence."
41. Eaton, "GOP Consultant Admits Using Influence."
42. Foer, "Paul Manafort."
43. Ibid.
44. Ibid.
45. Jack Anderson and Dale Van Atta, "Mobutu in Search of an Image Boost," *Washington Post* online, September 25, 1989, https://www.washingtonpost.com/archive/lifestyle/1989/09/25/mobutu-in-search-of-an-image-boost/d0626644-1a49-4414-82b2-70701894dfae.
46. Franklin Foer, "The Quiet American," Slate, last modified April 28, 2016, https://slate.com/news-and-politics/2016/04/paul-manafort-isnt-a-gop-retread-hes-made-a-career-of-reinventing-tyrants-and-despots.html.
47. K. Riva Levinson, "I Worked for Paul Manafort. He Always Lacked a Moral Compass," *Washington Post* online, November 1, 2017, https://www.washingtonpost.com/news/posteverything/wp/2017/11/01/i-worked-for-paul-manafort-he-always-lacked-a-moral-compass.
48. Ibid.
49. K. Riva Levinson, *Choosing the Hero: My Improbable Journey and the Rise of Africa's First Woman President* (Washington, DC: Kiwai Media, 2016), 75.
50. Ken Silverstein, "Paul Manafort, RIP: My First Hand, Very Personal and Painful Ordeal," August 19, 2016, https://washingtonbabylon.com/735-2.
51. Foer, "Paul Manafort."
52. Norman Kempster, "Angolan Rebel Vows to Attack U.S.-Run Firm; Savimbi, On Aid Tour, Calls Gulf Oil Facility Asset to Marxist Regime," *Los Angeles Times* online, February 1, 1986, https://www.latimes.com/archives/la-xpm-1986-02-01-mn-2925-story.html.
53. Casimiro Siona and Victoria Brittain, "Leader of UNITA Killed by Angolan Soldiers," *Irish Times* (Dublin) online, February 23, 2002, https://www.irishtimes.com/news/leader-of-unita-killed-by-angolan-soldiers-1.1051489.
54. Human Rights Watch online, *Human Rights Watch World Report 1989—Angola,* January 1, 1990, https://www.refworld.org/docid/467bb486c.html.
55. Ibid.
56. "Rebel Followers Say UNITA Chief Tortured and Killed Opponents," Associated Press, March 11, 1989; Craig R. Whitney with Jill Jolliffe, "Ex-Allies Say Angola Rebels Torture and Slay Dissenters," *New York Times*, March 11, 1989.
57. "Stamping Out 'Blood Diamonds,'" *New Zealand Herald* (Auckland) online, June 29, 2000, https://www.nzherald.co.nz/business/stamping-out-blood-diamonds/SO5EXITPKDUH26VC2DFFF6L6OI/#:~:text=LONDON%20%2D%20Representatives%20of%20diamond%2Dimporting,which%20bankroll%20wars%20across%20Africa.
58. Patrick E. Tyler and David B. Ottaway, "The Selling of Jonas Savimbi: Success and a $600,000 Tab," *Washington Post* online, February 9, 1986, https://www.washing

tonpost.com/archive/politics/1986/02/09/the-selling-of-jonas-savimbi-success-and
-a-600000-tab/d9fd8686-8f8d-497b-a3b4-7b636fec9b69/.

59. Art Levine, "Publicists of the Damned," *Spy*, February 1992, 60.

60. Tyler and Ottaway, "Selling of Jonas Savimbi."

61. Michael Hill, "Legacy of an Angolan Opportunist," *Baltimore Sun* online, March 3, 2003, https://www.baltimoresun.com/news/bs-xpm-2002-03-03-0203020255-story .html.

62. Tyler and Ottaway, "Selling of Jonas Savimbi."

63. Foer, "Paul Manafort."

64. Tyler and Ottaway, "Selling of Jonas Savimbi."

65. R. W. Apple Jr., "Red Carpet for a Rebel, or How a Star is Born," *New York Times* online, February 7, 1986, https://www.nytimes.com/1986/02/07/us/red-carpet-for-a -rebel-or-how-a-star-is-born.html.

66. "Doctor Jonas Savimbi Talked About the Fight for Angola's Independence," C-SPAN, January 31, 1986, https://www.c-span.org/video/?125966-1/angolian-liberation.

67. "Jonas Savimbi's Charisma, Brutality Still Haunt 10 Years On," Agence France Presse, February 21, 2012.

68. Hill, "Angolan Opportunist."

69. Foer, "Paul Manafort."

70. Phil McCombs, "The Salute to Savimbi," *Washington Post* online, February 1, 1986, https://www.washingtonpost.com/archive/lifestyle/1986/02/01/the-salute-to-sav imbi/b37b8411-a9fe-4cf3-8040-bb189e936d4a.

71. Tyler and Ottaway, "Selling of Jonas Savimbi."

72. Ibid.

73. Levine, "Publicists of the Damned."

74. George Gedda, "Washington Wire: From Afghanistan to Zaire, Chuck Robb's Been There," Associated Press, February 26, 1988.

75. Foer, "Paul Manafort."

76. Levine, "Publicists of the Damned."

77. Henri E. Cauvin, "Angola Shows Rebel's Body on Television," *New York Times* on-line, February 24, 2002, https://www.nytimes.com/2002/02/24/world/angola-shows -rebel-s-body-on-television.html.

78. Scott Peterson, "Long Rebel Siege of Isolated City Reflects Woes of Angola's Civil War," *Christian Science Monitor* online, November 9, 1993, https://www.csmonitor .com/1993/1109/09011.html.

79. "Modern Conflicts: Angola (1975–2002)," Political Economy Research Institute, University of Massachusetts, n.d., accessed April 12, 2023, https://peri.umass.edu/filead min/pdf/Angola.pdf.

80. Peterson, "Long Rebel Siege."

81. John Brady, *Bad Boy: The Life and Politics of Lee Atwater* (Reading, MA: Addison Wesley, 1997), 267–69.

82. Ibid., 268–69.
83. Ibid., 234, 284.
84. Ibid., 314–15, 319–20.
85. Ibid., 270.
86. Ibid.
87. Stefan Forbes and Noland Walker, "Boogie Man: The Lee Atwater Story," *Frontline*, 2008, https://www.pbs.org/wgbh/pages/frontline/atwater/etc/script.html.

Chapter 8

1. W. John Moore, "The Gravy Train," *National Journal* 24, no. 41 (October 10, 1992): 2294–98.
2. Ibid.
3. Ibid.
4. Burt Solomon, *The Washington Century: Three Families and the Shaping of the Nation's Capital* (New York: Harper Perennial, 2005), 239.
5. Neil A. Lewis, "Campaign Finance; Clinton's Coalition Proves Effective at Raising Money," *New York Times* online, March 3, 1992, https://www.nytimes.com/1992/03/03/us/1992-campaign-campaign-finance-clinton-s-coalition-proves-effective-raising.html.
6. Joseph C. Goulden, *The Money Lawyers: The No-Holds-Barred World of Today's Richest and Most Powerful Lawyers* (New York: Truman Talley Books, 2006), 58.
7. Moore, "Gravy Train."
8. Bill Clinton, Address on Health Care Reform, House Chamber, U.S. Capitol, September 22, 1993, https://millercenter.org/the-presidency/presidential-speeches/september-22-1993-address-health-care-reform.
9. Ibid.
10. Daniel Franklin, "Tommy Boggs and the Death of Health Care Reform," *Washington Monthly* online, April 1995, 31–37, https://archive.ph/y5JaJ#selection-347.0-353.11.
11. Clinton, Address on Health Care Reform.
12. *Well-Healed: Inside Lobbying for Health Care Reform* (Washington, DC: Center for Public Integrity, 1994), https://cloudfront-files-1.publicintegrity.org/legacy_projects/pdf_reports/WELL-HEALED.pdf.
13. Dana Priest, "Clinton Health Package Combines Cost Controls, Market Incentives," *Washington Post* online, September 5, 1993, https://www.washingtonpost.com/archive/politics/1993/09/05/clinton-health-package-combines-cost-controls-market-incentives/af9610ff-08f2-4609-ba1d-6ea388b9a6ba.
14. Luke Mullins, "The Making and Unmaking of Tony and Heather Podesta's Power Marriage," *Washingtonian* online, August 11, 2014, https://www.washingtonian.com/2014/08/11/the-making-and-unmaking-of-a-power-marriage/.
15. D'Vera Cohn, "Thousands at Rally Hear 'The Cry of the Earth,'" *Washington Post* online, April 23, 1990, https://www.washingtonpost.com/archive/politics/1990/04/23

/thousands-at-rally-hear-the-cry-of-the-earth/fe30ca17-6bbf-46e0-8b9c-e3abc9af
dcbd.

16. Kenneth Vogel, "Russia Scandal Befalls Two Brothers: John and Tony Podesta," *New York Times* online, November 10, 2017, https://www.nytimes.com/2017/11/10/us /politics/john-tony-podesta-mueller-russia-investigation.html.

17. Carol Felsenthal, "How the Podesta Brothers Rose from the 39th Ward to the White House," *Chicago* online, December 19, 2013, https://www.chicagomag.com/Chi cago-Magazine/Felsenthal-Files/December-2013/How-the-Podesta-Brothers-Rose -From-the-39th-Ward-to-the-White-House/.

18. Gerald M. Boyd, "Two Bush Aides Favor Bob Dole for 2nd Spot," *New York Times* on- line, June 26, 1988, https://www.nytimes.com/1988/06/26/us/top-bush-aides-favor -bob-dole-for-the-2d-spot.html.

19. Franklin, "Tommy Boggs."

20. Ibid.

21. Ibid.

22. Ibid.

23. Ibid.

24. Ibid.

25. Ibid.

26. Ibid.

27. Ibid.

28. Karen Tumulty, "John Dingell Sr.: A Legacy," *Time* online, September 9, 2009, https:// swampland.time.com/2009/09/09/john-dingell-sr-a-legacy.

29. Franklin, "Tommy Boggs."

30. David S. Broder, "Upstaging the President," *Washington Post* online, February 3, 1994, https://www.washingtonpost.com/archive/politics/1994/02/03/upstaging-the -president/0d298400-397c-450d-8e40-b0466e098dd7.

31. David Brooks, "The Cooper Concerns," Opinion, *New York Times* online, February 5, 2008, https://www.nytimes.com/2008/02/05/opinion/05brooks.html.

32. Stan Simpson, "Protesters Rally Against Alternative Health Plan," *Hartford (CT) Cou- rant* online, March 22, 1994, https://www.courant.com/1994/03/22/protesters-rally -against-alternative-health-plan.

33. David Broder and Haynes Johnson, *The System: The American Way of Politics at the Breaking Point* (Boston: Little, Brown, 1996), 207.

34. Sabin Russell, "In Health Reform Battle, Lobbyists Shoot to Kill: $100 Million So Far to Shape Debate," *San Francisco Chronicle*, August 18, 1994, A1.

35. Dan Diamond, "Pulse Check: 'Harry and Louise'—and Hillary," *Politico* online, last modified May 12, 2016, https://www.politico.com/story/2016/05/harry-louise-and -hillary-clinton-223139.

36. Michael Weisskopf, "Delivering a Defeat for Total Coverage," *Washington Post* online,

July 19, 1994, https://www.washingtonpost.com/archive/politics/1994/07/19/deliver ing-a-defeat-for-total-coverage/d7589844-1a82-4f13-a3ab-b707570d8ee4.

37. "1996 Democratic Party Platform," August 26, 1996, available at the American Presidency Project, https://www.presidency.ucsb.edu/documents/1996-democratic -party-platform.

38. "Excerpts from Platform Adopted at Democratic Convention," *New York Times* on-line, August 28, 1996, https://www.nytimes.com/1996/08/28/us/excerpts-from-plat form-adopted-at-democratic-convention.html.

39. William A. Niskanen, "The Clinton Regulatory Legacy," *Regulation* 24, no. 2 (Summer 2001): 42–44, https://www.cato.org/sites/cato.org/files/serials/files/regulation /2001/7/clinton.pdf.

40. Michael Smallberg, "How the Clinton Team Thwarted Effort to Regulate Derivatives," Project on Government Oversight, April 25, 2014, https://www.pogo.org/in vestigation/2014/04/how-clinton-team-thwarted-effort-to-regulate-derivatives.

41. "Financial Services Modernization Act of 1999 (Gramm-Leach-Bliley)," Federal Reserve History November 12, 1999, https://www.federalreservehistory.org/essays /gramm-leach-bliley-act.

42. Jim Zarroli, "Fact Check: Did Glass-Steagall Cause the 2008 Financial Crisis?," NPR online, October 14, 2015, https://www.npr.org/sections/thetwo-way /2015/10/14/448685233/fact-check-did-glass-steagall-cause-the-2008-financial -crisis; Smallberg, "How the Clinton Team."

43. Kim Phillips-Fein, *Invisible Hands: The Businessmen's Crusade Against the New Deal* (New York: W. W. Norton, 2009), 265.

44. David Vogel, *Fluctuating Fortunes: The Political Power of Business in America* (New York: Basic Books, 1989), 287.

45. Lee Drutman, *The Business of America Is Lobbying: How Corporations Became Politicized and Politics Became More Corporate* (Oxford: Oxford University Press, 2015), 61.

46. Mark Mizruchi, *The Fracturing of the American Corporate Elite* (Cambridge, MA: Harvard University Press, 2013), 8.

47. Jeffrey H. Birnbaum, "Merger Fever Infects Potomac Lobbying Firms in Spite of Fears That Public, Clients Will Suffer," *Wall Street Journal*, April 4, 1990.

48. Maralee Schwartz, "PR Firm Acquires Black, Manafort," *Washington Post* online, January 3, 1991, https://www.washingtonpost.com/archive/politics/1991/01/03/pr -firm-acquires-black-manafort/d31e37db-d7eb-4cf3-8ef6-749b9b73ecb7/.

49. Pamela Brogan, *The Torturers' Lobby: How Human Rights–Abusing Nations Are Represented in Washington* (Washington, DC: Center for Public Integrity, 1992), https:// cloudfront-files-1.publicintegrity.org/legacy_projects/pdf_reports/THETORTUR ERSLOBBY.pdf.

50. Franklin Foer, "The Quiet American," Slate, last modified April 28, 2016, https://

slate.com/news-and-politics/2016/04/paul-manafort-isnt-a-gop-retread-hes-made
-a-career-of-reinventing-tyrants-and-despots.html.

51. Michael Isikoff, "Top Trump Aide Lobbied for Pakistani Spy Front," Yahoo! News online, last modified April 18, 2016, https://www.yahoo.com/politics/top-trump-aide
-lobbied-for-1409744144007222.html.

52. Foer, "Quiet American."

53. "India Protests Visit by Human Rights Group Representatives," United Press International online, November 11, 1993, https://www.upi.com/Archives/1993/11/11/India
-protests-visit-by-human-rights-group-representatives/8561752994000; Foer, "Quiet
American."

54. Evan Thomas, "The Slickest Shop in Town," *Time* online, March 3, 1986, https://con
tent.time.com/time/subscriber/article/0,33009,960803,00.html.

55. Kenneth P. Vogel, "Paul Manafort's Wild and Lucrative Philippine Adventure," *Politico* online, last modified June 10, 2016, https://www.politico.com/magazine
/story/2016/06/2016-donald-trump-paul-manafort-ferinand-marcos-philippines
-1980s-213952/.

56. George Rau and Alexa Beattie, "Murder, Suicide Shatters Early Morning Calm," *Alexandria (VA) Gazette Packet*, March 26, 1996.

57. Charles W. Hall, "Alexandria Man Stalks, Kills Teacher," *Washington Post* online,
March 26, 1996, https://www.washingtonpost.com/archive/politics/1996/03/26/alex
andria-man-stalks-kills-teacher/69769bea-bfc0-4151-8d87-455b651fa145/.

58. Cheryl L. Tan, "Tougher Stalking Law Urged for Va.," *Washington Post* online, July 11,
1996, https://www.washingtonpost.com/archive/local/1996/07/11/tougher-stalking
-law-urged-for-va/568d1204-8141-46b7-b85e-163457ddb879/.

59. Hall, "Alexandria Man Stalks, Kills."

60. Rau and Beattie, "Murder, Suicide."

61. Ibid.

62. Tan, "Tougher Stalking Law Urged."

63. Vogel, *Fluctuating Fortunes*, 287.

64. Ibid.

65. Ibid.

Chapter 9

1. Brody Mullins, "The Rise and Fall of a K Street Renegade," *Wall Street Journal* online,
February 13, 2017, https://www.wsj.com/articles/the-rise-and-fall-of-a-k-street-ren
egade-1487001918.

2. Steven Malanga, "Why Queens Matters," *City Journal* online, Summer 2004, https://
www.city-journal.org/article/why-queens-matters.

3. Gwen Ifill, "Reporter's Notebook: Students Give Clinton a Skeptical Reception," *New
York Times* online, March 25, 1992, https://www.nytimes.com/1992/03/25/us/1992
-campaign-reporter-s-notebook-students-give-clinton-skeptical-reception.html.

4. Brody Mullins, "Rise and Fall of a K Street Renegade."

5. Ibid.

6. Robbie Diamond, "Can Biden's Green-Energy Czar Succeed?," *Washington Monthly* online, November 24, 2022, https://washingtonmonthly.com/2022/11/24/can-bidens-green-energy-czar-succeed/.

7. "Harold Ickes," National Park Service online, https://www.nps.gov/people/harold-ickes.htm.

8. John F. Harris, "Odd Man In," *Stanford* online, September/October 2000, https://stanfordmag.org/contents/odd-man-in.

9. Brody Mullins, "Rise and Fall of a K Street Renegade."

10. "J. Edgar Hoover: United States Goverment Official," in *Encyclopædia Britannica* online, last modified July 7, 2023, https://www.britannica.com/biography/J-Edgar-Hoover.

11. "In Memoriam: Harry Reid," GW Today, last modified December 29, 2021, https://gwtoday.gwu.edu/memoriam-harry-reid.

12. Matt Labash, "Roger Stone: Political Animal," *Weekly Standard*, November 5, 2007.

13. "Lobbying Firm Profile: Patton Boggs LLP, 1998," OpenSecrets online, last modified July 24, 2023, https://www.opensecrets.org/federal-lobbying/firms/summary?cycle=1998&id=D000022176.

14. "Lobbying Firm Profile: Patton Boggs LLP, 2003," OpenSecrets online, last modified July 24, 2023, https://www.opensecrets.org/federal-lobbying/firms/summary?cycle=2003&id=D000022176.

15. Ibid.

16. Brody Mullins, "Patton Boggs Tops on K St.," *Roll Call* online, February 24, 2004, https://rollcall.com/2004/02/24/patton-boggs-tops-on-k-st/.

17. Burt Solomon, *The Washington Century: Three Families and the Shaping of the Nation's Capital* (New York: Harper Perennial, 2005).

18. Spencer S. Hsu, "Ex-Justice Dept. Lawyer Caught in 'Most Serious' Internal Corruption Case in Recent Memory," *Washington Post* online, March 8, 2018, https://www.washingtonpost.com/local/public-safety/ex-justice-dept-lawyer-caught-in-most-serious-internal-corruption-case-in-recent-memory/2018/03/08/560071e2-2262-11e8-86f6-54bfff693d2b_story.html.

19. Spencer S. Hsu, "Ex-Justice Dept. Lawyer Offered to Sell Secret U.S. Whistleblower Lawsuits to Targets of the Complaints," *Washington Post* online, January 23, 2018, https://www.washingtonpost.com/local/public-safety/ex-justice-dept-lawyer-peddled-secret-us-whistleblower-suits-to-try-to-impress-his-bosses-with-new-clients/2018/01/24/49b7d934-e414-11e7-a65d-1ac0fd7f097e_story.html.

20. Greg Jaffe and Anne Marie Squeo, "Crusader Artillery Gun Is Quarry in Showdown with the Pentagon," *Wall Street Journal* online, May 4, 2011, https://www.wsj.com/articles/SB988922808939024392.

21. Jaffe and Squeo, "Crusader Artillery Gun Is Quarry."

22. Jaffe and Squeo, "Crusader Artillery Gun Is Quarry"; "Fact Sheet: The Debate over the

Crusader," CNN online, last modified May 10, 2002, https://edition.cnn.com/2002 /ALLPOLITICS/05/10/crusader.fact.sheet/.

23. Robert Dorr, "Review of Many Questions; Few Answers," *Aerospace America* online, January 2000; "Fact Sheet: The Debate over the Crusader."

24. Jaffe and Squeo, "Crusader Artillery Gun Is Quarry."

25. Dorr, "Review of Many Questions."

26. "Fact Sheet: Debate over the Crusader."

27. Jaime Holguin, "Rumsfeld Kills the Crusader," CBS News online, May 10, 2002, https://www.cbsnews.com/news/rumsfeld-kills-the-crusader-10-05-2002/.

28. Brady Mullins, "Rise and Fall of a K Street Renegade."

29. Solomon, *Washington Century.*

30. Rick Perlstein, *Reaganland: America's Right Turn 1976–1980* (New York: Simon & Schuster, 2020).

31. Solomon, *Washington Century.*

32. White House, "President Signs Campaign Finance Reform Act," press release, March 27, 2002, https://georgewbush-whitehouse.archives.gov/news/releases/2002 /03/20020327.html.

33. Tommy Boggs, interviewed by Robert Novak, *Novak Zone,* CNN, November 29, 2003, http://www.cnn.com/TRANSCRIPTS/0311/29/smn.06.html.

34. T. R. Goldman, "Two of a Kind: Flush with Cash, Connections," *Influence,* May 26, 2004.

35. Ibid.

36. Jennifer Lee, "Youth, Cash and Promise Are Brought Together," *New York Times* online, July 30, 2004, https://www.nytimes.com/2004/07/30/politics/campaign/youth -cash-and-promise-are-brought-together.html.

37. Ibid.

38. Ibid.

39. Goldman, "Two of a Kind."

40. Brody Mullins, "Donor Bundling Emerges as Major Ill in '08 Race," *Wall Street Journal* online, October 19, 2007, https://www.wsj.com/articles/SB119267248520862997.

41. T. Edward Nickens, "Where Waterfowling Is a Family Affair," *Garden & Gun* online, February/March 2020, https://gardenandgun.com/feature/where-waterfowling-is-a -family-affair/.

42. "Lobbying Firm Profile: Patton Boggs LLP, 2003."

43. Ibid.

44. Jennifer Frey, "A Double Dose of Heartache," *Washington Post* online, January 9, 2001, https://www.washingtonpost.com/archive/lifestyle/2001/01/09/a-double-dose-of -heartache/316cde6f-ef86-48e2-832b-445c880f4c41/.

45. Ibid.

46. Ibid.

47. Ibid.

48. Ibid.

49. Ibid.

50. Gary Gately, "A Drug's Dark Side," *Baltimore Sun* online, March 4, 2001, https://www.baltimoresun.com/news/bs-xpm-2001-03-04-0103060364-story.html.

51. Gately, "A Drug's Dark Side."

52. Frey, "Double Dose of Heartache."

53. Bart Stupak, "Safety of Accutane," clip from House Armed Services Subcommittee on Oversight and Investigations and the House Energy and Commerce Subcommittee on Oversight and Investigations, December 6, 2002, https://www.c-span.org/video/?174192-1/safety-accutane&event=174192&playEvent.

54. Ginger Gillenwater, "Congressman Turns up the Heat on the FDA over Accutane and Others," Lawyersandsettlements.com, February 23, 2008, https://www.lawyersandsettlements.com/features/accutane/accutane-suicide.html.

55. Frey, "Double Dose of Heartache."

56. *Accutane—Is This Acne Drug Treatment Linked to Depression and Suicide? Hearing before the Committee on Government Reform*, US House, 106th Cong., 2d sess. (December 5, 2000), https://www.govinfo.gov/content/pkg/CHRG-106hhrg73924/html/CHRG-106hhrg73924.htm.

57. Gately, "A Drug's Dark Side."

58. Frey, "Double Dose of Heartache."

59. Ibid.

60. John Flesher, Associated Press, "Congressman Links Acne Drug to Son's Suicide," *Daily Republican Register* (Mt. Carmel, IL), October 5, 2000, 6.

61. Stupak, "Safety of Accutane."

62. Frey, "Double Dose of Heartache."

63. Stupak, "Safety of Accutane."

64. Gilbert Cruz, "And the Earth Cried: Top 10 Environmental Disasters," *Time* online, May 3, 2010, https://content.time.com/time/specials/packages/article/0,28804,1986457_1986501_1986449,00.html.

65. "Review of Suspended Sentences Given in Baby Deaths," Associated Press, February 11, 1980.

66. Tony Micallef, "Daring to Break Silence," *Times of Malta* (Birkirkara) online, December 22, 2014, https://timesofmalta.com/articles/view/Daring-to-break-silence.549401.

67. "Review of Stanley Adams; Good Guys Finish Last," *Economist*, March 22, 1980.

68. "Blowing the Final Whistle," *Guardian* (US edition) online, November 25, 2001, https://www.theguardian.com/business/2001/nov/25/businessofresearch.research.

69. Micallef, "Daring to Break."

70. Stanley Adams, *Roche Versus Adams* (London: Fontana Press, 1985).

71. "A Song for Europe (TV Movie 1985)," IMDb, accessed May 1, 2023, https://www.imdb.com/title/tt0088964/?ref_=ttpl_ov_i.

72. Naftali Bendavid, "Vitamin Price-Fixing Draws Record $755 Million in Fines," *Chicago Tribune* online, May 21, 1999, https://www.chicagotribune.com/news/ct-xpm-1999-05-21-9905210013-story.html.

73. Ibid.

74. Michael J. Sniffen, Associated Press, "Vitamin Execs Sentenced in Price Fixing," *Los Angeles Times* online, April 7, 2000, https://www.latimes.com/archives/la-xpm-2000-apr-07-fi-16975-story.html.

75. Bendavid, "Vitamin Price-Fixing."

76. US Department of Justice, "F. Hoffmann-La Roche and BASF Agree to Pay Record Criminal Fines for Participating in International Vitamin Cartel—F. Hoffmann-La Roche Agrees to Pay $500 Million, Highest Criminal Fine Ever," press release, May 20, 1999, https://www.justice.gov/archive/atr/public/press_releases/1999/2450.htm#:~:text=Hoffmann%2DLa%20Roche%20Ltd%20today.

77. Bendavid, "Vitamin Price-Fixing."

78. US Department of Justice, "Former F. Hoffman-La Roche Executive Agrees to Plead Guilty for Participating in International Vitamin Cartel—Second Executive to Plead Guilty, Will Serve Jail Time and Pay $150,000 Fine," press release, August 19, 1999, https://www.justice.gov/archive/atr/public/press_releases/1999/2626.htm.

79. Russell Mokhiber, "Top 100 Corporate Criminals of the Decade," *Corporate Crime Reporter* online, https://www.corporatecrimereporter.com/top100.html.

80. "Drug Maker Roche Returning to Its Roots," AP News, accessed May 1, 2023, https://apnews.com/article/4a608296254251ce0d2d27eb8c518c14.

81. "Review of Heart Drug Pulled for Interactions," *Times Union* (Colonie, NY), June 9, 1998.

82. Lauran Neerbard, "Review of FDA Links New Parkinson's Drug to Deaths from Liver Failure," Associated Press, November 16, 1998.

83. "Xenical Commercial (1999)," YouTube, 1:00, uploaded by vhs vcr, June 29, 2016, https://www.youtube.com/watch?v=bpsz6mMRKDc; "Mel Gibson Expresses His Concern on the Danger of Losing Our Rights as Americans to Take Vitamins as We See Fit," YouTube, 1:15, uploaded by milealsa, March 27, 2007, https://www.google.com/search?q=mel+gibson+dietary+supplement+commercial&oq=Mel+Gibson+dietary+supp&aqs=chrome.2.69i57j33i10i160j33i10i22i29i30.6291j0j7&sourceid=chrome&ie=UTF-8#fpstate=ive&vld=cid:8f996263,vid:IV2olDA0w8U.

84. "Roche Names Abercrombie as New Head of North American Pharmaceuticals Operations," PR Newswire, January 8, 2001.

85. Lynne Lamberg, "M.D.s Must Warn That Acne Drug Can Cause Depression," *Psychiatric News* online, May 4, 2001, https://doi.org/10.1176/pn.36.9.0038.

86. Mark Benjamin and Dan Olmsted, "Two Studies Probe Suicide, Accutane Link," United Press International online, May 3, 2002, https://www.upi.com/Top_News/2002/05/03/Two-studies-probe-suicide-Accutane-link/85971020435113/.

87. Brody Mullins, "Rise and Fall of a K Street Renegade."

88. Ibid.
89. Ibid.
90. Robert Welliver et al., "Effectiveness of Oseltamivir in Preventing Influenza in Household Contacts: A Randomized Controlled Trial," *Journal of the American Medical Association* (*JAMA*) 285, no. 6 (February 14, 2001): 748–54, https://doi.org/10.1001/jama.285.6.748.
91. Brody Mullins, "Rise and Fall of a K Street Renegade."
92. David Vogel, *Fluctuating Fortunes: The Political Power of Business in America* (New York: Basic Books, 1989), 286–87.
93. Ibid.

Chapter 10

1. Rita Zeidner, "Lake Barcroft Offers Beach Living Inside the Beltway," *Washington Post* online, July 27, 2014, https://www.washingtonpost.com/realestate/where-we-live-lake-barcroft-offers-beach-living-inside-the-beltway/2014/06/25/72547b12-efef-11e3-9ebc-2ee6f81ed217_story.html.
2. Luke Mullins, "The Making and Unmaking of Tony and Heather Podesta's Power Marriage," *Washingtonian* online, August 11, 2014, https://www.washingtonian.com/2014/08/11/the-making-and-unmaking-of-a-power-marriage/.
3. Ibid.
4. Manuel Roig-Franzia, "Heather Podesta, a Storm in the Summer of a Lobbyist," *Washington Post* online, August 24, 2009, https://www.washingtonpost.com/wp-dyn/content/article/2009/08/23/AR2009082302381.html.
5. Luke Mullins, "Making and Unmaking of Tony and Heather."
6. Ibid.
7. Brody Mullins and Julie Bykowicz, "How Tony Podesta, a Washington Power Broker, Lost It All," *Wall Street Journal* online, April 18, 2018, https://www.wsj.com/articles/how-tony-podesta-a-washington-power-broker-lost-it-all-1524065781.
8. Luke Mullins, "Making and Unmaking of Tony and Heather."
9. Ibid.
10. Ibid.
11. Ibid.
12. Ibid.
13. Michael Barbaro and Ashley Parker, "A Glimpse of Lobbyists' Convention Exile," *New York Times* online, September 3, 2012, https://archive.nytimes.com/thecaucus.blogs.nytimes.com/2012/09/03/a-glimpse-of-lobbyists-convention-exile/.
14. Jessica Dawson, "Married, with Art," *Washington Post* online, September 23, 2004, https://www.washingtonpost.com/archive/lifestyle/2004/09/23/married-with-art/dee9a0d0-0f0d-4505-b0ef-2f0e1bd1e0e0/.
15. Alexander Burns and Kenneth Vogel, "Scarlet 'L': Lobbyists Mix with Pols," *Politico* online, last modified August 29, 2008, https://www.politico.com/story/2008/08/scarlet-l-lobbyists-mix-with-pols-012908.

16. Staff, "Best and Worst from the Denver Convention," Cox News Service, August 28, 2008.

17. John F. Harris, "President Chooses Podesta as Top Aide," *Washington Post* online, October 21, 1998, https://www.washingtonpost.com/wp-srv/politics/special/clinton /stories/podesta102198.htm.

18. Luke Mullins, "Making and Unmaking of Tony and Heather."

19. Ibid.

20. Robert Pear and John Broder, "In a Lobby-Happy Washington, Politics Can Be Even Thicker Than Blood," *New York Times* online, September 5, 2000, https://www .nytimes.com/2000/09/05/us/in-a-lobby-happy-washington-politics-can-be-even -thicker-than-blood.html.

21. John Donnelly, "The Fowl Bowl on Capitol Hill," *Washington Post* online, June 17, 1994, https://www.washingtonpost.com/archive/lifestyle/1994/06/17/the-fowl-bowl -on-capitol-hill/10c4609e-b0e6-4e61-af52-e823a0338eba/.

22. Ibid.

23. Bob Vandervoort, "A Chicken in Every Bowling Alley?," States News Service, June 16, 1994.

24. Shannon Brownlee, "Swallowing Ephedra," Salon, last modified June 7, 2000, https:// www.salon.com/2000/06/07/ephedra/.

25. "Mel Gibson Expresses His Concern on the Danger of Losing Our Rights as Americans to Take Vitamins as We See Fit," YouTube, 1:15, uploaded by milealsa, March 27, 2007, https://www.google.com/search?q=mel+gibson+dietary+supplement+commercial&o q=Mel+Gibson+dietaty+supp&aqs=chrome.2.69i57j33i10i160j33i10i22i29i30.6291j0j 7&sourceid=chrome&ie=UTF-8#fpstate=ive&vld=cid:8f996263,vid:IV2olDA0w8U.

26. Sara Miles, "Do *You* Know Tony Podesta?," *Wired* online, December 1, 1998, https:// www.wired.com/1998/12/podesta/.

27. "Update: Mortality Attributable to HIV Infection Among Persons Aged 25–44 Years—United States, 1991 and 1992," *Morbidity and Mortality Weekly Report* (*MMWR*) 42, no. 45 (November 19, 1993): 869–72, https://www.cdc.gov/mmwr/pre view/mmwrhtml/00022174.htm.

28. Ibid.

29. Paul Duggan, "1,000 Swarm FDA's Rockville Office to Demand Approval of Aids Drugs," *Washington Post* online, October 12, 1998, https://www.washingtonpost.com /archive/local/1988/10/12/1000-swarm-fdas-rockville-office-to-demand-approval -of-aids-drugs/eb77ac58-c872-4792-9c87-d758ad302773/.

30. Ibid.

31. Ibid.

32. Ibid.

33. Miles, "Do *You* Know Tony Podesta?"

34. Ibid.

35. Ibid.

36. Ibid.

37. Ibid.

38. Ibid.

39. White House, "Strengthening and Modernizing the FDA," press release, November 21, 1997, https://clintonwhitehouse5.archives.gov/WH/Work/112197.html#:~:text=Today%2C%20President%20Clinton%20signed%20into,FDA%20for%20the%2021st%20century.

40. "Remarks on Signing the Food and Drug Administration Modernization Act of 1997, November 21, 1997," in *Public Papers of the Presidents of the United States: William J. Clinton, 1997*, bk. 2, *July 1 to December 31, 1997* (Washington, DC: Government Printing Office, 1999), 1625, https://www.google.com/books/edition/Public_Papers _of_the_Presidents_of_the_U/vZN4mt0vba8C?hl=en&gbpv=1&bsq=model%20 for%20what%20America%20has%20to%20do%20in%20area%20after%20area%20 after%20area.

41. Miles, "Do *You* Know Tony Podesta?"

42. White House, Office of the Vice President, "Vice President Gore Names David Beier Domestic Policy Advisor," press release, April 10, 1998, https://clintonwhitehouse6. archives.gov/1998/04/1998-04-10-vp-names-new-domestic-policy-advisor.html.

43. Bill McAllister, "A Hit with the Gang," *Washington Post* online, December 24, 1998, https://www.washingtonpost.com/archive/politics/1998/12/24/a-hit-with-the -gang/3bced7e0-7d3e-4598-8eb4-7e293cf2d1d0/.

44. Miles, "Do *You* Know Tony Podesta?"

45. Ibid.

46. Pear and Broder, "In a Lobby-Happy Washington."

47. Luke Mullins, "Making and Unmaking of Tony and Heather."

48. Ibid.

49. Maria Puente, "Savvy Art Collectors Focus on Photos Market Zooms as Celebrities, Affluent Boomers Develop Affinity for Affordable Art," *USA Today*, March 23, 2001.

50. Dawson, "Married, with Art."

51. Luke Mullins, "Making and Unmaking of Tony and Heather."

52. Roig-Franzia, "Heather Podesta."

53. Ibid.

54. Dawson, "Married, with Art."

55. Ibid.

56. Luke Mullins, "Making and Unmaking of Tony and Heather."

57. Staff, "Washington's Most Influential Women," *National Journal*, July 12, 2012.

58. Brody Mullins and Bykowicz, "How Tony Podesta . . . Lost It All."

59. Mary Ann Akers, "Heard of the Hill," *Roll Call* online, October 5, 2004.

60. Mark Kukis, Kellie Lunney, and Gregg Sangillo, *National Journal*, June 11, 2005.

61. Brody Mullins and Bykowicz, "How Tony Podesta . . . Lost It All."

62. Luke Mullins, "Making and Unmaking of Tony and Heather."

63. Dawson, "Married, with Art."

64. Brody Mullins and Bykowicz, "How Tony Podesta . . . Lost It All."

65. Dawson, "Married, with Art."

66. Brody Mullins and Bykowicz, "How Tony Podesta . . . Lost It All."

67. Dawson, "Married, with Art."

68. Luke Mullins, "Making and Unmaking of Tony and Heather."

69. Amy Argetsinger and Roxanne Roberts, "Reliable Source," *Washington Post*, November 20, 2007.

70. Dawson, "Married, with Art."

71. Kenneth P. Vogel, "The Russia Inquiry Ended a Democratic Lobbyist's Career. He Wants It Back," *New York Times* online, July 8, 2021, https://www.nytimes .com/2021/07/08/us/politics/tony-podesta-lobbying-democrats.html.

72. Clara Grudberg, "Tony Podesta Had a Toilet Camera? Yes, Tony Podesta Had a Toilet Camera," *Washingtonian* online, July 12, 2021, https://www.washingtonian .com/2021/07/12/tony-podesta-had-a-toilet-camera-yes-tony-podesta-had-a-toilet -camera/.

73. Dawson, "Married, with Art."

74. Luke Mullins, "Making and Unmaking of Tony and Heather."

75. Ibid.

76. Roig-Franzia, "Heather Podesta."

77. Susan Schmidt and James V. Grimaldi, "The Fast Rise and Steep Fall of Jack Abramoff," *Washington Post* online, December 29, 2005, https://www.washingtonpost.com/ar. chive/politics/2005/12/29/the-fast-rise-and-steep-fall-of-jack-abramoff/56987391 -1b47-414d-866e-531bc2b0a603/.

78. Spencer S. Hsu, "DeLay Aide Sentenced to 20 Months in Abramoff Lobbying Scandal," *Washington Post* online, February 11, 2011, https://www.washingtonpost .com/national/delay-aide-sentenced-to-20-months-in-abramoff-lobbying-scan dal/2011/02/11/ABnQGtQ_story.html.

79. Schmidt and Grimaldi, "Fast Rise and Steep Fall."

80. Philip Shenon and David Stout, "Ney Pleads Guilty over Abramoff Bribes," *New York Times* online, October 13, 2006, https://www.nytimes.com/2006/10/13/wash ington/14neycnd.html.

81. Lawrence Hurley, "Court Upholds Former Congressional Staffer's Conviction," Reuters online, last modified August 12, 2014, https://www.reuters.com/article /us-usa-court-abramoff/court-upholds-former-cngressional-staffers-conviction -idUKKBN0GC1GC20140812.

82. US Department of Justice, "Former Lobbyist Jack Abramoff Sentenced to 48 Months in Prison on Charges Involving Corruption, Fraud, Conspiracy, and Tax Evasion," press release, September 4, 2008, https://www.justice.gov/archive/opa/pr/2008/Sep tember/08-crm-779.html.

83. Glen Justice, "For Lobbyist, a Seat of Power Came with a Plate," *New York Times*

online, July 6, 2005, https://www.nytimes.com/2005/07/06/politics/for-lobbyist-a-seat-of-power-came-with-a-plate.html.

84. William Branigin, Susan Schmidt, and James V. Grimaldi, "Abramoff Pleads Guilty to 3 Felony Counts," *Washington Post* online, January 3, 2006, https://www.washingtonpost.com/archive/business/technology/2006/01/03/abramoff-pleads-guilty-to-3-felony-charges/e21d6a67-51c3-49bb-9b3d-3a92887e3b86/.

85. US DOJ, "Former Lobbyist Jack Abramoff Sentenced to 48 Months in Prison."

86. Jessica Schneider and Caroline Kelly, "Washington Insider Jack Abramoff to Head Back to Prison, Prosecutors Say," CNN online, last modified June 25, 2020, https://www.cnn.com/2020/06/25/politics/jack-abramoff-back-to-prison/index.html.

87. Honest Leadership and Open Government Act of 2007, H.R. 2316, 110th Cong. (2007), https://www.congress.gov/bill/110th-congress/house-bill/2316.

88. Ibid.

89. Ibid.

90. Senate Rules Committee, "U.S. Senate Passes Comprehensive Lobbying and Ethics Reform Bill," press release, August 2, 2007, https://www.rules.senate.gov/news/minority-news/u-s-senate-passes-comprehensive-lobbying-and-ethics-reform-bill.

91. Isaac Arnsdorf, "The Lobbying Reform That Enriched Congress," *Politico* online, last modified July 3, 2016, https://www.politico.com/story/2016/06/the-lobbying-reform-that-enriched-congress-224849.

92. Brody Mullins and Bykowicz, "How Tony Podesta . . . Lost It All."

93. Steve Carlic, "Schumer: Democrats, If They Are the Victors, Better Act Fast," *Post-Standard* (Syracuse, NY) online, March 2, 2008, https://www.syracuse.com/news/2008/03/schumer_democrats_if_they_are.html.

94. Emily Heil and Elizabeth Brotherton, "Heard on The Hill," *Roll Call* online, March 25, 2009, https://rollcall.com/2004/10/05/heard-on-the-hill-star-wars/.

95. Brody Mullins and Bykowicz, "How Tony Podesta . . . Lost It All."

96. Jake Tapper, "Obama Ad Omits Lobbyist Reference," ABC News online, December 29, 2007, https://abcnews.go.com/Politics/Vote2008/story?id=4064444&page=1.

97. "Transcript of Second McCain, Obama Debate," CNN online, October 7, 2008, https://www.cnn.com/2008/POLITICS/10/07/presidential.debate.transcript/.

98. Peter Overby, "Obama Bans DNC from Taking Lobbyists' Money," NPR online, last modified June 6, 2008, https://www.npr.org/2008/06/06/91226631/obama-bans-dnc-from-taking-lobbyists-money.

99. Charles Babington, "Obama Finding Lobbyist Promise Is Hard to Keep," *Standard-Times* (New Bedford, MA) online, February 2, 2009, https://www.southcoasttoday.com/story/news/nation-world/2009/02/03/obama-finding-lobbyist-promise-is/52108904007/.

100. Brody Mullins, "Lobbyist Heather Podesta Draws a Parallel to Hester Prynne," *Wall Street Journal*, August 28, 2008.

101. Ibid.

102. Ibid.

103. Roig-Franzia, "Heather Podesta."

104. Brody Mullins, "Lobbyist Heather Podesta Draws a Parallel."

105. Roig-Franzia, "Heather Podesta."

106. Brody Mullins, "Lobbyist Heather Podesta Draws a Parallel."

107. Burns and Vogel, "Scarlet 'L'"

Chapter 11

1. Barack Obama, Inaugural Address, transcript of speech delivered in Washington, DC, January 21, 2009, https://obamawhitehouse.archives.gov/blog/2009/01/21/pres ident-Barack-obamas-inaugural-address.

2. "Healthcare System," Gallup online, https://news.gallup.com/poll/4708/healthcare -system.aspx.

3. "One Year Later, Health Care Reform Declared Dead Issue," *Tampa Bay (FL) Times* online, October 7, 2005, https://www.tampabay.com/archive/1994/09/27/one-year -later-health-care-reform-declared-dead-issue/.

4. White House, Office of the Press Secretary, "Remarks of President Barack Obama—Address to Joint Sessions of Congress," press release, February 24, 2009, https:// obamawhitehouse.archives.gov/the-press-office/remarks-president-barack-obama -address-joint-session-congress.

5. Lindsay Mark Lewis, *Political Mercenaries: The Inside Story of How Fundraisers Allowed Billionaires to Take Over Politics* (New York: St. Martin's Press, 2014), 228.

6. Ibid.

7. Joanna Breitstein and Walter Armstrong, "45 Under 45: The Change Generation," *Pharmaceutical Executive* online, June 1, 2008, https://www.pharmexec.com /view/45-under-45the-change-generation.

8. Sam Cage, "Roche's $46.8 Billion Genentech Deal Outshines Others," Reuters online, last modified March 12, 2009, https://www.reuters.com/article/us-roche-genentech-sb /roches-46-8-billion-genentech-deal-outshines-others-idUSTRE52B1DN20090312.

9. Ibid.

10. Andrew Pollack, "Roche Agrees to Buy Genentech for $46.8 Billion," *New York Times* online, March 12, 2009, https://www.nytimes.com/2009/03/13/business /worldbusiness/13drugs.html.

11. Tracey Staton, "Genentech Brand to Replace Roche in the US," *Fierce Pharma*, October 19, 2009, https://www.fiercepharma.com/pharma/genentech-brand-to-replace -roche-u-s.

12. Pollack, "Roche Agrees to Buy Genentech."

13. Nancy Waltzman, "Corporate Funded Nonprofit Works at Nexus of Politics and Entertainment," *Sunlight Foundation*, August 31, 2012, https://sunlightfoundation .com/2012/08/31/artists-and-athletes/.

14. Mary Yarrison, "Biden Boys Headline Artists & Athletes Alliance Fundraiser for

ServiceNation," *Washingtonian* online, January 21, 2013, https://www.washingtonian.com/2013/01/21/biden-boys-headline-artists-athletes-alliance-fundraiser-for-servicenation/.

15. Chris Frates, "Will Roche Get a Republican Leader?," *Politico* online, last modified May 7, 2009, https://www.politico.com/story/2009/05/will-roche-get-a-republican-leader-022237.

16. Ibid.

17. Ibid.

18. Ibid.

19. Chris Frates, "Roche Keeps Dem in Charge," *Politico* online, last modified May 19, 2009, https://www.politico.com/story/2009/05/roche-keeps-dem-in-charge-022742.

20. Alicia Mundy, "US House Panel Backs Exclusivity for Biologic Drugs," *Wall Street Journal* online, August 2, 2009, https://www.wsj.com/articles/SB124917341780899303.

21. "White House Stands Firm on 7-Year Biologics Exclusivity Period," *Inside Washington's FDA Week* 15, no. 25 (June 26, 2009).

22. Lisa Richwine, "Obama Seeks Path for Cheaper Generic Biotech Drugs," Reuters online, last modified February 26, 2009, https://www.reuters.com/article/us-obama-budget-generics-sb/obama-seeks-path-for-cheaper-generic-biotech-drugs-idUS TRE51P6YT20090226.

23. Mundy, "US House Panel Backs Exclusivity."

24. Chitra Sethi, "House Committee Supports 12-Year Data Exclusivity Period for Biologics," *International BioPharm*, August 3, 2009, https://www.biopharminternational.com/view/house-committee-supports-12-year-data-exclusivity-period-biologics.

25. Katie Kindelan, "Cuing Up the Latest Fight Over Generic Drugs," *Roll Call* online, March 17, 2009, https://rollcall.com/2009/03/17/cuing-up-the-latest-fight-over-generic-drugs/.

26. Maureen Groppe, "Obama Wants More Savings from Drug Makers," *Gannett News Service*, July 24, 2009.

27. John Wilkerson, "Waxman Suffers Unusual Defeat On Biosimilars," *Inside Washington's FDA Week* 15, no. 31 (August 7, 2009): 4, https://www.jstor.org/stable/26721454.

28. Ibid.

29. Ibid.

30. "US House Panel Adopts 12 Years' Biologicals Exclusivity," *Generics and Biosimilars Initiative*, January 10, 2009, https://www.gabionline.net/biosimilars/news/US-House-panel-adopts-12-years-biologicals-exclusivity.

31. Biotechnology Industry Organization, "Representative Eshoo Honored as BIO Legislator of the Year," press release, April 16, 2010, https://archive.bio.org/media/press-release/representative-eshoo-honored-bio-legislator-year-0.

32. Robert Pear, "In House, Many Spoke with One Voice: Lobbyists," *New York Times* online, November 14, 2009, https://www.nytimes.com/2009/11/15/us/politics/15health.html.

33. Ibid.
34. Ibid.
35. Ibid.
36. Ibid.
37. Ibid.
38. Ibid.
39. Ibid.
40. Ibid.
41. Ibid.
42. Ibid.

Chapter 12

1. *Politico* staff, "The Scenemakers: Jim Courtovich," *Politico* online, last modified July 23, 2010, https://www.politico.com/story/2010/07/the-scenemakers-040060.
2. Brody Mullins, "When the Party's Over: Washington's Premier Social Connector Fades from View," *Wall Street Journal* online, January 2, 2020, https://www.wsj.com /articles/when-the-partys-over-washingtons-premier-social-connector-fades-from -view-11577997343.
3. Mary Ann Akers, "Election Night Revelers Prepare to Party," *Washington Post*, November 3, 2008.
4. Mike Allen, *Politico* Playbook, last modified May 17, 2009, https://www.politico .com/tipsheets/playbook/2009/05/presented-by-the-us-travel-association-rummys -bible-verses-obama-i-dont-watch-cable-news-at-all-courics-profile-of-sec-gates -on-60-tonight-002365.
5. Ibid., last modified December 5, 2010, https://www.politico.com/tipsheets/play book/2010/12/potus-will-compromise-on-tax-cuts-for-rich-in-return-for-unemplo ment-extension-the-bernanke-is-on-the-60-minutes-billy-piper-goes-private-axe -at-gaucho-griffin-harris-roy-schwartz-bdays-002941.
6. Ibid., last modified May 17, 2009.
7. Ibid.
8. Ibid., last modified December 5, 2010.
9. Ibid.
10. Ibid.
11. Ibid., last modified October 17, 2011, https://www.politico.com/tipsheets/play book/2011/10/obama-begins-bus-tour-of-va-nc-world-series-jack-olivers-st-louis -cards-slight-favorite-over-president-bushs-texas-rangers-game-1-is-wed-jamal-en gaged-ken-baer-bday-003259.
12. *Politico* staff, "Scenemakers: Courtovich."
13. Brody Mullins, "When the Party's Over."
14. *Politico* staff, "Scenemakers: Courtovich."
15. Brody Mullins, "When the Party's Over."

16. Allen, *Politico* Playbook, last modified December 5, 2020.

17. Ibid., last modified May 23, 2020, https://www.politico.com/tipsheets/playbook /2010/05/what-the-west-wing-is-reading-gops-aloha-win-gibbs-hits-bp-transpar ency-kaine-blumenthal-statements-were-wrong-steele-uncomfortable-w-paul-civil -rights-words-rick-kleins-new-gig-002741.

18. Ibid., last modified May 18, 2008, https://www.politico.com/tipsheets/playbook /2008/05/mccain-could-lose-top-fund-raiser-in-lobbying-flap-clinton-obama-fi nanciers-start-merger-talks-001993.

19. Ibid.

20. Ibid., last modified May 22, 2011.

21. Chavie Lieber, "Meet the Man Who Fixes Retail CEO Disasters," *Racked*, July 1, 2014, https://www.racked.com/2014/7/1/7589259/crisis-management-plan-pr-firm-wash ington-dc-chip-wilson-lululemon.

22. Cleveland State University, "Remembering Former CSU President Dr. Claire A. Van Ummersen," press release, September 30, 2021, https://www.csuohio.edu/news/re membering-former-csu-president-dr-claire-van-ummersen.

23. "Top 40 Party Colleges," *Playboy*, January 1987.

24. *Boston Globe* staff, "Death Notices," *Boston Globe*, May 23, 1995.

25. Sam Howe Verhovek, "Politics: Bowing Out; Big Budget, Early Start and the Candidate Are Figured in the Collapse of Gramm's Bid," *New York Times* online, February 15, 1996, https://www.nytimes.com/1996/02/15/us/politics-bowing-big-budget-early -start-candidate-are-figured-collapse-gramm-s.html.

26. Ibid.

27. Richard L. Berke, "Candidates Seek Early Earful to Avoid a Rejection at Polls," *New York Times* online, October 9, 1995, https://www.nytimes.com/1995/10/09/us/candi dates-seek-early-earful-to-avoid-a-rejection-at-polls.html.

28. Howard Troxler, "Running Hard So as to Not Be Also-Rans," *St. Petersburg (FL) Times*, January 20, 1996, 1.

29. John King, "Political Notebook: Clinton's Ohio Pitch; RNC Tax Ads; Gramm vs Bu chanan," Associated Press, October 20, 1995.

30. Susan Feeney, "Forbes Tests Value of Door-to-Door New Hampshire Campaigning," *Dallas Morning News*, February 4, 1996.

31. David S. Broder, "Suddenly a Force in New Hampshire," *Washington Post* online, January 23, 1996, https://www.washingtonpost.com/archive/opinions/1996/01/23 /suddenly-a-force-in-new-hampshire/29199018-b41b-474e-a719-a0c0948b69fa/.

32. Michael Lewis, *Losers: The Road to Everyplace but the White House* (New York: Vin tage Books, 1998), 18.

33. Don Gonyea, "From the Start, Obama Struggled with Fallout from a Kind of Fake News," NPR online, January 10, 2017, https://www.npr.org/2017/01/10/509164679 /from-the-start-obama-struggled-with-fallout-from-a-kind-of-fake-news.

34. Ibid.

35. Solange Uwimana, "Beck Continues Never Ending Quest to Prove 'Death Panels' Really Are 'Coming,'" Media Matters for America, last modified April 13, 2011, https://www.mediamatters.org/glenn-beck/beck-continues-neverending-quest-prove-death-panels-really-are-coming.

36. 6ABC, "Suicide Note: 'D.C. Madam' Said She Didn't Want Prison," WPVI-TV online, last modified May 5, 2008, https:/6abc.com/archive/6122662/#:~:text=Deborah%20Palfrey%20was%20convicted%20of,David%20Vitter%2C%20a%20Louisiana%20Republican.

37. "*Hustler* Says It Revealed Senator's Link to Escort Service," CNN online, last modified July 10, 2007, https://www.cnn.com/2007/POLITICS/07/10/vitter.madam/index.html.

38. "New Woes for Senator Caught in Sex Scandal," CBS News online, last modified July 11, 2007, https://www.cbsnews.com/news/new-woes-for-senator-caught-in-sex-scandal/.

39. Adam Nossiter, "Senator Apologizes Again for Prostitution Link," *New York Times* online, July 17, 2017, https://www.nytimes.com/2007/07/17/us/17vitter.html.

40. "Vitter Raises Concerns About Cancer Treatment Rationing Practices at FDA," *Targeted News Service*, July 28, 2010.

41. "FDA Panel Urges Ending Approval of Breast-Cancer Drug," *Denver Post* online, July 20, 2010, https://www.denverpost.com/2010/07/20/fda-panel-urges-ending-approval-of-breast-cancer-drug.

42. Maggie Fox, "Avastin Battle Illustrates Washington's Health Care Pressures," *National Journal*, June 28, 2011.

43. Venable, "What Is Lobbying Under the LDA?," press release, January 2017, https://www.venable.com/files/Publication/7b6e0b31-c0ca-478e-bf13-718819dc51cd/Presentation/PublicationAttachment/de6f332e-b107-44b8-9191-790778162d15/What-is-Lobbying-Under-the-LDA.pdf.

44. Isaac Arnsdorf, "The Lobbying Reform That Enriched Congress," *Politico* online, last modified July 3, 2016, https://www.politico.com/story/2016/06/the-lobbying-reform-that-enriched-congress-224849.

45. Lee Fang, "Where Have All the Lobbyists Gone?," *Nation* online, February 19, 2014, https://www.thenation.com/article/archive/shadow-lobbying-complex/.

46. Brody Mullins, "The Rise and Fall of a K Street Renegade," *Wall Street Journal* online, February 13, 2017, https://www.wsj.com/articles/the-rise-and-fall-of-a-k-street-renegade-1487001918.

47. Ibid.

48. Ibid.

49. Ibid.

50. Ibid.

51. Lauren Schuker Blum and Craig Karmin, "Washington, D.C.: The New Boomtown,"

Wall Street Journal online, May 23, 2013, https://www.wsj.com/articles/SB100014241 2788732476700457848920224 7919668.

52. Ibid.

53. Ibid.

54. Veronica Toney, "Complete Guest List for the State Dinner in Honor of Prime Minister Lee Hsien Loong of Singapore," *Washington Post* online, August 2, 2016, https://www.washingtonpost.com/news/reliable-source/wp/2016/08/02/complete -guest-list-for-the-state-dinner-in-honor-of-prime-minister-lee-hsien-loong-of -singapore/.

55. National Media, "$6.3 Million in Political Advertising Airs on Corporate Scandals; National Media, Inc: Total Could Reach $50 Million by Election Day," press release, August 16, 2002.

56. Susan Glasser, "Covering Politics in a 'Post-Truth' America," *Politico* online, last modified December 13, 2016, https://www.politico.com/magazine/story/2016/12 /journalism-post-truth-trump-2016-election-politics-susan-glasser-214523/.

57. Ibid.

58. U.S. Senate Permanent Subcommittee on Investigations, "Senate Investigations Sub-committee Releases Levin-Coburn Report on the Financial Crisis," press release, April 13, 2011, https://www.hsgac.senate.gov/wp-content/uploads/imo/media/doc /PSIfinancialreportrelease041311.pdf.

59. "Congress Wants Say on Wall Street Pay," Associated Press, July 31, 2009, https:// www.redlandsdailyfacts.com/2009/07/31/congress-wants-say-on-wall-street-pay-2/.

60. Nicholas Schmidle, "The Kings of the Desert," *New Yorker*, April 6, 2015; Douwe Mi-edema, Shurna Robbins, and Sarah White, "In $22 Billion Saudi Family Feud, Who Knew What?" Reuters, June 10, 2011.

61. Margaret Coker, "A Saudi Family Feud Roils World Banks," *Wall Street Journal* online, October 22, 2009, https://www.wsj.com/articles/SB125616910974700325.

62. Brody Mullins, "Rise and Fall of a K Street Renegade."

63. Ibid.

64. Ibid.

Chapter 13

1. "Federal Trade Commission Building, Washington, DC," U.S. General Services Ad-ministration website, https://www.gsa.gov/real-estate/historic-preservation/explore -historic-buildings/find-a-building/all-historic-buildings/federal-trade-commis sion-building-washington-dc.

2. "Man Controlling Trade," Atlas Obscura, https://www.atlasobscura.com/places/man -controlling-trade.

3. Robert McMillan, "Inside the Cycleplex: The Weird, Wild World of Google Bikes," *Wired*, April 25, 2013, https://www.wired.com/2013/04/google-bikes/.

4. Google, "SEC Registration Statement," April 29, 2004, https://www.sec.gov/Archives/edgar/data/1288776/000119312504073639/ds1.htm.

5. Sara Miles, "Do *You* Know Tony Podesta?," *Wired* online, December 1, 1998, https://www.wired.com/1998/12/podesta/.

6. Ibid.

7. Ibid.

8. Ibid.

9. Kathleen Elkins, "Microsoft Co-Founders Bill Gates and Paul Allen Got 'Busted' in High School for Exploiting a Bug in the Computer System," CNBC online, last modified July 2, 2019, https://www.cnbc.com/2019/07/02/microsoft-co-founders-bill-gates-and-paul-allen-met-in-high-school.html.

10. Steve Lohr, "Judge Clears Antitrust Pact for Microsoft," *New York Times* online, August 22, 1995, https://www.nytimes.com/1995/08/22/business/judge-clears-antitrust-pact-for-microsoft.html.

11. John Burgess, "FTC Deadlocks Again in Microsoft Investigation," *Washington Post* online, July 23, 1993, https://www.washingtonpost.com/archive/business/1993/07/22/ftc-deadlocks-again-in-microsoft-investigation/dd8ce8ed-1d66-4c32-b5af-6334f422e364/.

12. Lohr, "Judge Clears Antitrust Pact."

13. Rajiv Chandrasekaran, "U.S., 20 States Sue Microsoft, Allege Abuses," *Washington Post* online, May 19, 1998, https://www.washingtonpost.com/wp-srv/business/longterm/microsoft/stories/1998/suits051998.htm.

14. Department of Justice, "Justice Department Files Antitrust Suit Against Microsoft for Unlawfully Monopolizing Computer Software Markets," press release, May 18, 1998, https://www.justice.gov/archive/atr/public/press_releases/1998/1764.htm.

15. Ibid.

16. "U.S., States Sue Microsoft for Antitrust—May 18, 1998," CNN Money, accessed February 12, 2021, https://money.cnn.com/1998/05/18/technology/microsoft_suit/.

17. "Microsoft's Teflon Bill," *Business Week*, November 30, 1998, https://www.bloomberg.com/news/articles/1998-11-29/microsofts-teflon-bill.

18. Chandrasekaran, "U.S., 20 States Sue Microsoft."

19. Steve Lohr, "Government Suit Against Microsoft Shaping Up as Battle for Public Opinion," *New York Times* online, May 20, 2023, https://archive.nytimes.com/www.nytimes.com/library/tech/98/05/biztech/articles/20microsoft.html.

20. Elizabeth Corcoran, "Microsoft Settles Case with Justice," *Washington Post* online, July 17, 1994, https://www.washingtonpost.com/archive/politics/1994/07/17/microsoft-settles-case-with-justice/dd31497e-612d-4ae9-9b22-9c3a428deaa2/.

21. Joel Brinkley and Steve Lohr, *U.S. V. Microsoft: The Inside Story of the Landmark Case* (New York: McGraw-Hill, 2001), 3.

22. Ibid., 4.

23. "Microsoft's Teflon Bill," *Business Week*, November 30, 1998, https://www.bloomberg.com/news/articles/1998-11-29/microsofts-teflon-bill.

24. Ibid.

25. Elizabeth Wasserman, "Gates Deposition Makes Judge Laugh in Court," *IDG News Service,* November 16, 1998, https://web.archive.org/web/19990902200311/http://www.infoworld.com/cgi-bin/displayStory.pl?981116.ecdeposition.htm.

26. Victor Luckerson, "'Crush Them': An Oral History of the Lawsuit That Upended Silicon Valley," *Ringer,* May 18, 2018, https://www.theringer.com/tech/2018/5/18/17362452/microsoft-antitrust-lawsuit-netscape-internet-explorer-20-years.

27. Wasserman, "Gates Deposition Makes Judge Laugh."

28. "Judge's Conduct Cited in Microsoft Decision," CNN online, June 29, 2001, http://www.cnn.com/2001/LAW/06/28/microsoft.judge/index.html.

29. John Wilke, "Microsoft Moves into Politics with Campaign Contributions," *Wall Street Journal,* January 22, 1999, https://www.wsj.com/articles/SB916101568108155500.

30. Dan Morgan and Juliet Eilperin, "Microsoft Targets Funding for Antitrust Office," *Washington Post* online, October 15, 1999, https://www.washingtonpost.com/wp-srv/business/longterm/microsoft/stories/1999/microsoft101599.htm.

31. Joel Brinkley, "'Unbiased' Ads for Microsoft Came at a Price," *New York Times* online, September 18, 1999, https://archive.nytimes.com/www.nytimes.com/library/tech/99/09/biztech/articles/18soft.html.

32. Ibid.

33. Ibid.

34. James Niccolai, "Ellison Defends Oracle's Investigation of Pro-Microsoft Groups," *IDG News Service,* June 29, 2000, https://www.computerworld.com/article/2595544/ellison-defends-oracle-s-investigation-of-pro-microsoft-groups.html.

35. Paul Thurrott, "Oracle Admits to Spying on Microsoft, Ellison Takes Responsibility," *ITPro Today,* June 28, 2000, https://www.itprotoday.com/windows-8/oracle-admits-spying-microsoft-ellison-takes-responsibility.

36. Sharon Pian Chan, "Long Antitrust Saga Ends for Microsoft," *Seattle Times* online, May 12, 2011, https://www.seattletimes.com/business/microsoft/long-antitrust-saga-ends-for-microsoft/.

37. Miles, "Do *You* Know Tony Podesta?"

38. "Google Search Statistics," Internet Live Stats, https://www.internetlivestats.com/google-search-statistics/.

39. Google, "Securities and Exchange Commission Filing," December 31, 2005, https://www.sec.gov/Archives/edgar/data/1288776/000119312506056598/d10k.htm.

40. Erick Schonfeld, "Counting the Google Millionaires," TechCrunch, November 12, 2007, https://techcrunch.com/2007/11/12/counting-the-google-millionaires/#:~:text=In%20the%201990s%2C%20we%20loved,worth%20more%20than%20%245%20million.

41. "Google Added to Merriam-Webster Dictionary," CIO, July 7, 2006, https://www.cio.com/article/258818/internet-google-added-to-merriam-webster-dictionary.html#:~:text=On%20Thursday%2C%20Google%27s%20uber%2Dcompany,the%20San%20Jose%20Mercury%20News.

42. Jeffrey Toobin, "Google's Moon Shot," *New Yorker* online, January 28, 2017, https://www.newyorker.com/magazine/2007/02/05/googles-moon-shot.

43. Andrew Ross Sorkin and Jeremy W. Peters, "Google to Acquire YouTube for $1.65 Billion," *New York Times* online, October 9, 2006, https://www.nytimes.com/2006/10/09/business/09cnd-deal.html#:~:text=Google%20announced%20this%20afternoon%20that,Yahoo%20and%20the%20News%20Corporation.

44. Ken Auletta, "The Search Party," *New Yorker* online, January 7, 2008, https://www.newyorker.com/magazine/2008/01/14/the-search-party.

45. Ibid.

46. "Online Extra: At SBC, It's All About 'Scale and Scope,'" *Bloomberg*, November 7, 2005, https://www.bloomberg.com/news/articles/2005-11-06/online-extra-at-sbc-its-all-about-scale-and-scope#xj4y7vzkg.

47. "Net Neutrality," Electronic Frontier Foundation, https://www.eff.org/issues/net-neutrality.

48. Auletta, "Search Party."

49. Arshad Mohammed and Sara Kehaulani Goo, "Google Is a Tourist in D.C., Brin Finds," *Washington Post* online, June 7, 2006, https://www.washingtonpost.com/archive/business/2006/06/07/google-is-a-tourist-in-dc-brin-finds/2ce2f66c-a394-4292-9222-e8a353b7a27a/.

50. Auletta, "Search Party."

51. Ibid.

52. Ibid.

53. Ibid.

54. "A Fighter Jet and Friends in Congress: How Google Got Access to a NASA Airfield," Tech Transparency Project, September 8, 2020.

55. Jon Brodkin, "What Google Bought in the Past 12 Months," Network World, May 31, 2017, https://www.networkworld.com/article/2290619/what-google-bought-in-the-past-12-months.html.

56. Ibid.

57. Rick Whiting, "Phone Home: Google Buys VoIP Company Gizmo5," *CRN*, November 13, 2009, https://www.crn.com/news/networking/221700052/phone-home-google-buys-voip-company-gizmo5.htm.

58. John Fontana, "Google Acquires Writely Online Word-Processing Application Provider," *Network World*, March 9, 2006, https://www.networkworld.com/article/2309524/google-acquires-writely-online-word-processing-application-provider.html#:~:text=Google%20buys%20Upstartle%2C%20maker%20of,Web%2Dbased%20collaborative%20document%20editor.&text=Google%2C%20which%20late%20last%20year,an%20online%20word%2Dprocessing%20application.

59. Antone Gonsalves, "Google Buys Maker Of 3D Modeling Software," *Information Week*, March 14, 2006, https://www.informationweek.com/it-life/google-buys-maker-of-3d-modeling-software.

60. "Google Buys Video Conferencing Software," *Information and Data Manager*, April 24, 2007, https://idm.net.au/blog/001444google-buys-video-conferencing-soft ware.

Chapter 14

1. Jim Puzzanghera and Jessica Guynn, "Google Ready to Pursue Its Agenda in Washington," *Los Angeles Times* online, January 24, 2009, https://www.latimes.com/ar chives/la-xpm-2009-jan-24-fi-google24-story.html.
2. Lauren Matison, "Last Look at the Inauguration: More Photos from Google's Party," *BizBash*, February 2, 2009, https://www.bizbash.com/production-strategy/experien tial-marketing-activations-sponsorships/media-gallery/13474788/last-look-at-the -inauguration-more-photos-from-googles-party.
3. Puzzanghera and Guynn, "Google Ready to Pursue Its Agenda."
4. Arshad Mohammed and Sara Kehaulani Goo, "Google Is a Tourist in D.C., Brin Finds," *Washington Post* online, June 7, 2006, https://www.washingtonpost.com /archive/business/2006/06/07/google-is-a-tourist-in-dc-brin-finds/2ce2f66c-a394 -4292-9222-e8a353b7a27a/.
5. Puzzanghera and Guynn, "Google Ready to Pursue Its Agenda."
6. Barack Obama, "Sen. Obama Delivers Remarks on Technology at Google, Mountain View, California," *Political Transcript Wire*, November 19, 2007.
7. David D. Kirkpatrick, "Campaign Pledge on Ethics Could Become Obstacle to Filling White House Jobs," *New York Times* online, November 5, 2008, https://www.nytimes .com/2008/11/06/us/politics/06lobby.html.
8. Peter Baker, "John D. Podesta," *New York Times* online, November 5, 2008, https:// www.nytimes.com/2008/11/06/us/politics/06podesta.html.
9. "Obama's 'Hope' Portrait Goes to Gallery," Associated Press, January 7, 2009, https:// www.nbcnews.com/id/wbna28545816.
10. Amy Argetsinger and Roxanne Roberts, "Fit for a T: New at the Portrait Gallery," *Washington Post*, January 7, 2009.
11. Ben Smith, "The 'Hope' Donation," *Politico* online, last modified January 26, 2009, https://www.politico.com/blogs/ben-smith/2009/01/the-hope-donation-015671.
12. White House visitor logs.
13. Robert Draper et al., "The 50 Most Powerful People in DC," *GQ* online, October 12, 2009, https://www.gq.com/gallery/50-most-powerful-people-in-dc.
14. Carrie Levine, "Fueling K Street; Lobbying; With Bills in House, Senate Needing to Be Reconciled, Energy, Climate Change Are Hot Topics for Lobbyists," Law.com, September 26, 2007.
15. "The Jolly Postman," *Hotline*, August 27, 2009.
16. Toby Harnden, "Review of *Vitriol Flows Fast as Power Couple Split*," *Times*, April 20, 2014.
17. David D. Kirkpatrick, "Campaign Pledge on Ethics Could Become Obstacle to Filling

White House Jobs," *New York Times* online, November 6, 2008, https://www.nytimes.com/2008/11/06/us/politics/06lobby.html.

18. Eric Lichtblau, "Lobbyist Says It's Not About Influence," *New York Times* online, July 2, 2010, sec. U.S. https://www.nytimes.com/2010/07/02/us/02podesta.html.

19. Manuel Roig-Franzia, "Heather Podesta, a Storm in the Summer of a Lobbyist," *Washington Post* online, August 24, 2009, https://www.washingtonpost.com/wp-dyn/content/article/2009/08/23/AR2009082302381.html.

20. "Google Enlisted Obama Officials to Lobby States on Driverless Cars," Campaign for Accountability, September 13, 2016, https://campaignforaccountability.org/google-enlisted-obama-officials-to-lobby-states-on-driverless-cars/.

21. Ben Brody, "The Grassroots Giant: How Google Became a Lobbying Powerhouse," *Protocol*, March 16, 2022, https://www.protocol.com/policy/google-sopa-pipa-lobbying.

22. Logan Whiteside, "Google Took Away This Perk. Employees Freaked Out," CNN online, last modified April 28, 2015, https://money.cnn.com/2015/04/28/technology/google-perks/index.html#:~:text=Google%27s%20Head%20of%20People%20Operations,became%20cheaper%20and%20more%20common.

23. David Moon, Patrick Ruffini, and David Segal, eds., *Hacking Politics: How Geeks, Progressives, the Tea Party, Gamers, Anarchists, and Suits Teamed Up to Defeat SOPA and Save the Internet* (New York: OR Books, 2013), 79.

24. "Obama Administration Responds to We the People Petitions on SOPA and Online Piracy," White House, January 14, 2012, https://obamawhitehouse.archives.gov/blog/2012/01/14/Obama-administration-responds-we-people-petitions-sopa-and-online-piracy.

25. Braden Goyette, "Wikipedia Blackout 101: What Exactly Are SOPA and PIPA?," *New York Daily News* online, January 18, 2012, https://www.nydailynews.com/news/national/wikipedia-sopa-pipa-article-1.1007847.

26. "SOPA Petition Gets Millions of Signatures as Internet Piracy Legislation Protests Continue," *Washington Post* online, January 20, 2012, https://www.washingtonpost.com/business/economy/sopa-petition-gets-millions-of-signatures-as-internet-piracy-legislation-protests-continue/2012/01/19/gIQAHaAyBQ_story.html.

27. Grant Gross, "Who Really Was Behind the SOPA Protests?," *IDG News Service*, February 3, 2012, https://www.computerworld.com/article/2732164/who-really-was-behind-the-sopa-protests-.html.

28. Chenda Ngak, "SOPA and PIPA Internet Blackout Aftermath, Staggering Numbers," CBS News online, last modified December 19, 2020, https://www.cbsnews.com/news/sopa-and-pipa-internet-blackout-aftermath-staggering-numbers/.

29. Ibid.

30. Ibid.

31. Kim Kardashian (@KimKardashian), "We must stop SOPA/PIPA to keep the web open & free," Twitter, January 18, 2012, 9:07 a.m., https://twitter.com/KimKardashian/status/159819209206022144?lang=bg.

32. Michael Cieply and Edward Wyatt, "Dodd Calls for Hollywood and Silicon Valley to Meet," *New York Times* online, January 20, 2012, https://www.nytimes.com/2012/01/20/technology/dodd-calls-for-hollywood-and-silicon-valley-to-meet.html.

33. Diane Bartz, "Update 2—Google Says US Probing Search Co's Market Practices," Reuters online, last modified June 24, 2011, https://www.reuters.com/article/google-antitrust-idCNN1E75N0O620110624.

34. Jessica Guynn and Jim Puzzanghera, "FTC Launches Investigation of Google," *Los Angeles Times* online, June 25, 2011, https://www.latimes.com/business/la-xpm-2011-jun-25-la-fi-google-ftc-20110625-story.html.

35. David Balto, "Internet Search Competition: Where's the Beef?" *AntitrustConnect* (blog). June 24, 2011, https://antitrustconnect.com/2011/06/24/internet-search-competition-wheres-the-beef/.

36. Geoffrey A. Manne, "What's Really Motivating the Pursuit of Google?," Main Justice, June 14, 2011.

37. Ibid.

38. Adam Thierer, "Searching in Vain for an Anti-Trust Case Against Google," *Forbes* online, June 30, 2011, https://www.forbes.com/sites/adamthierer/2011/06/30/searching-in-vain-for-an-anti-trust-case-against-google/?sh=6f86ed73a756.

39. Don Rachester and Daniel Oliver, "Government Shouldn't Regulate Google Searches," *Cedar Rapids (IA) Gazette*, October 21, 2012, 11A.

40. David Balto, "Handicapping Google Is No Good for Wisconsin Businesses and Consumers," WisPolitics.com, September 16, 2011.

41. Robert H. Bork, "Antitrust and Google," Perspective, *Chicago Tribune*, April 6, 2012, 19.

42. Brody Mullins and Jack Nicas, "Paying Professors: Inside Google's Academic Influence Campaign," *Wall Street Journal* online, July 14, 2017, https://www.wsj.com/articles/paying-professors-inside-googles-academic-influence-campaign-1499785286.

43. Ibid.

44. Ibid.

45. Ibid.

46. Geoffrey A. Manne and Joshua Wright, "Google and the Limits of Antitrust: The Case Against the Antitrust Case Against Google," George Mason University, June 2010.

47. David Balto and Brendan Coffman, "Using Antitrust Enforcement Prudently in High-Tech Markets; The Flaws of a Potential Antitrust Case Against Google," David A. Balto Law Offices, 2012.

48. Balto, "Internet Search Competition."

49. Eric Schmidt, Review of *Response of Eric Schmidt, Executive Chairman, Google Inc. Before the Senate Committee on the Judiciary Subcommittee on Antitrust, Competition Policy, and Consumer Rights*. Hearing on "The Power of Google: Serving Consumers or Threatening Competition?"

570 | Notes

50. Diane Bartz, "Microsoft Hires ex-FTC Google Expert as Lobbyist," Reuters online, last modified March 1, 2012, https://www.reuters.com/article/us-google-microsoft/microsoft-hires-ex-ftc-google-expert-as-lobbyist-idUSTRE82100B20120302.

51. Brody Mullins, Rolfe Winkler, and Brent Kendall, "Inside the U.S. Antitrust Probe of Google," *Wall Street Journal* online, March 19, 2015, https://www.wsj.com/articles/inside-the-u-s-antitrust-probe-of-google-1426793274.

52. Ibid.

53. Ibid.

54. Ibid.

55. Ryan Radia, "Google Is Many Things—But Not an Illegal Monopoly," *CNET*, October 25, 2012, https://www.cnet.com/tech/services-and-software/google-is-many-things-but-not-an-illegal-monopoly/.

56. Ed Black, "The Case Against the Case Against Google," *Daily Caller*, October 31, 2012.

Chapter 15

1. Anna Palmer and Byron Tau, "Power Broker Thomas Boggs Dies," *Politico* online, last modified September 16, 2014, https://www.politico.com/story/2014/09/tommy-boggs-110985.

2. Emily Heil, "Friends Mourn Tommy Boggs at His Old Table at the Palm," *Washington Post* online, September 17, 2014, https://www.washingtonpost.com/news/reliable-source/wp/2014/09/17/friends-mourn-tommy-boggs-at-his-old-table-at-the-palm/.

3. Palmer and Tau, "Power Broker Thomas Boggs Dies."

4. Adam Bernstein, "Lobbyist, Lawyer Thomas H. Boggs Jr. Dead at 73," *Washington Post* online, September 15, 2014, https://www.washingtonpost.com/local/obituaries/lobbyist-lawyer-thomas-boggs-dead-73/2014/09/15/f3117e48-3ce9-11e4-b0ea-8141703bbf6f_story.html.

5. Jennifer Smith and Elizabeth Williamson, "Lobbying Firm Patton Boggs Fights for Itself," *Wall Street Journal* online, March 9, 2014, https://www.wsj.com/articles/SB10001424052702304020104579429563392063526.

6. Steve Mufson, "Patton Boggs Becomes Mired in an Epic Legal Battle with Chevron over Jungle Oil Pits," *Washington Post* online, June 29, 2013, https://www.washingtonpost.com/business/economy/patton-boggs-becomes-mired-in-an-epic-legal-battle-with-chevron-over-jungle-oil-pits/2013/06/28/5933e834-cc91-11e2-8f6b-67f40e176f03_story.html.

7. Ibid.

8. Paul Barrett, "Fall of the House of Boggs," *Politico* online, last modified September 15, 2014, https://www.politico.com/magazine/story/2014/09/the-fall-of-the-house-of-boggs-110989/.

9. Barrett, "House of Boggs."

10. "Libya Pays $1.5 Billion to Settle Terrorism Claims," CNN online, October 31, 2018, https://www.cnn.com/2008/WORLD/africa/10/31/libya.payment/index.html.

11. Barrett, "House of Boggs."

12. Ibid.

13. Mufson, "Patton Boggs Becomes Mired in an Epic Legal Battle."

14. Barrett, "House of Boggs."

15. Ibid.

16. Ibid.

17. Ibid.

18. Mufson, "Patton Boggs Becomes Mired in an Epic Legal Battle."

19. Barrett, "House of Boggs."

20. Mufson, "Patton Boggs Becomes Mired in an Epic Legal Battle."

21. Ibid.

22. Ibid.

23. Elizabeth Olson, "After a Merger Falls Through, Patton Boggs Keeps Looking," *New York Times* online, https://archive.nytimes.com/dealbook.nytimes.com/2014/01/09/after-a-merger-fails-patton-boggs-still-seeks-partners/.

24. Casey Sullivan, "Washington Law Firm Patton Boggs Is in Merger Talks," *Washington Post* online, October 27, 2013, https://www.washingtonpost.com/business/economy/washington-law-firm-patton-boggs-is-in-merger-talks/2013/10/27/52622c3a-3f2f-11e3-ad86-5120269ae35b_story.html.

25. Catherine Ho, "Patton Boggs Lets Go 65 Attorneys and Staff; 23 in Washington," *Washington Post*, March 1, 2013, https://www.washingtonpost.com/blogs/capital-business/post/patton-boggs-lets-go-65-attorneys-and-staff-23-in-washington/2013/03/01/acc10ff2-82b5-11e2-a350-49866afab584_blog.html.

26. Jennifer Smith, "Law Firm Patton Boggs Lays Off 65," *Wall Street Journal*, March 1, 2013.

27. Ibid.

28. Catherine Ho, "Patton Boggs Loses Antitrust Attorney and Big Part of Health and Safety Practice," *Washington Post* online, July 13, 2014, https://www.washingtonpost.com/business/capitalbusiness/patton-boggs-loses-antitrust-attorney-and-big-part-of-health-and-safety-practice/2013/07/12/bc2e663e-e998-11e2-a301-ea5a8116d211_story.html.

29. Ibid.

30. Casey Sullivan, "Exclusive: Patton Boggs Details Merger Talks with Locke Lord to Partners," Reuters online, last modified November 12, 2013, https://www.reuters.com/article/us-usa-pattonboggsmerger/exclusive-patton-boggs-details-merger-talks-with-locke-lord-to-partners-idUSBRE9AC02N20131113.

31. Casey Sullivan and David Ingram, "Takeover Shores Up U.S. Lobbying Giant Patton Boggs," Reuters online, last modified May 23, 2014, https://www.reuters.com/article/us-patton-boggs-mergers/takeover-shores-up-u-s-lobbying-giant-patton-boggs-idUSBREA4N01K20140524.

32. Catherine Ho, "Patton Boggs Closes a New Jersey Office," *Washington Post* online, February 25, 2014, https://www.washingtonpost.com/business/capitalbusiness/patton -boggs-closes-a-new-jersey-office/2014/02/25/db72b828-9e34-11e3-b8d8-94577f f66b28_story.html.

33. Catherine Ho and Holly Yeager, "Patton Boggs to Merge with Squire Sanders," *Washington Post* online, May 23, 2014, https://www.washingtonpost.com/politics /patton-boggs-to-merge-with-squire-sanders/2014/05/23/1981b1b8-e2ab-11e3 -9743-bb9b59cde7b9_story.html.

34. Byron Tau, "Patton Boggs Merger Creates Giant," *Politico* online, last modified May 23, 2014, https://www.politico.com/story/2014/05/squire-patton-boggs-merger-107072.

35. Barrett, "House of Boggs."

36. Talia Buford, "Patton Boggs to Pay Chevron $15M," *Politico* online, last modified May 7, 2014, https://www.politico.com/story/2014/05/patton-boggs-chevron-ecuador-106448.

37. Catherine Ho, "Dentons Makes 'Serious Overture' to Patton Boggs," *Washington Post* online, April 3, 2014, https://www.washingtonpost.com/news/capital-business /wp/2014/04/03/dentons-makes-serious-overture-to-patton-boggs/.

38. Ho and Yeager, "Patton Boggs to Merge."

39. Tau, "Patton Boggs Merger."

40. Elizabeth Olson, "Powerful Law Firms Patton Boggs and Squire Sanders Will Join Forces," *New York Times* online, May 23, 2014, https://archive.nytimes.com/dealbook .nytimes.com/2014/05/23/patton-boggs-long-a-washington-powerhouse-to-merge/.

41. Squire Patton Boggs, "Squire Sanders and Patton Boggs Announce Agreement to Combine Firms," press release, May 23, 2014, https://www.squirepattonboggs.com /en/news/2014/05/squire-sanders-and-patton-boggs-announce-agreem2__.

42. Ho and Yeager, "Patton Boggs to Merge."

43. Anna Palmer and Byron Tau, "Exodus Hits Patton Boggs," *Politico* online, last modified June 4, 2014, https://www.politico.com/story/2014/06/exodus-hits-patton -boggs-107400.

44. Reid Wilson and Catherine Ho, "Three Top Republican Lawyers Leaving Patton Boggs to Establish Practice with Jones Day," *Washington Post* online, May 29, 2014, https://www.washingtonpost.com/politics/three-top-republican-lawyers-leaving -patton-boggs-to-establish-practice-with-jones-day/2014/05/29/bf8eab88-e77e -11e3-afc6-a1dd9407abcf_story.html.

45. Ibid.

46. "Top Lobbying Firms, 2014," OpenSecrets online, 2014, https://www.opensecrets .org/federal-lobbying/top-lobbying-firms?cycle=2014.

Chapter 16

1. Brody Mullins, "The Rise and Fall of a K Street Renegade," *Wall Street Journal* online, February 13, 2017, https://www.wsj.com/articles/the-rise-and-fall-of-a-k-street-ren egade-1487001918.

Notes | 573

2. Ibid.
3. Ibid.
4. Ibid.
5. Ibid.
6. Ibid.
7. Ibid.
8. Ibid.
9. Ibid.
10. "Police Report Supplement Regarding Death of Evan Morris," Federal Bureau of Investigation, Washington Field Office.
11. Brody Mullins, "Rise and Fall of a K Street Renegade."
12. "Police Report Supplement Regarding Death of Evan Morris,"
13. Brody Mullins, "Rise and Fall of a K Street Renegade."
14. Ibid.
15. Ibid.
16. Ibid.
17. Ibid.
18. Ibid.
19. "Police Report Supplement Regarding Death of Evan Morris."
20. Ibid.
21. Ibid.
22. Ibid.
23. Brody Mullins, "Rise and Fall of a K Street Renegade."
24. Ibid.

Chapter 17

1. Whitney Leaming, "Protesters Set Limo on Fire Outside the *Washington Post*" (video), *Washington Post* online, January 20, 2017, https://www.washingtonpost.com/video politics/protesters-set-limo-on-fire-outside-the-washington-post/2017/01/20/49096 b40-df58-11e6-8902-610fe486791c_video.html.
2. Donald J. Trump, Inaugural Address, transcript of speech delivered in Washington, DC, January 20, 2017, https://www.politico.com/story/2017/01/full-text-donald -trump-inauguration-speech-transcript-233907.
3. Anna Palmer, Jake Sherman, and Daniel Lippman, "Tony Podesta and the Podesta Group's GOPers," *Politico* Playbook, last modified January 22, 2017, https://www .politico.com/tipsheets/playbook/2017/01/first-in-playbook-next-up-for-trump -federal-workforce-freeze-and-mexico-city-abortion-policy-taking-stock-of-presi dent-trumps-first-full-day-sunday-best-bday-josh-earnest-218334.
4. Ibid.
5. Jeff Horwitz and Desmond Butler, "AP Sources: Manafort Tied to Undisclosed Foreign Lobbying," Associated Press online, August 17, 2016, https://apnews.com

/article/europe-lobbying-campaign-2016-events-united-states-presidential-election
-c01989a47ee5421593ba1b301ec07813.

6. Ibid.

7. Luke Mullins, "How Lobbying Has Changed in Donald Trump's Washington," *Washingtonian* online, March 10, 2019, https://www.washingtonian.com/2019/03/10/how-lobbying-has-changed-donald-trump-washington/.

8. Brody Mullins and Julie Bykowicz, "How Tony Podesta, a Washington Power Broker, Lost It All," *Wall Street Journal* online, April 18, 2018, https://www.wsj.com/articles/how-tony-podesta-a-washington-power-broker-lost-it-all-1524065781.

9. Horwitz and Butler, "Manafort Tied to Undisclosed Foreign Lobbying."

10. Jim Rutenberg, "The Untold Story of 'Russiagate' and the Road to War in Ukraine," *New York Times Magazine* online, November 2, 2022, https://www.nytimes.com/2022/11/02/magazine/russiagate-paul-manafort-ukraine-war.html.

11. Ibid.

12. Franklin Foer, "Paul Manafort, American Hustler," *Atlantic* online, March 2018, https://www.theatlantic.com/magazine/archive/2018/03/paul-manafort-american-hustler/550925.

13. Ibid.

14. Richard Stengel, "Businessman Adnan Khashoggi's High-Flying Realm," *Time* online, January 19, 1987, https://content.time.com/time/subscriber/article/0,33009,963261-1,00.html.

15. Foer, "Paul Manafort."

16. Ibid.

17. Ibid.

18. Ibid.

19. Dana Harris, "Nasso, Cohen Make Theirs Manhattan," *Variety* online, January 15, 2001, https://variety.com/2001/film/news/nasso-cohen-make-theirs-manhattan-1117792003; "Seagal Mob Saga Comes to an End," *Guardian* (US edition) online, February 18, 2004, https://www.theguardian.com/film/2004/feb/18/news1.

20. Foer, "Paul Manafort."

21. Ibid.

22. Ibid.

23. Steven Lee Myers, "Ukrainian Court Orders New Vote for Presidency, Citing Fraud," *New York Times* online, December 4, 2004, https://www.nytimes.com/2004/12/04/world/europe/ukrainian-court-orders-new-vote-for-presidency-citing-fraud.html.

24. Sharon LaFraniere and Kenneth P. Vogel, "Rick Gates Testifies He Committed Crimes with Paul Manafort," *New York Times* online, August 6, 2018, https://www.nytimes.com/2018/08/06/us/politics/rick-gates-manafort-trump-trial.html.

25. Embassy Kyiv, "Ukraine: Extreme Makeover for Party of Regions?," Wikileaks Cable: 06KIEV473_a, dated February 3, 2006, https://wikileaks.org/plusd/cables/06KIEV473_a.html.

26. Simon Shuster, "How Paul Manafort Helped Elect Russia's Man in Ukraine," *Time* online, October 31, 2017, https://time.com/5003623/paul-manafort-mueller-indict ment-ukraine-russia.

27. Franklin Foer, "The Quiet American," Slate, last modified April 28, 2016, https:// slate.com/news-and-politics/2016/04/paul-manafort-isnt-a-gop-retread-hes-made -a-career-of-reinventing-tyrants-and-despots.html.

28. Roman Kupchinsky, "Ukraine: Mystery Behind Yushchenko's Poisoning Continues," Radio Free Europe, September 18, 2006, https://www.rferl.org/a/1071434.html.

29. Embassy Kyiv, Ukraine: "Extreme Makeover for Party of Regions?"

30. Tom Balmforth, "Ukraine's Richest Man Announces His Holding's Exit from Media Business," Reuters online, last modified July 11, 2022, https://www.reuters.com/busi ness/media-telecom/ukraines-richest-man-announces-his-holdings-exit-media -business-2022-07-11/.

31. Josh Gerstein, "Previously Secret 'Alternative' Mueller Report Goes Public," *Politico* online, May 26, 2022, https://www.politico.com/news/2022/05/26/secret-alternative -mueller-report-goes-public-00035507.

32. *Team M Final*, November 16, 2018, https://s3.documentcloud.org/documents /22039718/051322_-_team_m_-_response.pdf.

33. Kenzi Abou-Sabe, Tom Winter, and Max Tucker, "What Did Ex-Trump Aide Paul Manafort Really Do in Ukraine?," NBC News online, last modified June 27, 2017, https://www.nbcnews.com/news/us-news/what-did-ex-trump-aide-paul-manafort -really-do-ukraine-n775431.

34. Foer, "Paul Manafort."

35. Foer, "Quiet American."

36. Ibid.

37. Rutenberg, "The Untold Story of 'Russiagate' and the Road to War in Ukraine."

38. Foer, "Quiet American."

39. Ibid.

40. Rutenberg, "The Untold Story of 'Russiagate' and the Road to War in Ukraine."

41. Zoe Tillman and Chris Geidner, "Here's the Evidence Paul Manafort Doesn't Want a Jury to See About His Work in Ukraine," BuzzFeed, July 26, 2018, https://www .buzzfeednews.com/article/zoetillman/heres-the-evidence-paul-manafort-doesnt -want-a-jury-to-see, https://www.documentcloud.org/documents/4619168-USA-v -Manafort-Motion-in-Limine-Exs-Part1#document/p9.

42. Foer, "Paul Manafort."

43. Ibid.

44. Rachel Weiner, "Paul Manafort Made More Than $60 Million in Ukraine, Prosecu tors Say," *Washington Post* online, July 30, 2018, https://www.washingtonpost.com /local/public-safety/paul-manafort-made-more-than-60-million-in-ukraine-prose cutors-say/2018/07/30/dfe5b47c-9417-11e8-810c-5fa705927d54_story.html.

45. Sarah Maslin Nir, "Take a Tour of Manafort's Multimillion-Dollar Homes, Going

Up for Sale," *New York Times* online, October 5, 2018, https://www.nytimes.com/2018/10/05/nyregion/paul-manafort-property-forfeiture.html; Nathan Layne, Karen Freifeld, and Amanda Becker, "Bank Sped Up Manafort Loan Approval as CEO Sought Trump Cabinet Job: Witness," Reuters online, last modified August 10, 2018, https://www.reuters.com/article/us-usa-trump-russia-manafort/bank-sped-up-manafort-loan-approval-as-ceo-sought-trump-cabinet-job-witness-idUSKBN1KV10C.

46. Lauren Lyons Cole and Tanza Loudenback, "All the Lavish Ways the FBI Says President Trump's Former Campaign Chairman Paul Manafort Spent His Hidden Millions," Business Insider, last modified October 31, 2017, https://www.businessinsider.in/finance/all-the-lavish-ways-the-fbi-says-president-trumps-former-campaign-chairman-paul-manafort-spent-his-hidden-millions/slidelist/61350075.cms.

47. Tierney McAfee, "'A Jacket for Every Treason': Internet Mocks Paul Manafort's $15,000 Ostrich Coat," *People* online, August 3, 2018, https://people.com/politics/paul-manafort-ostrich-leather-jacket.

48. Kenneth P. Vogel, "American Political Consultants in Ukraine," *Politico* online, last modified March 4, 2014, https://www.politico.com/gallery/2014/03/american-political-consultants-in-ukraine-001504.

49. Ellen Barry, "Former Ukraine Premier Is Jailed for 7 Years," *New York Times* online, October 11, 2011, https://www.nytimes.com/2011/10/12/world/europe/yulia-tymoshenko-sentenced-to-seven-years-in-prison.html.

50. Horwitz and Butler, "Manafort Tied to Undisclosed Foreign Lobbying."

51. "Foreign Agents Registration Act," US Department of Justice, https://www.justice.gov/nsd-fara.

52. United States of America v. Richard W. Gates III, Superseding Criminal Information, February 23, 2018.

Chapter 18

1. John Hooper, "'It's a Form of Addiction,'" *Guardian* (US edition) online, April 20, 2004, https://www.theguardian.com/culture/2004/apr/20/usa.world.

2. Brody Mullins and Julie Bykowicz, "How Tony Podesta, a Washington Power Broker, Lost It All," *Wall Street Journal* online, April 18, 2018, https://www.wsj.com/articles/how-tony-podesta-a-washington-power-broker-lost-it-all-1524065781.

3. The Reliable Source, "Heather and Tony Podesta, Married Superlobbyists and Art Collectors, Are Separating," *Washington Post* online, January 15, 2013, https://www.washingtonpost.com/blogs/reliable-source/post/2013/01/14/027e7402-5ec1-11e2-9940-6fc488f3fecd_blog.html.

4. Ibid.

5. Luke Mullins, "The Making and Unmaking of Tony and Heather Podesta's Power Marriage," *Washingtonian* online, August 11, 2014, https://www.washingtonian.com/2014/08/11/the-making-and-unmaking-of-a-power-marriage/.

6. The Reliable Source, "Surreal Estate: Heather Podesta's Kalorama Purchase," *Washington Post* online, December 2, 2021, https://www.washingtonpost.com/news/reliable-source/wp/2013/04/04/surreal-estate-heather-podestas-kalorama-purchase/.

7. Luke Mullins, "Making and Unmaking of Tony and Heather."

8. Ibid.

9. Ibid.

10. Anthony T. Podesta v. Heather Miller Podesta, "Complaint for Absolute Divorce and Other Relief," Superior Court of the District of Columbia, Family Court, April 2014.

11. Luke Mullins, "Making and Unmaking of Tony and Heather."

12. Ibid.

13. Anthony T. Podesta v. Heather Miller Podesta, "Counter Claim for Absolute Divorce," Superior Court of the District of Columbia, Family Court, April 3, 2014.

14. Ibid.

15. Anthony T. Podesta v. Heather Miller Podesta, "Complaint for Absolute Divorce and Other Relief," Superior Court of the District of Columbia, Family Court, April 2014.

16. Luke Mullins, "Making and Unmaking of Tony and Heather."

17. Anthony T. Podesta v. Heather Miller Podesta, "Answer to Complaint for Absolute Divorce and Other Relief," Superior Court of the District of Columbia, Family Court, April 23, 2014.

18. Luke Mullins, "Making and Unmaking of Tony and Heather."

19. Ibid.

20. Ibid.

21. Ibid.

22. Ibid.

23. Brody Mullins and Bykowicz, "How Tony Podesta . . . Lost It All."

24. Ibid.

25. Ibid.

26. Ibid.

27. Ibid.

28. Ibid.

29. Ibid.

30. Ibid.

31. Ibid.

32. Ibid.

33. John R. Emshwiller, "Financier Linked to Burkle and Clinton Is Charged," *Wall Street Journal* online, June 25, 2008, https://www.wsj.com/articles/SB121431648873899937.

34. Ibid.

35. Ibid.

36. Ibid.

37. Ibid.

38. Brody Mullins and Bykowicz, "How Tony Podesta . . . Lost It All."

39. Jeff Horwitz and Desmond Butler, "AP Sources: Manafort Tied to Undisclosed Foreign Lobbying," Associated Press online, August 17, 2016, https://apnews.com /article/europe-lobbying-campaign-2016-events-united-states-presidential-election -c01989a47ee5421593ba1b301ec07813.

40. Ibid.

41. Agreement between Podesta Group and Embassy of the Republic of Azerbaijan, FARA Registration, January 31, 2013, https://efile.fara.gov/docs/5926-Exhibit-AB -20130131-23.pdf.

42. Michael Isikoff, "Hillary Moneyman Highlights New Saudi Connection," Yahoo! News online, last modified October 16, 2015, https://www.yahoo.com/news/hillary -moneyman-highlights-new-saudi-connection-194828485.html.

43. Erin Quinn, "Rape, Murder, Famine—and $2.1 Million for K Street PR," Center for Public Integrity online, last modified July 14, 2016, https://publicintegrity.org/poli tics/rape-murder-famine-and-2-1-million-for-k-street-pr/.

44. "Top Lobbying Firms," OpenSecrets, 2015, https://www.opensecrets.org/federal-lob bying/top-lobbying-firms?cycle=2015.

45. Brody Mullins and Bykowicz, "How Tony Podesta . . . Lost It All."

46. "Lobbying Firm Profile: Podesta Group," OpenSecrets, 2015, https://www.opense crets.org/federal-lobbying/firms/summary?cycle=2015&id=D000022193.

47. Kenneth Vogel, "Trump Hones Attacks on Big Corporations, Donors and Media," Politico online, last modified October 1, 2016, https://www.politico.com/story/2016/10 /donald-trump-populism-corporatoins-donors-media-228995.

48. Rebecca Kaplan, "Donald Trump: The Hedge Fund Guys Are Getting Away with Murder," CBS News online, last modified August 23, 2015, https://www.cbsnews .com/news/donald-trump-the-hedge-fund-guys-are-getting-away-with-mur der/.

49. Jordyn Phelps, "Trump: 'I Don't Blame China' for Trade Imbalances,'" ABC News on- line, last modified November 9, 2017, https://abc7chicago.com/news/trump-i-dont -blame-china-for-trade-imbalances/2621610/.

50. Dan Merica and Eric Bradner, "Hillary Clinton Comes Out Against TPP Trade Deal," CNN online, last modified October 7, 2015, https://www.cnn.com/2015/10/07/poli tics/hillary-clinton-opposes-tpp/index.html.

51. Luke Harding, "What Are the Panama Papers? A Guide to History's Biggest Data Leak," Guardian (US edition) online, April 5, 2016, https://www.theguardian.com /news/2016/apr/03/what-you-need-to-know-about-the-panama-papers.

52. John R. Schindler, "Panama Papers Reveal Clinton's Kremlin Connection," Observer (New York) online, April 7, 2016, https://observer.com/2016/04/panama-papers-re veal-clintons-kremlin-connection/.

53. John Bennett, "Trump Questions Russia Lobbying by Clinton Campaign Chief's Brother," Roll Call online, April 3, 2017, https://rollcall.com/2017/04/03/trump-ques tions-russia-lobbying-by-clinton-campaign-chiefs-brother/.

Chapter 19

1. *Meet the Press with Chuck Todd*, June 26, 2016, NBC News online, transcript, https://www.nbcnews.com/meet-the-press/meet-press-june-26-2016-n599196.
2. Ibid.
3. Franklin Foer, "Paul Manafort, American Hustler," *Atlantic* online, March 2018, https://www.theatlantic.com/magazine/archive/2018/03/paul-manafort-american-hustler/550925.
4. Tyler Foggatt, "Manafort's Monster House in the Hamptons," *New Yorker* online, June 17, 2019, https://www.newyorker.com/magazine/2019/06/24/manaforts-monster-house-in-the-hamptons.
5. Foer, "Paul Manafort."
6. Ibid.
7. Ibid.
8. Ibid.
9. Ibid.
10. Ibid.
11. Paul Manafort, *Political Prisoner: Persecuted, Prosecuted, but Not Silenced* (New York: Skyhorse, 2022), 41.
12. Foer, "Paul Manafort."
13. Jeremy W. Peters and Alan Rappeport, "Republican Convention: Floor Fighting on Day 1," *New York Times* online, July 18, 2016, https://www.nytimes.com/2016/07/18/us/politics/republican-national-convention.html.
14. Foer, "Paul Manafort."
15. Ibid.
16. "Putin: Russia Helped Yanukovych to Flee Ukraine," BBC News online, last modified November 11, 2014, https://www.bbc.com/news/world-europe-29761799.
17. Andrew Kramer, "Ukraine's Ex-President Is Convicted of Treason," *New York Times* online, January 24, 2019, https://www.nytimes.com/2019/01/24/world/europe/viktor-yanukovych-russia-ukraine-treason.html.
18. William Booth, "Ukraine's Parliament Votes to Oust President; Former Prime Minister Is Freed from Prison," *Washington Post* online, February 22, 2014, https://www.washingtonpost.com/world/europe/ukraines-yanukovych-missing-as-protesters-take-control-of-presidential-residence-in-kiev/2014/02/22/802f7c6c-9bd2-11e3-ad71-e03637a299c0_story.html.
19. Foer, "Paul Manafort."
20. Ibid.
21. Ibid. Manafort denied wrongdoing in the case, which is still ongoing.
22. Ibid.
23. Steven Mufson, "Russian Tycoon Sues Former Trump Campaign Manager Manafort," *Washington Post*, January 10, 2018.
24. Foer, "Paul Manafort."

25. Ibid.

26. Ibid.

27. Manafort, *Political Prisoner*, 28.

28. Foer, "Paul Manafort."

29. Manafort, *Political Prisoner*, 38.

30. Michael Kranish, "'He's Better Than This,' Says Thomas Barrack, Trump's Loyal Whisperer," *Washington Post* online, October 11, 2017, https://www.washingtonpost .com/politics/hes-better-than-this-says-thomas-barrack-trumps-loyal-whisperer/20 17/10/10/067fc776-a215-11e7-8cfe-d5b912fabc99_story.html.

31. Glenn Thrush, "To Charm Trump, Paul Manafort Sold Himself as an Affordable Outsider," *New York Times* online, April 8, 2017, https://www.nytimes.com/2017/04/08 /us/to-charm-trump-paul-manafort-sold-himself-as-an-affordable-outsider.html.

32. Manafort, *Political Prisoner*, 351–53.

33. Ibid., 41.

34. Ibid., 44.

35. Ibid.

36. Thrush, "To Charm Trump, Paul Manafort Sold Himself."

37. Ibid.

38. Jill Colvin and Steve Peoples, "Trump Dumps Campaign Chief," Associated Press, June 12, 2016.

39. Ibid.

40. Alissa Priddle and Brent Snavely, "Mexico Bound? Ford Moving Two Key Models Out of Michigan," USA Today online, July 9, 2015, https://www.usatoday.com/story /money/cars/2015/07/09/ford-focus-cmax-mexico/29921307/.

41. Donald J. Trump (@realDonaldTrump), "Ford is MOVING jobs from Michigan to Mexico AGAIN!" Twitter post, July 14, 2015, 8:55 a.m., https://twitter.com/realDon aldTrump/status/620939800888127488.

42. Candice Choiap, "Trump Vows to Never Eat Oreos Again," Associated Press online, August 25, 2015, https://apnews.com/e9d785da80474fa3bb3b6b577e25db38/trump -vows-never-eat-oreos-again-citing-move-mexico.

43. Ibid.

44. Lesley Clark, "Donald Trump, 'World-Class Businessman'—and Business Critic," *McClatchy*, March 8, 2016.

45. "Road to the White House 2016: Donald Trump and Mike Pence at the New York Economic Club" (video and transcript of remarks delivered at the Economic Club of New York, September 15, 2016), https://www.c-span.org/video/?415315-1/donald -trump-mike-pence-york-economic-club.

46. Foer, "Paul Manafort."

47. Jonathan W. Martin and Jeremy W. Peters, "Donald Trump to Reshape Image, New Campaign Chief Tells G.O.P.," *New York Times* online, April 21, 2016, https://www

.nytimes.com/2016/04/22/us/politics/donald-trump-to-reshape-image-new-campaign-chief-tells-gop.html.

48. Andrew E. Kramer, Mike McIntire, and Barry Meier, "Secret Ledger in Ukraine Lists Cash for Donald Trump's Campaign Chief," *New York Times* online, August 14, 2016, https://www.nytimes.com/2016/08/15/us/politics/what-is-the-black-ledger.html.

49. Horwitz and Butler, "Manafort Tied to Undisclosed Foreign Lobbying."

50. Nolan D. McCaskill, Alex Isenstadt, and Shane Goldmacher, "Paul Manafort Resigns from Trump Campaign," *Politico* online, last modified August 19, 2016, https://www.politico.com/story/2016/08/paul-manafort-resigns-from-trump-campaign-227197.

51. Maggie Haberman and Jonathan Martin, "Paul Manafort Quits Donald Trump's Campaign After a Tumultuous Run," *New York Times* online, August 19, 2016, https://www.nytimes.com/2016/08/20/us/politics/paul-manafort-resigns-donald-trump.html.

52. D. McCaskill, Isenstadt, and Goldmacher, "Paul Manafort Resigns from Trump Campaign."

Chapter 20

1. Brody Mullins, "When the Party's Over: Washington's Premier Social Connector Fades from View," *Wall Street Journal* online, January 2, 2020, https://www.wsj.com/articles/when-the-partys-over-washingtons-premier-social-connector-fades-from-view-11577997343.

2. Ibid.

3. Ibid.

4. Ibid.

5. Ibid.

6. Ibid.

7. Ibid.

8. Ibid.

9. Ibid.

10. Ibid.

11. *Politico* staff, "The Scenemakers: Jim Courtovich," *Politico* online, last modified July 23, 2010, https://www.politico.com/story/2010/07/the-scenemakers-040060.

12. Brody Mullins, "When the Party's Over."

13. Mike Allen and Daniel Lippman, "Sphere's Hill House," *Politico* Playbook, last modified September 10, 2015, https://www.politico.com/playbook/2015/09/politico-playbook-september-10-2015-politico-50-210133.

14. Brody Mullins, "When the Party's Over."

15. Ibid.

16. Ibid.

17. Ibid.

18. Ibid.

19. Brody Mullins and Alex Leary, "Washington's Biggest Lobby, the U.S. Chamber of Commerce, Gets Shut Out," *Wall Street Journal* online, May 2, 2019, https://www.wsj.com/articles/washingtons-biggest-lobbyist-the-u-s-chamber-of-commerce-gets-shut-out-11556812302.

20. Julie Creswell, "Trump and U.S. Chamber of Commerce Pull No Punches on Trade Policy," *New York Times* online, July 11, 2016, https://www.nytimes.com/2016/07/12/business/us-chamber-of-commerce-donald-trump.html.

21. Nike Corasaniti, "Donald Trump Assails U.S. Chamber of Commerce over Trade," *New York Times* online, June 29, 2016, https://www.nytimes.com/2016/06/30/us/politics/donald-trump-us-chamber-of-commerce-trade.html.

22. Katie Thomas, "Wary Drug Makers Move to Fend Off Further Attacks Under Donald Trump," *New York Times* online, December 9, 2016, https://www.nytimes.com/2016/12/09/business/donald-trump-drug-prices-pharma-stocks.html.

23. Donald Trump (@realDonaldTrump), "Toyota Motor said will build a new plant in Baja, Mexico, to build Corolla cars for U.S. NO WAY! Build plant in U.S. or pay big border tax," Twitter, January 5, 2017, 1:14 p.m., https://twitter.com/realDonaldTrump/status/817071792711942145.

24. Luke Mullins, "How Lobbying Has Changed in Donald Trump's Washington," *Washingtonian* online, March 10, 2019, https://www.washingtonian.com/2019/03/10/how-lobbying-has-changed-donald-trump-washington/.

25. Shane Goldmacher et al., "Trump's Ex-Campaign Manager Starts Lobbying Firm," *Politico* online, last modified December 21, 2016, https://www.politico.com/story/2016/12/corey-lewandowski-consulting-firm-232888.

26. Steven Overly, "AT&T Paid Cohen $600K for Advice on Time Warner, Other Issues," *Politico* online, last modified May 10, 2018, https://www.politico.com/story/2018/05/10/cohen-trump-att-merger-time-warner-532022.

27. Beth Reinhardt and Jonathan O'Connell, "K Street's Newest Star Built Business on Dubious Claims of Trump Ties," *Washington Post* online, November 1, 2019, https://www.washingtonpost.com/investigations/k-streets-newest-star-built-business-on-dubious-claims-of-trump-ties/2019/11/01/f67de928-f5d9-11e9-829d-87b12c2f85dd_story.html.

28. Luke Mullins, "How Lobbying Has Changed."

29. Ibid.

30. Ibid.

31. Ibid.

32. Ibid.

33. Ibid.

34. Gabriel Sherman, "Inside Rupert Murdoch's Succession Drama," *Vanity Fair* online,

April 23, 2023, https://www.vanityfair.com/news/2023/04/rupert-murdoch-cover-story.

35. Brody Mullins and Julie Bykowicz, "Florida Lobbyist Thrives in Trump-era Washington," *Wall Street Journal* online, October 21, 2020, https://www.wsj.com/articles/florida-lobbyist-thrives-in-trump-era-washington-11603285219.

36. Ibid.

37. Paul Manafort, *Political Prisoner: Persecuted, Prosecuted, but Not Silenced* (New York: Skyhorse, 2022), 176–77.

38. Peter W. Stevenson, "Michael Flynn's Speech at the Republican National Convention Predicted His Demise Perfectly," *Washington Post* online, February 14, 2017, https://www.washingtonpost.com/news/the-fix/wp/2017/02/14/michael-flynns-speech-at-the-republican-national-convention-predicted-his-demise/.

39. Peter Baker and Matthew Rosenberg, "Michael Flynn Was Paid to Represent Turkey's Interests During Trump Campaign," *New York Times*, March 10, 2017.

40. Brody Mullins, "When the Party's Over."

41. Lt. Gen. Michael Flynn, "Our Ally Turkey Is in Crisis and Needs Our Support," *Hill* online, last modified November 8, 2016, https://thehill.com/blogs/pundits-blog/foreign-policy/305021-our-ally-turkey-is-in-crisis-and-needs-our-support/.

Chapter 21

1. Paul Manafort, *Political Prisoner: Persecuted, Prosecuted, but Not Silenced* (New York: Skyhorse, 2022), 162–63.

2. Jim Rutenberg, "The Untold Story of 'Russiagate' and the Road to War in Ukraine," *New York Times* online, November 2, 2022, https://www.nytimes.com/2022/11/02/magazine/russiagate-paul-manafort-ukraine-war.html.

3. Eric Tucker, "US Says Russia Was Given Trump Campaign Polling Data in 2016," Associated Press online, April 16, 2021, https://apnews.com/article/donald-trump-paul-manafort-russia-campaigns-konstantin-kilimnik-d2fdefdb37077e28eba135e21fce6ebf.

4. Manafort, *Political Prisoner*, 160.

5. Ibid., 162–63.

6. Ibid., 163.

7. Ibid., 164.

8. Ibid., 168

9. Ibid., 165.

10. Jeff Horwitz and Desmond Butler, "AP Sources: Manafort Tied to Undisclosed Foreign Lobbying," Associated Press online, August 17, 2016, https://apnews.com/article/europe-lobbying-campaign-2016-events-united-states-presidential-election-c01989a47ee5421593ba1b301ec07813.

11. Gregor Aisch, Jon Huang, and Cecilia Kang, "Dissecting the #Pizzagate Conspiracy

Theories," *New York Times* online, December 10, 2016, https://www.nytimes.com /interactive/2016/12/10/business/media/pizzagate.html.

12. Brody Mullins and Julie Bykowicz, "How Tony Podesta, a Washington Power Broker, Lost It All," *Wall Street Journal* online, April 18, 2018, https://www.wsj.com/articles /how-tony-podesta-a-washington-power-broker-lost-it-all-1524065781.

13. Ibid.

14. Megan R. Wilson, "Lobby Firm Heather Podesta + Partners Rebrands," *Hill* online, March 29, 2017, https://thehill.com/business-a-lobbying/business-a-lobbying /326279-lobby-firm-heather-podesta-partners-rebrands/.

15. Brody Mullins and Bykowicz, "How Tony Podesta . . . Lost It All."

16. Ibid.

17. Ibid.

18. Manafort, *Political Prisoner*, 180–81.

19. Ibid. 181–82.

20. United States vs. Paul J. Manafort Jr. and Richard W. Gates III in the U.S. District Court for the District of Columbia, "Indictment," October 30, 2017, https://www.jus tice.gov/file/1007271/download.

21. United States vs. Paul J. Manafort Jr. and Richard W. Gates III in the U.S. District Court for the Eastern District of Virginia, "Superseding Indictment," February 22, 2018, https://www.justice.gov/archives/sco/file/1038391/download.

22. Manafort, *Political Prisoner*, 182.

23. Brody Mullins and Bykowicz, "How Tony Podesta . . . Lost It All."

24. Ibid.

25. Ibid.

26. United States vs. Paul J. Manafort Jr. and Richard W. Gates III in the U.S. District Court for the District of Columbia, "Indictment."

27. Brody Mullins and Bykowicz, "How Tony Podesta . . . Lost It All."

28. Ibid.

29. Ibid.

30. Ibid.

31. Ibid.

32. Ibid.

33. Ibid.

34. Ibid.

35. Ibid.

36. Ibid.

37. Ibid.

38. Ibid.

39. Ibid.

40. Ibid.

41. Ibid.

Chapter 22

1. Paul Manafort, *Political Prisoner: Persecuted, Prosecuted, but Not Silenced* (New York: Skyhorse, 2022), 1–2.

2. Spencer S. Hsu, Ellen Nakashima, and Devlin Barrett, "Paul Manafort Ordered to Jail After Witness-Tampering Charges," *Washington Post* online, June 15, 2018, https://www.washingtonpost.com/local/public-safety/manafort-ordered-to-jail-after-witness-tampering-charges/2018/06/15/ccc526cc-6e68-11e8-afd5-778aca903bbe_story.html.

3. Manafort, *Political Prisoner*, 2.

4. Ibid.

5. Ibid., 3.

6. Ibid.

7. Ibid., 2–3.

8. Ibid., 3.

9. Ibid., 5.

10. Ibid.

11. Ibid., 7.

12. Ibid., 6.

13. Ibid., 6–7.

14. Ibid.

15. Ibid., 201–2.

16. Ibid., 202.

17. Ibid.

18. Ibid., 201–2.

19. Ibid., 204–5.

20. Ibid., 211.

21. Ibid., 211–12.

22. Ibid., 212.

23. Ibid., 211–12.

24. Donald J. Trump (@realDonaldTrump), "I feel very badly for Paul Manafort," Twitter, August 22, 2018, 9:21 a.m., https://twitter.com/realDonaldTrump/status/1032256443985084417.

25. Manafort, *Political Prisoner*, 205.

26. Ibid., 302–3.

27. Ibid., 291.

28. Ibid., 311, 313–14.

29. Bob Davis and Peter Nicholas, "Donald Trump Approves Tariffs on About $50 Billion of Chinese Goods," *Wall Street Journal* online, June 14, 2018, https://www.wsj.com/articles/donald-trump-approves-tariffs-on-about-50-billion-of-chinese-goods-1529016073.

30. Sarah Karlin-Smith, "Trump Finalizes Rule to Require Drug Prices in TV Ads,"

Politico online, last modified May 8, 2019, https://www.politico.com/story/2019/05/08/drug-prices-advertising-1310929.

31. Zeynep Ulku Kahveci, "Allow States and Victims to Fight Online Sex Trafficking Act (FOSTA): Senate Passes Bill Making Online Platforms Liable for Third-Party Content Enabling Illegal Sex-Trafficking," Jolt Digest (*Harvard Journal of Law and Technology*), last modified April 4, 2018, https://jolt.law.harvard.edu/digest/allow-states-and-victims-to-fight-online-sex-trafficking-act-fosta-senate-passes-bill-making-online-platforms-liable-for-third-party-content-enabling-illegal-sex-trafficking.

32. Brody Mullins and Ted Mann, "Google Axes Lobbyists Amid Growing Government Scrutiny," *Wall Street Journal* online, June 12, 2019, https://www.wsj.com/articles/google-facing-more-scrutiny-overhauls-lobbying-and-public-affairs-operations-11560331803.

33. Steve Peoples, Catherine Lucey, and Marcy Gordon, "Triumphant Trump Celebrates Tax Win—but Some Fear Backlash," Associated Press online, December 20, 2017, https://apnews.com/article/2d9e099660064f2b8a8fc2237b4e7e4e.

34. Department of Justice, "Justice Department and EPA File Complaint Against Norfolk Southern for Unlawful Discharge of Pollutants and Hazardous Substances in East Palestine Derailment," news release, March 31, 2023, https://www.justice.gov/opa/pr/justice-department-and-epa-file-complaint-against-norfolk-southern-unlawful-discharge.

35. Brody Mullins, "How Republicans and Big Business Broke Up," *Wall Street Journal* online, June 14, 2023, https://www.wsj.com/articles/republicans-corporations-donations-pacs-9b5b202b.

36. Business Roundtable, "Business Roundtable Redefines the Purpose of a Corporation to Promote 'An Economy That Serves All Americans,'" press release, August 19, 2019, https://www.businessroundtable.org/business-roundtable-redefines-the-purpose-of-a-corporation-to-promote-an-economy-that-serves-all-americans.

37. Rachel Weiner, Spencer S. Hsu, and Matt Zapotosky, "Paul Manafort Released from Prison, Granted Home Confinement Due to Coronavirus Fears," *Washington Post* online, May 13, 2020, https://www.washingtonpost.com/national-security/paul-manafort-granted-home-confinement-due-to-coronavirus-fears/2020/05/13/7746835c-8320-11ea-ae26-989cfce1c7c7_story.html.

38. Manafort, *Political Prisoner*, 315–16.

39. Ibid., 320–21.

40. Ibid., 321.

41. Ibid., 320–21.

Chapter 23

1. Officer Christopher L. Hampton, Charleston County Sheriff's Office, Charleston, SC, Incident report for case number 2020007694, June 6, 2020.

2. Ibid.

3. Ibid.

4. Ibid.

5. Ibid.

6. Ibid.

7. Ibid.

8. Ibid.

9. Ibid.

10. Brody Mullins, "The Rise and Fall of a K Street Renegade," *Wall Street Journal* online, February 13, 2017, https://www.wsj.com/articles/the-rise-and-fall-of-a-k-street-ren egade-1487001918.

11. Ibid.

12. Ibid.

13. Ibid.

14. Ibid.

15. Ibid.

16. Corporal Darren Botticelli, Sullivan's Island Police Department, Sullivan's Island, SC, Incident report for case number 17-00253, September 4, 2017.

17. Ibid.

18. Ibid.

19. Ibid.

20. Ibid.

21. Ibid.

22. Ibid.

23. Ibid.

24. Ibid.

25. Brody Mullins, "When the Party's Over: Washington's Premier Social Connector Fades from View," *Wall Street Journal* online, January 2, 2020, https://www.wsj.com /articles/when-the-partys-over-washingtons-premier-social-connector-fades-from -view-11577997343.

26. Ibid.

27. Ibid.

28. Ibid.

29. Woodland Drive LLC vs. James Courtovich in the U.S. District Court for the District of Columbia, "Complaint," April 26, 2018.

30. Brody Mullins, "When the Party's Over."

31. Pfc. Sydney De Nett, Sullivan's Island Police Department, Sullivan's Island, SC, Incident report for case number 19-00245, September 2, 2019.

32. Ibid.

33. Ibid.

34. Ibid.

Chapter 24

1. Paul Manafort, *Political Prisoner: Persecuted, Prosecuted, but Not Silenced* (New York: Skyhorse, 2022), 281–82.
2. Ibid., 324.
3. Ibid., 325
4. Ibid., 328.
5. Ibid., 332.
6. Ibid., 333.
7. Ibid.

Chapter 25

1. Kenneth P. Vogel, "The Russia Inquiry Ended a Democratic Lobbyist's Career. He Wants It Back," *New York Times* online, July 8, 2021, https://www.nytimes.com/2021/07/08/us/politics/tony-podesta-lobbying-democrats.html.
2. Ibid.
3. Ibid.
4. Ibid.
5. Ibid.
6. Thomas Byrne Edsall, *The New Politics of Inequality* (New York: W. W. Norton, 1984), 14.
7. Jacob Hacker and Paul Pierson, *Winner-Take-All Politics: How Washington Made the Rich Richer—and Turned Its Back on the Middle Class* (New York: Simon & Schuster, 2010), 41–72.
8. US Census Bureau, "Census Bureau Releases New Educational Attainment Data," news release, February 24, 2022, https://www.census.gov/newsroom/press-releases/2022/educational-attainment.html.
9. David Leonhardt, "'A Crisis Coming': The Twin Threats to American Democracy," *New York Times* online, September 17, 2020, https://www.nytimes.com/2022/09/17/us/american-democracy-threats.html.
10. Hacker and Pierson, *Winner-Take-All Politics*, 41–72.
11. Elizabeth Warren, "Warren, Hawley, Cortez Masto, Braun Introduce Bipartisan Bill to Claw Back Compensation from Failed Bank Executives," Elizabeth Warren, March 29, 2023, https://www.warren.senate.gov/newsroom/press-releases/warren-hawley-cortez-masto-braun-introduce-bipartisan-bill-to-claw-back-compensation-from-failed-bank-executives.
12. Office of Senator Chuck Grassley, "Senators Reintroduce Bill to Defend Cattle Producers and Nation's Food Supply," news release, February 9, 2023, https://www.grassley.senate.gov/news/news-releases/senators-reintroduce-bill-to-defend-cattle-producers-and-nations-food-supply.
13. Marco Rubio, "Sen. Marco Rubio: Amazon Should Face Unionization Drive Without Republican Support," Opinion Essay, *USA Today* online, March 12, 2021, https://

www.usatoday.com/story/opinion/2021/03/12/amazon-union-not-helping-work ing-class-economy-column/6947823002.

14. Jesus Jiménez and Brooks Barnes, "What We Know About the DeSantis-Disney Dispute," *New York Times,* May 19, 2023.

15. Mitchell Ferman, "Texas Bans Local, State Government Entities from Doing Business with Firms That 'Boycott' Fossil Fuels," *Texas Tribune* (Austin) online, August 24, 2022, https://www.texastribune.org/2022/08/24/texas-boycott-companies-fossil-fuels.

16. Brody Mullins, "How Republicans and Big Business Broke Up," *Wall Street Journal* online, June 14, 2023, https://www.wsj.com/articles/republicans-corporations-dona tions-pacs-9b5b202b.

17. Michael J. Barber, "Ideological Donors, Contribution Limits, and the Polarization of American Legislatures," *Journal of Politics* 78, no. 1 (January 2016): 296–310.

18. David Morgan, "Conservative Group Calls on Republicans to Disavow 'Left-Leaning' Companies," Reuters online, last modified September 23, 2022, https://www.reuters. com/world/us/us-house-republicans-unveil-agenda-ahead-nov-8-elections-2022 -09-23.

19. Brian Schwartz, "McCarthy, Scalise Go to War with U.S. Chamber After Group Backed Some Democrats in 2020 and 2022 Elections," CNBC online, last modified February 6, 2023, https://www.cnbc.com/2023/02/06/kevin-mccarthy-steve-scalise -no-plans-to-meet-chamber-of-commerce.html.

20. Matthew Boyle, "Exclusive—Kevin McCarthy: Chamber of Commerce 'Left' Republican Party 'A Long Time Ago,' Not Welcome Back," Breitbart News, last modified January 11, 2022, https://www.breitbart.com/politics/2022/01/11/exclusive-kevin -mccarthy-the-chamber-of-commerce-left-republican-party-a-long-time-ago-not -welcome-back.

21. Eleanor Mueller, "Union Membership Dropped to Record Low in 2022," *Politico* online, last modified January 19, 2023, https://www.politico.com/news/2023/01/19 /union-membership-drops-to-record-low-in-2022-00078525.

22. Justin McCarthy, "U.S. Approval of Labor Unions at Highest Point Since 1965," Gallup online, last modified August 30, 2022, https://news.gallup.com/poll/398303 /approval-labor-unions-highest-point-1965.aspx.

23. Lydia Saad, "More in U.S. See Unions Strengthening and Want It That Way," Gallup online, August 30, 2023, https://news.gallup.com/poll/510281/unions-strengthening .aspx.

Epilogue

1. Kelly Goles, "Congressional Cemetery—The Boggs Family," *In Custodia Legis* (blog), Library of Congress online, last modified October 6, 2021, https://blogs.loc.gov /law/2021/10/congressional-cemetery-the-boggs-family/.

2. Ivana Saric, "Paul Manafort Agrees to Pay $3.15 Million to Settle with DOJ," Axios, March 6, 2023.

3. Ibid.

4. Zachary Cohen, Holmes Lybrand, and Jackson Grigsby, "'Let's Get Right to the Violence': New Documentary Film Footage Shows Roger Stone pre–Election Day," CNN online, last modified September 27, 2022, https://www.cnn.com/2022/09/26/politics/roger-stone-january-6-documentary-film/index.html.

5. Ibid.

6. Betsy Woodruff Swan and Daniel Lippman, "Huawei Hiring Former Democratic Super Lobbyist Tony Podesta," *Politico* online, last modified July 23, 2021, https://www.politico.com/news/2021/07/23/huawei-hires-tony-podesta-500649.

7. Daniel Lippman, "Rick Gates, Who Flipped on Trump in Russia Probe, Seeks Redemption," *Politico* online, last modified October 28, 2020, https://www.politico.com/news/2020/10/28/rick-gates-redemption-432999.

8. Ibid.

9. Staff, "Powerful D.C. Lobbyist Linked to $7.7M Purchase of Rustic Canyon Lodge," *Real Deal* online, May 4, 2017.

10. Theodoric Meyer, "Former Podesta Group CEO Launches New Firm," *Politico* online, last modified November 16, 2017, https://www.politico.com/story/2017/11/16/podesta-group-ceo-kimberley-fritts-new-lobbying-firm-245557.

11. Bill Hutchinson, "Family of Ralph Nader's Niece Killed [in] Ethiopian Airlines Crash Files the First Lawsuit," ABC News online, last modified April 4, 2019, https://abcnews.go.com/International/lawsuits-filed-ethiopian-airlines-crash-family-consumer-advocate/story?id=62166217#:~:text=Samyo%20Stumo's%20uncle%20calls%20to%20ground%20all%20Boeing%20737%20Max%208%20airplanes.&text=The%20first%20lawsuit%20stemming%20from%20the%20Ethiopian%20Airlines%20crash,consumer%20advocate%20icon%20Ralph%20Nader.

12. "Boeing 737 Max: Indonesia Lifts Ban After 2018 Lion Air Crash," BBC News online, last modified December 29, 2021, https://www.bbc.com/news/business-59814571.

13. Rob Brunner, "Ralph Nader Is Opening Up About His Regrets," *Washingtonian* online, last modified November 3, 2019, https://www.washingtonian.com/2019/11/03/ralph-nader-is-opening-up-about-his-regrets/.

Index

ABC-TV, 29
Abel, Bess, 130
Abell, Rick, 98
Abercrombie, George, 234–38, 265, 276, 297, 305
Abercrombie, Neil, 122
Abramoff, Jack, 257–58, 259, 503
Abramoff, Jack, reforms following conviction
    of. See Honest Leadership and Open
    Government Act (2007)
ACA. See Affordable Care Act (2010)
Accutane (Roche), 227–31, 234
Acker, Neal, 97–98
Ackil, Josh, 345
Action for Children's Television Conference, 61
Adams, Sherman, 63
Adams, Stanley, 232
Adscape Media, 330
Affordable Care Act (2010), 10, 263–64, 270–76,
    292, 333
Afghanistan, foreign lobbying and, 175, 181
AFL-CIO, 338
Agnew, Spiro, 51
Ahmad Hamad Al Gosaibi & Brothers Co., 304–5
Ailes, Roger, 92
airline industry, Nader on, 144, 508
Akhmetov, Rinat, 393, 394
Al Assir, Abdul Rahman, 391–92
Albert, Carl, 20, 21–22, 49
Alcoa, 58
Alefantis, James, 421, 462
Alexander, Herbert, 132
Al Gosaibi family, 442
Ali, Muhammad, 158
Aliyev, Ilham, 420
Allbritton, Robert, 490
Allen, Paul, 316
Alptekin, Kamil Ekim, 457
Altman, Roger, 225

Amazon.com, 313, 353
American Airlines, 132, 254
American Bar Association, 52, 60
American Civil Liberties Union (ACLU), 159
American Conservative Union, 339
American Enterprise Institute, 56, 485
American Library Association, 157–58
Americans for Limited Government, 352
Americans with Disabilities Act (1990), 508
America Online, 313
Anderson, Jack (syndicated columnist), 84
Anderson, John (lobbyist), 402
Anderson, Stanton, 209–10, 450–51
Android, 330
Angola, foreign lobbying and, 176–83, 206
Antin, Norman, 373
antipiracy legislation, 337–45
anti–sex trafficking bill, 477–78
anti-stalking laws (Virginia), 211
antitrust investigations. See Federal Trade
    Commission (FTC); Google
Army, US, 220–22
Army Corps of Engineers, US, 120
Arrington, Richard, 162
Artists and Athletes Alliance, 269
The Art of the Deal (Trump), 104
Associated Press (AP), 461
Association of Trial Lawyers of America
    (ATLA), 195–98
AT&T, 223, 317, 324–30, 452, 506
Atlantic City, Trump casinos in, 121–24
"Attack on American Free Enterprise System"
    (Powell Memo), 52–57, 86, 351
Atwater, Joe, 89–90, 184–85
Atwater, Lee
    Bad Boy (Brady), 68
    Black, Manafort, Stone & Atwater (political
        consultants), 107, 116, 119

Atwater, Lee (*cont.*)
  Boogie Man (Rollins), 185
  Bush and work of, 67, 68, 116, 119
  characterization and tactics of, 68, 71,
    91–93 (*see also* Black Manafort, political
    consulting and conflicts of interest)
  death of, 66–69, 183–85
  early biographical information, 89–92
  lobbyist legacy of, 13, 66–72, 183–85
  presidential campaign (1988) and, 119,
    165–66, 170
  Reagan administration roles of, 107, 167
  Reagan's ascent and, 71–72, 96, 100–102
  Stone's and Manafort's introduction to, 94–99
  Thurmond campaign and, 88–91, 93
Auchter, Thorne, 114
"audience of one" strategy, 389, 453–56
auto industry
  environmental issues and, 143
  Nader and, 38–42 (*see also individual
    automobile companies*)
  self-driving vehicles and Google, 337
  Toyota Motor Corp., 451
Auto Safety Act. *see* National Traffic and Motor
  Vehicle Safety Act (1966)
Avastin (Genentech), 290–97
avian influenza pandemic scare, 235–37
Axelrod, David, 278

Babcock, George, 484
Bad Boy (Brady), 68
Bahamian government, foreign lobbying and,
  172
Baker, Howard, 110
Baker, James A., III, 66, 84–85, 176
Baldrige, Malcolm, Jr., 168
Ballard, Brian, 456
Balto, David, 347, 348, 351
Banca Privada d'Andorra, 449
Bank of America Corp., 46, 47, 423
banned books, 157–58
Bannon, Steve, 437
Barber, Michael, 500
Barber, Richard, 37
Barbour, Haley, 468
Barco, Cook, Patton & Blow, 44
Barrack, Tom, 432
Barry, Maryanne Trump, 121
Barthelemy, Sidney, 162
Barty, Billy, 116
Battle for Justice (Bronner), 162
Beck, Glenn, 292
Begich, Nick, 21, 22

Beier, David, 251
Bell, Tom, 209–10
Benenson, Joel, 397
Bethlehem Steel, 108, 127, 167–68
Biden, Hunter, 269
Biden, Joe
  Bork hearings and, 164
  Courtovich and, 301
  Google and, 357
  Huawei Technologies and, 508
  Morris and, 299
  Tamiflu and Strategic National Stockpile, 236
  as vice president, Ukraine policy, 407
Big Business. *see also* Big Pharma; Big Tech
  anticorporate uprising, Left-leaning
    Democrats (2019), 479
  consumer reform attempts, 9–10 (*see also*
    consumer advocacy)
  "countervailing forces" of, 8
  economic inequality resulting from, 11–12,
    497–98
  Founding Fathers on power of interest groups,
    6–9, 12, 38
  FTC and regulatory backlash, 59–65
  K Street's ascent (1980s), 12
  K Street's lobbying dynasties, 13–15
  New Right's ascent and PAC money, 94–99
  1970s change in, 6, 8–9, 10–11, 499, 502–3
  in nineteenth and early twentieth centuries,
    5–6
  Powell Memo and, 52–57, 86, 351
  Reagan's ascent and, 101–5
  Reagan's deregulatory agenda, 144
  Trump's anti-Big Business populism, 390,
    422–23, 434–35, 439–40, 449–56, 497–99,
    503
Big Government
  Clinton's right-leaning pivot on, 201–3
  consumer advocacy of 1960s and 1970s,
    38–42
  decentralization of federal power and, 59–65
  expansion of (1967–2007), 9
  expansion of, Hale Boggs's and, 43–44
  expansion of, post–World War II, 36–38
  Goldwater on, 73, 79–81, 92, 95, 96
  Reagan on, 10–11, 99, 113–15
  Trump's "Drain the Swamp" rhetoric, 390
Big Pharma. *See also* F. Hoffmann-La Roche Ltd.
  Avastin (Genentech), 290–97
  Biotechnology Industry Organization, 274,
    299
  FDA on vitamin regulation, 246–47
  FDA reform and Genentech, 247–52

Medicare Prescription Drug, Improvement, and Modernization Act (2003), 361–62
prescription drug prices and biologic drugs, 270–76

Big Tech. *see also* social media
anti–sex trafficking bill (Trump administration) and, 477–78
reputation of, 345 (*see also* Google)

Bing (Microsoft), 353

bin Salman, Mohammed, 449

Biotechnology Industry Organization, 274, 299

Black, Charlie. *see also* Black Manafort, political consulting and conflicts of interest; Young Republicans National Federation
Angola and Dole conflict, 180
Atwater's, Stone's, and Manafort's introduction to, 94–99
Atwater's friendship with, 69–70
Black, Manafort & Stone inception, 101, 106–10
Courtovich and, 287–89, 484
early biographical information, 92–93
Fox News inception and, 110–13
Google and, 351, 478
health care reform opposition, 194–95
lifestyle of, 115
lobbyist legacy of, 13, 505–6
presidential campaign (1988) work, 165–66, 170, 172
Prime Policy Group, 506
Reagan's ascent and, 71–72, 100–101
Stone's and Manafort's introduction to, 71
Trump and views of, 451–52, 506
Young & Rubicam acquisition of Black Manafort, 204–6, 208–10

Black, Ed, 353–54

Black, Manafort & Stone, 106–27. *see also* Black, Charlie; Manafort, Paul, Jr.; Stone, Roger; Young Republicans National Federation
Black, Manafort, Stone & Atwater (political consultants), 107, 116, 119
Black, Manafort, Stone & Kelly bipartisan model of, 124–25
Black, Manafort & Stone (corporate lobbyists), inception, 101, 107
Burson-Marsteller (Young & Rubicam) acquisition of, 203–12
culture and lifestyle, 108, 115–19, 125
early clients of, 106–9
Energy Department and Tosco, 109–10
health care reform opposition, 194–95
legacy of, 497
Manafort fired by (1995), 209–10, 391

Murdoch and Fox News inception, 108, 110–13
National Media split off from, 287
Reagan's government cuts and, 113–15
Reagan's Tax Reform Act of 1986 and, 125–27, 207
Senbet and, 207–8, 210–11
Trump's early work with, 108, 109, 119–24

Blackburn, Marsha, 499

Black Manafort, political consulting and conflicts of interest, 165–85
Atwater's death and, 183–85
foreign lobbying and, 172, 174–83 (*see also* Manafort, Paul, Jr.)
"grass tops" and grassroots tactics, 165–72, 182
HUD scandal and Manafort, 172–74, 245

"black ops" campaigns, 236, 295. *see also* shadow lobbying

blood diamonds, 178, 206

Bloomberg, 304

Blow, George, 147

Blumenthal, Richard, 317

Boehner, John, 327, 502

Boeing Co., 254, 417, 439, 451, 508

Boggs, Barbara (sister of Tommy Boggs), 21, 27, 30

Boggs, Barbara (wife of Tommy Boggs), 19, 20, 21, 25, 32, 47–48, 129, 359–60

Boggs, Charlie, 187

Boggs, Cokie. *see* Roberts, Corrine "Cokie" Boggs

Boggs, Douglas, 359

Boggs, Hale
Bill Clinton and, 187
controversies and investigation of, 23, 48–50, 130
death of, 19–23, 24–25, 50–51
early life of, 26–31
legacy of, 42–45, 47, 105, 360, 372, 505
as Speaker of the House, 48

Boggs, Lindy Claiborne, 21–23, 25–29, 30, 48, 50, 51

Boggs, Tommy, 19–38, 359–77
Bill Clinton's health care initiative and, 192, 194–98, 201
Bill Clinton's presidential election (1992) and, 186–88
campaign finance and PAC-spending role of, 128–34, 146–47
characterization of, 289, 297
duck hunting lodge of, 148–49, 226–27, 369
early lobbyist associates/work of, 32–38, 44–45, 72

Boggs, Tommy (*cont.*)
  family background and early life of, 23–31, 77
  father's death and legacy, 19–23, 24–25,
    42–45, 47–51, 105, 360, 372
  federal bailout (1979) and, 104, 105
  financial problems (2003–2014), 361–77
  government regulation undermined by, 105
  health decline and death of, 359–61, 368–69,
    377, 421
  "inside" tactics of, 109, 181 (*see also* "inside
    game" strategies)
  lawyer-lobbyist model of, 58–59, 61–63, 65
  lifestyle of, 298
  on lobbying influence, 222
  lobbying legacy of, 13, 218, 497, 505
  lobbyist registration by (1968), 45
  Morris and, 218, 219, 224, 226, 227, 265, 266,
    289
  offer to buy Podesta's firm, 244
  as political aide to Johnson, 31–32
  Reagan's Tax Reform Act of 1986 and, 125–27
Boies, David, 317, 319
Bongino, Dan, 476
Bono, Mary, 341
Boogie Man (Rollins), 185
Booker, Cory, 225
Boorstin, Robert, 340
Bopp, Michael, 381
Bork, Robert, 150–53, 160–64, 245, 246, 348
Boston University, 354
Botticelli, Darren, 488–89
Bourgeois, Louise, 255, 260, 409, 496
Bovim, Eric, 453
BP, 335
Brady, John, 68
Brand, Joe, 373
Brandeis, Louis, 12
Braun, Carol Moseley, 153
breast cancer, Avastin campaign and, 290–97
Breaux, John, 166
Brennan, William, Jr., 59
Bridges, Lloyd, 160
Brin, Sergey, 313–14, 322, 327, 328–29, 332, 339
Brinkley, David, 87
Brock, William, 168
Broder, David, 93, 200
Brokaw, Tom, 68
Bronner, Ethan, 162
Brooks, Jack, 196–97
Brown, Ron, 121, 184
Buchanan, John, 241
Buchanan, Pat, 288
Buffett, Warren, 335

"bundling," 223–27, 258
Bunn, David, 44
Burford Capital, 365
Burke, Margaret, 154–55
Burkle, Ron, 418
Burnett, Carol, 158
Burns, Mike, 400, 402–5
Burson-Marsteller, 203–12
Bush, George H. W.
  Americans with Disabilities Act, 508
  Atwater and, 67, 68, 116, 119
  Black Manafort and, 165–66, 170, 172, 180
  Clinton's pro-industry stance vs., 202
  inauguration of, 175–76
  presidential campaign (1980), 100, 102
  presidential campaign (1992), 188
  Savimba and, 180
  as US ambassador to UN, 20
Bush, George W.
  AT&T and, 325–26
  avian influenza pandemic scare, 235–37
  Black Manafort and, 108, 119
  "bundling" and McCain-Feingold Act, 223
  Microsoft and, 321
  Obama as successor to, 264
  Patton Boggs and defense contracts, 220–22
Bush, Jeb, 439, 451
Business-Industry Political Action Committee
  (BIPAC), 56, 95–96
The Business of America Is Lobbying (Drutman),
  9
Business Roundtable, 58

California
  Proposition 13, 86–87
  Reagan as governor of, 96
California Poultry Industry Federation, 246
campaign finance
  art sales by Tony Podesta as, 252
  Boggs's role in PAC-fueled spending, 128–34,
    146–49
  "bundling" and "soft money," 223–27, 258
  *Citizens United vs. The Federal Election
    Commission* (2010), 500–501
  Democrats and Coelho's role in, 135–46
  Democrats vs. Republicans (1980 election),
    134–35
  federal elections cost increase (1960–1980),
    131
  gift ban loophole, 243, 258–61, 268–70, 295
  health care reform opposition tactic, 198–99
  New Right's ascent and PAC money, 94–99
  1970s change in, 8–9

political action committees (PACs),
 dependency on, 499–502
political action committees (PACs), inception,
 55–57
 Powell Memo and, 55–57, 86, 351
 Super PACs, precursor to, 94
 Watergate and changes to, 131–34, 223
Campbell, Carroll, 66, 68
"capital-labor accord" of postwar era, 36
Capitol Building, January 6 attacks, 495, 497,
 505, 506
Carpenter, Liz, 22
Carrier Global Corp., 434
Carson, Rachel, 42
Carter, Jimmy, 59, 72, 85, 102, 114, 139
Carver, Paul, 75
Carville, James, 93, 216
Casey, William, 101
Casino Association of New Jersey, 121
Casino Jack (film), 257
Castellanos, Alex, 287, 288
Catholic Charities, 137
"cattle calls," 142
Center for American Progress, 241, 347
Center for Public Integrity, 191, 420
CFM Development Corporation, 172–74
Chain Bridge Bank, 425, 466–70
Chamber of Commerce, US, 35–36, 53–57,
 95–96, 338, 449–50, 501–2
Chang, David, 443
Charlton, Simon, 441–42, 491
Chase Manhattan Bank, 37
Chavez, Pablo, 328
Cheney, Dick, 66
Chesson, Scott, 424, 465
Chevron Corp., 364–66, 375, 379, 500
children, television advertising to, 61–65
Ciccone, Jim, 325–26, 328
Cincotta, Gale, 170–71
Citigroup Inc., 225, 367, 371
Citizens Choice, 57
Citizens United vs. The Federal Election
 Commission (2010), 500–501
Civil Aeronautics Board, 144
civil rights. see race
Civil Rights Act (1964), 37, 92, 151
Claiborne, Lindy. see Boggs, Lindy Claiborne
Claiborne, Thomas, 26
Claiborne, William Charles Cole (Virginia
 settler), 26
Claiborne, William (Virginia congressman),
 25–26
Clark, Kimberly, 441

Clark, Louise Caire, 201
Clarke, Yvette, 275
Clean Air Act (1970 amendments), 143
Clifford, Clark, 34–35, 63
Clinton, Bill
 anti–Vietnam War activism, 155
 corporate capitalism agenda and, 201–3
 FDA Modernization Act, 251
 Follieri and, 418–19
 health care reform plan of, 188–201, 264
  (see also health care reform, Clinton
  administration)
 John Podesta as chief of staff to, 241, 244
 lobbyist dynasties and administration of, 13
 McAuliffe and, 380
 Morris and, 216, 299
 presidential election (1992), 93, 186–88, 340
 presidential election (1996), 286
Clinton, Hillary
 Flynn on "lock her up," 456–57
 Follieri and, 418–19
 Google and, 333, 335
 and health care reform, Bill Clinton
  administration, 193
 McAuliffe and, 380
 Morris and, 226, 236, 237, 299
 Podesta's fund-raisers for, 242, 254, 256
 presidential campaign (2008), 419
 presidential campaign (2016), 380, 381,
  421–24, 427
 Senate campaign, 256
 Tony Podesta and, 463, 467
 as US senator, 335
Clinton Foundation, 299, 307, 484
CNN, issue advocacy and, 303, 304
coal industry, 43, 114, 335
Coats, Dan, 327
Coburn, Tom, 229
Coelho, Tony, 135–46, 508
Cogent Strategies, 508
Cognetta, Don, 468–70
Cohen, Michael, 147, 452, 476
Cohn, Roy, 119
Cole, Tom, 344
College Republicans of DC, 78, 90
Colt, Samuel, 5
Comcast Corp., 225, 324, 337
Comet Ping Pong, 421, 462–63
Commerce, Department of, 168
Commodity Futures Modernization Act (2000),
 202
Common Cause, 155, 172, 258
Competitive Enterprise Institute, 353

Compton, Erik, 378
Conference Board, 35
Congress, US. *see also* health care reform,
    Clinton administration; *individual names
    of US Representatives; individual names of
    US Senators*
    appropriations process as subversion, 63–65
    Boggs and early legislative influence, 58–59,
        61–63, 65
    committees and health care reform, Clinton
        administration, 196–98
    committees/subcommittees structure,
        inception of, 62–63
    consumer advocacy bill, 41
    House Commerce Committee and health care
        reform, Clinton administration, 198–99
    House Committee on Energy and Commerce
        and Waxman, 272–74
    House Judiciary Committee and health care
        reform, Clinton administration, 196–98
    House Native American Affairs subcommittee
        hearing and Trump, 121–22
    House of Representatives, Tommy Boggs's
        campaign for, 129–30
    Manafort and HUD scandal, 172–74, 245
    New Right's ascent in, 85–88, 93–94
    Senate and anti-Bork initiative, 150–53, 160–64
    Senate Commerce Committee and net
        neutrality, 328
    Senate Finance Committee and Russell Long,
        128–29
    Senate Judiciary Committee and Google, 340,
        342, 351
Congressional Quarterly, issue advocacy ads in, 302
Connally, John, 102
Conscience of a Conservative (Goldwater), 79, 92
Conservative Political Action Committee
    (CPAC), 179–80, 339
Constitution, US, "The Federalist No. 10"
    (Madison) on, 6–9, 12
consumer advocacy. *see also* Nader, Ralph
    auto industry and, 38–42
    Big Business reform attempts, 9–10
    influence of, in 1960s and early 1970s, 8–9
    protection agency, blocked plans, 65
    public interest movement, 42
Consumer Product Safety Act (1972), 43
Consumer Product Safety Commission, 42, 114
Conway, Kellyanne, 437
Cooper, Aaron, 338
Cooper, Jim, 199
Coors, Joseph, Sr., 56
Corcoran, Tommy "the Cork," 32–34, 35, 63

Corman, James, 139
Cottrell-Steward, Shannon, 379–80
"countervailing forces," 8
Courtovich, George, Jr. (Jim Courtovich's
    father), 283, 286
Courtovich, George (Jim Courtovich's brother),
    281–82, 286
Courtovich, Jim
    early biographical information, 280–84
    early political career, 284–88
    "Gaucho" parties of, 277–80
    "Hill House" of, 448–49, 458, 491
    legal investigations related to, 378–84, 480–92
    lifestyle and characterization of, 277–80, 300–301
    lobbyist legacy of, 13
    Morris's partnership with, 280, 287–97,
        305–11, 378–84, 440–49, 459, 482–86, 489
    reaction to book publication, 506–7
    SGR Government Relations and Lobbying,
        440, 442
    Sphere Consulting, 301–5, 308–11, 440, 445,
        448, 485–87
    as Trump ally, 439–40, 456–59
COVID pandemic, 12, 232
Covington & Burling, 44
Cox, Archibald, 132
Cranston, Alan, 171
Crawford, Jan, 442
Creighton, Susan, 354
Cruise, Tom, 192
Crusader, 220–22

Daily States (New Orleans), 27
Daimler-Benz, 484
Daley, Richard J., 154
Daschle, Tom, 226
David, Marta, 142
Davidson, Alan, 323–25, 326
Davis, Lanny, 146–47
DC Madam prostitution ring, 293
Dean, Howard, 225, 266
"death panels," 292–94
DeCavalcante crime family, 77
Defense, Department of, 33–34, 220–22, 329–30
DeFronzo, Donald, 76
DeLay, Tom, 257
Demeko, Vladimir, 396
Democratic lobbying dynasties. *see* Boggs,
    Tommy; Podesta, Tony
Democratic Party. *see also* campaign finance;
    individual names of Democratic politicians
    Black, Manafort, Stone & Kelly as lobbyists
        of, 124–25

business hostility, post–2008 financial crisis, 390 (*see also* Google; 2008 financial crisis)
Democratic Congressional Campaign Committee (DCCC) and Coelho, 135, 140–43, 145
Democratic control of Congress and White House (2008), 264
Democratic National Committee, infiltration of (*see* Watergate)
Democratic National Committee and Brown's chairmanship, 121, 184
Democratic National Convention (Chicago, 1968), 154
DNC Business Council, 265–66
early support of corporate capitalism, Clinton era, 190, 201–3
lobbying dynasties of, 13–15, 106 (*see also* Boggs, Tommy; Podesta, Tony)
net neutrality issue and, 325–27
New Democrats, Clinton's right-leaning pivot and, 201–3
Podesta's large donations to, 254, 261
Senatorial Campaign Committee and Morris, 226
Southern Democrats and New Right's ascent, 90–94
Deripaska, Oleg Vladimirovich, 430, 436
Desai, Deven, 349
DeSantis, Ron, 499
Devantery, Bob, 283
Devine, Tad, 397
Dewey, Thomas, 34
Dickerson, Nancy, 19–20
Dickerson, Wyatt, 19–20
dictators, lobbying for. *see* foreign lobbying
Dimon, Jamie, 501
Dingell, John, Jr., 198–99, 201
Dingell, John, Sr., 198
Dodd, Chris, 344
Dodd-Frank Wall Street Reform and Consumer Protection Act (2010), 10
Doggett, Lloyd, 93
Dolan, Terry, 94
Dole, Bob
 Black Manafort and, 165–66, 179, 180, 183
 health care reform opposition, 194–95
 presidential campaign (1988), 284
 presidential campaign (1996), 431
 as Senate majority leader, 286–87
 Stone and, 83
 Tony Podesta and, 246
Dollar Rent A Car, 335

Donaldson, John, 85, 392
Donna, Roberto, 240
Donner, Frederic, 38
Donohue, Thomas, 450
Donovan, Raymond, 168
"Don't Kill the Internet" (Google campaign), 341–45
Donziger, Steven, 365
DoubleClick, 314
Dow Chemical, 46
Dowd, Maureen, 442
Downing, Kevin, 494
Doyle, Mike, 344
"Drain the Swamp," 390
Drew, Elizabeth, 41, 142
Drummond, David, 352, 354, 356, 358
Drutman, Lee, 9
duck hunting incident, 148–49
Duffy, Joseph, 155, 192
Dukakis, Michael, 67, 70, 172, 183
DuPont, 34–35

Eastland, Terry, 160
East Palestine (Ohio), train crash in, 479
eBay Inc., 252, 338
economy. *see also* 2008 financial crisis
 corporate (*see* lobbying and corporate economy)
 federal bailout (1979) and Boggs, 104
 Golden Age of Capitalism, 36
 Great Society, 37, 42, 137
 gross domestic product (1947–1973), 36
 income gap, 11–12, 497–98
 of 1970s, change in business influence, 6, 8–9, 10–11
 Reagan on efficiency (vs. equity) of government, 10–11, 113–15 (*see also* Big Government)
 stagflation panic (1970s), 10, 47, 85–86
Edelman, R. David, 337
Edsall, Thomas, 10–11, 87, 93–94, 113
Edwards, Jim, 109–10
Eging, Mike, 264–65
Eisenhower, Dwight D., 63, 80, 99
Elhauge, Einer, 354
Eli Lilly and Company, 248, 336
Ellison, Larry, 320
El Paso Natural Gas Company, 33
Emanuel, Rahm, 278
employment. *see* economy; labor unions
Endangered Species Act (1973), 86
Endoxon, 330
Energy, Department of, 109–10

environmental issues
  Clean Air Act (1970 amendments), 143
  climate change, 335
  East Palestine (Ohio), train crash in, 479
  environmental group activism, 8–9, 42
  Environmental Protection Agency (EPA) and,
    25, 37, 45, 114
  Google employee incentives, 339
  Patton Boggs' duck hunting incident, 148–49
  Patton Boggs' work and (2000s), 362
  Reagan on, 114
Erdoğan, Tayyip, 457
Eshoo, Anna, 272–74, 329, 354, 355, 506
Esposito, Michael, 452–53
Ethiopia, foreign lobbying and, 458, 490
Europe, Roche controversies in, 227–34
European Centre for a Modern Ukraine, 398–
    408, 437. see also Ukraine lobbying scandal
European Union, Yanukovych and, 428–29
Evans, Rich, 74
Evinger, David, 470
exclusivity period (pharmaceuticals), 271–74
Export-Import Bank of the United States, 44
Exxon Mobil Corp., 109–10, 362

F. Hoffmann–La Roche Ltd. (Roche)
  controversies of 1970s–early 2000s, 227–34
  Morris hired as lobbyist for, 234–39
  pharmaceutical industry domination by, 248
  Switzerland headquarters of, 231, 232, 235,
    267, 380
  vitamin price-fixing scandal, 232–33, 247
Facebook, 337, 338, 455
Fairey, Shepard, 333
Falwell, Jerry, 87, 157, 158
Fannie Mae, 362
Federal Bureau of Investigation (FBI)
  Esposito investigation, 453
  on GM and Nader, 40
  Hale Boggs investigation, 23, 48–50, 130
  Manafort investigation, 460–62, 465–66
  Morris/Courtovich investigation, 4, 440,
    447–48, 459, 484, 486, 489
  Wertkin and, 219
Federal Coal Mine Health and Safety Act (1969),
    43
Federal Communications Commission (FCC),
    111–13, 325
Federal Election Commission (FEC), 56–57
Federal Housing Administration (FHA), 172–74
"The Federalist No. 10" (Madison), 6–9, 12
federal minimum wage, 43
Federal Register, 41–42

Federal Trade Commission Act (1914), 60, 354
Federal Trade Commission (FTC), 312–30
  Google antitrust charges, 352–58
  Google antitrust investigation, 345–52
  Google's hiring of Tony Podesta, 315–16, 321–30
  inception of, 312
  as independent agency, 346
  Microsoft investigation as warning to Google,
    315–23, 347
  Miller (former chairman) and Project Eagle, 346
  Reagan's cuts to, 114
  regulatory backlash to, 59–65
  Trump administration and, 455
Federal Water Pollution Control Act
    Amendments (1972), 43
Feingold, Russ, 222
Feinstein, Dianne, 259, 329, 354
Ferraro, Geraldine, 111
Ferrell, Jon, 309–11, 485–86
FHolding Ltd., 419
Financial Times, 304
Flahault, Hubert, 232
Fleming, Patrick, 458
Fluctuating Fortunes (Vogel), 143
Flynn, Michael, 456–58, 480, 487–88, 490
Flynn Intel Group, 457
Foer, Franklin, 73, 206
Follieri, Raffaello, 418–19
Food and Drug Administration (FDA). see also
    Big Pharma
  Accutane (Roche) and, 229–31, 234
  Avastin (Genentech), 290–97
  FDA Modernization Act (1997), 251
  Genentech and FDA reform, 247–52, 268
  Reagan and, 115
  vitamin regulation, 246–47
Footloose (film), 158–59
Forbes, Steve, 288
Ford, Gerald, 23, 49, 73, 84–85, 95, 433
Ford, Johnny, 162
Ford, William, 148
Ford Motor Co., 434
Foreign Agents Registration Act (FARA, 1938)
  Ethiopia and Courtovich's work, 490
  Flynn and, 457
  foreign lobbying image and, 419
  inception of, 175
  Ukraine lobbying campaign filing, 399–406,
    461, 464, 490
foreign lobbying. see also Ukraine lobbying
    scandal; individual names of countries
  by Black Manafort, and Young & Rubicam
    acquisition, 204–12

by Black Manafort, political consulting and
conflicts of interest, 172, 174–83
by Black Manafort during Reagan
administration, 107, 115
Boggs's work with, 419
Podesta's work with, 419–25
registration, FARA (*see* Foreign Agents
Registration Act (1938))
registration, Lobbying Disclosure Act (1995),
401–6
Fortress Investment Group, 336
Fowler, Mark, 112
Fox News
on Avastin and "death panels," 292–93
Black Manafort and inception of, 108, 110–13
Fox & Friends, 455
Murdoch and, 14, 108, 110–13, 322, 344, 455
News Corp, 344
fracking, 455
Franks, Martin, 142
Frantz, Douglas, 34–35
Freddie Mac, 362
Frenkil, Victor, 48
Friend, David, 76
Friends in High Places (Frantz and McKean),
34–35
Fritts, Kimberley
Cogent Strategies of, 508
Podesta Group and SunTrust resignation, 424
Podesta Group closure, 467–70
Podesta Group on FARA vs. LDA filing,
398–400, 402, 403, 405, 406
fund-raising. *See* campaign finance

Galbraith, John Kenneth, 8
Gallagher, Mike, 388
Gates, Bill, 315–23
Gates, Rick
Manafort and Ukraine lobbying scandal, 390,
391, 393, 394–97 (*see also* Ukraine lobbying
scandal)
Manafort as Trump's campaign manager, 428,
429, 435–37
Mueller investigation of, 406, 460–62, 466,
467, 507
plea deal of, 475
Podesta Group on FARA vs. LDA filing,
398–405, 406–8
Gates, Robert, 73
Gaubert, Thomas, 145
Genentech
Avastin campaign, 290–97
Courtovich investigation related to, 484–86, 489

Morris investigation, 1–4, 378–84, 506
Morris's and Courtovich's partnership,
investigation of, 308–11, 440–49, 459
prescription drug prices and lobby against
ACA, 270–76
General Electric Company, 34, 58, 96, 170,
203
General Mills, 64
General Motors (GM), 36, 38–42, 45, 53
generic drugs (exclusivity period of
pharmaceuticals), 271–74
GEO Group Inc., 456
George Mason University, 296, 348, 350–51
George Washington University Law School, 217
Gere, Richard, 192
Germany, American economy vs. (1970s), 47
"Get America's Business Online" (Google
program), 339–40
Giacometto, Leo, 323
Gibson, Dunn & Crutcher, 445–49
Gibson, Mel, 247
gift ban, 243, 258–61, 268–70, 295
Gilens, Martin, 9
Gingrich, Father (Boggs family priest), 22
Gingrich, Newt, 95, 189, 203, 244
Ginsberg, Benjamin, 278, 376
Giuliani, Rudy, 216
Glasser, Susan, 302
Glass-Steagall Act (1933), 202
GlaxoSmithKline, 237
Golden Age of Capitalism, 36
Goldman, T. R. (Ted), 132, 225–26
Goldman Sachs Group Inc., 303, 487
Goldwater, Barry, 73, 79–81, 92, 95, 96, 203
Gongadze, Georgy, 394
Goodyear Tire and Rubber Company, 132
Google, 331–58. *see also* YouTube
on antipiracy legislation, 337–45
as Big Tech, 345
Black fired by, 478
FTC's antitrust charges against, 352–58
FTC's antitrust investigation of, 345–52
Google News, 322
Microsoft investigation as warning to, 315–23,
347
net neutrality campaign of, 324–30, 332
NetPAC, 327–30
Obama and, 331–36, 358
Podesta fired by, 463
self-driving vehicles, 337
as Tony Podesta's client, 315–16, 321–30, 340,
342, 346, 354
Trump on, 455

"Google and the Limits of Antitrust" (Manne and Wright), 350–51
"Google Is Many Things—but Not an Illegal Monopoly" (Radia), 353
Gore, Al, Jr., 28, 199, 202, 216, 251, 252
Gore, Al, Sr., 28
Gore, Pauline, 28
Al Gosaibi family, 442
Graham, Bob, 166
Gramm, Phil, 93, 119, 166, 183, 286–88
Grassley, Chuck, 340, 348, 498–99
"grass tops" and grassroots tactics, 165–72, 182. see also Black Manafort, political consulting and conflicts of interest
Great Recession. see 2008 financial crisis
Great Society, 37, 42
Greenfield, Meg, 61
Gregg, Judd, 285
Griffin, Philip, 395
Griffis, Kevin, 404–5
Gross, Ken, 401, 403, 405, 406
Grove, Andy, 323
Gude, Gilbert, 130
Guerriero, Joseph "Pippi," 77
Guevara, Ernesto "Che," 178
Gülen, Fethullah, 457
Gursky, Andreas, 255
Guthrie, Savannah, 278

Hacker, Jacob, 11
Hacker Boat Company, 310, 447, 483–84
Haiti, foreign lobbying and, 14
Haldeman, H. R. "Bob," 83
Hampton, Christopher, 480–81
Harlow, Bryce, 58
Harriman, Averell, 34
Harris, John, 36
"Harry and Louise" campaign, 199–201, 245
Hartford Club, 199
Harvard Law School, 354
Harvard University, 195, 349
Hastert, Dennis, 154, 193, 327
Hastert, Josh, 327
Hatch, Orrin, 87
Hawley, Josh, 498, 499
Hawn, Goldie, 158
Hayden, Frederick, 236
Heald, Paul, 350
Healey, Jim, 125–27, 128, 210
Health and Human Services, Department of, 235–37
healthcare.gov website, 333
health care industry. see Affordable Care Act

(2010); Big Pharma; F. Hoffmann–La Roche Ltd. (Roche); health care reform, Clinton administration
health care reform, Clinton administration, 186–203
Clinton's presidential election (1992), 186–88
Democratic support of corporate capitalism as result of, 201–3
Democrats and Republicans in opposition to, 194–99
early opposition, by Republicans, 188–94
"Harry and Louise" campaign, 199–201, 245
public opinion of, 199–201, 245, 264
Health Insurance Association of America, 194, 199–201
Heath, Edward, 36
Heather Podesta + Partners, 464. see also Podesta, Heather Miller
Helms, Jesse, 93, 166
Heritage Foundation, 56
Hernandez, Carlos, 480–81
Hertz, 335
Hill, issue advocacy ads in, 302
"Hill House," 448–49, 458, 491. see also Courtovich, Jim
HIV/AIDS, 231, 249–50
Hoffmann-LaRoche, Fritz, 231. see also F. Hoffmann–La Roche Ltd. (Roche)
Holder, Eric, 305
Hollings, Fritz, 64
home ownership
National Affordable Housing Act, death of, 169–71
Patton Boggs' work and (2000s), 362
Proposition 13 (California), 86–87
Seabrook Apartments (New Jersey), 172–74
Truth in Lending Act (1968), 86
2008 housing crisis, 335–36 (see also 2008 financial crisis)
Honest Graft (Jackson), 135, 138, 142–45
Honest Leadership and Open Government Act (2007)
"consultants"/"strategists" vs. registered lobbyists following, 295–97
on gift ban, 243, 258–61, 268–70, 295
modern influence industry and, 297 (see also shadow lobbying)
Obama's anti-lobbyist ethos and, 261–62
on "wide-attended events," 279–80
Honeywell Corporation, 46
Hoover, J. Edgar, 48, 49, 217
Hope, Bob, 137
Hope (Obama portrait, Fairey), 333–34

Horton, Willie, 67, 70
Housing and Urban Development, Department of (HUD), 76, 172–74, 245
Hoyer, Steny, 121
Huawei Technologies, 506
Hull, William, 8
Human Rights Watch, 181
Humphrey, Hubert, 23, 51, 82, 140

Iacocca, Lee, 104, 108, 119
Iacuzio, Dominick, 237
IBM, 46, 252, 317
Icahn, Carl, 108, 115
Ickes, Harold, 216
Indian Gaming Regulatory Act (1988), 121–24
"In House, Many Spoke with One Voice" (Pear, New York Times), 275–76
Inouye, Daniel, 362
Inovo, 457
"inside game" strategies
    anti-Bork initiative example, 150–53
    Black Manafort's initial growth and, 109
    Google and antipiracy legislation, 337–39
    of late 1960s, 32–38
    "outside game" transition from, 14, 182, 296
        (see also lobbying and corporate economy; shadow lobbying)
    Podesta's and Google's use of, 315
insurance industry
    on health care reform, Clinton administration, 188–201 (see also health care reform, Clinton administration)
    mortgage insurance, 169–71
Interior, Department of, 121–24
Internal Revenue Service (IRS), 440–42, 466
International Brotherhood of Teamsters, 76
International Center for Law & Economics, 348, 350–51
International Consortium of Investigative Journalists, 423–24
"Internet Search Competition" (Balto), 347
Invariant, 464, 507. see also Podesta, Heather Miller
Invisible Hands (Phillips-Fein), 52
Isaacson, Walter, 476
issue advocacy advertising, 287, 289, 302

J. P. Morgan & Co., 5
Jackson, Amy Berman, 473
Jackson, Andrew, 26
Jackson, Brooks, 135, 138, 142–45
Jackson, Jesse, 207, 216
Jackson, Thomas Penfield, 319, 320

January 6 attacks, 495, 497, 505, 506
Japan, American economy vs. (1970s), 47
The Jenny Jones Show, 286
Johndroe, Gordon, 278
Johnson, Claudia Alta "Lady Bird," 28, 51
Johnson, Haynes, 200
Johnson, Lyndon B.
    Boggs family and, 21, 23–24, 29–32, 51, 372
    Civil Rights Act (1964), 92
    Clifford and, 34
    Corcoran and, 33
    Great Society, 37, 42, 137
    on health care reform, 189
    on National Traffic and Motor Vehicle Safety Act, 40
    presidential election (1964), 80, 154
    Tommy Boggs as political aide to, 31–32
Johnson, Matthew, 453
Johnson & Johnson, 108, 248
Johnston, J. Bennett, 163, 164
Jonas, John, 364, 375, 376
Jones, Robert Trent, Sr., 2
Jordan, Vernon, 216
JPMorgan Chase & Co., 225
judicial branch, Reagan's judicial nominations, 150–53, 160–64
Judis, John, 12
Justice, Department of. see also Federal Bureau of Investigation; Mueller, Robert
    Courtovich and, 305, 487, 489, 490
    FARA filing and, 405
    Flynn investigation, 457, 481, 487–88, 490
    Hale Boggs investigation, 48
    Microsoft settlement, 316–17
    Morris's suicide and, 3
    Podesta Group investigation, 464
    Quicken Loans investigation, 449
    Roche investigation, 232–33
    Trump administration and, 455

Kahn, Chip, 194
Kaiser, Henry, 33
Kaiser, Laurent, 236
Kalley, Terry, 294
Kaman Aerospace, 116
Kardashian, Kim, 343
Kashmiri American Council, 205
Kasich, John, 452
Katzenberg, Jeffrey, 225
Kauders, Andrew, 404–5
Kean, Tom, 120
Kearsarge Global Advisors, 445
Keene, David, 117

Kelly, Peter
  Angola and, 181
  at Black Manafort, 119, 124–25
  Black Manafort acquired by Young &
    Rubicam, 205, 208, 210
  health care reform and, 199
  presidential campaign (1988) and, 166
  Somalia and, 176
Kemp, Jack, 165–66, 170, 171
Kennedy, Edward "Ted"
  anti-Bork initiative of, 150–53, 160–64, 245
  on Hale Boggs's disappearance, 23
  Ickes and, 216
  presidential campaign of, 156
  Tommy Boggs and, 130
  Tony Podesta and, 252, 255
Kennedy, John F. (JFK)
  Boggs family and, 21, 23, 29–30
  "Camelot" of, 222
  Coelho influenced by, 129, 135, 145
  Corcoran and, 33
  presidential election (1960), 162
  Profiles in Courage, 20
  Stone's mock campaign for, 79
  Tommy Boggs influenced by, 130
Kennedy, Robert, 38
Kentz, Frederick, 378–80, 381–82, 383
Kenya, foreign lobbying and, 176, 206
Kerner, Otto, Jr., 154
Kerry, John, 225, 325, 331, 404
Kershaw, Clayton, 269
Kessler, Stephen, 410
Khashoggi, Adnan, 120, 391
Khashoggi, Jamal, 449
Kian, Bijan, 458
Kiddie Corps, 78
Kilimnik, Konstantin, 436, 460
King, Martin Luther, Jr., 162
King, Peter, 304–5
Kirkpatrick, Jeane, 180
Klain, Ron, 252, 357
Klein, Joel, 233, 317
Klein, Rick, 448
Klobuchar, Amy, 340
Koch, Charles, 501
Kohl, Herb, 348
Korologos, Tom, 164
Kovacevich, Adam, 339, 340, 346, 349
Krimm, Matt, 444
Kristol, William, 56
Krumholtz, Jack, 318
K Street. see lobbying and K Street
Kudlow, Larry, 155

Kushner, Jared, 424, 428
Kutler, Ed, 405
Kuzio, Taras, 393, 394, 396

Labor, Department of, 168
labor unions
  antipiracy legislation and, 338
  Bethlehem Steel and, 168
  "capital-labor accord" of postwar era, 36
  Manafort Brothers scandal and, 76
  New Right's ascent and, 87
  power of, in future, 502–3
  power of (1950s–1970s), 141
  power of (1960s and early 1970s), 8–9
  power of (1970s, late), 65
  Reagan on efficiency (vs. equity) of
    government, 10–11, 113–15
Laird, Melvin, 50
Lancaster, Burt, 158
Lane, Rick, 344
Lantos, Tom, 174
Laufman, David, 419
Lazerow, Andrew, 443
Leadership Conference on Civil Rights, 159, 336
Leahy, Patrick, 166, 240, 260, 262, 338, 361
Lear, Norman, 104, 156–57
Leavitt, Michael, 235, 237
Lee, Burton, 183
Lee, Ivy, 175
Lee, Mike, 342
Leibowitz, Jon, 315, 345–49, 352–58
Levin, Mark, 476
Levinson, Riva, 118, 176–77
Lewandowski, Corey, 434, 452
Lewinsky, Monica, 187, 216
Lewis, Eric, 305, 485, 486
Lewis, Lindsay, 266
Lewis, Michael, 288
LGBTQ issues, New Right's ascent and, 93
Liddy, G. Gordon, 83
Liebengood, Howard S., 506
Liebengood, Howie C., 506
Lieberman, Joe, 155
Limbaugh, Rush, 476
Lipsen, Linda, 25
lobbying and corporate economy, 186–212
  Black Manafort acquired by Burson-
    Marsteller (Young & Rubicam), 203–12
  corporate lobbyists' investment in new
    political candidates, 188
  health care reform attempt by Clinton
    administration, 186–203 (see also health
    care reform, Clinton administration)

lobbies as corporate profit centers, 238–39
mergers and acquisitions (shareholder
    primacy movement), 203
lobbying and K Street. *see also* foreign lobbying;
    "inside game" strategies; lobbying and
    corporate economy; lobbying regulation;
    lobbying tactics; "outside game" strategies;
    individual names of lobbyists
Boggs and early legislative influence, 58–59,
    61–63, 65
Democrat and Republican cooperation,
    against health care reform (Clinton
    administration), 190, 194–99, 201–3
FTC and regulatory backlash, 59–65
growth (1960s, early), 35
growth (1967–2007), 9
growth (1980s), 12, 65
growth (2000s), 305–6
growth (2002–2016), 296
Hull and first act of (1792), 8
issue advocacy advertising, 287, 289, 302
K Street and L'Enfant's design, 222
lobbying, defined, 8
lobbying dynasties of, 13–15 (*see also* Atwater,
    Lee; Black, Charlie; Boggs, Tommy; Manafort,
    Paul, Jr.; Podesta, Tony; Stone, Roger)
Manafort on "influence peddling," 174
modern influence industry, inception of, 297
    (*see also* Honest Leadership and Open
    Government Act (2007))
1980s, rising influence of, 12
Powell Memo and, 52–57, 86, 351
Trump and "audience of one" strategy, 389,
    453–56
Trump presidency and new lobbyists, 452–56
lobbying regulation. *see also* Foreign Agents
    Registration Act (FARA, 1938)
"consultants"/"strategists" vs. registered
    lobbyists, 295–97
Lobbying Disclosure Act (LDA, 1995), 401–6
McCain-Feingold Act (2002), 222–27
New York on disclosure, 123
lobbying tactics
"black ops," 236, 295
"bundling," 223–27, 258
gift ban loophole, 243, 258–61, 268–70, 295
issue advocacy, 289, 302
"poison pills," 198
shadow lobbying, 236, 280, 289–97, 305–11,
    345–54
"Speaker's Club," 142
Trump and "audience of one" strategy, 389,
    453–56

Locke Lord, 372
Lockerbie, Scotland terrorist bombing, 364
Lockheed Martin Corp., 418
Lockyer, Bill, 319
Lofgren, Zoe, 329, 354, 355
Long, Huey, 27
Long, Randall, 352
Long, Russell, 128, 147
Losers (Lewis), 288
Lott, Trent, 377
Louisiana. *see* Boggs, Hale
Lowery, Joseph, 162
Lowey, Nita, 216
"Loyal Bank," West Indies, 408, 429
Luetkemeyer, Blaine, 275
Lugar, Richard, 179
Lumpkin, Murray, 233
Lynd, Staughton, 46

Mack, Connie, 327
MacNeil, Robert, 72
Madison, James, 6–9, 12, 38
Magruder, Jeb, 81
Maiwurm, Jim, 374, 377, 508
"Make America Great Again," 390, 427, 436, 446,
    453, 456, 479
Maloney, Paul, 27
malpractice litigation, health care reform
    attempt and, 195–98
Manafort, Andrea, 427, 430–31, 433, 434
Manafort, Jessica, 430–31, 433, 434
Manafort, Kathy, 427, 431, 432, 472
Manafort, Paul, Jr., 172–79, 426–38. *see also*
    Young Republicans National Federation
Atwater's and Black's introduction to, 94–99
Black, Manafort & Stone inception, 101,
    106–8, 110
Black Manafort firing of (1995), 204–12, 391
Bush's 1988 presidential campaign, 172
characterization of, 97–99, 116–19,
    175–76 (*see also* Black Manafort, political
    consulting and conflicts of interest)
early biographical information, 74–78
Flynn and, 456
Ford campaign and, 73, 84–85, 95
foreign lobbying and conflicts of interest,
    175–79, 181 (*see also* foreign lobbying)
homes and lifestyle of (2000s), 397
HUD scandal, 172–74, 245
lifestyle and homes of, 397, 427, 430–31, 432
lobbyist legacy of, 13, 505, 507
"Paul tax," 175–76

Manafort, Paul, Jr. (*cont.*)
  Political Prisoner, 474
  prison release and pardon of, 479, 493–94
  Reagan's ascent and, 71–72, 99–102
  Stone's introduction to, 72–74
  trials and incarceration, 472–76
  as Trump's campaign manager (2016), 426–28,
    431–38
  Ukraine lobbying scandal and financial
    problems of, 428–31, 436–38 (*see also*
    Ukraine lobbying scandal)
  Young Republicans and control of, 73–74, 78
Manafort, Paul, Sr., 75–77
Manafort Brothers (New Britain, Connecticut),
  74–77
Manchester Union-Leader, 155–56
Mandel, Marvin, 130
Manhattan Pictures International, 392
Manion, Daniel, 159–60
Manne, Geoffrey A., 348, 350–51, 355
Mar-a-Lago, 120
Marathon Oil Corp., 336
Marcos, Ferdinand, 205, 206
Markey, Ed, 137
Marshall, Thurgood, 163
Mars Inc., 61
Mason, Julie, 459
Mattoon, Dan, 327, 335
McAuliffe, Terry, 380–81
McCain, John, 222, 431
McCain-Feingold Act (2002), 222–27
McCann, Madeleine, 462
McCarthy, Eugene, 154
McCarthy, Joseph, 119
McCarthy, Kevin, 73, 501–2
McCloskey, Pete, 82
McCormack, John, 48
McCormack, William, 30
McGahn, Don, 376
McGee, Palmer, 77
McGovern, George, 83, 156, 187
McInturff, Bill, 199–200
McKean, David, 33, 34–35
McLaughlin, Andrew, 333
McMinoway, Michael, 82–83
"meat markets," 142
media buying, 287, 302
Medicare Prescription Drug, Improvement, and
  Modernization Act (2003), 361–62
Meet the Press (NBC), 426–27
Melnick, Daniel, 158
Menendez, Robert, 404
Mercatus Center, George Mason University, 348

Mercury Public Affairs, 391, 398, 400–407,
  429–30, 437, 508. *see also* Ukraine lobbying
  scandal
mergers and acquisitions (shareholder primacy
  movement), 203. *see also* lobbying and
  corporate economy
Merrill, Steve, 285–86
Merrywood (Boggs family home), 19–20
Meskill, Thomas, 78
Michelin, 418
Mickelson, Phil, 2
Microsoft
  Bing, 353
  FTC investigation, 315–23, 347
  Long and, 352
  "soft money," 223
  YouTube bid by, 322
Miller, Arthur, 157
Miller, Bill, 80
Miller, George, 122
Miller, Heather. *See* Podesta, Heather Miller
Miller, James, III, 349
Mitsoff, Karen L., 210–11
Mobil Oil Corporation, 46
Mohawk Indians, 123
Mondale, Walter, 111
Mondeléz International Inc., 434
Moolenaar, John, 388
Moore, Walter, 249
Moral Majority, 87, 157
Morehead, Don, 363
Morocco, foreign lobbying and, 490
Morrell, Geoff, 388
Morris, Evan, 215–39, 263–76
  Boggs as mentor to, 13
  "bundling" by, 223–27, 258
  characterization and lifestyle of, 217–18,
    224–27, 264–70, 297–300, 443–44
  Congressional Record controversy, 274–76
  Courtovich's partnership with, 280, 287–97,
    305–11, 378–84, 440–49, 459, 482–86, 489
  early biographical information, 215–18
  financial settlements following death of, 506
  Genentech and Avastin campaign of, 290–97
  legal investigations of, 482–86, 489
  on Obama's health care reform, 263–64,
    270–74
  at Patton Boggs, 215, 218–27
  Roche history prior to Morris's career, 227–34
  as Roche lobbyist, 234–39
  as Roche vice president of government affairs
    promotion, 267–70
  suicide of, 1–4, 382–84, 443–44

Tamiflu and, 235–37, 264
Tommy Boggs's influence on, 265, 266
Morris, Tracy, 267, 306–7, 380, 382–83, 444–45, 448, 506
Mortgage Insurance Companies of America, 170
Mossack Fonseca, 423–24
Motion Picture Association of America, 344
Mueller, Robert
  Gates investigation, 406, 460–62, 466, 467, 507
  Manafort investigation, 406, 460–62, 473, 475–76, 493, 507
  Podesta investigation, 495, 496
  Russia/United States presidential election (2016) investigation, 480, 488, 490
  Stone investigation, 494
  Ukraine lobbying investigation, 399
Mullins, Brody, 482–86
Murdoch, Rupert, 14, 108, 110–13, 322, 344, 455. see also Fox News
Murphy, Richard T., 77
Murphy, Thomas, 45
Murray, Patty, 260
Musk, Elon, 335
Muskie, Edmund, 82, 130, 131, 155–56

NAACP, 67, 336
Nader, Ralph, 38–42, 59–65, 144, 222, 508
Napier, Lanham, 341–42
Napolitano, Janet, 255, 267
Nasso, Julius, 392
National Aeronautics and Space Administration (NASA), 329–30
National Affordable Housing Act, death of, 169–71
National Association of Manufacturers (NAM), 36, 57–58, 105
National Chamber Foundation, 55
National Conservative Political Action Committee, 94
National Enquirer, 103
National Highway Traffic Safety Administration, 114
National Journal, 302
National Labor Relations Board (NLRB), 115
National Media
  Courtovich's and Morris's partnership and, 289–97, 305–11
  investigation of, 445
"National Nanny" op-ed (Washington Post), 61–62
National People's Action, 170–71
National Poultry Federation, 246
National Resources, Department of (Maryland), 149

National Traffic and Motor Vehicle Safety Act (1966), 40–41, 43
National Union for the Total Independence of Angola (UNITA), 177–83
Navigator (Netscape), 317
NBC, 426–27
Neas, Ralph, 159
Neiman, Jeffrey, 505
NetJets, 335
net neutrality, 324–30
NetPAC, 327–30
Netscape, 317
Newberry, Ed, 366–68, 370–77, 508
New Deal
  equity principle of, 10, 113
  federal regulation expansion and, 36–38
  FTC and, 312
  Hale Boggs's legacy and, 25
  "New Deal Coalition," 27–28, 102–3, 360
Newhouse, Neil, 397
The New Politics of Inequality (Edsall), 10–11, 87, 93–94, 113
New Right, 10, 47, 80, 85–88, 90–99, 157–60. see also Young Republicans National Federation
News Corp, 344. see also Fox News
Newsom, Gavin, 225
New York Institute for Law and Society, 123
New York Post, Fox News and, 111
New York Times
  "In House, Many Spoke with One Voice" (Pear), 275–76
  " 'Unbiased' Ads for Microsoft Came at a Price," 320
Ney, Bob, 257
Nicaragua, foreign lobbying and, 175
Nicas, Jack, 350
Nigeria, foreign lobbying and, 176
Niskanen, William, 202
Nixon, Patricia, 51
Nixon, Richard, 62
  Boggs family and, 23, 30, 48–50
  on EPA, 37
  on FTC, 60
  on health care reform, 189
  presidential election (1974), 132
  Stone and, 81–84, 119, 217
  Watergate, 62, 72–73, 83–85, 131–34, 223
Norfolk Southern Corp., 478
North American Free Trade Agreement (NAFTA, 1994), 202
Northern Neck Regional Jail (Virginia), 473–75

Obama, Barack. *See also* Affordable Care Act
(2010)
  administration of, vs. Trump administration,
  453
  anti-lobbying ethos of, 242, 261–62, 313, 333,
  336
  on consumer reforms, 10
  Courtovich and, 301
  Follieri and, 419
  golf club membership of, 2
  Google and, 331–36, 358
  inauguration (2009), 263–64
  John Podesta as counselor to, 241
  lobbyist dynasties and administration of, 13
  Morris and, 236, 237, 299
  on prescription drug prices, 270–74
  presidential election (2008), 261–62, 418
  presidential election (2012), 354
  Ukraine policy, 396, 398, 404
  as US senator, 328, 332
Obama, Michelle, 299, 300, 334
Ocasio-Cortez, Alexandria, 479
Occupational Safety and Health Administration
  (OSHA), 25, 65, 114
O'Connell, Jonathan, 452
Office of Surface Mining Reclamation and
  Enforcement, 114
oil industry
  climate change, 335
  Patton Boggs' work and (2000s), 362
  Powder River Basin, 114
  Trump on fracking, 455
Okochi, Kaz, 240
Olin, John M., 56
Onassis, Jacqueline Kennedy, 19–20, 30
O'Neill, Tip, Jr., 49, 131–32, 134, 142
Oracle Corporation, 320, 335, 418, 468
Orange Revolution, 393, 396
"outside game" strategies
  anti-Bork initiative example, 153, 160–64
  defined, 153
  gift ban loophole, 243, 258–61, 268–70, 295
  Google and antipiracy legislation, 339–45
  "grass tops" and grassroots tactics, 165–72,
  182
  "Harry and Louise" and health care reform
  (Clinton administration), 199–201, 245
  "inside game" transition to, 14
  Tony Podesta and innovation of, 167, 243, 245
Owens, Nick, 458

Page, Benjamin I., 9
Page, Larry, 313–14, 322, 327, 339, 355–56

Pakistan, foreign lobbying and, 392
Palfrey, Deborah Jeane, 293
Palin, Sarah, 292, 339
"Panama Papers," 423–24
Pan American Airways, 33, 364
Pape, Stuart, 369
The Paradox of American Democracy (Judis), 12
Party of Regions (Ukraine), 394–98, 403–4, 437.
  see also Ukraine lobbying scandal
Pascrell, Bill, 275–76, 299
Pastrick, Scott, 108, 122
Pataki, George, 123
Patient Care Action Network, 291–93
Patton, Jim, Jr., 44, 147
Patton Boggs, 359–77. *see also* Boggs, Tommy
  culture and lifestyle, 147–49, 218–20
  financial problems (2003–2014), 361–74
  growth of (1980s–1990s), 146–47, 187
  "Harry and Louise" ad, 199–201, 245
  health care reform opposition, 194–98, 201
  mission of, 58
  Morris on staff at, 215, 218–27
  Morris's firing of (as Roche lobbyist), 266–67
  name of, 51
  Squire Patton Boggs merger, 374–77 (*see also*
  Squire Patton Boggs)
  Tosco and, 109
Paycheck Protection Program, 496
Payne, Donald, 275
Pear, Robert, 275
Peck, Gregory, 163, 164
Pelosi, Nancy
  ethics reform priority of, 258
  Google and, 342
  Podestas and, 240, 242, 254, 255, 496
  Tommy Boggs's eulogy by, 361
Pence, Mike, 487
People for the American Way (PAW), 156–60, 163
Perelman, Ron, 108, 115
Perlstein, Rick, 61, 96
Perot, H. Ross, 104
Pertschuk, Michael, 59–61, 62, 64
Peru, foreign lobbying and, 176
Peterson, Bruce, 173
Pfizer Inc., 227, 313
pharmaceutical industry. *see* Big Pharma
Philip Morris, 52
Philippines, foreign lobbying and, 176, 205, 206
Phillips, Howard, 179
Phillips, Kevin, 95
Phillips-Fein, Kim, 52
Phoenix Home Life Mutual Insurance Company,
  194

Pickens, T. Boone, 104
Pierson, Paul, 11
Pingree, Chellie, 258
PIPA (Preventing Real Online Threats to Economic Creativity and Theft of Intellectual Property Act), 337–45
Pirelli, 418, 471
"Pizzagate," 462–63
Plotkin, Kyle, 499
Podesta, Heather Miller
    art collection of, 241, 252–56, 260, 333–34, 336
    characterization of, 241–42
    divorce of, 409–13, 415–20
    early biographical information, 241, 253
    homes of, 254–55, 260
    lobbying firm of, 242, 336–37, 464, 507
    marriage to Tony Podesta, 240–43, 253–57
    Obama's election (2008) and, 261–62
    scarlet-letter-for-lobbyist stunt, 242, 261, 262
Podesta, John, Jr.
    as Bill Clinton's chief of staff, 241, 244
    Center for American Progress, 241
    early biographical information, 153, 156
    Obama and, 333, 335, 336
    "Pizzagate" and, 462
    Podesta & Associates, inception of, 191–93
    Tony Podesta's foreign lobbying work and, 421–22, 424
Podesta, John, Sr., 153
Podesta, Mary, 153, 244, 462
Podesta, Tony, 150–64, 240–62, 409–25
    on Abramoff scandal, 257, 258
    art collection of, 152, 241, 252–56, 260, 333–34, 336, 463, 468–70
    Avastin and, 290
    business growth of (1990s), 241, 244–47, 252
    business growth of (2007–2010), 334
    characterization of, 256–57, 297, 413–15
    Courtovich and, 449, 455, 458
    divorce of, 409–13, 415–20
    early biographical information, 153–56
    foreign lobbying work sought by, 419–25
    Genentech and FDA reform, 247–52, 268
    gift ban manipulation by, 258–61
    Google as client of, 315–16, 321–30, 340, 342, 346, 354
    homes of, 254–55, 260
    lobbyist legacy of, 13, 152, 164, 497
    marriage to first wife, 253
    marriage to Heather Podesta, 240–43, 253–57 (see also Podesta, Heather Miller)
    Morris's firing of, 305
    Obama and, 261–62, 333–37

"outside game" innovation by, 167, 243, 245
    as People for the American Way director, 156–60, 163
Podesta & Associates, inception of, 191–93
Podesta & Associates, podesta.com rebranding (1998), 252
Podesta Group, career after closing of, 495–97, 506
Podesta Group business name, 334
Podesta Group purchase offer and, 417, 465, 467–70
Podesta Group's loss of clients and eventual closing, 462–71
Republican lobbyists in firm of, 327
Sberbank as client of, 458
scarlet-letter-for-lobbyist stunt, 242, 261, 262
Ted Kennedy's anti-Bork initiative and, 150–53, 160–64
on Tommy Boggs's legacy, 376
Trump presidency and, 387–90
Ukraine lobbying scandal and, 390, 398–408, 420, 429–30, 437
Venice (Italy) retreats hosted by, 255, 416
"poison pills," 198
Poison Prevention Packaging Act (1970), 86
Political Mercenaries (Lewis), 266
Political Prisoner (Manafort), 474
Pompeo, Mike, 458
Popular Movement for the Liberation of Angola, 181
Porter, Bart, 83
Posicor (Roche), 233
Powder River Basin, 114
Powell, Lewis F., Jr., 52–57, 86, 151, 351
Preventing Real Online Threats to Economic Creativity and Theft of Intellectual Property Act (PROTECT IP Act, or PIPA), 337–45
Prime Policy Group, 506
Princeton University, 46
Procter & Gamble, 58
Profiles in Courage (Kennedy), 20
Project Eagle, 345–54
Proposition 13 (California), 86–87
Prudential Financial Inc., 336
public opinion
    of corporate America (1968–1970), 46–47
    health care and "Harry and Louise" campaign, 199–201, 245
    on health care reform (2008), 264
    of lobbyists (1980s), 245
    of National Affordable Housing Act, 170–71
Puck, Wolfgang, 246
Putin, Vladimir, 398, 424, 428–29, 473

al-Qahtani, Saud, 449
Qatar, Courtovich and, 448, 490, 506–7
Quayle, Dan, 66, 67, 70
Quicken Loans, 449

race
   Bork and, 162
   Civil Rights Act (1964), 37, 92, 151
   Thurmond and, 66, 88–91, 93
   2008 housing crisis, 335–36
   Young Republicans' influence on race issues,
      67, 70, 90–94
Rademaker, Steve, 402, 406
Radia, Ryan, 353
Raffetto, John, 192
Ramirez, Edith, 358
Rauschenberg, Robert, 252–53
Ravenel, Charles "Pug," 88–89
Rayburn, Sam, 24, 29, 30, 31
Raynes, Burt, 57–58
Reagan, Nancy, 101
Reagan, Ronald
   assassination attempt, 183
   Atwater in administration of, 185
   Bethlehem Steel and, 167–68
   on Big Government, 10, 99
   Black Manafort and, 125–27, 128–29, 207, 435
   Cold War and, 175
   end of second term, 165
   foreign lobby contribution rumor, 206
   government cuts by, 113–15
   judicial nominations, 150–53, 160–64
   presidential election (1980), 134
   Savimba and, 179, 180
   Trump's support of, 120
   Young Republicans and rise of, 67–69, 71, 73,
      84, 95–105
Reaganland (Perlstein), 61, 96
Reed, Linda, 69
Reid, Harry, 217, 225, 254, 342, 344, 361
Reinhardt, Beth, 452
religion. see New Right
Renner, Christopher, 357
Reno, Janet, 233
rental car companies, 335
Republican lobbying dynasties. see Atwater, Lee;
   Black, Charlie; Manafort, Paul, Jr.; Stone,
   Roger
Republican Party. see also campaign finance;
   Young Republicans National Federation;
   individual names of Republican politicians
   Goldwater's criticism of, 80 (see also
      Goldwater, Barry)

   on health care reform, Clinton administration,
      188–99
   lobbying dynasties of, 13–15 (see also Atwater,
      Lee; Black, Charlie; Black Manafort;
      Manafort, Paul; Stone, Roger)
   National Republican Congressional
      Committee (NRCC), 140, 146
   net neutrality issue and, 325–27
   New Right shift, 10, 47, 80, 85–88, 90–99,
      157–60 (see also Reagan, Ronald)
   Republican National Committee, Atwater's
      chairmanship, 67–69, 73, 183
   Tea Party movement, 342
Research Institute of America, 80
Reston, James, 80
Revlon, 115
Richardson, Bill, 240
Richardson, Elizabeth, 198
Ricker, Vernon, 148–49
"The Rise and Fall of a K Street Renegade"
   (Mullins, Wall Street Journal), 482–86
Rist, Pipilotti, 256
Rivers, Richard, 44
Robb, Chuck, 181
Roberts, Corrine "Cokie" Boggs, 29, 361
Robertson, Pat, 157, 158
Robert Trent Jones Golf Club (Gainesville,
   Virginia), 1–4, 378, 382–84, 483
Robyn, Dorothy, 253
Roche. see F. Hoffmann–La Roche Ltd.
Roche Family Foundation, 299
Rockefeller, John D. "Jay," 60, 200
Rockefeller, Nelson, 80
Roe v. Wade (1973), 151
Roll Call
   issue advocacy ads in, 302
   on Tommy Boggs as "King of K Street," 218
Rollins, Ed, 185
Romney, Mitt, 406
Roosevelt, Eleanor, 28
Roosevelt, Franklin Delano
   death of, 34
   Federal Housing Administration, 169
   Foreign Agents Registration Act (1938), 175
   on health care reform, 189
   Ickes family and, 216
   lobbyists' influence on, 32–33
   New Deal, 10, 27–28, 102–3, 113, 312, 360
Rosch, J. Thomas, 348
Rostenkowski, Dan, 125–27
Rove, Karl, 432
Royce, Ed, 448, 449, 458
Rubio, Marco, 499

Rudalevige, Andrew, 6
Rudman, Warren, 284
Russia
    Courtovich's work for, 300
    Manafort's fear of retribution, 397, 460–61
    Sberbank, 424, 458
    Ukraine's Party of Regions and (*see* Ukraine lobbying scandal)
    United States presidential election (2016) investigation, 473, 480, 488, 490
    Yanukovych in, 428–29

Salinger, J. D., 158
Salinger, Michael, 354
Salomon Brothers, 108, 115, 116, 127, 207
Sánchez, Linda, 225
Sanders, Bernie, 423
al-Sanea, Maan, 305
Saudi Arabia
    Courtovich's work for, 300, 304–5, 439, 441–42, 449, 491
    foreign lobbying by, 419, 420
    Podesta and American Public Relation Affairs Committee, 464
    Saudi Aramco, 422
    Tony Podesta's work for, 455
Savimbi, Jonas, 177–83, 206, 209
Sberbank, 424, 458
Scalise, Steve, 501
Schieffer, Bob, 278
Schindler, John R., 424
Schlesinger, Arthur M., Sr., 6
Schmidt, Eric, 327, 329, 332, 351, 356
Schmidt, Steve, 397
Schumer, Chuck, 226, 237–38, 242, 254, 331, 496
Schwarzenegger, Arnold, 68–69
Seabrook Apartments (New Jersey), 172–74
Seagal, Steven, 392
Sears, John, 71, 100–101
Securities and Exchange Commission, 314
Seidman, Ricki, 160
self-driving vehicles, 337
Senbet, Fasseha, 207–8, 210–11
September 11–related lawsuits, 364, 369–70, 373
Sessions, Jeff, 159
SGR Government Relations and Lobbying, 440, 442. *see also* Courtovich, Jim
shadow lobbying, 236, 280, 289–97, 305–11, 345–54
shareholder primacy movement, 203
Shelton, Johanna, 337, 354
Sherman Antitrust Act (1890), 317, 354
Shriver, Sargent, 130

Shultz, George P., 179
Siad Barre, Mohamed, 176
Silent Spring (Carson), 42
Silicon Valley. *see* Genentech; Google
Simon, Greg, 250–51
Simon, William, 56
Sisk, B. F., 138, 143, 145
Skadden Arps, 401
Smith, Bob, 280, 284
Smith, Lamar, 341, 342, 344
Smith, Megan, 333
social media. *see also individual names of social media outlets*
    antipiracy legislation and, 337, 338, 343–45
    "audience of one" strategy, 389, 453–56
    Avastin and, 293
    Courtovich's use of, 301
"soft money," 223–27
Solomon, Burt, 21, 25, 129
Somalia, foreign lobbying and, 176
Sonsini, Wilson, 351
Southern Christian Leadership Conference, 162
South Sudan, foreign lobbying and, 420–21
"Speaker's Club," 142
Specter, Arlen, 166
Spence, Floyd, 67
Sphere Consulting, 301–5, 308–11, 440, 445, 448, 485–87. *see also* Courtovich, Jim
Squire Patton Boggs, 374–77, 421, 452, 507, 508
St. Regis tribe, Mohawk Indians, 123
Stabile, John, 285
Staebler, Neil, 140
stagflation panic (1970s), 10, 47, 85–86
Stallman, Erik, 344
Standard & Poor's, 336
Standard Oil Company, 5, 34, 37, 60, 317
Stanford University, 46
Steinbeck, John, 158
Stephanopoulos, George, 216
Sternbach, Leo, 231
Stevens, Ted, 23, 328
Stewart, Maureen, 381
Stirling, Dave, 319
Stone, Ann "Bitsey," 81
Stone, Roger
    Atwater's and Black's introduction to, 94–99
    Atwater's friendship with, 185
    Black, Manafort & Stone inception, 101, 106–8
    Black Manafort's firing of, 204–12
    Bush's 1988 presidential campaign, 172
    characterization of, 79, 82–84, 97–99, 116–19, 123, 125 (*see also* Black Manafort, political consulting and conflicts of interest)

Stone, Roger (*cont.*)
  early biographical information, 78–81
  on foreign lobbying, 176
  "Jason Rainier" pseudonym, 82
  Kemp as client of, 165–66
  lobbyist legacy of, 13
  Manafort's introduction to, 72–74
  Nixon and, 81–84, 119, 217
  Reagan's ascent and, 71–72, 100–102
  Thurmond campaign and, 88–89
  Trump's pardon of, 494
  Trump's presidential campaign (2016) and,
    428, 432, 433
  in Ukraine, 398
  Young Republicans and control of, 73–74,
    78 (*see also* Young Republicans National
    Federation)
Stop Online Piracy Act (SOPA), 338–45
Strategic National Stockpile, 236–37
Stupak, Bart, Jr., 228, 234, 280
Stupak, Bart, Sr., 227–31, 280
Stupak, Ken, 228
Stupak, Laurie, 227–29, 231
Sullivan's Island (South Carolina) Police
  Department, 480–82, 488–89, 492
Sunoco, 335
SunTrust, 424
Sununu, John, 66
Supreme Court. *see* Bork, Robert; *individual
  names of cases*
Sweeney, Bill, 141
Sydnor, Eugene B., Jr., 53
The System (Broder and Johnson), 200

Taft, William Howard, 53, 80
Tamiflu (Roche), 235–37, 264
Target-Point Consulting, 292
Tasmar (Roche), 233–34
taxes
  1981 tax bill, 143
  Reagan on efficiency (vs. equity) of
    government, 10–11, 113–15
  Tax Reform Act of 1986 and, 125–27, 128–29,
    207
  2017 tax reform, 478
Tea Party movement, 342
tech sector. *see* Genentech; Google
televangelists, 157–58
television advertising
  to children, 61–65
  "Harry and Louise" and health care reform
    (Clinton administration), 199–201, 245
  media buying for, 287

Tennessee Valley Authority and Tellico Dam
  controversy, 86
Terekhova, Anna, 394
Theroux, David, 320
Thiel, Peter, 501
Thierer, Adam, 348
think tank scholarship. *see also individual names
  of think tanks*
  Google and Project Eagle, 345–54
  1970s change in, 8–9
  Powell Memo and, 52–57, 86, 351
This Week (ABC-TV), 29
Thomas, John, 249
Thurmond, Strom, 66, 88–89, 90, 91, 93
A Time for Truth (Simon), 56
Time Warner, 313
Tobacco Stick Lodge, 226–27, 369
Todd, Chuck, 426–27
Tommy the Cork (McKean), 33
"The Torturers' Lobby," 205
Tosco Corporation, 109–10
Toyota Motor Corp., 451
Trans-Pacific Partnership (TPP), 423
Trans World Airlines, 34, 115
Trautlein, Donald, 168
Treasury, Department of, 56, 175, 336, 449,
  460
Treaty of Detroit, 36
Tripadvisor Inc., 313, 353
Truman, Harry, 34, 189
Trump, Donald
  anti-Big Business populism of, 390, 422–23,
    434–35, 439–40, 449–56, 497–99, 503
  The Art of the Deal, 104
  "audience of one" strategy, 389, 453–56
  Black Manafort's early work with, 108, 109,
    119–24
  Black's views on, 451–52, 506
  Courtovich as ally of, 439–40, 456–59
  CPAC and, 339
  "Drain the Swamp," 390
  executive orders by, 453
  inauguration of, 387–90
  January 6 attacks and, 495, 497
  Kudlow and, 155
  lobbyists early influence on, 13
  "Make America Great Again," 390, 427, 436,
    440, 453, 456, 479
  Manafort pardoned by, 493–94
  on Manafort's conviction, 475–76
  presidential campaign (2016), 422, 426–28,
    431–38
  Sessions and, 159

Stone pardoned by, 494
Tony Podesta criticized by, 468
Trump, Ivanka, 428
Trump Princess (yacht), 120
Trump Shuttle (airline), 120
Trump Tower, 397, 432
Truth in Lending Act (1968), 86
Tumblr, 338
Tungsten LLC, 507
Turkey, Flynn and, 457, 487, 490
Turnipseed, Tom, 67, 70
20th Century Fox Film Co., 113
Twitter, 337, 338
2008 financial crisis
    Clinton administration deregulation and, 202
    Goldman Sachs and, 303
    housing crisis, 335–36
    lobbyists' revenue slump, 363–64
    Obama's advisory board for, 332
    Obama's health care plan, 270
    Obama's inaugural speech on (2009), 263–64
Tymoshenko, Yulia, 398
Tyrrell, James, Jr., 364–65, 371–75
Tyson Foods Inc., 246

Ukraine lobbying scandal, 460–71
    European Centre for a Modern Ukraine,
        398–408, 437
    FARA filing and, 390, 399–406, 461, 464, 490
    Manafort, investigation and indictment,
        460–62, 465–66
    Manafort, prison release, 479
    Manafort, trials and incarceration, 472–76
    Manafort's financial problems resulting from,
        428–31, 436–38
    Manafort's introduction to Ukrainian officials,
        390–94
    Manafort's telecommunications company
        investment, 427, 430, 436
    Mercury Public Affairs and, 391, 398, 400–
        407 (*see also* Weber, Vin)
    offshore payments ("Loyal Bank," West
        Indies), 408, 429
    Orange Revolution, 393, 396
    Party of Regions (Ukraine), 394–98, 403–4,
        437
    Podesta Group's loss of clients and eventual
        closure, 462–71
    Podesta's Ukraine campaign work related to,
        420
    Yanukovych's flight to Russia, 427–29
" 'Unbiased' Ads for Microsoft Came at a Price"
    (*New York Times*), 320

Union Pacific Railroad, 5
UNITA (National Union for the Total
    Independence of Angola), 177–83
United Automobile Workers, 36
United Defense LLC, 220–22
United Fruit Company, 33
United Nations, 20, 183, 421
United Steelworkers union, 168
University of California at Berkeley, 349
University of California at Santa Barbara, 47
University of Illinois, 350
Unsafe at Any Speed (Nader), 38
Urban League, 336
U.S. Steel, 5, 254
"Using Antitrust Enforcement Prudently in
    High-Tech Markets" (Balto), 351

Valis, Wayne, 105
Valium (Roche), 231, 233
Vance, J. D., 478, 499
Vander Jagt, Guy, 140, 146
Van Ummersen, Claire, 282
Verizon Communications Inc., 324
Verveer, Melanne, 193
Vietnam, foreign lobbying and, 422
Vietnam War, 46, 81, 154–55
Viguerie, Richard, 95
Vinson, Fred, 34
Virginia, anti-stalking laws, 211
vitamins
    regulation of, 246–47
    Roche and price-fixing scandal, 232–33, 247
Vitter, David, 293–94
Vogel, David, 41, 42, 102, 143
Voight, Jon, 388
Vonnegut, Kurt, 158

Wagner, Heidi, 268–70, 485
Wall Street Journal
    on Courtovich, 482–86
    issue advocacy and, 304–5
Walmart, 254, 362, 468
Warhol, Andy, 252–53
Warner-Lambert, 313
War Production Board, US, 33
Warren, Elizabeth, 498
The Washington Century (Solomon), 21, 25, 129
Washington Post
    "The FTC as National Nanny," 61–62
    issue advocacy and, 304
    Microsoft's ads in, 320
Washington Through a Purple Veil (Boggs), 22
Wasserman Schultz, Debbie, 294

Watergate, 62, 72–73, 83–85, 131–34, 223. *see also* campaign finance
Watt, James, 114
Waxman, Henry, 272–74
Weber, Vin
  Manafort investigation and, 461
  Manafort's payments to, 437
  Manafort's Ukraine lobbying campaign, FARA vs. LDA filing, 398, 400, 405, 406
  Manafort's Ukraine lobbying campaign, logistics, 390–91
  not charged in investigation, 496, 508
Weicker, Lowell, 64, 78
Weinberger, Caspar W., 179
Weissmann, Andrew, 474, 495–96
Welch, Jack, 203
Welliver, Robert, 236
Wells Fargo, 254, 367, 468
Wertheimer, Fred, 171–72
Wertkin, Jeffrey, 219
Westerfield, Divina, 119
Weyrich, Paul, 95
Whitacre, Ed, 324
White House Easter Egg Roll, 268–70
WikiLeaks, 462
Wikipedia, 343
Willhite, Debbie, 125
Williams, J. D., 132
Williams, Lynn, 168
Wilmer Hale, 371
Wilson, Joe, 275
Wilson, Woodrow, 60
Winner-Take-All Politics (Hacker and Pierson), 11
Wittig, Peter, 388
women lobbyists and staff. *see also* Fritts, Kimberley; Podesta, Heather Miller
  Black Manafort's treatment of, 108, 118, 125
  Morris's treatment of, 306
  Patton Boggs' treatment of, 148
  Tony Podesta's harassment accusation, 410–11
  Wagner at Roche, 268–70
Woods, Tiger, 2, 378, 450
World Health Organization, 231, 237

World War II
  "capital-labor accord" of postwar era, 36
  Corcoran's profiting from, 33–34
  federal regulation, postwar expansion of, 36–38
Wright, Jim, 139
Wright, Joshua, 350–51, 355
Wriston, Walter, 55

Xenical (Roche), 233–34

Yahoo!, 353
Yanukovych, Viktor. *see also* Ukraine lobbying scandal
  Manafort's and Podesta's lobbying registration, 398–99, 401, 403, 407
  Manafort's consulting to, 391, 394–97, 461
  Ukraine ouster of, 427–29
Yarowsky, Jonathan, 371
Yelp Inc., 313, 353
Yon, David, 90
Young, Andrew, 162
Young, Frank, 249
Young & Rubicam, 46, 203–12
Young Republicans National Federation, 66–105
  Atwater, biographical information, 89–92
  Atwater's death and legacy, 66–72
  Black, biographical information, 92–93
  Manafort, biographical information, 74–78
  Manafort and Ford campaign, 84–85
  Manafort's and Stone's introduction, 72–74
  New Right's rise and, 80, 85–88, 90–99
  Reagan and, 67–69, 71, 73, 84, 95–105
  Stone, biographical information, 78–81
  Stone and Nixon campaign, 81–84
  Stone and Thurmond campaign, 88–89
YouTube, 314, 322, 338
Yushchenko, Viktor, 393, 394

Zaire, foreign lobbying and, 14, 176
Zarris, George, 158
Zeleny, Jeff, 278, 303, 443, 490, 491, 508
Zeughauser, Peter, 367–68

About the Authors

Brody Mullins is an investigative reporter in the Washington, DC, bureau of the *Wall Street Journal*, where he covers business, lobbying, and campaign finance. He was part of the team that won the 2023 Pulitzer Prize for Investigative Reporting for revealing financial conflicts of interest among officials at fifty federal agencies who bought and sold stocks of companies they were tasked with regulating.

Luke Mullins is a contributing writer at *Politico* magazine, where he covers the people and institutions that control Washington's levers of power. He has been a senior writer at *Washingtonian* magazine, and he's also written for the *Atlantic*, *Esquire*, and *Mother Jones*, among other publications.